THE INDISPENSABLE PILL BOOK

The Pill Book gives you the answers to the questions millions of Americans are asking about the pills their physicians are prescribing for them and their families.

This newly revised, updated 5th edition of the 4-million–copy bestseller gives you the essentials about all the revolutionary new drugs and drug types.

Now, thanks to *The Pill Book,* the general public can easily understand and accurately identify the medicines their doctors prescribe. *The Pill Book* describes practically everything you should know about more than 1600 prescription drugs, including generic and brand names, usual doses, side effects, adverse reactions, cautions and warnings, overdose potential, interactions with other drugs, and much more.

It is based on the same information your physician and pharmacist rely on—information seldom available to patients. *The Pill Book* synthesizes the most important facts about each drug in a concise, readable entry. Warnings about drug use are given special prominence.

THE PILL BOOK
5th Edition

NO HOME SHOULD BE WITHOUT IT!

THE PILL BOOK

5th EDITION

BERT STERN

Producer

LAWRENCE D. CHILNICK

Editor-in-Chief

Text by

HAROLD M. SILVERMAN,

Pharm. D.

GILBERT I. SIMON,

Sc.D.

Additional Text
LAWRENCE D. CHILNICK

Consultants
IAN GINSBERG, R.Ph.
RAYMOND J. GIZIENSKI, R.Ph., M.S.

Photography
BENN MITCHELL

Production
MICHAEL HARKAVY
LISA JENIO

BANTAM BOOKS
NEW YORK · TORONTO · LONDON · SYDNEY · AUCKLAND

THE PILL BOOK

A Bantam Book

PUBLISHING HISTORY
Bantam edition published June 1979
Bantam revised edition / October 1982
Bantam 3rd revised edition / March 1986
Bantam 4th revised edition / February 1990
Bantam 5th revised edition / May 1992

*This revised edition was published simultaneously in
trade paperback and mass market paperback.*

Library of Congress Cataloging-in-Publication Data
Silverman, Harold M.
    The pill book / Bert Stern, producer; Lawrence D.
Chilnick, editor-in-chief; text by Harold M. Silverman,
Gilbert I. Simon; additional text, Lawrence D. Chilnick;
photography, Benn Mitchell.—5th ed.
        p.   cm.
    Includes index.
    ISBN 0-553-29463-6
    1.   Drugs—Dictionaries.   2.Drugs—Identification—
Pictorial works.   I. Simon, Gilbert I.   II. Chilnick,
Lawrence D.   III. Title.
RS51.S555   1992
615'.1—dc20
                                                    91-45258
                                                        CIP

*Published simultaneously in the United States
and Canada*

PRINTED IN THE UNITED STATES OF AMERICA

OPM   0   9   8   7

Contents

The purpose of this book is to provide educational information to the public concerning the majority of various types of prescription drugs which are presently utilized by physicians. It is not intended to be complete or exhaustive or in any respect a substitute for personal medical care. *Only a physician may prescribe these drugs and the exact dosage which should be taken.*

While every effort has been made to reproduce products on the cover and insert of this book in an exact fashion, certain variations of size or color may be expected as a result of the photographic process. Furthermore, pictures identified as brand name drugs should not be confused with their generic counterparts, and vice versa. *In any event, the reader should not rely upon the photographic image to identify any pills depicted herein, but should rely solely upon the physician's prescription as dispensed by the pharmacist.*

How to Use This Book

The Pill Book, like pills themselves, should be used with caution. Used properly, this book can save you money and perhaps your life.

Our book contains a section of life-size pictures of the drugs most often prescribed in the United States. *The Pill Book*'s product identification system is designed to help you check that the drug you're about to take is the right drug. Included are the most prescribed brand name drugs and some frequently prescribed generic versions of those drugs. Although many dosage forms are included, not all forms and available strengths of every drug have been shown.

Each drug has been reproduced as faithfully as possible. While every effort has been made to depict the products accurately, some variations of size or color may be expected as a result of the photographic process. (Birth control pill cases are shown reduced in size.) Readers should not rely solely upon the photographic image to identify any pills, but should check with their pharmacist if they have any questions about identification.

Most, although not all, drugs in the color section can be matched with the pill you have by checking to see if:

- The imprinted company logos (e.g., "Lilly," Roche) are the same.
- The product strengths (e.g., "250 mg.," "10 mg.") which are frequently printed on the pills are the same.
- Any product code numbers which may be imprinted directly on the pill are the same.

To find out more about the drugs depicted, check the descriptive material in the text (page numbers are given). The pill profiles provide a complete description of over 1600 generic and brand name drugs. These are the drugs most often prescribed to Americans. The descriptions will give you a detailed explanation of everything you need to know about your prescription. Most drugs are listed alphabetically under their generic classification; however, when a drug is a combination of 2 or more active ingredients, the listing is by major brand name. Every brand and generic name is cross-referenced in the index.

Each drug profile contains the following information:

Generic or Brand Name: The generic name, the common name or chemical description of the drug approved by the Food and Drug Administration, is listed along with the current brand names available for each generic drug.

Most prescription drugs are sold in more than one strength. Some, such as the oral contraceptive drugs, come in packages containing different numbers of pills. A few manufacturers reflect this fact by adding letters and/or numbers to the basic drug name; others do not. An example: Norlestrin 21 1/50, Norlestrin 21 2.5/50, Norlestrin 28 1/50, Norlestrin 28 2.5/50. (The numbers here refer to the number of tablets in each monthly supply—28 or 21—and the strength of medication found in the tablets.) Other drugs come in different strengths: This is often indicated by a notation such as "DS" (double strength) or "Forte" (stronger).

The Pill Book lists only generic or brand names (e.g., Norlestrin) where there are no differences in the basic ingredients. The amount of ingredient (strength) varies from product to product.

Type of Drug: Describes the general pharmacologic class of each drug: "antidepressant," "tranquilizer," "decongestant," "expectorant," and so on.

Prescribed for: The reasons for which a drug is most often prescribed. Most drugs are given for certain symptoms or conditions but a drug may also be prescribed in combination with another for a quite different reason. Check with your doctor if you are not sure why you have been given a certain pill.

General Information: Information on how the drug works, how long it takes for you to feel its effects, or a description of how this drug is similar to (or differs from) other drugs.

Cautions and Warnings: Any drug can be harmful if the patient is sensitive to any of its actions. The information given alerts you to possible allergic reactions and to certain physical conditions such as heart disease which should be taken into consideration if the drug is prescribed for you.

Pregnancy/Breast-feeding: Women who are pregnant or nursing newborn infants need the latest information on how their medicines can affect their babies. This section will help guide you on how to use medicines if you are or might be pregnant, and what to do if you must take a medicine during the time you are nursing your baby.

Seniors: Our bodies change as we grow older. As an older adult, you want information about how each drug affects you and what kind of reactions to expect. This section presents the special facts you need to know about every drug and how your reactions will differ from those of a younger person. It describes the symptoms you are more likely to develop just because you are older and how your doctor might adjust your drug dosage to take into account the changes in your body.

Possible Side Effects: Side effects are divided into two categories: those that are more common, and those that are less common (or rare), to help you better understand what to expect from your pills. If you are not sure whether you are experiencing an adverse reaction, ALWAYS call your doctor.

Drug Interactions: This section tells you what other drugs should not be taken at the same time as the drug under discussion. Drug interactions with other pills, alcohol, or other substances can cause death. Interactions are more common than overdoses. Obviously, it is important to be careful when taking alcohol with any medication or when taking several medications at the same time. Be sure to inform your doctor of any medication that you have been taking. Your pharmacist should also keep a record of all your prescription and nonprescription medicines. This listing, generally called a Patient Drug Profile, is used to review your record for any potential problems. You may want to keep your own drug profile and bring it to your pharmacist for review whenever a new medicine is added to it.

Food Interactions: This section includes information on

foods to avoid while taking a medication, whether or not to take your medicine with meals, and other important facts.

Usual Dose: The maximum and minimum amounts of a drug usually prescribed; however, you may be given different dosage instructions by your doctor. It is important to check with your doctor if you are confused about how often to take a pill and when, or why a different dosage than indicated in the book has been prescribed. You should not change the prescribed dosages for a drug you are taking without first calling your doctor. Dosages differ for different age groups, and this information is also given.

Overdosage: Symptoms of an overdose of drugs and the immediate steps to take in that event.

Special Information: Facts to help you take your medicine more safely, symptoms to watch for, what to do if you forget a dose of your medicine, and special instructions.

The Pill Book also suggests some questions you may want to ask your doctor or pharmacist about your medicine.

This book is a unique visual reference tool. Its use, however, is only intended to amplify the information given by your doctor and pharmacist.

If you read something in *The Pill Book* which does not jibe with your instructions, call your doctor. Any drug can have serious side effects if abused or used improperly.

In an Emergency!

Each year some 1.5 million people are poisoned in the United States; about 70,000 of the poisonings are drug related. In fact, drug overdose is a leading cause of fatal poisoning in this country, with about 7,000 deaths recorded each year. Sedatives, barbiturates, benzodiazepine tranquilizers, and topically applied medicines are responsible for the bulk of the drug-related poisonings or overdoses.

Although each of the product information descriptions in the 5th revised edition of *The Pill Book* has specific information on overdose management, there are also some general rules to remember if you are confronted with someone who has been poisoned.

Do the following:

1. Make sure the victim is breathing—call for medical help immediately.
2. When calling for help, the place to call is your local poison control center. The telephone number can be obtained from information; just ask for "poison control." When you call, be prepared to tell the person who answers:

• What was taken and how much.
• What the victim is doing (conscious or sleeping, vomiting, having convulsions, etc.).
• The approximate age and weight of the victim.
• Any chronic medical problems of the victim (such as diabetes, epilepsy, or high blood pressure), if you know them.
• What medicines, if any, the victim takes regularly.

5

3. Remove anything that could interfere with breathing. A person who has poor oxygen supply will turn blue (the fingernails or tongue change color first). If this happens, lay the victim on his or her back, open the collar, place one hand under the neck, and lift, pull, or push the victim's jaw so that it juts outward. This will open the airway between the mouth and lungs as wide as possible. If the victim is not breathing, begin mouth-to-mouth resuscitation.
4. If the victim is unconscious or having convulsions, call for medical help immediately. While waiting for the ambulance, lay the victim on the stomach and turn the head to one side. This will prevent inhalation of vomit should the victim throw up. Do not give an unconscious victim anything by mouth. Keep the victim warm.
5. If the victim is conscious, call for medical help and give the victim an 8-ounce glass of water to drink. This will dilute the poison.

Only a small percent of poisoning victims require hospitalization. Most can be treated with simple actions or need no treatment at all.

Depending on what was taken, you may be instructed to make the patient vomit. The best way to do this is to use Syrup of Ipecac, which can be purchased without a prescription at any pharmacy. Specific instructions on how much to give infants, children, or adults are printed on the label and will also be given by your poison control center. Remember, *do not* make the victim vomit unless you have been instructed to do so. Never make the victim vomit if the victim is unconscious, is having a convulsion, has a painful, burning feeling in the mouth or throat, or has swallowed a corrosive poison. (Corrosive poisons include bleach—liquid or powder—washing soda, drain cleaner, lye, oven cleaner, toilet bowl cleaner, and dishwasher detergent.) If a corrosive poison has been taken and the victim can still swallow, give milk or water to dilute the poison. The poison control center will give you further instructions.

If the victim has swallowed a petroleum derivative such as gasoline, kerosene, machine oil, lighter fluid, furniture polish, or cleaning fluids, do not do anything. Call the poison control center for instructions.

If the poison or chemical has spilled onto the skin, remove any clothing or jewelry that has been contaminated and wash the area with plenty of warm water for at least 15 minutes. Then wash the area thoroughly with soap and water. The poison control center will give you more instructions.

The best way to deal with a poisoning is to be ready for it. Do the following *now*:

1. Get the telephone number of your local poison control center and write it down with your other emergency phone numbers.
2. Decide which hospital you will go to, if necessary, and how you will get there.
3. Buy 1 ounce of Syrup of Ipecac from your pharmacy. The pharmacist will explain how to use it, if needed. Remember, this is a potent drug to be used only if directed.
4. Learn to give mouth-to-mouth resuscitation. You may have to use this on a victim of poisoning.

In order to reduce the possibility of poisoning, do the following:

1. Keep all medicine, household cleaners, disinfectants, insecticides, gardening products, and similar products out of the reach of young children, in a locked place.
2. Do not store poisonous materials in containers that have contained food.
3. Do not remove the labels from bottles so that the contents cannot be read.
4. Discard all medicines after you no longer need them.
5. Do not operate a car engine or other gasoline engine in an unventilated space. Do not use a propane heater indoors.
6. If you smell gas, call the gas company immediately.

Poison prevention is best achieved by common sense. If you follow the simple advice given in this chapter, you will have taken a giant step toward assuring household safety for you and your family members.

The Most Commonly Prescribed Drugs in the United States, Generic and Brand Names, with Complete Descriptions of Drugs and Their Effects

Generic Name

Acebutolol

Brand Name

Sectral

Type of Drug

Beta-adrenergic blocking agent.

Prescribed for

High blood pressure and abnormal heart rhythms. It may also be prescribed by your doctor to treat angina pectoris, anxiety, tremors, overactive thyroid, and mitral valve prolapse and to prevent second heart attacks in people.

General Information

Acebutolol is a relatively weak beta blocker and is given in larger doses than other beta-blocking drugs available in the United States. Otherwise, Acebutolol is remarkably similar to other beta blockers in its ability to lower blood pressure and treat abnormal heart rhythms and other conditions.

Cautions and Warnings

You should be cautious about taking Acebutolol if you have asthma, severe heart failure, very slow heart rate, or heart block because the drug can aggravate these conditions. Compared with the other beta blockers, Acebutolol has less of an effect on your pulse and bronchial muscles, and less of a rebound effect when the drug is discontinued, and it produces less tiredness, depression, and intolerance to exercise than other beta-blocking drugs.

People with angina who take Acebutolol for high blood pressure should have their drug dosage reduced gradually over 1 to 2 weeks rather than suddenly discontinued. This will avoid possible aggravation of the angina.

Acebutolol should be used with caution if you have liver disease, because your ability to eliminate the drug from your body will be impaired.

Pregnancy/Breast-feeding

Animal studies in which rats and rabbits were given amounts of medicine greater than normal human doses revealed no adverse effects of Acebutolol on the developing baby. However, Acebutolol should be avoided by pregnant women and women who might become pregnant while taking it. When the drug is considered essential by your doctor, the potential risk of taking the medicine must be carefully weighed against the benefit it might produce.

Small amounts of Acebutolol may pass into your breast milk. Nursing mothers taking this drug must observe their infants for possible drug-related side effects.

Seniors

Older adults may absorb more Acebutolol and may require only half as much medicine as younger adults to achieve the same effect. Your dosage of this drug must be adjusted to your individual needs by your doctor. Seniors may be more likely to suffer from cold hands and feet and reduced body temperature, chest pains, a general feeling of ill health, sudden difficulty breathing, sweating, or changes in heartbeat because of this medicine.

Possible Side Effects

Acebutolol side effects are relatively uncommon, usually develop early in the course of treatment, are relatively mild, and are rarely a reason to stop taking the medication. Side effects increase with increasing dosage and include dizziness, tingling of the scalp, nausea, vomiting, upset stomach, taste distortion, fatigue, sweating, male impotence, urinary difficulty, diarrhea, bile duct blockage, breathing difficulty, bronchial spasms, muscle weakness, cramps, dry eyes, blurred vision, skin rash, hair loss, and facial swelling. Like other beta blockers, Acebutolol can cause mental depression, confusion, disorientation, short-term memory loss, and emotional instability.

Rare side effects include aggravation of lupus erythematosus (a disease of the body's connective tissues), stuffy nose, chest pains, back or joint pains, colitis, drug allergy (fever, sore throat), and unusual bleeding or bruising.

Drug Interactions

Beta-blocking drugs may interact with surgical anesthetics to increase the risk of heart problems during surgery. Some anesthesiologists recommend stopping your beta blocker gradually 2 days before surgery.

Acebutolol may interfere with the normal signs of low blood sugar and can interfere with the action of oral antidiabetes medicines.

Taking Acebutolol together with Aspirin-containing drugs, Indomethacin, or Sulfinpyrazone can interfere with its blood-pressure-lowering effect.

The effects of Acebutolol may be increased by Molindone or by phenothiazine antipsychotic medicines with other antihypertensives like Clonidine, Diazoxide, Nifedipine, or Reserpine or with other drugs that can reduce blood pressure, like Nitroglycerin.

Cimetidine increases the amount of Acebutolol absorbed into the bloodstream from oral tablets.

Acebutolol may interfere with the effectiveness of some anti-asthma drugs, especially Ephedrine and Isoproterenol, and with Theophylline and Aminophylline.

The combination of Acebutolol and Phenytoin or digitalis drugs can result in excessive slowing of the heart and possible heart block.

Estrogen drugs can interfere with the blood-pressure-lowering effect of Acebutolol.

Food Interactions

Take this medicine with food if it upsets your stomach.

Usual Dose

Starting dose, 400 milligrams per day, taken all at once or in 2 divided doses. The daily dose may be gradually increased. Maintenance dose, 400 to 1200 milligrams per day.

Senior: Older adults may respond to lower doses of this drug than younger adults and should be treated more cautiously, beginning with 200 milligrams per day and increasing gradually up to a maximum of 800 milligrams per day.

Overdosage

Symptoms are changes in heartbeat (unusually slow, unusually fast, or irregular), severe dizziness or fainting, difficulty breathing, bluish-colored fingernails or palms of the hands, and seizures.

Special Information

Acebutolol is meant to be taken on a continuing basis. Do not stop taking it unless directed to do so by your doctor. Possible side effects of abrupt withdrawal of Acebutolol are chest pain, difficulty breathing, sweating, and unusually fast or irregular heartbeat.

Call your doctor at once if any of the following symptoms develop: back or joint pains, difficulty breathing, cold hands or feet, depression, skin rash, changes in heartbeat.

Call your doctor about the following side effects only if they persist or are bothersome: anxiety, diarrhea, constipation, sexual impotence, mild dizziness, headache, itching, nausea or vomiting, nightmares or vivid dreams, upset stomach, trouble sleeping, stuffed nose, frequent urination, unusual tiredness or weakness.

If you forget a dose of Acebutolol, take it as soon as you remember. If it is almost time for your next dose, skip the forgotten tablet. Do not double the dose.

Generic Name

Acetaminophen

Brand Names

Acephen	Genebs
Aceta	Halenol
Anacin-3, Children's Anacin-3	Liquiprin
APAP	Meda Tab
Arthritis Pain Formula	Myapap
Banesin	Neopap Supprettes
Bromo Seltzer	Oraphen-PD
Dapa	Panadol, Children's Panadol
Datril	Panex
Dolanex	Phenaphen
Genapap, Children's Genapap	St. Joseph Aspirin-Free for Children

Suppap   Tylenol, Children's Tylenol
Tapanol   Tylenol Extra Strength
Tempra

(Also available in generic form)

Type of Drug

Antipyretic analgesic.

Prescribed for

Symptomatic relief of pain and fever for people who cannot take Aspirin.

General Information

Acetaminophen is generally used to provide symptomatic relief from pain and fever associated with the common cold, flu, viral infections, or other disorders where pain or fever may be a problem. It is also used to relieve pain in people who are allergic to Aspirin, or those who cannot take Aspirin because of potential interactions with other drugs such as oral anticoagulants. It can be used to relieve pain from a variety of sources, including arthritis, headache, and tooth and periodontic pain, although it does not reduce inflammation.

Cautions and Warnings

Do not take Acetaminophen if you are allergic or sensitive to it. Do not take Acetaminophen for more than 10 consecutive days unless directed by your doctor. Do not take more than is prescribed for you or recommended on the package.

Use with caution if you have kidney or liver disease or virus infections of the liver.

Pregnancy/Breast-feeding

This drug appears safe for use during pregnancy when taken in usual doses. Taking continuous high doses of the drug may cause birth defects or interfere with your baby's development. Check with your doctor before taking it if you are, or might be, pregnant.

Small amounts of Acetaminophen may pass into breast milk. It is safe to breast-feed while taking this medicine.

Seniors

Seniors may take Acetaminophen according to package directions or as directed by their doctor.

Possible Side Effects

This drug is relatively free from side effects. For this reason it has become extremely popular, especially among those who cannot take Aspirin. Rarely, large doses or long-term use of Acetaminophen can cause rash, itching, fever, lowered blood sugar, stimulation, and/or yellowing of the skin or whites of the eyes. Other effects of overuse may include a change in the composition of your blood.

Usual Dose

Adult: 300 to 650 milligrams 4 to 6 times per day or 1000 milligrams 3 or 4 times per day. Avoid taking doses greater than 2.6 grams (8 of the 325-milligram tablets) per day for long periods of time.

Child (age 9 to 11): 400 to 480 milligrams 4 to 5 times per day.

Child (age 6 to 8): 320 milligrams 4 to 5 times per day.

Child (age 4 to 5): 240 milligrams 4 to 5 times per day.

Child (age 1 to 3): 120 to 160 milligrams 4 to 5 times per day.

Child (less than 1 year): 40 to 80 milligrams 4 to 5 times per day.

Overdosage

Symptoms are development of bluish color of the lips, fingertips, etc., rash; fever; stimulation; excitement; delirium; depression; nausea and vomiting; abdominal pain; diarrhea; yellowing of the skin and/or eyes; convulsions; and coma. Victims of Acetaminophen overdose should be made to vomit with Syrup of Ipecac and taken to a hospital emergency room. ALWAYS bring the medicine bottle.

Special Information

Unless abused, Acetaminophen is a beneficial, effective, and relatively nontoxic drug.

Generic Name

Acetaminophen with Codeine

Ingredients

Acetaminophen
Codeine Phosphate

Brand Names

Capital with Codeine   Tylenol with Codeine
Phenaphen with Codeine   Ty-Tab #3

(Also available in generic form)

Type of Drug

Narcotic analgesic combination.

Prescribed for

Relief of mild to moderate pain.

General Information

Acetaminophen with Codeine is generally prescribed for the patient who requires a greater analgesic effect than Acetaminophen alone can deliver and/or is allergic to Aspirin.

Acetaminophen with Codeine is probably not effective for arthritis or other pain caused by inflammation because the ingredient Acetaminophen does not reduce inflammation. Aspirin with Codeine will produce an anti-inflammatory effect; this is the major difference between these two products.

Cautions and Warnings

Do not take Acetaminophen with Codeine if you know you are allergic or sensitive to it. Use this drug with extreme caution if you suffer from asthma or other breathing problems or if you have kidney or liver disease or virus infections of the liver. Long-term use of Acetaminophen with Codeine may cause drug dependence or addiction.

Codeine is a respiratory depressant and affects the central nervous system, producing sleepiness, tiredness, and/or inability to concentrate. Be careful if you are driving, operating machinery, or performing other functions requiring concentration.

Pregnancy/Breast-feeding

High doses of Acetaminophen have caused some problems when used during pregnancy or breast-feeding. The regular use of Codeine may cause the unborn child to become addicted. If used during labor, it may cause breathing problems in the infant. If you are pregnant or suspect that you are pregnant, do not take this drug.

Both Acetaminophen and Codeine may pass into breast milk. Wait 4 to 6 hours after taking the medication before breast-feeding.

Seniors

Seniors may be sensitive to the depressant effects of Codeine in this combination. Take this drug product only according to your doctor's prescription.

Possible Side Effects

The most common side effects are light-headedness, dizziness, sleepiness, nausea, vomiting, loss of appetite, and sweating. If these effects occur, consider calling your doctor and asking him about lowering the dose of Codeine you are taking. Usually the side effects disappear if you simply lie down.

More serious side effects of Acetaminophen with Codeine are shallow breathing or difficulty in breathing.

Rarely, Acetaminophen with Codeine may cause euphoria (feeling high), weakness, sleepiness, headache, agitation, uncoordinated muscle movement, minor hallucinations, disorientation and visual disturbances, dry mouth, loss of appetite, constipation, flushing of the face, rapid heartbeat, palpitations, faintness, urinary difficulties or hesitancy, reduced sex drive and/or potency, itching, rashes, anemia, lowered blood sugar, or yellowing of the skin and/or whites of the eyes. Narcotic analgesics may aggravate convulsions in those who have had convulsions in the past.

Drug Interactions

Because of its depressant effect and potential effect on

breathing, Acetaminophen with Codeine should be taken with extreme care in combination with alcohol, sleeping medicine, tranquilizers, antihistamines, or other drugs producing sedation.

Food Interactions

Acetaminophen with Codeine is best taken with food or at least half a glass of water to prevent stomach upset.

Usual Dose

Adult: 1 to 2 tablets every 4 hours.

Child (age 6 to 12): 5 to 10 milligrams every 4 to 6 hours. Not to exceed 60 milligrams in 24 hours.

Child (age 2 to 6): 2.5 milligrams to 5 milligrams every 4 to 6 hours. Do not exceed 30 milligrams in 24 hours.

Overdosage

Symptoms are depression of respiration (breathing), extreme tiredness progressing to stupor and then coma, pinpointed pupils of the eyes, no response to stimulation such as a pin stick, cold and clammy skin, slowing down of the heart rate, lowering of blood pressure, yellowing of the skin and/or whites of the eyes, bluish color in skin of hands and feet, fever, excitement, delirium, convulsions, cardiac arrest, and liver toxicity (shown by nausea, vomiting, pain in the abdomen, and diarrhea). The patient should be made to vomit with Syrup of Ipecac and taken to a hospital emergency room immediately. ALWAYS bring the medicine bottle.

Special Information

If you forget to take a dose of Acetaminophen with Codeine, take it as soon as you remember. If it is almost time for your next dose, skip the forgotten dose and continue with your regular medication schedule. Do not take a double dose of this medication.

Generic Name

Acetazolamide

Brand Names

AK-Zol
Dazamide
Diamox

(Also available in generic form)

Type of Drug

Carbonic anhydrase inhibitor.

Prescribed for

Heart failure; glaucoma; prophylactic treatment of mountain sickness at high altitudes. This drug has also been used in treating some convulsive disorders, such as petit mal epilepsy and other unlocalized seizures.

General Information

Acetazolamide inhibits an enzyme in the body called carbonic anhydrase. This effect allows the drug to be used as a weak diuretic and as part of the treatment of glaucoma by helping to reduce pressure inside the eye. The same effect on carbonic anhydrase is thought to make Acetazolamide a useful drug in treating certain epileptic seizure disorders. The exact way in which the effect is produced is not understood.

Cautions and Warnings

Do not take Acetazolamide if you have serious kidney, liver, or Addison's disease. This drug should not be used by people with low blood sodium or potassium.

Pregnancy/Breast-feeding

High doses of this drug may cause birth defects or interfere with your baby's development. Check with your doctor before taking it if you are, or might be, pregnant. Acetazolamide has not caused problems among breast-feeding mothers, but check with your doctor about this.

Seniors

Take this medication according to your doctor's prescription.

Possible Side Effects

Side effects of short-term Acetazolamide therapy are usually minimal. Those which have been noted include tingling feeling in the arms, legs, lips, mouth, or anus; loss of appetite; increased frequency in urination (to be expected, since this drug has a weak diuretic effect); occasional drowsiness, and convulsion. Transient myopia has been reported.

Since this drug is chemically considered to be a sulfa drug it can cause all of the side effects of the sulfa drugs: fever, rash, the formation of drug crystals in the urine, and adverse effects of the drug.

Rare side effects of Acetazolamide are itching, rash, blood in stool or urine, increased blood sugar, convulsions, diarrhea, loss of weight, nausea, vomiting, constipation, weakness, nervousness, depression, dizziness, dry mouth, disorientation, muscle spasms, ringing in the ears, loss of taste or smell, and feelings of ill health.

Drug Interactions

Avoid over-the-counter drug products that contain stimulants or anticholinergics, which tend to aggravate glaucoma or cardiac disease. Ask your pharmacist about ingredients contained in the over-the-counter drugs.

Acetazolamide may increase the effect of Quinidine and predispose patients to Digitalis toxicity by increasing potassium losses.

Acetazolamide may inhibit or delay the absorption of Primidone (for seizures) into the bloodstream.

Avoid Aspirin while taking Acetazolamide, since Aspirin side effects can be enhanced by this combination.

Food Interactions

May be taken with food to minimize stomach upset. Acetazolamide may increase potassium loss. Take this drug with

foods that are rich in potassium, like apricots, bananas, orange juice, or raisins.

Usual Dose

250 milligrams to 1 gram per day, according to disease and
patient's condition.

Special Information

Acetazolamide may cause minor drowsiness and confusion,
particularly during the first 2 weeks of therapy. Take care
while performing tasks that require concentration, such as
driving or operating appliances or machinery.

   Call your doctor if you develop sore throat, fever, unusual
bleeding or bruises, tingling in the hands or feet, rash, or unusual pains. These can be signs of important drug side effects.

   If you forget a dose of Acetazolamide, take it as soon as
you remember. If it is almost time for your next dose, skip
the forgotten pill. Do not double the dosage.

Generic Name

Acyclovir

Brand Name

Zovirax Capsules/Ointment

Type of Drug

Antiviral; antiherpes.

Prescribed for

Treatment and prevention of serious, frequently recurring
herpes infections of the genitalia (sex organs), mucous
membrane tissues, and central nervous system. It is also
prescribed for varicella (chicken pox) in people whose immune systems are compromised.

General Information

Acyclovir is the only drug that can be taken by mouth that
can reduce the rate of growth of the herpes virus and its

relatives, Epstein-Barr virus, cytomegalovirus, and varicella-zoster. Other drugs, given by intravenous injection, may be used for these infections, but they are usually reserved for AIDS or cancer patients or others whose immune systems are compromised. Acyclovir does not cure herpes, but it does reduce pain associated with herpes and may help herpes sores heal faster. Acyclovir does not affect the viruses that cause the common cold.

Acyclovir works by interfering with the reproduction of viral DNA, slowing the growth of existing viruses. It has little effect on recurrent infection and will not prevent the infection from coming back once the herpes blisters have healed. The drug must be given by intravenous injection in a hospital or by mouth to treat both local and systemic symptoms. Local symptoms can be treated with the ointment alone. The capsules can be taken every day to reduce the number and severity of herpes attacks in people who usually suffer 10 or more a year and may be used to treat intermittent attacks as they occur, but the drug must be started as soon as possible to have the greatest effect.

Cautions and Warnings

Acyclovir ointment should not be applied to your skin if you have an allergic reaction to it or to the major component of the ointment base, Polyethylene Glycol. Acyclovir ointment should not be used to treat a herpes infection of the eye because it is not specifically made for that purpose. Some people develop tenderness, swelling, or bleeding of the gums while taking Acyclovir. Regular brushing, flossing, and gum massage may help prevent this.

High doses of Acyclovir taken over long periods of time have caused reduced sperm count in lab animals, but this effect has not yet been reported in men.

The ointment should not be applied inside the vagina because the Polyethylene Glycol base can irritate and cause swelling of those sensitive tissues.

Pregnancy/Breast-feeding

Acyclovir crosses into the circulation of a developing fetus. Very small amounts of the drug are absorbed into the blood after application in the ointment form. While there is no information to indicate that Acyclovir affects a developing baby, do not use this medication during pregnancy unless it is specifically prescribed by your doctor.

Acyclovir capsules and injections have been given to lab animals and found to cause no birth defects. However, Acyclovir has not been studied in pregnant women and should not be used unless the possible benefits clearly outweigh any possible adverse effects.

Acyclovir passes into breast milk at concentrations up to 4 times the concentration in blood, and Acyclovir has been found in the urine of a nursing infant. No drug side effects have been found in nursing babies, but mothers who must take this medicine should consider bottle-feeding their infants.

Seniors

Seniors with reduced kidney function should be given a lower oral dose than younger adults to account for normal reductions in kidney function that occur with aging.

Possible Side Effects

The ointment has few side effects, the most common of which are mild burning, irritation, rash, and itching. Women are 4 times more likely to experience burning than men, and it is more likely to occur when applied during an initial herpes attack than during a recurrent attack.

The most common side effects of Acyclovir capsules are dizziness, nausea, vomiting, and headache. Additional side effects that may be experienced by people taking the drug continuously are diarrhea and aching joints.

Acyclovir capsules may occasionally cause loss of appetite, fatigue, swelling and fluid retention, rash, leg pains, swollen lymph glands in the groin and elsewhere, sore throat, a bad taste in your mouth, sleeplessness, heart palpitations, menstrual abnormalities, superficial blood clots, hair loss, depression, fever, muscle cramps, and acne. Psychiatric side effects may occur if you are taking unusually high doses (these may be more common among immunocompromised patients and seniors).

Drug Interactions

Do not apply Acyclovir together with any other ointment or topical medicine.

Oral Probenecid may decrease the elimination of Acyclovir from your body and increase drug blood levels when the Acyclovir is taken by mouth or by injection.

Medicines which are toxic to the kidney may combine with Acyclovir to produce a more intense toxic reaction.

Food Interactions

Oral Acyclovir may be taken with food if it upsets your stomach.

Usual Dose

Capsules/Suspension:

For maximum benefit, treatment should be started as soon as possible. If you have kidney disease, your doctor will adjust your dose to account for the degree of functional loss.

Adult: For a genital herpes attack: 200 milligram every 4 hours, 5 times per day for 10 days. For recurrent infections: 400 milligrams twice a day or 200 milligrams 2 to 5 times a day. As suppressive therapy, for people who suffer from chronic herpes infection: 1 capsule 3 to 5 times per day, every day. For herpes zoster infections: 800 milligrams 5 times a day for 7 to 10 days.

Child: A specific child's dose has not been established, but Acyclovir has been given to children in doses as high as 36 milligrams per pound of body weight every day without any unusual side effects.

Ointment:

Apply the ointment every 3 hours, 6 times per day for 7 days, in sufficient quantity to cover all visible lesions. About ½ inch of Acyclovir ointment should cover about 4 square inches of skin lesions. Your doctor may prescribe a longer course of treatment to prevent the delayed formation of new lesions during the duration of an attack.

Overdosage

There is no information on Acyclovir overdose, but doses of up to 4.8 grams per day for 5 days have been taken without serious adverse effects.

The chance of experiencing toxic side effects from swallowing Acyclovir ointment is quite small because of the limited amount of drug contained in the ointment (only 50 milligrams per gram). Observe the overdose victim for side effects and call a poison control center for more detailed information and advice.

Special Information

Women with genital herpes have an increased risk of cervical cancer. Check with your doctor about the need for an annual pap smear.

Use a finger cot or rubber glove when applying the ointment to protect against inadvertently spreading the virus, and be sure to apply the medicine exactly as directed and to completely cover all lesions. If you skip several doses or a day or more of treatment, the therapy will not exert its maximum effect.

Keep affected areas clean and dry. Loose-fitting clothing will help to avoid irritating a healing herpes lesion.

Call your doctor if the drug does not relieve your condition, if side effects become severe or intolerable, or if you become pregnant or want to begin breast-feeding.

Herpes can be transmitted even if you don't have symptoms of active disease. To avoid transmitting the condition, do not have intercourse while visible herpes lesions are present. A condom should protect against transmission of the virus, but spermicidal products or diaphragms probably won't. Acyclovir alone also does not protect againt spreading the herpes virus.

Check with your dentist or doctor about how to take care of your teeth if you notice swelling or tenderness of the gums.

Generic Name

Albuterol

Brand Names

Proventil Inhaler/Repetabs
Ventolin Inhalation Aerosol/Tablets

Type of Drug

Bronchodilator.

Prescribed for

Asthma and bronchial spasms.

General Information

Albuterol is similar to other bronchodilator drugs like Meta-proterenol and Isoetharine, but it has a weaker effect on nerve receptors in the heart and blood vessels; for this reason it is somewhat safer for people with heart conditions.

Albuterol tablets begin to work within 30 minutes and continue working for about 4 hours. There is also a long-acting tablet preparation that continues to work for up to 12 hours. Albuterol inhalation begins working within 15 minutes and continues for 3 to 4 hours.

Cautions and Warnings

Albuterol should be used with caution by people with a history of angina, heart disease, high blood pressure, stroke or seizure, diabetes, thyroid disease, prostate disease, or glaucoma. Excessive use of Albuterol inhalants can lead to worsening of your asthmatic or other respiratory condition.

Pregnancy/Breast-feeding

This drug should be avoided by pregnant women and those who become pregnant while using it. It is not known if Albuterol causes birth defects in humans, but it has caused defects in pregnant-animal studies. When it is deemed essential, the potential risk of taking Albuterol must be carefully weighed against any benefit it might produce.

It is not known if Albuterol passes into breast milk. Nursing mothers must observe for any possible drug effect on their infants while taking Albuterol. You may want to consider using an alternate feeding method.

Seniors

Older adults are more sensitive to the effects of Albuterol. They should closely follow their doctors' directions and report any side effects at once.

Possible Side Effects

Albuterol's side effects are similar to those of other bronchodilators, except that its effects on the heart and blood vessels are not as pronounced. The most common side effects are restlessness, weakness, anxiety, fear, tension, sleeplessness, tremors, convulsions, dizziness, headache, flushing, loss of appetite, pallor, sweating, nausea, vomiting, and muscle cramps.

Less common side effects are angina, abnormal heart rhythms, heart palpitations, high blood pressure, and urinary difficulty.

Drug Interactions

Albuterol's effects may be increased by monoamine oxidase (MAO) inhibitor drugs, antidepressants, thyroid drugs, other bronchodilator drugs, and some antihistamines.

Albuterol is antagonized by the beta-blocking drugs (Propranolol and others.)

Albuterol may antagonize the effects of blood-pressure-lowering drugs, especially Reserpine, Methyldopa, and Guanethidine.

Food Interactions

Albuterol tablets are more effective taken on an empty stomach, 1 hour before or 2 hours after meals, but can be taken with food or meals if they upset your stomach. Do not inhale Albuterol if you have food or anything else in your mouth.

Usual Dose

Inhalation:
   Adult and child (age 12 and over): 2 puffs every 4 to 6 hours (each puff delivers 90 milligrams of Albuterol). Asthma brought on by exercise may be prevented by taking 2 puffs 15 minutes before the exercise is to begin.
Tablets:
   Adult: 6 to 16 milligrams per day in divided doses to start; the dosage may be slowly increased until it controls patient's asthma, to a maximum of 32 milligrams per day.
   Senior: 6 to 8 milligrams per day to start, but increase to the maximum daily adult dosage, if tolerated.
   Child (age 6 to 14 years): 2 to 6 milligrams 3 to 4 times per day.
   Child (age 2 to 5 years): up to 4 milligrams 3 times a day.

Overdosage

Overdose of Albuterol inhalation usually results in exaggerated side effects, including heart pains and high blood pressure, although the pressure may drop to a low level after a short period of elevation. People who inhale too much Albuterol should see a doctor, who may prescribe a beta-blocking drug, such as Atenolol or Metoprolol.

Overdose of Albuterol tablets is more likely to lead to side effects of changes in heart rate, palpitations, unusual heart rhythms, heart pains, high blood pressure, fever, chills, cold sweats, nausea, vomiting, and dilation of the pupils. Convulsions, sleeplessness, anxiety, and tremors may also develop, and the victim may collapse.

If the overdose was taken within the past half hour, give the victim Syrup of Ipecac to induce vomiting and remove any remaining medicine from the stomach. DO NOT GIVE SYRUP OF IPECAC IF THE VICTIM IS UNCONSCIOUS OR CONVULSING. If symptoms have already begun to develop, the victim may have to be taken to a hospital emergency room for treatment. ALWAYS bring the prescription bottle with you.

Special Information

If you are inhaling Albuterol, be sure to follow patient instructions that come with the product. The drug should be inhaled during the second half of your breath, since this will allow it to reach deeper down into your lungs. Wait about 5 minutes between puffs, if you use more than 1 puff per dose.

Do not take more Albuterol than prescribed by your doctor. Taking more than you need could actually result in worsening of your symptoms.

Call your doctor immediately if you develop chest pains, palpitations, rapid heart beat, muscle tremors, dizziness, headache, facial flushing, or urinary difficulty or if you continue to experience difficulty in breathing after using the medicine.

If a dose of Albuterol is forgotten, take it as soon as you remember. If it is almost time for your next dose, skip the forgotten one. Do not double up.

Brand Name

Aldactazide

Ingredients

Hydrochlorothiazide
Spironolactone

Other Brand Names

Alazide
Spironazide
Spironolactone with Hydrochlorothiazide
Spirozide

(Also available in generic form)

Type of Drug

Diuretic.

Prescribed for

High blood pressure or any condition where it is desirable
to eliminate excess water from the body.

General Information

Aldactazide is a combination of 2 diuretics. It is a convenient,
effective approach for the treatment of diseases where the
elimination of excess water is required. One of the ingredients in Aldactazide, Spironolactone, has the ability to hold
potassium in the body while producing a diuretic effect.
This balances off the other ingredient, Hydrochlorothiazide,
which normally causes a loss of body potassium.

  Combination drugs like Aldactazide should only be used
when you need the exact amount of ingredients contained
in the product and when your doctor feels you would benefit
from taking fewer pills per day.

Cautions and Warnings

Do not use Aldactazide if you have nonfunctioning kidneys,
if you may be allergic to this drug or any sulfa drug, or if
you have a history of allergy or bronchial asthma.

Do not take any potassium supplements together with Aldactazide unless specifically directed to do so by your doctor.

Pregnancy/Breast-feeding

Aldactazide may be used to treat specific conditions in pregnant women, but the decision to use this medication by pregnant women should be weighed carefully because the drug may cross the placental barrier into the blood of the unborn child. This drug may cause birth defects or interfere with your baby's development. Check with your doctor before taking it if you are, or might be, pregnant.

Both ingredients in Aldactazide can pass into breast milk. No problems have been found in nursing mothers taking Aldactazide, but be sure your baby doctor knows you are taking this medicine.

Seniors

Older adults are more sensitive to the effects of this drug, especially dizziness because of potassium loss. Follow your doctor's directions closely and report any side effects at once.

Possible Side Effects

Possible side effects include loss of appetite, drowsiness, lethargy, headache, gastrointestinal upset, and cramping and diarrhea.

Less common side effects are rash, mental confusion, fever, feeling of ill health, enlargement of the breasts, inability to achieve or maintain erection in males, irregular menstrual cycles or deepening of the voice in females, headache, tingling in the toes and fingers, restlessness, anemias or other effects on components of the blood, unusual sensitivity to sunlight, and dizziness when rising quickly from a sitting position. Aldactazide can also produce muscle spasms, gout, weakness, and blurred vision.

Drug Interactions

Aldactazide will increase the effect of other blood-pressure-lowering drugs. This is good and is the reason why many people with high blood pressure take more than one medicine.

The possibility of developing imbalances in body fluids (electrolytes) is increased if you take other medications such as Digitalis and adrenal corticosteroids while you are taking Aldactazide.

If you are taking an oral antidiabetic drug and begin taking Aldactazide, the antidiabetic dose may have to be altered.

Lithium Carbonate taken with Aldactazide should be monitored carefully as there may be an increased risk of Lithium toxicity.

Avoid over-the-counter cough, cold, or allergy remedies containing stimulant drugs that can aggravate your condition.

Aldactazide may interfere with the oral blood-thinning drugs (like Warfarin) by making the blood more concentrated (thicker).

Food Interactions

Take Aldactazide with food if it upsets your stomach.

Usual Dose

2 to 4 tablets per day, adjusted by your doctor until the desired therapeutic effect is achieved.

Overdosage

Signs can be tingling in the arms or legs, weakness, fatigue, changes in your heartbeat, a sickly feeling, dry mouth, restlessness, muscle pains or cramps, urinary difficulty, nausea, or vomiting. Take the overdose victim to a hospital emergency room for treatment at once. ALWAYS bring the prescription bottle and any remaining medicine.

Special Information

This drug may cause drowsiness or sleepiness. Be careful if you drive or operate machinery.

Call your doctor if you develop muscle or stomach cramps, nausea, diarrhea, unusual thirst, headache, rash, voice changes, breast enlargement, or unusual menstrual period.

If you forget a dose of Aldactazide, take it as soon as you remember. If it is almost time for your next dose, skip the forgotten dose and continue with your regular schedule. Do not take a double dose of Aldactazide, but call your doctor if you forget to take 2 or more doses in a row.

Generic Name
Allopurinol

Brand Name
Zyloprim

(Also available in generic form)

Type of Drug
Anti-gout medication.

Prescribed for
Gout or gouty arthritis. Allopurinol is also useful to help manage other conditions that may occur if too much uric acid is present in the body.

General Information
Unlike other anti-gout drugs that affect the elimination of uric acid from the body, Allopurinol acts on the system that manufactures uric acid in your body.

A high level of uric acid can mean that you have gout or that you have one of many other diseases, including various cancers and malignancies, or psoriasis. High uric acid levels can be caused by taking some drugs, including diuretic medicines. The fact that you have a high blood level of uric acid does not point to a specific disease.

Cautions and Warnings
Do not take this medication if you have ever developed a severe reaction to it. If you develop a rash or any other adverse effects while taking Allopurinol, stop taking the medication immediately and contact your doctor.

Allopurinol should be used by children only if they have high uric acid levels due to neoplastic disease.

Pregnancy/Breast-feeding

This drug may cause birth defects or interfere with your baby's development. Check with your doctor before taking it if you are, or might be, pregnant.

A nursing mother should not take this medication, since it will pass through the mother's milk into the child.

Seniors

No special precautions are required. Be sure to follow your doctor's directions and report any side effects at once.

Possible Side Effects

You may develop rash. Such rashes have been associated with severe, allergic, or sensitivity reactions to Allopurinol. If you develop an unusual rash or other sign of drug toxicity, stop taking this medication and contact your doctor.

Less common side effects are nausea, vomiting, diarrhea, intermittent stomach pains, effects on blood components, drowsiness or lack of ability to concentrate, and, rarely, effects on the eyes.

Other uncommon side effects are loss of hair, fever, chills, arthritis-like symptoms, itching, loosening of the fingernails, pain in the lower back, unexplained nosebleeds, numbness, tingling, or pain in the hands or feet.

Drug Interactions

Avoid taking Allopurinol with iron tablets or vitamins with iron: Allopurinol can cause iron to concentrate in your liver. Megadoses of Vitamin C may increase the possibility of kidney stone formation.

Interaction with drugs used to treat cancer is important and should be taken into account by your physician.

Allopurinol may interact with anticoagulant (blood-thinning) medications such as Dicumarol. The importance of this interaction is not yet known.

Food Interactions

Take each dose with a full glass of water and drink 10 to 12 glasses of water, juices, soda, or other liquids each day to avoid the formation of crystals in your urine and/or kidneys.

This drug may be taken with food to reduce upset stomach.

Usual Dose

Adult: 200 to 800 milligrams per day, depending on disease and patient's response.

Child (age 6 to 10): 300 milligrams per day.

Child (under age 6): 150 milligrams per day.

The dose should be reviewed periodically by your doctor to be sure that it is producing the desired therapeutic effect.

Special Information

Allopurinol can make you sleepy or make it difficult for you to concentrate: Take care while driving a car or using other equipment or machinery. Call your doctor at once if you develop rash, hives, itching, chills, fever, nausea, muscle aches, unusual tiredness, fever, or yellowing of the eyes or skin.

If you forget to take your regular dose of Allopurinol, take the missed dose as soon as possible. If it is time for your next regular dose, double this dose. For example, if your regular dose is 100 milligrams and you forget to take it, take 200 milligrams at the next usual dose time.

Generic Name

Alprazolam

Brand Name

Xanax

Type of Drug

Tranquilizer.

Prescribed for

Relief of symptoms of anxiety, tension, fatigue, and agitation.

General Information

Alprazolam is a member of the group of drugs known as benzodiazepines. These drugs are used either as antianxiety

agents, anticonvulsants, or sedatives (sleeping pills). They
exert their effects by relaxing the large skeletal muscles and
by a direct effect on the brain. In doing so, they can relax
you and make you either more tranquil or sleepier, depending upon which drug you use and how much you take.
Many doctors prefer the benzodiazepines to other drugs that
can be used for the same effects because benzodiazepines
tend to be safer, have fewer side effects, and are usually
as, if not more, effective. The benzodiazepines are generally
prescribed in any situation where they can be a useful
adjunct.

The benzodiazepines, including Alprazolam, can be abused
if taken for long periods of time, and it is possible to experience withdrawal symptoms if you stop taking the drug
abruptly. Withdrawal symptoms include tremor, muscle
cramp, stomach cramps, vomiting, insomnia, and
convulsions.

Cautions and Warnings

Do not take Alprazolam if you know you are sensitive or
allergic to this drug or other benzodiazepines such as Diazepam, Oxazepam, Chlorazepate, Temazepam, Halazepam,
Lorazepam, Prazepam, Flurazepam, and Clonazepam.

Alprazolam and other members of this group can aggravate narrow-angle glaucoma, but if you have open-angle
glaucoma you may take the drug. In any case, check with
your doctor.

Alprazolam can cause tiredness, drowsiness, inability to
concentrate, or similar symptoms. Be careful if you are driving, operating machinery, or performing other activities that
require concentration.

Pregnancy/Breast-feeding

This drug, like all members of the benzodiazepine family,
crosses into your developing baby's circulation and may
cause birth defects if taken during the first 3 months of
pregnancy. You should avoid taking this medication while
pregnant.

Benzodiazepines pass into breast milk. Since infants break
the drug down more slowly than adults, it is possible for
the medicine to accumulate and have an undesired effect on

the baby. Tell your doctor if you become pregnant or are nursing an infant.

Seniors

Older adults are more sensitive to the effects of the drug. They will require less of the drug. Follow your doctor's directions and report any side effects at once.

Possible Side Effects

The most common side effects are mild drowsiness during the first few days of therapy. If drowsiness persists, contact your doctor.

Less common side effects are confusion, depression, lethargy, disorientation, headache, inactivity, slurred speech, stupor, dizziness, tremor, constipation, dry mouth, nausea, inability to control urination, sexual difficulties, irregular menstrual cycle, changes in heart rhythm, lowered blood pressure, fluid retention, blurred or double vision, itching, rash, hiccups, nervousness, inability to fall asleep, and occasional liver dysfunction. If you experience any of these symptoms, stop taking the medicine and contact your doctor immediately.

Drug Interactions

Alprazolam is a central-nervous-system depressant. Avoid alcohol, other tranquilizers, narcotics, barbiturates, monoamine oxidase (MAO) inhibitors, antihistamines, and medicines used to relieve depression. Taking Alprazolam with these drugs may result in excessive depression, tiredness, sleepiness, difficulty breathing, or similar symptoms.

Smoking may reduce the effectiveness of Alprazolam by increasing the rate at which it is broken down by the body.

The effects of Alprazolam may be prolonged when taken together with Cimetidine.

Food Interactions

Alprazolam is best taken on an empty stomach but may be taken with food if it upsets your stomach.

Usual Dose

Adult: 0.75 to 4 milligrams per day.

The dose must be tailored to the individual needs of the patient. Debilitated patients will require less of the drug to control anxiety or tension.

Child: This drug should not be used.

Overdosage

Symptoms are confusion, sleepiness, lack of response to pain such as a pin stick, shallow breathing, lowered blood pressure, and coma. The patient should be taken to a hospital emergency room for treatment. ALWAYS bring the medicine bottle with you.

Special Information

If you forget a dose of Alprazolam, take it as soon as you remember. If it is almost time for your next dose, skip the forgotten pill and continue with your regular schedule. Do not take a double dose of Alprazolam.

Generic Name

Aminophylline

Brand Names

Phyllocontin
Truphylline Suppositories

(Also available in generic form)

Type of Drug

Xanthine bronchodilator.

Prescribed for

Relief of bronchial asthma and breathing difficulties associated with emphysema, bronchitis, and other diseases.

General Information

Aminophylline is one of several drugs known as xanthine derivatives, which are the mainstay of therapy for bronchial asthma and similar diseases. Other members of this group include Dyphylline, Oxtriphylline, and Theophylline. Although the dosage for each of these drugs is different, they all work by relaxing bronchial muscles and helping reverse spasms in these muscles.

Timed-release products allow Aminophylline to act continuously throughout the day. This permits you to decrease the total number of doses to be taken every day.

Cautions and Warnings

Do not take this medicine if you are allergic or sensitive to it or any other xanthine drug. Aminophylline can aggravate stomach ulcers or heart disease.

Pregnancy/Breast-feeding

Aminophylline passes into the circulation of the developing baby. It does not cause birth defects but may result in dangerous drug levels in the infant's bloodstream. Babies born of mothers taking this medication may be nervous, jittery, and irritable and may gag and vomit when fed. If you must use this medication to control asthma or other conditions, talk with your doctor about the relative risks of using this medication and the benefits it will produce for you.

Aminophylline passes into breast milk and may cause a nursing infant to have difficulty sleeping and be nervous or irritable.

Seniors

Older adults may take longer to clear this drug from their bodies than younger adults. Older adults with heart failure or other cardiac conditions, chronic lung disease, a virus infection with fever, or reduced liver function may require a lower dosage of this medication to account for the clearance effect.

Possible Side Effects

Possible side effects include nausea, vomiting, stomach pain, diarrhea, irritability, restlessness, difficulty sleeping, excitability, muscle twitching or spasms, palpitations, abnormal heart rhythms, changes in heart rate, low blood pressure, rapid breathing, and local irritation (if the suppository is used).

Infrequent side effects are vomiting blood, fever, headache, and dehydration.

Drug Interactions

Taking this drug together with another xanthine drug can increase side effects. Don't do it unless your doctor has directed you to.

Theophylline is often taken together with a stimulant like Ephedrine to treat asthma. Such combinations may result in excessive stimulation and should only be used if you are directed to do so by your doctor.

Erythromycin, flu vaccine, Allopurinol, and Cimetidine will increase the amount of Aminophylline in your blood and increase the chances for drug side effects.

Cigarette or marijuana smoking decreases the effectiveness of Aminophylline.

Food Interactions

This drug is best taken on an empty stomach, 1 hour before or 2 hours after meals. It may be taken with food or meals if it upsets your stomach.

Diet can influence the way this drug works in your body. For example, charcoal-broiled beef may increase the amount of Theophylline eliminated from your body through the urine. Low-carbohydrate/high-protein diets also produce this effect and may reduce Aminophylline's effectiveness.

Caffeine (another xanthine derivative) may add to drug side effects. Avoid large quantities of caffeine-containing foods, including coffee, cola beverages, tea, cocoa, and chocolate.

Usual Dose

Aminophylline dosage must be tailored to your specific needs and the severity of your disease. The best dose for you is the lowest dose that will control your symptoms.

Adult: 100 to 200 milligrams every 6 hours.

Child: 50 to 100 milligrams every 6 hours or 1 to 2.5 milligrams per pound of body weight every 6 hours.

Timed-release products: 1 to 3 times a day, based on your symptoms and response to treatment. Usual dose is 200 to 500 milligrams per day.

Overdosage

The first symptoms are loss of appetite, nausea, vomiting, difficulty sleeping, and restlessness, followed by unusual behavior patterns, frequent vomiting and extreme thirst with delirium, convulsions, and very high temperature. Some overdose victims collapse.

Overdoses of oral tablets or liquid rarely produce serious symptoms. Most often the overdose victim loses his/her appetite and experiences nausea, vomiting, and stimulation. Take the victim to a hospital emergency room at once for treatment. ALWAYS bring the medicine bottle with you.

Special Information

Even though it is necessary to keep a certain amount of Aminophylline in your blood, do not double the dose if you forget to take one. Skip the missed dose and go back to your regular schedule.

Generic Name
Amiodarone

Brand Name

Cordarone

Type of Drug

Antiarrhythmic.

Prescribed for

Abnormal heart rhythms.

General Information

Amiodarone should be prescribed only in situations where the abnormal rhythm is so severe as to be life-threatening, and it does not respond to other drug treatments. Amiodarone works by affecting the movement of nervous impulses within the heart.

Amiodarone may exert its effects 3 to 5 days after you start taking it and often takes 1 to 3 weeks to affect your heart. Since Amiodarone therapy is often started while you are in the hospital, especially if you are being switched from another antiarrhythmic drug to Amiodarone, your doctor will be able to closely monitor how well the drug is working for you. Amiodarone's antiarrhythmic effects can persist for weeks after you stop taking the drug.

Cautions and Warnings

Do not take Amiodarone if you are allergic or sensitive to it or if you have heart block.

Amiodarone can cause potentially fatal drug side effects. At high doses, 10 to 15 percent of people can develop lung and respiratory effects that have the potential of being fatal. Liver damage caused by Amiodarone can also be fatal.

Amiodarone can cause a heart block, a drastic slowing of electrical impulse movement between major areas of the heart, or extreme slowing of the heart rate. Amiodarone heart block occurs about as often as heart block caused by some other antiarrhythmic drugs, but its effects may last longer than those of the other drugs.

The majority of adults who take Amiodarone develop tiny deposits in the corneas of their eyes. These deposits may cause halos or blurred vision in up to 10 percent of people taking Amiodarone.

Amiodarone can cause a reduction in thyroid activity or worsen an already sluggish thyroid gland in 2 to 10 percent of people taking the drug.

Antiarrhythmic drugs are less effective and cause abnormal rhythms if blood potassium is low. Check with your doctor to see if you need extra potassium.

One-tenth of people taking Amiodarone can experience unusual sensitivity to the sun. Protect yourself by using an appropriate sunscreen product and reapplying it frequently.

Pregnancy/Breast-feeding

In animal studies, Amiodarone has been found to be toxic to a developing fetus in animal studies when given at a dose 18 times the maximum adult dose. Pregnant women should carefully review with their doctors both the benefits to be obtained by taking this drug and the potential dangers.

Amiodarone passes into mother's milk. Nursing mothers

who must take this drug should bottle-feed to avoid any possible complications in their babies.

Seniors

Amiodarone must be used with caution, regardless of your age. This drug is broken down in the liver, and a reduced dosage may be needed if you have poor liver function. Kidney function is not a factor in determining how much Amiodarone you need.

Possible Side Effects

About 75 percent of people taking 400 milligrams or more of Amiodarone every day develop drug side effects. As many as 10 percent of people have to stop taking the drug because of a side effect.

Common side effects include fatigue, a feeling of ill health, tremors, unusual involuntary movements, loss of coordination, an unusual walk, muscle weakness, dizziness, tingling in the hands or feet, reduced sex drive, sleeplessness or difficulty sleeping, headache, nervous system problems, nausea, vomiting, constipation, loss of appetite, abdominal pains, unusual sensitivity to bright light, dry eyes, halos.

Unusual sensitivity to the sun is the most common skin reaction to Amiodarone, but people taking this drug may develop a blue skin discoloration that may not go away completely when the drug is stopped. Other skin reactions are sun rashes, hair loss, and black-and-blue spots.

Amiodarone can cause heart failure, slowing of the heart rate, and abnormal rhythms. Up to 9 percent of people taking Amiodarone develop abnormalities in liver function.

Other side effects include inflammation of the lung or fibrous deposits in the lungs, changes in thyroid function, changes in taste or smell, bloating, unusual salivation, and changes in blood clotting.

Drug Interactions

Amiodarone increases the effects of Procainamide, Quinidine, Phenytoin, and Warfarin. These interactions can take from 3 days to several weeks to develop. The dosage of these drugs must be reduced drastically to take the interaction into account.

Amiodarone can interact with beta blockers and calcium channel blockers to cause unusual slowing of the heart.

Food Interactions

Amiodarone is poorly absorbed into the blood and should be taken on an empty stomach. Although food delays the absorption of Amiodarone into your bloodstream, the drug can be taken with food or meals if it upsets your stomach.

Usual Dose

The usual starting dose is 800 to 1600 milligrams per day, taken in 1 or 2 doses. Your dosage should be reduced to the lowest effective dose to minimize side effects. The usual maintenance dose is 400 milligrams per day.

Overdosage

Amiodarone overdose is generally not serious because the drug usually takes several days or weeks to exert an effect on the body. Anyone who has taken an overdose of Amiodarone should be taken to a hospital emergency room for treatment. ALWAYS remember to take the medicine bottle with you.

Special Information

Side effects are very common with Amiodarone. Three-fourths of people taking the drug will experience some drug-related problem. Call your doctor if you develop chest pains, difficulty breathing, or any other sign of changes in lung function, an abnormal heartbeat, bloating in your feet or legs, tremors, fever, chills, sore throat, unusual bleeding or bruising, changes in skin color, unusual sunburn, or any other unusual side effect.

Amiodarone can make you dizzy or light-headed. Take care while driving a car or performing any complex tasks.

If you take Amiodarone once a day and forget to take a dose, but remember within 12 hours, take it as soon as possible. If you don't remember until later, skip the forgotten dose and continue with your regular schedule.

If you take Amiodarone twice a day and remember within 6 hours of your regular dose, take it as soon as you remember. Call your doctor if you forget 2 or more doses in a row. Do not take a double dose of Amiodarone.

Generic Name
Amitriptyline

Brand Names
Elavil
Endep

(Also available in generic form)

Type of Drug
Antidepressant.

Prescribed for
Depression with or without symptoms of anxiety.

General Information
Amitriptyline and other members of this group are effective
in treating symptoms of depression. They can elevate mood,
increase physical activity and mental alertness, and improve
appetite and sleep patterns in a depressed patient. These
drugs are mild sedatives and therefore useful in treating
mild forms of depression associated with anxiety. You
should not expect instant results with this medicine: Results
are usually seen after 2 to 4 weeks. If symptoms are not
affected after 6 to 8 weeks, contact your doctor. Occasionally
this drug and other members of this group of drugs have
been used in treating nighttime bed-wetting in young children, but they do not produce long-lasting relief; therapy
with one of them for nighttime bed-wetting is of questionable value.

Cautions and Warnings
Do not take Amitriptyline if you are allergic or sensitive to
this or other members of this class of drug: Doxepin, Nortriptyline, Imipramine, Desipramine, and Protriptyline. The
drugs should not be used if you are recovering from a heart
attack.
   Amitriptyline may be taken with caution if you have a his-

tory of epilepsy or other convulsive disorders, difficulty in urination, glaucoma, heart disease, or thyroid disease.

Pregnancy/Breast-feeding

This drug, like other antidepressants, crosses into your developing baby's circulation and may cause birth defects if taken during the first 3 months of pregnancy. There have been reports of newborn infants suffering from heart, breathing, and urinary problems after their mothers had taken an antidepressant of this type immediately before delivery. You should avoid taking this medication while pregnant.

Antidepressants of this type are known to pass into breast milk and may affect a breast-feeding infant, although this has not been proven. Nursing mothers should consider alternate feeding methods if taking this medicine.

Seniors

Older adults are more sensitive to the effects of this drug and often require a lower dose than a younger adult to do the same job. Follow your doctor's directions and report any side effects at once.

Possible Side Effects

Possible side effects include changes in blood pressure (both high and low), abnormal heart rates, heart attack, confusion (especially in older adults), hallucinations, disorientation, delusions, anxiety, restlessness, excitement, numbness and tingling in the extremities, lack of coordination, muscle spasms or tremors, seizures and/or convulsions, dry mouth, blurred vision, constipation, inability to urinate, rash, itching, sensitivity to bright light or sunlight, retention of fluids, fever, allergy, changes in composition of blood, nausea, vomiting, loss of appetite, stomach upset, diarrhea, enlargement of the breasts in males and females, increased or decreased sex drive, and increased or decreased blood sugar.

Less common side effects include agitation, inability to sleep, nightmares, feeling of panic, a peculiar taste in the mouth, stomach cramps, black coloration of the tongue, yellowing eyes and/or skin, changes in liver function, increased or decreased weight, excessive perspiration, flushing, frequent urination, drowsiness, dizziness, weakness, headache, loss of hair, nausea, and not feeling well.

Drug Interactions

Interaction with monoamine oxidase (MAO) inhibitors can cause high fevers, convulsions, and occasionally death. Don't take MAO inhibitors until at least 2 weeks after Amitriptyline has been discontinued.

In patients who require concomitant use of Amitriptyline and an MAO inhibitor, close medical observation is warranted.

Amitriptyline interacts with Guanethidine and Clonidine, drugs used to treat high blood pressure: If your doctor prescribes Amitriptyline and you are taking medicine for high blood pressure, be sure to discuss this with him.

Amitriptyline increases the effects of barbiturates, tranquilizers, other sedative drugs, and alcohol. Don't drink alcoholic beverages if you take this medicine.

Taking Amitriptyline and thyroid medicine will enhance the effects of the thyroid medicine. The combination can cause abnormal heart rhythms. The combination of Amitriptyline and Reserpine may cause overstimulation.

Large doses of Vitamin C (Ascorbic Acid) and oral contraceptives can reduce the effect of Amitriptyline, as can smoking. Drugs such as Bicarbonate of Soda, Acetazolamide, Quinidine, or Procainamide will increase the effect of Amitriptyline. Ritalin and phenothiazine drugs such as Thorazine and Compazine block the metabolism of Amitriptyline, causing it to stay in the body longer. This can cause possible overdose.

The combination of Amitriptyline with large doses of the sleeping pill Ethchlorvynol has caused patients to experience passing delirium.

Food Interactions

Take this drug on an empty stomach. If it upsets your stomach you may take it with food.

Usual Dose

Adult: 25 milligrams 3 times per day, which may be increased to 150 milligrams per day if necessary. The medication must be tailored to the needs of the patient.

Adolescent and senior: lower doses are recommended—generally, 30 to 50 milligrams per day.

Overdosage

Symptoms are confusion, inability to concentrate, hallucinations, drowsiness, lowered body temperature, abnormal heart rate, heart failure, enlarged pupils of the eyes, convulsions, severely lowered blood pressure, stupor, and coma (as well as agitation, stiffening of body muscles, vomiting, and high fever). The patient should be taken to a hospital emergency room immediately. ALWAYS bring the medicine bottle.

Special Information

Avoid alcohol and other drugs that depress the nervous system while taking this antidepressant.

Do not stop taking this medicine unless your doctor has specifically told you to do so. Abruptly stopping this medicine may cause nausea, headache, and a sickly feeling.

This medicine can cause drowsiness, dizziness, and blurred vision. Be careful when driving or operating complicated machinery. Avoid exposure to the sun or sun lamps for long periods of time.

Call your doctor if dry mouth, difficulty urinating, or excessive sedation develops.

Do not double the dose if you forget to take one. Skip it and go back to you regular schedule.

Generic Name

Amoxapine

Brand Name

Asendin

Type of Drug

Antidepressant.

Prescribed for

Depression with or without symptoms of anxiety.

General Information

Amoxapine and other members of this group are effective in treating symptoms of depression. They can elevate mood, increase physical activity and mental alertness, and improve appetite and sleep patterns in a depressed patient. These drugs are mild sedatives and therefore useful in treating mild forms of depression associated with anxiety. You should not expect instant results with this medicine: Results are usually seen after 1 to 4 weeks. If symptoms are not affected after 6 to 8 weeks, contact your doctor. Occasionally this drug and other members of the group of drugs have been used in treating nighttime bed-wetting in young children, but they do not produce long-lasting relief; therapy with one of them for nighttime bed-wetting is of questionable value.

Cautions and Warnings

Do not take Amoxapine if you are allergic or sensitive to this or other members of this class of drug: Doxepin, Nortriptyline, Imipramine, Desipramine, and Amitriptyline. The drugs should not be used if you are recovering from a heart attack.

Amoxapine may be taken with caution if you have a history of epilepsy or other convulsive disorders, difficulty in urination, glaucoma, heart disease, or thyroid disease.

Pregnancy/Breast-feeding

This drug, like other antidepressants, crosses into your developing baby's circulation and may cause birth defects if taken during the first 3 months of pregnancy. There have been reports of newborn infants suffering from heart, breathing, and urinary problems after their mothers had taken an antidepressant of this type immediately before delivery. You should avoid taking this medication while pregnant.

Antidepressants of this type are known to pass into breast milk and may affect a breast-feeding infant, although this has not been proven. Nursing mothers should consider alternate feeding methods if taking this medicine.

Seniors

Older adults are more sensitive to the effects of this drug

and often require a lower dose than a younger adult to do the same job. Follow your doctor's directions and report any side effects at once.

Possible Side Effects

Possible side effects include changes in blood pressure (both high and low), abnormal heart rates, heart attack, confusion (especially in older adults), hallucinations, disorientation, delusions, anxiety, restlessness, excitement, numbness and tingling in the extremities, lack of coordination, muscle spasms or tremors, seizures and/or convulsions, dry mouth, blurred vision, constipation, inability to urinate, rash, itching, sensitivity to bright light or sunlight, retention of fluids, fever, allergy, changes in composition of blood, nausea, vomiting, loss of appetite, stomach upset, diarrhea, enlargement of the breasts in males and females, increased or decreased sex drive, and increased or decreased blood sugar.

Less common side effects include agitation, inability to sleep, nightmares, feelings of panic, a peculiar taste in the mouth, stomach cramps, black coloration of the tongue, yellowing eyes and/or skin, changes in liver function, increased or decreased weight, perspiration, flushing, frequent urination, drowsiness, dizziness, weakness, headache, loss of hair, nausea, and not feeling well.

Drug Interactions

Interaction with monoamine oxidase (MAO) inhibitors can cause high fevers, convulsions, and occasionally death. Don't take MAO inhibitors until at least 2 weeks after Amoxapine has been discontinued.

Certain patients may require concomitant use of Amoxapine and an MAO inhibitor, and in these situations close medical observation is warranted.

Amoxapine interacts with Guanethidine, a drug used to treat high blood pressure. If your doctor prescribes Amoxapine and you are taking medicine for high blood pressure, be sure to discuss this with him.

Amoxapine increases the effects of barbiturates, tranquilizers, other depressive drugs, and alcohol. Don't drink alcoholic beverages if you take this medicine.

Taking Amoxapine and thyroid medicine will enhance the effects of the thyroid medicine. The combination can cause abnormal heart rhythms.

Large doses of Vitamin C (Ascorbic Acid) can reduce the effect of Amoxapine. Drugs such as Bicarbonate of Soda or Acetazolamide will increase the effect of Amoxapine.

Food Interactions

This drug is best taken on an empty stomach, but can be taken with food if it upsets your stomach.

Usual Dose

Adult: 100 to 400 milligrams per day. Hospitalized patients may need up to 600 milligrams per day. The dose of this drug must be tailored to patient's need.

Senior: Lower doses are recommended: for people over 60 years of age, usually 50 to 300 milligrams per day.

Child (under age 16): This drug should not be used.

Overdosage

Symptoms are confusion, inability to concentrate, hallucinations, drowsiness, lowered body temperature, abnormal heart rate, heart failure, large pupils of the eyes, convulsions, severely lowered blood pressure, stupor, and coma (as well as agitation, stiffening of body muscles, vomiting, and high fever). The patient should be taken to a hospital emergency room immediately. ALWAYS bring the medicine bottle.

Special Information

Do not stop taking this medicine unless your doctor has specifically told you to do so. Abruptly stopping this medicine may cause nausea, headache, and a sickly feeling.

This medicine can cause drowsiness, dizziness, and blurred vision. Be careful when driving or operating complicated machinery.

Avoid exposure to the sun or sun lamps for long periods of time. Call your doctor if dry mouth, difficulty urinating, or excessive sedation develops.

If you forget to take a dose of Amoxapine, take it as soon

as you remember. If it is almost time for your next dose, skip the forgotten dose and continue with your regular schedule. Do not take a double dose of Amoxapine.

Type of Drug

Antacids

Brand Names

Aluminum Antacids

AlternaGel	Basaljel
Aluminum Hydroxide Gel	Dialume
Alu-Cap	Nephrox
Alu-Tab	Phosphaljel
Amphojel	Rolaids

Calcium Antacids

Alka-Mints	Dicarbosil
Amitone	Equilet
Anaids	Genalac
Calcilac	Glycate
Calcium Carbonate	Mallamint
Calglycine	Titracid
Chooz	Titralac
Diatrol	Tums
	Tums Extra Strength

Magnesium Antacids

Magnesium Oxide	Milk of Magnesia
Mag-Ox 400	Uro-Mag
Maox	

Sodium Bicarbonate Antacids

Bell/ans
Soda Mint
Sodium Bicarbonate

Aluminum + Magnesium Antacids

Alamag	Maalox TC
Algenic Alka	Magnagel
Algicon	Magnatril
Aludrox	Mintox
Kudrox	Riopan
Lowsium	Rulox
Maalox	WinGel

Aluminum + Magnesium + Sodium Antacids

Algenic Alka
Gaviscon

Calcium + Magnesium Antacids

Alkets	Marblen
Bicalma	Noralac
Bisodol	Spastosed

Calcium + Magnesium + Simethicone Antacids

Advanced Formula Di-Gel

Aluminum + Calcium + Magnesium Antacids

Camalox

Aluminum + Magnesium + Simethicone Antacids

Almacone	Maalox Plus
Alma-Mag	Mi-Acid
Anta Gel	Mintox Plus
Di-Gel	Mygel
Gelusil	Mylanta
Gelusil II	Mylanta II
Losotron Plus Liquid	Riopan Plus
Lowsium Plus	Simaal

Aluminum + Magnesium + Calcium + Simethicone Antacid

Tempo

Effervescent Powder or Tablet Antacids

Alka-Seltzer	Bisodol Powder
Alka-Seltzer with Aspirin	Bromo Seltzer
Citrocarbonate	Flavored Alka-Seltzer
ENO	

(Also available in generic form)

Type of Drug

Gastrointestinal acid antagonist.

Prescribed for

Relief of heartburn, acid indigestion, sour stomach, or other conditions related to an upset stomach. These drugs are also prescribed for excess acid in the stomach or intestine associated with ulcer, gastritis, esophagitis, and hiatal hernia. Antacid therapy will help these conditions to heal more quickly.

Aluminum antacids are prescribed for kidney failure patients to prevent phosphate from being absorbed into the body. Only Aluminum Hydroxide (any brand) and Basaljel have been shown to be useful as phosphate binders.

General Information

In spite of the large number of antacid products available on the market, there are basically only a few different kinds. All antacids work against stomach acid in the same way—by neutralizing the acid through a chemical reaction. The choice of an antacid is based upon its "neutralizing capacity," that is, how much acid is neutralized by a given amount of antacid. Sodium and calcium have the greatest capacity but should not be used for long-term or ulcer therapy because of the effects large amounts of sodium and calcium can have on your body. Of the other products, Magnesium Hydroxide has the greatest capacity. Next come mixtures of magnesium and aluminum compounds, Magnesium Trisilicate, Aluminum Hydroxide, and Aluminum Phosphates, in that order. The neutralizing capacity of an antacid product also depends upon how it is formulated, how much antacid is put in the mixture, and what the form of the mixture is. Antacid suspensions have greater neutralizing capacity than powders or tablets.

In most cases, the choice of an antacid product is based purely upon advertising, packaging, convenience, taste, or price. The similarity among so many products accounts for the vast amounts of advertising and promotion put behind antacid products.

Calcium antacids have been recommended as a source of supplemental calcium to prevent osteoporosis. Four to six tablets a day are needed to provide the proper amount of calcium. Although Tums has been widely recommended, any product listed in the section Calcium Antacids will do the job.

Cautions and Warnings

People with high blood pressure or heart failure, and those on low-sodium diets, must avoid antacids with a high sodium content. Many antacids are considered to be low in sodium, including Riopan. Your pharmacist can advise you which of these drugs are considered low-sodium antacids.

Sodium Bicarbonate is easily absorbed and may result in a condition called systemic alkalosis if it is taken for a long period of time. Magnesium antacids must be used with caution by patients with kidney disease.

Pregnancy/Breast-feeding

Antacids can be safely taken in moderation during pregnancy. Be sure your doctor knows you are taking antacids.

Antacids may be taken during breast-feeding.

Seniors

Seniors can safely use antacids without concern. Do not use excessive amounts of antacid unless so directed by your doctor.

Possible Side Effects

Possible side effects include diarrhea (magnesium products) and constipation (aluminum and calcium products). Aluminum/magnesium combinations are usually used to avoid affecting the bowel.

Kidney failure patients who take magnesium antacids may develop magnesium toxicity.

Calcium and sodium antacids may cause a rebound effect,

with more acid produced after the antacid is stopped than
before it was started.

Magnesium Trisilicate antacids used over long periods
may result in the development of silicate renal stones.

Drug Interactions

Antacids can interfere with the absorption of most drugs
into the body. Intake of antacids should be separated from
that of other oral drugs by 1 to 2 hours. Those drugs with
which antacids are known to interfere are anticholinergic
drugs, phenothiazines, Digoxin, Phenytoin, Isoniazid, Quinidine, Warfarin, iron-containing products, and tetracycline-
type antibiotics.

Food Interactions

Antacids are best taken on an empty stomach but may be
taken with food.

Usual Dose

The dose of antacids must be individualized to your requirement. For ulcers, antacids are given every hour for the first
2 weeks (during waking hours) and 1 to 3 hours after meals
and at bedtime thereafter.

Special Information

If you are using antacid tablets, be sure they are completely
chewed. Swallow with milk or water.

Aluminum antacids may cause speckling or add a whitish
coloration to the stool.

Severe stomach or abdominal pain, cramps, and nausea
may be a sign of appendicitis and cannot be treated with an
antacid.

Type of Drug

Antihistamine-Decongestant Combination Products

Brand Names

Ingredients: Azatadine + Pseudoephedrine

Trinalin

Ingredients: Brompheniramine + Phenylpropanolamine

Bromatapp
Dimaphen Time-Tabs
Dimetapp Extentabs

Ingredients: Chlorpheniramine + Pseudoephedrine

Anamine T.D.	Dura-Tap/PD
Brexin L.A.	Fedahist
Chlorafed	Isoclor
Chlordrine S.R.	Klerist D
Chlor-Trimeton	Kronofed-A
Decongestant	Myfedrine Plus
Codimal-L.A.	Napril
Cophene No. 2	ND Clear
Co-Pyronil 2	Novafed A
Dallergy-D	Pseudo-Chlor
Deconamine SR	Sudafed Plus
Denov	T-Dry
Duralex	

Ingredients: Chlorpheniramine + Phenylephrine

Alersule	Demazin
Coltab Children's	Histatab-Plus

Ingredients: Chlorpheniramine + Phenylpropanolamine

Allerest 12 Hour	Demazin
Chlor-Rest	Drize
Condrin L.A	Dura Vent/A
Conex D.A.	Gencold
Contac 12 Hour	Oragest S.R.
Dehist	Ornade

Resaid S.R.   Triaminic-12
Rhinolar-EX 12   Tri-Nefrin Extra Strength
Ru-Tuss II

Ingredients: Chlorpheniramine + Phenytoloxamine + Phenylephrine + Phenylpropanolamine

Decongestabs   New-Decongest
Histamic   Quadra-Hist
Naldecon   Tri-phen-chlor
Nalgest   Uni-Decon

Ingredients: Clemastine + Phenylpropanolamine

Tavist-D

Ingredients: Dexbrompheniramine + Pseudoephedrine

Dexaphen S.A.   Disophrol/Disophrol
Dexophed   Chronotabs
Disobrom   Drixoral
                               Resporal

(Also available in generic form)

Ingredients: Pseudoephedrine + Terfenadine

Seldane-D

Ingredients: Pseudoephedrine + Triprolidine

Actagen   Genac
Actifed   Trifed
Allerfrin   Tripodrine
Aprodine   Triposed
Cenafed Plus

(Also available in generic form)

Prescribed for

These products are prescribed to relieve symptoms of the common cold, allergy, or other upper respiratory condition, including sneezing, watery eyes, runny nose, itching or scratchy throat, and nasal congestion.

General Information

These products are among the hundreds of different cold and allergy remedies available on both a prescription-only and non-prescription basis. The basic formula that appears in each of these is always the same: an antihistamine to relieve allergy symptoms and a decongestant to treat the symptoms of either a cold or allergy.

Most of these products are taken several times a day, while others are taken once or twice a day because of their natural long-acting effect or the fact that they have been put into a special long-acting dosage form. Since nothing can cure a cold or allergy, the best you can hope to achieve from this or any other cold and allergy remedy is simply symptom relief.

Cautions and Warnings

The antihistamines in these products can cause drowsiness. Clemastine, the antihistamine ingredient in Tavist-D, and Terfenadine, the antihistamine ingredient in Seldane-D, are distinguishable from other products because they cause less drowsiness. The decongestant ingredient can cause you to become overly anxious and nervous and may interfere with sleep.

Pregnancy/Breast-feeding

The ingredients in these products have not been proven to be a cause of birth defects or other problems in pregnant women, although studies in animals have shown that some antihistamines, used mainly against nausea and vomiting, may cause birth defects. Do not take any of these products without your doctor's knowledge.

Small amounts of antihistamine or decongestant medicines pass into breast milk and may affect a nursing infant. Nursing mothers should either not take this medicine or use alternative feeding methods while taking it.

Seniors

Seniors are more sensitive to the side effects of these medications. Confusion, difficult or painful urination, dizziness, drowsiness, a faint feeling, dry mouth, nose, or throat, nightmares or excitement, nervousness, restlessness, or irritability are more likely to occur among older adults.

Possible Side Effects

Possible side effects include restlessness, sleeplessness, excitation, nervousness, drowsiness, sedation, dizziness, poor coordination, and upset stomach.

Less common side effects are low blood pressure, heart palpitations, chest pain, rapid heart beat and abnormal heart rhythm, anemia, fatigue, confusion, tremors, headache, irritability, a "high" feeling, tingling or heaviness in the hands, tingling in the feet or legs, blurred or double vision, convulsions, hysterical reactions, ringing or buzzing in the ears, fainting, changes in appetite (increase or decrease), nausea, vomiting, diarrhea or constipation, frequent urination, difficulty urinating, early periods, loss of sex drive, difficulty breathing, wheezing with chest tightness, stuffed nose, itching, rashes, unusual sensitivity to the sun, chills, excessive perspiration, and dry mouth, nose, or throat.

Drug Interactions

Interaction with alcoholic beverages, tranquilizers, antianxiety drugs, and narcotic-type pain relievers may lead to excessive drowsiness or difficulty concentrating.

These products should be avoided if you are taking a monoamine oxidase (MAO) inhibitor for depression or high blood pressure, because the MAO inhibitor may cause a very rapid rise in blood pressure or increase some side effects (dry mouth and nose, blurred vision, abnormal heart rhythms).

The decongestant portion of these products may interfere with the normal effects of blood-pressure-lowering medicines and can aggravate diabetes, heart disease, hyperthyroid disease, high blood pressure, a prostate condition, stomach ulcers, and urinary blockage.

Food Interactions

These drugs are best taken on an empty stomach but may be taken with food if they upset your stomach.

Usual Dose

One tablet or capsule every 4 to 12 hours, depending on the product.

Overdosage

The main symptoms of overdose are drowsiness, chills, dry mouth, fever, nausea, nervousness, irritability, rapid or irregular heartbeat, heart pains, and urinary difficulty. Most cases of overdose are not severe, but should be treated by inducing vomiting and then taking the victim to a hospital emergency room. ALWAYS bring the medicine container with you. Call your local poison control center for more information.

Special Information

Since the antihistamine component of these medicines can slow your central nervous system, you must take extra caution while doing anything that requires concentration, such as driving a car.

Call your doctor if your side effects are severe or gradually become intolerable. There are so many different cold and allergy products available to choose from that one is sure to be the right combination for you.

If you forget to take a dose of your medicine, take it as soon as you remember. If it is almost time for your next dose, skip the one you forgot and go back to your regular schedule. Do not take a double dose.

Generic Name

Aspirin, Buffered Aspirin

Brand Names

A.S.A.	Ecotrin Maximum Strength
Aspergum	Empirin
Bayer	Genprin
Bayer Children's Aspirin	Measurin
Bayer 8 Hour	Norwich Extra-Strength
Easprin	Verin
Ecotrin	ZORprin

Buffered Aspirin

Arthritis Pain Formula	Buffex
Alka-Seltzer	Buffinol
Ascriptin	Cama Arthritis Strength
Ascriptin A/D	Magnaprin Arthritis Strength
Ascriptin Extra Strength	Wesprin Buffered
Bufferin	

(Also available in generic form)

Type of Drug

Analgesic; anti-inflammatory.

Prescribed for

Mild to moderate pain; fever; inflammation of bones, joints, or other body tissues; reducing the probability that men who have had a stroke or TIA (oxygen shortage to the brain) because of a problem with blood coagulation will have another such attack. Aspirin may also be prescribed as an anticoagulant (blood-thinning) drug in people with unstable angina, and to protect against heart attack, although it has not been approved by the government for this purpose.

General Information

Aspirin is probably the closest thing we have to a wonder drug. It has been used for more than a century as a pain and fever remedy but is now used for its effect on the blood as well.

Aspirin is the standard against which all other drugs are compared for pain relief and for reduction of inflammation. Chemically, Aspirin is a member of the group called salicylates. Other salicylates include Sodium Salicylate, Sodium Thiosalicylate, Choline Salicylate, and Magnesium Salicylate (Trilisate). These drugs are no more effective than regular Aspirin, although 2 of them (Choline Salicylate and Magnesium Salicylate) may be a little less irritating to the stomach. They are all more expensive than Aspirin.

Scientists have discovered how Aspirin works. It reduces fever by causing the blood vessels in the skin to open, thereby allowing heat from our body to leave more rapidly. Its effects on pain and inflammation are thought to be related to its ability to prevent the manufacture of complex body hormones called prostaglandins. Of all the salicylates, Aspirin has the greatest effect on prostaglandin production.

Many people find that they can take Buffered Aspirin but not regular Aspirin. The addition of antacids to Aspirin can be important to patients who must take large doses of Aspirin for chronic arthritis or other conditions. In many cases, Aspirin is the only effective drug and it can be tolerated only with the antacids present.

Cautions and Warnings

People with liver damage should avoid Aspirin. People who are allergic to Aspirin may also be allergic to drugs such as Indomethacin, Sulindac, Ibuprofen, Fenoprofen, Naproxen, Tolmetin, and Meclofenamate Sodium or to products containing tartrazine (a commonly used orange dye and food coloring). People with asthma and/or nasal polyps are more likely to be allergic to Aspirin.

Reye's syndrome is a life-threatening condition characterized by vomiting and stupor or dullness and may develop in children with influenza (flu) or chicken pox if treated with Aspirin or other Salicylates. Because of this, the U.S. Surgeon General, Centers for Disease Control, and pediatric physicians' associations advise against the use of Aspirin or other salicylates in children under age 17. Acetaminophen-containing products are suggested instead.

Aspirin can interfere with normal blood coagulation and should be avoided for 1 week before surgery for this reason. It would be wise to ask your surgeon or dentist their recommendation before taking Aspirin for pain after surgery.

Pregnancy/Breast-feeding

Check with your doctor before taking any Aspirin-containing product during pregnancy. Aspirin can cause bleeding problems in the developing fetus during the last 2 weeks of pregnancy. Taking Aspirin during the last 3 months of pregnancy may lead to a low-birth-weight infant, prolong labor, and extend the length of pregnancy; it can also cause bleeding in the mother before, during, or after delivery.

Aspirin has not caused any problems among nursing mothers or their infants.

Seniors

Aspirin, especially in the larger doses that an older adult may take to treat arthritis and rheumatic conditions, may be irritating to the stomach.

Possible Side Effects

Possible side effects include nausea, upset stomach, heartburn, loss of appetite, and loss of small amounts of blood in the stool. Aspirin may contribute to the formation of a stomach ulcer and bleeding.

Drug Interactions

People taking anticoagulants (blood-thinning drugs) should avoid Aspirin. The effect of the anticoagulant will be increased.

Aspirin may increase the possibility of stomach ulcer when taken together with adrenal corticosteroids, Phenylbutazone, or alcoholic beverages.

Aspirin will counteract the uric-acid-eliminating effect of Probenecid and Sulfinpyrazone.

Food Interactions

Since Aspirin can cause upset stomach or bleeding, take each dose with food, milk, or a glass of water.

Usual Dose

Adult: for aches, pains, and fever, 325 to 650 milligrams every 4 hours; for arthritis and rheumatic conditions, up to 5200 milligrams (16 325-milligram tablets) per day; for rheumatic fever, up to 7800 milligrams (24 325-milligram tablets) per day; to prevent heart attack, stroke, or TIA in men, 325 milligrams 2 to 4 times per day.

Child: not recommended for children age 16 or younger. Consult your doctor for more information.

Overdosage

Symptoms of mild overdosage are rapid and deep breathing, nausea, vomiting, dizziness, ringing or buzzing in the ears, flushing, sweating, thirst, headache, drowsiness, diarrhea, and rapid heartbeat.

Severe overdosage may cause fever, excitement, confusion, convulsions, coma, or bleeding.

The initial treatment of Aspirin overdose involves making the patient vomit to remove any Aspirin remaining in the stomach. Further therapy depends on how the situation develops and what must be done to maintain the patient. DO NOT INDUCE VOMITING UNTIL YOU HAVE SPOKEN WITH YOUR DOCTOR OR POISON CONTROL CENTER. If in doubt, go to a hospital emergency room.

Special Information

Contact your doctor if you develop a continuous stomach pain or a ringing or buzzing in the ears.

If you take Aspirin on a regular basis and forget to take a dose, take it as soon as you remember. If it is almost time for your next dose, skip the forgotten dose and continue with your regular schedule.

Generic Name

Aspirin with Codeine

Brand Names

Aspirin with Codeine
Empirin with Codeine

(Also available in generic form)

Type of Drug

Narcotic analgesic.

Prescribed for

Relief of mild to moderate pain.

General Information

Aspirin with Codeine is one of many combination products containing narcotics and analgesics. These products often contain barbiturates or tranquilizers, and Acetaminophen may be substituted for Aspirin and/or Caffeine may be omitted.

Cautions and Warnings

Do not take Codeine if you know you are allergic or sensitive to it. Use this drug with extreme caution if you suffer from asthma or other breathing problems. Long-term use of this drug may cause drug dependence or addiction. Codeine is a respiratory depressant and affects the central nervous system, producing sleepiness, tiredness, and/or inability to concentrate.

Do not take this product if you are allergic to Aspirin, any salicylate, or a nonsteroidal anti-inflammatory drug (NSAID). Check with your doctor or pharmacist if you are not sure. This and all other Aspirin-containing products should not be taken by children under age 17.

Pregnancy/Breast-feeding

Check with your doctor before taking any Aspirin-containing product during pregnancy. Aspirin can cause bleeding problems in the developing fetus during the last 2 weeks of pregnancy. Taking Aspirin during the last 3 months of pregnancy may lead to a low-birth-weight infant, prolong labor, and extend the length of pregnancy; it can also cause bleeding in the mother before, during, or after delivery.

Codeine has not been associated with birth defects, but taking too much Codeine, or any other narcotic, during pregnancy can lead to the birth of a drug-dependent infant and can lead to drug withdrawal symptoms in the baby. All narcotics, including Codeine, can cause breathing problems in the newborn if taken just before delivery.

Aspirin with Codeine has not caused any problems among nursing mothers or their infants.

Seniors

The Codeine in this combination product may have more of a depressant effect on seniors than on younger adults. Other effects that may be more prominent are dizziness, light-headedness, or fainting when rising suddenly from a sitting or lying position.

Possible Side Effects

The most frequent side effects are light-headedness, dizziness, sleepiness, nausea, vomiting, loss of appetite, and sweating. If these occur, consider calling your doctor and asking him about lowering the dose of Codeine you are taking. Usually the side effects disappear if you simply lie down.

More serious side effects of Aspirin with Codeine are shallow breathing or difficulty in breathing.

Less common side effects include euphoria (feeling "high"), weakness, sleepiness, headache, agitation, uncoordinated muscle movement, minor hallucinations, disorientation and visual disturbances, dry mouth, loss of appetite, constipation, flushing of the face, rapid heartbeat, palpitations, faintness, urinary difficulties or hesitancy, reduced sex drive and/or potency, itching, rashes, anemia, lowered blood sugar, and yellowing of the skin and/or whites of the eyes. Narcotic analgesics may aggravate convulsions in those who have had convulsions in the past.

Drug Interactions

Interaction with alcohol, tranquilizers, barbiturates, or sleeping pills produces tiredness, sleepiness, or inability to concentrate and seriously increases the depressive effect of Aspirin with Codeine.

The Aspirin component of Aspirin with Codeine can affect anticoagulant (blood-thinning) therapy. Be sure to discuss this with your doctor so that the proper dosage adjustment can be made.

Interaction with adrenal corticol steroids, Phenylbutazone, or alcohol can cause severe stomach irritation with possible bleeding.

Food Interactions

Take with food or half a glass of water to prevent stomach upset.

Usual Dose

1 to 2 tablets 3 to 4 times per day.

Overdosage

Symptoms are depression of respiration (breathing), extreme tiredness progressing to stupor and then coma, pinpointed pupils of the eyes, no response to stimulation such as a pin stick, cold and clammy skin, slowing down of the heartbeat, lowering of blood pressure, convulsions, and cardiac arrest. The patient should be taken to a hospital emergency room immediately. ALWAYS bring the medicine bottle.

Special Information

Drowsiness may occur: Be careful when driving or operating hazardous machinery.

If you forget a dose of Aspirin with Codeine, take it as soon as you remember. If it is almost time for your next dose, skip the one you forgot and continue with your regular schedule. Do not take a double dose of Aspirin with Codeine.

Generic Name

Astemizole

Brand Name

Hismanal

Type of Drug

Antihistamine.

Prescribed for

Seasonal allergy, stuffed and runny nose, itching of the eyes, scratchy throat caused by allergies, and other symptoms of allergy, such as rash, itching, or hives.

General Information

Astemizole is a non-sedating antihistamine. It may be used by people who find other antihistamines unacceptable because of the drowsiness and tiredness they cause. Astemizole appears to work in exactly the same way as Chlorpheniramine and other widely used antihistamines.

Cautions and Warnings

Astemizole should not be taken by people who have had an allergic reaction to it in the past. People with asthma or other deep-breathing problems, glaucoma (pressure in the eye), or stomach ulcer or other stomach problems should avoid Astemizole because it may aggravate these problems.

Pregnancy/Breast-feeding

Astemizole has been studied in lab animals and found to cause no damage to a developing fetus. Nevertheless, this drug should be used by a pregnant woman only if it is absolutely necessary.

Nursing mothers should avoid using this drug. Temporarily suspend breast-feeding if you must use Astemizole.

Seniors

Older adults may be more sensitive to the side effects of Astemizole and should be treated with the minimum effective dose, 10 milligrams per day.

Possible Side Effects

Occasional side effects include headache; nervousness; weakness; upset stomach; nausea; vomiting; dry mouth, nose, or throat; cough; stuffed nose; nervousness; weakness; change in bowel habits; sore throat; and nosebleeds. In scientific studies Astemizole was found to cause the same amount of drowsiness as a placebo (inactive pill) and about half of the other antihistamines sold in the United States. Most commonly used antihistamines cause more sedation than Astemizole.

Less common side effects of Astemizole include hair loss, allergic reactions, depression, sleeplessness, menstrual irregularities, muscle aches, sweating, tingling in the hands or feet, frequent urination, and visual disturbances. A few people taking this drug have developed liver damage.

Drug Interactions

Antihistamines may decrease the effects of oral anticoagulant (blood-thinning) drugs.

Food Interactions

Astemizole should be taken 1 hour before or 2 hours after food or meals.

Usual Dose

Adult and child (over age 12): 10 milligrams once a day. Your doctor may prescribe 30 milligrams on the first day, 20 milligrams on the second day, and 10 milligrams a day thereafter to increase the speed with which the drug takes effect.

Child (under 12): not recommended.

Overdosage

Astemizole overdose is likely to cause exaggerated side effects. People who have taken an Astemizole overdose should be given Syrup of Ipecac to cause vomiting and taken to a hospital emergency room for treatment. ALWAYS remember to bring the prescription bottle with you.

Special Information

You should report any unusual side effects to your doctor.

Astemizole's only disadvantage is its cost. Equally effective antihistamines are sold without a prescription and can be purchased for relatively little money. This drug is sold by prescription only and is rather costly when compared to over-the-counter products.

If you forget to take a dose of Astemizole, take it as soon as you remember. If it is almost time for your next dose, skip the forgotten dose and continue with your regular schedule. Do not take a double dose of Astemizole.

Generic Name

Atenolol

Brand Name

Tenormin

Type of Drug

Beta-adrenergic blocking agent.

Prescribed for

High blood pressure and angina. It may also be prescribed by your doctor to treat severe headaches, abnormal heart rhythms, overactive thyroid, and mitral valve prolapse and to prevent second heart attacks in people who have already had one.

General Information

Atenolol is much like Metoprolol, another beta blocker with specific effects on the heart and less specific effects on the blood vessels and respiratory tract than Propranolol, the first beta blocker available in the United States. It is thought that beta blockers lower blood pressure by affecting body hormone systems and the heart, but the exact mechanism is not known. Atenolol and Metoprolol cause fewer side effects than Propranolol because of the specific nature of their effect on the heart.

Cautions and Warnings

You should be cautious about taking Atenolol if you have asthma, severe heart failure, very slow heart rate, or heart block because the drug can aggravate these conditions. Compared with the other beta blockers, Atenolol has less of an effect on your pulse and bronchial muscles and less of a rebound effect when the drug is discontinued, and it produces less tiredness, depression, and intolerance to exercise than other beta-blocking drugs.

People with angina who take Atenolol for high blood pressure should have their drug dosage reduced gradually over 1 to 2 weeks rather than suddenly discontinued. This will avoid possible aggravation of the angina.

Atenolol should be used with caution if you have liver disease because your ability to eliminate the drug from your body will be impaired.

Pregnancy/Breast-feeding

Animal studies in which rats were given 150 times the human dose of Atenolol revealed no adverse effects of Atenolol on the developing baby. However, Atenolol should be avoided by pregnant women or women who might become pregnant while taking it. When the drug is considered essential by your doctor, the potential risk of taking the medicine must be carefully weighed against the benefit it might produce.

Small amounts of Atenolol may pass into your breast milk. Nursing mothers taking this drug must observe their infants for possible drug-related side effects.

Seniors

Senior citizens may be more or less sensitive to the effects of Atenolol than young adults and require a different dose to achieve the same effect. Your dosage of this drug must be adjusted to your individual needs by your doctor. Seniors may be more likely to suffer from cold hands and feet and reduced body temperature, chest pains, a general feeling of ill health, sudden difficulty breathing, sweating, or changes in heartbeat because of this medicine.

Possible Side Effects

Atenolol side effects are relatively uncommon, usually develop early in the course of treatment, are relatively mild, and are rarely a reason to stop taking the medication. Side effects increase with increasing dosage and include dizziness, tingling of the scalp, nausea, vomiting, upset stomach, taste distortion, fatigue, sweating, male impotence, urinary difficulty, diarrhea, bile duct blockage, breathing difficulty, bronchial spasms, muscle weakness, cramps, dry eyes, blurred vision, skin rash, hair loss, and facial swelling. Like other beta blockers, Atenolol can cause mental depression, disorientation, short-term memory loss, and emotional instability.

Rare side effects include aggravation of lupus erythematosus (a disease of the body's connective tissues), stuffy nose, chest pains, colitis, drug allergy (fever, sore throat), and unusual bleeding or bruising.

Drug Interactions

Beta-blocking drugs may interact with surgical anesthetics to increase the risk of heart problems during surgery. Some anesthesiologists recommend stopping your beta blocker gradually 2 days before surgery.

Atenolol may interfere with the normal signs of low blood sugar and can interfere with the action of Insulin or oral antidiabetes medicines.

Taking Atenolol together with Aspirin-containing drugs, Indomethacin, or Sulfinpyrazone can interfere with its blood-pressure-lowering effect.

The effects of Atenolol may be increased by Phenothiazine antipsychotic medicines with other antihypertensives like Clonidine, Diazoxide, Nifedipine, Reserpine, or with other drugs that can reduce blood pressure, like Nitroglycerin.

Atenolol may interfere with the effectiveness of some anti-asthma drugs, especially Ephedrine and Isoproterenol, and with Theophylline or Aminophylline.

The combination of Atenolol and Phenytoin or digitalis drugs can result in excessive slowing of the heart and possible heart block.

Estrogen drugs can interfere with the blood-pressure-lowering effect of Atenolol.

Food Interactions

Take this medicine with food if it upsets your stomach.

Usual Dose

Starting dose, 50 milligrams per day, taken all at once. The daily dose may be gradually increased up to 200 milligrams. Maintenance dose, 50 to 200 milligrams given once a day. People with kidney disease may need only 50 milligrams every other day.

Senior: Older adults may respond to lower doses of this drug than younger adults and should be treated more cautiously.

Overdosage

Symptoms are changes in heartbeat (unusually slow, unusually fast, or irregular), severe dizziness or fainting, difficult breathing, bluish-colored fingernails or palms of the hands, and seizures. Take the overdose victim to a hospital emergency room for treatment. ALWAYS remember to bring the medicine bottle with you.

Special Information

Atenolol is meant to be taken on a continuing basis. Do not stop taking it unless directed to do so by your doctor. Possible side effects of abrupt withdrawal of Atenolol are chest pain, difficulty breathing, sweating, and unusually fast or irregular heartbeat.

Call your doctor at once if any of the following symptoms develop: back or joint pains, difficulty breathing, cold hands or feet, depression, skin rash, changes in heartbeat.

Call your doctor about the following side effects only if they persist or are bothersome: anxiety, diarrhea, constipation, sexual impotence, mild dizziness, headache, itching, nausea or vomiting, nightmares or vivid dreams, upset stomach, trouble sleeping, stuffed nose, frequent urination, unusual tiredness or weakness.

If you forget to take a dose of Atenolol, take it as soon as possible. If it is within 8 hours of your next dose, go back to your regular dose schedule and skip the missed dose.

Generic Name

Azatadine Maleate

Brand Name

Optimine

Type of Drug

Antihistamine.

Prescribed for

Seasonal allergy, stuffed and runny nose, itching of the eyes, scratching of the throat caused by allergy, and other allergic symptoms such as itching, rash, or hives.

General Information

Antihistamines, including Azatadine, generally act by blocking the release of histamine from the cell at the H_1 histamine receptor site. Antihistamines work by drying up the secretions of the nose, throat, and eyes.

Cautions and Warnings

Azatadine Maleate should not be used if you are allergic to this drug. It should be avoided or used with extreme care if you have narrow-angle glaucoma (pressure in the eye), stomach ulcer or other stomach problems, enlarged prostate, or problems passing urine. It should not be used by people who have deep-breathing problems such as asthma.

Use with care if you have a history of thyroid disease, heart disease, high blood pressure, or diabetes.

Pregnancy/Breast-feeding

Azatadine has not been proven to be a cause of birth defects or other problems in pregnant women, although studies in animals have shown that some other antihistamines (Meclizine and Cyclizine), used mainly against nausea and vomiting, may cause birth defects. Do not take any antihistamine without your doctor's knowledge.

Small amounts of antihistamine medicines pass into breast milk and may affect a nursing infant. Nursing mothers should avoid antihistamines or use alternative feeding methods while taking the medicine.

Seniors

Seniors are more sensitive to antihistamine side effects. Confusion, difficult or painful urination, dizziness, drowsiness, a faint feeling, nightmares or excitement, nervousness, restlessness, irritability, and dry mouth, nose, or throat are more likely to occur among older adults.

Possible Side Effects

Occasionally seen are itching, rash, sensitivity to light, excessive perspiration, chills, lowering of blood pressure, headache, rapid heartbeat, sleeplessness, dizziness, disturbed coordination, confusion, restlessness, nervousness, irritability, euphoria (feeling high), tingling of the hands and feet, blurred vision, double vision, ringing in the ears, stomach upset, loss of appetite, nausea, vomiting, constipation, diarrhea, difficulty in urination, tightness of the chest, wheezing, nasal stuffiness, and dryness of the mouth, nose, and throat.

Drug Interactions

Azatadine Maleate should not be taken with monoamine oxidase (MAO) inhibitors.

Interactions with tranquilizers, sedatives, and sleeping medication will increase the effect of these drugs; it is extremely important that you discuss this with your doctor so that doses of these drugs can be properly adjusted.

Be extremely cautious when drinking alcohol while taking Azatadine Maleate, which will enhance the intoxicating effect of the alcohol. Alcohol also has a sedative effect.

Usual Dose

1 to 2 milligrams twice per day.

Overdosage

Symptoms are depression or stimulation (especially in children), dry mouth, fixed or dilated pupils, flushing of the skin, and stomach upset. Take the patient to a hospital emergency room immediately if you cannot make him or her vomit. ALWAYS bring the medicine bottle.

Special Information

Antihistamines produce a depressing effect: Be extremely cautious when driving or operating heavy equipment.

If you forget a dose of Azatadine, take it as soon as you remember. If it is almost time for your next dose, skip the forgotten dose and continue with your regular schedule. Do not take a double dose of Azatadine.

Generic Name

Beclomethasone

Brand Names

Beclovent Inhalation Aerosol	Vancenase Nasal Inhaler
Beconase Inhalation Aerosol	Vancenase AQ Nasal Spray
Beconase AQ Nasal Spray	Vanceril Inhaler

Type of Drug

Adrenal corticosteroid.

Prescribed for

Treatment of chronic asthma.

General Information

Beclomethasone is used as an inhaler by mouth and as an intranasal product to relieve symptoms associated with seasonal allergy. It works by reducing inflammation of the mucosal lining within the bronchi, thereby making it easier to breathe. This drug should not be used for more than 3 weeks if it has not worked within that time. Beclomethasone will not work immediately, as a decongestant would; it may take several days to exert its effect.

Cautions and Warnings

Do not use this drug if you are allergic to Beclomethasone. This drug cannot be used as the primary treatment of severe asthma. It is only for people who usually take Prednisone, or another adrenal corticosteroid, by mouth and those who are taking other asthma drugs but are still having asthmatic attacks.

Even though this drug is taken by inhaling directly into the lungs or nose, it should be considered a potent adrenal corticosteroid drug. During periods of severe stress, you may have to go back to taking steroid drugs by mouth if Beclomethasone does not control your asthma.

Pregnancy/Breast-feeding

Large amounts of Beclomethasone used during pregnancy or breast-feeding may slow the growth of newborn babies. This drug may cause birth defects or interfere with your baby's development. Check with your doctor before taking it if you are, or might be, pregnant.

This medicine may pass into breast milk and cause unwanted effects in nursing infants.

Seniors

Older adults may use this medication without special precautions. Be sure your doctor knows if you suffer from bone disease, colitis, diabetes, bowel disease, glaucoma, fungus infection, heart disease, herpes infection, high blood pressure, high blood cholesterol, kidney disease, liver disease, or underactive thyroid.

Possible Side Effects

Possible side effects include dry mouth and hoarseness.

Rarely, deaths have occurred in patients taking adrenal corticosteroid tablets or syrup who are switched to Beclomethasone by inhalation due to failure of the adrenal gland. This is a rare complication and usually results from stopping the liquid or tablets too quickly. They must be stopped gradually over a long period of time.

This drug can also cause rash or spasm of the bronchial muscles.

Usual Dose

Intranasal inhalation:
    Adult and child (over age 12): 1 inhalation in each nostril 2 to 4 times per day.
    Child (under age 12): not recommended.
Oral inhalation:
    Adult and child (over age 12): 6 to 20 inhalations per day.
    Child (age 6 to 12): 3 to 10 inhalations per day.

Special Information

People using both Beclomethasone and a bronchodilator by inhalation should use the bronchodilator first, wait a few minutes, then use the Beclomethasone. This will allow more Beclomethasone to be absorbed.

This drug is for preventive therapy only and will not affect an asthma attack. Beclomethasone must be inhaled regularly, as directed. Wait at least 1 minute between inhalations.

Dry mouth or hoarseness may be reduced by rinsing your mouth after each use of the inhaler.

Shake well before each use.

If you forget a dose of Beclomethasone, take it as soon as you remember. If it is almost time for your next dose, skip the forgotten dose and continue with your regular schedule. Do not take a double dose of Beclomethasone.

Generic Name
Benazepril Hydrochloride

Brand Name
Lotensin

Type of Drug
Antihypertensive.

Prescribed for
High blood pressure. This medicine may be taken alone or with a thiazide-type diuretic. Other members of the same drug class (ACE inhibitors) are used to treat heart failure.

General Information
This medicine belongs to a class of drugs, the ACE inhibitors, that work by preventing the conversion of a potent hormone called Angiotensin 1. This directly affects the production of other hormones and enzymes that participate in the regulation of blood pressure. Benazepril begins working about an hour after you take it.

Some people taking Benazepril with a diuretic experience a rapid blood-pressure drop. To prevent this from happening, your doctor may tell you to stop taking the diuretic 2 or 3 days before starting Benazepril; he or she may have you start the diuretic again if your blood pressure is not controlled by Benazepril alone.

Cautions and Warnings
Benazepril should not be taken if you have had an allergic reaction to it in the past. It can, rarely, cause very low blood pressure, and it can affect your kidneys, especially if you have congestive heart failure. It is advisable for your doctor to check your urine for changes during the first few months of treatment. Benazepril can raise your blood potassium level and can affect white-blood-cell count, possibly increasing your susceptibility to infection. Dosage adjustment is necessary if you have reduced kidney function, but is not needed if you have liver disease.

Pregnancy/Breast-feeding

ACE inhibitors have caused low blood pressure, kidney failure, slow formation of the skull, and death in developing fetuses when taken during the last 6 months of pregnancy. The specific effect of Benazepril is not known. Therefore, it should be used with caution by women who are, or might become, pregnant.

Small amounts of Benazepril will pass into breast milk. The effect on a nursing infant is likely to be minimal because of the very small amount received. Nursing mothers who must take this drug should consider an alternative feeding method.

Seniors

Older adults may be more sensitive to the effects of this drug than younger adults. The dosage of Benazepril must be individualized to your needs.

Possible Side Effects

Dizziness, tiredness, headache, nausea, and cough are most common.

Less common side effects include itching, fever, chest pain, stomach pain, low blood pressure, heart palpitations, sleeping difficulty, tingling in the hands or feet, nausea, vomiting, anxiety, sleeplessness, nervousness, reduced sex drive, muscle cramps or weakness, impotence, arthritis, muscle aches, asthma, bronchitis, sinus irritation, breathing difficulty, weakness, sweating, kidney problems, urinary infection, and swelling of the arms, legs, lips, face, and throat.

Drug Interactions

The blood-pressure-lowering effect of Benazepril is additive with diuretic drugs and beta-blockers. Any other drug that causes a rapid blood pressure drop should be used with caution if you are taking Benazepril. Benazepril may increase potassium levels in your blood, especially when taken with Dyazide or other potassium-sparing diuretics. Benazepril may increase the effects of Lithium; this combination should be used with caution.

Food Interactions

Benazepril may be taken without regard to food or meals. You may take it with food if it upsets your stomach.

Usual Dose

10 to 40 milligrams once or twice per day. People with poor kidney function may need less medicine to lower blood pressure.

Overdosage

The principal effect of Benazepril overdose is a rapid drop in blood pressure, as evidenced by dizziness or fainting. Take the overdose victim to a hospital emergency room immediately. ALWAYS remember to bring the medicine bottle.

Special Information

Call your doctor if you develop swelling of the face or throat, if you have sudden difficulty breathing, or if you develop a sore throat, mouth sores, abnormal heartbeat, chest pain, a persistent rash, or loss of taste perception.

You may get dizzy if you rise to your feet quickly from a sitting or lying position.

Avoid strenuous exercise and/or very hot weather because heavy sweating or dehydration can cause a rapid blood pressure drop.

Avoid nonprescription diet pills, decongestants, and stimulants that can raise blood pressure.

If you take Benazepril once a day and forget to take a dose, take it as soon as you remember. If it is almost time for your next dose, skip the one you forgot and continue with your regular schedule. Do not take a double dose.

If you take Benazepril twice a day and forget a dose, take it as soon as you remember. If it is almost time for your next dose, take one dose as soon as you remember and another in 5 or 6 hours, then go back to your regular schedule.

Generic Name

Benztropine Mesylate

Brand Name

Cogentin

(Also available in generic form)

Type of Drug

Anticholinergic.

Prescribed for

Treatment of Parkinson's disease or prevention or control of muscle spasms caused by other drugs, particularly phenothiazine drugs.

General Information

Benztropine Mesylate has an action on the body similar to that of Atropine Sulfate, but side effects are less frequent and less severe. It is an anticholinergic and has the ability to reduce muscle spasms. This property makes the drug useful in treating Parkinson's disease and other diseases associated with spasms of skeletal muscles.

Cautions and Warnings

Benztropine Mesylate should be used with caution if you have narrow-angle glaucoma, stomach ulcers, heart disease, obstructions in the gastrointestinal tract, prostatitis, or myasthenia gravis.

Pregnancy/Breast-feeding

Drugs of this type have not been proven to be a cause of birth defects or of other problems in pregnant women. However, women who are, or may become, pregnant while taking this medication should discuss the possibility of birth defects with their doctor and other therapies that may be substituted for this medicine.

This medication may reduce the amount of breast milk produced by a nursing mother. Infants are also particularly sensitive to Benztropine. Alternative feeding methods should be used.

Seniors

Seniors taking this medication on a regular basis may be more sensitive to drug side effects, including a predisposition to developing glaucoma and confusion, disorientation, agitation, and hallucinations.

Possible Side Effects

Possible side effects include difficulty in urination, constipation, blurred vision, and increased sensitivity to strong light. The effects may increase if Benztropine Mesylate is taken with antihistamines, phenothiazines, antidepressants, or other anticholinergic drugs.

Drug Interactions

Interaction with other anticholinergic drugs, including tricyclic antidepressants or phenothiazine drugs, may cause severe stomach upset or unusual abdominal pain. If this happens, contact your doctor.

Avoid over-the-counter remedies that contain Atropine or similar drugs. Your pharmacist can tell you the ingredients of over-the-counter drugs.

This drug should be used with caution by people taking barbiturates. Use alcoholic beverages with care while taking this drug.

This drug may reduce the absorption and therefore the effect of some drugs, including Levodopa, Haloperidol, and phenothiazines.

Food Interactions

This medicine is best taken on an empty stomach but may be taken with food if it upsets your stomach.

Usual Dose

0.5 to 6 milligrams per day, depending upon the disease being treated and patient's response.

Overdosage

Signs of drug overdose include clumsiness or unsteadiness;

severe drowsiness; severely dry mouth, nose, or throat; hallucinations; mood changes; difficulty breathing; rapid heartbeat; and unusually warm and dry skin. Overdose victims
should be taken to a hospital emergency room at once. AL-
WAYS bring the medicine bottle.

Special Information

Side effects of dry mouth, constipation, and sensitivity to
bright lights can be easily relieved with candy or gum, a
stool softener like Docusate, and sunglasses.

This medicine will reduce your tolerance to hot weather
because it makes you sweat less. Be careful not to become
overheated in hot weather because of the chance of developing heat stroke.

If you forget to take a dose of Benztropine, take it as soon
as you remember. If it is within 2 hours of your next regular
dose, go back to the regular schedule and skip the missed
dose.

Generic Name

Bepridil Hydrochloride

Brand Name

Vascor

Type of Drug

Calcium channel blocker.

Prescribed for

Prevention of angina-type heart pains.

General Information

Bepridil is one of several calcium channel blockers to be
marketed in the United States. These drugs work by blocking
the passage of calcium into heart and smooth muscle. Since
calcium is an essential factor in muscle contraction, any
drug that affects calcium in this way will interfere with the
contraction of these muscles. When this happens, the

amount of oxygen used by the muscles is also reduced. Therefore, Bepridil is used to treat angina, a type of heart pain related to poor oxygen supply to the heart muscles. Bepridil affects the movement of calcium only into muscle cells. It does not have any affect on calcium in the blood.

Cautions and Warnings

Do not take this drug if you have had an allergic reaction to it. It should be used with extreme caution if you have a history of problems related to heart rhythm.

Bepridil has caused serious derangement of heart rhythm and has affected white-blood-cell counts. Because of these cautions, Bepridil is usually reserved only for people who do not respond to other treatments.

Use Bepridil with caution if you have heart failure, since the drug can worsen the condition. Abruptly stopping this medication can cause increased chest pain. If you must stop, the drug dose should be gradually reduced.

People with serious liver disorders should use this product with care because it is primarily eliminated from the body by breakdown in the liver. Drug dosage should be reduced.

People with kidney problems need to have their Bepridil dosage adjusted because the drug's breakdown products pass out of the body through the kidneys.

Pregnancy/Breast-feeding

Bepridil has been found to affect the development of animal fetuses in laboratory studies. It has not caused human birth defects. Pregnant women, or those who might become pregnant while taking this drug, should not take it without their doctor's approval. When the drug is considered essential by your doctor, the potential risk of taking the medicine must be carefully weighed against the benefit it might produce.

Bepridil passes into breast milk. This drug has caused no problems among breast-fed infants. If you must take Bepridil, you should consider the potential effect on your infant before breast-feeding while taking this medicine.

Seniors

No problems have been reported in older adults. However, older adults are likely to have age-related reduction in kidney and/or liver function. This factor should be taken into account by your doctor when determining the dosage of this medication. Follow your doctor's directions and report any side effects at once. Older adults require more frequent monitoring by their doctors after treatment has started.

Possible Side Effects

Possible side effects include light-headedness, dizziness, drowsiness, nervousness, hand tremors, headache, stomach cramps, upset stomach, diarrhea, and appetite changes.

Less common side effects are swelling in the arms and legs, heart palpitations, very slow or very rapid heartbeat, depression, memory loss, tingling in the hands or feet, paranoia, psychosis, hallucinations, visual disturbances, loss of balance, difficulty sleeping, ringing or buzzing in the ears, anxiety, constipation, dry mouth, stomach gas, itching, rash, skin irritation, stuffed or runny nose, chest congestion, flu symptoms, sore throat, difficulty breathing, wheezing, sweating, reduced sex drive or poor performance, cough and respiratory infections, fever, joint pain, muscle weakness and pain, high blood pressure, flushing, abnormal heart rhythms, changes in how you taste food, and behavior changes.

Drug Interactions

Bepridil may interact with the beta-blocking drugs to cause heart failure, very low blood pressure, or an increased incidence of angina pain. However, in many cases these drugs have been taken together with no problem.

Bepridil may, in rare instances, increase the effects of anticoagulant (blood-thinning) drugs.

Bepridil may increase the amount of digoxin in the blood.

Additional drug interactions occur with other members of this class but have not been seen with Bepridil.

Food Interactions

Taking Bepridil with food has a minor effect on the absorption of the drug, but you may take it with food if it upsets your stomach.

Usual Dose

200 to 400 milligrams per day in 2 doses. Do not stop taking
this drug abruptly. The dosage should be gradually reduced
over a period of time.

Overdosage

Overdose of Bepridil can cause nausea, dizziness, weakness,
drowsiness, confusion, slurred speech, very low blood pressure, reduced heart efficiency, and unusual heart rhythms.
Victims of a Bepridil overdose should be taken to a hospital
emergency room for treatment. ALWAYS bring the medicine
bottle.

Special Information

Call your doctor if you develop swelling in the arms or legs,
difficulty breathing, abnormal heartbeat, increased heart
pains, dizziness, constipation, nausea, light-headedness, or
very low blood pressure.

   If you forget to take a dose of Bepridil, take it as soon as
you remember. If it is almost time for your next regularly
scheduled dose, skip the forgotten dose and continue with
your regular schedule. Do not take a double dose.

Generic Name

Betaxolol

Brand Names

Betoptic Sterile Ophthalmic Solution
Kerlone Tablets

Type of Drug

Beta-adrenergic blocking agent.

Prescribed for

High blood pressure; glaucoma.

General Information

Betaxolol is a member of the same group of drugs as Propanolol, Metoprolol, and the other beta blockers. It was used as an eyedrop for glaucoma for some time before it was introduced as an oral blood-pressure-lowering product. Other drugs have been studied more extensively than Betaxolol, but it is very similar to Acebutolol and Metoprolol in many ways.

When applied to the eye, Betaxolol eyedrops work in the same way as the other beta-blocker eyedrops, Timolol and Levobunolol. It reduces fluid pressure inside the eye by reducing the production of eye fluids and slightly increasing the rate at which fluids flow through and leave the eye. Beta-blocking eyedrops produce a greater drop in eye pressure than either Pilocarpine or Epinephrine but may be combined with these or other drugs to produce a more pronounced drop in eye pressure.

Betaxolol eyedrops differ from Timolol eyedrops in that they do not have an important effect on lung function or heart rate; thus, Betaxolol may be used by people who cannot use Timolol or Levobunolol because of the possible effect of those drugs on heart or lung function.

Betaxolol eyedrops should not be used by people who cannot take oral beta-blocking drugs, such as Propranolol.

Studies have shown Betaxolol tablets to be very effective for treating the heart pain called angina. They have also been used to treat high blood pressure.

Cautions and Warnings

Betaxolol should not be used if you have heart failure, heart block, or a very slow heart rate. Your doctor should give careful consideration to the use of Betaxolol if you have diabetes or overactive thyroid because Betaxolol may mask important signs of low blood sugar or overactive thyroid. Poor pulmonary (lung) function should be considered as a possible reason to avoid this drug, even though its effect on lung function is minimal when compared to that of the other beta blockers.

Pregnancy/Breast-feeding

It is not known if Betaxolol crosses into the blood circulation of a developing baby, but it has not been found to cause birth defects. Pregnant women, or those who might become pregnant while taking this drug, should not take it without their doctors' approval. When the drug is considered essential by your doctor, the potential risk of taking the medicine must be carefully weighed against the benefit it might produce.

It is generally recommended that women who must take any beta blocker not breast-feed because of the possibility of drug effects on the nursing infant.

Seniors

Older adults may be more or less sensitive to the effects of this medication. Your dosage of Betaxolol should start at 5 milligrams a day instead of 10 and increase gradually. It must be adjusted to your individual needs by your doctor. Seniors may be more likely to suffer from cold hands and feet and reduced body temperature, chest pains, a general feeling of ill health, sudden difficulty breathing, sweating, or changes in heartbeat because of this medicine.

Older adults may use Betaxolol eyedrops without special precautions. Some older adults may have weaker eyelid muscles. This creates a small reservoir for the eyedrops and may actually increase the drug's effect by keeping it in contact with your eye for a longer period. Your doctor may take this into account when determining the proper drug dosage.

Possible Side Effects

Betaxolol may decrease the heart rate; aggravate or worsen congestive heart failure; or produce low blood pressure, tingling in the extremities, light-headedness, mental depression, reduced sex drive and/or performance, difficulty sleeping, weakness, and tiredness. It can also produce visual disturbances, hallucinations, disorientation, and loss of short-term memory. People taking Betaxolol may experience nausea, vomiting, upset stomach, abdominal cramps and diarrhea, or constipation. If you are allergic to Betaxolol, you may show typical reactions associated with drug allergies, including sore throat, fever, difficulty breathing, and various effects on the blood system. Betaxolol may induce spasm of muscles in the bronchi, which will aggravate any existing asthma or respiratory disease.

Occasionally, people taking Betaxolol may experience

emotional instability, become detached, or show unusual personality change. Betaxolol may cause adverse effects on the blood system.

The more common side effects of Betaxolol eyedrops include tearing, stinging, and redness or inflammation of the eye.

Rare eyedrop side effects include sleeplessness, confusion, depression, very slow heartbeat, and increased sensitivity to bright lights.

Drug Interactions

Betaxolol's effectiveness in lowering blood pressure may be reduced by any of the nonsteroidal anti-inflammatory drugs (NSAIDs), estrogens, Theophylline, or Aminophylline.

The drug's effectiveness may be increased by Cimetidine, Molindone, Nicorette, or phenothiazine antipsychotic medicines or by stopping cigarette smoking.

It is not recommended that beta blockers be taken with monoamine oxidase (MAO) inhibitor drugs because of a possible sudden increase in blood pressure.

Beta blockers should be stopped gradually 2 days before surgery because of possible interaction with the surgical anesthetics.

Betaxolol tablets may cause increased effectiveness of Insulin or oral antidiabetic drugs. If you are diabetic, discuss the situation with your doctor. A reduction in dosage of your antidiabetic drug may be required.

Betaxolol may reduce the effectiveness of Digitalis on your heart. Any dose of Digitalis will have to be altered if you are taking Betaxolol. If you are taking Digitalis for a purpose other than heart failure, the effectiveness of the Digitalis may be increased by Betaxolol and the dose of Digitalis reduced.

Betaxolol may interact with other drugs to cause lowering of blood pressure. This interaction often has positive effects in the treatment of patients with high blood pressure.

Do not self-medicate with over-the-counter drugs for colds, coughs, or allergy that may contain stimulants that will aggravate certain types of heart disease and high blood pressure or other ingredients that may antagonize the effects of Betaxolol. Check with your doctor or pharmacist before taking any over-the-counter medication.

Betaxolol eyedrops should be used with caution if you are

taking a beta-blocking drug by mouth. If Betaxolol is absorbed into your bloodstream, it can increase the effects of the oral drug on your body and also increase the chance for drug side effects.

Food Interactions

Take Betaxolol tablets with food if they upset your stomach. The eyedrops may be used at any time.

Usual Dose

Eyedrops: 1 drop in the affected eye twice a day.

Tablets: 5 to 20 milligrams once a day. People with kidney failure should take 5 milligrams to start and then 5 to 20 milligrams once every 2 weeks.

Overdosage

Symptoms are slowed heart rate, heart failure, lowered blood pressure, and spasms of the bronchial muscles that make it difficult to breathe. The overdosed patient should be taken to a hospital emergency room where proper therapy can be given. ALWAYS bring the medicine bottle with you.

Special Information

Call your doctor if you develop breathing problems, wheezing or chest pain, confusion, swelling in the arms and/or legs, heart failure, hallucinations, yellow coloration in the skin or eyes, irregular heartbeat, depression, back or joint pain, or rash or if other side effects are persistent or particularly bothersome.

There have been reports of serious effects when Betaxolol is stopped abruptly. The dose should be lowered gradually over a period of 2 weeks.

It is best to take your Betaxolol tablets at the same time every day. But, if you forget to take them, take the forgotten dose as soon as possible. If it is within 8 hours of your next dose, skip the forgotten dose and go back to your regular schedule. Do not take a double dose.

If you forget to take a dose of Betaxolol eyedrops, take it as soon as you remember. If it is almost time for your next regularly scheduled dose, skip the one you forgot and continue with your regular schedule. Do not take a double dose.

To administer the eyedrops, lie down or tilt your head backward and look at the ceiling. Hold the dropper above your eye and drop the medicine inside your lower lid while looking up. To prevent possible infection, don't allow the dropper to touch your fingers, eyelids, or any surface. Release the lower lid and keep your eye open. Don't blink for about 30 seconds. Press gently on the bridge of your nose at the inside corner of your eye for about a minute. This will help circulate the medicine around your eye. Wait at least 5 minutes before using any other eyedrops.

Generic Name

Bitolterol Mesylate

Brand Name

Tornalate

Type of Drug

Bronchodilator.

Prescribed for

Asthma and bronchospasm.

General Information

Bitolterol is currently available only as an inhalation. It may be taken in combination with other medicines to control your asthma. The drug starts working 3 to 4 minutes after it is taken and continues to work for 5 to 8 hours. It can be used only when needed to treat an asthmatic attack or on a regular basis to prevent an attack.

Cautions and Warnings

Bitolterol should be used with caution if you have had angina, heart disease, high blood pressure, a history of stroke or seizures, diabetes, prostate disease, or glaucoma.

Pregnancy/Breast-feeding

Bitolterol should be used by a pregnant or breast-feeding

woman only when it is absolutely necessary. The potential benefit of using this medicine must be weighed against the potential, but unknown, hazard it can pose to your baby.

Seniors

Older adults are more sensitive to the effects of this drug. They should closely follow their doctor's directions and report any side effects at once.

Possible Side Effects

Bitolterol's side effects are similar to those associated with other bronchodilator drugs. The most common side effects are restlessness, weakness, anxiety, fear, tension, sleeplessness, tremors, convulsions, dizziness, headache, flushing, loss of appetite, pallor, sweating, nausea, vomiting, and muscle cramps.

Less common side effects include angina, abnormal heart rhythms, heart palpitations, high blood pressure, and urinary difficulty. Bitolterol has been associated with abnormalities in blood tests for the liver and white blood cells and with tests for urine protein, but the true importance of this reaction is not known.

Drug Interactions

Bitolterol's effects may be enhanced by monoamine oxidase (MAO) inhibitor drugs, antidepressants, thyroid drugs, other bronchodilators, and some antihistamines. It is antagonized by the beta-blocking drugs (Propranolol and others).

Bitolterol may antagonize the effects of blood-pressure-lowering drugs, especially Reserpine, Methyldopa, and Guanethidine.

Food Interactions

Bitolterol does not interact with food, since it is only taken by inhalation into the lungs.

Usual Dose

To treat an attack: 2 inhalations at an interval of at least 1 to 3 minutes, followed by a third inhalation, if needed.

To prevent an attack: 2 inhalations every 8 hours.

Overdosage

Bitolterol overdosage can result in exaggerated side effects, including heart pains and high blood pressure, although the pressure can drop to a low level after a short period of elevation. People who inhale too much Bitolterol should see a doctor, who may prescribe a beta-blocking drug like Atenolol or Metoprolol to counter the bronchodilator's effects.

Special Information

Be sure to follow your doctor's directions for using Bitolterol and do not take more than 4 inhalations of Bitolterol over an 8-hour period. Using more than is prescribed can lead to drug tolerance and actually cause your condition to worsen.

The drug should be inhaled during the second half of your breath. This allows the medicine to reach more deeply into your lungs.

Call your doctor at once if you develop chest pains, rapid heartbeat, palpitations, muscle tremors, dizziness, headache, facial flushing, or urinary difficulty or if you still have trouble breathing after using the medicine.

If you are using this drug to prevent an asthma attack and you forget a dose, take it as soon as you remember. If it is almost time for your next dose, skip the forgotten dose and continue with your regular schedule. Do NOT take a double dose.

Generic Name

Brompheniramine Maleate

Brand Names

Diamine T. D.   Dimetane Extentabs
Dimetane   Veltane

(Also available in generic form)

Type of Drug

Antihistamine.

Prescribed for

Seasonal allergy, stuffed and runny nose, itching of the eyes, scratchy throat caused by allergy, and other allergic symptoms, such as itching, rash, or hives.

General Information

Antihistamines, including Brompheniramine, generally act by antagonizing histamine at the site where histamine works. This site is often called the histamine receptor. Antihistamines work by drying up the secretions of the nose, throat, and eyes.

Cautions and Warnings

Brompheniramine Maleate should not be used if you are allergic to this drug. It should be avoided or used with extreme care if you have narrow-angle glaucoma (pressure in the eye), stomach ulcer or other stomach problems, enlarged prostate, or problems passing urine. It should not be used by people who have deep-breathing problems such as asthma.

Use with care if you have a history of thyroid disease, heart disease, high blood pressure, or diabetes.

Pregnancy/Breast-feeding

Brompheniramine has not been proven to be a cause of birth defects or other problems in pregnant women, although studies in animals have shown that some antihistamines (Meclizine and Cyclizine), used mainly against nausea and vomiting, may cause birth defects. Do not take any antihistamine without your doctor's knowledge.

Small amounts of antihistamine medicines pass into breast milk and may affect a nursing infant. Nursing mothers should avoid antihistamines or use alternative feeding methods while taking the medicine.

Seniors

Seniors are more sensitive to antihistamine side effects. Confusion, difficult or painful urination, dizziness, drowsiness, a faint feeling, nightmares or excitement, nervousness, restlessness, irritability, or dry mouth, nose, or throat are more likely to occur among older adults.

Possible Side Effects

Occasionally seen are itching, rash, sensitivity to light, perspiration, chills, lowering of blood pressure, headache, rapid heartbeat, sleeplessness, dizziness, disturbed coordination, confusion, restlessness, nervousness, irritability, euphoria (feeling "high"), tingling of the hands and feet, blurred vision, double vision, ringing in the ears, stomach upset, loss of appetite, nausea, vomiting, constipation, diarrhea, difficulty in urination, tightness of the chest, wheezing, nasal stuffiness, and dryness of the mouth, nose, and throat.

Drug Interactions

Brompheniramine Maleate should not be taken with monoamine oxidase (MAO) inhibitors.

Interaction with tranquilizers, sedatives, and sleeping medication will increase the effects of these drugs; it is extremely important that you discuss this with your doctor so that the doses of these drugs can be properly adjusted.

Be extremely cautious when drinking alcohol while taking Brompheniramine Maleate, which will enhance the intoxicating effect of the alcohol. Alcohol also has a sedative effect.

Usual Dose

Adult: 4 milligrams 3 to 4 times per day.

Child (age 6 to 12): 2 to 4 milligrams 3 to 4 times per day. Do not exceed 12 milligrams per day.

Child (under age 6): ¼ milligram per pound per day in divided doses.

Timed-release doses:

Adult: 8 to 12 milligrams at bedtime or every 8 to 12 hours during the day.

Child (age 6 to 12): 8 milligrams during the day or at bedtime.

Overdosage

Symptoms of overdose are depression or stimulation (especially in children), dry mouth, fixed or dilated pupils, flushing of the skin, and stomach upset. Take the patient to a hospital emergency room immediately, if you cannot make him or her vomit. ALWAYS bring the medicine bottle.

Special Information

Antihistamines produce a depressing effect: Be extremely cautious when driving or operating heavy equipment.

If you forget a dose of Brompheniramine, take it as soon as you remember. If it is almost time for your next dose, skip the forgotten dose and continue with your regular schedule. Do not take a double dose of Brompheniramine.

Generic Name

Bumetanide

Brand Name

Bumex

Type of Drug

Diuretic.

Prescribed for

Congestive heart failure, cirrhosis of the liver, kidney dysfunction, high blood pressure, and other conditions where it may be desirable to rid the body of excess fluid.

General Information

Bumetanide is a potent diuretic that works in the same way as Furosemide and Ethacrynic Acid. Not only do these drugs affect the same part of the kidney as the more commonly used thiazide diuretics, they also affect the portion of the kidney known as the Loop of Henle. This double action makes Bumetanide and the other "loop" diuretics extremely powerful drugs. All 3 loop diuretics can be used for the same purposes, but their doses are quite different. One milligram of Bumetanide is equivalent to about 40 milligrams of Furosemide and about 50 milligrams of Ethacrynic Acid.

Cautions and Warnings

Excessive amounts of Bumetanide can lead to dehydration and severe imbalances in your body levels of potassium, sodium, and chloride. Warning signs of dehydration are dry mouth, excessive thirst, loss of appetite, weakness, lethargy, drowsiness, restlessness, tingling in the hands or feet, muscle weakness, pain or cramps, low blood pressure, reduced urinary volume, rapid heartbeat, abnormal heart rhythms, nausea, and vomiting.

Do not use Bumetanide if you have had an allergic reaction to it in the past. People who are allergic to or cannot tolerate Furosemide may receive a prescription for Bumetanide as an alternative diuretic.

People with severe kidney or liver disease who take this medicine should maintain close contact with their doctor because the drug can accentuate some conditions affecting these organs.

Pregnancy/Breast-feeding

In animals given doses between 3.4 and 3400 times the maximum human dose, some effect was shown on developing embryos. Bumetanide has not caused adverse effects on developing infants and may even be prescribed to treat severe pregnancy-induced high blood pressure when other treatments fail. In general, though, this drug should be avoided by pregnant women or women who may become pregnant while using it. In those situations where it is deemed essential, the potential risk of taking Bumetanide must be carefully weighed against any benefit it might produce.

It is not known if Bumetanide passes into breast milk. It is recommended that women taking Bumetanide use alternative feeding methods.

Seniors

Older adults may be more sensitive to Bumetanide side effects than younger adults and should be treated with doses at the low end of the recommended range.

Possible Side Effects

Possible side effects include loss of appetite, nausea, vomiting, diarrhea, inflammation of the pancreas, yellowing of the skin or whites of the eyes, dizziness, headache, blurred vision, ringing or buzzing in the ears, and reduction of blood-platelet and white-blood-cell levels.

Other side effects include worsening of liver or kidney disease, abdominal pains, dry mouth, impotence, muscle weakness or cramps, arthritis-like pains in the joints, low blood pressure, changes in heart rhythm, and chest pains. The loop diuretics have been associated with mild ear congestion, diminished hearing, and hearing loss, but these are rare and usually only follow rapid intravenous injection of these drugs.

Drug Interactions

Because Bumetanide may enhance the effects of drugs that lower blood pressure, this interaction is beneficial and is often used to treat high blood pressure.

Bumetanide increases the side effects of Lithium by interfering with the elimination of that drug from the body.

Alcohol, barbiturate-type sleeping pills, and narcotic pain relievers can cause excessive low blood pressure when taken with potent diuretics like Bumetanide.

The possibility of losing body potassium with Bumetanide is increased by combining it with Digoxin (for the heart) and adrenal corticosteroids (for inflammation). Potassium loss also increases the chances of Digoxin side effects.

Probenecid reduces the effectiveness of Bumetanide by interfering with its action on the kidneys. Indomethacin and other nonsteroidal anti-inflammatory drugs such as Naproxen, Sulindac, and Ibuprofen may also reduce Bumetanide effectiveness.

People taking Bumetanide for high blood pressure or heart failure should take care to avoid nonprescription medicines that might aggravate those conditions, such as decongestants, cold and allergy treatments, and diet pills, all of which can contain stimulants. If you are unsure about which medicine to choose, ask your pharmacist.

Food Interactions

Bumetanide may cause hypokalemia (loss of body potassium), a complication that can be avoided by adding foods high in potassium to your diet. Some potassium-rich foods are tomatoes, citrus fruits, melons, and bananas. Hypokalemia can also be prevented by taking a potassium supplement in pill, powder, or liquid form.

Bumetanide may be taken with food if it upsets your stomach.

Usual Dose

0.5 to 2 milligrams per day. It may also be taken every other day for 3 to 4 consecutive days followed by 1 to 2 medicine-free days.

Overdosage

The major symptoms of overdose are related to the potent diuretic effect of Bumetanide: lethargy, weakness, dizziness, confusion, cramps, loss of appetite, and vomiting. Victims of Bumetanide overdose should be taken to a hospital emergency room for treatment. ALWAYS bring the medicine bottle with you.

Special Information

Take your daily dose no later than 10:00 A.M. If taken later in the day, this potent diuretic could interfere with your sleep by keeping you up to go to the bathroom.

Call your doctor if any warning signs of dehydration develop while you are taking Bumetanide. The warning signs are dry mouth, excessive thirst, loss of appetite, weakness, lethargy, drowsiness, restlessness, tingling in the hands or feet, muscle weakness, pain or cramps, low blood pressure, reduced urinary volume, rapid heartbeat, abnormal heart rhythms, nausea, and vomiting.

Take a missed dose as soon as you remember, but don't double the dose of Bumetanide.

Generic Name

Bupropion Hydrochloride

Brand Name

Wellbutrin

Type of Drug

Antidepressant.

Prescribed for

Depression.

General Information

Bupropion is generally not prescribed for the treatment of severe or major depression until after other drugs have been tried because of the higher-than-usual chance of developing seizures while taking it. Bupropion is chemically different from other antidepressants and chemically similar to Diethylpropion, an appetite suppressant.

Bupropion is not likely to work until you have taken it for 3 to 4 weeks. The drug takes about 2 weeks to clear from your system after you have stopped taking it.

Cautions and Warnings

People with seizure disorders, people who have had a seizure in the past, and people with eating disorders should be very careful about taking Bupropion because of the greatly increased chance of having a seizure while taking it. The chance of developing a seizure increases by about 10 times when the daily dosage is between 450 and 600 milligrams a day.

People with a history of heart disease or heart attack should take this drug with caution because of possible drug side effects.

Many people taking Bupropion experience some restlessness, agitation, anxiety, and sleeplessness, especially soon after they start taking the drug. Some even require sleeping pills to counter this effect, and others find the stimulation so severe that they have to stop taking Bupropion.

People taking Bupropion may experience hallucinations, delusions, and psychotic episodes. Dosage reduction or drug withdrawal is usually necessary to minimize these reactions. One-quarter of the people who take Bupropion lose their appetites and 5 or more pounds of body weight. Most other antidepressants cause weight gain. People who have lost weight because of their depression should be cautious about taking Bupropion.

If you are taking Bupropion and switch to a monoamine oxidase (MAO) inhibitor antidepressant, at least 2 weeks should elapse between the time you stop taking Bupropion and start the other antidepressant. The same thing applies if you are switching from an MAO inhibitor to Bupropion.

Bupropion has caused liver damage in animals and should

be used with caution by people with a history of liver disease.

People with kidney disease require less medication to produce a desired effect because the drug passes out of the body almost exclusively through the kidneys.

People with a history of drug abuse should probably be treated with a different antidepressant because they experience mild stimulation while taking Bupropion and may require a larger-than-usual dose. However, they are still susceptible to seizures at the higher doses. Severely depressed individuals are more likely to attempt suicide; they should not be given a large number of Bupropion tablets until they improve because of the chance they will swallow the whole bottle in a suicide attempt.

Pregnancy/Breast-feeding

As with all drug products, pregnant women, or those who might become pregnant, should not use Bupropion unless its advantages have been carefully weighed against the possible dangers of taking this drug while pregnant.

Bupropion passes into breast milk and may cause serious reactions in nursing babies. Nursing mothers who must use Bupropion should bottle-feed their babies.

Seniors

No problems have been reported in older adults. However, older adults are likely to have age-related reduction in kidney and/or liver function. This factor should be taken into account by your doctor when determining the dosage of this drug.

Possible Side Effects

The most common side effects of Bupropion are dry mouth, sleeplessness, headaches or migraines, nausea, vomiting, constipation, and tremors. About 1 in 10 people who take this drug have to stop it because side effects are intolerable.

Other side effects include appetite changes, weight loss, upset stomach, diarrhea, menstrual complaints, impotence, urinary difficulties, excessive sweating, sedation, slowing of movements, salivation, muscle spasms, warmth, uncontrolled muscle movements, dizziness, rapid heartbeat, abnormal heart rhythms, blood-pressure changes, heart palpitations, fainting, itching, redness and rash, agitation, confusion, hostility, loss of concentration, loss of sex drive, anxiety, delusions, a "high" feeling, fatigue, joint pains, fever or chills, respiratory infections, and visual, taste, and hearing disturbances. Many other side effects have been reported with Bupropion, but their link to the drug is not well established.

Drug Interactions

Bupropion may increase the rate at which the body breaks down Carbamazepine, Cimetidine, Phenobarbital, or Phenytoin. Dosage adjustments may be needed if the combination continues to be used.

People taking Levodopa experience more Bupropion side effects than other people. Levodopa users should have their Bupropion dosages increased more slowly and gradually than others.

Phenelzine, an MAO inhibitor antidepressant, increases the toxic effects of Bupropion.

The combination of Bupropion and any other drug that can increase the chance of seizures (including tricyclic antidepressants, Haloperidol, Lithium, Loxapine, Molindone, phenothiazine tranquilizers, or thioxanthene tranquilizers) should be avoided because of the much-improved chance of having a seizure.

Food Interactions

Bupropion may be taken with food if it upsets your stomach.

Usual Dose

200 to 300 milligrams per day.

Overdosage

Overdose symptoms are likely to be exaggerated drug side effects. Most people who take a Bupropion overdose recover without a problem. Bupropion overdose victims should be taken to a hospital emergency room for treatment. ALWAYS bring the medicine bottle with you.

Special Information

Do not stop taking Bupropion without your doctor's permission. Suddenly stopping the medicine may precipitate a drug withdrawal reaction and drug side effects.

Call your doctor if you become agitated or excited, restless, or confused; if you have trouble sleeping; if you have a fast or abnormal heart rhythm, severe headache, seizure, or skin rash; if you faint; or if symptoms are unusually persistent or severe.

The daily dose should be taken in 3 or 4 equal doses each day. The total dose should not be more than 450 milligrams, and single doses should not be greater than 150 milligrams.

People taking Bupropion must be careful when performing tasks requiring concentration and coordination because of the chance that the drug will make them tired, dizzy, or lightheaded.

Alcohol, tranquilizers, or other nervous-system depressants will increase the depressant effects of this drug. Alcohol also increases the chances of a seizure.

If you take Bupropion 3 or more times a day and forget a dose, take it as soon as you remember. If it is almost time for your next dose, take one dose as soon as you remember and another in 3 or 4 hours, then go back to your regular schedule. Do not take a double dose.

Generic Name

Buspirone

Brand Name

BuSpar

Type of Drug

Minor tranquilizer; antianxiety drug.

Prescribed for

Anxiety.

General Information

This drug is chemically different from the benzodiazepines, the most widely prescribed antianxiety drugs, but it has a potent antianxiety effect. Although it is approved by the United States Food and Drug Administration for short-term relief of anxiety, it appears that the drug can be safely used for longer periods of time (more than 4 weeks). Buspirone's exact effect on the body is not known, but it seems to lack the danger of drug addiction associated with other antianxiety drugs, including the benzodiazepines, and does not severely depress the nervous system or act as an anticonvulsant or muscle relaxant, as other antianxiety drugs do. Minor improvement will show after only 7 to 10 days of drug treatment, but the maximum effect does not occur until 3 to 4 weeks after starting treatment.

Cautions and Warnings

Although Buspirone has not shown any potential for drug dependence, you should be aware of the possibility that this might still happen.

Pregnancy/Breast-feeding

Buspirone has not been found to cause birth defects. Nevertheless, pregnant women, or those who might become pregnant while taking this drug, should not take it without their doctors' approval. When the drug is considered essential by your doctor, the potential risk of taking the medicine must be carefully weighed against the benefit it might produce.

This drug passes into breast milk, but has caused no problems among breast-fed infants. You must consider the potential effect on the nursing infant if breast-feeding while taking this medicine.

Seniors

Several hundred older adults participated in drug evaluation studies without any unusual problems. However, the effect of this drug in older adults is not well known and special problems may surface as time passes and the use of Buspirone becomes more widespread.

Possible Side Effects

The most common side effects are dizziness, nausea, headache, fatigue, nervousness, light-headedness, and excitement.

Other common side effects are heart palpitations, muscle aches and pains, tremors, skin rash, sweating, and clamminess.

Less common side effects are sleeplessness, chest pain, rapid heartbeat, low blood pressure, fainting, stroke, heart attack, heart failure, dream disturbances, difficulty concentrating, a drug "high," anger, hostility, depression, depersonalization and disassociation, intolerance to noise, intolerance to cold temperatures, fearfulness, loss of interest, hallucinations, suicidal tendencies, claustrophobia, stupor, and slurred speech.

Other side effects include ringing or buzzing in the ears, a "roaring" sensation in the head, sore throat, red and itchy eyes, changes in taste and smell, inner ear problems, eye pain, intolerance to bright lights, dry mouth, stomach or intestinal upset or cramps, diarrhea, constipation, stomach gas, changes in appetite, excess salivation, urinary difficulty, menstrual irregularity, pelvic inflammatory disease, bedwetting, muscle cramps and spasms, numbness, tingling in the hands and feet, poor coordination, involuntary movements, slowed reaction time, rapid breathing, shortness of breath, chest congestion, changes in sex drive, itching, facial swelling, flushing, easy bruising, hair loss, dry skin, blisters, fever, a feeling of ill health, bleeding disturbance, and voice loss.

Rare side effects are very slow heartbeat, high blood pressure, seizures and psychotic reactions, blurred vision, stuffed nose, pressure on the eyes, thyroid abnormalities, irritable colon, bleeding from the rectum, burning of the tongue, periodic spotting, painful urination, muscle weakness, nosebleeds, delayed ejaculation and impotence (men), thinning of the nails, and hiccups.

Drug Interactions

The combination of Buspirone with monoamine oxidase (MAO) inhibitor drugs may produce very high blood pressure and can be dangerous.

The effects of Buspirone together with other drugs that work in the central nervous system are not known. Do not take other tranquilizers, antianxiety, or psychoactive drugs with Buspirone unless prescribed by a doctor who knows your complete medication history.

The combination of Buspirone and Trazodone may cause liver inflammation.

Food Interactions

Food can affect the amount of drug absorbed into the bloodstream and the rate at which the drug is absorbed. This drug can be taken either with or without food. For the most consistent results, always take your dose at the same time of day in the same way (i.e., with or without food).

Usual Dose

15 to 60 milligrams per day in 3 divided doses.

Overdosage

Symptoms of overdose are nausea, vomiting, dizziness, drowsiness, pinpoint pupils, and upset stomach. To date, no deaths have been caused by Buspirone overdose. There is no specific antidote for Buspirone overdose. Take the victim to a hospital emergency room for treatment. ALWAYS bring the medicine bottle with you.

Special Information

Buspirone can cause nervous system depression. Be careful while driving or operating complex equipment.

Studies have shown that Buspirone does not increase the depressant effect of alcohol. Nevertheless, it would be wise for you to avoid alcoholic beverages while taking this, or any other, central-nervous-system drug product.

Contact your doctor if you develop any intolerable side effects. About 1 out of 10 people who were included in drug studies had to stop taking Buspirone because of drug side effects. Especially important are uncontrolled or repeated movements of the head, face, neck, or other body parts.

If you miss a dose of Buspirone, take it as soon as you remember. If it is almost time for your next dose, skip the missed dose and go back to your regular dose schedule. Do not take a double dose of Buspirone.

Brand Name

Capozide

Ingredients
Captopril
Hydrochlorothiazide

Type of Drug
Antihypertensive combination.

Prescribed for
High blood pressure; heart failure.

General Information
This medicine is a combination of a thiazide diuretic and a member of a class of blood-pressure-lowering drugs known as the ACE inhibitors. ACE inhibitors work by preventing the conversion of a potent hormone called Angiotensin 1. This directly affects the production of other hormones and enzymes that participate in the regulation of blood pressure. The blood-pressure-lowering effects of the 2 drugs combine to produce a result greater than could be expected from either ingredient. These effects also work together to relieve symptoms of heart failure.

Cautions and Warnings
This drug can cause kidney problems, especially loss of protein in the urine. Patients taking Capozide should have the amount of protein in the urine measured during the first month of treatment and monthly for the next few months. The drug can also cause a reduction in white-blood-cell count, leading to a potential for increased susceptibility to infection. Capozide should be used with caution by people who have kidney disease or diseases of the immune/colla-

gen system (particularly lupus erythematosus) or who have taken other drugs that affect the white-blood-cell count.

Do not take this combination if you are allergic to either ingredient or to sulfa drugs. You may be sensitive to Hydrochlorothiazide if you have a history of allergy or bronchial asthma.

Pregnancy/Breast-feeding

Animal studies show that Captopril may cause birth defects. Hydrochlorothiazide crosses into the developing baby's blood system and can cause jaundice, blood problems, and low potassium. Women who are, or might become, pregnant while taking this drug should discuss the matter with their doctor.

It is not known if Captopril passes into breast milk and if it will affect a nursing infant. Hydrochlorothiazide passes into breast milk, but no problems have been reported in nursing infants.

Seniors

Older adults may be *less* sensitive to the blood-pressure-lowering effects of this drug combination than younger adults, but they may be *more* sensitive to its side effects. Dosage must be individualized to your needs.

Possible Side Effects

Dizziness, tiredness, headache, diarrhea, rash (usually mild), and cough are the most common side effects.

Less common drug side effects are itching, fever, temporary loss of taste perception, stomach irritation, chest pain, low blood pressure, heart palpitations, difficulty sleeping, tingling in the hands or feet, nausea, vomiting, jaundice and liver damage, excessive sweating, muscle cramps, (male) impotence, and muscle weakness. Some people experience unusual reactions after taking the first dose of the drug, which can include facial flushing and swelling, swelling of the arms and legs, and closing of the throat.

The Hydrochlorothiazide ingredient can cause a loss of body potassium. Signs of low potassium are dry mouth, thirst, weakness, lethargy, drowsiness, restlessness, muscle pains or cramps, muscle tiredness, low blood pressure, low urine production, abnormal heart rate, and upset stomach.

Drug Interactions

The blood-pressure-lowering effect of Capozide is additive with diuretic drugs and the beta blockers. Other drugs that cause rapid drops in blood pressure should be used with extreme caution because of a possible severe drop when taken together with Capozide.

The Captopril portion of this combination may increase potassium levels in your blood, especially when given with potassium-sparing diuretics and/or potassium supplements.

People taking oral antidiabetic drugs who start taking Capozide may have to have their antidiabetic dosage adjusted.

The chance of Lithium toxicity may be increased by Hydrochlorothiazide.

Food Interactions

This drug is best taken on an empty stomach, usually 1 hour before or 2 hours after meals.

The Hydrochlorothiazide ingredient in Capozide can cause a loss of body potassium. Your doctor may prescribe a potassium-rich diet or a potassium supplement, although the Captopril ingredient can counteract the Hydrochlorothiazide.

Usual Dose

Adult: 1 tablet 2 or 3 times a day. People with poor kidney function have to take less of the medicine to achieve reduced blood pressure.

Child: as determined by body weight and individual response.

Overdosage

The primary effect of Capozide overdosage is a rapid drop in blood pressure, as evidenced by dizziness or fainting. Take the overdose victim to a hospital emergency room immediately. ALWAYS remember to bring the medicine bottle

Special Information

Call your doctor if you develop fever, sore throat, mouth

sores, abnormal heartbeat, or chest pain or if you have persistent rash or loss of taste perception.

Capozide may cause dizziness when you quickly rise from a lying or sitting position.

Avoid strenuous exercise and/or very hot weather because heavy sweating and/or dehydration can cause a rapid drop in blood pressure.

Do not stop taking this medicine without your doctor's knowledge.

Avoid nonprescription medicines such a diet pills, decongestants, and stimulants that can raise your blood pressure.

If you forget a dose of Capozide, take it as soon as you remember. If it is almost time for your next dose, skip the one you forgot and continue with your regular schedule. Do not take a double dose.

Generic Name

Captopril

Brand Name

Capoten

Type of Drug

Antihypertensive; ACE inhibitor.

Prescribed for

High blood pressure or congestive heart failure. Low doses may be used to treat mild to moderate high blood pressure. Captopril may be taken alone or together with a diuretic drug. Captopril is widely used in the treatment of congestive heart failure.

Captopril has been studied as a treatment for rheumatoid arthritis.

General Information

This drug was the first member of a class of drugs, called the ACE inhibitors, that work by preventing the conversion of a potent hormone called Angiotensin 1. This directly affects the production of other hormones and enzymes that participate in the regulation of blood pressure. The effect is to lower blood pressure relatively quickly, within 1 to 1½ hours after taking the medicine. Captopril plays a role in treating heart failure because it dilates (opens) blood vessels and eases the work of the heart.

Cautions and Warnings

This drug can cause kidney disease, especially loss of protein in the urine. Patients should have the amount of protein in their urine measured during the first month and monthly for a few months afterward. The drug can also cause reduction in the white-blood-cell count, and this can result in increased susceptibility to infection. Captopril should be used with caution by people who have kidney disease or diseases of the immune/collagen system (particularly lupus erythematosus) or who have taken other drugs that affect the white-blood-cell count.

Pregnancy/Breast-feeding

Animal studies show that Captopril may cause birth defects. Women who are, or might become, pregnant while taking Captopril should discuss the matter thoroughly with their doctor.

Captopril passes into breast milk in concentrations about 1 percent of those found in blood. The effect of this drug on nursing infants is not known.

Seniors

Older adults may be *less* sensitive to the blood-pressure-lowering effects of Captopril than younger adults, but they may be *more* sensitive to drug side effects. Dosage must be individualized to your needs.

Possible Side Effects

Possible side effects include rash (usually mild), itching, fever, loss of taste perception (which usually returns in 2 to 3 months), and gastric irritation.

Less common side effects are those on the kidney, including protein in the urine, kidney failure, excessive or frequent urination, and reduction in the amount of urine produced; adverse effect on the blood system, especially white blood cells; swelling of the face, mucous membranes of the mouth, or arms and legs, and flushing or pale color of skin. Captopril may also cause low blood pressure and adverse effects on the heart (chest pain, abnormal heart-beats, spasms of blood vessels, heart failure).

Drug Interactions

The blood pressure effect of Captopril is additive with di-uretic drugs. Some other hypertensive drugs can cause se-vere blood pressure drops when used with large amounts of Captopril. They should be used with extreme caution. Beta-adrenergic blocking drugs may add some blood-pressure-lowering effect to Captopril.

Captopril may increase serum potassium, especially if given with potassium-sparing diuretics and/or potassium supplements.

Avoid over-the-counter cough, cold, and allergy remedies containing drugs that may aggravate your condition.

Aspirin or Indomethacin may decrease or completely abol-ish the blood-pressure-lowering effect of Captopril.

Food Interactions

Do not take this medicine with food or meals. It must be taken at least 1 hour before or 2 hours after meals.

Usual Dose

Adult: 75 milligrams per day to start. Dose may be in-creased up to 450 milligrams per day, if needed. The dose of this medicine must be tailored to your needs.

Child: about 0.15 milligrams per pound of body weight 3 times a day.

People with poor kidney function have to take less medicine.

Overdosage

The primary effect of Captopril overdosage is very low blood pressure. A person who has taken a Captopril overdose must be taken to a hospital emergency room for treatment. ALWAYS bring the medicine bottle with you.

Special Information

Call your doctor if you develop fever, sore throat, mouth sores, abnormal heartbeat, or chest pain or if you have persistent rash, or loss of taste perception.

This drug may cause dizziness when you rise quickly from sitting or lying down.

Avoid strenuous exercise and/or very hot weather because heavy sweating and/or dehydration can cause a rapid drop in blood pressure.

If you are taking this medicine for high blood pressure, be certain to avoid nonprescription drugs such as diet pills, decongestants, and stimulants that can raise blood pressure.

Do not abruptly stop taking this medication. If you forget to take a dose, do not double your next dose. Skip the forgotten dose and go back to your regular dose schedule.

Generic Name

Carbamazepine

Brand Names

Epitol
Tegretol

(Also available in generic form)

Type of Drug

Anticonvulsant.

Prescribed for

Seizure disorders and trigeminal neuralgia. It is also prescribed for diabetes insipidus (a hormonal disease leading to severe water retention), some psychiatric disorders, and alcoholism.

General Information

Carbamazepine was first approved for the relief of severe pain associated with trigeminal neuralgia. Over the years, though, it has gained much greater acceptance for seizure control, especially for people who are not controlled by Phenytoin, Phenobarbital, or Primidone or who have suffered severe side effects from these medicines.

This drug is not a simple pain reliever and should not be taken for everyday aches and pains. It has some potentially fatal side effects.

Cautions and Warnings

This drug should not be used if you have a history of bone marrow depression or if you are sensitive or allergic to this drug or to the tricyclic antidepressants. Monoamine oxidase (MAO) inhibitors should be discontinued 2 weeks before Carbamazepine treatment is begun.

Carbamazepine can cause severe, life-threatening blood reactions. Your doctor should have a complete blood count done before you start taking this medicine and repeat that examination weekly during the first 3 months of treatment and then every month for the next 2 or 3 years.

Carbamazepine may aggravate glaucoma and should be used with caution by people with this condition.

Pregnancy/Breast-feeding

This drug has caused birth defects in lab animals. However, the exact effect of Carbamazepine on a developing fetus is not known. Women taking this drug for a seizure problem should continue taking the drug because of the possibility of causing a seizure by stopping the drug, which could be dangerous for the unborn child. If possible, anticonvulsant drugs should be stopped before the pregnancy begins.

Carbamazepine passes into breast milk in concentrations of about 60 percent of the concentrations in the mother's bloodstream and can affect a nursing infant. Do not nurse your baby if you must take this drug. You can ask your doctor if it will be safe to discontinue the medication during the time you will be nursing your newborn baby.

Seniors

Older adults are more likely to develop Carbamazepine-induced heart problems, psychosis, confusion, or agitation.

Possible Side Effects

The most frequent side effects of Carbamazepine are dizziness, drowsiness, unsteadiness, nausea, and vomiting. Other common side effects are blurred or double vision, confusion or hostility, headache, and severe water retention.

Less common side effects are mood and behavior changes (especially in children), confusion, hives, itching or skin rash, and allergic reaction.

Rare side effects are chest pain, fainting, trouble breathing, continuous back-and-forth eye movements, slurred speech, depression, restlessness, nervousness, muscle rigidity, ringing or buzzing in the ears, trembling, uncontrolled body movement, hallucinations, darkening of the stool or urine, yellowing of the eyes or skin, mouth sores, unusual bleeding or bruising, unusual tiredness or weakness, changes in your pattern of urination (frequent, or a sudden decrease of urine production), swelling of the feet or lower legs, numbness, tingling, pain or weakness in the hands or feet, pain, tenderness, a bluish color of the leg or foot, and swollen glands.

Drug Interactions

Carbamazepine blood levels may be increased by Cimetidine, Diltiazem, Isoniazid, Propoxyphene, Erythromycin, Mexilitene, Troleandomycin, or Verapamil, leading to drug toxicity.

Women taking oral contraceptives may experience breakthrough bleeding with Carbamazepine.

Phenobarbital, Phenytoin or Primidone can reduce the amount of Carbamazepine in the blood. Charcoal tablets or powder decrease the amount of Carbamazepine absorbed into the blood.

Carbamazepine decreases the effect of Warfarin (an anticoagulant drug) and Theophylline (for asthma). People taking this combination may need more of these medicines to retain the desired effects. Other drugs counteracted by Carbamazepine are Cyclosporine, Dacarbazine, digitalis drugs, Disopyramide, Doxycycline, Levothyroxine, and Quinidine.

Taking Carbamazepine together with antidepressants or antipsychotic drugs can increase the depressant effects of Carbamazepine.

Food Interactions

Carbamazepine may be taken with food if it causes upset stomach.

Usual Dose

Adult and child (over age 12): 200 to 1200 milligrams per day, depending on the condition being treated. The usual maintenance dose is 400 to 800 milligrams per day in 2 divided doses.

Child (age 6 to 12): 200 to 1000 milligrams per day, or 10 to 15 milligrams per pound of body weight per day, divided into 3 or 4 equal doses.

Overdosage

Carbamazepine is a potentially lethal drug. The lowest known single lethal dose was 60 grams. Adults have survived single doses of 30 grams and children have survived single doses of 5 to 10 grams.

Overdose symptoms appear 1 to 3 hours after the drug is taken. The most prominent effects are irregularity or difficulty in breathing, rapid heartbeat, changes in blood pressure, shock, loss of consciousness or coma, convulsions, muscle twitching, restlessness, uncontrolled body movements, drooping eyelids, psychotic mood changes, nausea, vomiting, and reduced urination.

The overdose victim must be taken to a hospital emergency room immediately. Successful treatment depends on prompt elimination of the drug from the body. ALWAYS bring the medicine bottle with you.

Special Information

Carbamazepine can cause dizziness and drowsiness. Take care while driving or operating any mechanical equipment.

Call your doctor at once if you develop a yellow coloration of the eyes or skin, unusual bleeding or bruising, abdominal pain, pale stools, dark urine, impotence (men), mood changes, nervous system symptoms, swelling, fever, chills, sore throat, or mouth sores. These may be signs of a potentially fatal drug side effect.

Do not abruptly stop taking Carbamazepine without your physician's advice. If you forget to take a dose, however, skip the missed dose and go back to your regular dose schedule. If you miss more than 1 dose in a day, check with your doctor.

Generic Name

Carprofen

Brand Name
Rimadyl

Type of Drug
Nonsteroidal anti-inflammatory.

Prescribed for
Rheumatoid and gouty arthritis; osteoarthritis.

General Information
Carprofen is one of many nonsteroidal anti-inflammatory drugs (NSAIDs) sold in the United States to reduce inflammation, relieve pain and fever, and relieve menstrual cramps and discomfort. The choice of one member of this group over another often depends on your individual response to a specific drug. Because of this, it is common to try several of these drugs before you find the one that is right for you. Carprofen should be reserved for people who cannot tolerate, or do not respond to, other NSAIDs. Carprofen starts working in about 1 hour and will last for about 6 hours.

Cautions and Warnings
Do not take this product if you are allergic to Aspirin or to any other NSAID. This drug can worsen stomach ulcers or cause a new ulcer to develop. It should be used with caution if you have kidney disease.

Pregnancy/Breast-feeding
This drug may cross into the blood circulation of a developing baby. It has not been found to cause birth defects. Nevertheless, pregnant women, or those who might become

pregnant while taking this drug, should not take it without their doctors' approval. When the drug is considered essential by your doctor, the potential risk of taking the medicine must be carefully weighed against the benefit it might produce.

This drug may pass into breast milk, but it has caused no problems among breast-fed infants. You must consider the potential effect on the nursing infant if breast-feeding while taking this medicine.

Seniors

Older adults are more sensitive to the stomach, kidney, and liver effects of this drug. Some doctors recommend that persons 70 years of age and older take half the usual dose. Follow your doctor's directions and report any side effects at once.

Possible Side Effects

The most frequent side effects are upset stomach, dizziness, headache, drowsiness, ringing in the ears, and rash.

Other side effects include heartburn, nausea, vomiting, bloating, stomach gas or pain, diarrhea, constipation, dark stools, nervousness, sleeplessness, depression, confusion, tremor, loss of appetite, fatigue, itching, double or blurred vision, dry or irritated eyes, heart failure, palpitations, abnormal heart rhythms, anemia or other changes in the composition of your blood, changes in liver function, hair loss, tingling in the hands or feet, fever, enlarged breasts, blood in the urine, urinary irritation, thirst, frequent urination, kidney damage, low blood sugar, asthma, difficulty breathing, skin rash, itching, swelling, and black-and-blue marks.

Drug Interactions

Aspirin causes this drug to be eliminated from the body more rapidly than it usually is.

This drug may increase the effectiveness of Lithium and anticoagulant (blood-thinning), antidiabetes, and antiseizure drugs.

People taking Methotrexate should not take Carprofen or any other NSAID. Four people have died from taking Methotrexate and an NSAID.

Carprofen may reduce the effects of beta-blocking drugs like Propranolol, Atenolol, and others.

Carprofen may increase the effects of sulfa drugs, antidiabetes drugs, and Phenytoin or other drugs for seizure disorders.

Food Interactions

You may take this drug with food if it upsets your stomach.

Usual Dose

300 to 600 milligrams per day. Seniors and people with kidney problems should start with a lower dosage.

Overdosage

Symptoms of overdose may include drowsiness, dizziness, confusion, disorientation, lethargy, tingling in the hands or feet, numbness, nausea, vomiting, upset stomach, stomach pains, headache, ringing or buzzing in the ears, sweating, and blurred vision. Take the victim to a hospital emergency room at once for treatment. ALWAYS bring the medicine bottle with you.

Special Information

Avoid Aspirin and alcoholic beverages while taking this medication. You may become dizzy or drowsy while taking this medicine; be careful while driving or operating complex equipment.

Call your doctor if you develop a skin rash, itching, swelling, visual disturbances, black stools, or a persistent headache while taking this medication.

If you forget to take a dose of Carprofen, take it as soon as you remember. If it is almost time for your next dose, skip the forgotten dose and continue with your regular schedule.

Generic Name

Carteolol Hydrochloride

Brand Name

Cartrol

Type of Drug

Beta-adrenergic blocking agent.

Prescribed for

High blood pressure; angina pectoris (a specific type of chest pain).

General Information

This drug is quite similar to Propranolol, the original beta-blocking agent. It has not been studied in as many kinds of conditions as Propranolol and most of the other beta-blocking drugs. Carteolol is very useful because it can be taken once a day. When used for high blood pressure, it is often given with a diuretic such as Hydrochlorothiazide, but it may be taken by itself.

Cautions and Warnings

Carteolol should be used with care if you have a history of asthma or other upper respiratory disease or of heart failure. It should not be used if your heart rate is consistently very slow. You should stop taking the drug several days before major surgery, if possible; do not do this without telling your doctor. Carteolol can hide some symptoms of diabetes or thyroid disease.

Pregnancy/Breast-feeding

Carteolol crosses into the blood circulation of a developing fetus. It has not been found to cause birth defects. Pregnant women, or those who might become pregnant while taking this drug, should not take it without their doctors' approval. When the drug is considered essential by your doctor, the potential risk of taking the medicine must be carefully weighed against the benefit it might produce.

It is not known if Carteolol passes into breast milk. In general, women taking a beta blocker are strongly urged to not breast-feed their babies because of possible drug side effects.

Seniors

A variety of factors may make older adults more or less sensitive to the effects of this medication. Your dosage of this drug must be adjusted to your individual needs by your doctor. Seniors may be more likely to suffer from cold hands and feet and reduced body temperature, chest pains, a general feeling of ill health, sudden difficulty breathing, sweating, or changes in heartbeat because of this medicine.

Possible Side Effects

Carteolol may decrease the heart rate, worsen congestive heart failure, and produce lowered blood pressure, tingling in the extremities, light-headedness, anxiety, nervousness, vivid dreams, dizziness, fainting, weakness, and tiredness. It may also produce a mental depression that is reversible when the drug is withdrawn, visual disturbances, disorientation, and short-term memory loss. Patients taking Carteolol may experience stuffed nose, dry eyes, nausea, vomiting, stomach upset, abdominal cramps and diarrhea, constipation, frequent urination, or reduced sex drive and/or performance. If you are allergic to this drug, you may show typical reactions associated with drug allergies, including difficulty in breathing, and various effects on the blood system. Carteolol may induce bronchospasms (spasms of muscles in the bronchi), which will make any existing asthmatic condition or severe upper respiratory disease worse.

Occasionally, patients taking Carteolol may experience emotional instability or a feeling of detachment or of personality change, or the drug may produce unusual effects on the blood system.

Drug Interactions

Carteolol's effectiveness in lowering blood pressure may be reduced by any of the nonsteroidal anti-inflammatory drugs (NSAIDs), estrogens, Theophylline, or Aminophylline.

The drug's effectiveness may be increased by Cimetidine, Molindone, Nicorette, or phenothiazine antipsychotic medicines or by stopping cigarette smoking.

It is not recommended that beta blockers be taken with monoamine oxidase (MAO) inhibitor drugs because of a possible sudden increase in blood pressure.

Beta blockers should be stopped gradually 2 days before surgery because of possible interaction with the surgical anesthetics.

Carteolol may increase the effectiveness of Insulin or oral antidiabetes drugs. If you are diabetic, discuss the situation with your doctor; a reduction in dose of antidiabetic medication will probably be made.

Carteolol may reduce the effectiveness of Digitalis and related drugs (Digoxin, Digitoxin) on your heart. Your Digitalis dose will have to be altered. If you are taking Digitalis for a purpose other than congestive heart failure, the effectiveness of the Digitalis may be increased by Carteolol, and the dose of Digitalis may have to be reduced.

Carteolol may interact with certain other drugs to lower blood pressure. This interaction often has positive results in the treatment of patients with high blood pressure.

Do not self-medicate with over-the-counter cold, cough, or allergy remedies that may contain stimulants that will aggravate certain types of heart disease and high blood pressure or other ingredients that may antagonize the effects of Carteolol. Double-check with your doctor or pharmacist before taking any over-the-counter medication.

Food Interactions

Take this medicine with food if it upsets your stomach.

Usual Dose

2.5 to 10 milligrams once a day. Doses above 10 milligrams a day are not likely to improve the drug's effect.

Patients with bad kidneys may take their medication dosage as infrequently as once every 72 hours.

Overdosage

Symptoms are slowed heart rate, heart failure, lowered blood pressure, and spasms of the bronchial muscles that make it difficult to breath. The overdosed patient should be taken to a hospital emergency room where proper therapy can be given. ALWAYS bring the medicine bottle with you.

Special Information

Carteolol may be taken at any time, without regard to meals. Since this drug is taken only once a day, be sure to take it at the same time every day.

Do not stop taking the drug abruptly unless your doctor

tells you to, or serious heart pain and other effects can occur.

Call your doctor if you have trouble breathing when you exert yourself or are lying down; if you have a nighttime cough; if you develop swollen ankles, arms, or legs, joint pain, fever, chills, rash, chest pain, confusion, depression, or irregular heartbeat; or if your side effects are particularly persistent or intolerable.

If you forget to take a dose of Carteolol, take it as soon as possible. However, if it is within 8 hours of your next dose, skip the forgotten dose and go back to your regular schedule. Do not take a double dose.

Type of Drug

Cephalosporin Antibiotics

Brand Names

Generic Name: Cefaclor

Ceclor

Generic Name: Cefadroxil

Duricef
Ultracef

(Also available in generic form)

Generic Name: Cefixime

Suprax

Generic Name: Cefuroxime Axetil

Ceftin

Generic Name: Cephalexin

Keflet
Keflex

Generic Name: Cephalexin Hydrochloride

Keftab

(Also available in generic form)

Generic Name: Cephradine

Anspor
Velosef

(Also available in generic form)

Prescribed for

Infections caused by organisms sensitive to the antibiotic.

General Information

All of these antibiotics are related to the first member of the family, Cephalosporin A. Cephalosporin A was isolated from a microorganism discovered in the sea near Sardinia in 1948. Over the years, researchers have manipulated the basic cephalosporin chemical structure, which is similar to that of penicillin, to produce more than 20 different antibiotic drugs. These drugs are differentiated from one another by the variety of bacteria they kill and how they are taken. The cephalosporin antibiotics included in The Pill Book can be taken orally, as a liquid, tablet, or capsule. Injectable cephalosporins are not included.

Cautions and Warnings

A small number of people with an allergy to penicillin may also be allergic to a cephalosporin. Be sure your doctor knows about your penicillin allergy. The most common allergic reaction to a cephalosporin is a hivelike condition with redness over large areas of the body.

Prolonged or repeated use of a cephalosporin antibiotic can lead to the overgrowth of a fungus or bacteria that is not susceptible to the antibiotic and can cause a secondary infection.

Several of the injectable cephalosporins can interfere with blood coagulation after very high doses. This problem has not occurred with any of the oral products.

The dosage of some cephalosporins must be adjusted for people with poor kidney function.

Pregnancy/Breast-feeding

These drugs are considered to be relatively safe for pregnant women, but there are few reports of pregnant women who have actually taken cephalosporin antibiotics. These drugs should be taken only if the potential benefit outweighs any harm they could cause.

Small amounts of all of the cephalosporin antibiotics will pass into breast milk. Nursing mothers should temporarily discontinue breast-feeding while taking cephalosporin antibiotics.

Seniors

Seniors may take oral cephalosporin antibiotics without special precautions. Be sure to report any unusual side effects to your doctor.

Possible Side Effects

Most cephalosporin side effects are quite mild. The most common are abdominal pains and gas, upset stomach, nausea, vomiting, diarrhea, itching, and rashes.

Less common are headache, dizziness, tiredness, tingling in the hands or feet, seizures, confusion, drug allergy, fever, joint pains, chest tightness, redness, muscle aches and swelling, loss of appetite, and changes in taste perception. Colitis may develop during treatment because of changes in the normal microorganisms found in the gastrointestinal tract.

Cefaclor may cause serum sickness (a combination of fever, joint pains, and rash).

Cephalosporins may cause changes in some blood cells, but this problem is not generally seen with those drugs that can be taken orally. Some cephalosporins have caused kidney problems, liver inflammation, and jaundice, but these are also rarely a problem with oral cephalosporins.

Drug Interactions

The cephalosporins should not be taken together with Erythromycin or Tetracycline because of conflicting antibacterial action.

Probenecid may increase blood levels of the cephalosporins by preventing their elimination through the kidneys.

Food Interactions

Food interferes with the absorption of Cephalexin and Cefaclor into the blood. These drugs should be taken on an empty stomach, 1 hour before or 2 hours after meals, but may be taken with food if they upset your stomach.

Cefadroxil, Cefixime, Cefuroxime, and Cephradine may be taken without regard to food or meals.

Usual Dose

Cefaclor:
Adult: 250 to 500 milligrams every 8 hours.
Child: 3 to 6 milligrams per pound of body weight every 8 hours.
Cefadroxil:
Adult: 1 to 2 grams per day in 1 or 2 doses.
Child: 13 milligrams per pound of body weight per day in 1 or 2 doses.
Cefixime:
Adult: 400 milligrams per day in 1 or 2 doses.
Child: 3½ milligrams per pound of body weight per day in 1 or 2 doses.
Cefuroxime:
Adult and child (over age 12): 125 to 500 milligrams every 12 hours.
Child (under age 12) *and infant:* 125 to 250 milligrams every 12 hours.
Cephalexin:
Adult: 250 to 1000 milligrams every 6 hours. Some urinary infections may be treated with 500 milligrams every 12 hours.
Child: 11 to 23 milligrams per pound of body weight per day. The dose may be increased to 46 milligrams per pound of body weight to treat middle ear infections.
Cephradine:
Adult: 250 to 500 milligrams every 6 to 12 hours.
Child (over 9 months of age): 11 to 45 milligrams per pound of body weight per day in 2 or 4 doses.

Overdosage

The most common symptoms of a cephalosporin overdose are nausea, vomiting, and upset stomach. These symptoms can be treated with milk or an antacid. Cephalosporin overdoses are generally not serious, but you may contact a hospital emergency room or local poison information center to learn more about this problem.

Special Information

The cephalosporins, like all antibiotics, will make you feel better within 2 or 3 days after you begin taking them. However, to obtain the maximum benefit from any antibiotic, you must take the full daily dose of antibiotic prescribed by your doctor for the 7 to 10 days of your prescription.

If you miss a dose of a cephalosporin antibiotic, and it is almost time for your next dose, and you take the medicine once a day, take the dose you forgot right away and your next one 10 to 12 hours later. Then go back to your regular schedule.

If you take the medicine 2 times a day, take the dose you forgot right away and the next dose 5 to 6 hours later. Then go back to your regular schedule.

If you take the medicine 3 or more times a day, take the dose you missed right away and your next dose 2 to 4 hours later. Then go back to your regular schedule.

Most of the liquid forms of these antibiotics must be kept in the refrigerator to maintain their strength. Only Cefixime liquid does not require refrigeration and may be kept at room temperature.

The cephalosporins may interfere with the "Clinitest" test for sugar in the urine. They do not interfere with enzyme-based tests like Tes-Tape and Clinistix.

Generic Name

Chlordiazepoxide

Brand Names

Libritabs   Mitran
Librium   Reposans-10

(Also available in generic form)

Type of Drug

Minor tranquilizer.

Prescribed for

Relief of symptoms of anxiety, tension, fatigue, or agitation.

General Information

Chlordiazepoxide is a member of the group of drugs known as benzodiazepines. These drugs are used as antianxiety agents, anticonvulsants, or sedatives (sleeping pills). They exert their effect by relaxing the large skeletal muscles and by a direct effect on the brain. In doing so, they can relax you and make you either more tranquil or sleepier, depending on the drug and how much you use. Many doctors prefer Chlordiazepoxide and the other members of this class to other drugs that can be used for the same effect. Their reason is that the benzodiazepines tend to be safer, have fewer side effects, and are usually as, if not more, effective.

These drugs are generally used in any situation where they can be a useful adjunct.

Benzodiazepine tranquilizing drugs can be abused if taken for long periods of time and it is possible to develop withdrawal symptoms if you discontinue the therapy abruptly. Withdrawal symptoms include tremor, muscle cramps, stomach cramps, vomiting, insomnia, agitation, sweating, and even convulsions.

Cautions and Warnings

Do not take Chlordiazepoxide if you know you are sensitive or allergic to this drug or to other benzodiazepines such as Diazepam, Oxazepam, Clorazepate, Lorazepam, Prazepam, Flurazepam, Clonazepam, and Temazepam.

Chlordiazepoxide and other members of this drug group may aggravate narrow-angle glaucoma, but if you have open-angle glaucoma you may take the drugs. In this case, check this information with your doctor.

Pregnancy/Breast-feeding

This drug, like all members of the benzodiazepine family, crosses into your developing baby's circulation and may cause birth defects if taken during the first 3 months of pregnancy. You should avoid taking this medication while pregnant.

Members of the benzodiazepine family pass into breast milk. Since infants break the drug down more slowly than adults, it is possible for the medicine to accumulate and have an undesired effect on the baby.

Seniors

Older adults are more sensitive to the effects of this drug, especially dizziness and drowsiness. Closely follow your doctor's directions and report any side effects at once.

Possible Side Effects

The most common side effect is mild drowsiness during the first few days of therapy. If drowsiness persists, contact your doctor.

Less common side effects are confusion, depression, lethargy, disorientation, headache, inactivity, slurred speech, stupor, dizziness, tremor, constipation, dry mouth, nausea, inability to control urination, changes in sex drive, irregular menstrual cycle, changes in heart rhythm, lowered blood pressure, retention of fluids, blurred or double vision, itching, rash, hiccups, nervousness, inability to fall asleep, and, occasionally, liver dysfunction. If you experience any of these reactions, stop taking the medicine and contact your doctor immediately.

Drug Interactions

Chlordiazepoxide is a central-nervous-system depressant. Avoid alcohol, tranquilizers, narcotics, barbiturates, monoamine oxidase (MAO) inhibitors, antihistamines, and other medicines used to relieve depression.

Smoking may reduce the effectiveness of Chlordiazepoxide.

The effects of Chlordiazepoxide may be prolonged when it is taken together with Cimetidine.

Food Interactions

This drug is best taken on an empty stomach, but may be taken with food if it upsets your stomach.

Usual Dose

Adult: 5 to 100 milligrams per day. This tremendous range in dosage exists because of varying response of individuals, related to age, weight, severity of disease, and other characteristics.

Child (over age 6): This drug may be given if it is deemed appropriate by the physician. Initial dose, lowest available (5 milligrams 2 to 4 times per day). The dose may later be increased in some children to 30 to 40 milligrams per day. The dose must be individualized to obtain maximum benefit.

Overdosage

Symptoms of overdose are confusion, sleep or sleepiness, lack of response to pain such as a pin stick, shallow breathing, lowered blood pressure, and coma. The patient should be taken to a hospital emergency room immediately. ALWAYS bring the medicine bottle.

Special Information

Chlordiazepoxide can cause tiredness, drowsiness, inability to concentrate, or similar symptoms. Be careful if you are driving, operating machinery, or performing other activities that require concentration.

If you forget to take a dose of Chlordiazepoxide, take it as soon as you remember. If it is almost time for your next dose do not double up, but skip the missed dose and go back to your usual dose schedule. Do not take a double dose of Chlordiazepoxide.

Generic Name

Chlorhexidine Gluconate

Brand Name

Peridex Oral Rinse

Type of Drug

Oral disinfectant.

Prescribed for

Swelling and redness of the gums. It is also prescribed for severe gum disease as part of an overall treatment program. It may be used to treat or prevent mouth infections after periodontal surgery and in cancer patients, to reduce dental plaque, and to treat minor ulcers inside the mouth. Chlorhexidine may also be prescribed for gum irritations caused by ill-fitting dentures.

General Information

Chlorhexidine Gluconate kills bacteria that contribute to gum redness, swelling, and bleeding. Chlorhexidine is absorbed by the tissues it comes into contact with and is slowly released over a 24-hour period after you have rinsed with it, providing a continuous anti-bacterial effect.

Cautions and Warnings

People who have experienced an allergic reaction to Chlorhexidine skin disinfectants should avoid this product.

Chlorhexidine rinse is not recommended for children under age 18.

Chlorhexidine Gluconate may permanently discolor tooth-filling edges. People with front-tooth fillings should be careful about using this product because it can create the need for cosmetic treatment of the front teeth.

Pregnancy/Breast-feeding

There are no reports of adverse effects of Chlorhexidine on developing fetuses. Also, animal studies have revealed no problems with the drug. Pregnant women, or whose who might become pregnant while using the drug, should use Chlorhexidine mouthwash only after considering the possible risks and potential benefits of the treatment.

It is not known if Chlorhexidine passes into breast milk. No problems have been found in nursing mothers or in laboratory animal studies.

Seniors

Older adults may use this product without restriction.

Possible Side Effects

The most common side effects of Chlorhexidine are tooth staining and temporary taste alterations.

Chlorhexidine may also cause minor mouth irritation and tissue loss, especially in children.

Drug Interactions

Do not mix Chlorhexidine with any oral drug product.

Food Interactions

Do not dilute Chlorhexidine rinse with any food or liquid. To get the maximum benefit from each treatment, do not eat or drink for several hours after using Chlorhexidine rinse.

Usual Dose

Adult (over 18 years): Rinse for 30 seconds twice a day after flossing and brushing your teeth.

For denture irritation: Soak your dentures twice a day for 1 to 2 minutes. Rinse your mouth for 30 seconds twice a day. Or, you may be asked to brush your dentures and gums with Chlorhexidine rinse 2 times a day.

Overdosage

Small children swallowing 1 or 2 ounces of Chlorhexidine rinse may develop upset stomach or signs of alcohol intoxication (the product is 11.6% alcohol). If a small child (22 pounds or less) swallows 4 ounces or more, or if signs of drunkenness develop, take the victim to a hospital emergency room.

Special Information

Do not use Chlorhexidine except under the supervision of a dentist, who will remove tartar and other tooth deposits before Chlorhexidine use.

Chlorhexidine rinse should be used after flossing and brushing your teeth. Rinse your mouth completely before using Chlorhexidine rinse. Swish the rinse in your mouth for 30 seconds and spit it out. Do not swallow the rinse. Do not rinse with water immediately after a Chlorhexidine rinse because this will increase the product's bitter taste.

If you forget a dose of Chlorhexidine, take it as soon as

you remember. If it is almost time for your next dose, skip the dose you forgot and continue with your regular schedule. Do not take a double dose of Chlorhexidine rinse.

Generic Name

Chlorpheniramine Maleate

Brand Names

Aller-Chlor	Chlor-Trimeton
Chlo-Amine	Chlor-Trimeton Repetabs
Chlorate	Pfeiffer's Allergy
Chlor-Pro	Phenetron
Chlorspan-12	Telachlor
Chlortab	Teldrin

(Also available in generic form)

Type of Drug

Antihistamine.

Prescribed for

Seasonal allergy, stuffed and runny nose, itching of the eyes, scratching of the throat caused by allergy, and other allergic symptoms, such as itching, rash, or hives.

General Information

Antihistamines, including Chlorpheniramine, generally act by antagonizing histamine at the site where histamine works. This site is often called the H_1 histamine receptor. Antihistamines work by drying up the secretions of the nose, throat, and eyes.

Cautions and Warnings

Chlorpheniramine Maleate should not be used if you are allergic to it. This drug should be avoided or used with extreme care if you have narrow-angle glaucoma (pressure in the eye), stomach ulcer or other stomach problems, enlarged prostate, or problems passing urine. It should not be used by people who have deep-breathing problems such as asthma.

Use with care if you have a history of thyroid disease, heart disease, high blood pressure, or diabetes.

Pregnancy/Breast-feeding

Chlorpheniramine Maleate has not been proven to be a cause of birth defects or other problems in pregnant women, although studies in animals have shown that some antihistamines (Meclizine and Cyclizine), used mainly against nausea and vomiting, may cause birth defects. Do not take any antihistamine without your doctor's knowledge.

Small amounts of antihistamine medicines pass into breast milk and may affect a nursing infant. Nursing mothers should avoid antihistamines or use alternative feeding methods while taking the medicine.

Seniors

Seniors are more sensitive to antihistamine side effects. Confusion, difficult or painful urination, dizziness, drowsiness, a faint feeling, nightmares or excitement, nervousness, restlessness, irritability, and dry mouth, nose, and throat are more likely to occur among older adults.

Possible Side Effects

Occasionally seen are itching, rash, sensitivity to light, perspiration, chills, lowering of blood pressure, headache, rapid heartbeat, sleeplessness, dizziness, disturbed coordination, confusion, restlessness, nervousness, irritability, euphoria (feeling high), tingling of the hands and feet, blurred vision, double vision, ringing in the ears, stomach upset, loss of appetite, nausea, vomiting, constipation, diarrhea, difficulty in urination, tightness of the chest, wheezing, nasal stuffiness, and dryness of the mouth, nose, and throat. Young children develop nervousness, irritability, tension, and anxiety.

Drug Interactions

Chlorpheniramine Maleate should not be taken with monoamine oxidase (MAO) inhibitors.

Interaction with tranquilizers, benzodiazepines, sedatives,

and sleeping medications will increase the effect of these drugs; it is extremely important that you discuss this with your doctor so that the doses of these drugs can be properly adjusted.

Be extremely cautious when drinking alcohol while taking Chlorpheniramine Maleate, which will enhance the intoxicating effect of alcohol. Alcohol also has a sedative effect.

Usual Dose

Adult: 4-milligram tablet 3 to 4 times per day.
Child (age 6 to 12): 2-milligram tablet 3 to 4 times per day.
Timed-release doses (capsules or tablets):
Adult: 8 to 12 milligrams at bedtime or every 8 to 10 hours during the day.
Child (age 6 to 12): 8 milligrams during the day or at bedtime.

Overdosage

Symptoms of overdose are depression or stimulation (especially in children), dry mouth, fixed or dilated pupils, flushing of the skin, and stomach upset. Take the patient to a hospital emergency room immediately if you cannot make him or her vomit. ALWAYS bring the medicine bottle.

Special Information

Antihistamines produce a depressing effect: Be extremely cautious when driving or operating heavy equipment.

If you forget a dose of Chlorpheniramine, take it as soon as you remember. If it is almost time for your next dose, skip the one you forgot and continue with your regular schedule. Don't take a double dose.

Generic Name

Chlorpromazine

Brand Name

Thorazine

(Also available in generic form)

Type of Drug

Phenothiazine antipsychotic.

Prescribed for

Psychotic disorders, moderate to severe depression with anxiety, control of agitation or aggressiveness of disturbed children, alcohol withdrawal symptoms, intractable pain, and senility. Chlorpromazine may also be used to relieve nausea, vomiting, hiccups, restlessness, and apprehension before surgery or other special therapy.

General Information

Chlorpromazine and other members of the phenothiazine group act on a portion of the brain called the hypothalamus. They affect parts of the hypothalamus that control metabolism, body temperature, alertness, muscle tone, hormone balance, and vomiting and may be used to treat problems related to any of these functions. Chlorpromazine is available in suppositories and liquid forms for those who have trouble swallowing tablets.

Cautions and Warnings

Chlorpromazine should not be taken if you are allergic to any of the drugs in the broad classification known as phenothiazine drugs. Do not take Chlorpromazine if you have any blood, liver, kidney, or heart disease; very low blood pressure; or Parkinson's disease. This medication is a tranquilizer and can have a sedative effect, especially during the first few days of therapy.

This drug should be used with caution and under strict

supervision of your doctor if you have glaucoma, epilepsy, ulcers, or difficulty passing urine.

Pregnancy/Breast-feeding

Infants born to women taking this medication have experienced drug side effects (liver jaundice, nervous-system effects) immediately after birth. Check with your doctor about taking this medicine if you are, or might become, pregnant.

This drug may pass into breast milk and affect a nursing infant. Consider alternative feeding methods if you must take this medicine.

Seniors

Older adults are more sensitive to the effects of this medication than younger adults and usually require a lower dosage to achieve a desired effect. Also, older adults are more likely to develop drug side effects. Some experts feel that seniors should be treated with one-half to one-quarter the usual adult dose.

Possible Side Effects

The most common side effect is drowsiness, especially during the first or second week of therapy. If the drowsiness becomes troublesome, contact your doctor. Do not allow the liquid forms of this medicine to come in contact with your skin. This can cause contact reactions.

Chlorpromazine can cause jaundice (yellowing of the whites of the eyes or skin), usually in 2 to 4 weeks. The jaundice usually goes away when the drug is discontinued, but there have been cases when it did not. If you notice this effect, or if you develop symptoms such as fever and general not feelings of ill health, contact your doctor immediately.

Less frequent side effects are changes in components of the blood including anemias, raised or lowered blood pressure, abnormal heart rates, heart attack, and faintness or dizziness.

Phenothiazines can produce extrapyramidal effects, such as spasm of the neck muscles, rolling back of the eyes, convulsions, difficulty in swallowing, and symptoms associated with Parkinson's disease. These effects look very serious but disappear after the drug has been withdrawn; however, symptoms of the face, tongue, and jaw may persist for as long as several years, especially in older adults with a history of brain damage. If you experience extrapyramidal effects contact your doctor immediately.

Chlorpromazine may cause an unusual increase in psychotic symptoms or may cause paranoid reactions, tiredness, lethargy, restlessness, hyperactivity, confusion at night, bizarre dreams, inability to sleep, depression, and euphoria. Other reactions are itching, swelling, unusual sensitivity to bright lights, red skin, and rash. There have been cases of breast enlargement, false positive pregnancy tests, changes in menstrual flow in females, and impotence and changes in sex drive in males, as well as stuffy nose, headache, nausea, vomiting, loss of appetite, change in body temperature, loss of facial color, excessive salivation, excessive perspiration, constipation, diarrhea, changes in urine and stool habits, worsening of glaucoma, blurred vision, weakening of eyelid muscles, spasms in bronchial and other muscles, increased appetite, excessive thirst, and changes in the coloration of skin, particularly in exposed areas.

Drug Interactions

Chlorpromazine should be taken with caution in combination with barbiturates, sleeping pills, narcotics, other tranquilizers, or any other medication that may produce a sedative effect. Avoid alcohol.

Usual Dose

Adult: 30 to 1000 milligrams or more per day, individualized according to disease and patient's response.

Child: 0.25 milligram per pound of body weight every 4 to 6 hours, up to 200 milligrams or more per day (by various routes including rectal suppositories), depending on disease, age, and response to therapy.

Overdosage

Symptoms of overdose are depression, extreme weakness, tiredness, desire to go to sleep, coma, lowered blood pressure, uncontrolled muscle spasms, agitation, restlessness, convulsions, fever, dry mouth, and abnormal heart rhythms.

The patient should be taken to a hospital emergency room immediately. ALWAYS bring the medicine bottle.

Special Information

This medication may cause drowsiness. Use caution when driving or operating complex equipment and avoid alcoholic beverages while taking the medicine.

The drug may also cause unusual sensitivity to the sun and can turn your urine reddish-brown to pink.

If dizziness occurs, avoid sudden changes in posture and avoid climbing stairs.

Use caution in hot weather. This medicine may make you more prone to heat stroke.

If you are using the sustained release capsules, do not chew them or break them: swallow them whole.

If you forget to take a dose of Chlorpromazine, take it as soon as you remember. If you are taking 1 dose per day and forget to take the dose, skip the missed dose and continue your regular dose schedule the next day. If you take more than 1 dose per day, do not double your dose, but skip the missed dose and continue with your regular schedule.

Generic Name

Chlorpropamide

Brand Name

Diabinese

(Also available in generic form)

Type of Drug

Oral antidiabetic.

Prescribed for

Diabetes mellitus (sugar in the urine).

General Information

Chlorpropamide is one of several oral antidiabetic drugs that work by stimulating the production and release of Insulin from the pancreas. The action of these agents is also related to improved Insulin sensitivity of peripheral tissues. The primary difference between these drugs lies in the duration of action. Because they do not lower blood sugar directly, they require some function of pancreas cells.

Cautions and Warnings

Mild stress such as infection, minor surgery, or emotional upset reduces the effectiveness of Chlorpropamide. Remember that while you are taking this drug you should be under your doctor's continuous care.

Chlorpropamide is an aid to, not a substitute for, a diet. Diet remains of primary importance in the treatment of your diabetes. Follow the diet plan your doctor has prescribed for you.

Chlorpropamide and similar drugs are not oral Insulin, nor are they a substitute for Insulin. They do not lower blood sugar by themselves.

This drug should not be used if you have serious liver, kidney, or endocrine disease.

Pregnancy/Breast-feeding

This drug may cause birth defects or interfere with your baby's development. Check with your doctor before taking it if you are, or might be, pregnant. For control of diabetes in pregnant women, the use of Insulin and diet is recommended.

Nursing women who must take this drug should find an alternative method of feeding their children.

Seniors

Older adults with reduced kidney function may be more sensitive to drug side effects because of a reduced ability to eliminate it from the body. Low blood sugar, the major sign of drug overdose, may be more difficult to identify in older adults than in younger adults. Also, low blood sugar is more likely to be a cause of nervous-system side effects in older adults. Older adults taking antidiabetes drugs must keep in close touch with their doctors and closely follow their directions.

Possible Side Effects

Common side effects are loss of appetite, nausea, vomiting, stomach upset. At times, you may experience weakness or tingling in the hands and feet. These effects can be eliminated by reducing the daily dose of Chlorpropamide or, if necessary, by switching to a different oral antidiabetic drug. This decision must be made by your doctor.

Chlorpropamide may produce abnormally low levels of blood sugar when too much is taken for your immediate requirements. (Other factors that may cause lowering of blood sugar are liver or kidney disease, malnutrition, age, drinking alcohol, and disease of the glands.)

Less commonly, Chlorpropamide may cause a yellowing of the whites of the eyes or skin, itching, rash, or changes in the results of laboratory tests made by your doctor. Usually these reactions will disappear in time. If they persist you should contact your doctor.

Drug Interactions

Thiazide diuretics may lessen the effect of Chlorpropamide, while Insulin, sulfa drugs, Oxyphenbutazone, Phenylbutazone, and monoamine oxidase (MAO) inhibitor drugs prolong and enhance the action of Chlorpropamide.

Interaction with alcoholic beverages may cause flushing of the face and body, throbbing pain in the head and neck, difficult breathing, nausea, vomiting, sweating, thirst, chest pains, palpitations, lowered blood pressure, weakness, dizziness, blurred vision, and confusion. If you experience these reactions, contact your doctor immediately.

Because of the stimulant ingredients in many over-the-counter drug products for the relief of coughs, colds, and allergies, avoid them unless your doctor advises otherwise.

Response to Chlorpropamide may be reduced if a betablocking agent such as Propranolol is given to the same patient.

Food Interactions

This medicine is best taken on an empty stomach, but may be taken with food. Dietary management is an important part of the treatment of diabetes. Be sure to follow your doctor's directions about the foods you should avoid.

Usual Dosage

Adult: 250 milligrams daily.
Senior: 100 to 250 milligrams daily.
For severe cases: 500 milligrams daily.

Overdosage

A mild overdose of Chlorpropamide lowers the blood sugar, which can be treated by consuming sugar in such forms as candy and orange juice. A patient with a more serious overdose should be taken to a hospital emergency room immediately. ALWAYS bring the medicine bottle.

Special Information

The treatment of diabetes is your responsibility. You should follow all instructions about diet, body weight, exercise, and personal hygiene and take all measures to avoid infection. If you are not feeling well, or if you have symptoms such as itching, rash, yellowing of the skin or eyes, abnormally light-colored stools, a low-grade fever, sore throat, or diarrhea, contact your doctor immediately.

Do not discontinue taking this medication unless advised to do so by your physician.

If you forget a dose of Chlorpropamide, take it as soon as you remember. If you don't remember until the next day, skip the forgotten dose and continue with your regular schedule.

Generic Name

Chlorzoxazone

Brand Names

Paraflex
Parafon Forte DSC

(Also available in generic form)

Type of Drug

Skeletal muscle relaxant.

Prescribed for

Relief of pain and spasm of muscular conditions, including lower back pain, strains, sprains, or muscle bruises.

General Information

Chlorzoxazone is one of several drugs used to treat the aches and pains associated with muscle aches, strains, or a bad back. It gives only temporary relief and is not a substitute for other types of therapy, such as rest, surgery, or physical therapy.

Chlorzoxazone acts primarily at the spinal cord level and on areas of the brain. It does not directly relax tense muscles.

A half-strength tablet is also available in generic form or as the brand Paraflex.

Cautions and Warnings

Do not take Chlorzoxazone if you are allergic to it. Do not take more than the exact amount of medication prescribed.

Pregnancy/Breast-feeding

This drug has not been found to cause birth defects. Nevertheless, pregnant women, or those who might become pregnant while taking this drug, should not take it without their doctors' approval.

It is not known if Chlorzoxazone passes into breast milk, but it has not caused problems among breast-fed infants. Consider the potential effect on your nursing infant if breast-feeding while taking this medicine.

Seniors

Older adults with severe liver disease are more sensitive to the effects of this drug. Follow your doctor's directions and report any side effects at once.

Possible Side Effects

The major side effects are stomach upset and other gastrointestinal problems. Chlorzoxazone has been associated with bleeding from the stomach, drowsiness, dizziness, lightheadedness, feelings of ill health, and overstimulation.

Less commonly, Chlorzoxazone has been associated with liver disease.

Drug Interactions

The depressive effects of Chlozoxazone may be enhanced by taking it together with alcohol, tranquilizers, sleeping pills, or other nervous system depressants. Avoid these combinations.

Food Interactions

Take this drug with food if it upsets your stomach. Chlorzoxazone may be crushed and mixed with food.

Usual Dose

Adult: 250 to 750 milligrams 3 to 4 times per day.
Child: 125 to 500 milligrams 3 to 4 times per day.

Overdosage

Symptoms of massive overdosage are sleepiness; weakness; tiredness; turning blue of lips, fingertips, or other areas; and signs of liver damage, such as nausea, vomiting, diarrhea, and severe abdominal pain. Contact your doctor immediately or go to a hospital emergency room where appropriate therapy can be provided. ALWAYS bring the medicine bottle.

Special Information

Chlorzoxazone can make you sleepy, dull your senses, or disturb your concentration, so be extremely careful while driving or operating equipment or machinery. Drinking alcoholic beverages further complicates this problem and enhances the drug's sedative effects.

A breakdown product of Chlorzoxazone can turn your urine orange to purple-red: This is not dangerous.

Call your doctor if you develop dryness, drowsiness, weakness, or breathing difficulty.

If you forget to take a dose of Chlorzoxazone, take it as soon as you remember. If it is almost time for your next regularly scheduled dose, skip the forgotten dose and continue with your regular schedule. Do not take a double dose.

Generic Name

Cholestyramine

Brand Name
Questran Powder

Type of Drug
Antihyperlipidemic (blood-fat reducer).

Prescribed for
High blood cholesterol; itching associated with bile duct obstruction; some forms of colitis; pesticide poisoning.

General Information
This medication reduces blood cholesterol by removing bile acids from the biliary system. Since cholesterol is used by the body to make bile acids and bile acids are necessary for the digestion of dietary fats, the only way the body can continue to digest fats is to make more bile acids from cholesterol, resulting in a lowering of blood cholesterol levels. The medicine works entirely within the bowel and is never absorbed into the bloodstream.

Cautions and Warnings
Do not use Cholestyramine if you are sensitive to it or to a similar drug product, Colestipol.

Pregnancy/Breast-feeding
The safety of using this medication during pregnancy is not known. If you are pregnant and must use this medication, talk to your doctor about the potential benefit to be gained versus other treatments for your condition.

The medicine is not absorbed into your blood and will not affect a nursing infant. However, it can affect the amounts of vitamins and other nutrients absorbed, possibly making your milk less nutritious. You may want to consider alternative methods or supplemental feedings for your infant.

Seniors

Older adults are more likely to suffer side effects from this medication, especially those relating to the bowel.

Possible Side Effects

The most common side effect is constipation, which may be severe and result in a bowel impaction. Hemorrhoids may be worsened.

Less frequent side effects are abdominal pain and bloating, bleeding in the stomach or intestine, gas, nausea, vomiting, diarrhea, heartburn, and appetite loss. Your stool may have an unusual appearance because of high fat level.

Other side effects include vitamin A and D deficiency, rashes, irritation of the tongue and anus, osteoporosis, black stools, stomach ulcers, dental bleeding, hiccups, a sour taste, pancreas inflammation, ulcer attack, gallbladder attack, bleeding, black-and-blue marks, itching and rash, backache, muscle and joint pains, arthritis, headache, anxiety, dizziness, fatigue, ringing or buzzing in the ears, fainting, tingling in the hands or feet, blood in the urine, frequent or painful urination, an unusual urine odor, eye irritation, weight changes, increased sex drive, swollen glands, swelling of the arms or legs, and shortness of breath.

Drug Interactions

This medication interferes with the absorption of virtually all other medicines taken by mouth. Some drugs for which this effect has been proven are Cephalexin, Chenodiol, Clindamycin, corticosteroids, digitalis drugs, iron, Penicillins, Phenobarbital, Phenylbutazone, Tetracycline, thiazide diuretics, thyroid drugs, Trimethoprim, Warfarin, and Vitamins A, D, E, and K. Take other medicines at least 1 hour before or 4 to 6 hours after you take Cholestyramine.

Food Interactions

Take this medication before meals. It should be mixed with water, juice, applesauce, or crushed pineapple.

Usual Dose

1 packet taken 1 to 6 times a day.

Overdosage

The most severe effect of Cholestyramine overdose is bowel impaction. Take the overdose victim to a hospital emergency room for evaluation and treatment. ALWAYS bring the medicine container with you.

Special Information

Do not swallow the powder in its dry form; mix the contents of each packet with 2 to 6 ounces of water or a noncarbonated beverage and drink as a liquid. The powder may also be mixed with soups or fruit sources like applesauce or crushed pineapple.

Constipation, stomach gas, nausea, and heartburn may occur and then disappear with continued use of this medication. Call your doctor if these side effects continue or if you develop unusual problems such as bleeding from the gums or rectum.

If you forget to take a dose, take it as soon as possible. Do not double any doses. If it is almost time for your next dose, skip the missed dose and go back to your regular dose schedule.

Generic Name

Cimetidine

Brand Name

Tagamet

Type of Drug

Antiulcer; histamine H_2 antagonist.

Prescribed for

Ulcers of the stomach and upper intestine (duodenum). It is also prescribed for other conditions characterized by the production of large amounts of gastric fluids. Surgeons may prescribe Cimetidine during a surgical procedure when it is desirable for the production of stomach acid to be stopped completely.

General Information

Cimetidine was the first histamine H_2 antagonist to be released in the United States. It works against ulcers and other gastrointestinal conditions by actually turning off the system that produces stomach acid.

Cautions and Warnings

Do not take Cimetidine if you have had an allergic reaction to it in the past. Cimetidine has a mild antiandrogen effect. This is probably the reason why some people experience painful, swollen breasts after taking this medicine for a month or more.

Pregnancy/Breast-feeding

Studies with laboratory animals have revealed no damage to a developing fetus, although Cimetidine does pass into the developing baby's circulation. It is recommended that Cimetidine be avoided by pregnant women and women who might become pregnant while using it. In those situations where it is deemed essential, Cimetidine's potential risk must be carefully weighed against any benefit it might produce.

Cimetidine is known to pass into breast milk. No problems among nursing infants have been reported, but nursing mothers must consider the possibility of a drug effect while nursing their infants.

Seniors

Older adults respond well to Cimetidine but may need less medication than younger adults to achieve the desired response, since the drug is eliminated through the kidneys and kidney function tends to decline with age. Older adults may be more susceptible to some side effects of this drug, especially confusion.

Possible Side Effects

Most people taking Cimetidine do not experience serious drug side effects. The most common side effects of Cimetidine are mild diarrhea, muscle pains and cramps, dizziness, skin rash, nausea and vomiting, headache, confusion, and drowsiness. Rarely, the medicine has an effect on white blood cells or blood platelets. Some symptoms of these effects are unusual bleeding or bruising, unusual tiredness, and weakness. Other rare side effects are impotence (men) and painful swollen breasts.

Drug Interactions

The effects of Cimetidine may be reduced if the drug is taken together with an antacid. This minor interaction may be avoided by separating Cimetidine from doses of antacid by about 3 hours.

Cimetidine may increase the effects of a variety of drugs, possibly leading to drug toxicity. Cimetidine exerts this effect by preventing the drugs' breakdown or elimination from the body. The drugs so affected by Cimetidine include alcohol, antidepressants, antidiabetes drugs, Aminophylline, bone marrow depressants used in cancer treatment, Alprazolam, caffeine, Carbamazepine, Chlordiazepoxide, Diazepam and other similar minor tranquilizers, Cyclosporine, Flurazepam, Labetalol, Lidocaine, Mexilitene, Metoprolol, Metronidazole, Phenytoin and Procainamide, Propranolol, Nifedipine, Quinidine, Theophylline, Triazolam, Warfarin (a blood-thinning drug).

Enteric-coated tablets should not be taken with Cimetidine. The change in stomach acidity will cause the tablets to disintegrate prematurely in the stomach.

Cimetidine may inhibit the absorption of Ketoconazole into the bloodstream.

Food Interactions

Cimetidine should be taken with food or meals and at bedtime to achieve maximum effect from the drug.

Usual Dose

The usual adult dosage is 400 to 800 milligrams at bedtime, 300 milligrams 4 times a day with meals and at bedtime, or 400 milligrams twice a day. You should not exceed 2400 milligrams per day. However, smaller doses may be as effective for seniors or patients with impaired kidney function.

Overdosage

There is little information on Cimetidine overdosage. Overdose victims might be expected to show exaggerated side effect symptoms, but little else is known. Your local poison center may advise giving the victim Syrup of Ipecac to cause vomiting and remove any remaining drug from the stomach. Victims who have definite symptoms should be taken to a hospital emergency room for observation and possible treatment. ALWAYS remember to bring the prescription bottle with you.

Special Information

You must take this medicine exactly as directed and follow your doctor's instructions for diet and other treatments in order to get the maximum benefit from it. Cigarettes are known to be associated with stomach ulcers and will reverse the effect of Cimetidine on stomach acid.

Call your doctor at once if any unusual side effects develop. Especially important are unusual bleeding or bruising, unusual tiredness, diarrhea, dizziness, rash, or hallucinations. Black, tarry stools or vomiting "coffee-ground" material may indicate your ulcer is bleeding.

If you miss a dose of Cimetidine, take it as soon as possible. If it is almost time for your next dose, skip the missed dose and go back to your usual dose schedule. Do not double the dose.

Generic Name

Cinoxacin

Brand Name

Cinobac

Type of Drug

Urinary anti-infective.

Prescribed for

Urinary tract infections in adults caused by susceptible microorganisms.

General Information

Cinoxacin treats urinary infections by interfering with DNA reproduction in those bacteria.

Cautions and Warnings

People who are allergic to other quinolone antibacterials (Ciprofloxacin, Nalidixic Acid, and Norfloxacin) are also likely to be allergic to Cinoxacin.

This drug should not be used by infants or children because of the possibility that it could affect their development.

Pregnancy/Breast-feeding

Cinoxacin crosses the placenta into the developing fetus and has affected laboratory animal fetuses. Cinoxacin should not be used by pregnant women or women who might become pregnant.

Other members of this group of drugs pass into breast milk, but it is not known if Cinoxacin shares this property. It is not recommended in nursing mothers because it has caused permanent changes in some joints and connective tissues of immature animals and could affect infant development.

Seniors

Seniors are likely to require a reduced dosage of Cinoxacin because of the normal tendency to reduced kidney function in older adults.

Possible Side Effects

The most common side effects of Cinoxacin are nausea, headache, dizziness, rash, itching, and redness.

Less common side effects of Cinoxacin include vomiting, appetite loss, abdominal cramps, diarrhea, altered taste sensations, burning in the area surrounding the rectum, sleeplessness, confusion, drowsiness, tingling sensations, blurred vision, ringing or buzzing in the ears, sensitivity to the sun or bright light, and drug reactions. Cinoxacin may also affect some laboratory tests that reflect liver and kidney function.

Drug Interactions

Probenecid blocks the excretion of Cinoxacin through the kidneys, causing the drug to accumulate in the body.

Food Interactions

You should take Cinoxacin with food, unless otherwise directed by your doctor.

Usual Dose

1 gram per day, divided in 2 or 4 doses, for 14 days.
  For preventive treatment: 250 milligrams at bedtime.
  Dosages are reduced for people with reduced kidney function.

Overdosage

The most likely effects of Cinoxacin overdose are exaggerated drug side effects. Take the victim to a hospital emergency room for treatment. ALWAYS bring the bottle for identification.

Special Information

Call your doctor if you become dizzy while taking Cinoxacin. Your eyes may be more sensitive to bright light while taking this medicine. This is a normal side effect of Cinoxacin.
  If you take Cinoxacin twice a day and forget a dose, take it as soon as you remember. If it is almost time for your next dose, take one dose as soon as you remember and another in 5 or 6 hours, then go back to your regular schedule.
  If you take it 3 or 4 times a day and forget a dose, take it as soon as you remember. If it is almost time for your next dose, take one dose as soon as you remember and another in 3 or 4 hours, then go back to your regular schedule.

Generic Name

Ciprofloxacin

Brand Names

Cipro Tablets
Ciloxan Eyedrops

Type of Drug

Anti-infective.

Prescribed for

Lower respiratory infections, skin infections, bone and joint infections, eye infections, treating and preventing urinary infections, infectious diarrhea, lung infections in people with cystic fibrosis, bronchitis, pneumonia, prostate infection, and traveler's diarrhea. This medicine does not work against the common cold, flu, or other virus infections.

General Information

Ciprofloxacin is a member of the class of antibacterial drugs called fluoroquinolones. This widely used drug works against many organisms that traditional treatments like antibiotics have trouble killing. Ciprofloxacin is also available as eyedrops to treat ocular infections. Ciprofloxacin is chemically related to an older antibacterial called Nalidixic Acid, but works better than that drug against urinary infections. Research conducted after the drug was first approved for marketing has shown that it can be used to treat a wide variety of infections all over the body.

Cautions and Warnings

Do not take Ciprofloxacin if you have had an allergic reaction to it in the past, or if you have had a reaction to a related medication like Nalidixic Acid. Severe, possibly fatal allergic reactions can occur as soon as after the first dose of medicine. Ciprofloxacin is eliminated by the kidneys; the drug dose must be adjusted in the presence of kidney failure.

This drug may cause increased pressure on parts of the brain, leading to convulsions and psychotic reactions. This can also cause restlessness, light-headedness, confusion, and hallucinations. Ciprofloxacin should be used with caution in people with seizure disorder or other conditions of the nervous system.

Prolonged use of Ciprofloxacin, as with any other anti-infective, can lead to fungal overgrowth.

Pregnancy/Breast-feeding

Pregnant women should not take this medication unless the

risks have been weighed against the possible benefits of its use. Animal studies have shown that this drug may reduce your chances for a successful pregnancy.

Ciprofloxacin may pass into breast milk. Nursing mothers should avoid taking it unless it is absolutely necessary because of the chance that the drug might pass into breast milk. Be sure your doctor knows if you are breast-feeding.

Seniors

Studies in healthy seniors showed that Ciprofloxacin was released from their bodies more slowly than from the bodies of younger adults because of decreased kidney function. Ciprofloxacin dosage must be adjusted according to kidney function. Since most seniors have lost some kidney function, your doctor will take this factor into account and give you a lower daily dosage of Ciprofloxacin.

Older adults may use Ciprofloxacin eyedrops without special precautions. Some older adults may have weaker eyelid muscles. This creates a small reservoir for the eyedrops and may actually increase the drug's effect by keeping it in contact with your eye for a longer period. Your doctor may take this into account when determining the proper drug dosage.

Possible Side Effects

The most common side effects of Ciprofloxacin are nausea, vomiting, diarrhea, abdominal pain, headache, and rash.

Other side effects are dry mouth, fatigue, drowsiness, feelings of ill health, depression, difficulty sleeping, seizures, psychotic reactions, hallucinations, tingling in the hands or feet, allergic reactions, diarrhea, colitis, fever, vomiting, hearing and visual disturbances (such as blurred or double vision), changes in color perception, halos around lights, and sensitivity to bright light.

Rare side effects include vaginal irritation, high blood pressure, upset stomach, constipation, heartburn, stomach gas, colitis, confusion, itching, skin peeling, and severe skin reactions.

Drug Interactions

Antacids will decrease the amount of Ciprofloxacin absorbed

into the blood. If you must take them, separate your antacid dosage from your Ciprofloxacin dosage by at least 2 hours.

Probenecid and Azlocillin may decrease the amount of Ciprofloxacin released through your kidneys and may increase the chance of drug side effects.

Anticancer drugs may decrease the amount of Ciprofloxacin in your blood.

Nitrofurantoin may antagonize Ciprofloxacin's antibacterial effects. Do not take these drugs together.

Ciprofloxacin may increase the amount of Theophylline in the blood, leading to increased drug side effects and possible drug toxicity.

Ciprofloxacin may increase the effects of anticoagulant (blood-thinning) drugs and can increase the kidney toxicity of Cyclosporine, which is used to prevent rejection in kidney and other organ transplants.

This drug increases the effects of caffeine on your body.

Food Interactions

Take this medicine with a full glass of water. You may take it with food if it upsets your stomach. Food slows the rate at which the drug is absorbed into the blood, but does not affect the total amount absorbed into the blood.

Usual Dose

Oral tablets (adults only): 500 to 1500 milligrams per day. Daily dosage is adjusted in the presence of kidney failure.

Eyedrops: 1 or 2 drops in the affected eye several times a day as directed by the doctor.

Overdosage

The symptoms of Ciprofloxacin overdose are the same as those found under "Possible Side Effects." Overdose victims should be taken to a hospital emergency room for treatment of those symptoms. However, you may induce vomiting with Syrup of Ipecac to remove excess medication from the victim's stomach. Consult the local poison control center or hospital emergency room for specific instructions.

Special Information

Take each dose with a full glass of water and be sure to

drink at least 8 glasses of water a day while taking Ciprofloxacin. This will promote removal of the drug from your system and help to avoid side effects.

Call your doctor if you faint or if you develop facial swelling, itching, rash, difficulty breathing, convulsions, depression, visual disturbances, dizziness, headache, light-headedness, or any intolerable side effect.

It is essential that you take this medicine according to your doctor's directions. Do not stop taking it if you begin to feel better a few days after you start treatment, unless directed to do so by your doctor.

Since Ciprofloxacin can cause visual changes, dizziness, drowsiness, or light-headedness, it can affect your ability to drive a car or do other things requiring full concentration and attention.

If you forget to take a dose of Ciprofloxacin, take it as soon as you remember. If it is almost time for your next regularly scheduled dose, skip the forgotten dose and continue with your regular schedule. Do not take a double dose.

To administer eyedrops, lie down or tilt your head backward and look at the ceiling. Hold the dropper above your eye, hold out your lower lid to make a small pouch, and drop the medicine inside while looking up. Release the lower lid and keep your eye open. Don't blink for about 40 seconds. Press gently on the bridge of your nose at the inside corner of your eye for about a minute to help circulate the medicine around your eye. To avoid infection, don't touch the dropper tip to your finger or eyelid. Wait 5 minutes before using another eyedrop or ointment.

If you forget a dose of Ciprofloxacin eyedrops, take it as soon as you remember. If it is almost time for your next dose, take the forgotten dose as soon as you remember and then go back to your regular schedule. Do not take a double dose.

Call your doctor at once if your stinging, itching or burning, redness, irritation, swelling, or pain gets worse or if you start having trouble seeing.

Generic Name

Clemastine

Brand Name

Tavist/Tavist-1

Type of Drug

Antihistamine.

Prescribed for

Seasonal allergy, stuffed and runny nose, itching of the eyes, scratchy throat caused by allergies, and other allergic symptoms, such as rash, itching, or hives.

General Information

Clemastine is distinguished from most other antihistamines in that it is somewhat less sedating. It works in exactly the same way as Chlorpheniramine and other widely used antihistamines.

Cautions and Warnings

Clemastine should not be taken if you have had an allergic reaction to it in the past. People with asthma or other deep-breathing problems, glaucoma (pressure in the eye), stomach ulcer, or other stomach problems should avoid this drug because its side effects may aggravate these problems.

Pregnancy/Breast-feeding

Antihistamines have not been proven to be a cause of birth defects or other problems in pregnant women, although studies in animals have shown that some antihistamines (Meclizine and Cyclizine), used mainly against nausea and vomiting, may cause birth defects. Do not take any antihistamine without your doctor's knowledge.

Small amounts of antihistamine medicines pass into breast milk and may affect a nursing infant. Nursing mothers should avoid antihistamines or use alternative feeding methods while taking the medicine.

Seniors

Seniors are more sensitive to antihistamine side effects. Confusion, difficult or painful urination, dizziness, drowsiness, a faint feeling, dry mouth, nose, or throat, nightmares or excitement, nervousness, restlessness, and irritability are more likely to occur among older adults.

Possible Side Effects

The most common side effects are headache, nervousness, weakness, upset stomach, nausea, vomiting, cough, stuffed nose, change in bowel habits, sore throat, nosebleeds, and dry mouth, nose, or throat.

Less common side effects include drowsiness, hair loss, allergic reactions, depression, sleeplessness, menstrual irregularities, muscle aches, sweating, tingling in the hands or feet, frequent urination, and visual disturbances.

Drug Interactions

Taking Clemastine with alcohol, tranquilizers, sleeping pills, or other nervous-system depressants can increase the depressant effects of Clemastine.

The effects of oral anticoagulant (blood-thinning) drugs may be decreased by antihistamines. Do not take this combination without your doctor's knowledge.

Monoamine oxidase (MAO) inhibitor drugs (for depression or high blood pressure) may increase the drying and other effects of Clemastine. The combination may also increase urinary difficulty.

Food Interactions

Clemastine should be taken 1 hour before or 2 hours after food or meals, but may be taken with food if it upsets your stomach.

Usual Dose

Adult and child (over age 12): 1.34 milligrams 2 times a day to 2.68 milligrams 3 times a day. Do not take more than 8.04 milligrams (7 tablets of Tavist-1 or 3½ tablets of Tavist).
Child (under age 12): not recommended.

Overdosage

Clemastine overdose is likely to cause exaggerated side effects. A person who has taken a Clemastine overdose should be given Syrup of Ipecac to induce vomiting and taken to a hospital emergency room for treatment. ALWAYS remember to bring the prescription bottle with you.

Special Information

Clemastine can make it difficult for you to concentrate and perform complex tasks like driving a car. Be sure to report any unusual side effects to your doctor.

If you forget to take a dose of Clemastine, take it as soon as you remember. If it is almost time for your next dose, skip the forgotten dose and continue with your regular schedule. Do not take a double dose of Clemastine.

Generic Name

Clindamycin

Brand Names

Cleocin Hydrochloride Capsules
Cleocin T Gel/Lotion/Topical Solution

Type of Drug

Antibiotic.

Prescribed for

Serious infections caused by bacteria that are generally found to be susceptible to this drug.

General Information

This is one of the few drugs given by mouth that is effective against anaerobic organisms: bacteria that grow only in the absence of oxygen and are frequently found in infected wounds, lung abscesses, abdominal infections, and infections of the female genital tract. It is also effective against the organisms usually treated by Penicillin or Erythromycin.

Clindamycin may be useful for treating certain skin or soft tissue infections where susceptible organisms are present.

Cautions and Warnings

Do not take Clindamycin if you are allergic to it or to Lincomycin, another antibiotic drug. It may cause a severe intestinal irritation called colitis, which may be fatal. Because of this, Clindamycin should be reserved for serious infections due to organisms known to be affected by it. It should not be taken for the casual treatment of colds or other moderate infections or for infections that can be successfully treated with other drugs. If you develop severe diarrhea or stomach pains, call your doctor at once.

Pregnancy/Breast-feeding

This drug crosses into the blood circulation of a developing baby. It has not been found to cause birth defects. Nevertheless, pregnant women or those who might become pregnant while taking this drug should not take it without their doctor's approval. When the drug is considered essential by your doctor, the potential risk of taking the medicine must be carefully weighed against the benefit it might produce.

This drug passes into breast milk, but has caused no problems among breast-fed infants. You must consider the potential effect on the nursing infant if breast-feeding while taking this medicine.

Seniors

Older adults may take this medication without special consideration.

Possible Side Effects

Possible side effects include stomach pain, nausea, vomiting, diarrhea, and pain when swallowing.

Less common side effects are itching and rash or more serious signs of drug sensitivity, such as difficulty in breathing; yellowing of the skin or whites of the eyes; occasional effects on components of the blood; and joint pain.

Drug Interactions

Clindamycin may antagonize Erythromycin; these drugs should not be taken together.

Food Interactions

Take this medication with a full glass of water or food to prevent irritation of the stomach or intestine.

Usual Dose

Adult: 150 to 450 milligrams every 6 hours.

Child: 4 to 11 milligrams per pound of body weight per day in divided doses. No child should be given less than 37.5 milligrams 3 times per day, regardless of weight.

Topical lotion: Apply enough to cover the affected area(s) lightly.

Special Information

Unsupervised use of this drug or other antibiotics can cause secondary infections from susceptible organisms such as fungi. As with any antibiotic treatment, take this drug for the full course of therapy as indicated by your physician.

If you miss an oral dose of Clindamycin, take it as soon as possible. If it is almost time for your next dose, double that dose and go back to your regular dose schedule.

Generic Name

Clofibrate

Brand Name

Atromid-S

(Also available in generic form)

Type of Drug

Antihyperlipidemic (blood-fat reducer).

Prescribed for

Reduction of high blood levels of triglycerides and cholesterol in patients who do not respond to diet, weight control, and exercise measures to control their diabetes. Clofibrate has also been used to treat a condition known as diabetes insipidus, but it has been mostly replaced by other medicines.

General Information

Although we don't know exactly how Clofibrate works, we do know that it works on both blood cholesterol and triglycerides by interfering with the natural systems that make those blood fats and by increasing the rate at which they are removed from the body. It is generally much more effective in reducing blood triglycerides than cholesterol.

Lower blood-fat levels are considered beneficial in reducing the chances of developing heart disease, but people with high cholesterol and low triglycerides should not take Clofibrate because it is not the most effective treatment for high cholesterol.

Clofibrate is only part of the therapy for high blood levels of cholesterol and/or triglycerides. Diet and weight control are also very important. You must remember that taking this medicine is not a substitute for other activities or dietary restrictions which have been prescribed for you by your doctor.

Cautions and Warnings

Clofibrate causes liver cancer in rats and may do the same to people. It should be used with caution if you are allergic to the drug or if you have cirrhosis of the liver, heart disease, gall stones, liver disease, an under-active thyroid, or stomach ulcer. People with kidney disease may take Clofibrate as long as their daily dosage is calibrated for their degree of kidney function loss.

Clofibrate has not been shown to reduce the number of deaths from heart disease; therefore, this drug should be used only by patients whose diets and other activities have not solved their triglyceride or cholesterol problems.

Pregnancy/Breast-feeding

Women who are pregnant should not take this drug because large concentrations of Clofibrate pass into the developing fetus. If you plan to become pregnant, stop taking Clofibrate several months before you expect to become pregnant.

It is not known if Clofibrate passes into breast milk, but it should not be taken by nursing mothers because the drug can cause serious effects on nursing infants.

Seniors

Older adults generally take this medicine without restriction. Normal losses of kidney function that are expected with advancing age may require your doctor to adjust your daily dosage of Clofibrate.

Possible Side Effects

The most frequent side effects of Clofibrate are diarrhea and nausea. Other gastrointestinal reactions, such as loose stools, stomach upset, stomach gas, and abdominal pain, may also occur.

Less frequent side effects include headache, dizziness, tiredness, cramped muscles, aching and weakness, rash, itching, brittle hair, loss of hair, abnormal heart rhythms, blood clots in the lungs or veins, enlargement of the liver, gallstones (especially in patients who have taken Clofibrate for a long time), decreased sex drive, and sexual impotence.

If you suffer from angina pectoris, a specific type of chest pain, Clofibrate may increase this pain. This drug may cause you to produce smaller amounts of urine than usual, and it has been associated with blood in the urine, tiredness, weakness, drowsiness, and mildly increased appetite and weight gain. Clofibrate has been accused of causing stomach ulcers, stomach bleeding, arthritis-like symptoms, uncontrollable muscle spasms, increased perspiration, blurred vision, breast enlargement, and some effects on the blood.

An early (1978) study of Clofibrate suggested that taking it regularly for many years increases the chances of dying from noncardiac causes, but this inference has not been confirmed by more recent work.

Drug Interactions

If you are taking an anticoagulant and get a new prescription for Clofibrate, your anticoagulant dose will have to be reduced by up to one-half. It is absolutely essential that your doctor knows you are taking both drugs so that the proper dose adjustments can be made.

The effect of Chenodiol may be decreased when it is taken together with Clofibrate.

Clofibrate may increase the effect of oral antidiabetes drugs and can increase the effects of any drug used to treat diabetes insipidus, including Carbamazepine, Chlorpropamide, Desmopressin, some diuretics, and hormone replacement products.

Oral contraceptive drugs can alter the effectiveness of Clofibrate. Probenecid can increase the effectiveness and side effects of Clofibrate.

The combination of Furosemide and Clofibrate can result in an increased effect of both drugs. This interaction can lead to stiffness, muscle pain, and excess urination.

Clofibrate can interfere with a number of blood tests. Make sure your doctor knows you are taking the drug before any blood tests are taken.

Food Interactions

This drug may be taken with food or milk if it causes upset stomach.

Usual Dose

1500 to 2000 milligrams per day in divided doses.

Overdosage

Overdose symptoms are most likely to be exaggerated drug side effects. Take the overdose victim to a hospital emergency room for treatment. ALWAYS bring the medicine bottle with you.

Special Information

Call your doctor if you develop chest pains, difficulty breathing, abnormal heart rates, severe stomach pains with nausea and vomiting, fever and chills, sore throat, blood in the urine, swelling of the legs, weight gain, or change in urine habits, or if other side effects become intolerable.

Follow your diet and limit your intake of alcoholic beverages.

Clofibrate capsules are covered with soft gelatin that must

be protected from heat and moisture. The capsules should not be stored in the refrigerator or in a bathroom medicine chest, where there may be a lot of heat or moisture in the air; store them in a dresser or night table, where room temperature is normal.

Regular visits to your doctor are necessary while taking Clofibrate to be sure the drug is still working and to be screened with blood counts and liver function tests, which may uncover possible drug side effects.

If you miss a dose, take it as soon as possible. If it is almost time for your next dose, skip the missed dose and go back to your regular dose schedule. Do not double any doses.

Generic Name

Clomipramine

Brand name

Anafranil

Type of Drug

Antidepressant.

Prescribed for

Obsessive-compulsive disorder with or without depression. It may also be used for narcolepsy.

General Information

Clomipramine is a tricyclic antidepressant. It and other members of this group of drugs are effective in treating depressive illness, but Clomipramine is the only member of the group used to treat obsessive-compulsive symptoms that cause marked distress, are time-consuming, or interfere with a person's ability to function socially or in the workplace. It is not known how Clomipramine produces its effect, but the drug interferes with the action of a neurohormone called serotonin.

Cautions and Warnings

Do not take Clomipramine if you are allergic or sensitive to it or to other members of this group of drugs. It should not be used if you are recovering from a heart attack, and it should be used with caution if you have a history of epilepsy or other convulsive disorders, urinary difficulties, glaucoma, heart disease, or thyroid disease. Do not stop taking this medicine without your doctor's knowledge, or you may become nauseated, weak, and headachy or have vivid dreams.

Pregnancy/Breast-feeding

There are no reports of Clomipramine use by pregnant women, but other members of this group have caused birth difficulties and birth defects. Animal studies of Clomipramine have produced inconclusive results. Pregnant women, or those who might become pregnant while using the drug, should not use Clomipramine unless absolutely necessary and with their doctors' knowledge and approval.

Small amounts of Clomipramine may pass into breast milk and may affect a nursing infant. Nursing mothers who must take Clomipramine should consider bottle-feeding.

Seniors

Older adults are more sensitive to the therapeutic and side effects of this drug and may require a smaller dose of Clomipramine and more gradual dose increases. Follow your doctor's directions and report any side effects at once.

Possible Side Effects

Possible side effects include blood pressure changes (high and low), abnormal heart rates, heart attack, confusion (especially in older adults), hallucinations, disorientation, delusions, anxiety, restlessness, excitement, numbness and tingling in the hands and feet, lack of coordination, muscle spasms, tremors, convulsions or seizures, dry mouth, blurred vision, constipation, urinary difficulty, rash, itching, sensitivity to bright lights or sunlight, fluid retention, fever, allergic reactions, changes in blood composition, nausea, vomiting, appetite loss, upset stomach, diarrhea, painful breast enlargement in men and women, changes in sex drives, and changes in blood sugar.

Less common side effects are agitation, sleeping difficulties, nightmares, panic, peculiar taste sensations, stomach cramps, discoloration of the tongue, yellowing of the eyes and/or skin, liver function changes, weight changes, perspiration, flushing, urinary frequency, drowsiness, dizziness, weakness, headache, hair loss, and feelings of ill health.

Drug Interactions

Clomipramine increases the effects of alcohol and other nervous-system depressants.

This drug may interact with antihistamines to produce exaggerated drug side effects (dry mouth, blurred vision, constipation, urinary difficulty, sensitivity to bright light or sun).

Clomipramine may increase the effects of Cyclobenzaprine, Haloperidol, Loxapine, Molindone, Pimozide, anticoagulant (blood-thinning) drugs, anticonvulsants, thyroid hormones and antithyroid drugs, phenothiazines, or thioxanthenes.

The effects of nasal decongestants like Naphazoline, Oxymetazoline, Phenylephrine, and Xylometazoline may be increased by Clomipramine.

Monoamine oxidase (MAO) inhibitors and antidepressants may produce high fevers, severe convulsions, very high blood pressure, and death. However, this combination of drugs may be used, under your doctor's direct supervision, to control severe depression that does not respond to other treatments.

Barbiturates and Carbamazepine may counteract the effects of antidepressants like Clomipramine.

Fluoxetine, Ranitidine, Cimetidine, Methylphenidate, Estramustine, estrogens, and birth control pills may increase the effects and side effects of Clomipramine.

Clomipramine may counteract the effects of Clonidine, Guanadrel, and Guanethidine.

Food Interactions

Take Clomipramine with food or meals to reduce upset stomach.

Usual Dose

Adult: 25 to 250 milligrams per day.
Child: 25 to 100 milligrams per day.
After the dose has been determined, the total daily dose may be taken at bedtime to minimize daytime sedation.

Overdosage

Overdose symptoms are confusion, difficulty concentrating, hallucinations, drowsiness, low body temperature, changes in heart rate, heart failure, enlarged pupils, convulsions, very low blood pressure, stupor, and coma. Take the overdose victim to an emergency room at once. ALWAYS bring the medicine bottle.

Special Information

Clomipramine can cause blurred vision, drowsiness, and dizziness. Take care when driving or operating complicated equipment.

Do not stop taking Clomipramine without your doctor's knowledge. Abruptly stopping this medicine can produce nausea, headache, and a feeling of ill health.

Avoid exposure to the sun or bright lights and call your doctor if dry mouth, urinary difficulty, or excessive sedation develops.

If you take Clomipramine once a day and forget to take a dose, take it as soon as you remember. If it is almost time for your next dose, skip the one you forgot and continue with your regular schedule. Do not take a double dose.

If you take Clomipramine twice a day and forget a dose, take it as soon as you remember. If it is almost time for your next dose, take one dose as soon as you remember and another in 5 or 6 hours, then go back to your regular schedule.

If you take Clomipramine 3 times a day and forget a dose, take it as soon as you remember. If it is almost time for your next dose, take one dose as soon as you remember and another in 3 or 4 hours, then go back to your regular schedule.

Generic Name

Clonazepam

Brand Name
Klonopin

Type of Drug
Anticonvulsant.

Prescribed for
Control of petit mal and other seizures. Clonazepam has also been used to treat panic attacks.

General Information
Clonazepam is a member of the family of drugs known as benzodiazepines. Other members of the family include Diazepam, Chlordiazepoxide, Flurazepam, and Triazolam. Clonazepam is used only to control petit mal seizures in people who have not responded to other drug treatments, such as Ethosuximide. Clonazepam is generally considered a safe and effective treatment for such seizures and shares many of the same side effects, precautions, and interactions as its benzodiazepine cousins. People commonly develop tolerance to the effects of Clonazepam within about 3 months of starting on it. This happens because of the body's natural tendency to increase its efficiency in breaking the drug down and eliminating it from the circulation. Your doctor may have to periodically increase your Clonazepam dosage to maintain the drug's effect.

Cautions and Warnings
When stopping Clonazepam treatments, it is essential that the drug be discontinued gradually over a period of time to allow for safe withdrawal. Abrupt discontinuation of any benzodiazepine, including Clonazepam, may lead to drug withdrawal symptoms. In the case of Clonazepam, the withdrawal symptoms can include severe seizures. Other symptoms include tremors, abdominal cramps, muscle cramps, vomiting, and sweating.

Clonazepam should be used with caution if you have a chronic respiratory illness because the drug tends to increase salivation and other respiratory secretions and can make breathing more labored.

Pregnancy/Breast-feeding

Clonazepam should be avoided by women who may become pregnant while using it and by pregnant and nursing mothers. It will cross into the developing infant and can affect the developing infant. In those situations where the drug is deemed essential, the potential risk of the drug must be carefully weighed against any benefit it might produce.

Some reports suggest a strong association between the use of anticonvulsant drugs and birth defects. Although most of the information pertains to Phenytoin and Phenobarbital, not Clonazepam, other reports indicate a general association between anticonvulsant drug treatments and birth defects. It is possible that the epileptic condition itself or genetic factors common to people with seizure disorders may also figure in the higher incidence of birth defects.

Mothers taking Clonazepam should not breast-feed because of the possibility that the drug will pass into their breast milk and affect the baby. Use an alternative feeding method.

Seniors

Older adults are more sensitive to the effects of this drug, especially dizziness and drowsiness. Follow your doctor's directions and report any side effects at once.

Possible Side Effects

Possible side effects include drowsiness, poor muscle control, and behavior changes.

Less common side effects are abnormal eye movements, loss of voice and/or the ability to express a thought, double vision, coma, a glassy-eyed appearance, headache, temporary paralysis, labored breathing, shortness of breath, slurred speech, tremors, dizziness, fainting, confusion, depression, forgetfulness, hallucination, increased sex drive, hysteria, sleeplessness, psychosis, suicidal acts, chest congestion, stuffy nose, heart palpitations, hair loss, hairiness, rash, swelling of the face or ankles, changes in appetite and body weight (increased or decreased), coated tongue, constipation, diarrhea, involuntary passing of feces, dry mouth, stomach irritation, nausea, sore gums, difficulty urinating, pain on urination, bed-wetting, getting up at night to urinate, muscle weakness or pain, reduced red- and white-blood-cell and platelet levels, enlarged liver, liver inflammation, dehydration, a deterioration in general health, fever, and swollen lymph glands.

Drug Interactions

The depressant effects of Clonazepam are increased by tranquilizers, sleeping pills, narcotic pain relievers, antihistamines, alcohol, monoamine oxidase (MAO) inhibitors, antidepressants, and other anticonvulsants.

The combination of Valproic Acid and Clonazepam may produce severe petit mal seizures.

Phenobarbital or Phenytoin may reduce Clonazepam effectiveness by increasing the rate at which it is eliminated from the body.

Clonazepam treatment may increase the requirement for other anticonvulsant drugs because of its effects on people who suffer from multiple types of seizures.

Smoking may reduce Clonazepam's effectiveness.

Food Interactions

Clonazepam is best taken on an empty stomach but may be taken with food if it upsets your stomach.

Usual Dose

Adult and child (over age 10): 0.5 milligram 3 times per day to start. The dose is increased in steps of 0.5 to 1 milligram every 3 days until seizures are controlled or side effects develop. The maximum daily dose is 20 milligrams.

Infant and child (up to age 10, or 66 pounds): 0.004 to 0.013 milligram per pound of body weight per day to start. The dosage can be gradually increased to a maximum of 0.045 to 0.09 milligram per pound of body weight.

The dosage of Clonazepam must be reduced in people with impaired kidney function because this drug is primarily released from the body via the kidneys.

Overdosage

Clonazepam overdose will cause confusion, coma, poor reflexes, sleepiness, low blood pressure, labored breathing, and other depressive effects. If the overdose is discovered immediately, it may be helpful to make the victim vomit with Syrup of Ipecac to remove any remaining medicine from the stomach. All victims of Clonazepam overdose *must* be taken to a hospital emergency room for treatment. ALWAYS bring the prescription bottle with you.

Special Information

Clonazepam may interfere with your ability to drive a car or perform other complex tasks because it can cause drowsiness and difficulty concentrating.

Your doctor should perform periodic blood counts and liver-function tests while you are taking this drug to check for possible adverse drug effects.

Do not suddenly stop taking the medicine, since doing so could result in severe seizures. The dosage must be discontinued gradually by your doctor.

If you miss a dose, and it is within an hour or so of that dose time, take it right away. Otherwise skip the missed dose and go back to your regular dose schedule. Do not double any dose.

Carry identification or wear a bracelet indicating that you suffer from a seizure disorder for which you take Clonazepam.

Generic Name

Clonidine

Brand Name

Catapres Tablets
Catapres-TTS Transdermal Patch

(Tablets also available in generic form)

Type of Drug

Antihypertensive.

Prescribed for

High blood pressure. Clonidine has also been used in the treatment of nicotine dependence, Tourette's syndrome, migraine headaches, Methadone/opiate detoxification, and withdrawal from alcohol and benzodiazepines (e.g., Valium).

General Information

Clonidine acts in the brain by causing the dilation of certain blood vessels, thereby decreasing blood pressure. The drug produces its effect very quickly, causing a decline in blood pressure within 1 hour. If you abruptly stop taking Clonidine you may experience an unusual increase in blood pressure with symptoms of agitation, headache, and nervousness. These effects can be reversed by simply resuming therapy or by taking another drug to lower the blood pressure. Under no circumstances should you stop taking Clonidine without your doctor's knowledge. People who abruptly stop taking this medication may suffer severe reactions and even die. Be sure you always have an adequate supply on hand.

Cautions and Warnings

Some people develop a tolerance to their usual dose of Clonidine. If this happens to you, your blood pressure may increase, and you will require a change in the Clonidine dose.

Pregnancy/Breast-feeding

Animal studies have shown this drug to be potentially damaging to a developing fetus in doses as low as one-third the maximum human dose. Pregnant women, and those who might become pregnant, should avoid this drug.

Clonidine passes into breast milk, but no effects on nursing infants have been noted. Nursing mothers should avoid this drug or use an alternative feeding method.

Seniors

Older adults are more susceptible to the effects of this drug and should be given lower than normal doses.

Possible Side Effects

The most common side effects are dry mouth, drowsiness, sedation, constipation, dizziness, headache, and fatigue. These effects tend to diminish as you continue taking the drug.

Infrequent side effects include loss of appetite, not feeling well, nausea, vomiting, weight gain, breast enlargement, various effects on the heart, changes in dream patterns, nightmares, difficulty sleeping, nervousness, restlessness, anxiety, mental depression, rash, hives, itching, thinning or loss of scalp hair, difficulty urinating, impotence, and dryness and burning of the eyes.

Drug Interactions

Clonidine has a depressive effect and will increase the depressive effects of alcohol, barbiturates, sedatives, and tranquilizers. Avoid them.

Antidepressants, appetite suppressants, estrogens, stimulants, Indocin, and other NSAIDs (nonsteroidal anti-inflammatory drugs) may counteract the effects of Clonidine.

Food Interactions

Clonidine is best taken on an empty stomach but may be taken with food if it upsets your stomach.

Usual Dose

The starting dose of 0.1 milligram twice per day may be raised by 0.1 to 0.2 milligram per day until maximum control is achieved. The dose must be tailored to your individual needs. It is recommended that no one take more than 2.4 milligrams per day.

Opiate detoxification: up to 0.008 milligram per pound of body weight in divided doses.

Transdermal patch: 0.1-milligram patch applied every 7 days. Two 0.3-milligram patches have not been shown to increase effectiveness.

Overdosage

Symptoms are severe lowering of blood pressure, weakness, and vomiting. The patient should be taken to a hospital emergency room immediately. ALWAYS bring the medicine bottle.

Special Information

Clonidine causes drowsiness in about 35 percent of those who take it: Be extremely careful while driving or operating any sort of appliance or machinery. The effect is prominent during the first few weeks of therapy, then tends to decrease.

Avoid taking nonprescription cough and cold medicines unless so directed by your doctor.

Apply the patch to a hairless area of skin like the upper arm or torso. Use a different skin site each time. If the patch becomes loose during the 7 days, apply the specially supplied adhesive directly over the patch. If the patch falls off apply a new one. The patch should not be removed for bathing.

If you miss a dose of the oral medication, take it as soon as possible and go back to your regular dose schedule. If you miss 2 or more doses in a row, consult your doctor. Missing 2 or more doses could cause your blood pressure to go up and severe adverse effects to occur.

Generic Name

Clorazepate Dipotassium

Brand Name

Tranxene/Tranxene-SD

(Also available in generic form)

Type of Drug

Tranquilizer.

Prescribed for

Relief of symptoms of anxiety, tension, fatigue, or agitation. Clorazepate is also utilized to treat seizures and alcohol withdrawal.

General Information

Clorazepate is a member of the group of drugs known as benzodiazepines. These drugs are widely used as antianxiety agents, anticonvulsants, or sedatives (sleeping pills). They exert their effects by relaxing the large skeletal muscles and by increasing, in the brain, the effects of an amino acid known as GABA, which slows nerve transmission. In doing so, they can relax you and make you either more tranquil or sleepier, depending on the drug and how much you use. Many doctors prefer Clorazepate and the other members of this class to other drugs that can be used for the same effect. Their reason is that the benzodiazepines tend to be safer, have fewer side effects, and are usually as, if not more, effective.

These drugs are generally used in any situation where they can be a useful adjunct.

Benzodiazepine tranquilizing drugs can be abused if taken for long periods of time, and it is possible to develop withdrawal symptoms if you discontinue the therapy abruptly. Withdrawal symptoms include tremor, muscle cramps, stomach cramps, vomiting, insomnia, agitation, sweating, and even convulsions.

Cautions and Warnings

Do not take Clorazepate if you know you are sensitive or allergic to it or to other benzodiazepines such as Chlordiazepoxide, Diazepam, Oxazepam, Lorazepam, Prazepam, Flurazepam, Clonazepam, and Temazepam. Clorazepate and other members of this drug group may aggravate narrow-angle glaucoma, but if you have open-angle glaucoma you may take these drugs. In any case, check this information with your doctor.

Pregnancy/Breast-feeding

Avoid taking this drug during the first 3 months of pregnancy except under strict supervision by your doctor. Drugs similar to Clorazepate have been shown to affect a newborn baby, causing sucking difficulties, lethargy, and poor muscle tone.

The baby may become dependent on Clorazepate if the drug is used continuously during pregnancy. If the drug is used during the last weeks of pregnancy or during breast-feeding, the baby may be over-tired or short of breath or have a low heartbeat.

Use during labor may cause weakness in the newborn.

Seniors

Older adults are more sensitive to the effects of this drug. Follow your doctor's directions and report any side effects at once.

Possible Side Effects

The most common side effects are mild drowsiness during the first few days of therapy, especially in older adults or the debilitated. If drowsiness persists, contact your doctor.

Less common side effects are confusion, depression, lethargy, disorientation, headache, inactivity, slurred speech, stupor, dizziness, tremor, constipation, dry mouth, nausea, inability to control urination, changes in sex drive and performance, irregular menstrual cycle, changes in heart rhythm, lowered blood pressure, retention of fluids, blurred or double vision, itching, rash, hiccups, nervousness, inability to fall asleep, and, occasionally, liver dysfunction. If you experience any of these reactions, stop taking the medicine and contact your doctor immediately.

Drug Interactions

Clorazepate is a central-nervous-system depressant. Avoid alcohol, tranquilizers, narcotics, barbiturates, monoamine oxidase (MAO) inhibitors, antihistamines, and other medicines used to relieve depression.

Smoking may reduce the effectiveness of Clorazepate.

The effects of Clorazepate may be prolonged when it is taken together with Cimetidine.

Food Interactions

This drug is best taken on an empty stomach but may be taken with food if it upsets your stomach.

Usual Dose

15 to 60 milligrams daily; average dose, 30 milligrams in

divided quantities. The dose must be adjusted to individual response for the patient to receive the maximum effect.

Tranxene-SD, a long-acting form of Clorazepate, may be given as a single dose, either 11.25 or 22.5 milligrams once every 24 hours.

Overdosage

Symptoms are confusion, sleep or sleepiness, lack of response to pain (such as a pin stick), shallow breathing, lowered blood pressure, and coma. The patient should be taken to a hospital emergency room immediately. ALWAYS bring the medicine bottle.

Special Information

Clorazepate can cause tiredness, drowsiness, inability to concentrate, or similar symptoms. Be careful if you are driving, operating machinery, or performing other activities that require concentration.

If you miss a dose, take it as soon as you remember. If it is almost time for your next dose, skip the missed dose and go back to your regular dose schedule. Do not double any doses.

Generic Name

Clotrimazole

Brand Names

Gyne-Lotrimin Vaginal Cream/Tablets
Lotrimin Cream/Lotion/Solution
Mycelex Cream/Solution/Troches
Mycelex-G Vaginal Cream/Tablets

(Also available in generic form)

Type of Drug

Antifungal.

Prescribed for

Fungus infections of the mouth, skin, and vaginal tract.

General Information

Clotrimazole is one of a group of the newer antifungal drugs available in the United States, although it has been available in other parts of the world for some time. This drug is especially useful against a wide variety of fungus organisms that other drugs do not affect.

Cautions and Warnings

If Clotrimazole causes local itching and/or irritation, stop using it. Do not use in the eyes.

Pregnancy/Breast-feeding

No studies of this medication have been done in pregnant women and no reports of human birth defects exist, but animal studies show that high doses of the drug can cause problems in a developing fetus. Pregnant women, or women who might become pregnant while using this drug, should talk to their doctor about the risk of taking this medicine versus the benefits it can provide. Women who are in the first 3 months of pregnancy should use this drug only if directed to do so by their doctors.

This drug is poorly absorbed into the bloodstream and not likely to pass into breast milk. Nursing mothers need not worry about adverse effects on their infants while taking Clotrimazole.

Seniors

Seniors may use this medication without restriction.

Possible Side Effects

Side effects do not occur very often and are usually mild.

Cream or solution: redness, stinging, blistering, peeling, itching and swelling of local areas.

Vaginal tablets: mild burning, skin rash, mild cramps, frequent urination, burning or itching in a sexual partner.

Oral tablets: stomach cramps or pain, diarrhea, nausea, vomiting.

Food Interactions

The oral form of Clotrimazole is best taken on an empty

stomach, but you may take it with food, just as long as you allow the tablet to dissolve in your mouth like a lozenge.

Usual Dose

Topical cream or solution: apply to affected areas, morning and night.

Vaginal cream: one applicatorful at bedtime for 7 to 14 days.

Vaginal tablets: 1 tablet inserted into the vagina at bedtime for 7 days, or 2 tablets a day for 3 days.

Lozenges: 1 lozenge 5 times a day for 2 weeks or more.

Special Information

If treating a vaginal infection, you should refrain from sexual activity or be sure that your partner wears a condom until the treatment is finished. Call your doctor if burning or itching develops or if the condition does not show improvement in 7 days.

Dissolve the oral troche slowly in the mouth. Do not swallow it.

This medicine must be taken on consecutive days. If you forget to take a dose of oral Clotrimazole, take it as soon as you remember. Do not double any doses.

Generic Name

Clozapine

Brand Name

Clozaril

Type of Drug

Antipsychotic.

Prescribed for

Severely ill schizophrenics who do not respond to other medicines.

General Information

Clozapine is a unique antipsychotic that has the capacity to treat people who either don't respond to other drugs or suffer from severe side effects of those drugs. It works by a mechanism that differs from those of other antipsychotic drugs.

The problem with Clozapine is that a very small number of people who take it develop a rapid drop in white-blood-cell count called *agranulocytosis*. This effect usually reverses itself when the drug is stopped, but the patient must stop taking the drug AS SOON AS IT IS DISCOVERED. It is essential that blood samples be taken every week or so to watch for this effect.

Cautions and Warnings

People with a history of diseases affecting the white blood cells or who are taking other drugs that could affect white blood cells should not use Clozapine because they may be more susceptible to agranulocytosis. There is no easy way to know who is likely to develop agranulocytosis from Clozapine. A disproportionately large number of people who have developed Clozapine-related agranulocytosis in the United States are Eastern European Jews, but the association is not very strong. Most cases of agranulocytosis occur within between week 4 and week 10 of treatment.

About 5% of people taking the drug experience a seizure in the first year of treatment. Seizure is most likely at higher drug doses. People with heart disease should be carefully monitored while on Clozapine because of possible cardiac risks.

Some people taking antipsychotic drugs develop a group of potentially irreversible, uncontrollable movements. This has not been reported with Clozapine and is seen as a major advantage of the drug. However, there is still a possibility that this set of symptoms could occur with Clozapine.

Clozapine patients may develop a fever during the first few weeks of treatment. Generally, the fever is not important, but it may occasionally be necessary to stop treatment because of a persistent fever. This decision is made by the supervising doctor.

Clozapine should be used with caution by people with

glaucoma or prostate problems or with liver, kidney, or heart disease.

This drug may interfere with mental or physical abilities because of the sedation it usually causes in the first few weeks of treatment.

Pregnancy/Breast-feeding

This drug should be used during pregnancy only if necessary and the benefits of the drug have been weighed against its possible risks.

Clozapine may pass into breast milk. Nursing mothers who must take this drug should bottle-feed their babies.

Seniors

Older adults may be more likely to experience some of Clozapine's side effects (such as dizziness on rapidly rising from a sitting or lying position, confusion, excitement) than younger adults. Older men are also more likely to have prostate problems, a cause for caution with Clozapine.

Possible Side Effects

The most common side effects are rapid or irregular heartbeats, low blood pressure, dizziness on rapidly rising from a sitting or lying position, and fever in the first 3 weeks of treatment.

Less frequent side effects include agitation, restlessness, confusion, blurred vision, electocardiogram changes, high blood pressure, dizziness, severe headaches, and fainting.

Rare side effects include agranulocytosis and other changes in blood components, absence of movement, severe muscle stiffness, tremors, impotence, difficulty sleeping, depression, seizures, tardive dyskinesia (characterized by lip smacking or puckering, puffing of the cheeks, rapid tongue movement, and uncontrolled chewing motions), and neuroleptic malignant syndrome (characterized by convulsions, difficulty breathing, rapid heartbeat or irregular pulse, fever, blood-pressure changes, sweating, loss of bladder control, severe muscle stiffness, pale skin, and unusual tiredness. If these symptoms occur, take the patient to a hospital emergency room immediately for treatment. ALWAYS bring the medicine bottle with you.

Drug Interactions

Clozapine's anticholinergic effects (blurred vision, dry mouth, confusion) may be enhanced by other anticholinergic drugs, such as the antidepressants.

Drugs that reduce blood pressure may enhance the blood-pressure-lowering effects of Clozapine.

Alcohol and other nervous-system depressants, including benzodiazepines and other antianxiety drugs, may enhance Clozapine's sedative actions. There is at least one known case of a patient dying while taking a combination of Diazepam and Clozapine.

Clozapine may increase blood levels of Digoxin, Warfarin, Heparin, or Phenytoin.

The combination of Lithium and Clozapine may cause seizures, confusion, and neuroleptic malignant syndrome (see "Possible Side Effects").

Cigarette smoking may increase the rate at which the liver breaks down Clozapine, altering dosage requirements. This is usually only a problem if a person changes his or her smoking habits while taking the drug.

Food Interactions

Clozapine may be taken without regard to food or meals.

Usual Dose

25 milligrams twice a day to start, with gradual dosage increases to 900 milligrams daily, although no more than 600 milligrams daily is usually required.

Overdosage

Usual symptoms of overdose are changes in heart rhythm, unusual excitement, nervousness, restlessness, hallucinations, severe drowsiness, excessive salivation, dizziness or fainting, slow or irregular breathing, and rapid or irregular heartbeat. Any victim of a Clozapine overdose must be taken to a hospital emergency room immediately. ALWAYS take the medicine bottle with you.

Special Information

Regular blood tests are necessary to monitor blood composition for any changes that might be caused by Clozapine.

Call your doctor at once if you develop lethargy or weakness, a flu-like infection, sore throat, a sickly feeling, mouth ulcers, or dry mouth that lasts for more than 2 weeks. Dry mouth, a common side effect of Clozapine, may be countered by using gum, candy, ice, or a saliva substitute.

Do not stop taking Clozapine without your doctor's knowledge and approval. A gradual dosage reduction may be needed.

Avoid alcohol or any other nervous-system depressant while taking Clozapine.

Some of the side effects of Clozapine (drowsiness, blurred vision, or seizures) may interfere with the performance of complex tasks or those that require intense concentration, like driving or operating equipment.

Be aware, while taking Clozapine, that rapidly rising from a sitting or lying position may cause you to become dizzy.

If you take Clozapine twice a day and forget a dose, take it as soon as you remember. If it is almost time for your next dose, take one dose as soon as you remember and another in 5 or 6 hours, then go back to your regular schedule. Do not take a double dose.

If you take Clozapine 3 times a day and forget a dose, take it as soon as you remember. If it is almost time for your next dose, take one dose as soon as you remember and another in 3 or 4 hours, then go back to your regular schedule. Do not take a double dose of Clozapine.

Generic Name

Codeine

(Available only in generic form)

Type of Drug

Narcotic analgesic/cough suppressant combination.

Prescribed for

Relief of moderate pain and as a cough suppressant.

General Information

Codeine is a narcotic drug with some pain-relieving and cough-suppressing activity. As an analgesic it is useful for mild to moderate pain. 30 to 60 milligrams of Codeine is approximately equal in pain-relieving effect to 2 Aspirin tablets (650 milligrams). Codeine may be less active than Aspirin for types of pain associated with inflammation, since Aspirin reduces inflammation and Codeine does not. Codeine suppresses the cough reflex but does not cure the underlying cause of the cough. In fact, sometimes it may not be desirable to overly suppress a cough, because cough suppression reduces your ability to naturally eliminate excess mucus produced during a cold or allergy attack. Other narcotic cough suppressants are stronger than Codeine, but Codeine remains the best cough medicine available today.

Cautions and Warnings

Do not take Codeine if you know you are allergic or sensitive to it. Use this drug with extreme caution if you suffer from asthma or other breathing problems. Long-term use of this drug may cause drug dependence or addiction.

Pregnancy/Breast-feeding

No studies of this medication have been done in women and no reports of human birth defects exist, but animal studies show that high doses of the drug can cause problems in a developing fetus. Pregnant women, or women who might become pregnant while using this drug, should talk to their doctor about the risk of taking this medicine versus the benefits it can provide.

This drug passes into breast milk, but no problems in nursing infants have been seen. Breast-feeding women should consider the possibility of adverse effects on their nursing infant. Choose another feeding method if you must take this medicine.

Seniors

Seniors are more likely to be sensitive to side effects of this drug and should be treated with smaller dosages than younger adults.

Possible Side Effects

The most frequent side effects are light-headedness, dizziness, sleepiness, nausea, vomiting, loss of appetite, and sweating. If these occur, consider calling your doctor and asking him about lowering the dose of Codeine you are taking. Usually the side effects disappear if you simply lie down.

More serious side effects of Codeine are shallow breathing or difficulty in breathing.

Less common side effects are euphoria (feeling high), sleepiness, headache, agitation, uncoordinated muscle movement, minor hallucinations, disorientation and visual disturbances, dry mouth, loss of appetite, constipation, flushing of the face, rapid heartbeat, palpitations, faintness, urinary difficulties or hesitancy, reduced sex drive and/or potency, itching, rashes, anemia, lowered blood sugar, and yellowing of the skin and/or whites of the eyes. Narcotic analgesics may aggravate convulsions in those who have had convulsions in the past.

Drug Interactions

Because of its depressant effect and potential effect on breathing, Codeine should be taken with extreme care in combination with alcohol, sleeping medicine, tranquilizers, or other depressant drugs.

Food Interactions

Codeine may be taken with food to reduce stomach upset.

Usual Dose

Adult: 15 to 60 milligrams 4 times per day for relief of pain; 10 to 20 milligrams every few hours as needed to suppress cough.

Child: 1 to 2 milligrams per pound of body weight in divided doses for relief of pain; 0.5 to 0.75 milligram per pound of body weight in divided doses to suppress cough.

Overdosage

Symptoms are depression of respiration (breathing), extreme tiredness progressing to stupor and then coma, pinpointed pupils of the eyes, no response to stimulation such

as a pin stick, cold and clammy skin, slowing down of the
heartbeat, lowering of blood pressure, convulsions, and cardiac arrest. The patient should be taken to a hospital emergency room immediately. ALWAYS bring the medicine
bottle.

Special Information

Codeine is a respiratory depressant and affects the central
nervous system, producing sleepiness, tiredness, and/or inability to concentrate. Be careful if you are driving, operating machinery, or performing other functions requiring
concentration.

Avoid alcohol while taking Codeine.

Call your doctor if you develop constipation or dry mouth.

If you forget a dose of Codeine, take it as soon as you
remember. If it is almost time for your next dose, skip the
one you forgot and continue with your regular schedule. Do
not take a double dose of Codeine.

Generic Name

Colchicine

(Available only in generic form)

Type of Drug

Reduces the inflammatory response to gout.

Prescribed for

Gouty arthritis. It may also be prescribed for Mediterrane-
an Fever, calcium deposits, amyloidosis, Paget's disease of
bone, and nerve problems associated with multiple
sclerosis.

General Information

While no one knows exactly how Colchicine works, it appears to affect gout by reducing the body's inflammatory
response to gout. Unlike drugs that affect uric-acid levels,
Colchicine will not block the progression of gout to chronic

gouty arthritis, but it will relieve the pain of acute attacks
and lessen the frequency and severity of attacks.

Cautions and Warnings

Do not use Colchicine if you suffer from a serious kidney,
liver, stomach, or cardiac disorder.

Safety and effectiveness for use by children has not been
established.

Periodic blood counts should be done when you are taking
Colchicine for long periods of time.

Pregnancy/Breast-feeding

Colchicine can harm the fetus; use by pregnant women
should be considered only when the benefits clearly outweigh the potential hazards to the fetus.

Colchicine may pass into breast milk. No problems with
nursing infants are known to exist, but you should consider
the possibility of a reaction while taking this medicine.

Seniors

Older adults are more likely to develop drug side effects and
should use this drug with caution.

Possible Side Effects

Possible side effects include vomiting, diarrhea, stomach
pain, nausea, hair loss, skin rash, and loss of appetite.

Less commonly, disorders of the blood may occur in patients undergoing long-term Colchicine therapy.

Drug Interactions

Colchicine has been shown to cause poor absorption of Vitamin B_{12}, a condition that is reversible.

Colchicine may increase sensitivity to central-nervous-system depressants such as tranquilizers and alcohol.

The following drugs can reduce Colchicine's effectiveness:
anticancer drugs, Bumetanide, Diazoxide, thiazide diuretics,
Ethacrynic Acid, Furosemide, Mecamylamine, Pyrazinamide,
and Triamterene.

Taking Phenylbutazone together with Colchicine increases
the chance of drug side effects.

Food Interactions

This drug may be taken without regard to food or meals.

Usual Dose

To relieve an acute attack of gout: 1 to 1.2 milligrams. This dose may be followed by 0.5 to 1.2 milligrams every 1 to 2 hours until pain is relieved or nausea, vomiting, or diarrhea occurs. The total amount usually needed to control pain and inflammation during an attack varies from 4 to 8 milligrams.

To prevent gout attacks: 0.3 to 1.8 milligrams daily.

Overdosage

Symptoms may include nausea, vomiting, stomach pain, diarrhea (which may be severe and bloody), and burning sensations in the throat, stomach, and skin. If you think you are experiencing an overdose, contact your doctor immediately, or go to a hospital emergency room. ALWAYS bring the medicine bottle with you.

Special Information

Notify your doctor if you experience skin rash, sore throat, fever, unusual bleeding or bruising, tiredness, and numbness or tingling.

Stop taking Colchicine as soon as gout pain is relieved or at the first sign of nausea, vomiting, stomach pain, or diarrhea. If you experience these side effects, contact your doctor.

If you are regularly taking Colchicine and you forget to take a dose, take it as soon as possible. Do not double any doses.

Generic Name

Colestipol

Brand Name

Colestid Granules

Type of Drug

Antihyperlipidemic (blood-fat reducer).

Prescribed for

High blood cholesterol; itching associated with bile duct obstruction; some forms of colitis; pesticide poisoning.

General Information

This medication reduces blood cholesterol by removing bile acids from the biliary system. Since cholesterol is used by the body to make bile acids and bile acids are necessary for the digestion of dietary fats, the only way the body can continue to digest fats is to make more bile acids from cholesterol, resulting in a lowering of blood cholesterol levels. The medicine works entirely within the bowel and is never absorbed into the bloodstream.

In some kinds of hyperlipidemia, Colestipol may be more effective in lowering total blood cholesterol than Clofibrate. There are 6 different types of hyperlipidemia. Check with your doctor as to the kind you have and the proper drug treatment for your condition.

Cautions and Warnings

Do not use Colestipol if you are sensitive to it or to a similar drug product, Cholestyramine.

Pregnancy/Breast-feeding

The safety of using this medication during pregnancy is not known. If you are pregnant and must use this medication, talk to your doctor about the potential benefit to be gained versus other treatments for your condition.

The medicine is not absorbed into your blood and will not affect a nursing infant. However, it can affect the amounts of vitamins and other nutrients absorbed, possibly making your milk less nutritious. You may want to consider alternative methods or supplemental feedings for your infant.

Seniors

Older adults are more likely to suffer side effects from this medication, especially those relating to the bowel.

Possible Side Effects

The most common side effect is constipation, which may be severe and result in a bowel impaction. Hemorrhoids may be worsened.

Less frequent side effects are abdominal pain and bloating, bleeding in the stomach or intestine, belching, gas, nausea, vomiting, diarrhea, heartburn, and appetite loss. Your stool may have an unusual appearance because of a high fat level.

Other side effects include Vitamin A and D deficiency, rashes, irritation of the tongue and anus, osteoporosis, black stools, stomach ulcers, dental bleeding, hiccups, a sour taste, pancreas inflammation, ulcer attack, gallbladder attack, bleeding, black-and-blue marks, itching and rash, backache, muscle and joint pains, arthritis, headache, anxiety, dizziness, fatigue, ringing or buzzing in the ears, fainting, tingling in the hands or feet, blood in the urine, frequent or painful urination, an unusual urine odor, eye irritation, weight changes, increased sex drive, swollen glands, swelling of the arms or legs, and shortness of breath.

Drug Interactions

This medication interferes with the absorption of virtually all other medicines taken by mouth. Some drugs for which this effect has been proven are: Cephalexin, Chenodiol, Clindamycin, corticosteroids, digitalis drugs, iron, Penicillins, Phenobarbital, Phenylbutazone, Tetracycline, thiazide diuretics, thyroid drugs, Trimethoprim, Warfarin, and Vitamins A, D, E, and K. Take other medicines at least 1 hour before or 4 to 6 hours after Colestipol.

Food Interactions

Take this medication before meals. It may be mixed with soda, water, juice, applesauce, or crushed pineapple.

Usual Dose

15 to 30 grams (3 to 6 packets) per day in 2 to 4 divided doses.

Overdosage

The most severe effect of Colestipol overdose is bowel impaction. Take the overdose victim to a hospital emergency room for evaluation and treatment. ALWAYS bring the medicine container with you.

Special Information

Do not swallow the granules in their dry form. Prepare each packet of powder by mixing it with a soup, cereal, or pulpy fruit. Alternatively, the powder may be added to a glass of 6 ounces or more of a liquid, such as a carbonated beverage. Some of the drug may stick to the sides of the glass; this material should be rinsed with water or juice and drunk.

Constipation, stomach gas, nausea, and heartburn may occur and then disappear with continued use of this medication. Call your doctor if these side effects continue or if you develop unusual problems such as bleeding from the gums or rectum.

If you miss a dose, skip it and continue on your regular dose schedule. Do not double any doses.

Brand Name

Combipres

Ingredients

Chlorthalidone
Clonidine

Type of Drug

Antihypertensive.

Prescribed for

High blood pressure.

General Information

This drug is a combination of 2 effective antihypertensive drugs. One of them works by causing the dilation of certain blood vessels. The other is a diuretic that lowers blood pressure through its effect on body ions (sodium and potassium). Although it is convenient to take the 2 drugs in 1 tablet, it may not be in your best interest. If you need more or less of one of the ingredients than are available in the Combipres tablets, you must take the drugs as separate pills. Often, doctors are able to lower your blood pressure most effectively by manipulating the doses of one drug or the other.

Cautions and Warnings

Do not take Combipres if you are allergic to either of the ingredients or to sulfa-type drugs.

Some people develop a tolerance to the effect of one of the ingredients in this product. If this happens, your blood pressure may increase and you may require a change of dose or medicine.

Pregnancy/Breast-feeding

This drug should not be taken by women who are or might become pregnant. Chlorthalidone, if used during pregnancy, may cause side effects (jaundice, blood problems, low potassium) in the newborn infant.

Chlorthalidone passes into breast milk. Nursing mothers should use an alternative feeding method.

Seniors

Older adults may be more likely to be sensitive to this drug's effects and should be treated with a lower dosage than younger adults.

Possible Side Effects

One of the ingredients in this drug can cause hypokalemia (loss of potassium). The signs of this problem are dryness of the mouth, weakness, lethargy, drowsiness, restlessness, muscle pains or cramps, muscular tiredness, stomach upset, nausea and vomiting, and abnormal heart rhythms. To prevent or treat hypokalemia, potassium supplements, in the form of tablets, powders, or liquids, are given every day. You may increase your potassium intake naturally by eating more bananas, citrus fruits, melons, or tomatoes.

Combipres may also cause constipation or headache.

Less common side effects include loss of appetite, feeling of ill health, nausea, vomiting, weight gain, breast enlargement, adverse effects on the heart, changes in dream patterns, nightmares, difficulty sleeping, anxiety, depression, rash, hives, itching, thinning or loss of hair, dryness or burning of the eyes, and sexual impotence. Other possible adverse effects from this combination are tingling of the toes or fingers, changes in blood composition, sensitivity to sunlight, difficulty in breathing, drug allergy, dizziness when rising quickly from a sitting or lying position, muscle spasms, weariness, and blurred vision.

Drug Interactions

Combipres may interact with Digitalis to cause abnormal heart rhythms.

The effect of an oral antidiabetic medicine may be altered by Combipres.

People taking Lithium drugs should be careful about also taking Combipres since the combination may lead to Lithium toxicity.

Avoid alcohol, barbiturates, sedatives, and tranquilizers while taking Combipres. Their action may be increased by one of the ingredients in Combipres.

Food Interactions

You may take this medicine without regard to food, although medicine is, generally, best taken on an empty stomach.

Usual Dose

2 tablets per day (of either strength). The dose of this drug must be tailored to your individual needs for maximum effectiveness.

Overdosage

Symptoms are excessive urination, fatigue, and extreme lowering of blood pressure. The patient should be taken immediately to a hospital emergency room. ALWAYS bring the medicine bottle.

Special Information

Avoid over-the-counter drugs containing stimulant drugs. If you are unsure about which ones to avoid, ask your pharmacist.

One of the ingredients in Combipres causes drowsiness in about 35 percent of those who take it. Be extremely careful while driving or operating any equipment. This effect is most prominent during the first few weeks of therapy.

Do not suddenly stop taking this medication.

If you forget a dose of Combipres, take it as soon as you remember. If it is almost time for your next dose, skip the one you forgot and continue with your regular schedule. Do not take a double dose of Combipres.

Generic Name

Contraceptives

Brand Names

Low-Dose Estrogen/Low-Dose Progestin
Single-Phase Combinations

Brevicon	Nelova 0.535 E
Genora 0.5/35	Nelova 1/35 E
Genora 1/35	Nelova 1/50 M
Genora 1/50	Norcept E 1/35
Loestrin 1.5/30	Norethin 1/50 M
Loestrin 1/20	Norinyl 1+35
Loestrin Fe 1.5/30	Norinyl 1+50
Loestrin Fe 1/20	Ortho-Novum 1/35
Modicon	Ortho-Novum 1/50
NEE 1/35 E	Ovcon-35

Low-Dose Estrogen/Intermediate-Dose Progestin
Single-Phase Combinations

Demulen 1/35	Lo/Ovral
Levlen	Nordette

Regular-Dose Estrogen/Low-Dose Progestin
Single-Phase Combinations

Norlestrin 1/50
Norlestrin Fe 1/50
Ovcon-50

Regular-Dose Estrogen/Intermediate-Dose Progestin
Single-Phase Combinations

Demulen 1/50
Norlestrin 2.5/50
Norlestrin Fe 2.5/50

Regular-Dose Estrogen/High-Dose Progestin
Single-Phase Combination

Ovral

Low-Dose Estrogen/Low-Dose Progestin 2-Phase Combinations

Nelova 10/11
Ortho-Novum 10/11

Low-Dose Estrogen/Low-Dose Progestin 3-Phase Combinations

Ortho-Novum 7/7/7   Tri-Norinyl
Tri Levlen   TriPhasil

Low-Dose Progestin Mini-Pill

Ovrette

High-Dose Progestin Mini-Pills

Micronor
Nor-Q.D.

Implant Systems

Levonorgestrel Implant   Progesterone Intrauterine
Norplant System   Insert
                               Progestasert

Type of Drug

Contraceptive.

Prescribed for

Prevention of pregnancy. Postcoital (morning-after) pill;
endometriosis; excessive menstruation; cyclic withdrawal
bleeding.

General Information

Oral contraceptives ("the Pill") are synthetic hormones, either Progestin alone or Progestin combined with Estrogen. These hormones are similar to natural female hormones that control the menstrual cycle and prepare a woman's body to accept a fertilized egg. The natural hormones cannot be used as contraceptives because very large doses would be needed. Once a fertilized egg is accepted (implanted in the womb) no more eggs may be released from the ovaries until the pregnancy is over. Oral contraceptives interfere with these natural processes; they may not allow sperm to reach the unfertilized egg, not allow the acceptance of a fertilized egg, and/or not allow ovulation (the release of an unfertilized egg).

Oral contraceptives provide a very high-rated protection from pregnancy. They are from 97 to 99 percent effective, depending upon which product is used and your compliance with taking it regularly. Using no contraceptive at all is only about 20 to 40 percent effective.

The many different combination products available contain different amounts of Estrogen and Progestin. Products containing the least amount of Estrogen may be less effective in some women than others. In general, the product that contains the lowest amount of hormones but is effective and keeps side effects to a minimum is preferred.

The mini-pill, a Progestin-only product, may cause irregular menstrual cycles and may be less effective than combination products. Mini-pills may be used in older women or women who should avoid Estrogens (see "Cautions and Warnings").

Single-phase products provide a fixed amount of Estrogen and Progestin throughout the entire pill cycle.

In the 2-phase combination, the amount of Progestin first increases and then decreases. This is supposed to allow normal changes to take place in the uterus. The amount of Estrogen remains at a steady low level throughout the cycle. The newest combination products are triple-phase in design. Throughout the cycle, the Estrogen portion remains the same, but the Progestin changes to create a wave pattern in 3 parts. The 3-phase products are supposed to act like normal hormones and reduce breakthrough bleeding. Breakthrough bleeding may be seen with the older combination products beginning with the eighth through sixteenth days. The amount of Estrogen in these new products is considered to be in the low category.

Levonorgestrel Implants provide effective contraception for up to 5 years after implantation in the skin of your upper arm by your doctor. They can be removed at any time, reversing the contraceptive effect, but should be replaced by your doctor at least once every 5 years. The intrauterine insert provides a continuous flow of Progestin, and effective contraception, for about 1 year. The medicines contained in both of these systems are of the same type as the Progestin-only mini pills and can be associated with many of the same side side effects and precautions as the oral pills.

Every woman taking or thinking of using one of these contraceptives, whether it is a pill or an implantable device, should be fully aware of the problems associated with this type of contraception. The highest risk is in women over 35 who smoke and have high blood pressure.

Cautions and Warnings

You should not use oral contraceptives if you are or might be pregnant or if you have or have had blood clots of the veins or arteries, stroke, a disease affecting blood coagulation, known or suspected cancer of the breast or sex organs, liver cancer, or irregular or scanty menstrual periods.

Your doctor should carefully consider the risks of contraceptive products if you are physically immobile or if you have asthma, cardiac insufficiency, epilepsy, migraine headaches, kidney problems, a strong family history of breast cancer, benign breast disease, diabetes, endometriosis, gallbladder disease or gallstones, liver problems (including jaundice), high blood cholesterol, high blood pressure, estrogen or progestin intolerance, depression, tuberculosis, or varicose veins.

There is an increased risk of heart attack in women who take oral contraceptives for more than 10 years or who are between age 40 and 49; this remains even after the medication is stopped. Smokers who use oral contraceptives have a 5 times greater chance of having a heart attack as non-smoking Pill users and a 10 to 12 times greater chance of heart attack than non-smoking, non-Pill users.

Women who should avoid Estrogen-containing products are those with a history of headaches, high blood pressure, and varicose veins. Older women and women who have experienced side effects from Estrogen also should not take Estrogen products.

Progestin-only products also carry an increased risk of blood clotting problems, but the exact risk is not well understood.

Pregnancy/Breast-feeding

Oral contraceptives cause birth defects or interfere with your baby's development. They are not considered safe for use during pregnancy.

Oral contraceptives reduce the amount of breast milk you make and can affect its quality. Some of the hormone passes into your breast milk, but the effect on a nursing infant is not known. Do not breast-feed while you are taking oral contraceptives.

Possible Side Effects

Nausea, abdominal cramps, bloating, vaginal bleeding, change in menstrual flow, possible infertility after coming off the Pill, breast tenderness, weight change, headaches, rash, vaginal itching and burning, general vaginal infection, nervousness, dizziness, formation of eye cataract, changes in sex drive, changes in appetite, loss of hair.

Rarely, women who take oral contraceptives are more likely to develop several serious conditions including the formation of blood clots in the deep veins, stroke, heart attack, liver cancer, gallbladder disease, and high blood pressure. Women who smoke cigarettes are much more likely to develop some of these adverse effects.

Drug Interactions

Interaction with Rifampin decreases the effectiveness of oral contraceptives. The same may be true of barbiturates, Phenylbutazone, Phenytoin, Ampicillin, Neomycin, Penicillin V, Tetracycline, Chloramphenicol, sulfa drugs, Nitrofurantoin, tranquilizers, and antimigraine medication.

Another interaction reduces the effect of anticoagulant (blood-thinning) drugs. Discuss this with your doctor.

The Pill can increase blood cholesterol (fat) levels, and can interfere with blood tests for thyroid function and blood sugar.

Usual Dose

The first day of bleeding is the first day of the menstrual

cycle. At the start, 1 tablet, beginning on the fifth day of the menstrual cycle, is taken every day for 20 to 21 days according to the number of contraceptive tablets supplied by the manufacturer. If 7 days after taking the last tablet menstrual flow has not begun, begin the next month's cycle of pills. Progestin-only mini-pills are taken every day, 365 days a year.

Overdosage

Overdosage may cause nausea and withdrawal bleeding in adult females. Accidental overdosage in children who take their mothers' pills has not caused serious adverse effects; however, overdose victims should be taken to a hospital emergency emergency room for evaluation and treatment. ALWAYS bring the medicine bottle with you.

Special Information

Use an alternative method of birth control during the first 3 weeks you are taking the Pill.

Call your doctor at once if you develop sudden, severe abnominal pains, severe or sudden headaches, pains in the chest, groin or leg (especially the calf), sudden slurring of your speech, visual changes, weakness, numbness or unexplained arm or leg pains; if you start coughing up blood; if you lose coordiantion; or if you become suddenly short of breath.

Other problems that may develop and require medical attention are bulging eyes, double vision, loss of eyesight, changes in vaginal bleeding patterns, fainting, frequent or painful urination, a gradual increase in blood pressure, breast lumps or secretions, mental depression, yellow eyes or skin, skin rash, redness or irritation, upper abdominal swellin, pain or tenderness, an unusual or dark-colored mole, thick, white vaginal discharge, or vaginal itching or tenderness. Other symptoms that may develop while taking contraceptive products require medical attention only if they are unusually bothersome or persistent.

See your doctor every 6 to 12 months to check on your progress.

Some manufacturers have included 7 blank or 7 iron pills in their packages, to be taken on days when the Pill is not taken. These pills have the number 28 as part of the brand name and a pill should be taken every day.

For the single or 2-phase pills: If you forget to take the Pill for 1 day, take 2 pills the following day. If you miss 2 consecutive days, take 2 pills for the next 2 days. Then continue to take 1 pill daily. If you miss 3 consecutive days, don't take any Pills for the next 7 days and use another form of contraception; then start a new cycle.

For the 3-phase pills: If you forget to take the Pill for 1 day, take 2 pills the following day and then continue with your regular dose. If you miss 2 consecutive days, take 2 pills for the next 2 days. Then continue to take 1 pill daily. If you forget to take the Pill for 3 days in a row, stop taking the medicine and use an alternate means of contraception until your period comes. ALWAYS use a backup contraceptive method for the remainder of your cycle if you forget even one 3-phase pill.

Forgetting to take the Pill reduces your protection: If you keep forgetting to take it, you should use another means of birth control.

If you must take any medication listed in the "Drug Interactions" section, use a backup contraceptive method during that cycle.

It is important to maintain good dental hygiene while taking this drug and to use extra care when using your toothbrush or dental floss because of the chance that the drug will make you more susceptible to some infections. See your dentist regularly while taking a contraceptive product. Check with your dentist if you notice swelling or bleeding of your gums.

You may be more sensitive to the sun while taking oral contraceptives.

You may become intolerant to contact lenses because of minor changes in the shape of your eyes.

All oral contraceptive prescriptions must come with a "patient package insert" for you to read. It gives detailed information about the drug and is required by federal law.

Type of Drug

Corticosteroid Aerosols/Creams/Gels/Lotions/Ointments/Topical Solutions

Brand Names

Generic Name: Aclometasone Dipropionate

Aclovate Cream/Ointment

Generic Name: Amcinonide

Cyclocort Cream/Lotion/Ointment

Generic Name: Betamethasone

Alphatrex Cream/Lotion/Ointment
Betatrex Cream/Lotion/Ointment
Beta-Val Cream/Lotion/Ointment
Dermabet Cream
Diprolene Cream/Ointment
Diprosone Aerosol/Cream/Lotion/Ointment
Maxivate Cream/Lotion/Ointment
Uticort Cream/Gel/Lotion
Valisone Cream/Lotion/Ointment

Generic Name: Clobetasol Propionate

Temovate Cream/Ointment

Generic Name: Clocortolone Pivalate

Cloderm Cream

Generic Name: Desonide

DesOwen Cream/Ointment
Tridesilon Cream/Ointment

Generic Name: Dexamethasone

Aeroseb-Dex Aerosol
Decaderm Gel
Decaspray Aerosol

Generic Name: Desoximetasone

Topicort Emollient Cream/Gel/Ointment
Topicort-LP Emollient Cream

(Also available in generic form)

Generic Name: Diflorasone Diacetate

Florone Cream/Ointment   Maxiflor Cream/Ointment
Florone E Cream   Psorcon Ointment

Generic Name: Fluocinolone Acetonide

Fluonid Topical Solution   Synalar-HP Cream
Flurosyn Cream/Ointment   Synemol Cream
Synalar Cream/Ointment/
  Topical Solution

(Also available in generic form)

Generic Name: Fluocinonide

Lidex Cream/Ointment   Vasoderm Cream
Lidex-E Cream   Vasoderm-E Cream

(Also available in generic form)

Generic Name: Flurandrenolide

Cordran Lotion/Ointment/Tape
Cordran SP Cream

(Also available in generic form)

Generic Name: Fluticasone Propionate

Cutivate Cream/Ointment

Generic Name: Halcinonide

Halog Cream/Ointment
Halog-E Cream

Generic Name: Halobetasol Propionate

Ultravate Cream/Ointment

Generic Name: Hydrocortisone

Acticort Lotion
Aeroseb-HC Aerosol
Ala-Cort Cream/Lotion
Ala-Scalp Lotion
Alphaderm Cream
Anusol-HC Cream
Bactine Hydrocortisone
   Cream
CaldeCort Cream
Cetacort Lotion
CortaGel
Cortaid Lotion
Cort-Dome Cream/Lotion
Cortef Feminine Itch Cream
Corticaine Cream
Cortizone-5 Cream/Ointment
Cortril Ointment
Delcort Cream/Lotion
Dermacort Cream/Lotion
DermiCort Cream/Lotion
Dermolate Anti-Itch Cream

Dermtex HC with Aloe
   Cream
FoilleCort Cream
Gynecort Cream
Hi-Cor Cream
Hycort Cream/Ointment
HydroTex Cream/Ointment
Hytone Cream/Lotion/
   Ointment
Lacticare-HC Lotion
Lanacort Cream/Ointment
Locoid Cream/Ointment
Nutracort Cream/Lotion
Penecort Cream
S-T Cort Cream/Lotion
Synacort Cream
Tega-Cort Lotion
Tega-Cort Forte Lotion
Texacort Solution
U-Cort Cream
Westcort Cream/Ointment

(Also available in generic form)

Generic Name: Methylprednisolone

Medrol Acetate Topical Ointment

Generic Name: Mometasone Furoate

Elocon Cream/Lotion/Ointment

(Also available in generic form)

Generic Name: Triamcinolone Acetonide

Aristocort Cream/Ointment
Aristocort A Cream/Ointment
Flutex Cream/Ointment
Kenalog Aerosol/Cream/
   Lotion/Ointment

Kenalog-H Cream
Triacet Cream
Triderm Cream

(Also available in generic form)

Prescribed for

Relief of inflammation in a local area, itching, or other dermatological (skin) problems.

General Information

Topical (applied to the skin) corticosteroids are used to relieve the symptoms of any itching, rash, or inflammation of the skin; they do not treat the underlying cause of the skin problem. They exert this effect by interfering with natural body mechanisms that produce the rash, itching, or inflammation. If you use one of these drugs without finding the cause of the problem, the condition may return after you stop using the drug. You should not use a topical corticosteroid without your doctor's consent because it could cover an important reaction, one that may be valuable to your doctor in treating you.

Cautions and Warnings

You should not use a topical corticosteroid if you have a viral disease of the skin (such as herpes), fungal infection of the skin (such as athlete's foot), or tuberculosis of the skin, nor should one be used in the ear if the eardrum has been perforated. Do not use one of these drugs if you have a history of allergies to any of the components of the aerosol, cream, gel, lotion, ointment, or topical solution.

Using a topical corticosteroid for prolonged periods around the eyes can cause cataracts or glaucoma.

Pregnancy/Breast-feeding

Studies have shown that corticosteroids applied to the skin in large amounts or over long periods of time can be the cause of birth defects. Pregnant women, or those who might become pregnant, should not use this medicine unless they are under a doctor's care.

Corticosteroid drugs taken by mouth pass into breast milk, and large drug doses may interfere with the growth of a nursing infant. Steroids applied to the skin are not likely to cause problems, but you should not use the medicine unless under a dcotor's care.

Seniors

Older adults are more likely to develop high blood pressure and older women are more susceptible to osteoporosis (bone degeneration) associated with large doses of medicines in this class while taking corticosteroids by mouth. However, these effects are unlikely with a steroid applied to the skin.

Possible Side Effects

Burning sensations, itching, irritation, dryness, and secondary infection.

Drug Interactions

None known.

Special Information

Clean the skin before applying a topical corticosteroid, to prevent secondary infection. Apply in a very thin film (effectiveness is based on contact area and not on the thickness of the layer applied).

Flurandrenolide tape comes with specific directions for use; follow them carefully.

If you forget to take a dose of a topical corticosteroid, take it a soon as you remember. If it is almost time for your next regularly scheduled dose, skip the one you forgot and continue with your regular schedule. Do not take a double dose.

Brand Name

Cortisporin Otic Solution

Ingredients

Hydrocortisone
Neomycin Sulfate
Polymyxin-B

Other Brand Names

AK-Spore H.C. Otic
Cortatrigen Modified Ear
　Drops
Drotic

Ortega Otic M
Otocort Sterile Ear Solution
Otomycin-Hpn Otic

(Also available in generic form)

Type of Drug

Steroidal antibiotic combination product.

Prescribed for

Superficial infections, inflammation, itching, and other problems involving the outer ear.

General Information

Cortisporin Otic contains a steroid drug to reduce inflammation and 2 antibiotics to treat local infections. This combination can be quite useful for local infections and inflammations of the ear because of its dual method of action and its relatively broad, nonspecific applicability.

Cautions and Warnings

This product is specifically designed to be used in the ear. It can be very damaging if accidentally placed into your eye.

Pregnancy/Breast-feeding

Pregnant and breast-feeding women may use this product with no restriction.

Seniors

Older adults may use this product with no restriction.

Possible Side Effects

Local irritation such as itching or burning can occur if you are sensitive or allergic to one of the ingredients in this drug.

Usual Dose

2 to 4 drops in the affected ear 3 to 4 times per day.

Overdosage

The chance of experiencing adverse effects from swallowing Cortisporin Otic Solution is small because of the small amount of medicine in the bottle. Call a hospital emergency room or a poison control center for more information.

Special Information

Use only when specifically prescribed by a physician. Overuse of this or similar products can result in the growth of other organisms such as fungi. If new infections or new problems appear during the time you are using this medication, stop using the drug and contact your doctor.

If your forget a dose of Cortisporin, take it as soon as you remember. If it is almost time for your next dose, skip the forgotten dose and continue with your regular schedule. Do not take a double dose.

Generic Name

Cromolyn Sodium

Brand Names

Intal Capsules/Inhaler/Nebulizer Solution
Nasalcrom Nasal Solution
Gastrocrom Capsules
Opticrom 4%

Type of Drug

Allergy preventive.

Prescribed for

Prevention of severe allergic reactions including various types of asthma, runny nose, and mastocytosis. Cromolyn is also used to treat food allergies, eczema, dermatitis, chronic itching, and hay fever. It may be used to treat and prevent chronic inflammatory bowel disease; however, other drug products are more effective for this use. Cromolyn eyedrops are used to treat conjunctivitis and other allergic responses in the eye.

General Information

Cromolyn prevents allergy, asthma, and other conditions by stabilizing mast cells, which are a key component to developing any allergic reaction because they release histamine. Cromolyn prevents the release of histamine and other potent chemicals from the mast cells. The drug works only in the areas to which it is applied; it is not absorbed into the blood in any appreciable amount. Even the oral capsules, which one would normally expect to be absorbed into the blood, are swallowed to treat gastrointestinal-tract allergies. Cromolyn products must be used on a regular basis to be effective in reducing the frequency and intensity of allergic reactions and their consequences.

Cautions and Warnings

Cromolyn should never be used to treat an acute allergy attack. It is intended only to prevent or reduce the number of allergic attacks and their intensity. On rare occasions, people have experienced severe allergic attacks after taking Cromolyn. People allergic to Cromolyn should not take any product containing that ingredient.

People with kidney or liver disease should have their dosages reduced.

Pregnancy/Breast-feeding

There are no reports of birth defects in animal studies with Cromolyn or of individual cases of birth defects associated with this drug. As with all drug products, pregnant women, or those who might become pregnant while taking the drug, should not use Cromolyn unless its advantages have been carefully weighed against the possible dangers of taking it while pregnant.

It is not known if Cromolyn passes into breast milk. No drug-related problems have been known to occur. Nursing mothers who use Cromolyn should exercise caution.

Seniors

No problems have been reported in older adults. However, older adults are likely to have age-related reduction in kidney and/or liver function. Your doctor should take this factor into account when determining your Cromolyn dosage.

Possible Side Effects

The most common side effect of Cromolyn is skin rash and itching. Other reactions to the inhaler, nasal solution, and eyedrops include local irritation (nasal stinging or sneezing, tearing, cough, stuffed nose), urinary difficulty, dizziness, headache, joint swelling, a bad taste in the mouth, nosebleeds, abdominal pain, and nausea.

Severe drug reactions—consisting of coughing, difficulty swallowing, hives, itching, difficulty breathing, or swelling of the eyelids, lips, or face—are rare.

Most reactions reported after the oral capsules are minor and could be symptoms of the disease; headache and diarrhea are the most common. A variety of other side effects to oral Cromolyn capsules have been reported but could not be conclusively tied to the drug.

Drug Interactions

None known.

Food Interactions

Inhaled or swallowed Cromolyn products should not be mixed with any food, juice, or milk. The nasal and eye products may be taken without regard to food or meals.

Usual Dose

Inhaled capsules or solution:
   Adult and child (age 2 and over): 20 milligrams 4 times a day to start. (Children under age 2 may inhale Cromolyn if their allergies are severe.)
Aerosol:
   Adult and child (age 5 and over): Up to 2 sprays 4 times a day, spaced equally throughout the day. The contents of a single capsule or 2 aerosol puffs may be inhaled up to 1 hour before exercise to prevent exercise asthma.
Nasal solution:
   Adult and child (age 6 and over): 1 spray in each nostril up to 6 times a day at regular intervals. Blow your nose first and inhale the solution through your nose.
Oral capsules:
   Adult: 2 capsules a half hour before meals and at bedtime.
   Child (age 2 to 12): 1 capsule (100 milligrams) 4 times per

day a half hour before meals and at bedtime, up to about 15–20 milligrams per pound of body weight per day in 4 equal doses.

Child (under age 2): about 10 milligrams per pound of body weight per day divided into 4 equal doses. This product is recommended in infants and young children only if absolutely necessary.

Eyedrops:

Adult and child (age 4 and over): 1 to 2 drops in each eye up to 6 times a day at regular intervals.

Overdosage

No action is necessary other than medical observation. Call your local poison control center or hospital emergency room for more information.

Special Information

Cromolyn is taken to prevent or minimize severe allergic reactions. It is imperative that you take Cromolyn products on a regular basis to provide equal protection throughout the day.

If you are taking Cromolyn to prevent seasonal allergic problems, it is essential that you start taking the medicine before you come into contact with the cause of the allergy and continue treatment throughout the period you will be exposed to the allergy source.

Cromolyn oral capsules should be opened and mixed with about 4 ounces of hot water. Stir until the powder is completely dissolved and fill the rest of the glass with cold water. Drink the water without mixing it with food, juice, or milk.

People should not wear soft contact lenses while taking Cromolyn eyedrops. The lenses may be replaced a few hours after you stop taking the drug.

Call your doctor if you develop wheezing, coughing, severe drug reaction (see "Possible Side Effects"), or skin rash. Other side effects should be reported if they are severe or particularly bothersome.

Call your doctor if your symptoms do not improve or get worse while you are taking this drug.

If you forget a dose of Cromolyn, take it as soon as you

remember and space the remaining doses equally throughout the rest of the day. Do not take a double dose of this
drug.

Generic Name

Cyclobenzaprine

Brand Name

Flexeril
(Also available in generic form)

Type of Drug

Muscle relaxant.

Prescribed for

Relieving serious muscle spasms associated with acute painful muscle conditions.

General Information

This drug is used as a part of the treatment for severe
muscle spasms. Physical therapy, rest, and other medical
measures may also be employed. Cyclobenzaprine is not
effective for relieving muscle spasms caused by disorders
of the central nervous system. The drug starts working an
hour after you take it and reaches maximum effect after 1
to 2 weeks of continuous use.

Cautions and Warnings

Do not take Cyclobenzaprine if you are or may be allergic
to it.
   Cyclobenzaprine should not be taken for a few weeks following a heart attack or by people with abnormal heart
rhythms, heart failure, heart block, or hyperthyroidism (an
overactive thyroid).
   Cyclobenzaprine inhibits the flow of saliva and may increase the chances for dental cavities or gum disease.

Pregnancy/Breast-feeding

Animal studies have shown no evidence that Cyclobenzaprine harms a developing fetus. Nevertheless, Cyclobenzaprine should not be taken by a woman who is or might become pregnant unless the potential benefits have been weighed against the possibility that the drug might cause a problem.

It is not known if Cyclobenzaprine passes into breast milk, but other drugs with a similar chemical structure do find their way into breast milk. Nursing mothers who must take this drug should consider bottle-feeding.

Seniors

Older adults are more likely to be sensitive to the effects of Cyclobenzaprine. Be sure to report any unusual or bothersome side effects to your doctor.

Possible Side Effects

The most common side effects of Cyclobenzaprine are drowsiness, dry mouth, and dizziness.

Less common side effects are muscle weakness, fatigue, nausea, constipation, upset stomach, unpleasant taste, blurred vision, headache, nervousness, and confusion.

Other side effects that may occur are rapid heartbeat, fainting, abnormal heart rhythms, low blood pressure, heart palpitations, disorientation, sleeplessness, depression, abnormal sensations, anxiety, agitation, abnormal thoughts and dreams, hallucinations, excitement, vomiting, loss of appetite, stomach irritation and pains, diarrhea, stomach gas, thirst, temporary loss of taste sensation, urinary changes, hepatitis, yellowing of the eyes or skin, sweating, skin rash, itching, muscle twitching, local weakness, and swelling of the face and tongue.

Many other side effects have been reported by people taking Cyclobenzaprine, but their relationship to the drug has never been established. Report anything unusual to your doctor.

High doses of Cyclobenzaprine may cause temporary confusion, disturbed concentration, hallucinations, agitation, hyperactive reflexes, muscle rigidity, vomiting, or high fever.

Drug Interactions

The effects of alcohol, sedatives, or other nervous-system depressant may be increased by Cyclobenzaprine.

Cyclobenzaprine may increase specific side effects of other drugs. Known as anticholinergic effects, these include blurred vision, constipation, urinary difficulty, dry mouth, confusion, and drowsiness.

The combination of Cyclobenzaprine with a monoamine oxidase (MAO) inhibitor-type antidepressant can produce very high fever, convulsions, and possibly death. Do not take these drugs within 14 days of each other.

This drug may increase the effects of Haloperidol, Loxapine, Molindone, Pimozide, anticoagulant (blood-thinning) drugs, anticonvulsants, thyroid hormones, antithyroid drugs, phenothiazines, and thioxanthenes. The effects of nasal decongestants like Naphazoline, Oxymetazoline, Phenylephrine, and Xylometazoline may be increased by Cyclobenzaprine.

Barbiturates and Carbamazepine may counteract the effects of antidepressants like Cyclobenzaprine, Fluoxetine, Ranitidine, Cimetidine, Methylphenidate, Estramustine, estrogens, and birth control pills may increase the effects and side effects of Cyclobenzaprine.

Cyclobenzaprine may counteract the effects of Clonidine, Guanadrel, and Guanethidine.

Food Interactions

Cyclobenzaprine may be taken without regard to food or meals.

Usual Dose

10 milligrams 3 times a day.

Overdosage

Overdose may cause drowsiness, low body temperature, rapid or irregular heartbeat and other kinds of abnormal heart rhythms, heart failure, dilated pupils, convulsions, very low blood pressure, stupor, and coma. Sweating has been reported. Overdose victims must be taken to a hospital emergency room as soon as possible for treatment. ALWAYS bring the medicine bottle with you.

Special Information

Cyclobenzaprine causes drowsiness, dizziness, or blurred vision in more than 40% of people who take it. These side effects can interfere with your ability to perform complex tasks like driving or operate complicated equipment.

Avoid alcohol, sedatives, and other nervous-system depressants while taking Cyclobenzaprine.

Call your doctor if you develop any of the following symptoms: skin rash, hives or itching, urinary problems, clumsiness, confusion, depression, convulsions, yellow eyes or skin, swelling of the face, lips, or tongue. Other side effects should be reported if they are unusually persistent or bothersome.

If you take Cyclobenzaprine once a day and forget to take a dose, take it as soon as you remember. If it is almost time for your next dose, skip the one you forgot and continue with your regular schedule. Do not take a double dose.

If you take Cyclobenzaprine twice a day and forget a dose, take it as soon as you remember. If it is almost time for your next dose, take one dose as soon as you remember and another in 5 or 6 hours, then go back to your regular schedule. Do not take a double dose.

If you take Cyclobenzaprine 3 times a day and forget a dose, take it as soon as you remember. If it is almost time for your next dose, take one dose as soon as you remember and another in 3 or 4 hours, then go back to your regular schedule. Do not take a double dose.

Generic Name

Cyclosporine

Brand Name

Sandimmune Ampuls/Oral Solution

Type of Drug

Immunosuppressant.

Prescribed for

Prevention of the body's rejection of a transplanted kidney, heart, or liver, together with corticosteroids. Cyclosporine is also used for bone-marrow, heart-lung, and pancreas transplants.

Many researchers think that Cyclosporine may help in the treatment of other immunologic diseases such as diabetes, psoriasis, myasthenia gravis, multiple sclerosis, rheumatoid arthritis, lupus, and others. The drug is not approved by the FDA for treating these conditions.

General Information

Cyclosporine was the first drug approved in the United States in over 20 years to prevent rejection of transplanted organs. A product of fungus metabolism, Cyclosporine was proved a potent immunosuppressant in 1972. First given to human kidney- and bone-marrow-transplant patients in 1978, it selectively inhibits cells known as T-lymphocytes, which, as an integral part of the body's defense mechanism, actually destroy invading cells. Cyclosporine also prevents the production of a compound known as interlukein-II, which activates T-lymphocyte cells.

Cautions and Warnings

This drug should be prescribed only by doctors experienced in immunosuppressive therapy and the care of organ-transplant patients. It is always used with adrenal corticosteroid drugs. Cyclosporine should not be given with other immunosuppressants since oversuppression of the immune system can result in lymphoma or extreme susceptibility to infection.

The oral form of the drug is poorly and erratically absorbed into the bloodstream. Because of this, it must be taken in doses 3 times larger than the injectable dose. People taking this drug orally over a period of time should have their blood checked for Cyclosporine levels so that the dose can be adjusted, if necessary.

Pregnancy/Breast-feeding

This drug should be avoided by pregnant women or women who may become pregnant while using it. In those situations where it is deemed essential, the potential risk of the drug must be carefully weighed against any benefit it might produce.

Cyclosporine passes into breast milk. Even though no problems have been noted in nursing infants, mothers who take this medicine should use an alternative feeding method.

Seniors

Older adults are likely to have age-related decreases in kidney function and may, therefore, be more susceptible to the kidney toxicity associated with this drug. Otherwise, older adults can take Cyclosporine without special restrictions.

Possible Side Effects

Cyclosporine is known to be extremely toxic to the kidneys. This effect is seen in 25 percent of all kidney transplants, 38 percent of heart transplants, and 37 percent of liver transplants where the drug is used. Mild toxicity is generally seen 2 to 3 months after the transplant and is often reversed by reducing the Cyclosporine dose.

Severe toxicity usually develops soon after transplantation and may be difficult to differentiate from organ rejection. Drug toxicity responds to a reduction in Cyclosporine dosage, while rejection does not. If the toxic effect does not respond to dosage reduction, your doctor will probably switch you to a different drug. All people treated with Cyclosporine should be tested periodically for kidney function.

Liver toxicity is much less common than kidney toxicity, but still occurs in many people receiving Cyclosporine. Liver toxicity is usually present in 4 percent of kidney transplants, 7 percent of heart transplants, and 4 percent of liver transplants, usually during the first month of therapy, when doses tend to be the highest.

Lymphoma may develop in people whose immune systems are excessively suppressed. Almost 85 percent of all people treated with this medicine will develop an infection, compared with 94 percent on other forms of immunosuppressive therapy.

Other frequent Cyclosporine side effects are high blood pressure, increased hair growth, growth of the gums, tremors, cramps, acne, brittle hair or fingernails, convulsions, headache, confusion, diarrhea, nausea and vomiting, tingling in the hands or feet, facial flushing, reduction in blood counts of white cells and platelets, sinus inflammation, swollen and painful male breasts, drug allergy, conjunctivitis (red-eye), fluid retention and swelling, ringing or buzzing in the ears, hearing loss, high blood sugar, muscle pains.

Rare side effects include blood in the urine, heart attack, itching, anxiety, depression, lethargy, weakness, mouth sores, difficulty swallowing, intestinal bleeding, constipation, pancreas inflammation, night sweats, chest pain, joint pains, visual disturbances, weight loss.

Drug Interactions

Cyclosporine should be used carefully with other drugs known to be toxic to the kidneys, including nonsteroidal antiinflammatory drugs (NSAIDs). Lovastatin may interact with Cyclosporine to cause acute kidney failure.

Phenytoin, for seizure disorders, reduces Cyclosporine blood levels.

Excessive immunosuppression may result from the use of Cyclosporine with another immunosuppressant other than a corticosteroid.

Cyclosporine's effect and the chance of drug side effects are increased when it is taken together with male hormones, Cimetidine, Danazol, Diltiazem, Erythromycin, Ketoconazole, or Miconazole.

Cyclosporine increases blood potassium. Excessive blood potassium levels can be reached if Cyclosporine is taken together with Enalapril, Lisinopril, a potassium-sparing diuretic (like Spironolactone), salt substitutes, potassium supplements, or (low-salt) foods high in potassium.

People taking Cyclosporine should be vaccinated only after specific discussions with your doctor. Cyclosporine prevents the body from responding in the normal way to vaccines. You must wait for a period of several months to several years after stopping the medicine before vaccination can be considered again.

Food Interactions

The oral form of this drug comes in an oily base derived

from castor oil. You should mix it in a glass (not a paper or plastic cup) with whole milk, chocolate milk, or orange juice at room temperature to make it taste better. Drink immediately after mixing, add more of the diluent, and drink the diluent to be sure that the entire dose has been taken.

Cyclosporine is best taken on an empty stomach but may be taken with food if it upsets your stomach.

Usual Dose

Adult and Adolescent: The usual oral dose of Cyclosporine is 6 to 8 milligrams per pound of body weight per day, given 4 to 12 hours before the transplant operation. This dosage is continued after the operation for a week or 2 and then gradually reduced (5 percent per week) to 2.25 to 4.5 milligrams per pound of body weight.

Child: Children may require larger and more frequent doses because they release the drug from their bodies faster than adolescents or adults.

Use the method described in "Food Interactions" to take the drug. Injectable Cyclosporine is given to people who can't take or tolerate the oral form, in one-third the dose of the oral liquid.

Overdosage

Victims of Cyclosporine overdose can be expected to develop drug side effects and symptoms of extreme immunosuppression. Patients taking an overdose of this drug must be made to vomit with Syrup of Ipecac (available at any pharmacy) to remove any remaining drug from the stomach. Call your doctor or a poison control center before doing this. If you must go to a hospital emergency room, ALWAYS bring the medicine bottle.

Special Information

Call your doctor at the first sign of fever, sore throat, tiredness, weakness, nervousness, unusual bleeding, or bruising, tender, swollen gums, convulsions, irregular heartbeat, confusion, numbness or tingling of your hands, feet or lips, difficulty breathing, severe stomach pains with nausea, or bloody urine. Other drug effects (shaking or trembling of the hands, increased hair growth, acne, headache, leg cramps, nausea, or vomiting) are less serious but should be brought to your doctor's attention if they are unusually bothersome or persistent.

It is important to maintain good dental hygiene while taking Cyclosporine and to use extra care when using your toothbrush or dental floss because of the chance that the drug will make you more susceptible to dental infections. Cyclosporine can cause swollen gums and suppresses the normal body systems that fight infection. See your dentist regularly while taking this medicine.

This medicine should be continued as long as prescribed by the doctor. Do not stop taking it because of side effects or other problems. If you cannot tolerate the oral form, it can be given by injection.

Do not keep the oral liquid in the refrigerator. After the bottle is opened, use the medicine within 2 months.

If you forget to take a dose of Cyclosporine, take it as soon as you remember if it is within 12 hours of your regular dose. If not, skip the forgotten dose and continue with your regular schedule. Do not take a double dose.

Generic Name

Cyproheptadine Hydrochloride

Brand Name

Periactin

(Also available in generic form)

Type of Drug

Phenothiazine-type antihistamine.

Prescribed for

Relief of symptoms associated with allergies, drug allergies, colds or upper respiratory infections, infection or itching of the extremities, insect bites, and general itching. It has also been used to stimulate appetite and for the treatment of headaches.

General Information

Cyproheptadine Hydrochloride is an antihistamine. Any effect it exerts is due to its ability to counteract the effects of histamine, a chemical released by the body as part of allergic or sensitivity reactions. Histamine is also released as a part of the body's reaction to the common cold or similar respiratory infections. Cyproheptadine Hydrochloride is especially useful in treating symptoms of allergy, itching, and the common cold. It has also been reported to cause weight gain and has even been tried as an appetite stimulant.

Cautions and Warnings

Do not take Cyproheptadine Hydrochloride if you are allergic to it or to other phenothiazine-type drugs such as Chlorpromazine and Prochlorperazine. Signs of allergies to the phenothiazines include sore throat, fever, unusual bleeding or bruising, rash, blurred vision, and yellowing of the skin.

Although this drug is usually not a problem for people with heart, liver, and stomach problems, they would do well to avoid taking it.

Pregnancy/Breast-feeding

Antihistamines have not been proven to be a cause of birth defects or other problems in pregnant women, although studies in animals have shown that some antihistamines (Meclizine and Cyclizine), used mainly against nausea and vomiting, may cause birth defects. Do not take any antihistamine without your doctor's knowledge.

Small amounts of antihistamine medicines pass into breast milk and may affect a nursing infant. Nursing mothers should avoid antihistamines or use alternative feeding methods while taking the medicine.

Seniors

Seniors are more sensitive to antihistamine side effects. Confusion, difficult or painful urination, dizziness, drowsiness, a faint feeling, nightmares or excitement, nervousness, restlessness, irritability, and dry mouth, nose, and throat are more likely to occur among older adults.

Possible Side Effects

The most frequent side effects are sedation, sleeplessness, dizziness, and disturbed coordination.

Less common side effects are itching, rash, drug allergy, sensitivity to sunlight, excessive perspiration, chills, and dryness of the mouth, nose, and throat.

Other possible side effects include lowered blood pressure, headache, palpitations, rapid heartbeat, effects on the blood system, confusion, restlessness, excitation, nervousness, irritability, sleeplessness, euphoria, tingling in the hands and feet, blurred vision, double vision, ringing in the ears, convulsions, stomach upset, loss of appetite, vomiting, nausea, diarrhea, constipation, thickening of mucus and other bronchial secretions resulting in tightness in the chest, wheezing, and stuffy nose. Cyproheptadine Hydrochloride may also produce adverse effects common to the phenothiazine class of drugs, such as tremors, a spastic, uncontrollable motion, and, rarely, a form of jaundice (yellowing of the skin and eyes).

Drug Interactions

Alcohol will increase the drowsiness or sleepiness that can be produced by Cyproheptadine Hydrochloride, so avoid drinking excessive amounts of alcoholic beverages. Taking Cyproheptadine Hydrochloride with another sedative, tranquilizer, barbiturate, or hypnotic drug can increase drowsiness and other symptoms of depression.

Cyproheptadine Hydrochloride can influence the effectiveness of any high blood pressure medicine you are taking.

If you have Parkinson's disease, you probably should not be taking this type of antihistamine: It is known to produce specific adverse drug effects in people with Parkinson's disease.

A monoamine oxidase (MAO) inhibitor may interact with Cyproheptadine Hydrochloride to prolong the drying effect of the antihistamine, causing dry mouth and blurred vision.

Usual Dose

Adult: 4 to 20 milligrams daily.
Child (age 7 to 14): 4 milligrams 2 to 3 times per day.
Child (age 2 to 6): 2 to 3 milligrams per day.

The maximum daily dose for adults is 32 milligrams; for children age 7 to 14, 16 milligrams; for children age 2 to 6, 12 milligrams.

Overdosage

Symptoms are depression or stimulation (especially in children), dry mouth, fixed or dilated pupils, flushing of the skin, and stomach upset. Take the patient to a hospital emergency room immediately. ALWAYS bring the medicine container to the hospital. Do not induce vomiting. After having taken this drug the patient might breathe in the vomit, causing serious lung damage.

Special Information

Cyproheptadine Hydrochloride can produce sleepiness. Be careful if you are driving or operating hazardous machinery.

The liquid form of this medicine is very bitter. To improve the taste you can mix it with fruit juice, milk, or a carbonated beverage.

If you forget to take a dose of Cypropheptadine, take it as soon as you remember. If it's almost time for your next dose, skip the one you forgot and continue with your regular schedule. Do not take a double dose of Cyproheptadine.

Generic Name

Dantrolene Sodium

Brand Name

Dantrium

Type of Drug

Muscle relaxant.

Prescribed for

Muscle spasticity resulting from spinal cord injuries, stroke, cerebral palsy, multiple sclerosis, or other forms of major nerve damage.

General Information

Dantrolene is an effective muscle relaxant for specialized or severe kinds of muscle injury or spasm. It should not be used to treat spasms associated with arthritis or other medical conditions or to treat routine muscle spasms or injuries associated with athletic or other physical activity because of the possibility of severe side effects. The intravenous form of this drug is used to treat or prevent very high body temperatures that sometimes occur during or after surgery.

Cautions and Warnings

This drug can cause liver damage and should be used with caution by people with a history of liver problems. People with no history of liver problems should use it only if necessary. Liver damage is more common with higher drug doses. Abnormal liver function is likely to develop between the third and twelfth month of Dantrolene treatment, but can occur at any time. Women over 35 and people taking other drugs that may be toxic to the liver are more likely to suffer liver damage while taking Dantrolene. Your doctor should test your liver function every 1½ months while you are taking this drug.

Dantrolene should be used with caution if you are allergic to it or if you have a pulmonary (lung) condition or severe heart disease.

Pregnancy/Breast-feeding

It is not known if Dantrolene affects a developing fetus, although it is toxic to developing animal fetuses. If you are or might be pregnant, do not take this drug without your doctor's knowledge.

Nursing mothers who must take Dantrolene should bottle-feed their babies.

Seniors

Seniors may take Dantrolene without any special restrictions. Be sure to observe all of the other cautions and special conditions pertaining to Dantrolene. Women and people over 35 are most likely to develop liver problems with Dantrolene.

Possible Side Effects

The most common side effects of Dantrolene are drowsiness, weakness, dizziness, fatigue, and a general feeling of poor health. These side effects are generally mild, occur early in treatment, and can be avoided by starting with a lower dose and gradually increasing the dose over time. Diarrhea, also a common side effect, may be so severe that it causes you to stop taking the drug. If the diarrhea starts again when you start taking the medicine, your doctor should try a different treatment.

Other side effects are constipation, stomach bleeding, loss of appetite, swallowing difficulty, abdominal cramps and stomach irritation, hepatitis, speech disturbances, seizure, headache, light-headedness, visual disturbances, double vision, taste changes, sleeplessness, depression, confusion, nervousness, rapid heartbeat, blood pressure changes, increased frequency of urination, blood or drug crystals in the urine, impotence, loss of urinary control, increased frequency of nighttime urination, urinary difficulty or pain on urination, an acne-like rash and other skin eruptions, itching, unusual hair growth, sweating, muscle and backaches, chills and fever, breathing difficulty, excess tear formation, chest pain, tenderness, changes in skin color, and swelling of the feet or legs.

Drug Interactions

The combination of estrogens and Dantrolene has been associated with a higher incidence of liver damage in women over 35; avoid this combination.

Tranquilizers and other nervous-system depressants can cause excessive drowsiness when taken together with Dantrolene.

Warfarin and Clofibrate increase the amount of Dantrolene in the blood and may increase drug side effects.

Tolbutamide decreases the amount of Dantrolene in the blood and may reduce the drug's effectiveness.

Food Interactions

Dantrolene may be taken without regard to food or meals. It may be mixed with juice or another liquid to mask the taste if you can't swallow the capsules. If you do mix Dantrolene with another liquid, drink it immediately after mixing.

Because this drug can cause difficulty swallowing, be careful when eating; choking has been reported.

Usual Dose

Adult: 25 milligrams once a day to start, gradually increased to 400 milligrams a day. For treatment before surgery, 2 to 4 milligrams per pound of body weight a day.

Child (age 5 and over): about ½ milligram per pound of body weight twice a day, gradually increased to a maximum of about 6 milligrams per pound every day, or 400 milligrams per day.

Overdosage

There is no known antidote for Dantrolene overdose. Overdose victims must be taken to a hospital emergency room as soon as possible. ALWAYS take the medicine bottle with you.

Special Information

Call your doctor if you develop severe diarrhea or constipation; difficulty breathing; skin rash; itching; bloody, black, or tarry stools; dark or bloody urine; confusion; convulsions;, chest pain; pain; tenderness; changes in skin color; swelling of the feet or legs; or a yellowish discoloration of the skin or eyes.

This drug causes drowsiness, dizziness, or light-headedness. Take care when driving or doing anything else that requires concentration.

Alcohol, tranquilizers, and other nervous-system depressants will increase the depressant effects of Dantrolene.

Dantrolene may make you unusually sensitive to the sun.

If you take Dantrolene once a day and forget to take a dose, take it as soon as you remember. If it is almost time for your next dose, skip the one you forgot and continue with your regular schedule. Do not take a double dose.

If you take it twice a day and forget a dose, take it as soon as you remember. If it is almost time for your next dose, take one dose as soon as you remember and another in 5 or 6 hours, then go back to your regular schedule. Do not take a double dose.

If you take Dantrolene 3 or more times a day and forget a dose, take it as soon as you remember. If it is almost time for your next dose, take one dose as soon as you remember and another in 3 or 4 hours, then go back to your regular schedule. Do not take a double dose.

Generic Name

Demeclocycline

Brand Name

Declomycin

Type of Drug

Broad-spectrum antibiotic effective against gram-positive and gram-negative organisms. It belongs to the general class of antibiotics known as Tetracycline.

Prescribed for

Bacterial infections such as gonorrhea; infections of the mouth, gums, and teeth; Rocky Mountain spotted fever and other fevers caused by ticks and lice; urinary tract infections; and respiratory system infections such as pneumonia and bronchitis. These diseases are produced by gram-positive and gram-negative organisms such as diplococci, staphylococci, streptococci, gonococci, *E. coli*, and *Shigella.*

Demeclocycline has also been used successfully to treat some skin infections, but it is not considered the first-choice antibiotic for the treatment of general skin infections or wounds.

Demeclocycline has been used experimentally to treat the disease syndrome of inappropriate antidiuretic hormone (SIADH), where excess amounts of antidiuretic hormone are produced by the body.

General Information

Demeclocycline works by interfering with the normal growth

cycle of the invading bacteria, preventing them from reproducing and thus allowing the body's normal defenses to fight off the infection. This process is referred to as bacteriostatic action. Demeclocycline has also been used along with other medicines to treat amoebic infections of the intestinal tract, known as amoebic dysentery.

Demeclocycline has been successfully used for the treatment of adolescent acne, in small doses over a long period of time. Adverse effects or toxicity in this type of therapy are almost unheard of.

Since the action of this antibiotic depends on its concentration within the invading bacteria, it is imperative that you completely follow your doctor's directions.

Cautions and Warnings

Demeclocycline should not be given to people with known liver disease or kidney or urine excretion problems. You should avoid taking high doses of Demeclocycline or undergoing extended Demeclocycline therapy if you will be exposed to sunlight for a long period, because this antibiotic can interfere with your body's normal sun-screening mechanism, possibly causing a severe sunburn.

If you have a known history of allergy to Demeclocycline, you should avoid taking this drug or other drugs within this category, such as Aureomycin, Terramycin, Rondomycin, Vibramycin, Tetracycline, and Minocycline.

Pregnancy/Breast-feeding

You should not use Demeclocycline if you are pregnant, especially during the last 4-and-a-half months. Do not use while breast-feeding because Demeclocycline may have an adverse effect on the formation of an infant's bones and teeth. Demeclocycline, when used in children, has been shown to interfere with the development of the long bones and may retard growth. Exceptions would be when Demeclocycline is the only effective antibiotic available and all risk factors have been known to the patient.

Seniors

Older adults, especially those with poor kidney function,

may be more likely to develop side effects if they take this drug for a long period of time.

Possible Side Effects

As with other antibiotics, the common side effects of Demeclocycline are stomach upset, nausea, vomiting, diarrhea, and rash.

Less common side effects include hairy tongue and itching and irritation of the anal and/or vaginal region. If these symptoms appear, consult your physician immediately. Periodic physical examinations and laboratory tests should be given to patients who are on long-term Demeclocycline.

Less common side effects are loss of appetite, peeling of the skin, sensitivity to the sun, fever, chills, anemia, possible brown spotting of the skin, decrease in kidney function, weakness, thirst, excessive urination, and damage to the liver.

Drug Interactions

Demeclocycline (a bacteriostatic drug) may interfere with the action of bactericidal agents such as Penicillin. It is not advisable to take both during the same course of therapy.

Don't take multivitamin products containing minerals at the same time as Demeclocycline, or you may reduce the antibiotic's effectiveness. You should take these 2 medicines at least 2 hours apart.

People receiving anticoagulation therapy (blood-thinning agents) should consult their doctor because Demeclocycline will interfere with this form of therapy. An adjustment in the anticoagulant dosage may be required.

Food Interactions

The antibacterial effect of Demeclocycline is neutralized when taken with food; some dairy products, including milk and cheese; and antacids.

Usual Dose

Adult: 600 milligrams per day.

Child (age 8 and over): 3 to 6 milligrams per pound per day.

Child (under age 8): should avoid Demeclocycline because

it has been shown to produce serious discoloration of the permanent teeth.

Take on an empty stomach 1 hour before or 2 hours after meals.

Special Information

Do *not* take this drug after the expiration date on the label. The decomposition of Demeclocycline produces a highly toxic substance that can cause serious kidney damage. Demeclocycline can be stored at room temperature.

If you forget to take a dose of Demeclocycline, take it as soon as you remember. If it is almost time for your next dose and you take 2 doses per day, take the missed dose and then the next dose 5 to 6 hours later. If you take 4 doses per day, double your next dose or take the missed dose and then the next dose 2 to 4 hours later. Go back to your regular dose schedule after making up for the missed dose.

Generic Name

Desipramine

Brand Names

Norpramin
Pertofrane

Type of Drug

Antidepressant.

Prescribed for

Depression with or without symptoms of anxiety.

General Information

Desipramine and other members of this group are effective in treating symptoms of depression. They can elevate mood, increase physical activity and mental alertness, and improve appetite and sleep patterns in a depressed patient. These drugs are mild sedatives and therefore useful in treating mild forms of depression associated with anxiety. You should not expect instant results with this medicine: Benefits are usually seen after 1 to 4 weeks. If symptoms are not affected after 6 to 8 weeks, contact your doctor. Occasionally this drug and other members of the group of drugs have been used in treating nighttime bed-wetting in young children, but they do not produce long-lasting relief, and therapy with one of them for nighttime bed-wetting is of questionable value.

Cautions and Warnings

Do not take Desipramine if you are allergic or sensitive to this or other members of this class of drug: Doxepin, Nortriptyline, Imipramine, Protriptyline, and Amitriptyline. These drugs should not be used if you are recovering from a heart attack.

Desipramine may be taken with caution if you have a history of epilepsy or other convulsive disorders, difficulty in urination, glaucoma, heart disease, or thyroid disease.

Pregnancy/Breast-feeding

This drug, like other antidepressants, crosses into your developing baby's circulation and may cause birth defects if taken during the first 3 months of pregnancy. There have been reports of newborn infants suffering from heart, breathing, and urinary problems after their mothers had taken an antidepressant of this type immediately before the delivery. You should avoid taking this medication while pregnant.

Antidepressants of this type are known to pass into breast milk and may affect a breast-feeding infant, although this has not been proven. Nursing mothers should consider alternative feeding methods if taking this medicine.

Seniors

Older adults are more sensitive to the effects of this drug and often require a lower dose than a younger adult to do the same job. Follow your doctor's directions and report any side effects at once.

Possible Side Effects

Possible side effects include changes in blood pressure (both high and low), abnormal heart rates, heart attack, confusion, especially in elderly patients, hallucinations, disorientation, delusions, anxiety, restlessness, excitement, numbness and tingling in the extremities, lack of coordination, muscle spasms or tremors, seizures and/or convulsions, dry mouth, blurred vision, constipation, inability to urinate, rash, itching, sensitivity to bright light or sunlight, retention of fluids, fever, allergy, changes in composition of blood, nausea, vomiting, loss of appetite, stomach upset, diarrhea, enlargement of the breasts in males and females, increased or decreased sex drive, and increase or decrease of blood sugar.

Less common side effects are agitation, inability to sleep, nightmares, feeling of panic, peculiar taste in the mouth, stomach cramps, black coloration of the tongue, yellowing eyes and/or skin, changes in liver function, increased or decreased weight, perspiration, flushing, frequent urination, drowsiness, dizziness, weakness, headache, loss of hair, nausea, and not feeling well.

Drug Interactions

Interaction with monoamine oxidase (MAO) inhibitors can cause high fevers, convulsions, and occasionally death. Don't take MAO inhibitors until at least 2 weeks after Desipramine has been discontinued. Certain patients may require concomitant use of Desipramine and an MAO inhibitor; in these cases close medical observation is warranted.

Desipramine interacts with Guanethidine, a drug used to treat high blood pressure: If your doctor prescribes Desipramine and you are taking medicine for high blood pressure, be sure to discuss this with him.

Desipramine increases the effects of barbiturates, tranquilizers, other depressive drugs, and alcohol. Don't drink alcohol while taking this medicine.

Taking Desipramine and a thyroid medicine will enhance the effects of the latter. The combination can cause abnormal heart rhythms.

Large doses of Vitamin C (Ascorbic Acid) can reduce the effect of Desipramine. Drugs such as Bicarbonate of Soda or Acetazolamide will increase the effect of Desipramine.

Food Interactions

This drug is best taken on an empty stomach but may be taken with food if it upsets your stomach.

Usual Dose

Adult: 75 to 300 milligrams per day. The dose of this drug must be tailored to patient's need. Patients taking high doses of this drug should have regular heart examinations to check for side effects.

Adolescent and senior: Lower doses are recommended, usually 25 to 150 milligrams per day.

Child (under age 12): This drug should not be used.

Overdosage

Symptoms are confusion, inability to concentrate, hallucinations, drowsiness, lowered body temperature, abnormal heart rate, heart failure, large pupils of the eyes, convulsions, severely lowered blood pressure, stupor, and coma (as well as agitation, stiffening of body muscles, vomiting, and high fever). The patient should be taken to a hospital emergency room immediately. ALWAYS bring the medicine bottle.

Special Information

Avoid alcohol and other drugs that depress the nervous system while taking this antidepressant.

Do not stop taking this medicine unless your doctor has specifically told you to do so. Abruptly stopping this medicine may cause nausea, headache, and a sickly feeling.

This medicine can cause drowsiness, dizziness, and blurred vision. Be careful when driving or operating complicated machinery.

Avoid exposure to the sun or sun lamps for long periods of time.

Call your doctor if dry mouth, difficulty urinating, or excessive sedation develops.

If you take more than 1 dose of Desipramine per day and forget to take a dose, take the missed dose as soon as possible. If it is almost time for your next dose, skip the missed dose and continue your usual dose schedule.

If you take Desipramine once a day and don't remember until the next day, skip the forgotten dose and continue with your regular schedule. Do not double any doses.

Generic Name

Dexchlorpheniramine Maleate

Brand Names

Dexchlor   Polaramine
Poladex

(Also available in generic form)

Type of Drug

Antihistamine.

Prescribed for

Seasonal allergy, stuffed and runny nose, itching of the eyes, scratchy throat caused by allergy, and other allergic symptoms, such as itching, rash, or hives.

General Information

Antihistamines generally, and Dexchlorpheniramine Maleate specifically, act by antagonizing at the site where histamine works. This site is often called the H_1 histamine receptor. Antihistamines work by drying up the secretions of the nose, throat, and eyes.

Cautions and Warnings

Dexchlorpheniramine Maleate should not be used if you are allergic to this drug. It should be avoided or used with extreme care if you have narrow-angle glaucoma (pressure in the eye), stomach ulcer or other stomach problems, enlarged prostate, or problems passing urine. It should not be used by people who have deep-breathing problems such as asthma.

Use with care if you have a history of thyroid disease, heart disease, high blood pressure, or diabetes.

Pregnancy/Breast-feeding

Dexchlorpheniramine has not been proven to be a cause of birth defects or other problems in pregnant women, although studies in animals have shown that some antihistamines (Meclizine and Cyclizine), used mainly against nausea and vomiting, may cause birth defects. Do not take any antihistamine without your doctor's knowledge.

Small amounts of antihistamine medicines pass into breast milk and may affect a nursing infant. Nursing mothers should avoid antihistamines or use alternative feeding methods while taking the medicine.

Seniors

Seniors are most sensitive to antihistamine side effects. Confusion, difficult or painful urination, dizziness, drowsiness, a faint feeling, nightmares or excitement, nervousness, restlessness, irritability, and dry mouth, nose, or throat are more likely to occur among older adults.

Possible Side Effects

Occasional side effects are itching, rash, sensitivity to light, excessive perspiration, chills, lowering of blood pressure, headache, rapid heartbeat, sleeplessness, dizziness, disturbed coordination, confusion, restlessness, nervousness, irritability, euphoria (feeling high), tingling of the hands and feet, blurred vision, double vision, ringing in the ears, stomach upset, loss of appetite, nausea, vomiting, constipation, diarrhea, difficulty in urination, tightness of the chest, wheezing, nasal stuffiness, and dryness of mouth, nose, and throat.

Drug Interactions

Dexchlorpheniramine Maleate should not be taken with monoamine oxidase (MAO) inhibitors.

Interaction with tranquilizers, sedatives, and sleeping medication will increase the effects of these drugs. It is extremely important that you discuss this with your doctor so that the doses of these drugs can be properly adjusted.

Be extremely cautious when drinking alcohol while taking Dexchlorpheniramine Maleate, which will enhance the intoxicating effect of the alcohol. Alcohol also has a sedative effect.

Usual Dose

Adult: 2 milligrams every 4 to 6 hours. Repeat-action tablets: 4 to 6 milligrams every 8 to 10 hours and at bedtime.

Child (age 6 to 12): 1 milligram every 4 to 6 hours. Repeat-action tablets: 4 milligrams once a day and at bedtime.

Child (age 2 to 5): 0.5 milligram every 4 to 6 hours. Do not use the repeat-action tablets.

Overdosage

Symptoms are depression or stimulation (especially in children), dry mouth, fixed or dilated pupils, flushing of the skin, and stomach upset. Take the patient to a hospital emergency room immediately, if you cannot make him or her vomit. ALWAYS bring the medicine bottle.

Special Information

Antihistamines produce a depressing effect: Be extremely cautious when driving or operating heavy equipment.

If you forget a dose of Dexchlorpheniramine Maleate, take it as soon as you remember. If it is almost time for your next dose, skip the forgotten dose and continue with your regular schedule. Do not take a double dose.

Generic Name

Dextroamphetamine (D-Amphetamine)

Brand Names

Dexedrine   Spancap
Oxydess

(Also available in generic form)

Type of Drug

Central-nervous-system stimulant.

Prescribed for

Short-term (a couple of months) aid to diet control; abnormal behavioral syndrome in children; narcolepsy (uncontrollable and unpredictable desire to sleep).

General Information

When taking this medicine as part of a weight control program it is usual to experience a decrease in drug effectiveness because your body is breaking down the drug faster. Do not increase the amount of drug you are taking: Simply stop taking the medicine.

The use of D-Amphetamine (as well as other drugs) in the treatment of minimal brain dysfunction in children is extremely controversial and must be judged by a physician qualified to treat the disorder. Children whose problems are judged to have been produced by their surroundings or by primary psychiatric disorders may not be helped by D-Amphetamine.

Cautions and Warnings

D-Amphetamine is highly abusable and addictive. It must be used with extreme caution. People with arteriosclerosis (hardening of the arteries), heart disease, high blood pressure, thyroid disease, or glaucoma or who are sensitive or allergic to any amphetamine should not take this medication.

Pregnancy/Breast-feeding

Amphetamines should be avoided by women who are or might become pregnant. Amphetamine use early in pregnancy has been associated with some birth defects, and animal studies suggest that amphetamines can be the source of other birth defects as well. Infants born to mothers taking amphetamines have a lower birth weight and an increased risk of premature delivery. They may experience drug withdrawal symptoms immediately after birth.

It is not known if amphetamines pass into breast milk. The potential risk of affecting your nursing infant must be taken into account when deciding to breast-feed while on an amphetamine diet pill.

Seniors

Older adults are more sensitive to the effects of this drug. Follow your doctor's directions and report any side effects at once.

Possible Side Effects

Possible side effects include palpitations, restlessness, over-stimulation, dizziness, sleeplessness, increased blood pressure, and rapid heartbeat.

Less common side effects are euphoria, hallucinations, muscle spasms and tremors, headache, dryness of the mouth, unpleasant taste, diarrhea, constipation, stomach upset, itching, loss of sex drive, and, rarely, psychotic drug reactions.

Drug Interactions

D-Amphetamine should not be given at the same time as, or within 14 days following the use of, a monoamine oxidase (MAO) inhibitor. This may cause severe lowering of blood pressure.

D-Amphetamine may decrease the effectiveness of Guanethidine.

If D-Amphetamine is taken with Insulin, Insulin requirements may be altered.

Food Interactions

Take this medicine with food if it upsets your stomach.

Usual Dose

For narcolepsy: 5 to 60 milligrams per day, depending on individual need.

For abnormal behavior syndrome: 2.5 to 40 milligrams per day, depending on child's age and response to the drug.

For weight control: 5 to 30 milligrams per day in divided doses one-half to 1 hour before meals; or, as a long-acting dose, once in the morning.

Overdosage

Symptoms are tremors, muscle spasms, restlessness, exaggerated reflexes, rapid breathing, hallucinations, confusion, panic, and overaggressive behavior, followed by depression and exhaustion after the central-nervous-system stimulation wears off, as well as abnormal heart rhythms, changes in blood pressure, nausea, vomiting, diarrhea, convulsions, and coma. The patient should be taken to a hospital emer-

gency room immediately. ALWAYS bring the medicine
container.

Special Information

Take this medicine at least 6 to 8 hours before you plan to
go to sleep, or it will interfere with a sound and restful
night's sleep.

Do not crush or chew the sustained-release formulations.

If you miss a dose, take it as early as possible to avoid
sleeping problems. If you take 1 dose per day, it may be
best to skip the missed dose and resume your dose schedule
the next day.

If you take 2 to 3 doses per day and you remember the
missed dose within an hour or so, take it right away. If you
remember too late, skip the missed dose and go back to
your regular dose schedule the next day. Do not double any
doses.

Generic Name

Diazepam

Brand Names

Valium
Valrelease
Zetran

(Also available in generic form)

Type of Drug

Minor tranquilizer.

Prescribed for

Relief of symptoms of anxiety, tension, fatigue, or agitation.

General Information

Diazepam is a member of the group of drugs known as benzodiazepines. These drugs are used as antianxiety agents,
anticonvulsants, or sedatives (sleeping pills). They exert

their effects by relaxing the large skeletal muscles and by a direct effect on the brain. In doing so, they can relax you and make you either more tranquil or sleepier, depending on the drug and how much you use. Many doctors prefer Diazepam and the other members of this class to other drugs that can be used for the same effect. Their reason is that the benzodiazepines tend to be safer, have fewer side effects, and are usually as, if not more, effective.

These drugs are generally used in any situation where they can be a useful adjunct.

Benzodiazepine tranquilizing drugs can be abused if taken for long periods of time, and it is possible to develop withdrawal symptoms if you discontinue the therapy abruptly. Withdrawal symptoms include tremor, muscle cramps, stomach cramps, vomiting, insomnia, agitation, sweating, and even convulsions.

Cautions and Warnings

Do not take Diazepam if you know you are sensitive or allergic to this drug or to other benzodiazepines such as Chlordiazepoxide, Oxazepam, Clorazepate, Lorazepam, Prazepam, Flurazepam, Clonazepam, and Temazepam.

Diazepam and other members of this drug group may aggravate narrow-angle glaucoma, but if you have open-angle glaucoma you may take the drugs. In any case, check this information with your doctor.

Pregnancy/Breast-feeding

Avoid taking this drug during the first 3 months of pregnancy except under strict supervision of your doctor. Taken during the first 3 months of pregnancy, Diazepam has been shown to increase the chance of birth defects. The baby may become dependent on Diazepam if it is used continually during pregnancy. If used during the last weeks of pregnancy or during breast-feeding, the baby may be over-tired or short of breath or have a low heartbeat. Use during labor may cause weakness in the newborn.

Members of the benzodiazepine family pass into breast milk. Since infants break the drug down more slowly than adults, it is possible for the medicine to accumulate and have an undesired effect on the baby.

Seniors

Older adults are more sensitive to the effects of this drug, especially dizziness and drowsiness. Follow your doctor's directions and report any side effects at once.

Possible Side Effects

The most common side effect is mild drowsiness during the first few days of therapy. If drowsiness persists, contact your doctor.

Less common side effects are confusion, depression, lethargy, disorientation, headache, inactivity, slurred speech, stupor, dizziness, tremor, constipation, dry mouth, nausea, inability to control urination, changes in sex drive, irregular menstrual cycle, changes in heart rhythm, lowered blood pressure, retention of fluids, blurred or double vision, itching, rash, hiccups, nervousness, inability to fall asleep, and occasionally, liver dysfunction. If you experience any of these reactions, stop taking the medicine and contact your doctor immediately.

Drug Interactions

Diazepam is a central-nervous-system depressant. Avoid alcohol, tranquilizers, narcotics, barbiturates, monoamine oxidase (MAO) inhibitors, antihistamines, and other medicines used to relieve depression.

Smoking may reduce the effectiveness of Diazepam.

The effects of Diazepam may be prolonged when it is taken together with Cimetidine.

Usual Dose

Adult: 2 to 40 milligrams per day as individualized for maximum benefit, depending on symptoms and response to treatment.

Senior: Less of the drug is usually required to control tension and anxiety.

Child (6 months and over): 1 to 2.5 milligrams 3 to 4 times per day; possibly more if needed to control anxiety and tension.

Infant (under 6 months): This drug should not be used.

Overdosage

Symptoms are confusion, sleep or sleepiness, lack of response to pain such as a pin stick, shallow breathing, lowered blood pressure, and coma. The patient should be taken to a hospital emergency room immediately. ALWAYS bring the medicine bottle.

Special Information

Diazepam can cause tiredness, drowsiness, inability to concentrate, or similar symptoms. Be careful if you are driving, operating machinery, or performing other activities that require concentration.

Do not crush or chew the sustained-release preparation (Valrelease).

If you miss a dose and it is within an hour or so of your usual dose time, take it right away. If over an hour has passed, skip the missed dose and go back to your regular dose schedule. Do not double any doses.

Generic Name

Diclofenac

Brand Name

Voltaren

Type of Drug

Nonsteroidal anti-inflammatory.

Prescribed for

Rheumatoid arthritis and osteoarthritis.

General Information

Diclofenac is one of many nonsteroidal anti-inflammatory drugs (NSAIDs) sold in the United States to reduce inflammation, relieve pain and fever, and relieve menstrual cramps and discomfort. The choice of one member of this group over another often depends on your individual response to a specific drug. Because of this, it is common to try several of these drugs before you find the one that is right for you. Diclofenac starts working in about 30 minutes and will remain effective for about 3 hours. Diclofenac is used all over the world and holds the distinction of having been one of the most widely prescribed NSAIDs in the world before it was approved in the United States in 1988.

Cautions and Warnings

Do not take this product if you are allergic to Aspirin or to any other NSAID. This drug can worsen stomach ulcers or cause a new ulcer to develop. It should be used with caution if you have kidney disease. Diclofenac may cause liver inflammation.

Pregnancy/Breast-feeding

This drug may cross into the blood circulation of a developing baby. It has not been found to cause birth defects. Pregnant women, or those who might become pregnant while taking this drug, should not take it without their doctor's approval. When the drug is considered essential by your doctor, the potential risk of taking the medicine must be carefully weighed against the benefit it might produce.

This drug passes into breast milk, but has caused no problems among breast-fed infants. You must consider the potential effect on the nursing infant if breast-feeding while taking this medicine.

Seniors

Older adults are more sensitive to the stomach, kidney, and liver effects of this drug. Some doctors recommend that persons 70 years of age and older take half the usual dose, although Diclofenac's rapid elimination from the body may make it more useful for older adults. Follow your doctor's directions and report any side effects at once.

Possible Side Effects

The most common side effects are upset stomach, dizziness, headache, drowsiness, and ringing in the ears.

Other side effects include heartburn, nausea, vomiting, bloating, stomach gas or pain, diarrhea, constipation, dark stools, nervousness, sleeplessness, depression, confusion, tremor, loss of appetite, fatigue, itching, rash, double or blurred vision, dry or irritated eyes, heart failure, palpitations, abnormal heart rhythms, anemia or other changes in the composition of your blood, changes in liver function, hair loss, tingling in the hands or feet, fever, enlarged breasts, blood in the urine, urinary tract irritation, thirst, frequent urination, kidney damage, low blood sugar, asthma, difficulty breathing, skin rash, itching, swelling, and black-and-blue marks.

Drug Interactions

Aspirin causes this drug to be eliminated from the body more rapidly than normal. Avoid Aspirin while taking this medication.

Do not take Diclofenac together with Methotrexate, which is used to treat cancers and severe rheumatoid arthritis.

This drug may increase the effectiveness of anticoagulant (blood-thinning) drugs. It can increase blood-clotting time by 3 to 4 minutes.

Taking Diclofenac together with a thiazide diuretic increases the chances for kidney failure.

Diclofenac may increase the effects of sulfa drugs, antidiabetes drugs, and Phenytoin or other drugs for seizure disorders.

Food Interactions

You may take this drug with food if it upsets your stomach.

Usual Dose

Adult: 100 to 200 milligrams per day divided into 2, 3, or 4 doses.

Senior: probably should start with one-half to one-third the usual dose.

Overdosage

Symptoms may include drowsiness, dizziness, confusion, disorientation, lethargy, tingling in the hands or feet, numbness, nausea, vomiting, upset stomach, stomach pains, headache, ringing or buzzing in the ears, sweating, and blurred vision. Take the victim to a hospital emergency room at once for treatment. ALWAYS bring the medicine bottle with you.

Special Information

Avoid alcoholic beverages while taking this medication.

You may become dizzy or drowsy while taking this medicine. Be careful while driving or operating complex equipment.

Call your doctor if you develop a skin rash, itching, swelling, visual disturbances, black stools, or a persistent headache while taking this medication.

If you forget to take a dose of Diclofenac, take it as soon as you remember. If it is almost time for your next dose, skip the forgotten dose and continue with your regular schedule.

Generic Name

Diethylpropion Hydrochloride

Brand Names

Tenuate	Tepanil
Tenuate Dospan	Tepanil Ten-Tab

(Also available in generic form)

Type of Drug

Nonamphetamine appetite depressant.

Prescribed for

Suppression of appetite and treatment of obesity.

General Information

Although Diethylpropion Hydrochloride is not an amphetamine, it can produce the same adverse effects as the amphetamine appetite suppressants.

Cautions and Warnings

Do not use Diethylpropion Hydrochloride if you have heart disease, high blood pressure, thyroid disease, or glaucoma or if you are sensitive or allergic to this or similar drugs. Furthermore, do not use this medication if you are emotionally agitated or have a history of drug abuse.

Pregnancy/Breast-feeding

Other drugs similar to Diethylpropion Hydrochloride have caused birth defects. However, in animal and human studies, Diethylpropion Hydrochloride has not been shown to cause these effects. Check with your doctor before taking it if you are, or might be, pregnant.

This medicine passes into breast milk and can affect a nursing infant.

Seniors

Older adults should not take this medicine unless prescribed by a doctor. It can aggravate diabetes and high blood pressure, conditions common to older adults.

Possible Side Effects

Common side effects are a false sense of well-being, nervousness, overstimulation, restlessness, and trouble sleeping.

Other side effects are palpitations, high blood pressure, drowsiness, sedation, weakness, dizziness, tremor, headache, dry mouth, nausea, vomiting, diarrhea and other intestinal disturbances, rash, itching, changes in sex drive, hair loss, muscle pain, difficulty in passing urine, sweating, chills, blurred vision, and fever.

Usual Dose

25 milligrams 3 times per day, 1 hour before meals; an additional tablet may be given in midevening if needed to suppress the desire for midnight snacks.

Sustained-release tablets or capsules of 75 milligrams (Tenuate Dospan, Tepanil Ten-Tab): 1 per day, usually in midmorning.

Overdosage

Symptoms are restlessness, tremor, shallow breathing, confusion, hallucinations, and fever, followed by fatigue and depression, with additional symptoms such as high or possibly low blood pressure, cold and clammy skin, nausea, vomiting, diarrhea, and stomach cramps. The patient should be taken to a hospital emergency room immediately. ALWAYS bring the medicine bottle.

Special Information

Use this drug for no more than 12 weeks as an adjunct to diet, under strict supervision of your doctor.

Medicine alone will not take off weight. You must limit and modify your food intake, preferably under medical supervision.

This drug can cause dry mouth, which can be relieved by sugarless candy, gum, or shaved ice.

Do not crush or chew sustained-release products.

The long-acting preparations should be taken at least 10 to 14 hours before your bedtime to help avoid sleeping troubles.

If you forget to take a dose of Diethylpropion Hydrochloride, take it as soon as you remember. If it is almost time for your next regularly scheduled dose, skip the one you forgot and continue with your regular schedule. Do not take a double dose.

Generic Name

Diflunisal

Brand Name

Dolobid

Type of Drug

Nonsteroidal anti-inflammatory.

Prescribed for

Relief of mild or moderate pain, rheumatoid arthritis, osteoarthritis.

General Information

This drug is derived from salicylic acid but is chemically different from Aspirin. It reduces pain and inflammation but we do not know exactly how the medicine works. Part of the drug's action may be due to its ability to inhibit a hormone called prostaglandin, a property it shares with other nonsteroidal anti-inflammatory drugs (NSAIDs). It is quickly absorbed into the bloodstream and produces pain relief in about 1 hour. Its maximum effect is seen within 2 to 3 hours. People taking Diflunisal generally have a good pain-relieving effect 8 to 12 hours after taking their medicine. Usually it takes 3 to 4 days of therapy to reach an acceptable level of pain relief.

A single 500-milligram tablet of Diflunisal is about equal in its ability to relieve pain to 650 milligrams of Aspirin or Acetaminophen (2 regular tablets) or to 1 tablet of Darvon-N 100. Two 500-milligram tablets of Diflunisal are about equal to 600 milligrams of Acetaminophen with 60 milligrams of Codeine (Tylenol with Codeine £4) in pain relief.

Cautions and Warnings

People who are allergic to Diflunisal, Aspirin, or other NSAIDs and those with a history of asthma attacks brought on by another NSAID or by Aspirin should not take Diflunisal.

This medicine can cause gastrointestinal bleeding. People with a history of active gastrointestinal bleeding should be cautious about taking Diflunisal.

This drug can affect blood clotting at high doses and should be avoided by people with clotting problems and those taking Warfarin.

People with heart problems who use this medicine may find their arms and legs or feet become swollen.

Pregnancy/Breast-feeding

This drug crosses into the blood circulation of a developing baby. It has not been found to cause birth defects, but may affect a developing infant's heart during the last 3 months of pregnancy. Pregnant women, or those who might become pregnant while taking this drug, should not take it without their doctors' approval. When the drug is considered essential by your doctor, the potential risk of taking the medicine must be carefully weighed against the benefit it might produce.

This drug passes into breast milk, but has caused no problems among breast-fed infants. You should either stop breast-feeding while taking this medicine or use an alternative feeding method.

Seniors

Older adults, especially those with poor kidney function, may be more susceptible to the side effects of this drug.

Possible Side Effects

Common side effects include diarrhea, stomach gas, headache, sleeplessness, and rash.

Less common side effects are nausea, upset stomach, vomiting, constipation, stomach ulcers, gastrointestinal bleeding, loss of appetite, hepatitis, gallbladder attacks, painful urination, poor kidney function, kidney inflammation, blood and protein in the urine, dizziness, fainting, nervousness, depression, hallucinations, confusion, disorientation, tingling in the hands or feet, light-headedness, itching, sweating, dry nose and mouth, heart palpitations, chest pain, difficulty breathing, and muscle cramps.

A small number of people taking Diflunisal have experienced severe allergic reactions, including closing of the throat, fever and chills, changes in liver function, jaundice, and kidney failure. These people must be treated in a hospital emergency room or doctor's office.

Severe dermatologic reactions like erythema multiforme and Stevens-Johnson syndrome have occurred to people taking this medication.

Drug Interactions

Diflunisal can increase the effects of oral anticoagulant drugs such as Warfarin. You may take this combination, but your doctor may have to adjust your anticoagulant dose to take this effect into account.

The combination of Diflunisal and a thiazide diuretic increases the amount of diuretic in your blood.

Taking antacids together with Diflunisal may decrease the amount of Diflunisal absorbed into the bloodstream. This effect is especially important if you take antacids on a continuous basis for hyperacidity or an ulcer.

Diflunisal increases the amount of Acetaminophen in your blood by about 50 percent. It also increases the amount of Indomethacin in your blood; the combination of Indomethacin and Diflunisal has resulted in a fatal gastrointestinal hemorrhage.

Food Interactions

Take this medicine with food if it upsets your stomach.

Usual Dose

500 to 1000 milligrams to start, then 250 to 500 milligrams every 8 to 12 hours. Do not take more than 1500 milligrams per day.

Overdosage

People have died from an overdose of 15 grams of Diflunisal. The most common signs of overdose are drowsiness, nausea, vomiting, diarrhea, rapid breathing, rapid heartbeat, sweating, ringing or buzzing in the ears, disorientation, stupor, and coma.

Take the victim to a hospital emergency room at once for treatment. ALWAYS remember to bring the medicine bottle with you.

Special Information

Do not take any nonprescription products with Aspirin or Acetaminophen while taking Diflunisal, unless directed to do so by your doctor.

Do not crush or chew the tablets.

Contact your doctor if you develop any unusual side effects or if side effects become intolerable.

If you forget to take a dose of Diflunisal, take it as soon as you remember. If it is almost time for your next regularly scheduled dose, skip the one you forgot and continue with your regular schedule. Do not take a double dose.

Type of Drug

Digitalis Glycosides

Brand Names

Generic Name: Digitoxin

Crystodigin

(Also available in generic form)

Generic Name: Digoxin

Lanoxicaps
Lanoxin

(Also available in generic form)

Prescribed for

Congestive heart failure and other heart abnormalities.

General Information

Digitalis glycosides directly affect the myocardium (heart muscle), depending on the dose you are taking. They improve your heart's pumping ability or helps to control its beating rhythm. Patients with heart problems very often notice swelling of the feet, ankles, and hands. Digitalis drugs improve this symptom by improving drug circulation.

Digitoxin is more useful than Digoxin in patients who have kidney problems. Digitoxin is not removed from the body by the kidneys, but mostly by the liver.

These medications are generally used for long periods of time.

Cautions and Warnings

Do not use these drugs if you know you are allergic or sensitive to digitalis. Long-term use of a digitalis drug can cause the body to lose potassium, especially since digitalis drugs are generally used in combination with diuretic drugs. For this reason, be sure to eat a well-balanced diet and emphasize foods that are high in potassium such as bananas, citrus fruits, melons, and tomatoes.

Pregnancy/Breast-feeding

Digitalis drugs cross into the blood circulation of a developing baby. They have not been found to cause birth defects. Nevertheless, pregnant women, or those who might become pregnant while taking one of these drugs, should not take it without their doctors' approval. When the drug is considered essential by your doctor, the potential risk of taking the medicine must be carefully weighed against the benefit it might produce.

Digitalis drugs pass into breast milk, but have caused no problems among breast-fed infants. You must consider the potential effect on the nursing infant if breast-feeding while taking one of these medicines.

Seniors

Older adults are more sensitive to the effects of digitalis drugs, especially loss of appetite. Follow your doctor's directions and report any side effects at once.

Possible Side Effects

The most common side effects are loss of appetite, nausea, vomiting, diarrhea, and blurred or disturbed vision. If you experience any of these problems, discuss them with your doctor immediately.

Enlargement of the breasts has been reported after long-term use of a digitalis drug, but this is uncommon. Allergy or sensitivity to digitalis drugs is also uncommon.

Drug Interactions

Barbiturates, Phenytoin, antidiabetic drugs, Phenylbutazone, and Rifampin will counteract the effectiveness of a digitalis drug by stimulating its breakdown by your liver.

The absorption of a digitalis drug into your bloodstream is reduced by taking it together with antacids, kaolin-pectin mixtures, Cholestyramine, or Colestipol. Other drugs that can prevent digitalis drugs from being absorbed are oral Kanamycin, Metoclopramide, and oral Neomycin.

Drugs that may increase the effect of a digitalis drug are

anticholinergic drugs, Erythromycin and Tetracycline, Hydroxychloroquine, Nifedipine, and Verapamil.

Low blood potassium, a common side effect of thiazide diuretics, Furosemide, Ethacrynic Acid, and Bumetanide, will increase a digitalis drug's effect and increase the chance of developing a toxic side effect.

Spironolactone can either increase or decrease the effect of a digitalis drug. The effect is unpredictable.

Quinidine may increase the amount of a digitalis drug in your blood by 2 to 3 times, beginning 1 to 3 days after the Quinidine is started.

The effects of a digitalis drug on your heart may be additive to those of the Ephedrine, Epinephrine, and other stimulants; beta blockers; calcium salts; Procainamide; and Rauwolfia drugs.

Thyroid drugs will change your digitalis drug requirement. Your doctor will have to make a dosage adjustment if you start taking a thyroid drug.

Food Interactions

Take each day's dose after your morning meal.

Usual Dose

Digitoxin:
Adult: The first dose—known as the digitalizing dose—is 2 milligrams over about 3 days, or 0.4 milligram per day for 4 days. Maintenance dose ranges from 0.05 to 0.03 milligram daily.
Senior: lower doses, because seniors are more sensitive to adverse effects.
Infant and child: The first dose depends on age but can be from 0.01 milligram per pound to 0.02 milligram per pound. Maintenance dose is one-tenth the first dose.

Digoxin:
Adult: The first dose—known as the digitalizing dose—is 1 to 1.5 milligrams. Maintenance dose ranges from 0.125 to 0.5 milligram.
Senior: lower doses, because seniors are more sensitive to adverse effects.
Infant and child: substantially lower dose.

Overdosage

Symptoms are loss of appetite, nausea, vomiting, diarrhea, headache, weakness, apathy, blurred vision, yellow or green spots before the eyes, yellowing of the skin and eyes, or changes in heartbeat. Contact your doctor immediately if any of these symptoms appear. An early sign of overdose in children is change in heart rhythm. Vomiting, diarrhea, and eye trouble are frequently seen in older people.

Special Information

Do not stop taking this medicine unless your doctor tells you to.

Avoid nonprescription medicine containing stimulants. Your pharmacist can tell you which nonprescription medicine is safe for you.

Call your doctor if you develop loss of appetite, stomach pains, nausea or vomiting, diarrhea, unusual tiredness or weakness, visual disturbances, or mental depression.

There are considerable variations among digitalis drug tablets made by different manufacturers. Do not change brands without telling your doctor.

If you forget to take a dose of a digitalis drug, do not take the forgotten dose. Skip the dose and go back to your regular schedule. Do not take a double dose. Call your doctor if you forget to take your medicine for 2 or more days.

Generic Name

Diltiazem Hydrochloride

Brand Name

Cardizem
Cardizem-SR

Type of Drug

Calcium channel blocker.

Prescribed for

Angina pectoris; high blood pressure; prevention of a reoccurrence of some kinds of heart attack.

General Information

Diltiazem Hydrochloride is one of several calcium channel blockers marketed in the United States. These drugs work by slowing the passage of calcium into muscle cells. This causes muscles in the blood vessels that supply your heart to open wider, allowing more blood to reach heart tissues. The drugs also decrease muscle spasm in those blood vessels. Diltiazem Hydrochloride also reduces the speed at which electrical impulses are carried through heart tissue, adding to its ability to slow the heart and prevent the pain of angina. This drug can help to reduce high blood pressure by causing blood vessels throughout the body to widen, allowing blood to flow more easily through them, especially when combined with a diuretic, beta blocker, or other blood-pressure-lowering drug.

Cautions and Warnings

Diltiazem Hydrochloride can slow your heart and interfere with normal electrical conduction. For people with a condition called sick sinus syndrome, this can result in temporary heart stoppage; most people will not develop this effect.

   Diltiazem Hydrochloride can cause severe liver damage and should be taken with caution if you have had hepatitis or any other liver condition. Caution should also be exercised if you have a history of kidney problems, although no clear tendency toward causing kidney damage exists.

Pregnancy/Breast-feeding

Animal studies with Diltiazem Hydrochloride have revealed a definite potential to harm a developing fetus, usually at doses greater than the usual human dose. As doses are increased, adverse effects become more frequent and more severe. Diltiazem Hydrochloride should not be taken by pregnant women or women who may become pregnant while using it. In those situations where it is deemed essential, the potential risk of the drug must be carefully weighed against any benefit it might produce.

Nursing mothers should use an alternative feeding method, since Diltiazem Hydrochloride passes into breast milk. Diltiazem Hydrochloride's safety in children has not been established.

Seniors

Older adults are more sensitive to the effects of this drug because it takes longer to pass out of their bodies. Follow your doctor's directions and report any side effects at once.

Possible Side Effects

Possible side effects include abnormal heart rhythms, headache, fatigue, nausea, rash, and fluid accumulation in the hands, legs, or feet.

Less common side effects are low blood pressure, dizziness, fainting, changes in heart rate (increase or decrease), heart failure, light-headedness, nervousness, tingling in the hands or feet, hallucinations, temporary memory loss, difficulty sleeping, weakness, diarrhea, vomiting, constipation, upset stomach, itching, unusual sensitivity to sunlight, painful or stiff joints, liver inflammation, and increased urination, especially at night.

Drug Interactions

Taking Diltiazem Hydrochloride together with a beta-blocking drug for high blood pressure is usually well tolerated, but may lead to heart failure in people with already weakened hearts.

Calcium channel blockers, including Diltiazem Hydrochloride, may add to the effects of Digoxin, although this effect is not observed with any consistency and only affects people with a large amount of Digoxin already in their systems.

Food Interactions

Diltiazem Hydrochloride is best taken on an empty stomach, at least 1 hour before or 2 hours after meals.

Usual Dose

30 to 60 milligrams 4 times per day.

Overdosage

The 2 major symptoms of Diltiazem Hydrochloride overdose are very low blood pressure and reduced heart rate. Patients poisoned with this drug must be made to vomit within 30 minutes of the actual dose with Syrup of Ipecac (available at any pharmacy) to remove the drug from the stomach. If overdose symptoms have developed or more than 30 minutes have passed, vomiting is of little value. You must go to a hospital emergency room for treatment. ALWAYS bring the medicine bottle.

Special Information

Call your doctor if you develop any of the following symptoms: swelling of the hands, legs, or feet, severe dizziness, constipation or nausea, or very low blood pressure.

If you forget to take a dose of Diltiazem Hydrochloride, take it as soon as you remember. If it is almost time for your next regularly scheduled dose, skip the one you forgot and continue with your regular schedule. Do not take a double dose.

Generic Name

Dimenhydrinate

Brand Names

Calm-X	Nico-Vert
Dimetabs	Tega-Vert
Dramamine	Triptone
Marmine	

(Also available in generic form)

Type of Drug

Antihistamine.

Prescribed for

Prevention or treatment of nausea, vomiting, or dizziness associated with motion sickness.

General Information

Dimenhydrinate is a mixture of Diphenhydramine, an anti-histamine, and another ingredient, although the antihistamine is believed to be the active ingredient. Dimenhydrinate depresses middle-ear function, but the way in which it actually prevents nausea, vomiting, or dizziness is not known. Dimenhydrinate tablets and liquid are available without a prescription.

Cautions and Warnings

People with a prostate condition, some types of stomach ulcers, bladder problems, difficulty urinating, glaucoma, asthma, or abnormal heart rhythms should use Dimenhydrinate only while under a doctor's care.

Because it controls nausea and vomiting, Dimenhydrinate can hide the symptoms of overdose of other medicines or the symptoms of appendicitis. Your doctor may have difficulty reaching an accurate diagnosis in these conditions unless he or she knows you are taking Dimenhydrinate.

Pregnancy/Breast-feeding

Antihistamines have not been proven to be a cause of birth defects or other problems in pregnant women, although studies in animals have shown that some antihistamines (Meclizine and Cyclizine), used mainly against nausea and vomiting, may cause birth defects. Do not take any antihistamine without your doctor's knowledge.

Small amounts of antihistamines pass into breast milk and may affect a nursing infant. Dimenhydrinate may inhibit milk production. Nursing mothers should avoid antihistamines or use alternative feeding methods while taking the medicine.

Seniors

Seniors are more sensitive to antihistamine side effects.

Possible Side Effects

The most common side effect of Dimenhydrinate is dizziness. Other, less frequent, side effects are blurred vision, difficult or painful urination, increased sensitivity to the sun, loss of appetite, nightmares, rash, ringing or buzzing in the ears, and dry mouth, nose, or throat.

Drug Interactions

Taking Dimenhydrinate together with alcoholic beverages, other antihistamines, tranquilizers, or other nervous-system depressants can result in excessive dizziness, drowsiness, or other signs of nervous-system depression.

Food Interactions

Take this medicine with food or milk if it upsets your stomach.

Usual Dose

Adult: 50 to 100 milligrams (1 to 2 tablets or 4 to 8 teaspoons) every 4 to 6 hours.

Child (age 6 to 12): 25 to 50 milligrams (½ or 1 tablet or 2 to 4 teaspoons) every 6 to 8 hours. No more than 3 doses a day.

Child (age 2 to 5): up to 25 milligrams (½ tablet or 2 teaspoons) every 6 to 8 hours. No more than 3 doses a day.

Child (under age 2): See your doctor.

Overdosage

The usual effect of an overdose is drowsiness, clumsiness, and unsteadiness. A faint feeling, facial flushing, and dry mouth, nose, and throat can also occur. Convulsions, coma, and breathing difficulty can develop after a massive overdose of Dimenhydrinate.

Overdose victims should be taken to a hospital emergency room for treatment. ALWAYS remember to bring the medicine bottle with you.

Special Information

For maximum effectiveness against motion sickness, take your dose of Dimenhydrinate 1 to 2 hours before traveling. Dimenhydrinate may still be effective if taken 30 minutes before traveling.

Dimenhydrinate and other antihistamines can cause dry mouth, nose, or throat. Sugarless candy, gum, or ice chips can relieve this symptom, which is only temporary. Contact your doctor if excessive dryness lasts more than 2 weeks.

If you forget to take a dose of Dimenhydrinate, take it as soon as you remember. If it is almost time for your next regularly scheduled dose, skip the one you forgot and continue with your regular schedule. Do not take a double dose.

Generic Name

Diphenhydramine Hydrochloride

Brand Names

Aller Max	Hydramyn
Banophen	Nervine Nighttime Sleep-Aid
Belix	Nidryl
Benadryl	Nordryl
Benylin Cough	Nytol
Bydramine	Phendry
Compōz	Sleep-Eze 3
Diphen Cough	Sominex 2
Dormarex-2	Tusstat
Genahist	Twilite
Hydramine	

(Also available in generic form)

Type of Drug

Antihistamine.

Prescribed for

Seasonal allergy, stuffed and runny nose, itching of the eyes, scratchy throat caused by allergy, and other allergic symptoms, such as itching, rash, or hives. In addition, Diphenhydramine Hydrochloride has been used for motion sickness and, with other drugs, for Parkinson's disease and as a nighttime aid.

General Information

Antihistamines generally, and Diphenhydramine Hydrochloride specifically, act by antagonizing histamine at the site of the H_1 histamine receptor. Antihistamines work by drying up the secretions of the nose, throat, and eyes. They relieve itch and will help you go to sleep.

Cautions and Warnings

Diphenhydramine Hydrochloride should not be used if you are allergic to this drug. It should be avoided or used with extreme care if you have narrow-angle glaucoma (pressure in the eye), stomach ulcer or other stomach problems, enlarged prostate, or problems passing urine. It should not be used by people who have deep-breathing problems such as asthma.

Use with care if you have a history of thyroid disease, heart disease, high blood pressure, or diabetes.

Pregnancy/Breast-feeding

Antihistamines have not been proven to be a cause of birth defects or other problems in pregnant women, although studies in animals have shown that some antihistamines (Meclizine and Cyclizine), used mainly against nausea and vomiting, may cause birth defects. Do not take any antihistamine without your doctor's knowledge.

Small amounts of antihistamine medicines pass into breast milk and may affect a nursing infant. Nursing mothers should avoid antihistamines or use alternative feeding methods while taking the medicine.

Seniors

Seniors are more sensitive to antihistamine side effects. Confusion, difficult or painful urination, dizziness, drowsiness, a faint feeling, nightmares or excitement, nervousness, restlessness, irritability, and dry mouth, nose, or throat are more likely to occur among older adults.

Possible Side Effects

Occasional side effects are itching, rash, sensitivity to light, perspiration, chills, lowering of blood pressure, headache, rapid heartbeat, sleeplessness, dizziness, disturbed coordination, confusion, restlessness, nervousness, irritability, euphoria (feeling high), tingling of the hands and feet, blurred vision, double vision, ringing in the ears, stomach upset, loss of appetite, nausea, vomiting, constipation, diarrhea, difficulty in urination, tightness of the chest, wheezing, nasal stuffiness, and dry mouth, nose, and throat.

Drug Interactions

Diphenhydramine Hydrochloride should not be taken with monoamine oxidase (MAO) inhibitors.

Interaction with tranquilizers, sedatives, and sleeping medication will increase the effects of these drugs; it is extremely important that you discuss this with your doctor so that doses of these drugs can be properly adjusted.

Be extremely cautious when drinking alcohol while taking Diphenhydramine Hydrochloride, which will enhance the intoxicating effect of the alcohol. Alcohol also has a sedative effect.

Food Interactions

Take this drug with food if it upsets your stomach.

Usual Dose

Adult: 25 to 50 milligrams 3 to 4 times times per day.

Child (over 20 pounds): 12.5 to 25 milligrams 3 to 4 times per day.

For sleep: 25 to 50 milligrams at bedtime.

Overdosage

Symptoms are depression or stimulation (especially in children), dry mouth, fixed or dilated pupils, flushing of the skin, and stomach upset. Take the patient to a hospital emergency room immediately, if you cannot make him or her vomit. ALWAYS bring the medicine bottle.

Special Information

Diphenhydramine Hydrochloride produces a depressant effect: Be extremely cautious when driving or operating heavy equipment.

If you forget to take a dose of Diphenhydramine Hydrochloride, take it as soon as you remember. If it is almost time for your next regularly scheduled dose, skip the one you forgot and continue with your regular schedule. Do not take a double dose.

Generic Name

Dipivefrin

Brand Name

Propine Eyedrops

Type of Drug

Antiglaucoma treatment.

Prescribed for

Glaucoma.

General Information

When applied to the eye, Dipivefrin is converted to Epinephrine, one of the cornerstone drugs of glaucoma treatment. It provides the same effect on glaucoma as Epinephrine, but has fewer side effects. Dipivefrin may be used in combination with Pilocarpine Ophthalmic Solution or a beta-blocker eyedrop to produce a greater drop in eye pressure. The drug starts working about a half hour after it is applied and has its maximum effect at about 1 hour.

Cautions and Warnings

Use this product with care if you have reacted to Dipivefrin in the past. Interestingly, people who have reacted to Epinephrine eyedrops in the past are not likely to react to Dipivefrin and can probably use this product; this is because of the conversion step that must take place.

Dipivefrin eyedrops contain sulfite preservatives. Be careful if you are sensitive to sulfites.

Pregnancy/Breast-feeding

As with all drug products, pregnant women, or those who might become pregnant, should not use Dipivefrin unless the advantages of the product have been carefully weighed against the possible dangers of taking it while pregnant.

It is not known if this drug passes into breast milk. No drug-related problems have been known to occur. Nursing mothers who use Dipivefrin should exercise caution.

Seniors

Older adults may use Dipivefrin without any special precautions. Some older adults may have weaker eyelid muscles. This creates a small reservoir for the eyedrops and may actually increase the drug's effect by keeping it in contact with the eye for a longer period. Your doctor may take this into account when determining the proper drug dosage.

Possible Side Effects

You may feel some burning or stinging on applying the eyedrops. Rarely, it is possible to experience conjunctivitis, drug allergies, rapid heartbeat, abnormal heart rhythms, and high blood pressure.

Drug Interactions

Dipivefrin eyedrops are often prescribed with other antiglaucoma medicines.

Usual Dose

One drop in the eye every 12 hours.

Overdosage

Possible symptoms are rapid heartbeat, excitement, and sleeplessness. Call your local poison control center or hospital emergency room for more information.

Special Information

To administer eyedrops, lie down or tilt your head backward and look at the ceiling. Hold the dropper above your eye, hold out your lower lid to make a small pouch, and drop the medicine inside while looking up. Release the lower lid and keep your eye open. Don't blink for about 30 seconds. Press gently on the bridge of your nose at the inside corner of your eye for about a minute to help circulate the medicine around your eye. To prevent infection, don't touch the dropper tip to your finger or eyelid. Wait 5 minutes before using any other eyedrop or ointment.

If you forget a dose of Dipivefrin, take it as soon as you remember. If it is almost time for your next dose, take one dose as soon as you remember and then go back to your regular schedule. Do not take a double dose.

Generic Name

Disopyramide

Brand Names

Napamide
Norpace
Norpace CR

(Also available in generic form)

Type of Drug

Antiarrhythmic.

Prescribed for

Abnormal heart rhythms.

General Information

Disopyramide slows the rate at which nerve impulses are carried through heart muscle, reducing the response of heart muscle to those impulses. It acts on the heart similarly to the more widely used antiarrhythmic medicines, Procainamide Hydrochloride and Quinidine Sulfate. Disopyramide is often used as an alternative for people who do not respond to other antiarrhythmic drugs. It may be prescribed for people who have had a heart attack (infarction) because it helps infarcted areas to respond more like adjacent, healthy heart tissue to nerve impulses.

Cautions and Warnings

This drug can exacerbate heart failure or produce severe reductions in blood pressure. It should be used only in combination with another antiarrhythmic agent or beta blocker, such as Propranolol Hydrochloride, when single-drug treatment has not been effective or the arrhythmia may be life-threatening.

In rare instances, Disopyramide has caused a reduction in blood-sugar levels. Because of this, the drug should be used with caution by diabetics, older adults (who are more susceptible to this effect), and people with poor kidney or liver function. Blood-sugar levels should be measured periodically in people with heart failure or liver or kidney disease, those who are malnourished, and those taking a beta-blocking drug.

Disopyramide should be used with caution by people who have severe difficulty urinating (especially men with a severe prostate condition), glaucoma, or myasthenia gravis.

Pregnancy/Breast-feeding

Do not take this drug if you are pregnant or planning to become pregnant while using it, because it will pass from mother to child. If Disopyramide is considered essential, discuss the potential risks of taking it with your doctor.

Nursing women should not take Disopyramide because it passes into breast milk.

Seniors

Older adults are more sensitive to the effects of this drug, especially urinary difficulty and dry mouth. Follow your doctor's directions and report any side effects at once.

Possible Side Effects

Heart failure, low blood pressure, and urinary difficulty are the most serious side effects of this drug. Other frequent side effects are dry mouth, constipation, blurred vision, frequent urination, dizziness, fatigue, headache, nervousness, difficulty breathing, chest pain, nausea, stomach bloating, gas, stomach pain, loss of appetite, diarrhea, vomiting, itching, rashes, muscle weakness, generalized aches and pains, a feeling of ill health, low blood levels of potassium, increases in blood cholesterol and triglyceride levels, and dry nose, eyes, and throat.

Less common side effects are male impotence, painful urination, stomach pain, reduction in heart activity, anemia (reduced levels of blood hemoglobin and hematocrit), reduced white-blood-cell counts (rare), sleeplessness, depression, psychotic reactions (rare), liver inflammation and jaundice, numbness and tingling in the hands or feet, elevated blood urea nitrogen (BUN) and creatinine (blood tests for kidney function), low blood sugar, fever, swollen, painful male breasts, drug allergy, and glaucoma.

Drug Interactions

Phenytoin and Rifampin may increase the rate at which your body removes Disopyramide from the blood. Your doctor may need to alter your Disopyramide dose if this combination is used. Other drugs known to increase drug breakdown by the liver, such as barbiturates and Primidone, may also have this effect.

Food Interactions

Disopyramide may cause symptoms of low blood sugar: anxiety, chills, cold sweats, drowsiness, excessive hunger, nausea, nervousness, rapid pulse, shakiness, unusual weakness, tiredness, or cool, pale skin. If this happens to you, eat some chocolate candy or other high-sugar food and call your doctor at once.

Disopyramide should be taken 1 hour before or 2 hours after meals.

Usual Dose

Adult: 200 to 300 milligrams every 6 hours. In severe cases, 400 milligrams every 4 hours may be required. The long-acting preparation is taken every 12 hours.

Patient with reduced kidney function: reduced dosage, depending on the degree of kidney failure present.

Patient with liver failure: 400 milligrams per day.

Child: 2.5 to 14 milligrams per pound of body weight per day, depending on age and condition.

Overdosage

Symptoms are breathing difficulty, abnormal heart rhythms, and unconsciousness. In severe cases, overdose can lead to death. Patients taking an overdose of this drug must be made to vomit with Syrup of Ipecac (available at any pharmacy) to remove any remaining drug from the stomach. Call your doctor or a poison control center before doing this. If you must go to a hospital emergency room, ALWAYS bring the medicine bottle. Prompt and vigorous treatment can make the difference between life and death in severe overdose cases.

Special Information

Disopyramide can cause dry mouth, urinary difficulty, constipation, and blurred vision. Call your doctor if these symptoms become severe or intolerable, but don't stop taking this medicine without your doctor's knowledge and approval.

If Disopyramide is required for a child and capsules are not appropriate, your pharmacist, with your doctor's permission, can make a liquid product. Do not do this at home, because Disopyramide requires special preparation. The liquid should be refrigerated and protected from light and should be thrown away after 30 days.

If you forget to take a dose of Disopyramide, take it as soon as possible. However, if it is within 4 hours of your next dose, skip the forgotten dose and go back to your schedule. Do not take a double dose.

Brand Name

Donnatal Capsules/Elixir/Tablets

Ingredients

Atropine Sulfate   Phenobarbital
Hyoscyamine Hydrobromide   Scopolamine Hydrobromide

(Liquids also contain alcohol)

Other Brand Names

Barophen Elixir   Malatal Tablets
Donnamor Elixir   Relaxadon Tablets
Donnapine Tablets   Spasmolin Capsules/Tablets
Donna-Sed Elixir   Spasquid Elixir
Hyosophen Elixir/Tablets   Susano Elixir/Tablets

(Also available in generic form)

The following products contain the same ingredients in different concentrations:
Barbidonna Elixir/Tablets
Kinesed Tablets
Spasmophen Elixir/Tablets

(Also available in generic form)

Type of Drug

Anticholinergic combination.

Prescribed for

Symptomatic relief of stomach spasm and other forms of cramps. Donnatal may also be prescribed for the treatment of motion sickness.

The actions of this drug should be considered as "possibly effective." There is considerable doubt among medical experts that this drug produces the effects claimed for it.

General Information

Donnatal is a mild antispasmodic sedative drug. It is used only to relieve symptoms, not to treat the cause of the symptoms. In addition to the brand names listed above, there are 40 to 50 other anticholinergic combinations with the same properties. All are used to relieve cramps, and all are about equally effective. Some have additional ingredients to reduce or absorb excess gas in the stomach, to coat the stomach, or to control diarrhea.

Cautions and Warnings

Donnatal should not be used by people with glaucoma, rapid heartbeat, severe intestinal disease such as ulcerating colitis, serious kidney or liver disease, or a history of allergy to any of the ingredients of this drug. Donnatal and other drugs of this class can reduce the patient's ability to sweat. Therefore if you take this type of medication, avoid extended heavy exercise and the excessive high temperature of summer.

Pregnancy/Breast-feeding

This drug may cause birth defects or interfere with your baby's development. Check with your doctor before taking it if you are, or might be, pregnant. Regular use of Donnatal during the last 3 months of pregnancy may cause drug dependency of the newborn. Labor may be prolonged, delivery may be delayed, and the newborn may have breathing problems if Donnatal is used.

Breast-feeding while using Donnatal may cause increased tiredness, shortness of breath, or a slow heartbeat in the baby. Donnatal may decrease the flow of breast milk. Nursing mothers should use alternative feeding methods.

Seniors

Older adults are more sensitive to the effects of this drug, especially excitement, confusion, drowsiness, agitation, constipation, dry mouth, and urinary problems. Memory may be impaired and glaucoma worsened. Follow your doctor's directions and report any side effects at once.

Possible Side Effects

The most common side effects are blurred vision, dry mouth, difficulty in urination, flushing, and dry skin.

Infrequent side effects include rapid or unusual heartbeat, increased sensitivity to strong light, loss of taste sensation, headache, difficulty in passing urine, nervousness, tiredness, weakness, dizziness, inability to sleep, nausea, vomiting, fever, stuffy nose, heartburn, loss of sex drive, decreased sweating, constipation, bloated feeling, and allergic reactions, such as fever and rash.

Drug Interactions

Although Donnatal contains only a small amount of Phenobarbital, it is wise to avoid excessive amounts of alcohol or other drugs that have a sedative effect. Be careful when driving or operating equipment. Other Phenobarbital interactions are probably not important, but are possible with anticoagulants, adrenal corticosteroids, tranquilizers, narcotics, sleeping pills, Digitalis or other cardiac glycosides, and antihistamines.

Some phenothiazine drugs, tranquilizers, antidepressants, and narcotics may increase the side effects of the Atropine Sulfate contained in Donnatal, causing dry mouth, difficulty in urination, and constipation.

Food Interactions

Take this drug about 30 to 60 minutes before meals.

Usual Dose

Adult: 1 to 2 tablets, capsules, or teaspoons 3 to 4 times per day.
Child: half the adult dose, if necessary.

Overdosage

Symptoms are dry mouth, difficulty in swallowing, thirst, blurred vision, sensitivity to strong light, flushed, hot dry skin, rash, fever, abnormal heart rate, high blood pressure, difficulty in urination, restlessness, confusion, delirium, and difficulty in breathing. The patient should be taken to a hospital emergency room immediately. ALWAYS bring the medicine bottle.

Special Information

Dry mouth from Donnatal can be relieved by chewing gum or sucking hard candy or ice chips; constipation can be treated with a stool-softening laxative.

Donnatal is also available in a longer-acting preparation called Donnatal Extentabs.

If you forget to take a dose of Donnatal, take it as soon as you remember. If it is almost time for your next regularly scheduled dose, skip the one you forgot and continue with your regular schedule. Do not take a double dose.

Generic Name

Doxazosin Mesylate

Brand Name

Cardura

Type of Drug

Antihypertensive.

Prescribed for

High blood pressure.

General Information

Doxazosin works by opening blood vessels and reducing pressure in them. The maximum blood-pressure-lowering effect of Doxazosin takes place between 2 and 6 hours after the dose has been taken. There is no difference in response between different races and between older and younger adults. A small amount of Doxazosin passes out of the body in feces; the rest is broken down in the liver. Almost none passes out of the body via the kidneys.

Cautions and Warnings

People allergic or sensitive to Prazosin or Terazosin should avoid Doxazosin because of the chance that they will react to that drug as well.

Some people taking Terazosin and Prazosin, drugs similar to Doxazosin, experience a small but important increase in blood-cholesterol levels. Doxazosin may slightly reduce cholesterol levels and increase the HDL/LDL (important blood fats) ratio, a positive step for people with a blood-cholesterol problem. People with an already-high blood-cholesterol level should discuss this problem with their doctors.

Doxazosin can cause dizziness and fainting, especially after the first dose in Doxazosin therapy and in doses exceeding 4 milligrams a day. This effect is called "postural hypotension." It can be minimized by limiting the first dose of Doxazosin to 1 milligram at bedtime. Postural hypotension occurs in about 1 percent of people taking Doxazosin and can reoccur if the drug is stopped for a few days and then restarted.

Doxazosin should be taken with caution if you have liver disease because the drug is eliminated from your system almost exclusively via the liver.

Animal studies have shown that Doxazosin is toxic to the heart and causes loss of testicular function. These effects have not been seen in people taking the drug.

Pregnancy/Breast-feeding

There are have been no studies of Doxazosin in pregnant women. The safety of Doxazosin use during pregnancy is not known. Doxazosin should be used only when the drug's potential benefits outweigh its potential dangers if taken during pregnancy.

Animal studies have shown that Doxazosin passes into breast milk. Nursing mothers who must take this medication should bottle-feed their babies.

Seniors

Older adults with liver conditions may be more sensitive to the effects of Doxazosin. Report any unusual side effects to your doctor.

Possible Side Effects

The most common side effects are dizziness and headache.

Less common side effects are heart palpitations; abnormal heart rhythms; chest pain; nausea; vomiting; dry mouth; constipation; diarrhea; stomach pains and discomfort; stomach gas; breathing difficulty; sore throat; runny nose; nosebleeds; pain in the shoulder, neck, back, arms, or legs; arthritis; muscle pain; gout; visual disturbances; fainting; ringing or buzzing in the ears; depression; loss of sex drive; nervousness; tingling in the hands or feet; anxiety; sleep disturbances; sleepiness; muscle weakness; muscle stiffness; frequent urination; loss of urinary control; sweating; itching; rash; swelling in the arms, legs, or face; and facial flushing.

Rare side effects include dizziness when rising from a sitting or lying position, rapid heartbeat, sinus irritation, common cold symptoms, bronchitis, flu symptoms, coughing, hair loss, weight loss, and fever.

Drug Interactions

Doxazosin may interact with Nitroglycerin or calcium-channel-blocking drugs to increase the chances of dizziness and fainting.

The blood-pressure-lowering effect of Doxazosin may be reduced by Indomethacin.

Other blood-pressure-lowering drugs (diuretics, calcium channel blockers, beta blockers, etc.) increase the blood-pressure-lowering effect of Doxazosin.

Food Interactions

Doxazosin may be taken without regard to food or meals.

Usual Dose

The usual starting dose of Doxazosin is 1 milligram at bedtime. The dosage may be increased to a total of 16 milligrams per day. Doxazosin may be taken once or twice a day.

Overdosage

Doxazosin overdose may produce drowsiness, poor reflexes, and very reduced blood pressure. Overdose victims should be taken to a hospital emergency room at once. ALWAYS remember to bring the prescription bottle with you.

Special Information

Take this drug exactly as prescribed. Do not stop taking Doxazosin unless directed to do so by your doctor. Avoid nonprescription drugs that contain stimulants because they can increase your blood pressure. Your pharmacist will be able to tell you what you can and cannot take.

Doxazosin can cause dizziness, headache, and drowsiness, especially 2 to 6 hours after you take your first drug dose. Before driving or doing anything that requires intense concentration, wait several hours after taking this medicine. You may take your Doxazosin at bedtime to avoid this problem.

If you forget to take a dose of Doxazosin, take it as soon as you remember. If it is almost time for your next dose, skip the forgotten dose and continue with your regular medication schedule.

Generic Name

Doxepin Hydrochloride

Brand Name

Sinequan

(Also available in generic form)

Type of Drug

Antidepressant.

Prescribed for

Primary depression or depression secondary to disorders such as alcoholism, major organic diseases such as cancer, or other illnesses that may have a strong psychological impact on a patient.

General Information

Doxepin Hydrochloride and other members of this group
are effective in treating symptoms of depression. They can
elevate your mood, increase physical activity and mental
alertness, and improve appetite and sleep patterns in a depressed patient. The drugs are mild sedatives and therefore
useful in treating mild forms of depression associated with
anxiety. You should not expect instant results with this medicine: Benefits are usually seen after 1 to 4 weeks of therapy.
If symptoms are not changed after 6 to 8 weeks, contact
your doctor.

Cautions and Warnings

Unlike other tricyclic antidepressants, Doxepin Hydrochloride should not be given to children under age 12 and cannot
be used to treat nighttime bed-wetting.

Do not take Doxepin Hydrochloride if you are allergic or
sensitive to this or other members of this class of drug:
Imipramine, Nortriptyline, Amitriptyline, Desipramine, and
Protriptyline. The drugs should not be used if you are recovering from a heart attack. Doxepin Hydrochloride may be
taken with caution if you have a history of epilepsy or other
convulsive disorders, difficulty in urination, glaucoma, heart
disease, or thyroid disease.

Pregnancy/Breast-feeding

This drug, like other antidepressants, crosses into your developing baby's circulation and may cause birth defects if
taken during the first 3 months of pregnancy. There have
been reports of newborn infants suffering from heart,
breathing, and urinary problems after their mothers had
taken an antidepressant of this type immediately before delivery. You should avoid taking this medication while
pregnant.

Antidepressants of this type are known to pass into breast
milk and may affect a breast-feeding infant, although this
has not been proven. Nursing mothers should consider alternative feeding methods if taking this medicine.

Seniors

Older adults are more sensitive to the effects of this drug

and often require a lower dose than a younger adult to do the same job. Follow your doctor's directions and report any side effects at once.

Possible Side Effects

Possible side effects include changes in blood pressure (both high and low), abnormal heart rate, heart attack, confusion, especially in elderly patients, hallucinations, disorientation, delusions, anxiety, restlessness, excitement, numbness and tingling in the extremities, lack of coordination, muscle spasm or tremors, seizures and/or convulsions, dry mouth, blurred vision, constipation, inability to urinate, rash, itching, sensitivity to bright light or sunlight, changes in composition of blood, nausea, vomiting, loss of appetite, stomach upset, diarrhea, enlargement of the breasts in males and females, increased or decreased sex drive, and increased or decreased blood sugar.

Less common side effects include agitation, inability to sleep, nightmares, feeling of panic, peculiar taste in the mouth, stomach cramps, black coloration of the tongue, yellowing eyes and/or skin, changes in liver function, increased or decreased weight, excessive perspiration, flushing, frequent urination, drowsiness, dizziness, weakness, headache, loss of hair, nausea, and not feeling well.

Drug Interactions

Interaction with monoamine oxidase (MAO) inhibitors can cause high fevers, convulsions, and, occasionally, death. Don't take MAO inhibitors until at least 2 weeks after Doxepin Hydrochloride has been discontinued. Certain patients may require concomitant use of Doxepin Hydrochloride and an MAO inhibitor, and in these cases close medical observation is warranted.

Doxepin Hydrochloride interacts with Guanethidine and Clonidine, drugs used to treat high blood pressure: If your doctor prescribes Doxepin Hydrochloride and you are taking medicine for high blood pressure, be sure to discuss this with him or her.

Doxepin Hydrochloride increases the effects of barbiturates, tranquilizers, other depressive drugs, and alcohol. Don't drink alcoholic beverages if you take Doxepin Hydrochloride.

Taking Doxepin Hydrochloride and thyroid medicine will enhance the effects of the thyroid medicine. The combination can cause abnormal heart rhythms. The combination of Doxepin Hydrochloride and Reserpine may cause overstimulation.

Large doses of Vitamin C (Ascorbic Acid), oral contraceptives, and smoking can reduce the effect of Doxepin Hydrochloride.

Drugs such as Bicarbonate of Soda, Acetazolamide, Quinidine, and Procainamide will increase the effect of Doxepin Hydrochloride.

Ritalin and phenothiazine drugs such as Thorazine and Compazine block the metabolism of Doxepin Hydrochloride, causing it to stay in the body longer. This can cause possible overdose.

The combination of Doxepin Hydrochloride with large doses of the sleeping pill Ethchlorvynol has caused patients to experience passing delirium.

Food Interactions

This drug is best taken on an empty stomach, but you can take it with food if it upsets your stomach.

Usual Dose

Adult: Initial dose is a moderate 10 to 25 milligrams 3 times per day; the low dose reduces drowsiness during the first few days. The doctor may then increase or decrease the dose according to individual response, giving 50 to 300 milligrams per day.

Child (under age 12): This drug should not be used.

Overdosage

Symptoms are confusion, inability to concentrate, hallucinations, drowsiness, lowered body temperature, abnormal heart rate, heart failure, large pupils of the eyes, convulsions, severely lowered blood pressure, stupor, and coma (as well as agitation, stiffening of body muscles, vomiting, and high fever). The patient should be taken to a hospital emergency room immediately. ALWAYS bring the medicine bottle.

Special Information

Doxepin Hydrochloride can cause drowsiness, dizziness, and blurred vision. Be careful when driving or operating complicated machinery.

Do not stop taking this medicine without first discussing it with your doctor, since stopping may cause you to become nauseated, weak, and headachy.

Liquid Doxepin Hydrochloride should not be diluted until just before use. Dilute in about 4 ounces of water or juice just before you take it. Do not mix with grape juice.

Avoid exposure to the sun or sun lamps for long periods of time.

Call your doctor if dry mouth, difficulty urinating, or excessive sedation develops.

If you take Doxepin Hydrochloride several times a day and forget a dose, take it as soon as you remember. If it is almost time for your next regularly scheduled dose, skip the one you forgot and continue with your regular schedule.

If you take it once a day at bedtime and forget, don't take it when you get up and go back to your regular schedule. Call your doctor if you skip 2 or more days of medication. Never take a double dose.

Generic Name

Doxycycline

Brand Names

Doryx	Vibramycin
Doxy-Caps	Vibra-Tabs
Doxychel	

Type of Drug

Broad-spectrum antibiotic effective against gram-positive and gram-negative organisms; tetracycline-type antibiotic.

Prescribed for

Bacterial infections such as gonorrhea; infections of the mouth, gums, and teeth; pelvic inflammatory disease; Rocky

Mountain spotted fever and other fevers caused by ticks and lice; urinary tract infections; and respiratory system infections such as pneumonia and bronchitis.

These diseases may be produced by gram-positive or gram-negative organisms such as diplococci, staphylococci, streptococci, gonococci, *E. coli*, and *Shigella*.

Doxycycline has also been used successfully to treat some skin infections, but is not considered the first-choice antibiotic for the treatment of general skin infections or wounds. It may be used to prevent "traveler's diarrhea."

General Information

Doxycycline works by interfering with the normal growth cycle of the invading bacteria, preventing them from reproducing and thus allowing the body's normal defenses to fight off the infection. This process is referred to as bacteriostatic action. Doxycycline has also been used along with other medicines to treat amoebic infections of the intestinal tract, known as amoebic dysentery. It is also prescribed for diseases caused by ticks, fleas, and lice.

Doxycycline has been successfully used for the treatment of adolescent acne, in small doses over a long period of time. Adverse effects or toxicity in this type of therapy are almost unheard of.

Since the action of this antibiotic depends on its concentration within the invading bacteria, it is imperative that you completely follow the doctor's directions.

Cautions and Warnings

In general, children up to age 8 should avoid Doxycycline because it has been shown to produce serious discoloration of the permanent teeth. Doxycycline when used in children has been shown to interfere with the development of long bones and may retard growth. Exceptions would be when Doxycycline is the only effective antibiotic available and all risk factors have been made known to the patient.

Doxycycline should not be given to people with known liver disease.

You should avoid taking high doses of Doxycycline therapy if you will be exposed to sunlight for a long period because this antibiotic may interfere with your body's normal sun-screening mechanism, possibly causing severe sunburn.

If you have a known history of allergy to Doxycycline you should avoid taking this drug or other drugs within this category, such as Aureomycin, Terramycin, Rondomycin, Vibramycin, Demeclocycline, Tetracycline, and Minocycline.

Pregnancy/Breast-feeding

You should not use Doxycycline if you are pregnant. Doxycycline is not recommended for use during the last half of pregnancy or during breast-feeding, when the infant's bones and teeth are being formed.

Nursing mothers should not take this medication.

Seniors

This drug may be taken without special precautions.

Possible Side Effects

As with other antibiotics, the common side effects of Doxycycline are stomach upset, nausea, vomiting, diarrhea, and rash. Less common side effects include hairy tongue and itching and irritation of the anal and/or vaginal region. If these symptoms appear, consult your physician immediately. Periodic physical examinations and laboratory tests should be given to patients who are on long-term Doxycycline.

Less common side effects are loss of appetite, peeling of the skin, sensitivity to the sun, fever, chills, anemia, possible brown spotting of the skin, decrease in kidney function, and damage to the liver.

Drug Interactions

Doxycycline (a bacteriostatic drug) may interfere with the action of bactericidal agents such as Penicillin. It is not advisable to take both.

Don't take multivitamin products containing minerals at the same time as Doxycycline, or you will reduce the antibiotic's effectiveness. Space the taking of these medicines at least 2 hours apart.

People receiving anticoagulation therapy (blood-thinning agents) should consult their doctor, since Doxycycline will interfere with this form of therapy. An adjustment in the anticoagulant dosage may be required.

Anticonvulsant drugs such as Carbamazepine, Phenytoin, and barbiturates may increase the elimination of Doxycycline from the body, requiring higher or more frequent doses of the antibiotic.

Food Interactions

You may take Doxycycline with food or milk to reduce stomach upset.

Usual Dose

Adult and child (101 pounds and over): first day, 200 milligrams given as 100 milligrams every 12 hours. Maintenance, 100 milligrams per day in 1 to 2 doses. The maintenance dose may be doubled for severe infections.

Child (under 101 pounds): first day, 2 milligrams per pound of body weight divided in 2 doses. Maintenance, 1 milligram per pound as a single daily dose. Double the maintenance dose for severe infections.

For gonorrhea: 300 milligrams in one dose and then a second 300-milligram dose in 1 hour.

For syphilis: 300 milligrams a day for not less than 10 days.

An increased incidence of side effects is observed if the dose is over 200 milligrams per day.

Special Information

Do *not* take after the expiration date on the label.

Doxycycline can be stored at room temperature.

If you forget a dose of Doxycycline, take it as soon as possible. Space the next 2 doses 10 to 12 hours apart if you usually take it once a day and then go back to your regular schedule. If you take the medicine twice a day, space the next 2 doses 5 to 6 hours apart, then go back to your regular schedule.

Generic Name

Dronabinol

Brand Name

Marinol

Type of Drug

Antinauseant.

Prescribed for

Relief of nausea and vomiting associated with cancer chemotherapy. Dronabinol has been studied as a treatment for glaucoma.

General Information

Dronabinol is the first legal form of marijuana available to the American public. The psychoactive chemical ingredient in marijuana, it is also known as delta-9-THC. It has been studied for several years as an antinauseant in people receiving cancer chemotherapy who have not responded to other antinausea drugs. Dronabinol has all of the psychological effects of marijuana and is, therefore, considered to be a highly abusable drug. Its ability to cause personality changes, feelings of detachment, hallucinations, and euphoria has made Dronabinol relatively unacceptable among older adults and others who feel they must be in control of their environment at all times. Younger adults have reported greater success rate with Dronabinol, probably because they are able to tolerate these effects.

   Most people start on Dronabinol while in the hospital because the doctor needs to monitor closely their response to the medication and possible adverse effects.

Cautions and Warnings

Dronabinol should not be used to treat nausea and vomiting caused by anything other than cancer chemotherapy. It should not be used by people who are allergic to it, to marijuana, or to sesame oil. Dronabinol has a profound effect on its users' mental status; it will impair your ability to operate complex equipment, or engage in any activity that requires intense concentration, sound judgment, and coordination.

Like other abusable drugs, Dronabinol produces a definite set of withdrawal symptoms. Tolerance to the drug's effects develops after a month of use. Withdrawal symptoms can develop within 12 hours of the drug's discontinuation and include restlessness, sleeplessness, and irritability. Within a day after the drug has been stopped, stuffy nose, hot flashes, sweating, loose stools, hiccups, and appetite loss may be evident. The symptoms will subside within 4 days.

Dronabinol should be used with caution by people with a manic-depressive or schizophrenic history because of the possibility that Dronabinol will aggravate the underlying disease.

Dronabinol causes reduced fertility in animal studies and may have a similar effect on women. It may also affect the potency of male sperm, actually reducing the number of sperm produced.

Pregnancy/Breast-feeding

Studies of Dronabinol in pregnant animals taking doses 10 to 400 times the human dose have shown no adverse effects on the developing fetus. However, Dronabinol should not be taken by a pregnant woman unless it is absolutely necessary.

Dronabinol passes into breast milk and can affect a nursing infant. Nursing mothers either should not use the drug or should use an alternative feeding method.

Seniors

Older adults are more sensitive to the effects of this drug. Follow your doctor's directions and report any side effects at once.

Possible Side Effects

The most frequent side effects are drowsiness, a "high" feeling (easy laughing, elation, and heightened awareness), dizziness, anxiety, muddled thinking, perceptual difficulties, poor coordination, irritability, a weird feeling, depression, weakness, sluggishness, headache, hallucinations, memory lapse, loss of muscle coordination, unsteadiness, paranoia, depersonalization, disorientation and confusion, rapid heart-beat, and dizziness when rising from a sitting or lying position.

Less common side effects are difficulty talking, flushing of the face, perspiring, nightmares, ringing or buzzing in the ears, speech slurring, fainting, diarrhea, loss of ability to control bowel movement, and muscle pains.

Drug Interactions

Dronabinol will increase the psychological effects of alcoholic beverages, tranquilizers, sleeping pills, sedatives, and other depressants. It will also enhance the effects of other psychoactive drugs.

Usual Dose

5 to 15 milligrams 1 to 3 hours before starting chemotherapy treatment, repeated every 2 to 4 hours after chemotherapy has been given, for a total of 4 to 6 doses per day. The daily dose may be increased up to 30 milligrams a day if needed, but psychiatric side effects increase dramatically at higher doses.

Overdosage

Overdosage symptoms can occur at usual doses or at higher doses taken if the drug is being abused. The primary symptoms of overdosage are the psychiatric symptoms listed under "Possible Side Effects." No deaths have been caused by either marijuana or Dronabinol. Dronabinol treatment may be restarted at lower doses if other antinauseants are ineffective.

Special Information

Dronabinol may impair your ability to drive a car, to perform complex tasks, or to operate complex equipment.

Dronabinol can cause acute psychiatric or psychological effects; you should be aware of this possibility while taking the drug. Be sure to remain in close contact with your doctor and call him or her if any such side effects develop.

Dronabinol capsules must be stored in the refrigerator.

If you forget to take a dose of Dronabinol, take it as soon as you remember. If it is almost time for your next regularly

scheduled dose, skip the one you forgot and continue with
your regular schedule. Do not take a double dose.

Brand Name

Dyazide

Ingredients

Hydrochlorothiazide
Triamterene

Other Brand Name

The following product contains the same ingredients in different concentrations:
Maxzide

(Both Dyazide and Maxzide are also available in generic
form)

Type of Drug

Diuretic.

Prescribed for

High blood pressure or any condition where it is desirable
to eliminate excess water from the body.

General Information

Dyazide is a combination of 2 diuretics and is a convenient,
effective approach for the treatment of diseases where the
elimination of excess water is required. One of the ingredients, Triamterene, has the ability to hold potassium in the
body while producing a diuretic effect. This balances off
the other ingredient, Hydrochlorothiazide, which normally
causes a loss of body potassium. Combination drugs like
Dyazide should be used only when you need the exact
amounts of ingredients in the product and when your doctor
feels you would benefit from taking fewer pills each day.

Cautions and Warnings

Do not use Dyazide if you have nonfunctioning kidneys, if you may be allergic to this drug or any sulfa drug, or if you have a history of allergy or bronchial asthma.

Do not take any potassium supplements together with Dyazide unless specifically directed to do so by your doctor.

Pregnancy/Breast-feeding

Dyazide may be used to treat specific conditions in pregnant women, but the decision to use this medication by pregnant women should be weighed carefully because the drug may cross the placental barrier into the blood of the unborn child.

Dyazide may appear in the breast milk of nursing mothers. Be sure your baby doctor knows you are taking Dyazide.

Seniors

Older adults are more sensitive to the effects of this drug, especially dizziness because of potassium loss. Closely follow your doctor's directions and report any side effects at once.

Possible Side Effects

Possible side effects include loss of appetite, drowsiness, lethargy, headache, gastrointestinal upset, cramping, and diarrhea.

Less common side effects are rash, mental confusion, fever, feeling of ill health, inability to achieve or maintain erection in males, bright red tongue, burning inflamed feeling in the tongue, headache, tingling in the toes and fingers, restlessness, anemias or other effects on components of the blood, unusual sensitivity to sunlight, and dizziness when rising quickly from a sitting position. Dyazide can also produce muscle spasms, gout, weakness, and blurred vision.

Drug Interactions

Dyazide will increase the effect of other blood-pressure-lowering drugs. This is good and is the reason why many people with high blood pressure take more than one medicine.

The possibility of developing imbalances in body fluids (electrolytes) is increased if you take other medications such as Digitalis and adrenal corticosteroids while you are taking Dyazide.

If you are taking an oral antidiabetic drug and begin taking Dyazide, the antidiabetic dose may have to be altered.

Lithium Carbonate should not be taken with Dyazide because the combination may increase the risk of Lithium toxicity.

Avoid over-the-counter cough, cold, or allergy remedies containing stimulant drugs that can aggravate your condition.

Food Interactions

Take this drug with food if it upsets your stomach.

Usual Dose

1 capsule twice per day.

Overdosage

Signs can be tingling in the arms or legs, weakness, fatigue, changes in your heartbeat, a sickly feeling, dry mouth, restlessness, muscle pains or cramps, urinary difficulty, nausea, or vomiting. Take the overdose victim to a hospital emergency room for treatment at once. ALWAYS bring the prescription bottle and any remaining medicine.

Special Information

Take Dyazide exactly as prescribed.

Call your doctor if you develop muscle or stomach cramps, drowsiness, nausea, diarrhea, unusual thirst, headache, or rash.

If you forget to take a dose of Dyazide, take it as soon as you remember. If it is almost time for your next regularly scheduled dose, skip the one you forgot and continue with your regular schedule. Do not take a double dose.

Generic Name

Dyphylline

Brand Names

Dilor Elixir/Tablets   Lufylline Elixir/Tablets
Dyphlex Tablets   Neothylline Tablets

(Also available in generic form)

Type of Drug

Bronchodilator.

Prescribed for

Relief of bronchial asthma and breathing difficulty associated with emphysema, bronchitis, and other diseases.

General Information

Dyphylline is one of several drugs, known as xanthine derivatives, that are the mainstay of therapy for bronchial asthma
and similar diseases. Other members of this group include
Aminophylline, Oxtriphylline, and Theophylline. Although
the dosage for each of these drugs is different, they all work
by relaxing bronchial muscles and helping reverse spasms
in these muscles.

Timed-release products allow Dyphylline to act continuously throughout the day. This permits you to decrease the
total number of doses to be taken every day.

Cautions and Warnings

Do not take this medicine if you are allergic or sensitive
to it or any other xanthine drug. Dyphylline can aggravate
stomach ulcers or heart disease.

Pregnancy/Breast-feeding

Dyphylline passes into the circulation of the developing
baby. It does not cause birth defects but may result in dangerous drug levels in the infant's bloodstream. Babies born
of mothers taking this medication may be nervous, jittery,
and irritable and may gag and vomit when fed. Women who

must use this medication to control asthma or other conditions should talk with their doctor about the relative risks of using this medication and the benefits it will produce for them.

Very large quantities of Dyphylline pass into breast milk and may cause a nursing infant to have difficulty sleeping and be nervous or irritable. Use an alternative feeding method if you must take this medicine.

Seniors

Older adults may take longer to clear this drug from their bodies than younger adults. Older adults with heart failure or other cardiac conditions, chronic lung disease, a virus infection with fever, or reduced liver function may require a lower dosage of this medication to account for the clearance effect.

Possible Side Effects

Possible side effects include nausea, vomiting, stomach pain, diarrhea, irritability, restlessness, difficulty sleeping, excitability, muscle twitching or spasms, palpitations, abnormal heart rhythms, changes in heart rate, low blood pressure, rapid breathing, and local irritation (if the suppository is used).

Infrequent side effects are vomiting blood, fever, headache, and dehydration.

Drug Interactions

Taking this drug together with another xanthine drug can increase side effects. Don't do it unless your doctor has directed you to.

Theophylline is often taken together with a stimulant like Ephedrine to treat asthma. Such combinations may result in excessive stimulation; you should use them only if directed by your doctor.

Erythromycin, flu vaccine, Allopurinol, and Cimetidine will increase the amount of Dyphylline in your blood and increase the chances for drug side effects.

Cigarette or marijuana smoking decreases the effectiveness of Dyphylline.

Food Interactions

This drug is best taken on an empty stomach, 1 hour before or 2 hours after meals. It may be taken with food or meals if it upsets your stomach.

Diet can influence the way this drug works in your body. For example, charcoal-broiled beef may increase the amount of Dyphylline eliminated from your body through the urine. Low-carbohydrate/high-protein diets also produce this effect and may reduce Dyphylline's effectiveness.

Caffeine (another xanthine derivative) may add to drug side effects. Avoid large quantities of caffeine-containing foods, including coffee, cola beverages, tea, cocoa, and chocolate.

Usual Dose

Up to 7 milligrams per pound of body weight 4 times a day.

Dyphylline dosage must be tailored to your specific needs and the severity of your disease. The best dose for you is the lowest dose that will control your symptoms.

Overdosage

The first symptoms are loss of appetite, nausea, vomiting, difficulty sleeping, and restlessness, followed by unusual behavior patterns, frequent vomiting, and extreme thirst with delirium, convulsions, and very high temperature. Some overdose victims collapse.

Overdoses of oral tablets or liquid rarely produce serious symptoms. Most often, the overdose victim loses his or her appetite or experiences nausea, vomiting, and stimulation. Take the victim to a hospital emergency room at once for treatment. ALWAYS bring the medicine bottle with you.

Special Information

If you forget to take a dose of Dyphylline, take it as soon as you remember. If it is almost time for your next regularly scheduled dose, skip the one you forgot and continue with your regular schedule. Do not take a double dose.

Generic Name

Econazole Nitrate

Brand Name

Spectazole Cream

Type of Drug

Antifungal.

Prescribed for

Fungus infections of the skin, including those responsible for athlete's foot and many other common infections.

General information

This drug is similar to another antifungal agent, Miconazole Nitrate. However, unlike Miconazole Nitrate, Econazole Nitrate is available only as a cream for application to the skin. Very small amounts of Econazole Nitrate are absorbed into the bloodstream, but quite a bit of the drug penetrates to the middle and inner layers of the skin, where it can kill fungus organisms that may have penetrated to deeper layers.

Cautions and Warnings

This product is generally safe, but belongs to a family known to cause liver damage. Therefore, the long-term application of this product to large areas of skin might produce an adverse effect on the liver.

Pregnancy/Breast-feeding

When the drug was given by mouth to pregnant animals in doses 10 to 40 times the amount normally applied to the skin, Econazole Nitrate was found to be toxic to the developing fetus. Because of this, Econazole Nitrate should be avoided by women during the first 3 months of pregnancy. It should be used during the last 6 months of pregnancy only if absolutely necessary.

It is not known if Econazole Nitrate passes into human breast milk. However, animals given this drug by mouth did show passage of the drug and its breakdown products into milk. As a precaution, nursing mothers either should not use the drug or should change the method of feeding their children.

Seniors

Older adults may take this medicine without restriction.

Possible Side Effects

Possible side effects include burning, itching, stinging, and redness in the areas to which the cream has been applied.

Drug Interactions

None known.

Usual Dose

Apply enough of the cream to cover affected areas once or twice a day.

Overdosage

This cream should not be swallowed. If it is swallowed, the victim may be nauseated and have an upset stomach. Other possible effects are drowsiness and liver inflammation and damage. Little is known about Econazole Nitrate overdose; you should call your local poison control center for more information.

Special Information

Clean the affected areas before applying Econazole Nitrate cream, unless otherwise directed by your doctor.

Call your doctor if the affected area burns, stings, or becomes red after you use this product.

This product is quite effective and can be expected to relieve symptoms within a day or two after you begin using it. Follow your doctor's directions for the complete 2-to-4-week course of treatment to gain maximum benefit from the product. Stopping it too soon may not completely eliminate the fungus and can lead to a relapse.

If you forget to take a dose of Econazole Nitrate, apply it as soon as you remember. If it is almost time for your next regularly scheduled dose, skip the one you forgot and continue with your regular schedule. Do not apply a double dose.

Generic Name

Enalapril

Brand Name

Vasotec

Type of Drug

Antihypertensive.

Prescribed for

High blood pressure in adults or children; heart failure; diabetic kidney disease. This medicine may be taken alone or with a thiazide-type diuretic.

General Information

Enalapril belongs to a class of drugs known as ACE inhibitors, which reduce blood pressure by preventing the conversion of a potent hormone called Angiotensin 1. This directly affects the production of other hormones and enzymes which participate in the regulation of blood pressure. The effect is to lower blood pressure within 1 to 1¼ hours after taking the medicine. They may treat heart failure by dilating blood vessels and reducing the amount of work the heart has to do to pump blood throughout the body. Some people, if taking Enalapril with a diuretic, experience a rapid blood pressure drop. To prevent this from happening, your doctor may tell you to stop the diuretic 2 or 3 days before starting Enalapril and start again if your blood pressure is not controlled by Enalapril alone.

Cautions and Warnings

This drug can cause kidney problems, especially loss of protein in the urine. Patients taking Enalapril should have the amount of protein in the urine measured during the first month of treatment and monthly for the next few months. The drug can also cause a reduction in white-blood-cell count, leading to a potential for increased susceptibility to infection. Enalapril should be used with caution by people who have kidney disease or diseases of the immune/collagen system (particularly lupus erythematosus) or who have taken other drugs that affect the white-blood-cell count.

Pregnancy/Breast-feeding

ACE inhibitors pass into the developing fetus and are generally associated with some birth defects if taken during the last 6 months of pregnancy. The specific effect of Enalapril on the developing fetus is not known, but studies have shown that it can affect a developing animal fetus. Enalapril should be used with caution by women who are or might become pregnant.

Small amounts of Enalapril passes into the breast milk and may affect a nursing infant. Nursing mothers should not use this medication.

Seniors

Older adults may be *less* sensitive to the blood-pressure-lowering effects of this drug than younger adults, but they may be *more* sensitive to its side effects. Dosage must be individualized to your needs.

Possible Side Effects

Chest pain, low blood pressure, angina pains, dizziness (especially when rising from a sitting or lying postion), fainting, tiredness, headache, nausea, vomiting, diarrhea, urinary infections, rash (usually mild), bronchitis, cough, difficulty breathing, and weakness are the most common side effects.

Less common drug side effects are heart palpitations, abnormal heart rhythms, heart attack, stroke, rapid heartbeat, sleeping difficulty, tingling in the hands or feet, confusion, depression, muscle weakness or cramps, nervousness, changes in taste perception, appetite loss, constipation, decreased urination, dry mouth, upset and irritated stomach, bloody stool, irritation of the tongue, hepatitis (including yellowing of the skin or eyes), abdominal pains, respiratory infection, hair loss, sweating, skin rashes, flushing, itching, blurred vision, conjunctivitis, dry eyes, tearing, ringing or buzzing in the ears, hearing loss, arthritis, muscle or joint pains, kidney problems, pneumonia, asthma, sore throat, and hoarseness. Swelling of the face, arms, legs, mucous membranes, throat, or tongue may occur and should be reported to your doctor.

Drug Interactions

The blood-pressure-lowering effect of Enalapril is additive with diuretic drugs and beta blockers. Other drugs that cause rapid drops in blood pressure should be used with extreme caution because of a possible severe drop when taken together with Enalapril.

Antacids and Indomethacin may interfere with Enalapril's blood-pressure-lowering effects.

Enalapril may increase potassium levels in your blood, especially when taken together with Dyazide or other potassium-sparing diuretics. It may also increase blood levels of Digoxin or Lithium. Your doctor may reduce the dosage of those drugs to account for this interaction.

Food Interactions

Enalapril may be taken without regard to food or meals.

Usual Dose

½ to 40 milligrams once a day. Some people may take their total daily dosage in 2 divided doses. People with poor kidney function have to take less medicine to achieve reduced blood pressure.

Overdosage

The primary effect of Enalapril overdosage is a rapid drop in blood pressure, as evidenced by dizziness or fainting. Take the overdose victim to a hospital emergency room immediately. ALWAYS remember to bring the medicine bottle.

Special Information

Call your doctor if you develop a sore throat, mouth sores, abnormal heartbeat, chest pain, swelling of the face, eyes, lips, or tongue, a persistent rash, or loss of taste perception.

You may get dizzy if you rise to your feet quickly from a sitting or lying position.

Avoid strenuous exercise and/or very hot weather because heavy sweating and/or dehydration can cause a rapid drop in blood pressure.

Do not stop taking this medicine without your doctor's knowledge.

Avoid nonprescription medicines such as diet pills, decongestants, and stimulants that can raise your blood pressure.

If you forget to take a dose of Enalapril, take it as soon as you remember. If it is almost time for your next regularly scheduled dose, skip the one you forgot and continue with your regular schedule. Do not take a double dose.

Brand Name

Entex LA

Ingredients

Guaifenesin
Phenylpropanolamine

Other Brand Names

Ami-Tex LA	Phenylfenesin L.A.
Dura-Vent	PPA/Guaifenesin
Enomine LA	Rymed TR
Guipax	Tega D & E SR
Nolex LA	Vanex-LA

Type of Drug

Decongestant-expectorant combination.

Prescribed for

Relief of some symptoms of the common cold, allergy, or other upper respiratory condition, including nasal congestion and stuffiness and runny nose. The ingredient Guaifenesin is supposed to help loosen thick mucus that may contribute to your feeling of chest congestion, but the effectiveness of this and other expectorant drugs has not been established.

General Information

Entex LA and its generic equivalent products are only a few of the several hundred cold and allergy remedies available on both a prescription-only and a nonprescription basis. There are a variety of different formulas employed in these products, such as the combination used in Entex LA. The decongestant ingredient, Phenylpropanolamine, will produce the most dramatic effect in reducing congestion and stuffiness. The expectorant, Guaifenesin, may help relieve chest congestion. There are other products using this same general formula—an expectorant plus a decongestant—on the market, but they use different decongestants or a combination of decongestants in combination with the expectorant Guaifenesin.

These products should not be used over extended periods to treat a persistent or chronic cough, especially one that may be caused by cigarette smoking, asthma, or emphysema. Information on other decongestant-expectorant combinations can be obtained from your pharmacist.

Since nothing can cure a cold or an allergy, the best you can hope to achieve from taking this or any other cold or allergy remedy is symptom relief.

Cautions and Warnings

Entex LA can cause you to become over-anxious and nervous and may interfere with your sleep.

Do not use these products if you have diabetes, heart disease, high blood pressure, thyroid disease, glaucoma, or a prostate condition.

Pregnancy/Breast-feeding

Entex LA should be avoided by pregnant women or women who may become pregnant while using it. Discuss the potential risks with your doctor.

Nursing mothers must observe for any possible drug effects on their infants while taking Entex LA, since the decongestant Phenylpropanolamine may pass into breast milk.

Seniors

Older adults are more sensitive to the effects of this drug. Follow your doctor's directions and report any side effects at once.

Possible Side Effects

Possible side effects include fear, anxiety, restlessness, sleeplessness, tenseness, excitation, nervousness, dizziness, drowsiness, headaches, tremors, hallucinations, psychological disturbances, and convulsions.

Less common are nausea, vomiting, upset stomach, low blood pressure, heart palpitations, chest pain, rapid heartbeat, abnormal heart rhythms, irritability, feeling "high," eye irritation and tearing, hysterical reactions, reduced appetite, difficulty urinating in men with a prostate condition, weakness, loss of facial color, and breathing difficulty.

Drug Interactions

This product should be avoided if you are taking a monoamine oxidase (MAO) inhibitor for depression or high blood pressure because the MAO inhibitor may cause a very rapid rise in blood pressure or increase some side effects (dry mouth and nose, blurred vision, abnormal heart rhythms).

The decongestant portion of this product may interfere with the normal effects of blood-pressure-lowering medicines. It can also aggravate diabetes, heart disease, hyperthyroid disease, high blood pressure, a prostate condition, stomach ulcers, and urinary blockage.

Food Interactions

Take this medicine with food if it causes an upset stomach.

Usual Dose

1 tablet (Entex LA) or capsule (Dura-Vent) 2 times per day.

Overdosage

The main symptoms of overdose are sedation, sleepiness, sweating, and increased blood pressure. Hallucinations, convulsions, and nervous-system depression are particularly prominent in older adults, and breathing may become more difficult. Most cases of overdose are not severe. Patients taking an overdose of this drug must be made to vomit with Syrup of Ipecac (available at any pharmacy) to remove any remaining drug from the stomach. Call your doctor or a poison control center before doing this. If you must go to a hospital emergency room, ALWAYS bring the medicine bottle.

Special Information

Call your doctor if your side effects are severe or gradually become intolerable.

If you forget to take a dose of Entex LA, take it as soon as you remember. If it is almost time for your next regularly scheduled dose, skip the one you forgot and continue with your regular schedule. Do not take a double dose.

Brand Name

Equagesic

Ingredients

Aspirin
Meprobamate

Other Brand Names

Epromate	Meprogesic-Q
Equazine-M	Micrainin

(Also available in generic form)

Type of Drug

Analgesic combination.

Prescribed for

Pain relief in patients who suffer muscle spasms, sprains, strains, or bad backs.

General Information

Equagesic is a combination product containing a tranquilizer (Meprobamate) and Aspirin; it is used for the relief of pain associated with muscle spasms. The tranquilizer in this combination opens it to many drug interactions, especially with other tranquilizers or depressant drugs, which can result in habituation and possible drug dependence. Equagesic may be effective in providing temporary relief from pain and muscle spasm. If you are taking Equagesic, you must follow any other instructions your doctor gives you to help treat the basic problem.

Cautions and Warnings

Do not take Equagesic if you are allergic to any of the ingredients contained in it.

Pregnancy/Breast-feeding

This drug crosses into the blood circulation of a developing baby. It has not been found to cause birth defects, although the Meprobamate ingredient increases the chance of birth defects if taken during the first 3 months of pregnancy. Pregnant women, or those who might become pregnant while taking this drug, should not take it without their doctors' approval. When the drug is considered essential by your doctor, the potential risk of taking the medicine must be carefully weighed against the benefit it might produce.

This drug passes into breast milk, but has caused no problems among breast-fed infants. You must consider the potential effect on the nursing infant if breast-feeding while taking this medicine.

Seniors

Older adults are more sensitive to the effects of Equagesic. Follow your doctor's directions and report any side effects at once.

Possible Side Effects

The most frequent side effects are nausea, vomiting, stomach upset, dizziness, drowsiness. Less frequent: allergy, itching, rash, fever, fluid in the arms and/or legs, occasional fainting spells, and spasms of bronchial muscles leading to difficulty in breathing.

Less commonly, people taking Equagesic have occasionally experienced effects on components of the blood system. Equagesic has also caused blurred vision.

Drug Interactions

Meprobamate may cause sleepiness, drowsiness, or, in high doses, difficulty in breathing. Avoid interaction with other drugs that produce the same effect, for example, barbiturates, narcotics, tranquilizers, sleeping pills, and some antihistamines. Do not drink alcoholic beverages with Equagesic, because the depressive effect of the alcohol will be increased.

If you are taking an anticoagulant (blood-thinning medication) and have been given a new prescription for Equagesic, be sure that your doctor is aware that there is Aspirin in Equagesic. Aspirin affects the ability of your blood to clot and can necessitate a change in the dose of your anticoagulant.

Food Interactions

If you experience stomach upset with Equagesic, take each dose with food or water.

Usual Dose

1 or 2 tablets 3 to 4 times per day as needed for the relief of pain associated with skeletal muscle spasms.

Overdosage

Equagesic overdoses are serious. Symptoms are drowsiness, feeling of light-headedness, desire to go to sleep, nausea, and vomiting. The patient should be taken to a hospital emergency room immediately. ALWAYS bring the medicine bottle.

Special Information

If you forget to take a dose of Equagesic, take it as soon as you remember. If it is almost time for your next regularly scheduled dose, skip the one you forgot and continue with your regular schedule. Do not take a double dose.

Generic Name

Ergoloid Mesylates

Brand Names

Gerimal
Hydergine
Hydergine-LC

(Also available in generic form)

Type of Drug

Psychotherapeutic.

Prescribed for

Alzheimer's disease; depression, confusion, forgetfulness,
antisocial behavior, and dizziness in older adults.

General Information

Ergoloid Mesylates has improved the supply of blood to the
brain in test animals and reduces heart rate and muscle tone
in blood vessels. Some studies have shown the drug to be
very effective in relieving mild symptoms of mental impair-
ment, while others have found it to be only moderately effective. It has been most beneficial in patients whose
symptoms are due to the effects of high blood pressure in
the brain.

Cautions and Warnings

Do not use this drug if you are allergic or sensitive to Ergoloid Mesylates or any of its derivatives.

Pregnancy/Breast-feeding

This drug may interfere with your baby's development.
Check with your doctor before taking it if you are or might
be pregnant.

Seniors

Older adults are more likely to develop some drug side effects, especially hypothermia (low body temperature).

Possible Side Effects

Ergoloid Mesylates does not produce serious side effects. Since some forms of this drug are taken under the tongue, you may experience some irritation, nausea, or stomach upset. Some other side effects are drowsiness, slow heartbeat, and rash.

Usual Dose

1 milligram 3 times a day.

Overdosage

Symptoms are blurred vision, dizziness, fainting, flushing, headache, loss of appetite, nausea, vomiting, stomach cramps, and stuffed nose. Take the victim to a hospital emergency room for treatment. ALWAYS remember to take the medicine bottle with you.

Special Information

The results of this drug are gradual. Frequently they are not seen for 3 to 4 weeks.

Dissolve sublingual tablets under the tongue: They are not effective if swallowed whole.

If you forget to take a dose of Ergoloid Mesylates, do not take the forgotten dose. Skip the dose and go back to your regular schedule. Do not take a double dose. Call your doctor if you forget to take your medicine for 2 or more days.

Generic Name

Erythromycin

Brand Names

Capsules and Tablets

E-Base	Erypar
E.E.S. 400	EryPed
E-Mycin	Ery-Tab
Eramycin	Erythrocin
ERYC	Erythromycin Base

Erythromycin Estolate   PCE Distertab
Erythromycin Ethyl-   Pediamycin
   succinate   Pfizer-E
Erythromycin Stearate   Robimycin Robitabs
Ethril   Wyamycin S
Ilosone

(Also available in generic form)

Eye Ointments

AK-Mycin
Ilotycin

(Also available in generic form)

Topical Ointments and Solutions

Akne-Mycin   Erymax
A/T/S   E-Solve 2
C-Solve 2   ETS-2%
Erycette   Staticin
Eryderm 2%   T-Stat 2%

(Also available in generic form)

Type of Drug

Bacteriostatic antibiotic, effective against gram-positive organisms such as streptococcus, staphylococcus, and gonococcus.

Prescribed for

Infections of the upper and lower respiratory tract; infections of the mouth, gums, and teeth; infections of the nose, ears, and sinuses. It may be used for mild to moderate skin infections, but it is not considered the antibiotic of choice. It can also be effective against amoebas of the intestinal tract, which cause amoebic dysentery and legionnaire's disease.

Erythromycin is a relatively safe antibiotic. It is used instead of Penicillin for mild to moderate infections in people who are allergic to the penicillin class of antibiotics.

Erythromycin eye ointment is used to prevent newborn gonococcal or chlamydial infections of the eye. Erythromycin topical solution and ointment are used to control acne.

Note: Erythromycin is not the antibiotic of choice for severe infections.

General Information

Erythromycin works by interfering with the normal growth cycle of the invading bacteria, preventing them from reproducing and thus allowing the body's normal defenses to fight off the infection. This process is referred to as bacteriostatic action.

Erythromycin is absorbed from the gastrointestinal tract, but it is deactivated by the acid content of the stomach. Because of this, the tablet form of this drug is formulated in such a way as to bypass the stomach and dissolve in the intestine.

Erythromycin is used primarily for infections of the mouth, nose, ears, sinuses, throat, and lungs. It can also be used to treat venereal disease and pelvic inflammatory disease in people who have allergies and/or sensitivity to the penicillin class of antibiotics.

Because the action of this antibiotic depends on its concentration within the invading bacteria, it is imperative that you follow the doctor's directions regarding the spacing of the doses as well as the number of days you should continue taking the medication. The effect of the antibiotic is severely reduced if these instructions are not followed.

Cautions and Warnings

Erythromycin is excreted primarily through the liver. People with liver disease or damage should exercise caution. Those on long-term therapy with Erythromycin are advised to have periodic blood tests.

Erythromycin is available in a variety of formulations. One formula, Erythromycin Estolate, has occasionally produced fatigue, nausea, vomiting, abdominal cramps, and fever.

If you are susceptible to stomach problems, Erythromycin may cause mild to moderate stomach upset. Discontinuing the drug will reverse this condition.

Pregnancy/Breast-feeding

Pregnant and breast-feeding women may use this product with no restriction.

Seniors

Older adults may use this product with no restriction.

Possible Side Effects

The most common side effects are nausea, vomiting, stomach cramps, diarrhea.

Less common side effects are hairy tongue, itching, and irritation of the anal and/or vaginal region. If any of these symptoms appear, consult your physician immediately.

Erythromycin should not be given to people with known sensitivity to this antibiotic. It may cause a yellowing of the skin and eyes. If this occurs, discontinue the drug and notify your doctor immediately.

Drug Interactions

Erythromycin is relatively free of interactions with other medicines. However, there seems to be a neutralizing effect between it and Lincomycin and Clindamycin.

Erythromycin interferes with the elimination of Theophylline from the body. This may cause toxic effects of Theophylline overdose.

Food Interactions

Food in the stomach will decrease the absorption rate of some Erythromycin products. In general, Erythromycin is best taken on an empty stomach.

Usual Dose

Adult: 250 to 500 milligrams every 6 hours.

Child: 50 to 200 milligrams per pound of body weight per day in divided doses, depending upon age, weight, and severity of infection.

Take 1 hour before or 2 hours after meals.

Eye ointment: 1/2-inch ribbon, 2 to 3 times per day.

Topical solution: Apply morning and night.

Doses of E.E.S., Pediamycin and Wyamycin are 60 percent higher, due to different chemical composition of the Erythromycin formulation.

Special Information

Erythromycin products should be stored at room temperature, except for oral liquids and topical liquids. These should be kept in the refrigerator.

If you forget a dose of oral Erythromycin, take it as soon as you remember. If it is almost time for your next dose, space the next 2 doses over 4 to 6 hours, then go back to your regular schedule.

Generic Name

Estazolam

Brand Name

ProSom

Type of Drug

Sedative.

Prescribed for

Short-term treatment of insomnia or sleeplessness, frequent nighttime awakening, and waking too early in the morning.

General Information

Estazolam, which is used only as a sleep inducer, is a member of the group of drugs known as the benzodiazepines. Characterized by Diazepam (Valium), other benzodiazepine drugs are used as antianxiety agents, anticonvulsants, and sedatives (sleeping pills). They exert their effects by relaxing large skeletal muscles and by, in the brain, increasing the effect of an amino acid known as GABA, which slows nerve transmission. Benzodiazepines make it easier to go to sleep and decrease the number of times you wake up during the night.

Estazolam is similar to Temazepam, another benzodiazepine sedative, in that it takes about 2 hours to reach its highest blood levels and lasts for 8 to 12 hours. It produces less hangover than other sleeping pills but more than some of the very short-acting products. Some people who use Estazolam on a regular basis may find that they still get up early in the morning.

Benzodiazepines can be abused if taken for long periods of time, and it is possible for a person taking a benzodiazepine drug to develop drug-withdrawal symptoms if the drug is suddenly discontinued. Withdrawal symptoms include convulsions, tremors, muscle cramps, insomnia, agitation, diarrhea, vomiting, sweating, and convulsions.

Cautions and Warnings

Estazolam is not intended for children under age 18.

Clinical depression may be increased by Estazolam or other drugs with an ability to depress the nervous system. Intentional overdosage is more common among depressed people who take sleeping pills than those who do not.

Pregnancy/Breast-feeding

This drug may not be used by pregnant women or women who may become pregnant while using it. Animal studies have shown that it passes easily into the blood system of a developing baby and can affect it.

Estazolam and the products of its metabolism pass into breast milk and can affect a nursing infant. The drug should not be taken by nursing mothers.

Seniors

Older adults are more susceptible to drug side effects than are younger adults and should take the lowest possible dosage of Estazolam, although doses lower than 1 milligram are often not effective in older adults.

Possible Side Effects

Drowsiness, headache, dizziness, nervousness, poor muscle coordination, light-headedness, daytime tiredness, muscle weakness, slowness of movements, hangover, nausea, and vomiting.

Less common side effects are a "high" feeling, rapid heartbeat, confusion, temporary memory loss, upset stomach, cramps and pain, depression, and blurred or double vision.

The least-often experienced adverse effects of Estazolam

are constipation, changes in taste perception, appetite
changes, stuffy nose, nosebleeds, common cold symptoms,
asthma, sore throat, cough, breathing problems, diarrhea,
dry mouth, allergic reactions, fainting, abnormal heart
rhythms, itching, acne, dry skin, sensitivity to the sun, rash,
nightmares or strange dreams, difficulty sleeping, tingling in
the hands or feet, ringing or buzzing in the ears, ear or eye
pains, double vision and other visual disturbances, menstrual cramps, frequent urination and other urinary difficulties, blood in the urine, discharge from the penis or vagina,
poor control of the urinary function, lower back and other
pains, muscle spasms and pain, fever, swollen breasts, and
weight changes.

Drug Interactions

As with all other benzodiazepines, the effects of Estazolam
may be enhanced if it is taken together with an alcoholic
beverage, antihistamine, tranquilizer, barbiturate, anticonvulsant medicine, antidepressant, or monoamine oxidase
(MAO) inhibitor drug (most often prescribed for severe
depression).

Oral contraceptives, Cimetidine, and Disulfiram may increase the effect of Estazolam by interfering with the drug's
breakdown in the liver. Estazolam's effect may also be increased by Probenecid.

Cigarette smoking, Rifampin, and Theophylline may reduce the effect of Estazolam on your body.

The effectiveness of Levodopa may be increased by benzodiazepine drugs, including Estazolam.

Estazolam may increase the amount of Phenytoin or Digoxin in your blood.

Food Interactions

Estazolam may be taken with food if it upsets your stomach.

Usual Dose

Adult: 1 to 2 milligrams about 60 minutes before you want
to go to sleep.

Senior: 0.5 to 1 milligram to start. Dosage should be increased with special care.

Overdosage

The most common symptoms of Estazolam overdose are
confusion, sleepiness, depression, loss of muscle coordination, and slurred speech. Coma may develop if the overdose
is particularly large. Overdose symptoms can develop if a
single dose of only 4 times the maximum daily dose is taken.
Patients taking an overdose of this drug must be made to
vomit with Syrup of Ipecac (available at any pharmacy) to
remove any remaining drug from the stomach. Call your
doctor or a poison control center before doing this. If 30
minutes have passed since the overdose was taken or symptoms have begun to develop, the victim must be taken immediately to a hospital emergency room for treatment.
ALWAYS bring the medicine bottle.

Special Information

Never take more of this medication than your doctor has
prescribed. If you have been taking Estazolam for several
months and decide to stop using it, your daily dosage
should be gradually reduced rather than stopped all at once,
to avoid drug-withdrawal symptoms.

People taking this drug must be careful when performing
tasks requiring concentration and coordination because of
the chance that the drug will make them tired, dizzy, or light-
headed.

If you take Estazolam for 3 or more weeks, you may experience some withdrawal symptoms when you stop taking
the drug. Talk with your doctor about the best way to discontinue the drug.

If you forget to take a dose of Estazolam, and you remember within about an hour of your regular time, take it as
soon as you remember. If you do not remember until later,
skip the forgotten dose and go back to your regular schedule. Do not take a double dose.

Type of Drug

Estrogen

Brand Names

Generic Name: Chlorotrianisene

TACE Capsules

Generic Name: Conjugated Estrogens

Premarin Tablets/Vaginal Cream

Generic Name: Dienestrol

DV Vaginal Cream
Ortho Dienestrol Cream

Generic Name: Diethylstilbestrol

Diethylstilbestrol Tablets

Generic Name: Estradiol

Estrace Tablets/Vaginal Cream
Estraderm Transdermal System

Generic Name: Esterified Estrogens

Estratab
Menest Tablets

Generic Name: Estropipate

Ogen Tablets/Vaginal Cream

Generic Name: Ethinyl Estradiol

Estinyl Tablets
Feminone Tablets

Generic Name: Quinestrol

Estrovis

Prescribed for

Moderate to severe symptoms associated with menopause
and the prevention of postmenopausal osteoporosis. Esto-

gens are also prescribed for ovarian failure, breast cancer (in selected women and men), advanced cancer of the prostate, osteoporosis, abnormal bleeding of the uterus, vaginal irritation, female castration, and birth control. There is no evidence that these drugs are effective for nervous symptoms or depression occurring during menopause: They should not be used to treat this condition; they should be used only to replace the estrogen that is naturally absent after menopause. Estrogens should not be used during pregnancy to prevent a possible miscarriage; they don't work for this purpose and are dangerous to the fetus.

General Information

Because of the potential development of secondary disease after a long period of taking any estrogen, the decision to take these medications regularly over a long period of time should be made cautiously by you and your doctor.

Estrogens are natural body substances that have specific effects on the human body, including growth and maintenance of the female reproductive system and all of the sex characteristics that make a woman a woman. Among other specific actions, estrogens promote growth and development of all parts of the reproductive system and breasts; they affect the release of hormones from the pituitary (master) gland that controls the opening of the capillaries (the smallest blood vessels); they can cause fluid retention; they affect protein breakdown in the body; they prevent ovulation and breast engorgement in women after they give birth; and they continue in the shaping and maintenance of the skeleton through their influence on calcium in the body.

Many therapeutic uses of estrogen are merely applications of the natural activity of the hormone. The differences between the various products lie in the specific estrogenic substances they contain, their dose, and, in some cases, the fact that they affect one part of the body more than another. For the most part, however, the products are interchangeable, so long as differences in dosage are taken into account.

Cautions and Warnings

Estrogens have been reported to increase the risk of some cancers in postmenopausal women taking this type of drug for prolonged periods of time; the risk tends to depend upon the duration of treatment and the dose of the estrogen being taken. When long-term estrogen therapy is indicated for the treatment of menopausal symptoms, the lowest effective dose should be used. If you have to take an estrogen for an extended period of time, you should see your doctor at least twice a year so that he can assess your current condition and your need to continue the drug therapy.

Post-menopausal women taking estrogens have a 2 to 3 times greater chance of developing gall-bladder disease than women who don't take an estrogen product.

If you are taking an estrogen product and experience recurrent, abnormal, or persistent vaginal bleeding, contact your doctor immediately.

If you have active thrombophlebitis or any other disorder associated with the formation of blood clots, you probably should not take this drug. If you feel that you have a disorder associated with blood clots, and you have been taking an estrogen or a similar product, you should contact your doctor immediately so that he or she can evaluate your situation and decide whether or not to stop the drug therapy.

Prolonged continuous administration of estrogen substances to certain animal species has increased the frequency of cancer in these animals, and there is evidence that these drugs may increase the risk of various cancers in humans. This drug should be taken with caution by women with a strong family history of breast cancer or those who have breast nodules, fibrocystic disease of the breast, or abnormal mammograms.

It is possible that women taking estrogens for extended periods of time may experience some of the same development of long-term adverse effects as women who have taken oral contraceptives for extended periods of time. These long-term problems may include the development of various disorders associated with the development of blood clots, liver cancer or other liver tumors, high blood pressure, glucose intolerance (symptoms similar to diabetes) or worsening of the disease in diabetic patients, unusual sensitivity to the sun, and high blood levels of calcium in certain classes of patients.

Vaginal estrogen creams may stimulate bleeding of the uterus, breast tenderness, and vaginal discharge, and withdrawal bleeding can occur if the product is suddenly stopped. Women with endometriosis may experience heavy vaginal bleeding.

Pregnancy/Breast-feeding

If you are pregnant do not use any estrogen. If used during the earlier stages of pregnancy, estrogens can seriously damage the developing fetus.

Estrogens may reduce the flow of breast milk. The effects of estrogens on nursing infants are not predictable.

Seniors

Estrogens may be taken without special precaution by most seniors, but the risk of some side effects increases with age, especially if you smoke.

Possible Side Effects

The most common side effects include enlargement or tenderness of the breasts, swelling of the ankles and legs, loss of appetite, weight changes, retention of water, nausea, vomiting, abdominal cramps, feeling of bloatedness, and, with the estrogen patch, skin rash, irritation, and redness.

Less common side effects are bleeding gums, breakthrough vaginal bleeding, vaginal spotting, changes in menstrual flow, painful menstruation, premenstrual syndrome, no menstrual period during and after estrogen use, enlargement of uterine fibroids, vaginal infection with candida, cystitis-like syndrome, mild diarrhea, jaundice or yellowing of the skin or whites of the eyes, rash, loss of scalp hair, and development of new hairy areas. Lesions of the eye and contact-lens intolerance have also been associated with estrogen therapy. You may experience migraine headache, mild dizziness, depression, and increased sex drive (women) or decreased sex drive (men).

Other side effects include stroke, blood-clot formation, dribbling or sudden passage of urine, loss of coordination, chest pains, leg pains, difficulty breathing, slurred speech, and vision changes. Men who receive large estrogen doses as part of the treatment of prostate cancer are at a greater risk for heart attack, phlebitis, and blood clots in the lungs.

Drug Interactions

Phenytoin, Ethotoin, and Mephenytoin may interfere with estrogen effects.

Estrogens may reduce your requirement for oral anticoagulant (blood-thinning) drugs, an adjustment your doctor can make with a simple blood test.

Estrogens increase the amount of calcium absorbed from the stomach. This interaction is used in treating osteoporosis.

Estrogens may increase the side effects of antidepressants and phenothiazine tranquilizers. Low estrogen doses may increase phenothiazine effectiveness.

Estrogens may increase the amount of Cyclosporine (used in organ transplants) and adrenal corticosteroid drugs in your blood. Dosage adjustments of the non-estrogen drugs may be needed.

Estrogen increases the toxic effects of other drugs on the liver, especially in women over 35 and people with pre-existing liver disease.

Rifampin, barbiturates, and other drugs that stimulate the liver to break down drugs may reduce the amount of estrogen in the blood.

Estrogens may interfere with the actions of Tamoxifen and Bromocriptine.

Women, especially those over 35, who smoke cigarettes and take an estrogen have a much greater chance of developing stroke, hardening of the arteries, or blood clots in the lungs. The risk increases as age and tobacco use increase.

Estrogens interfere with many diagnostic tests. Make sure your doctor knows you are taking an estrogen before doing any blood tests or other diagnostic procedures.

Food Interactions

This drug may be taken with food to reduce nausea and upset stomach.

Usual Dose

Oral tablets: The usual daily dose of estrogen depends on the disease being treated and individual patient response.
Chlorotrianisene: 12 to 200 milligrams.
Conjugated Estrogens: 0.3 to 3.75 milligrams.
Diethylstilbestrol: 1 to 15 milligrams a day.

Esterified Estrogens: 0.3 to 30 milligrams.
Estradiol: 1 to 30 milligrams.
Estropipate: 0.625 to 7.5 milligrams.
Ethinyl Estradiol: 0.02 to 0.5 milligrams.
Quinestrol: 100 micrograms once a day for 7 days, then
100 to 200 micrograms a week.

Skin patches:
Estradiol: 1 (0.05 or 0.1 milligram) patch twice a week for
3 weeks; rest 1 week, then start again.

Vaginal creams: The lowest possible dosage should be
used, and your doctor should re-evaluate your need for an
estrogen vaginal cream every 3 to 6 months. The medicine
should not be suddenly stopped because of the chance of
developing unpredicted or breakthrough vaginal bleeding.
Conjugated Estrogens: 2 to 4 grams a day for 3 weeks;
rest 1 week, then start again.
Dienestrol: 1 applicatorful 1 or 2 times a day for 1 to 2
weeks, then half the original dose for 1 or 2 weeks, then 1
applicatorful 1 to 3 times a week.
Estradiol: 2 to 4 grams a day for 2 weeks, half the starting
dose for another 2 weeks, then 1 gram 1 to 3 times a week.
Estropipate: 2 to 4 grams a day for 3 weeks; rest 1 week,
then start again.

Overdosage

Overdose may cause nausea and withdrawal bleeding in
adult women. Accidental overdoses in children have not resulted in serious adverse side effects. Call your local poison
center or hospital emergency room for information.

Special Information

Call your doctor if you develop breast pain or tenderness,
swelling of the feet and lower legs, rapid weight gain, chest
pain, difficulty breathing, pain in the groin or calves, unusual
vaginal bleeding, missed menstrual period, lumps in the
breast, sudden severe headaches, dizziness or fainting, disturbances in speech or vision, weakness or numbness in the
arms or legs, abdominal pains, depression, yellowing of the
skin or whites of the eyes, or jerky or involuntary muscle
movements. Call your doctor if you think you are pregnant.

Women using a vaginal estrogen cream who start to bleed or develop breast tenderness or other vaginal discharge should contact their doctors at once.

Women who smoke cigarettes and take estrogens have a greater chance of cardiovascular side effects, including stroke and blood clotting.

Estrogen skin patches should be applied to a clean, dry, non-oily, hairless area of intact skin, preferably on the abdomen. Do not apply to your breasts, waist, or other area where tight-fitting clothes can loosen the patch from your skin. The application site should be rotated to prevent irritation, and each site should have a 7-day patch-free period.

It is important to maintain good dental hygiene while taking this drug and to use extra care when using your toothbrush or dental floss because of the chance that your estrogen will make you more susceptible to some infections. Dental work should be completed prior to starting on any estrogen.

Vaginal estrogen creams should be inserted high into the vagina, about two-thirds of the length of the applicator.

Some of these products contain tartrazine, a dye widely used to color pharmaceutical products. If you are allergic to tartrazine or have asthma you should avoid tartrazine-containing products. Check with your pharmacist to find out if your estrogen product contains tartrazine.

If you forget a dose of your estrogen, take it as soon as you remember. If it is almost time for your next dose, skip the forgotten dose and continue with your regular schedule. Do not take a double dose of an estrogen.

Generic Name

Ethacrynic Acid

Brand Name

Edecrin

Type of Drug

Diuretic.

Prescribed for

Congestive heart failure, cirrhosis of the liver, kidney dysfunction, high blood pressure, and other conditions where it
may be desirable to rid the body of excess fluid.

General Information

Ethacrynic Acid is a potent diuretic that works in the same
way as Furosemide and Bumetanide. Not only do these
drugs affect the same part of the kidney as the more commonly used thiazide-type diuretics, they also affect the portion of the kidney known as the Loop of Henle. This double
action makes Ethacrynic Acid and the other "loop" diuretics
extremely potent drugs. All 3 loop diuretics can be used for
the same purposes, but their doses are quite different.

Cautions and Warnings

Excessive quantities of Ethacrynic Acid can lead to dehydration and severe imbalance in your body levels of potassium,
sodium, and chloride. Warning signs of dehydration are dry
mouth, excessive thirst, loss of appetite, weakness, lethargy,
drowsiness, restlessness, tingling in the hands or feet, muscle weakness, pain or cramps, low blood pressure, reduced
urine volume, rapid heartbeat, abnormal heart rhythms, nausea, and vomiting.

Do not use Ethacrynic Acid if you have had an allergic
reaction to it in the past. People who are allergic to or cannot
tolerate Ethacrynic Acid may receive a prescription for Bumetanide as an alternative diuretic.

People with severe kidney or liver disease who take this
medicine should maintain close contact with their doctor because the drug can accentuate some conditions affecting
these organs.

Pregnancy/Breast-feeding

Ethacrynic Acid is not recommended during pregnancy because it may cause abnormalities in the developing baby.
Pregnant women who require a potent diuretic may be given
Furosemide or Bumetanide, but only under the supervision
of a doctor.

It is not known if Ethacrynic Acid passes into breast milk.
Nursing mothers who take this drug must watch for any

possible drug effects on their infants while taking this medication; however, it is recommended that women taking Ethacrynic Acid use alternative feeding methods.

Seniors

Older adults may be more sensitive to Ethacrynic Acid side effects than younger adults and should be treated with doses at the low end of the recommended range.

Possible Side Effects

Loss of appetite, nausea, vomiting, diarrhea, inflammation of the pancreas, yellowing of the skin or whites of the eyes, dizziness, headaches, blurred vision, ringing or buzzing in the ears, and reduction of blood-platelet and white-blood-cell levels.

Less common side effects are worsening of liver or kidney disease, abdominal pains, dry mouth, impotence, muscle weakness or cramps, arthritislike pains in the joints, low blood pressure, changes in heart rhythm, and chest pains. The loop diuretics have been associated with a sense of fullness in the ears, diminished hearing, and hearing loss, but these side effects are rare and usually only follow rapid intravenous injection of these drugs.

Drug Interactions

Ethacrynic Acid may increase the effects of blood-pressure-lowering drugs. This is a beneficial interaction that doctors may use in treating high blood pressure.

Ethacrynic Acid increases the side effects of Lithium by interfering with the elimination of that drug from the body.

Alcohol, barbiturate-type sleeping pills, and narcotic pain relievers can cause excessive low blood pressure when taken with potent diuretics like Ethacrynic Acid.

The possibility of losing body potassium with Ethacrynic Acid is accentuated by combining it with Digoxin (for the heart) and the adrenal corticosteroids (for inflammation). Also, potassium loss increases the chances of Digoxin side effects.

Probenecid reduces the effectiveness of Ethacrynic Acid by interfering with its action on the kidneys. Indomethacin and other nonsteroidal anti-inflammatory drugs (NSAIDs) like Naproxen, Sulindac, and Ibuprofen may also reduce Ethacrynic Acid effectiveness.

People taking Ethacrynic Acid for high blood pressure or heart failure should take care to avoid nonprescription medicines that might aggravate their condition, such as decongestants, cold and allergy treatments, and diet pills, all of which can contain stimulants. If you are unsure about which medicine to choose, ask your pharmacist.

Food Interactions

Ethacrynic Acid may cause hypokalemia (loss of body potassium), a complication that can be avoided by adding foods rich in potassium to your diet. Some potassium-rich foods are tomatoes, citrus fruits, melons, and bananas. You can also prevent hypokalemia by taking a potassium supplement in pill, powder, or liquid form. Ethacrynic Acid may be taken with food or meals if it upsets your stomach.

Usual Dose

Adult: 50 to 200 milligrams taken every day or every other day.

Child: starting dose, 25 milligrams. Increase slowly.

Overdosage

The major symptoms of overdose are related to the potent diuretic effect of Ethacrynic Acid: lethargy, weakness, dizziness, confusion, cramps, loss of appetite, and vomiting. Victims of Ethacrynic Acid overdose should be taken to a hospital emergency room for treatment. ALWAYS remember to bring the medicine bottle with you.

Special Information

Take your daily dose no later than 10 A.M.. If taken later in the day, this potent diuretic could interfere with your sleep by keeping you up to go to the bathroom.

Call your doctor if any warning signs of dehydration develop while you are taking Ethacrynic Acid. They are dry mouth, excessive thirst, loss of appetite, weakness, lethargy, drowsiness, restlessness, tingling in the hands or feet, muscle weakness, pain, or cramps, low blood pressure, reduced urinary volume, rapid heartbeat, abnormal heart rhythms, nausea, and vomiting.

If you forget to take a dose of Ethacrynic Acid, take it as soon as you remember. If it is almost time for your next regularly scheduled dose, skip the one you forgot and continue with your regular schedule. Do not take a double dose.

Generic Name

Ethosuximide

Brand Name

Zarontin

Type of Drug

Anticonvulsant.

Prescribed for

Control of petit mal seizures.

General Information

Ethosuximide and the other succinimide-type anticonvulsants control petit mal seizures (sometimes known as absence seizures) by slowing the transmission of impulses through certain areas of the brain. The succinimides are the first choice of treatment for this type of seizure, which may then be treated by Clonazepam if the succinimides are not sufficient.

Cautions and Warnings

Ethosuximide may be associated with severe reductions in white-blood-cell and platelet counts. Your doctor should perform periodic blood counts while you are taking this medicine.

In patients with grand mal and petit mal, succinimide-type anticonvulsants, when used alone, may increase the number of grand mal seizures, necessitating more medicine to control those seizures.

Abrupt withdrawal of any anticonvulsant may lead to severe seizures. It is important that your dosage be gradually reduced by your doctor.

Pregnancy/Breast-feeding

This drug should be avoided by women who are or might become pregnant while using it because it will cross into the developing infant, and possible adverse effects on the infant are not known. In those situations where the drug is deemed essential, the potential risk of the drug must be carefully weighed against any benefit it might produce.

Recent reports suggest a strong association between the use of anticonvulsant drugs and birth defects. Although most of the information pertains to Phenytoin and Phenobarbital, not Ethosuximide, other reports indicate a general association between all anticonvulsant-drug treatments and birth defects. It is possible that the epileptic condition itself or genetic factors common to people with seizure disorders may also figure in the higher incidence of birth defects.

Mothers taking Ethosuximide should not breast-feed because of the possibility that the drug will pass into their breast milk and affect the baby. Use an alternative feeding method.

Seniors

Older adults may take this drug without restriction. Be sure to follow your doctor's directions.

Possible Side Effects

Nausea, vomiting, upset stomach, stomach cramps and pain, loss of appetite, diarrhea, constipation, weight loss, drowsiness, dizziness, and poor muscle control.

Less common side effects are reductions in white-blood-cell and platelet counts, nervousness, hyperactivity, sleeplessness, irritability, headache, blurred vision, unusual sensitivity to bright lights, hiccups, a euphoric feeling, a dreamlike state, lack of energy, fatigue, confusion, mental instability, mental slowness, depression, sleep disturbances, nightmares, loss of the ability to concentrate, aggressiveness, constant concern with well-being and health, paranoid psychosis, suicidal tendencies, increased sex drive, rash, itching, frequent urination, kidney damage, blood in the urine, swelling around the eyes, hair loss, hairiness, muscle weakness, nearsightedness, vaginal bleeding, and swelling of the tongue and/or gums.

Drug Interactions

The depressant effects of Ethosuximide are increased by tranquilizers, sleeping pills, narcotic pain relievers, antihistamines, alcohol, monoamine oxidase (MAO) inhibitors, antidepressants, and other anticonvulsants.

Ethosuximide may increase the action of Phenytoin by increasing the blood levels of that drug. Your doctor should be sure that your dosages of the 2 drugs are appropriate to your condition.

Carbamazepine, another medicine prescribed to treat seizure disorders, may interfere with Ethosuximide action by increasing the rate at which it is removed from the body.

The action of Ethosuximide may be increased by Isoniazid, prescribed to prevent tuberculosis, and by Valproic Acid, another anticonvulsant drug, possibly leading to an increase in drug side effects when both drugs are taken together.

Food Interactions

Ethosuximide is best taken on an empty stomach but may be taken with food if it upsets your stomach.

Usual Dose

Adult and child (over age 6): 500 milligrams per day to start.
Child (age 3 to 6): 250 milligrams per day to start.

The dose is increased in steps of 250 milligrams every 4 to 7 days until seizures are controlled or side effects develop. The maximum daily dose is 1500 milligrams.

Dosage adjustments may be required for people with reduced kidney or liver function.

Overdosage

Ethosuximide overdose will cause exaggerated side effects. If the overdose is discovered immediately, it may be helpful to make the victim vomit with Syrup of Ipecac to remove any remaining medicine from the stomach. But all victims of Ethosuximide overdose must be taken to a hospital emer-

gency room for treatment. ALWAYS bring the prescription
bottle with you.

Special Information

Call your doctor if side effects become intolerable. Especially
important are sore throat, joint pains, unexplained fever,
rashes, unusual bleeding or bruising, drowsiness, dizziness,
and blurred vision. Be sure to tell your doctor if you become
pregnant while taking this medicine.

Ethosuximide may interfere with your ability to drive a
car or perform other complex tasks because it can cause
drowsiness and difficulty concentrating.

Your doctor should perform periodic blood counts while you
are taking this drug to check for possible adverse drug effects.

Do not suddenly stop taking the medicine, since this can
result in severe seizures. The dosage must be discontinued
gradually by your doctor.

Carry identification or wear a bracelet indicating that you
suffer from a seizure disorder for which you take
Ethosuximide.

If you forget to take a dose of Ethosuximide and remember within 4 hours, take it as soon as possible, then go back
to your regular schedule. Do not take a double dose.

Generic Name

Etodolac

Brand Name

Lodine

Type of Drug

Nonsteroidal anti-inflammatory.

Prescribed for

Arthritis.

General Information

Etodolac is one of many nonsteroidal anti-inflammatory
drugs (NSAIDs) available in the United States for the treat-

ment of pain and osteoarthritis. Many people find they must try several of these NSAIDs before they find the one that is right for their condition. Etodolac must be taken for several days before it exerts any effect, and it will take 2 to 3 weeks for the maximum effect to develop.

As a group, NSAIDs reduce inflammation and ease pain via the same mechanism and share many side effects, the most common of which are stomach upset and irritation. In fact, most people taking Etodolac experience upset stomach, gas, and other gastro-intestinal symptoms early in therapy. Many doctors also prescribe NSAIDs to treat mild to moderate pain, menstrual cramps and pain, dental pain, and strains and sprains. Check with your doctor before using Etodolac for any of these purposes.

Cautions and Warnings

Do not use Etodolac if you have had an allergic reaction to it or to any other NSAID. Also, people allergic to Aspirin should not take Etodolac.

People with reduced kidney function should receive lower than the usual dose because their ability to remove the drug from the body is impaired. Also, their kidney function should be monitored by periodic measurements of blood creatinine levels.

Etodolac may cause fluid retention and high blood pressure. It should be used with caution by people with hypertension or heart failure.

Pregnancy/Breast-feeding

Animal studies indicate that Etodolac may cause some birth defects. It should be avoided by pregnant women, women who may become pregnant while using it, and nursing mothers, since this drug may pass into breast milk. In those situations where it is deemed essential, the potential risk of the drug must be carefully weighed against any benefit it might produce.

Seniors

Older patients may be treated with the same starting dose as younger patients, but are more likely to be affected by drug side effects if the daily dosage is increased. Report any unusual effects to your doctor at once.

Possible Side Effects

Most people who take Etodolac experience only mild side effects that pass with time. About 1 in 10 people studied with Etodolac stopped taking it because of side effect problems. Among the most common are nausea, vomiting, and diarrhea, which may be severe. Other possible side effects are heartburn, stomach pain and discomfort, stomach ulcer, bleeding in the stomach or intestines, liver inflammation and jaundice, dizziness, headache, and rashes.

Less common side effects are light-headedness, nervousness, tension, fainting, tingling in the hands or feet, muscle weakness and aches, tiredness, a feeling of ill health, difficulty sleeping, drowsiness, strange dreams, confusion, loss of the ability to concentrate, depression, personality changes, stuffy nose, changes in taste perception, heart failure, low blood pressure, fluid retention, cystitis, urinary infection, changes in kidney function, nosebleeds, hemorrhage, easy bruising, reduction in the count of some white blood cells, itching, hair loss, appetite and body-weight changes, increased sugar in the blood or urine, increased need for Insulin in diabetic patients, flushing or sweating, menstrual difficulty, and vaginal bleeding.

Drug Interactions

Etodolac may enhance the activity of oral anticoagulants (blood-thinning agents), Phenytoin and other antiseizure drugs, oral antidiabetes drugs, and sulfa drugs by increasing the amounts of these agents in the bloodstream. People taking Etodolac in combination with any of these medications may require a reduction in the dosage of the latter.

Aspirin reduces the effectiveness of Etodolac. These drugs should never be taken together.

Antacids reduce the total amount of Etodolac in the blood by 15 to 20 percent, but rarely interfere with the drug's effectiveness.

Food Interactions

Etodolac may be taken with food or meals if it upsets your stomach. If your stomach is still irritated, your dosage may have to be reduced, or you may have to change to another NSAID.

Usual Dose

200 to 400 milligrams every 6 to 8 hours. Do not take more than 1200 milligrams a day.

Overdosage

The primary symptom of overdose is acute stomach and intestinal distress. Symptoms generally develop within an hour of the overdose and resolve on their own within another 24 hours. Patients taking an overdose of this drug must be made to vomit with Syrup of Ipecac (available at any pharmacy) to remove any remaining drug from the stomach if the overdose was taken within the past hour. Call your doctor or a poison control center before doing this. If more than an hour has passed, go to a hospital emergency room. ALWAYS bring the medicine bottle.

Special Information

Etodolac may cause blurred vision or drowsiness. Because of this, you should be especially careful while driving or doing anything else that requires concentration.

Call your doctor if you develop severe stomach or intestinal irritation, sudden weight gain, rash, itching, swelling, black or tarry bowel movements, or intense headaches.

If you take Etodolac twice a day and forget a dose, take it as soon as you remember. If it is almost time for your next dose, take one dose as soon as you remember and another in 5 or 6 hours, then go back to your regular schedule. Do not take a double dose.

If you take Etodolac 3 or more times a day and forget a dose, take it as soon as you remember. If it is almost time for your next dose, take one dose as soon as you remember and another in 3 or 4 hours, then go back to your regular schedule. Do not take a double dose.

Generic Name

Famotidine

Brand Name

Pepcid

Type of Drug

Antiulcer; histamine H_2 antagonist.

Prescribed for

Ulcers of the stomach and upper intestine (duodenum). It is also prescribed for other conditions characterized by the production of large amounts of gastric fluids.

General Information

Famotidine works against ulcers and other gastrointestinal conditions by actually turning off the system that produces stomach acid.

Cautions and Warnings

Do not take Famotidine if you have had an allergic reaction to it in the past.

Pregnancy/Breast-feeding

Although studies with laboratory animals have revealed no damage to a developing fetus, it is recommended that Famotidine be avoided by pregnant women or women who might become pregnant while using it. In those situations where it is deemed essential, Famotidine's potential risk must be carefully weighed against any benefit it might produce.

Famotidine may pass into breast milk. Animal studies revealed that nursing infants experienced growth problems. No problems have been identified in nursing human babies, but breast-feeding mothers must consider the possibility of a drug effect while nursing their infants.

Seniors

Older adults respond well to Famotidine but may need less

medication than a younger adult to achieve the desired response, since the drug is eliminated through the kidneys, and kidney function tends to decline with age. Older adults may be more susceptible to some drug side effects.

Possible Side Effects

The most common side effects of Famotidine are mild diarrhea, dizziness, and constipation.

Less common side effects are anxiety, decrease in sexual drive, headache, drowsiness, dry mouth or skin, joint or muscle pains, loss of appetite, depression, nausea or vomiting, ringing or buzzing in the ears, skin rash or itching, stomach pains, temporary hair loss, and changes in taste perception.

Rarely, the medicine has caused fever, swelling of the eyelids, chest tightness, rapid heartbeat, unusual bleeding or bruising, and unusual tiredness or weakness.

Drug Interactions

Enteric-coated tablets should not be taken with Famotidine. The change in stomach acidity will cause the tablets to disintegrate prematurely in the stomach.

Famotidine may inhibit the absorption of Ketoconazole into the bloodstream.

Vitamin B_{12} absorption may be inhibited by Famotidine.

Food Interactions

Famotidine may be taken on an empty stomach or with food or meals. Food may slightly increase the amount of drug absorbed, but this difference is of no consequence.

Usual Dose

The usual adult dosage is either 20 to 40 milligrams at bedtime, or 20 milligrams twice a day.

Overdosage

There is little information on Famotidine overdosage. Overdose victims might be expected to show exaggerated side effect symptoms, but little else is known. Your local poison control center may advise giving the victim Syrup of Ipecac to cause vomiting and remove any remaining drug from the stomach. Victims who have definite symptoms should be taken to a hospital emergency room for observation and possible treatment. ALWAYS remember to bring the prescription bottle with you.

Special Information

You must take this medicine exactly as directed and follow your doctor's instructions for diet and other treatments in order to get the maximum benefit from it. Cigarettes are known to be associated with stomach ulcers and will reverse effect of Famotidine on stomach acid.

Call your doctor at once if any unusual side effects develop. Especially important are unusual bleeding or bruising, unusual tiredness, diarrhea, dizziness, or rash. Black, tarry stools or vomiting "coffee-ground" material may indicate your ulcer is bleeding.

If you forget to take a dose of Famotidine, take it as soon as you remember. If it is almost time for your next regularly scheduled dose, skip the one you forgot and continue with your regular schedule. Do not take a double dose.

Generic Name

Felodipine

Brand Name

Plendil

Type of Drug

Calcium channel blocker.

Prescribed for

High blood pressure.

Other calcium channel blockers have also been prescribed to treat angina pectoris, Prinzmetal's angina, asthma, to prevent migraine headaches and other conditions.

General Information

Felodipine is a member of one of the most widely prescribed

drug categories in the United States. Its once-daily dosage
schedule makes Felodipine a natural for treating high blood
pressure. It works by blocking the passage of calcium into
heart and smooth muscle tissue, especially the smooth muscle found in arteries. Since calcium is an essential factor in
muscle contraction, any drug that affects calcium in this way
will interfere with the contraction of these muscles. This
causes the veins to dilate, reducing blood pressure. Also,
the amount of oxygen used by the muscles is reduced.
Therefore, Felodipine is also useful in the treatment of angina, a type of heart pain related to poor oxygen supply to
the heart muscles. Felodipine also dilates (opens) the vessels
that supply blood to the heart muscles and prevents spasm
of these arteries. Felodipine affects the movement of calcium only into muscle cells. It does not have any affect on
calcium in the blood.

Cautions and Warnings

Felodipine should not be taken if you have had an allergic
reaction to it in the past.

On rare occasions, Felodipine may cause very low blood
pressure in some people. This may lead to stimulation of
the heart and rapid heartbeat and can worsen angina pains
in some people.

Patients taking a beta-blocking drug who begin taking Felodipine may develop heart failure or increased angina pain.
Angina pain may also increase at the time when your Felodipine dosage is increased.

People with severe liver disease break down Felodipine
much more slowly than people with less severe disease or
normal livers. Your doctor should take this factor into account when determining your Felodipine dosage.

Pregnancy/Breast-feeding

Animal studies with Felodipine have shown that it crosses
into the blood circulation of the developing fetus and has
caused some birth defects. Women who are or might become pregnant while taking this drug should not take it without their doctors' approval. The potential risk of taking
Felodipine must be carefully weighed against the benefit it
might produce.

It is not known if Felodipine passes into breast milk, but it has caused no problems among breast-fed infants. You must consider the potential effect on the nursing infant if you breast-feed while taking this medicine.

Seniors

Older adults, especially those with liver disease, are more sensitive to the effects of this drug because it takes longer to pass out of their bodies. Follow your doctor's directions and report any side effects at once.

Possible Side Effects

The most common side effects are swelling in the feet and legs and headache. Side effects are more common with higher doses and increasing age.

Less common side effects include flushing, dizziness, respiratory infections, muscle weakness and cramps, cough, tingling in the hands or feet, upset stomach, abdominal pains, chest pains, nausea, constipation, diarrhea, heart palpitations, sore throat, runny nose, back pain, and rash.

Rare side effects include facial swelling and a feeling of warmth, rapid heartbeat, heart attack, very low blood pressure, fainting, angina pains, abnormal heart rhythms, vomiting, dry mouth, stomach gas, anemia, muscle joint and bone pain, depression, anxiety, sleeplessness, irritability and nervousness, daytime tiredness, bronchitis, flu-like symptoms, sinus irritation, breathing difficulty, nosebleeds, sneezing, itching, redness, bruising, sweating, blurred vision, ringing or buzzing in the ears, swelling of the gums, decreased sex drive, loss of sexual ability, painful urination, and frequent and urgent urination.

Drug Interactions

Felodipine may increase the amount of beta-blocking drug in the bloodstream. This can lead to heart failure, very low blood pressure, or an increased incidence of angina pain. However, in many cases these drugs have been taken together with no problem.

Felodipine increases the blood-pressure effects of other blood-pressure-lowering drugs. Drug combinations are often used to treat hypertension.

Cimetidine and Ranitidine increase the amount of Felodipine in the blood and may account for a slight increase in the drug's effect.

Felodipine may increase the effects of Digoxin.

Other calcium channel blockers can increase the effects of Theophylline (for asthma and other respiratory problems) and oral anticoagulant (blood-thinning) drugs. They can also interact with Quinidine (for abnormal heart rhythm) to produce low blood pressure, very slow heart rate, abnormal heart rhythms, and swelling in the arms or legs. Felodipine, as a member of the same drug class, may interact in the same way.

Food Interactions

Felodipine can be taken without regard to food or meals. You may take it with food if it upsets your stomach. Taking Felodipine with concentrated grapefruit juice results in twice as much as normal of the drug being absorbed into the blood; avoid the combination.

Usual Dose

5 to 10 milligrams per day. No patient should take more than 20 milligrams per day.

Do not stop taking Felodipine abruptly. The dosage should be gradually reduced over a period of time.

Overdosage

Overdose of Felodipine can cause low blood pressure. If you think you have taken an overdose of Felodipine, call your doctor or go to a hospital emergency room. ALWAYS bring the medicine bottle.

Special Information

Call your doctor if you develop constipation, nausea, very low blood pressure, swelling in the hands or feet, difficulty breathing, increased heart pains, dizziness, or light-headedness or if other side effects are particularly bothersome or persistent.

Be sure to continue taking your medicine and follow any instructions for diet restriction or other treatments to help maintain a lower blood pressure. High blood pressure is a condition with few recognizable symptoms; it may seem to you that you are taking medicine for no good reason. Call your doctor or pharmacist if you have any questions.

Do not break or crush Felodipine tablets.

It is important to maintain good dental hygiene while taking Felodipine and to use extra care when using your toothbrush or dental floss because of the chance that the drug will make you more susceptible to some infections.

If you forget to take a dose of Felodipine, take it as soon as you remember. If it is almost time for your next regularly scheduled dose, skip the forgotten dose and continue with your regular schedule. Do not take a double dose.

Generic Name

Fenoprofen Calcium

Brand Name

Nalfon

Type of Drug

Nonsteroidal anti-inflammatory.

Prescribed for

Relief of pain and inflammation of joints and muscles; arthritis, both rheumatoid and osteoarthritis; mild to moderate pain of menstrual cramps; dental surgery and extractions; and athletic injuries such as sprains and strains.

General Information

Fenoprofen Calcium is one of several nonsteroidal anti-inflammatory drugs (NSAIDs) used to reduce inflammation, relieve pain, or reduce fever. NSAIDs share the same side effects and may be used by patients who cannot tolerate Aspirin. The choice of one of these drugs over another depends on disease response, side effects seen in a particular patient, convenience of times to be taken, and cost. Different drugs or different doses of the same drug may be tried to produce the greatest effectiveness with the fewest side effects.

Cautions and Warnings

Do not take Fenoprofen Calcium if you are allergic or sensitive to this drug, Aspirin, or other NSAIDs. Fenoprofen Calcium may cause stomach ulcers. This drug should not be used by patients with severe kidney disease.

Pregnancy/Breast-feeding

This drug crosses into the blood circulation of a developing baby. It has not been found to cause birth defects. Pregnant women, or those who might become pregnant while taking this drug, should not take it without their doctor's approval. When the drug is considered essential by your doctor, the potential risk of taking the medicine must be carefully weighed against the benefit it might produce.

This drug passes into breast milk, but has caused no problems among breast-fed infants. You must consider the potential effect on the nursing infant if breast-feeding while taking this medicine.

Seniors

Older adults are more sensitive to the stomach, kidney, and liver effects of this drug. Some doctors recommend that persons 70 and older take half the usual dose. Follow your doctor's directions and report any side effects at once.

Possible Side Effects

The most frequent side effects are stomach upset, dizziness, headache, drowsiness, ringing in the ears.

Other side effects include heartburn, nausea, vomiting, bloating, gas in the stomach, stomach pain, diarrhea, constipation, dark stool, nervousness, insomnia, depression, confusion, tremor, loss of appetite, fatigue, itching, rash, double vision, abnormal heart rhythm, anemia or other changes in the composition of the blood, changes in liver function, loss of hair, tingling in the hands and feet, fever, breast enlargement, lowered blood sugar, and effects on the kidneys. If symptoms appear, stop taking the medicine and see your doctor immediately.

Drug Interactions

Fenoprofen Calcium increases the action of Phenytoin, sulfa drugs, drugs used to control diabetes, and drugs used to thin the blood. If you are taking any of these medicines, be sure to discuss it with your doctor, who will probably change the dose of the other drug.

An adjustment in the dose of Fenoprofen Calcium may be needed if you take Phenobarbital.

Food Interactions

Take this medicine with food if it upsets your stomach.

Usual Dose

Adult: 300 to 600 milligrams 4 times per day to start. Mild to moderate pain: 200 milligrams every 4 to 6 hours.

Child: not recommended.

For arthritis: 300 to 600 milligrams 3 to 4 times per day; up to 3200 milligrams per day.

Overdosage

Symptoms may include drowsiness, dizziness, confusion, disorientation, lethargy, tingling in the hands or feet, numbness, nausea, vomiting, upset stomach, stomach pains, headache, ringing or buzzing in the ears, sweating and blurred vision, low blood pressure, and rapid heartbeat. Take the victim to a hospital emergency room at once for treatment. ALWAYS bring the medicine bottle with you.

Special Information

Avoid Aspirin and alcoholic beverages while taking this medication.

You may become dizzy or drowsy while taking this medicine. Be careful while driving or operating complex equipment.

Call your doctor if you develop a skin rash, itching, swelling, visual disturbances, black stools, or a persistent headache while taking this medication.

If you forget to take a dose of Fenoprofen Calcium, take it as soon as you remember. If it is almost time for your next regularly scheduled dose, skip the one you forgot and continue with your regular schedule. Do not take a double dose.

Generic Name

Ferrous Sulfate

Brand Names

Feosol	Ferralyn Lanacaps
Fer-In-Sol	Ferra TD
Fer Iron	Mol-Iron
Fero-Gradumet	Slow FE
Ferospace	

(Also available in generic form)

Type of Drug

Iron-containing product.

Prescribed for

Iron deficiency of the blood.

General Information

Ferrous Sulfate is used to treat anemias due to iron deficiency. Other anemias will not be affected by this drug. Ferrous Sulfate works by being incorporated into red blood cells, where it can help carry oxygen throughout the body. Iron is absorbed only in a small section of the gastrointestinal tract called the duodenum. Sustained-release preparations of iron should be used only to help minimize the stomach discomfort that Ferrous Sulfate can cause, since any drug that passes the duodenum (in the upper part of the small intestine) cannot be absorbed.

Other drugs may also provide a source of iron to treat iron deficiency anemia. The iron in these products may be combined with other vitamins or with special extracts, as in the product Triniscon, where iron is combined with Vitamin B_{12}, Folic Acid, and Intrinsic Factor.

Cautions and Warnings

Do not take Ferrous Sulfate if you have a history of stomach upset, peptic ulcer, or ulcerative colitis.

Pregnancy/Breast-feeding

This drug has been found to be safe for use during pregnancy and breast-feeding. But remember, you should check with your doctor before taking any drug if you are pregnant.

Seniors

Older adults may require larger doses than younger adults to correct an iron deficiency because the ability to absorb iron decreases with age.

Possible Side Effects

Possible side effects include stomach upset and irritation, nausea, diarrhea, and constipation.

Drug Interactions

Ferrous Sulfate will interfere with the absorption of oral Tetracycline. Separate the doses by at least 2 hours.

Antacids will interfere with the absorption of iron; again, separate doses by 2 hours.

In either case, avoid taking iron supplements (unless absolutely necessary) until your other medical condition clears up.

Food Interactions

Iron salts and iron-containing products are best absorbed on an empty stomach, but if they upset your stomach, take with meals or immediately after meals.

Usual Dose

1 to 3 tablets per day.

Overdosage

Symptoms appear after 30 minutes to several hours: lethargy (tiredness), vomiting, diarrhea, stomach upset, change in pulse to weak and rapid, and lowered blood pressure—or, after massive doses, shock, black and tarry stools due to massive bleeding in the stomach or intestine, and pneumonia. Quickly induce vomiting and feed the patient eggs and milk until he or she can be taken to a hospital for stomach pumping. Be sure to call a doctor right away. The patient

must be taken to the hospital as soon as possible, since
stomach pumping should not be performed after the first
hour of iron ingestion because there is a danger of perforation of the stomach wall. In the hospital emergency room
measures to treat shock, loss of water, loss of blood, and
respiratory failure may be necessary. ALWAYS bring the
medicine bottle.

Special Information

Iron salts impart a black color to stools and are slightly constipating. If stools become black and tarry in consistency,
however, there may be some bleeding in the stomach or
intestine. Discuss it with your doctor.

If you forget to take a dose of Ferrous Sulfate, take it as
soon as you remember. If it is almost time for your next
regularly scheduled dose, skip the one you forgot and continue with your regular schedule. Do not take a double dose.

Brand Name

Fiorinal

Ingredients

Aspirin
Butalbital
Caffeine

Other Brand Names

Butalbital Compound   Lanorinal
Fiorgen PF   Marnal
Isollyl Improved

(Also available in generic form)

Type of Drug

Nonnarcotic analgesic combination.

Prescribed for

Relief of headache pain or other types of pain.

General Information

Fiorinal is one of many combination products containing a barbiturate and an analgesic. These products often also contain a tranquilizer or a narcotic. Products such as Esgic' and Fioricet substitute Acetaminophen for Aspirin.

Cautions and Warnings

Fiorinal can cause drug dependence or addiction. Use this drug with caution if you have asthma or problems in breathing.

The Aspirin component in this drug can interfere with the normal coagulation of blood. This is especially important if you are taking blood-thinning medication.

Pregnancy/Breast-feeding

There is an increased chance of birth defects while using Fiorinal during pregnancy. Fiorinal may be required to be used if a serious situation arises which threatens the mother's life.

Regularly using Fiorinal during the last 3 months of pregnancy may cause drug dependency of the newborn. Pregnant women using Fiorinal may experience prolonged labor and delayed delivery, and breathing problems may afflict the newborn. If taken during the last 2 weeks of pregnancy, Fiorinal may cause bleeding problems in the newborn child. Problems may also be seen in the mother herself, including bleeding.

Breast-feeding while using Fiorinal may cause increased tiredness, shortness of breath, or a slow heartbeat in the baby.

Caffeine can cause birth defects in animals but has not been shown to cause problems in humans.

Seniors

The Butalbital in this combination product may have more of a depressant effect on seniors than on younger adults. Other effects that may be more prominent are dizziness, light-headedness, or fainting when rising suddenly from a sitting or lying position.

Possible Side Effects

Major side effects are light-headedness, dizziness, sedation, nausea, vomiting, sweating, stomach upset, loss of appetite, and (possible) mild stimulation.

Less common side effects include weakness, headache, sleeplessness, agitation, tremor, uncoordinated muscle movements, mild hallucinations, disorientation, visual disturbances, feeling high, dry mouth, loss of appetite, constipation, flushing of the face, changes in heart rate, palpitations, faintness, difficulty in urination, skin rashes, itching, confusion, rapid breathing, and diarrhea.

Drug Interactions

Interaction with alcohol, tranquilizers, barbiturates, sleeping pills, or other drugs that produce depression can cause tiredness, drowsiness, and inability to concentrate.

Interaction with Prednisone, steroids, Phenylbutazone, or alcohol can irritate your stomach.

The dose of anticoagulant (blood-thinning) drugs will have to be changed by your physician if you begin taking Fiorinal, which contains Aspirin.

Food Interactions

Take with a full glass of water or with food to reduce the possibility of stomach upset.

Usual Dose

1 to 2 tablets or capsules every 4 hours or as needed. Maximum of 6 doses per day.

Overdosage

Symptoms are difficulty in breathing, nervousness progressing to stupor or coma, pinpointed pupils of the eyes, cold clammy skin and lowered heart rate and/or blood pressure, nausea, vomiting, dizziness, ringing in the ears, flushing, sweating and thirst. The patient should be taken to a hospital emergency room immediately. ALWAYS bring the medicine bottle.

Special Information

This drug may cause drowsiness, affecting your ability to drive a car or operate complicated machinery.

If you forget to take a dose of Fiorinal, take it as soon as you remember. If it is almost time for your next regularly scheduled dose, skip the one you forgot and continue with your regular schedule. Do not take a double dose.

Brand Name

Fiorinal with Codeine

Ingredients

Aspirin   Caffeine
Butalbital   Codeine Phosphate

(Also available in generic form)

Type of Drug

Narcotic analgesic combination.

Prescribed for

Relief of headache pain or other types of pain.

General Information

Fiorinal with Codeine is one of many combination products containing a barbiturate and an analgesic. These products often also contain a tranquilizer or a narcotic, and Acetaminophen may be substituted for Aspirin.

Cautions and Warnings

Fiorinal with Codeine can cause drug dependence or addiction. Use this drug with caution if you have asthma or problems in breathing.

The Aspirin component in this drug can interfere with the normal coagulation of blood. This is especially important if you are taking blood-thinning medication.

Pregnancy/Breast-feeding

There is an increased chance of birth defects while using Fiorinal with Codeine during pregnancy. Fiorinal with Codeine may be required to be used if a serious situation arises which threatens the mother's life.

Regularly using Fiorinal with Codeine during the last 3 months of pregnancy may cause drug dependency of the newborn. Pregnant women using Fiorinal with Codeine may experience prolonged labor and delayed delivery, and breathing problems may afflict the newborn. If taken during the last 2 weeks of pregnancy, Fiorinal with Codeine may cause bleeding problems in the newborn child. Problems may also be seen in the mother herself, including bleeding.

Breast-feeding while using Fiorinal with Codeine may cause increased tiredness, shortness of breath, or a slow heartbeat in the baby.

Caffeine can cause birth defects in animals but has not been shown to cause problems in humans.

Codeine can cause addiction in the unborn child if used regularly during pregnancy.

Seniors

The Codeine and Butalbital in this combination product may have more of a depressant effect on seniors than on younger adults. Other effects that may be more prominent are dizziness, light-headedness or fainting when rising suddenly from a sitting or lying position.

Possible Side Effects

Major side effects are light-headedness, dizziness, sedation, nausea, vomiting, sweating, stomach upset, loss of appetite, and (possible) mild stimulation.

Less common side effects include weakness, headache, sleeplessness, agitation, tremor, uncoordinated muscle movements, mild hallucinations, disorientation, visual disturbances, feeling high, dry mouth, loss of appetite, constipation, flushing of the face, changes in heart rate, palpitations, faintness, difficulty in urination, rashes, itching, confusion, rapid breathing, and diarrhea.

Drug Interactions

Interaction with alcohol, tranquilizers, barbiturates, sleeping pills, or other drugs that produce depression can cause tiredness, drowsiness, and inability to concentrate.

Interaction with Prednisone, steroids, Phenylbutazone, or alcohol can irritate your stomach.

The dose of anticoagulant (blood-thinning) drugs will have to be changed by your physician if you begin taking Fiorinal with Codeine, which contains Aspirin.

Food Interactions

Take with a full glass of water or with food to reduce the possibility of stomach upset.

Usual Dose

1 to 2 tablets or capsules every 4 hours or as needed. Maximum of 6 doses per day.

Overdosage

Symptoms are difficulty in breathing, nervousness progressing to stupor or coma, pinpointed pupils of the eyes, cold clammy skin and lowered heart rate and/or blood pressure, nausea, vomiting, dizziness, ringing in the ears, flushing, sweating, and thirst. The patient should be taken to a hospital emergency room immediately. ALWAYS bring the medicine bottle.

Special Information

Fiorinal with Codeine may cause drowsiness, affecting your ability to drive a car or operate complicated machinery.

If you forget to take a dose of Fiorinal with Codeine, take it as soon as you remember. If it is almost time for your next regularly scheduled dose, skip the one you forgot and continue with your regular schedule. Do not take a double dose.

Generic Name

Flecainide

Brand Name
Tambocor

Type of Drug
Antiarrhythmic.

Prescribed for
Abnormal heart rhythm.

General Information
Flecainide is prescribed for situations where the abnormal rhythm is so severe as to be life-threatening and does not respond to other drug treatments. Flecainide, like other antiarrhythmic drugs, works by affecting the movement of nervous impulses within the heart.

Flecainide's effects may not become apparent for 3 to 4 days after you start taking it. Since Flecainide therapy is often started while you are in the hospital, especially if you are being switched from another antiarrhythmic drug to Flecainide, your doctor will be able to closely monitor how well the drug is working for you.

Cautions and Warnings
Do not take Flecainide if you are allergic or sensitive to it or if you have heart block.

Flecainide can cause new arrhythmias or worsen others that already exist in 7 percent of people who take this drug. The chance of Flecainide causing or worsening arrhythmias increases with certain kinds of underlying heart disease and an increasing dose of the drug. Flecainide may cause or worsen heart failure in about 5 percent of people taking the drug because it tends to reduce the force and rate of each heartbeat.

Flecainide is broken down extensively in the liver. People with poor liver function should not take Flecainide unless the benefits of taking it clearly outweigh the possible risks of drug toxicity.

Pregnancy/Breast-feeding

Animal studies have shown Flecainide to damage a developing fetus at doses 4 times the normal human dose, although it is not known if Flecainide passes into the blood circulation of a developing baby. Pregnant women should carefully review the benefits to be obtained by taking this drug versus the potential dangers with their doctors. It is not known if Flecainide will affect the labor and delivery process.

It is not known if Flecainide passes into mother's milk. Nursing mothers who must take this drug should use bottle-feeding to avoid any potential complications in their babies.

Seniors

Older adults with reduced kidney and/or liver function are more likely to develop drug side effects and require a lower dosage than people with normal liver and kidneys.

Possible Side Effects

The most common side effects of Flecainide are dizziness, light-headedness, faintness, unsteadiness, visual disturbances (blurred vision, spots before the eyes), difficulty breathing, headache, nausea, fatigue, heart palpitations, chest pain, tremors, weakness, constipation, bloating, and abdominal pain.

Less common side effects are new or worsened heart arrhythmias or heart failure, heart block, slowed heart rate, vomiting, diarrhea, upset stomach, loss of appetite, stomach gas, a bad taste in your mouth, dry mouth, tingling in the hands or feet, partial or temporary paralysis, loss of muscle control, flushing, sweating, ringing or buzzing in the ears, anxiety, sleeplessness, depression, feeling sick, twitching, weakness, convulsions, speech disorders, stupor, memory loss, personality loss, nightmares, a feeling of apathy, eye pain, unusual sensitivity to bright light, sagging eyelids, reduced white-blood-cell or blood-platelet counts, male impotence, reduced sex drive, frequent urination, urinary difficulty, itching, rash, fever, muscle aches, closing of the throat, and swollen lips, tongue, and mouth.

Drug Interactions

The combination of Propranolol and Flecainide can cause an exaggerated decrease in heart rate. Other drugs that slow the heart may also interact with Flecainide to produce an excessive slowing of heart rate.

The passing of Flecainide out of your body through the kidneys is affected by the acid nature of your urine. Less acidity increases the amount of drug released, and more acidity, such as can occur with megadoses of Vitamin C, decreases the amount you release. Extreme changes in urine acid content can expose you to increased side effects (more acid) or loss of drug effect (less acid).

Food Interactions

Flecainide can be taken without regard to food or meals.

Usual Dose

The usual starting dose for all patients is 100 milligrams every 12 hours. Your doctor can increase your dose by 50 milligrams each time every several days, if needed. The maximum dose of Flecainide depends on your response to the drug, your kidney function, and the specific arrhythmia being treated, but can go up to 600 milligrams a day.

Overdosage

The effects of Flecainide overdosage are changes in heart function. Victims of Flecainide overdose should be taken to a hospital emergency room for treatment. ALWAYS remember to bring the medicine bottle with you.

Special Information

Flecainide can make you dizzy, light-headed, or disoriented. Take care while driving a car or performing any complex tasks.

Call your doctor if you develop chest pains, an abnormal heartbeat, difficulty breathing, bloating in your feet or legs, tremors, fever, chills, sore throat, unusual bleeding or bruis-

ing, yellowing of the whites of your eyes, or any other side
effect that you feel is intolerable.

If you forget to take a dose of Flecainide and remember
within 6 hours, take it as soon as possible. If you don't remember until later, skip the forgotten dose and continue
with your regular schedule. Do not take a double dose of
Flecainide.

Generic Name

Fluconazole

Brand Name

Diflucan

Type of Drug

Antifungal.

Prescribed for

Fungal infections of the blood, mouth, throat, and central
nervous system.

General Information

Fluconazole is an antifungal agent that is effective against
a broad variety of fungal organisms. It works by inhibiting
important enzyme systems in the organisms it attacks. Fluconazole's effectiveness against Candida and Cryptococcus
has made this drug an important contributor in the fight
against AIDS and the fungal infections that inflict many AIDS
victims.

Cautions and Warnings

People who are or have been allergic to Fluconazole should
not take this drug. People who are allergic to similar antifun-
gals (Ketoconazole, Miconazole, and Itraconazole) may also
be allergic to Fluconazole, but cross-reactions may not
occur.

On rare occasions, Fluconazole causes liver damage. The
drug should be used with caution in people with pre-existing

liver disease. In studies with laboratory animals, Fluconazole caused an increase in liver tumors.

Skin rash may be a sign of drug toxicity. Report any skin rashes, especially ones that don't heal readily, to your doctor.

Pregnancy/Breast-feeding

Animal studies with Fluconazole show very specific effects on the developing fetus that have not been seen in humans. These are attributable to a specific effect that the drug has on rats and which does not occur in humans. Pregnant women should not use Fluconazole unless the possible risks of treatment have first been weighed against the benefits of taking the drug while pregnant.

It is not known if Fluconazole passes into breast milk. Nursing mothers who must take this drug should consider alternative feeding methods.

Seniors

Older adults are more likely to have lost some kidney function and may require dosage adjustment based on that loss.

Possible Side Effects

Side effects are, generally, more common among AIDS patients, but they follow the same pattern for all people taking this drug.

Most commonly, people taking Fluconazole experience nausea, headache, skin rash, vomiting, abdominal pain, and diarrhea. Fluconazole may cause some liver toxicity, as measured by increases in specific lab tests. These changes in lab values are more common in people with AIDS or cancer, who are more likely to be taking several drugs, some of which may also be toxic to the liver. The medicines most likely to be involved in this reaction are Rifampin, Phenytoin, Isoniazid, Valproic Acid, and oral antidiabetes agents. People with AIDS or cancer who take Fluconazole for fungus infections rarely develop severe liver or skin problems, but they may occur.

Drug Interactions

Cimetidine and Rifampin may reduce blood levels of Fluconazole, which can reduce the drug's effectiveness. Higher doses of Fluconazole may be necessary to offset this effect.

Fluconazole may increase the amount of oral antidiabetes drugs in the blood, causing low blood sugar. Cyclosporine, Phenytoin, and Warfarin are similarly affected. Dosage adjustments of these drugs may be required to offset the effect of Fluconazole.

Fluconazole may interfere with the effectiveness of oral contaceptive drugs.

Food Interactions

Fluconzole may be taken without regard to food or meals.

Usual Dose

Adult and child (over age 13): 100 to 400 milligrams taken once daily.

Child (age 3 to 13): up to about 3 milligrams per pound of body weight per day.

Overdosage

Symptoms of a very large Fluconazole overdose may include breathing difficulty, lethargy, excess tearing, droopy eyelids, excess salivation, loss of bladder control, convulsions, and blue discoloration of the skin under the nails. Overdose victims should be taken to a hospital emergency room for treatment. ALWAYS bring the medicine bottle with you.

Special Information

Regular visits to your doctor are necessary to permit monitoring of liver function and your general progress.

Call your doctor if you develop reddening, loosening, blistering or peeling of the skin, darkening of the urine, yellow discoloration of the skin or eyes, loss of appetite, or abdominal pain (especially on the right side). Other symptoms need be reported only if they are bothersome or persistent.

If you forget to take a dose of Fluconazole, take it as soon as you remember. If it is almost time for your next dose, skip the one you forgot and continue with your regular schedule. Do not take a double dose.

Generic Name

Flucytosine

Brand Name

Ancobon

Type of Drug

Antifungal.

Prescribed for

Serious blood-borne fungal infections.

General Information

Flucytosine is meant for fungal infections (Candida, chro-
momycoses, and Cryptococcus) carried in the blood that affect the urinary tract, respiratory tract, central nervous
system, heart, and other organs. It is not meant for fungus
infections of the skin like common athlete's foot.

Cautions and Warnings

Do not take this drug if you are allergic to it. Flucytosine can
worsen bone marrow depression in people whose immune
systems are already compromised. Liver and kidney function
and blood composition should be monitored during the time
you are taking this drug.

Pregnancy/Breast-feeding

This drug causes birth defects in rats and mice, but the effect
appears to be species-specific. It crosses the placenta, but no
problems have been seen in pregnant women. Flucytosine
should be used by pregnant women only if the benefit to be
gained from taking the drug outweighs potential harm to
the developing fetus.

It is not known if Flucytosine passes into breast milk; no
problems with this drug have been seen in nursing infants.

Seniors

Older adults are likely to have some loss of kidney function and are likely to require dosage adjustment based on that loss of kidney function.

Possible Side Effects

Chest pains, breathing difficulties, rash, itching, sensitivity to the sun or bright lights, abdominal pain, diarrhea, loss of appetite, dry mouth, duodenal ulcers, severe bowel irritation, stomach bleeding, liver dysfunction, yellowing of the skin or whites of the eyes, interference with kidney function, kidney failure, anemia, reduced white-blood-cell counts and other changes in the composition of the blood, headache, hearing loss, confusion, shaking, fever, dizziness, weakness, sedation or tiredness, hallucinations, psychosis, heart attack, reduction in the amount of sugar, and potassium in the blood.

Drug Interactions

Amphotericin B increases the effectiveness of Flucytosine; this combination is often used.

Flucytosine may interfere with some routine blood tests.

Food Interactions

Take Flucytosine with food if it upsets your stomach.

Usual Dose

22 to 66 milligrams per pound every day in divided doses.

Overdosage

There is little experience with Flucytosine overdose, but it would be usual for an overdose of Flucytosine to cause exaggerated drug side effects.

Special Information

Take the capsules a few at a time over 15 minutes to avoid nausea while taking your regular dose of Flucytosine.

Call your doctor if any of the following symptoms develop: unusual tiredness or weakness; yellow skin or eyes; skin rash, redness, or itching; sore throat and fever; or unusual bleeding or bruising. Other side effects need to be reported only if they become excessive or bothersome.

It is important to maintain good dental hygiene while taking Flucytosine and use extra care when using your toothbrush or dental floss because of the chance that Flucytosine will make you more susceptible to some infections. Dental work should be completed prior to starting on this drug.

If you forget a dose, take it as soon as you remember. If it is almost time for your next dose, take one dose as soon as you remember and another in 3 or 4 hours, then go back to your regular schedule. Do not take a double dose of Flucytosine.

Generic Name

Flunisolide

Brand Names

AeroBid Inhaler
Nasalide Spray

Type of Drug

Adrenal corticosteroid.

Prescribed for

Chronic asthma or other respiratory condition. It also relieves symptoms of seasonal inflammation of the nasal membranes.

General Information

The Flunisolide used in this product works in the same way as other adrenal corticosteroids applied to the skin or taken by mouth as a tablet. Flunisolide inhaler relieves the symptoms of asthma for people who require regular steroid treatment by mouth. Using the aerosol generally allows a reduction in the oral dose or elimination of oral steroids all together. Flunisolide works by reducing the inflammation of the mucosal lining within the bronchi, making it easier to breathe. This product should be used only as part of a preventive therapy program. It will not treat an asthma attack. The nasal inhaler acts directly in the nose, reducing inflammation. This relieves the symptoms of seasonal rhinitis.

Cautions and Warnings

Flunisolide oral inhalation should not be used if your asthma can be controlled by other steroid medicines. It is meant only for people taking Prednisone or another steroid by mouth and other asthma medicines who still do not have their asthma under control. Do not use a Flunisolide inhaler if you are allergic to it or to any other steroid drug. During stressful periods, you may have to go back to taking steroids by mouth if your asthma is not controlled.

Pregnancy/Breast-feeding

Large amounts of Flunisolide used during pregnancy may slow the growth of a developing baby. Steroids can cause birth defects or interfere with the developing fetus. Check with your doctor if you are, or might be, pregnant.

Flunisolide may pass into breast milk and cause unwanted effects in a nursing infant.

Seniors

Older adults may use this medicine without special precaution. Be sure your doctor knows if you have any bone disease, colitis, diabetes, bowel disease, glaucoma, fungus infection, heart disease, herpes infection, high blood pressure, high blood cholesterol, kidney disease, or underactive thyroid.

Possible Side Effects

The most common side effects are dry mouth and hoarseness.

Less common side effects are fungus infections of the mouth or throat.

Rarely, deaths due to failure of the adrenal gland have occurred during the process of switching from an oral product. Aerosol Flunisolide is given in a much smaller dose than the oral tablets, reducing the chance for side effects. However, if the drug is used in very large amounts for a long period of time, you may develop a variety of other side effects. Information on those can be found under Prednisone.

Drug Interactions

None known.

Food Interactions

Do not use this product if you have any food in your mouth.

Usual Dose

Oral:
Adult: 2 inhalations (0.5 milligrams) 2 times a day, morning and evening. Do not take more than 8 inhalations a day. Allow at least 1 minute between inhalations. People with more severe asthma may start out with a higher dose.
Child (age 6 to 15): 2 inhalations twice a day, morning and night.
Child (under age 6): not recommended.
Nasal:
Adult: 2 sprays (0.5 milligrams) in each nostril 2 times a day up to 8 times per day in each nostril.
Child (age 6 to 15): 1 spray in each nostril 3 times a day or 2 sprays 2 times per day.
Child (under age 6): not recommended.

Special Information

Follow the instructions that come with your inhaler. Do not exceed the maximum dose per day.

If you use a bronchodilator inhaler (Isoproterenol, Metaproterenol, etc.) at the same time as your Flunisolide inhaler, use the bronchodilator first to open your bronchial tree and increase the amount of Flunisolide that gets into your lungs.

If you forget a dose of Flunisolide and remember within an hour of the normal time, use it right away. If you don't remember until later skip the forgotten dose and go back to your regular schedule. Do not take a double dose.

Generic Name

Fluoxetine Hydrochloride

Brand Name

Prozac

Type of Drug

Antidepressant.

Prescribed for

Depression.

General Information

Fluoxetine Hydrochloride is chemically unrelated to the older tricyclic and tetracyclic antidepressant medicines. It works by allowing the passage of a neurohormone, serotonin, into nervous system cells. The drug is effective in treating common symptoms of depression. It can help improve your mood and mental alertness, increase physical activity, and improve sleep patterns. The drug takes about 4 weeks to work and stays in the body for several weeks, even after you stop taking it. This may be important when your doctor starts or stops treatment.

Unlike other antidepressants, Fluoxetine Hydrochloride can cause people taking the drug to experience weight loss. This is particularly true in underweight depressed people. In one study, 13 percent of people taking this drug lost more than 5 percent of their body weight. This property of the drug earned a lot of publicity during its initial period of evaluation, but the drug has not been studied as a weight-loss treatment.

Cautions and Warnings

Do not take Fluoxetine Hydrochloride if you are allergic to it. Allergies to other antidepressants should not prevent you from taking Fluoxetine Hydrochloride because the drug is chemically different from other antidepressants.

People with severe liver or kidney disease should be cautious about taking this drug and should be treated with doses that are lower than normal.

Pregnancy/Breast-feeding

Animal studies have shown no evidence that Fluoxetine Hydrochloride will harm a developing fetus. However, there is no information showing that this drug is safe to take during pregnancy. Do not take this drug if you are, or might be-

come, pregnant without first seeing your doctor and reviewing the benefits of therapy against the risk of taking
Fluoxetine Hydrochloride.

It is not known if Fluoxetine Hydrochloride passes into
breast milk.

Seniors

Fluoxetine Hydrochloride has been studied in older adults.
Several hundred seniors took the drug during its study
phase without any unusual adverse effect, but any person
with liver or kidney disease, problems that are more common among seniors, must receive a lower dose than an otherwise healthy person. Be sure to report any unusual side
effects to your doctor.

Possible Side Effects

The most common side effects of Fluoxetine Hydrochloride
are anxiety, nervousness, sleeplessness, drowsiness, tiredness, weakness, tremors, sweating, dizziness, light-
headedness, dry mouth, upset or irritated stomach, appetite
loss, nausea, vomiting, diarrhea, stomach gas, rash, and
itching.

Less common side effects include changes in sex drive,
abnormal ejaculation, impotence, abnormal dreams, difficulty concentrating, increased appetite, acne, hair loss, dry
skin, chest pains, allergy, runny nose, bronchitis, abnormal
heart rhythms, bleeding, blood pressure changes, headaches, fainting when rising suddenly from a sitting position,
bone pain, bursitis, twitching, breast pain, fibrocystic disease of the breast, cystitis, urinary pain, double vision, eye
or ear pain, conjunctivitis, anemia, swelling, low blood
sugar, and low thyroid activity.

In addition, many other side effects affecting virtually
every body system have been reported by people taking this
medicine. They are too numerous to mention here but are
considered infrequent or rare and affect only a small number
of people.

In studies of the drug before it was released in the United
States, 15 percent of people taking it had to stop because
of drug side effects. Be sure to report anything unusual to
your doctor at once.

Drug Interactions

Fluoxetine Hydrochloride may prolong the effects of Diazepam and other benzodiazepine-type drugs in your body.

Little is known about taking Fluoxetine Hydrochloride and other nervous-system-active agents together. Report any unusual occurrences to your doctor. At least 2 weeks should elapse between taking Fluoxetine Hydrochloride and a monoamine oxidase (MAO) inhibitor drug.

People taking Warfarin or Digoxin may experience an increase in that drug's effect if they start taking Fluoxetine Hydrochloride. Your doctor will have to reevaluate your Warfarin or Digoxin dosage.

People taking Tryptophan and Fluoxetine Hydrochloride together may develop agitation, restlessness, and upset stomach.

Food Interactions

Fluoxetine Hydrochloride may be taken without regard to food or meals.

Usual Dose

20 to 80 milligrams per day. Seniors, people with kidney or liver disease, and those taking several different medicines should take a lower dosage.

Overdosage

Two people have died after taking a Fluoxetine Hydrochloride overdose. Symptoms of overdose may include seizures, nausea, vomiting, agitation, restlessness, and nervous system excitation. There is no specific antidote for Fluoxetine Hydrochloride overdose.

Any person suspected of having taken a Fluoxetine Hydrochloride overdose should be taken to a hospital emergency room for treatment at once. ALWAYS take the medicine bottle with you.

Special Information

Fluoxetine Hydrochloride can make you dizzy or drowsy. Take care when driving or doing other tasks that require alertness and concentration.

Be sure your doctor knows if you are pregnant, breast-feeding, taking other medications, or drinking alcohol while taking this drug. Notify your doctor of any unusual side effects, if rash or hives develop, if you become excessively nervous or anxious while taking Fluoxetine Hydrochloride, or if you lose your appetite (especially if you are already underweight).

If you forget a dose of Fluoxetine Hydrochloride, take it as soon as you remember. If it is almost time for your next dose, skip the forgotten dose and continue with your regular schedule. Do not take a double dose of Fluoxetine Hydrochloride.

Generic Name

Fluoxymesterone

Brand Names

Halotestin

(Also available in generic form)

Type of Drug

Androgenic (male) hormone.

Prescribed for

Diseases in which male hormone replacement or augmentation is needed; male menopause.

General Information

This is a member of the androgenic, or male, hormone group, which includes Testosterone, Methyl Testosterone, Calusterone, and Dromostanolone Propionate. (The last two are used primarily to treat breast cancer in women.)

Cautions and Warnings

Females taking any androgenic drug should be careful to watch for deepening of the voice, oily skin, acne, hairiness, increased libido, and menstrual irregularities, effects related to the so-called virilizing effects of these hormones.

Virilization is a sign that the drug is starting to produce changes in secondary sex characteristics. The drugs should be avoided if possible by young boys who have not gone through puberty.

Men with unusually high blood levels of calcium, known or suspected cancer of the prostate, prostate destruction or disease, cancer of the breast, or liver, heart, or kidney disease should not use this medication.

Pregnancy/Breast-feeding

Fluoxymesterone is not recommended for use during pregnancy or breast-feeding. Fluoxymesterone may cause unwanted problems in babies, such as the development of male features in female babies.

Seniors

Older men treated with this medicine run an increased risk of prostate enlargement or prostate cancer.

Possible Side Effects

In males: inhibition of testicle function, impotence, chronic erection of the penis, enlargement of the breast.

In females: unusual hairiness, baldness in a pattern similar to that seen in men, deepening of the voice, enlargement of the clitoris. These changes are usually irreversible once they have occurred. Females also experience increases in blood calcium and menstrual irregularities.

In both sexes: changes in libido, flushing of the skin, acne, habituation, excitation, chills, sleeplessness, water retention, nausea, vomiting, diarrhea. Symptoms resembling stomach ulcer may develop. Fluoxymesterone may affect levels of blood cholesterol.

Drug Interactions

Fluoxymesterone may increase the effect of an oral anticoagulant; dosage of the anticoagulant may have to be decreased. It may also have an effect on the glucose tolerance test, a blood test used to screen for diabetes mellitus.

Food Interactions

Take Fluoxymesterone with meals if the drug upsets your stomach.

Usual Dose

2 to 30 milligrams per day, depending upon the disease being treated and the patient's response.

Special Information

Fluoxymesterone and other androgens are potent drugs. They must be taken only under the close supervision of your doctor and never used casually. The dosage and clinical effects of the drug vary widely and require constant monitoring.

If you forget to take a dose of Fluoxymesterone, take it as soon as you remember. If it is almost time for your next regularly scheduled dose, skip the one you forgot and continue with your regular schedule. Do not take a double dose.

Generic Name

Fluphenazine Hydrochloride

Brand Names

Permitil
Prolixin

Type of Drug

Phenothiazine antipsychotic.

Prescribed for

Psychotic disorders; moderate to severe depression with anxiety; control of agitation or aggressiveness of disturbed children; alcohol withdrawal symptoms; intractable pain; senility.

General Information

Fluphenazine Hydrochloride and other members of the phenothiazine group act on a portion of the brain called the hypothalamus. The drugs affect parts of the hypothalamus that control metabolism, body temperature, alertness, muscle tone, hormone balance, and vomiting and may be used to treat problems related to any of these functions.

Cautions and Warnings

Fluphenazine Hydrochloride should not be taken if you are
allergic to one of the drugs in the broad classification of
phenothiazine drugs. Do not take it if you have very low
blood pressure, Parkinson's disease, or blood, liver, kidney,
or heart disease. This medication is a tranquilizer and can
have a depressive effect, especially during the first few days
of therapy.

Pregnancy/Breast-feeding

Infants born to women taking this medication have experienced drug side effects (liver jaundice, nervous-system effects) immediately after birth. Check with your doctor about
taking this medicine if you are or might become pregnant.

This drug may pass into breast milk and affect a nursing
infant. Consider alternative feeding methods if you must
take this medicine.

Seniors

Older adults are more sensitive to the effects of this medication than younger adults and usually require a lower dosage
to achieve a desired effect. Also, older adults are more likely
to develop drug side effects. Some experts feel that older
patients should be treated with one-half to one-quarter the
usual adult dose.

Possible Side Effects

The most common side effect is drowsiness, especially during the first or second week of therapy. If the drowsiness
becomes troublesome, contact your doctor.

This drug can cause jaundice (yellowing of the whites of
the eyes or skin), usually in 2 to 4 weeks. The jaundice usually goes away when the drug is discontinued, but there
have been cases when it did not. If you notice this effect or
if you develop symptoms such as fever and generally not
feeling well, contact your doctor immediately.

Less frequently, changes in components of the blood
occur, including anemias, raised or lowered blood pressure,
abnormal heart rate, heart attack, and feeling faint or dizzy.

Phenothiazines can produce extrapyramidal effects, such
as spasms of the neck muscles, severe stiffness of the back

muscles, rolling back of the eyes, convulsions, difficulty in swallowing, and symptoms associated with Parkinson's disease. These effects look very serious, but disappear after the drug has been withdrawn; however, symptoms of the face, tongue, and jaw may persist for as long as several years, especially in older adults with a history of brain damage. If you experience extrapyramidal effects, contact your doctor immediately.

Fluphenazine Hydrochloride may cause an unusual increase in psychotic symptoms or may cause paranoid reactions, tiredness, lethargy, restlessness, hyperactivity, confusion at night, bizarre dreams, inability to sleep, depression, and euphoria. Other reactions are itching, swelling, unusual sensitivity to bright lights, red skin, and rash. There have been cases of breast enlargement, false positive pregnancy tests, changes in menstrual flow in females, and impotence and changes in sex drive in males. Fluphenazine Hydrochloride may also cause dry mouth, stuffy nose, headache, nausea, vomiting, loss of appetite, change in body temperature, loss of facial color, excessive salivation, excessive perspiration, constipation, diarrhea, changes in urine and stool habits, worsening of glaucoma, blurred vision, weakening of eyelid muscles, and spasms in bronchial and other muscles, as well as increased appetite, fatigue, excessive thirst, and changes in the coloration of skin, particularly in exposed areas.

Drug Interactions

Fluphenazine Hydrochloride should be taken with caution in combination with barbiturates, sleeping pills, narcotics, or any other medication which may produce a depressive effect. Avoid alcohol.

Usual Dose

Adult: 0.5 to 10 milligrams per day in divided doses. (The lowest effective dose should be used.) Few people will require more than 3 milligrams per day, although some have required 20 milligrams or more per day.

Senior: Older patients usually require lower doses of this drug than younger adults because they metabolize it more slowly.

Overdosage

Symptoms are depression, extreme weakness, tiredness, desire to go to sleep, coma, lowered blood pressure, uncontrolled muscle spasms, agitation, restlessness, convulsions, fever, dry mouth, and abnormal heart rhythms. The patient should be taken to a hospital emergency room immediately. ALWAYS bring the medicine bottle.

Special Information

This medication may cause drowsiness. Use caution when driving or operating complex equipment, and avoid alcoholic beverages while taking the medicine.

The drug may also cause unusual sensitivity to the sun and can turn your urine reddish-brown to pink.

If dizziness occurs, avoid sudden changes in posture and avoid climbing stairs.

Use caution in hot weather. This medicine may make you more prone to heat stroke.

If you take Fluphenazine Hydrochloride once a day and forget your dose, take it as soon as possible. If you don't remember until the next day, skip the forgotten dose and continue with your regular schedule.

If you take the medicine more than once a day and forget a dose, take the forgotten dose as soon as possible. If it is almost time for your next dose, skip the forgotten dose and go on with your regular schedule.

Generic Name

Flurazepam

Brand Name

Dalmane

(Also available in generic form)

Type of Drug

Sedative (sleeping medicine).

Prescribed for

Insomnia or sleeplessness, frequent nighttime awakening, or waking up too early in the morning.

General Information

Flurazepam is a member of the group of drugs known as benzodiazepines. These drugs are used as antianxiety agents, anticonvulsants, or sedatives (sleeping pills). They exert their effects by relaxing the large skeletal muscles and by a direct effect on the brain. In doing so, they can relax you and make you either more tranquil or sleepier, depending on the drug and how much you use. Many doctors prefer Flurazepam and the other members of this class to other drugs that can be used for the same effect. Their reason is that the benzodiazepines tend to be safer, have fewer side effects, and are usually as, if not more, effective.

These drugs are generally used in any situation where they can be a useful adjunct.

Benzodiazepine tranquilizing drugs can be abused if taken for long periods of time, and it is possible to develop withdrawal symptoms if you discontinue the therapy abruptly. Withdrawal symptoms include convulsions, tremor, muscle cramps, stomach cramps, insomnia, agitation, diarrhea, vomiting, and sweating.

Cautions and Warnings

Do not take Flurazepam if you know you are sensitive or allergic to this drug or to other benzodiazepines, such as Chlordiazepoxide, Oxazepam, Clorazepate, Diazepam, Lorazepam, Prazepam, Clonazepam, and Temazepam.

Flurazepam and other members of this drug group may aggravate narrow-angle glaucoma, but if you have open-angle glaucoma you may take the drugs. In any case, check this information with your doctor.

Pregnancy/Breast-feeding

Avoid taking this drug during the first 3 months of pregnancy except under strict supervision of your doctor.

The baby may become dependent on Flurazepam if the drug is used continually during pregnancy. If used during the last weeks of pregnancy or during breast-feeding the baby may be over-tired, be short of breath, or have a slow heartbeat.

Use during labor may cause weakness in the newborn.

Seniors

Older adults are more sensitive to the effects of this drug, especially dizziness and drowsiness. Follow your doctor's directions and report any side effects at once.

Possible Side Effects

The most common side effect is mild drowsiness during the first few days of therapy, especially in older adults or the debilitated. If drowsiness persists, contact your doctor.

Less common side effects are confusion, depression, lethargy, disorientation, headache, lack of activity, slurred speech, stupor, dizziness, tremor, constipation, dry mouth, nausea, inability to control urination, changes in sex drive, irregular menstrual cycle, changes in heart rhythm, lowered blood pressure, retention of fluids, blurred or double vision, itching, rash, hiccups, nervousness, inability to fall asleep, and (occasional) liver dysfunction. If you experience any of these reactions stop taking the medicine and contact your doctor immediately.

Drug Interactions

Flurazepam is a central-nervous-system depressant. Avoid alcohol, tranquilizers, narcotics, sleeping pills, barbiturates, monoamine oxidase (MAO) inhibitors, antihistamines, and other medicines used to relieve anxiety.

Cimetidine may increase the effect of Flurazepam.

Food Interactions

Flurazepam is best taken on an empty stomach, but may be taken with food if it upsets your stomach.

Usual Dose

Adult: 15 to 30 milligrams at bedtime. Must be individualized for maximum benefit.

Senior: Initiate therapy with 15 milligrams at bedtime.

Overdosage

Symptoms are confusion, sleep or sleepiness, lack of response to pain such as a pin stick, shallow breathing, lowered blood pressure, and coma. The patient should be taken to a hospital emergency room immediately. ALWAYS bring the medicine bottle.

Special Information

Flurazepam can cause tiredness, drowsiness, inability to concentrate, or similar symptoms. Be careful if you are driving, operating machinery, or performing other activities that require concentration.

Your sleep may be disturbed for 1 or 2 nights after you stop taking the medication regularly.

If you forget to take a dose of Flurazepam and you remember within about an hour of your regular time, take it right away. If you do not remember until later, skip the forgotten dose and go back to your regular schedule. Do not take a double dose.

Generic Name

Flurbiprofen

Brand Name

Ansaid

Type of Drug

Nonsteroidal anti-inflammatory.

Prescribed for

Rheumatoid and osteoarthritis.

General Information

Flurbiprofen is one of many nonsteroidal anti-inflammatory drugs (NSAIDs) sold in the United States to reduce inflammation, relieve pain and fever, and relieve menstrual cramps and discomfort. The choice of one member of this group over another often depends on your individual response to a specific drug. It is common to try several of these drugs before you find the one that is right for you. People who cannot tolerate or do not respond to other NSAIDs may respond to Flurbiprofen.

Cautions and Warnings

Do not take this product if you are allergic to Aspirin or any other NSAID. This drug can worsen a stomach ulcer or cause a new ulcer to develop. It should be used with caution if you have kidney disease.

Pregnancy/Breast-feeding

Flurbiprofen may cross into the blood circulation of a developing baby. It has not been found to cause birth defects. Pregnant women or those who might become pregnant while taking Flurbiprofen should not take it without their doctors' approval. When the drug is considered essential by your doctor, the potential risk of taking the medicine must be carefully weighed against the benefit it might produce.

Flurbiprofen may pass into breast milk but has caused no problems among breast-fed infants. You must consider the potential effect on the nursing infant if you are breast-feeding while taking this medicine.

Seniors

Older adults are more sensitive to the stomach, kidney, and liver effects of this drug. Some doctors recommend that persons 70 years of age and older take one half the usual dose. Follow your doctor's directions and report any side effects at once.

Possible Side Effects

The most frequent side effects are upset stomach, dizziness, headache, drowsiness, ringing in the ears, and rash.

Other side effects include heartburn, nausea, vomiting, bloating, stomach gas or pain, diarrhea, constipation, dark stools, nervousness, sleeplessness, depression, confusion, tremor, loss of appetite, fatigue, itching, double or blurred vision, dry or irritated eyes, heart failure, palpitations, abnormal heart rhythms, anemia or other changes in the composition of the blood, changes in liver function, hair loss, tingling in the hands or feet, fever, enlarged breasts, blood in the urine, urinary irritation, thirst, frequent urination, kidney damage, low blood sugar, asthma, difficulty breathing, skin rash, itching, swelling, and black and blue marks.

Drug Interactions

Aspirin causes this drug to be eliminated from the body more rapidly than normal.

Flurbiprofen may increase the effectiveness of Lithium and sulfa, anticoagulant (blood-thinning), antidiabetes, and anti-seizure drugs.

People taking Methotrexate should not take Flurbiprofen or any other NSAID. Four people have died from combining Methotrexate and an NSAID.

Flurbiprofen may reduce the effects of beta-blocking drugs such as Propranolol and Atenolol.

Food Interactions

You may take this drug with food if it upsets your stomach.

Usual Dose

200 to 300 milligrams per day. Seniors and those with kidney problems should start with a lower dose.

Overdosage

Symptoms may include drowsiness, dizziness, confusion, disorientation, lethargy, tingling in the hands or feet, numbness, nausea, vomiting, upset stomach, stomach pains, headache, ringing or buzzing in the ears, sweating, and blurred vision. Take the victim to a hospital emergency room at once for treatment. ALWAYS bring the medicine bottle with you.

Special Information

Avoid Aspirin and alcoholic beverages while taking this medication.

You may become dizzy or drowsy while taking this medicine. Be careful while driving or operating complex equipment.

Call your doctor if any of the following symptoms develop: skin rash, itching, swelling, visual disturbances, black stools, or a persistent headache.

If you forget to take a dose of Flurbiprofen, take it as soon as you remember. If it is almost time for your next dose, skip the forgotten dose and continue with your regular schedule.

Generic Name

Fosinopril

Brand Name

Monopril

Type of Drug

Antihypertensive.

Prescribed for

High blood pressure. This medicine may be taken alone or with a thiazide-type diuretic.

General Information

Fosinopril belongs to a class of drugs, the ACE inhibitors, that work by preventing the conversion of a potent hormone called Angiotensin 1. This directly affects the production of other hormones and enzymes that are a part of the system which regulates blood pressure. It begins working about an hour after you take the medicine. Some people taking Fosinopril with a diuretic experience a rapid blood pressure drop. To prevent this from happening, your doctor may tell you to stop the diuretic 2 or 3 days before starting Fosinopril and start again if your blood pressure is not controlled by Fosinopril alone.

Cautions and Warnings

Fosinopril, like the other ACE inhibitors, can affect your kidneys. It is advisable for your doctor to check your urine for abnormalities during the first few months of treatment. It can also affect your white-blood-cell count, possibly increasing your susceptibility to infection. The drug should be used with caution if you have kidney disease or a disease of the immune/collagen system (particularly lupus erythematosus) or who have taken other drugs that can affect white-blood-cell count.

People with impaired liver function do not clear the drug from their bodies as fast as those with normal livers and may accumulate a large amount of drug in their bloodstream.

Pregnancy/Breast-feeding

ACE inhibitors pass into the developing fetus and are generally associated with some birth defects if taken during the last 6 months of pregnancy. The specific effect of Fosinopril on the developing fetus is not known, but studies have shown that it can develop a developing animal fetus. Fosinopril should be used with caution by women who are or might become pregnant.

Fosinopril passes into breast milk and may affect a nursing infant. Nursing mothers should not use this medication.

Seniors

Older adults may be less sensitive to the blood-pressure-lowering effects of this drug than younger adults but more sensitive to drug side effects. Fosinopril dosage must be individualized to your needs.

Possible Side Effects

Cough, dizziness (especially when rising rapidly from a sitting or lying position), tiredness, headache, nausea, vomiting, and diarrhea are most common.

Less common side effects include confusion, shortness of breath, constipation, dry mouth, chest pain, heart attack, low blood pressure, heart palpitations, angina pains, stroke, sleeping difficulty, stomach gas with pain, heartburn, weight changes, frequent urination, liver damage and jaundice (yellow discoloration of the skin or whites of the eyes), sweating, flushing, unusual sensitivity to the sun, itching, rash, memory disturbances, tremor, mood changes, reduced sex drive, muscle cramps, fainting, muscle or joint aches, ringing or buzzing in the ears, visual disturbances, eye pain, and nosebleeds. Swelling of the face, extremities, lips, tongue, or throat is rare but should be reported to your doctor.

Drug Interactions

The blood-pressure-lowering effect of Fosinopril is additive with diuretic drugs and beta blockers. Any other drug that causes a rapid blood pressure drop should be used with caution if you are taking Fosinopril.

Antacids and Indomethacin may interfere with Fosinopril's blood-pressure-lowering effects.

Fosinopril may increase potassium levels in your blood, especially when taken together with Dyazide or other potassiumsparing diuretics. It may also increase blood levels of Digoxin or Lithium. Your doctor may reduce the dosage of those drugs to account for this interaction.

Food Interactions

Food interferes with the rate at which Fosinopril is absorbed into the blood, but does not interfere with its effect on your body. You may take it with food if it upsets your stomach.

Usual Dose

10 to 80 milligrams daily.

Overdosage

The principal effect of Fosinopril overdose is a rapid drop in blood pressure, as evidenced by dizziness or fainting. Take the overdose victim to a hospital emergency room immediately. ALWAYS remember to bring the medicine bottle.

Special Information

Call your doctor if you develop a sore throat, mouth sores, abnormal heartbeat, chest pain, swelling of the face, eyes, lips or tongue, a persistent rash, or loss of taste perception. You may get dizzy if you rise to your feet quickly from a sitting or lying position.

Avoid strenuous exercise and/or very hot weather because heavy sweating or dehydration (as well as vomiting and diarrhea) can cause a rapid blood pressure drop.

Avoid non-prescription diet pills, decongestants, or stimulants that can raise blood pressure.

If you take Fosinopril once a day and forget to take a dose, take it as soon as you remember. If it is almost time for your next dose, skip the one you forgot and continue with your regular schedule. Do not take a double dose.

If you take Fosinopril twice a day and forget a dose, take it as soon as you remember. If it is almost time for your next dose, take one dose as soon as you remember and another in 5 or 6 hours, then go back to your regular schedule.

Generic Name

Furosemide

Brand Names

Fumide
Lasix

(Also available in generic form)

Type of Drug

Diuretic.

Prescribed for

Congestive heart failure, cirrhosis of the liver, kidney dysfunction, high blood pressure, and other conditions where it may be desirable to rid the body of excess fluid.

General Information

Furosemide causes the production of urine by affecting the kidneys. It may also cause lowered blood pressure. Furosemide is particularly useful as a very strong drug with great diuretic potential, when a drug with less diuretic potential would fail to produce the desired therapeutic effect.

Cautions and Warnings

If given in excessive quantities, Furosemide will cause depletion of water and electrolytes. It should not be taken without constant medical supervision and without the dose being adjusted to your particular needs. You should not take this drug if your production of urine has been decreased abnormally by some type of kidney disease, or if you feel you may be allergic to it or have experienced an allergic reaction to it in the past.

Excessive use of Furosemide will result in dehydration or reduction in blood volume and may cause circulatory collapse and other related problems, particularly in older adults. In addition, because of the potent effect that this drug has on the electrolytes in the blood—potassium, sodium, carbon dioxide, and others—frequent laboratory evaluations of these electrolytes should be performed during the few months of therapy and periodically afterward.

Pregnancy/Breast-feeding

Although Furosemide has been used to treat specific conditions in pregnancy, it should generally not be used to treat a pregnant woman because of its potential effects on the unborn child. Although this effect has not been seen in humans, Furosemide can cause kidney problems in unborn animals if given to animals during pregnancy. If your doctor feels that your case warrants the use of Furosemide, the decision to use this drug must be made by you and your doctor based on the potential benefits derived from this drug as opposed to the potential problems that may be associated with its use.

If you must take this drug during the period that you are nursing a newborn baby, you should stop nursing and feed the baby prepared formulas.

Seniors

Older adults are more sensitive to the effects of this drug. Follow your doctor's directions and report any side effects at once.

Possible Side Effects

If you are taking Furosemide you should be aware that changes may develop in potassium and other electrolyte concentrations in your body. In the case of hypokalemia (lowered potassium) produced by Furosemide, you may observe these warning signs: dryness of the mouth, thirst,

weakness, lethargy, drowsiness, restlessness, muscle pains
or cramps, muscular tiredness, low blood pressure, decreased frequency of urination and decreased amount of
urine produced, abnormal heart rate, and stomach upset,
including nausea and vomiting. To treat this, potassium supplements are given in the form of tablets, liquids, or powders, or consumption of potassium-rich foods such as
bananas, citrus fruits, melons, and tomatoes is increased.

Furosemide may alter the metabolism of sugar in your
body. If you have diabetes mellitus, you may develop high
blood sugar or sugar in the urine while you are taking the
drug. To treat this problem, the dose of drugs that you are
taking to treat your diabetes will have to be altered.

In addition, people taking Furosemide have experienced
one or more of the following side effects: abdominal discomfort, nausea, vomiting, diarrhea, rash, dizziness, light-
headedness, weakness, headache, blurred vision, fatigue,
jaundice (yellowing of the skin or whites of the eyes), acute
attacks of gout, ringing in the ears, reversible periodic im-
pairment in hearing. There have also been some reported
cases of irreversible hearing loss.

Other side effects are dermatitis, unusual skin reactions,
tingling in the extremities, postural hypotension (or dizziness on rising quickly from a sitting or lying position), and
anemia of various types. Rare side effects include a sweet
taste in the mouth, burning feeling in the stomach and/or
mouth, thirst, increased perspiration, and frequent urination.

Drug Interactions

Furosemide will increase (potentiate) the action of other
blood-pressure-lowering drugs. This is beneficial and is frequently used to help lower blood pressure in patients with
hypertension.

The possibility of developing electrolyte imbalances in
body fluids is increased if you take other medications such
as Digitalis and adrenal corticosteroids while you are taking
Furosemide.

If you are taking Furosemide because of congestive heart
failure and are also taking Digitalis, loss of potassium may
significantly affect the toxicity of Digitalis.

If you are taking an oral antidiabetic drug and begin taking
Furosemide, the antidiabetic dose may have to be altered.

If you are taking Lithium Carbonate, you should probably not take a diuretic, which, by reducing the elimination of Lithium from the blood, adds a high risk of Lithium toxicity.

Interaction with aminoglycoside antibiotics may cause periodic hearing losses; make sure your doctor knows you are taking Furosemide before he or she gives you an injection of an aminoglycoside.

If you are taking high doses of Aspirin to treat arthritis or similar diseases, and you begin to take Furosemide, you may have to lower the dose of Aspirin because of the effect Furosemide has on passage of Aspirin through the kidneys.

If you are taking Furosemide for the treatment of high blood pressure or congestive heart failure, avoid over-the-counter drug products for the treatment of coughs, colds, and allergies which may contain stimulant drugs. Check with your pharmacist, who can give you accurate information about any over-the-counter drug and its potential interactions with Furosemide.

Food Interactions

Foods that are high in potassium, including bananas, citrus fruits, melons, and tomatoes, should be given high priority in your daily diet.

Usual Dose

Adult: 20 to 80 milligrams per day, depending on disease and patient's response. Doses of 600 milligrams per day or even more have been prescribed.

Infant and child: 4 to 5 milligrams per pound of body weight daily in a single dose. If therapy is not successful, the dose may be increased by steps of 2 to 5 milligrams, but not to more than 14 to 15 milligrams per day.

Maintenance doses are adjusted to the minimum effective level.

Special Information

If the amount of urine you produce each day is dropping or if you suffer from significant loss of appetite, muscle weakness, tiredness, or nausea while taking this drug, contact your doctor immediately.

Furosemide is usually taken once a day, after breakfast. If

a second dose is needed, it should be taken no later than 2 in the afternoon. This is to avoid waking up during the night to urinate.

If you forget to take a dose of Furosemide, take it as soon as you remember. If it is almost time for your next regularly scheduled dose, skip the one you forgot and continue with your regular schedule. Do not take a double dose.

Generic Name

Gemfibrozil

Brand Name

Lopid

Type of Drug

Antihyperlipidemic (blood-fat reducer).

Prescribed for

People with excessively high levels of blood triglycerides.

General Information

Gemfibrozil consistently reduces blood triglyceride levels, but is usually prescribed only for people with very high blood-fat levels who have not responded to dietary changes or other therapies. Normal levels range between 50 and 200 milligrams. People with very high levels of blood triglycerides are likely to have severe abdominal pains and pancreas inflammation. Gemfibrozil usually has little effect on blood-cholesterol levels, although it may reduce blood cholesterol in some people.

Gemfibrozil works by affecting the breakdown of body fats and by reducing the amount of triglyceride manufactured by the liver. However, it is not known if these 2 mechanisms are solely responsible for the drug's effect on triglyceride levels.

Cautions and Warnings

Gemfibrozil should not be taken by people with severe liver

or kidney disease or by those who have had allergic reactions to the drug. Gemfibrozil users may have an increased chance of developing gallbladder disease and should realize that this drug, like other blood-fat reducers (including Clofibrate and Probucol), has not been proven to reduce the chances of fatal heart attacks.

Long-term studies in which male rats were given between 1 and 10 times the maximum human dose showed a definite increase in liver tumors, both cancerous and noncancerous. Other studies of male rats, in which 3 to 10 times the human dose was given for 10 weeks, showed that the drug reduced sperm activity, although this effect has not been reported in humans.

Pregnancy/Breast-feeding

There have been no Gemfibrozil studies involving pregnant women. However, it should be avoided by pregnant women or women who may become pregnant while using it. In those situations where its use is considered essential, the potential risk of the drug must be carefully weighed against any benefit it might produce.

Because of the tumor-stimulating effect of Gemfibrozil, it is recommended that nursing mothers consider bottle-feeding while taking this drug.

Seniors

Older adults may be more likely to develop drug side effects because the drug primarily passes out of the body through your kidneys and kidney function declines with age.

Possible Side Effects

The most common side effects are abdominal and stomach pains and gas, diarrhea, nausea, and vomiting.

Less common side effects are rash and itching, dizziness, blurred vision, anemia, reduced levels of certain white blood cells, increased blood sugar, and muscle pains, especially in the arms and legs. Other adverse reactions are dry mouth, constipation, loss of appetite, upset stomach, sleeplessness, tingling in the hands or feet, ringing or buzzing in the ears, back pains, painful muscles and/or joints, swollen joints, fatigue, a feeling of ill health, reduction in blood potassium, and abnormal liver function. People taking this drug may be more susceptible to the common cold or other viral or bacterial infections.

Drug Interactions

Gemfibrozil increases the effects of oral anticoagulant (blood-thinning) drugs; your doctor will have to reduce your anticoagulant dosage when Gemfibrozil treatment is started.

Food Interactions

Follow your doctor's instructions for dietary restrictions.

Gemfibrozil is best taken on an empty stomach 30 minutes before meals, but may be taken with food if it upsets your stomach.

Usual Dose

900 to 1500 milligrams per day, in 2 divided doses taken 20 minutes before breakfast and the evening meal.

Overdosage

There are no reports of Gemfibrozil overdosage, but victims might be expected to develop exaggerated versions of the drug's side effects. Patients taking an overdose of this drug must be made to vomit with Syrup of Ipecac (available at any pharmacy) to remove any remaining drug from the stomach. Call your doctor or a poison control center before doing this. If you must go to a hospital emergency room, ALWAYS bring the medicine bottle.

Special Information

Your doctor should perform periodic blood counts during the first year of Gemfibrozil treatment to check for anemia or other blood effects. Liver-function tests are also necessary. Blood-sugar levels should be checked periodically while you are taking Gemfibrozil, especially if you are diabetic or have a family history of diabetes.

Gemfibrozil may cause dizziness or blurred vision. Use caution while driving or doing anything else that requires concentration and alertness.

Call your doctor if any drug side effects become severe or intolerable, especially diarrhea, nausea, vomiting, or stomach pains and/or gas. These may disappear by reducing the drug dose.

If you forget to take a dose of Gemfibrozil, take it as soon as you remember. If it is almost time for your next regularly scheduled dose, skip the one you forgot and continue with your regular schedule. Do not take a double dose.

Generic Name

Glipizide

Brand Name

Glucotrol

Type of Drug

Oral antidiabetic.

Prescribed for

Diabetes mellitus (high sugar levels in the blood and urine) that develops during adulthood.

General Information

Glipizide is a "second-generation" antidiabetes drug that was sold in Europe and Canada for several years before the FDA approved its use in the United States. It belongs to the same chemical class as earlier oral antidiabetic drugs, but is more potent, so that less medication is required to accomplish the same effect as the other products. Other minor differences between the first- and second-generation drugs are not considered clinically important. Glipizide and the other second-generation antidiabetes drug, Glyburide, offer no advantage over first-generation agents (Acetohexamide, Chlorpropamide, Tolazamide, and Tolbutamide) available in the United States.

The major differences among all antidiabetes drugs are in the time it takes for the drugs' action to begin and the duration of their effect. All oral antidiabetes drugs work by stimulating the cells in the pancreas that release Insulin into the blood to increase their production. These antidiabetics require a functioning pancreas to produce their effect. However, they may be used together with Insulin injections in certain cases.

Cautions and Warnings

Mild stress, such as infection, minor surgery, or emotional upset, reduces the effectiveness of Glipizide. Remember that while you are taking this medication, you should be under your doctor's continuous care.

The long-term (several years) use of oral antidiabetes drugs has been associated with more heart disease than has treatment with diet or diet plus Insulin. For this reason, many physicians consider diet or diet plus Insulin to be superior to an oral antidiabetes drug.

Glipizide is an aid to, not a substitute for, dietary control. Dietary restriction is still of primary importance in treating diabetes. Follow the diet plan your doctor has prescribed.

Glipizide and the other oral antidiabetes drugs are not oral Insulin, nor are they a substitute for Insulin; they do not lower blood sugar by themselves.

Treating diabetes is your responsibility. Following all of your doctor's instructions with regard to diet, body weight, exercise, personal hygiene, and measures to avoid infection is of paramount importance.

Glipizide should not be used if you have severe kidney, liver, or endocrine (hormone) system disease.

Pregnancy/Breast-feeding

This drug should be avoided by pregnant women and by those who may become pregnant while using it. In those situations where it is deemed essential, the potential risk of the drug must be carefully weighed against any benefit it might produce. Bear in mind that diabetic mothers are known to be 3 to 4 times more likely to have children with birth defects than are nondiabetic women.

If you are pregnant or nursing, attempts should be made to control your diabetes with diet and/or Insulin during this time. If you take Glipizide during pregnancy, it should be stopped at least 1 month before the expected birth date to avoid very low blood sugar in your newborn baby.

This drug may pass into breast milk. Nursing mothers who

must take this drug should consider alternative feeding methods.

Seniors

Older adults with reduced kidney function may be more sensitive to drug side effects because of a reduced ability to eliminate it from the body. Low blood sugar, the major sign of drug overdose, may be more difficult to identify in older adults than in younger adults. Also, low blood sugar is more likely to be a cause of nervous system side effects in older adults.

Older adults taking antidiabetes drugs must keep in close touch with their doctor and closely follow his/her directions.

Possible Side Effects

The most common side effects are appetite loss, nausea, vomiting, heartburn, and upset stomach. You may experience tingling in your hands or feet and itching and rash. These effects can be treated by reducing the daily Glipizide dose or switching to another antidiabetes drug.

Less commonly, Glipizide can produce abnormally low blood-sugar levels if too much is taken. Other factors that can contribute to low blood sugar are age, kidney or liver disease, malnutrition, consumption of alcoholic beverages, and glandular disorders.

Glipizide may produce liver inflammation, shown by a yellow discoloration of your skin or the whites of your eyes, but this is rare. Other side effects are relatively infrequent, but can include weakness, fatigue, dizziness, headache, loss of some kidney function, mild reduction in levels of white blood cells and platelets (involved in clotting), and drug allergy (itching and rash).

Drug Interactions

The action of Glipizide may be enhanced by Insulin, sulfa drugs, Oxyphenbutazone, Phenylbutazone, Clofibrate, Aspirin and other salicylates, Probenecid, Dicumarol, Bishydroxycoumarin, Warfarin, Phenyramidol, and monoamine oxidase (MAO) inhibitor drugs, requiring a reduction in Glipizide dosage.

Thiazide-type diuretics, corticosteroids, phenothiazine tranquilizers, drugs for underactive thyroids, estrogens, oral contraceptives, Phenytoin, Nicotinic Acid, calcium channel blockers, Isoniazid, and the stimulant ingredients added for their decongestant effects to many nonprescription cough, cold, and allergy medicines can increase blood-sugar levels, calling for a possible increase in Glipizide dosage. Check with your doctor or pharmacist before taking any such over-the-counter products.

Beta blockers, prescribed for high blood pressure and some forms of heart disease, may counteract the effects of oral antidiabetes drugs. The outward signs of low blood sugar may also be reversed by these drugs.

Alcoholic beverages can either increase or decrease blood-sugar levels and should be avoided. Also, alcoholic beverages can interact with this medication to cause flushing of the face and body, throbbing pain in the head and neck, breathing difficulty, nausea, vomiting, sweating, chest pains, thirst, low blood pressure, heart palpitations, weakness, dizziness, blurred vision, and confusion. Contact your doctor at once if you experience any of these symptoms.

Food Interactions

Dietary restriction is an essential part of the treatment of diabetes. Be sure to follow the diet your doctor prescribes. Glipizide is best taken on an empty stomach but may be taken with food if it upsets your stomach.

Usual Dose

5 milligrams once per day.

Overdosage

Mild Glipizide overdosage lowers blood sugar and can be treated by consuming sugar in such forms as candy and orange juice. More serious overdosage must be treated in a hospital emergency room. ALWAYS bring the prescription bottle with you.

Special Information

This medicine should not be discontinued without your doctor's knowledge and advice. It should be taken as a part of a program for the treatment of your condition, including diet, exercise, personal hygiene, measures to avoid infection, and periodic testing of your urine for sugar and ketones. Your doctor may also want you to measure blood sugar periodically, which can be conveniently accomplished at home using an appropriate device.

Contact your doctor if you are not feeling well or if you develop symptoms such as yellowing of the skin or whites of the eyes, an abnormally light-colored stool, low-grade fever, unusual bleeding or bruising, sore throat, or diarrhea.

Abnormally low blood sugar may be evidenced by fatigue, hunger, profuse sweating, and numbness in your hands or feet.

Abnormally high blood sugar may be evidenced by excessive thirst and/or frequent urination, and very high levels of sugar or ketones in your urine.

If you forget to take a dose of Glipizide, take it as soon as you remember. If it is almost time for your next regularly scheduled dose, skip the one you forgot and continue with your regular schedule. Do not take a double dose.

Generic Name

Glyburide

Brand Names

DiaBeta
Micronase

Type of Drug

Oral antidiabetic.

Prescribed for

Diabetes mellitus (high sugar levels in the blood and urine) that develops during adulthood.

General Information

Glyburide is a "second-generation" antidiabetes drug that was sold in Europe and Canada for several years before the

FDA approved its use in the United States. It belongs to the same chemical class as earlier oral antidiabetic drugs, but is more potent, so that less medication is required to accomplish the same effect as the other products. Other minor differences between the first- and second-generation drugs are not considered clinically important. Glyburide and the other second-generation antidiabetes drug, Glipizide, offer no advantage over first-generation agents (Acetohexamide, Chlorpropamide, Tolazamide, and Tolbutamide) available in the United States.

The major differences among all antidiabetes drugs are in the time it takes for the drugs' action to begin and the duration of their effect. All currently available antidiabetes drugs work by stimulating the cells in the pancreas that release Insulin into the blood to increase their production. These antidiabetics require a functioning pancreas to produce their effect. However, they may be used together with Insulin in certain cases.

Cautions and Warnings

Mild stress, such as infection, minor surgery, or emotional upset, reduces the effectiveness of Glyburide. Remember that while you are taking this medication, you should be under your doctor's continuous care.

The long-term (several years) use of oral antidiabetes drugs has been associated with more heart disease than has treatment with diet or diet plus Insulin. For this reason, many physicians consider diet or diet plus Insulin to be superior to an oral antidiabetes drug.

Glyburide is an aid to, not a substitute for, dietary control. Dietary restriction is still of primary importance in treating diabetes. Follow the diet plan your doctor has prescribed.

Glyburide and the other oral antidiabetes drugs are not oral Insulin, nor are they a substitute for Insulin. They do not lower blood sugar on their own.

Treating diabetes is your responsibility. Following all of your doctor's instructions with regard to diet, body weight, exercise, personal hygiene, and measures to avoid infection is of paramount importance.

Glyburide should not be used if you have severe kidney, liver, or endocrine (hormone) system disease.

Pregnancy/Breast-feeding

Unlike the older oral antidiabetes drugs, Glyburide has been tested in animals and found to produce no damage to the developing fetus. Other oral antidiabetes drugs produce birth defects, but the exact relationship is unclear because children of diabetic mothers are 3 to 4 times more prone to birth defects than are children of nondiabetic women. Nevertheless, there is no corresponding proof of safety in humans, and Glyburide should be taken with extreme caution if you are pregnant, might become pregnant during its use, or are nursing. Attempts should be made to control your diabetes with diet and/or Insulin during this time. If you take Glyburide during pregnancy, it should be stopped at least 2 weeks before the expected birth to avoid very low blood sugar in the newborn baby.

This drug may pass into breast milk. Nursing mothers who must take this medicine should consider alternative feeding methods.

Seniors

Older adults with reduced kidney function may be more sensitive to drug side effects because of a reduced ability to eliminate it from the body. Low blood sugar, the major sign of drug overdose, may be more difficult to identify in older adults than in younger adults. Also, low blood sugar is more likely to be a cause of nervous-system side effects in older adults.

Older adults taking antidiabetes drugs must keep in close touch with their doctors and closely follow their directions.

Possible Side Effects

The most common side effects are appetite loss, nausea, vomiting, heartburn, and upset stomach. You may experience tingling in your hands or feet and itching and rash. These effects can be treated by reducing the daily Glyburide dose or switching to another antidiabetes drug.

Less commonly, Glyburide can produce abnormally low blood-sugar levels if too much is taken. Other factors that can contribute to low blood sugar are age, kidney or liver disease, malnutrition, consumption of alcoholic beverages, and glandular disorders.

Glyburide may produce liver inflammation shown by a yellow discoloration of your skin or the whites of your eyes, but this is rare. Other side effects are relatively infrequent, but can include weakness, fatigue, dizziness, headache, loss of some kidney function, mild reduction in levels of white blood cells and platelets (involved in clotting), and drug allergy (itching and rash).

Drug Interactions

The action of Glyburide may be enhanced by Insulin, sulfa drugs, Oxyphenbutazone, Phenylbutazone, Clofibrate, Aspirin and other salicylates, Probenecid, Dicumarol, Bishydroxycoumarin, Warfarin, Phenyramidol, and monoamine oxidase (MAO) inhibitor drugs, requiring a reduction in Glyburide dosage.

Thiazide-type diuretics, corticosteroids, phenothiazine tranquilizers, drugs for underactive thyroids, estrogens, oral contraceptives, Phenytoin, Nicotinic Acid, calcium channel blockers, Isoniazid, and the stimulant ingredients added for their decongestant effects to many nonprescription cough, cold, and allergy medicines can increase blood-sugar levels, calling for a possible increase in Glyburide dosage. Check with your doctor or pharmacist before taking any such over-the-counter products.

Beta blockers, prescribed for high blood pressure and some forms of heart disease, may counteract the effects of oral antidiabetes drugs. The outward signs of low blood sugar may also be reversed by these drugs.

Alcoholic beverages can either increase or decrease blood-sugar levels and should be avoided. Also, alcoholic beverages can interact with this medication to cause flushing of the face and body, throbbing pain in the head and neck, breathing difficulty, nausea, vomiting, sweating, chest pains, thirst, low blood pressure, heart palpitations, weakness, dizziness, blurred vision, and confusion. Contact your doctor at once if you experience any of these symptoms.

Food Interactions

This medicine is best taken on an empty stomach, but may be taken with food. Dietary management is an important part of the treatment of diabetes. Be sure to follow your doctor's directions about the foods you should avoid.

Usual Dose

2.5 to 20 milligrams once per day, usually with breakfast or the first main meal.

Overdosage

Mild Glyburide overdosage lowers blood sugar and can be treated by consuming sugar in such forms as candy and orange juice. More serious overdosage must be treated in a hospital emergency room. ALWAYS bring the prescription bottle with you.

Special Information

This medicine should not be discontinued without your doctor's knowledge and advice. It should be taken as a part of a program for the treatment of your condition, including diet, exercise, personal hygiene, measures to avoid infection, and periodic testing of your urine for sugar and ketones. Your doctor may also want you to measure blood sugar periodically, which can be conveniently accomplished at home using an appropriate device.

Contact your doctor if you are not feeling well or if you develop symptoms such as yellowing of the skin or whites of the eyes, an abnormally light-colored stool, low-grade fever, unusual bleeding or bruising, sore throat, or diarrhea.

Abnormally low blood sugar may be evidenced by fatigue, hunger, profuse sweating, and numbness in your hands or feet.

Abnormally high blood sugar may be evidenced by excessive thirst and/or frequent urination and very high levels of sugar or ketones in your urine.

If you forget to take a dose of Glyburide, take it as soon as you remember. If it is almost time for your next regularly scheduled dose, skip the one you forgot and continue with your regular schedule. Do not take a double dose.

Generic Name

Guanabenz Acetate

Brand Name
Wytensin

Type of Drug
Antihypertensive.

Prescribed for
High blood pressure.

General Information
This drug works by stimulating certain nerve receptors in the central nervous system, resulting in a lessening of general nervous-system stimulation by the brain. The immediate blood-pressure reduction occurs without a major effect on blood vessels. However, chronic use of Guanabenz Acetate can result in widening of blood vessels and a slight reduction in pulse rate. It can be taken alone or in combination with a thiazide diuretic.

Cautions and Warnings
Do not take Guanabenz Acetate if you are sensitive to it.

Pregnancy/Breast-feeding
Reports of the effects of this drug in pregnant women have yielded conflicting results. Because it may adversely affect a developing baby, this drug should be avoided by pregnant women or women who may become pregnant while using it. In those situations where it is deemed essential, the potential risk of the drug must be carefully weighed against any benefit it might produce.

Nursing mothers should not use this drug, since it is not known if it passes into breast milk. Consider an alternative feeding method if you must take Guanabenz Acetate.

Seniors
Older adults are more sensitive to the sedative and blood-

pressure-lowering effects of this drug. Follow your doctor's directions and report any side effects at once.

Possible Side Effects

The incidence and severity of side effects increase with increases in the daily dosage. The side effects are drowsiness, sedation, dry mouth, dizziness, weakness, and headache.

Less common side effects are chest pains, swelling in the hands, legs, or feet, heart palpitations and abnormal heart rhythms, stomach and abdominal anxiety, pains and discomfort, nausea, diarrhea, vomiting, constipation, anxiety, poor muscle control, depression, difficulty sleeping, stuffy nose, blurred vision, muscle aches and pains, difficulty breathing, frequent urination, male impotence, unusual taste in the mouth, and swollen and painful male breasts.

Drug Interactions

The effect of this drug is increased by taking it together with other blood-pressure-lowering agents. Its sedative effects will be increased by taking it together with tranquilizers, sleeping pills, or other nervous-system depressants.

People taking Guanabenz Acetate for high blood pressure should avoid nonprescription medicines that might aggravate hypertension, such as decongestants, cold and allergy treatments, and diet pills, all of which may contain stimulants. If you are unsure about which medicine to choose, ask your pharmacist.

Food Interactions

This drug is best taken on an empty stomach but may be taken with food if it upsets your stomach.

Usual Dose

4 milligrams 2 times per day to start, with a gradual increase to a maximum of 32 milligrams twice per day, although doses this large are rarely needed.

Overdosage

Guanabenz Acetate overdose will cause sleepiness, lethargy, low blood pressure, irritability, pinpoint pupils, and reduced heart rate. Patients taking an overdose of this drug must be made to vomit with Syrup of Ipecac (available at any pharmacy) to remove any remaining drug from the stomach. Call your doctor or a poison control center before doing this. If you must go to a hospital emergency room, ALWAYS bring the medicine bottle.

Special Information

Take this drug exactly as prescribed for maximum benefit. If any side effects become severe or intolerable, contact your doctor, who may reduce your daily dosage to eliminate the side effect.

If you forget to take a dose of Guanabenz Acetate, take it as soon as you remember. If it is almost time for your next regularly scheduled dose, skip the one you forgot and continue with your regular schedule. Do not take a double dose. Call your doctor if you miss 2 or more consecutive doses.

Generic Name

Guanadrel Sulfate

Brand Name

Hylorel

Type of Drug

Antihypertensive.

Prescribed for

High blood pressure.

General Information

This drug is similar to Guanethidine Sulfate and works by preventing the release of the neurohormone norepinephrine from nervous-system storage sites. This relaxes blood-vessel muscles and lowers blood pressure by preventing blood-vessel constriction. Guanadrel Sulfate is usually taken with other medicines, such as diuretics.

Cautions and Warnings

Guanadrel Sulfate must not be taken by people who are sensitive or allergic to its effects, who have heart failure (the drug can cause you to retain salt and water), or who have a tumor of the adrenal glands known as pheochromocytoma. Asthmatics and people with stomach ulcers may find their conditions are worsened by this drug.

Pregnancy/Breast-feeding

This drug should be avoided by pregnant women or women who may become pregnant while using it. In those situations where it is deemed essential, the potential risk of the drug must be carefully weighed against any benefit it might produce.

Nursing mothers should watch for any possible drug effect on their infants while taking this medication. It is not known if Guanadrel Sulfate passes into breast milk.

Seniors

Older adults are more sensitive to the blood-pressure-lowering effects of this drug. Follow your doctor's directions and report any side effects at once.

Possible Side Effects

Difficulty breathing with or without physical exertion, heart palpitations, chest pains, coughing, fatigue, headache, feeling faint, drowsiness, visual disturbances, tingling in the hands or feet, confusion, increased bowel movements, gas pains, indigestion, constipation, loss of appetite, inflammation of the tongue, nausea, vomiting, frequent urination, a feeling that you need to urinate, nighttime urination, male impotence, aching arms or legs, leg cramps, and excessive changes in body weight (up or down), fluid retention and swelling in the arms, legs, or feet.

Other side effects are psychological changes, depression, difficulty sleeping, fainting, dry mouth, dry throat, blood in the urine, joint pains or inflammation, backache, and neckache.

Drug Interactions

Guanadrel Sulfate should be discontinued 2 to 3 days before

surgery to avoid potentially severe interaction with anesthetic agents.

It should not be taken together with monoamine oxidase (MAO) inhibitor drugs or within a week of MAO inhibitor therapy because of the possible enhancement of MAO side effects.

The effects of Guanadrel Sulfate may be reversed by tricyclic antidepressant drugs, Ephedrine, Phenylpropanolamine, and the phenothiazine tranquilizers.

Avoid nonprescription medicines that might aggravate your condition, such as decongestants, cold and allergy treatments, asthma remedies, and diet pills, all of which may contain stimulants. If you are unsure about which medicine to choose, ask your pharmacist.

Guanadrel Sulfate's effects may be increased by beta-blocking drugs and Reserpine.

Alcoholic beverages are likely to increase the chances of dizziness and fainting associated with Guanadrel Sulfate.

Food Interactions

This drug is best taken on an empty stomach but may be taken with food if it upsets your stomach.

Usual Dose

5 milligrams twice per day to start. The daily dosage will be increased in small steps until blood-pressure control is achieved or side effects become intolerable. Most people require between 20 and 75 milligrams per day. Larger daily amounts may be required but should be divided into 3 or 4 doses per day.

Overdosage

Extreme dizziness and blurred vision are the hallmarks of Guanadrel Sulfate overdose. Lie down until the symptoms subside. If the symptoms are more severe and include a rapid drop in blood pressure, take the victim to the hospital at once for treatment. ALWAYS bring the prescription bottle with you.

Special Information

It may seem odd, but Guanadrel Sulfate is available only in

a 10-milligram or 25-milligram tablet. If you are required to take 5 milligrams twice a day, you must break a 10-milligram tablet in half. This tablet is designed for this.

Guanadrel Sulfate frequently causes weakness and dizziness in someone who has been sitting or lying down and then rises quickly. This is more likely to happen early in the morning, during hot weather, if you have been sitting or reclining for a long period of time, or if you have been drinking alcoholic beverages. You can minimize this reaction by getting up as slowly as possible. When you get up from lying down, sit on the edge of your bed for several minutes with your feet dangling, then stand slowly. Call your doctor if the problem continues; your daily drug dosage may have to be reduced.

People taking this drug for long periods of time may become tolerant to its effects. If this happens, your doctor will increase your daily dose slightly to achieve the same degree of blood-pressure control.

If you forget to take a dose of Guanadrel Sulfate, take it as soon as you remember. If it is almost time for your next regularly scheduled dose, skip the one you forgot and continue with your regular schedule. Do not take a double dose.

Generic Name
Guanethidine Monosulfate

Brand Name
Ismelin Sulfate

(Also available in generic form)

Type of Drug
Antihypertensive.

Prescribed for
High blood pressure.

General Information
Guanethidine Monosulfate affects the section of the ner-

vous system which controls pressure in the major blood vessels. Its blood-pressure-lowering effect is enhanced when taken along with other medicines, such as diuretics.

Cautions and Warnings

Patients who may be allergic to this drug, who are taking a monoamine oxidase (MAO) inhibitor, or who also have a tumor called a pheochromocytoma should not take Guanethidine Monosulfate.

Pregnancy/Breast-feeding

This drug may cross into the blood circulation of a developing baby. It has not been found to cause birth defects. Pregnant women, or those who might become pregnant while taking this drug, should not take it without their doctors' approval. When the drug is considered essential by your doctor, the potential risk of taking the medicine must be carefully weighed against the benefit it might produce.

This drug has caused no problems among breast-fed infants. You must consider the potential effect on the nursing infant if breast-feeding while taking this medicine.

Seniors

Older adults are more sensitive to the blood-pressure-lowering effects of this drug. Follow your doctor's directions and report any side effects at once.

Possible Side Effects

Dizziness, weakness, especially on rising quickly from a sitting or prone position, slowed heartbeat, increased bowel movements, possibly severe diarrhea, male impotence (difficult ejaculation), retention of fluid in the body.

Less common side effects are difficulty in breathing, fatigue, nausea, vomiting, increased frequency of nighttime urination, difficulty in controlling urinary function, itching, rash, loss of scalp hair, dry mouth, involuntary lowering of eyelids, blurred vision, muscle aches and spasms, mental depression, chest pains (angina pectoris), tingling in the chest, stuffy nose, weight gain, asthma in some patients. This drug may affect kidney function.

Drug Interactions

Guanethidine Monosulfate may interact with digitalis drugs to slow heart rates excessively. When taken with other bloodpressure-lowering drugs it can lower pressure excessively. Otherwise, this is a useful interaction that is sometimes used in treating hypertension (high blood pressure).

Drugs with stimulant properties (such as antidepressants and decongestants), oral contraceptives, and some antipsychotic drugs (such as phenothiazines) may reduce the effectiveness of Guanethidine Monosulfate. The drug should not be taken together with MAO inhibitors, which should be stopped at least 1 week before taking Guanethidine Monosulfate.

Avoid over-the-counter cough, cold, or allergy medicines which may contain stimulants. Check with your doctor or pharmacist before combining these medicines.

Guanethidine should be taken with caution if you also take an antidiabetes drug. The combination will increase antidiabetic activity and may cause your blood sugar to be too low.

Food Interactions

This medicine is best taken on an empty stomach, but you may take it with food if it upsets your stomach.

Usual Dose

Adult: 10 milligrams per day to start. Dose is adjusted according to patient's need. Average daily dose is 25 to 50 milligrams.

Child: 0.09 milligrams per pound of body weight per day. Maximum daily dose is 1.36 milligrams per pound of body weight.

Overdosage

Symptoms are basically exaggerated or prolonged side effects, including dizziness, weakness, slowed heartbeat, and possible diarrhea. Call your doctor immediately if the symptoms appear or if you think you have these symptoms.

Special Information

Do not stop taking this medication unless specifically directed to. Call your doctor if you develop frequent diarrhea or are often dizzy or faint.

Alcoholic beverages, heat, and strenuous exercise may increase the chances of dizziness or faintness developing.

If you forget to take a dose of Guanethidine Monosulfate, take it as soon as you remember. If it is almost time for your next regularly scheduled dose, skip the one you forgot and continue with your regular schedule. Do not take a double dose.

Generic Name

Guanfacine Hydrochloride

Brand Name

Tenex

Type of Drug

Antihypertensive.

Prescribed for

High blood pressure; heroin withdrawal.

General Information

Guanfacine works by stimulating a particular portion of the nervous system that dilates or widens blood vessels. Because the studies of Guanfacine were conducted only in people taking a thiazide-type diuretic, the drug is recommended for use only in combination with one of those drugs. Guanfacine's effect is long-acting; it can be taken only once a day (usually at bedtime, to take advantage of the drug's side effect of producing sleepiness).

Cautions and Warnings

People who are allergic to Guanfacine should not use this drug.

People with kidney function loss should have their dosages adjusted by the doctor because the drug passes out of the body primarily through the kidneys.

Pregnancy/Breast-feeding

Animal studies indicate that Guanfacine, in high doses, may be toxic to a developing baby. As with all drug products, pregnant women or those who might become pregnant should not use this drug unless the advantages of the product have been carefully weighed against the possible dangers of taking it while pregnant.

It is not known if Guanfacine passes into breast milk; no drug-related problems have been known to occur. Nursing mothers who must use it should exercise caution.

Seniors

Older adults may be more sensitive to the sedative and blood-pressure-lowering effects of Guanfacine because of expected age-related losses of kidney function. This factor should be taken into account by your doctor when determining your daily dosage of Guanfacine.

Possible Side Effects

Guanfacine may cause sedation, especially when treatment is first started. Like most Guanfacine side effects, the frequency with which drowsiness occurs tends to increase with increased drug dosage and to become less severe as you continue to take the drug.

Other common side effects include dry mouth, weakness, dizziness, headache, constipation, and sleeplessness.

Less common side effects include heart palpitations, chest pain, slow heartbeat, abdominal pain, diarrhea, upset stomach, difficulty swallowing, nausea, memory loss, confusion, depression, loss of sex drive, runny nose, taste changes, ringing or buzzing in the ears, conjunctivitis, eye irritation, blurring and other visual disturbances, leg cramps, unusually slow movements, breathing difficulty, itching, rash, redness, sweating, testicle disorders, poor urinary control, a feeling of ill health, and tingling in the hands or feet.

Drug Interactions

Alcohol or any other nervous-system depressant will increase the sedative effects of Guanfacine.

Indomethacin, Ibuprofen, and other nonsteroidal anti-inflammatory pain relievers (NSAIDs) may decrease Guanfacine's effectiveness.

Estrogen drugs may cause fluid retention, which increases blood pressure.

Any medication that lowers blood pressure will increase the blood-pressure-lowering effect of Guanfacine.

Stimulants, including those used in non-prescription decongestants and diet pills, can antagonize Guanfacine's effect.

Food Interactions

Guanfacine may be taken with food if it upsets your stomach.

Usual Dose

Adult and child (over age 12): 1 to 3 milligrams a day, taken at bedtime. Doses above 3 milligrams a day are rarely used because side effects increase dramatically above that level.

Overdosage

Overdose symptoms are likely to be drowsiness, slow heartbeat, and weakness. Overdose victims should be taken to a hospital emergency room for treatment. ALWAYS bring the medicine bottle with you.

Special Information

High blood pressure is usually a symptomless condition. Be sure to continue taking your medicine even if you feel perfectly healthy. If the medicine causes problems, don't stop taking it on your own.

Call your doctor if you develop breathing difficulty; slow heartbeat; extreme dizziness; dry mouth that lasts more than 2 weeks and does not respond to gum, candy, or saliva substitutes; dry, itchy, or burning eyes; sex-drive loss; headache; nausea or vomiting; sleeping difficulty; or unusual tiredness or weakness during the daytime. You may also want to call the doctor if other side effects become bothersome or extremely persistent.

People taking this drug must be careful when performing tasks reguiring concentration and coordination because of the chance that the drug will make them tired, dizzy, or light-headed.

Abruptly stopping Guanfacine treatment can result in a rebound increase in blood pressure after 2 to 4 days.

Visit your doctor regularly to check on your progress, and be sure to follow your doctor's directions for diet, salt restriction, and other non-drug ways to help control your blood pressure.

If you forget to take a dose, take it as soon as you remember. If it is almost time for your next dose, skip the one you forgot and continue with your regular schedule. Do not take a double dose. Call your doctor if you forget to take 2 or more doses in a row.

Generic Name
Halazepam

Brand Name
Paxipam

Type of Drug
Minor tranquilizer.

Prescribed for
Relief of symptoms of anxiety, tension, fatigue, and agitation.

General Information
Halazepam is a member of the group of drugs known as benzodiazepines. These drugs are used as antianxiety agents, anticonvulsants, or sedatives (sleeping pills.) They exert their effects by relaxing the large skeletal muscles and by a direct effect on the brain. In doing so, they can relax you and make you either more tranquil or sleepier, depending upon which drug you use and how much you take. Many doctors prefer the benzodiazepines to other drugs that can be used for the same effects. Their reason is that these drugs tend to be safer, have fewer side effects, and are usually as, if not more, effective. The benzodiazepines are gen-

erally prescribed in any situation where they can be a useful adjunct.

The benzodiazepines, including Halazepam, can be abused if taken for long periods of time, and it is possible to experience withdrawal symptoms if you stop taking the drug abruptly. Withdrawal symptoms include tremor, muscle cramps, stomach cramps, vomiting, insomnia, and convulsions.

Cautions and Warnings

Do not take Halazepam if you know you are sensitive or allergic to this drug or other benzodiazepines such as Diazepam, Oxazepam, Chlorazepate, Lorazepam, Prazepam, Flurazepam, Temazepam, and Clonazepam. Halazepam and other members of this group can aggravate narrow-angle glaucoma, but if you have open-angle glaucoma you may take the drug.

Pregnancy/Breast-feeding

This drug may cause birth defects or interfere with your baby's development. Check with your doctor before taking it if you are, or might be, pregnant.

If Halazepam is used during breast-feeding the baby may be overtired, be short of breath, or have a slow heartbeat.

Seniors

Older adults are more sensitive to the effects of this drug, especially dizziness and drowsiness, and require a lower daily dose, usually 20 to 40 milligrams. Follow your doctor's directions and report any side effects at once.

Possible Side Effects

The most common side effect is mild drowsiness during the first few days of therapy. If drowsiness persists, contact your doctor.

Less common side effects are confusion, depression, lethargy, disorientation, headache, inactivity, slurred speech, stupor, dizziness, tremor, constipation, dry mouth, nausea, inability to control urination, changes in sex drive, irregular menstrual cycle, changes in heart rhythm, lowered blood pressure, fluid retention, blurred or double vision, itching, rash, hiccups, nervousness, inability to fall asleep, and occasional liver dysfunction. If you experience any of these symptoms, stop taking the medicine and contact your doctor immediately.

Drug Interactions

Halazepam is a central-nervous-system depressant. Avoid alcohol, other tranquilizers, narcotics, barbiturates, monoamine oxidase (MAO) inhibitors, antihistamines, and medicine used to relieve depression. Taking Halazepam with these drugs may result in excessive depression, tiredness, sleepiness, difficulty breathing, or similar symptoms.

Smoking may reduce the effectiveness of Halazepam by increasing the rate at which it is broken down in the body.

The effects of Halazepam may be prolonged when it is taken together with Cimetidine.

Food Interactions

Halazepam is best taken on an empty stomach but may be taken with food if it upsets your stomach.

Usual Dose

The dose must be tailored to the individual needs of the patient.

Adult: 60 to 160 milligrams per day.

Senior and debilitated patient: require less of the drug to control anxiety and tension.

Child: This drug should not be used.

Overdosage

Symptoms are confusion, sleepiness, lack of response to pain such as a pin stick, shallow breathing, lowered blood pressure, and coma. The patient should be taken to a hospital emergency room. ALWAYS bring the medicine bottle.

Special Information

Halazepam can cause tiredness, drowsiness, inability to concentrate, or similar symptoms. Be careful if you are driving, operating machinery, or performing other activities that require concentration.

Tell your doctor if you become pregnant or are nursing an infant.

If you forget to take a dose of Halazepam and you remember within about an hour of your regular time, take it right away. If you do not remember until later, skip the forgotten dose and go back to your regular schedule. Do not take a double dose.

Generic Name
Haloperidol

Brand Name
Haldol

(Also available in generic form)

Type of Drug
Butyrophenone antipsychotic.

Prescribed for
Psychotic disorders, including Gilles de la Tourette's syndrome; short-term treatment of hyperactive children.

General Information
Haloperidol is one of many nonphenothiazine agents used in the treatment of psychosis. The drugs in this group are usually about equally effective when given in therapeutically equivalent doses. The major differences are in type and severity of side effects. Some patients may respond well to one and not at all to another; this variability is not easily explained and is thought to result from inborn biochemical differences.

Cautions and Warnings
Haloperidol should not be used by patients who are allergic to it. Patients with very low blood pressure, Parkinson's disease, or blood, liver, or kidney disease should avoid this drug.

Pregnancy/Breast-feeding

Avoid this drug if you are pregnant. Haloperidol has not been studied in pregnant women; however, serious problems have been seen in pregnant animals given large amounts of Haloperidol.

Nursing baby animals have also shown problems, such as tiredness and body movement problems. Haloperidol is not recommended during nursing.

Seniors

Older adults are more sensitive to the effects of this medication than younger adults and usually require a lower dosage to achieve a desired effect. Also, older adults are more likely to develop drug side effects. Some experts feel that seniors should be treated with one-half to one-quarter the usual adult dose.

Possible Side Effects

The most common side effect is drowsiness, especially during the first or second week of therapy. If the drowsiness becomes troublesome, contact your doctor.

Less commonly, Haloperidol can cause jaundice (yellowing of the whites of the eyes or skin), usually in 2 to 4 weeks. The jaundice usually goes away when the drug is discontinued, but there have been cases when it did not. If you notice this effect or if you develop fever and generally do not feel well, contact your doctor immediately. Other less common side effects are changes in components of the blood including anemias, raised or lowered blood pressure, abnormal heartbeat, heart attack, feeling faint or dizzy.

Butyrophenone drugs can produce extrapyramidal effects, such as spasms of the neck muscles, severe stiffness of the back muscles, rolling back of the eyes, convulsions, difficulty in swallowing, and symptoms associated with Parkinson's disease. These effects look very serious but disappear after the drug has been withdrawn; however, symptoms of the face, tongue, and jaw may persist for several years, especially in the older adults with a long history of brain disease. If you experience these extrapyramidal effects contact your doctor immediately.

Haloperidol may cause an unusual increase in psychotic

symptoms or may cause paranoid reactions, tiredness, lethargy, restlessness, hyperactivity, confusion at night, bizarre dreams, inability to sleep, depression, or euphoria. Other reactions are itching, swelling, unusual sensitivity to bright lights, red skin, and rash. There have been cases of breast enlargement, false positive pregnancy tests, changes in menstrual flow in females, and impotence and changes in sex drive in males.

Haloperidol may also cause dry mouth, stuffy nose, headache, nausea, vomiting, loss of appetite, change in body temperature, loss of facial color, excessive salivation, excessive perspiration, constipation, diarrhea, changes in urine and stool habits, worsening of glaucoma, blurred vision, weakening of eyelid muscles, and spasms of bronchial and other muscles, as well as increased appetite, fatigue, excessive thirst, and changes in the coloration of skin, particularly in exposed areas.

Drug Interactions

Haloperidol should be taken with caution in combination with barbiturates, sleeping pills, narcotics, or any other medication which produces a depressive effect. Avoid alcohol.

Haloperidol may increase the need for anticonvulsant medicine in patients who must take both drugs. It may interfere with oral anticoagulant drugs. Any dosage adjustment necessary can easily be made by your doctor.

Food Interactions

This medicine is best taken on an empty stomach, but you may take it with food if it upsets your stomach.

Usual Dose

Adult: 0.5 to 2 milligrams 2 to 3 times per day. Dose may be increased according to patient's need up to 100 milligrams per day.

Child: not recommended.

Overdosage

Symptoms are depression, extreme weakness, tiredness, desire to go to sleep, comas, lowered blood pressure, uncontrolled muscle spasms, agitation, restlessness, convulsions, fever, dry mouth, and abnormal heart rhythms. The patient should be taken to a hospital emergency room immediately. ALWAYS bring the medicine bottle.

Special Information

This medication may cause drowsiness. Use caution when driving or operating complex equipment and avoid alcoholic beverages while taking the medicine.

The drug may cause unusual sensitivity to the sun and can turn your urine reddish-brown to pink.

If dizziness occurs, avoid sudden changes in posture and avoid climbing stairs.

Use caution in hot weather. This medicine may make you more prone to heat stroke.

If you forget to take a dose of Haloperidol, take it as soon as you remember. Take the rest of the day's doses evenly spaced throughout the day. Do not take a double dose.

Generic Name

Hydralazine Hydrochloride

Brand Names

Alazine
Apresoline

(Also available in generic form)

Type of Drug

Antihypertensive.

Prescribed for

Aortic insufficiency; congestive heart failure; essential hypertension (high blood pressure); heart valve replacement.

General Information

Although the mechanism of action is not completely understood, it is felt that Hydralazine Hydrochloride lowers blood pressure by enlarging the blood vessels throughout the body. This also helps to improve heart functions and blood flow to the kidneys and brain.

Cautions and Warnings

Long-term administration of large doses of Hydralazine Hydrochloride may produce an arthritislike syndrome in some people, although symptoms of this problem usually disappear when the drug is discontinued. Fever, chest pain, not feeling well, or other unexplained symptoms should be reported to your doctor.

Pregnancy/Breast-feeding

This drug crosses into the blood circulation of a developing baby. It has not been found to cause human birth defects. Nevertheless, pregnant women, or those who might become pregnant while taking this drug, should not take it without their doctors' approval. When the drug is considered essential by your doctor, the potential risk of taking the medicine must be carefully weighed against the benefit it might produce.

This drug passes into breast milk, but has caused no problems among breast-fed infants. You must consider the potential effect on the nursing infant if breast-feeding while taking this medicine.

Seniors

Older adults are more sensitive to the blood-pressure-lowering effects of this drug and to the drug's side effects, especially low body temperature. Follow your doctor's directions and report any side effects at once.

Possible Side Effects

Common side effects include headache, loss of appetite, nausea, vomiting, diarrhea, rapid heartbeat, and chest pain.

Less common side effects are stuffy nose, flushing, tearing in the eyes, itching and redness of the eyes, numbness and tingling of the hands and feet, dizziness, tremors, muscle cramps, depression, disorientation, anxiety, itching, rash, fever, chills, (occasional) hepatitis, constipation, difficulty in urination, and adverse effects on the normal composition of the blood.

Drug Interactions

Hydralazine Hydrochloride should be used with caution by patients who are taking a monoamine oxidase (MAO) inhibitor.

Nonsteroidal anti-inflammatory drugs, especially Indomethacin, estrogens, and drugs with stimulant properties, will reduce the effects of Hydralazine.

The combination of Hydralazine with other blood-pressure-lowering drugs can produce very low blood pressure.

Do not self-medicate with over-the-counter cough, cold, or allergy remedies whose stimulant ingredients will increase blood pressure.

Food Interactions

Hydralazine Hydrochloride may antagonize Vitamin B_6 (pyridoxine), which can result in peripheral neuropathy, including tremors and tingling and numbness of the fingers, toes, or other extremities. If these occur, your doctor may consider pyridoxine supplementation.

Take Hydralazine Hydrochloride with food.

Usual Dose

As with other antihypertensive drugs, dosage is tailored to your needs.

Adult: Most people begin with 40 milligrams per day for the first few days, then increase to 100 milligrams per day for the rest of the first week. Dose increases until the maximum effect is seen.

Child: 0.34 milligrams per pound of body weight per day and up to 200 milligrams per day.

Overdosage

If symptoms of extreme lowering of blood pressure, rapid heartbeat, headache, generalized skin flushing, chest pains, and poor heart rhythms appear, contact your doctor immediately.

Special Information

Take this medicine exactly as prescribed.

If you forget to take a dose of Hydralazine Hydrochloride, take it as soon as you remember. If it is almost time for your next regularly scheduled dose, skip the one you forgot and continue with your regular schedule. Do not take a double dose.

Generic Name

Hydroxyzine

Brand Names

Anxanil   Hydroxyzine Pamoate
Atarax   Vistaril
Hydroxyzine Hydrochloride

(Also available in generic form)

Type of Drug

Antihistamine.

Prescribed for

Nausea and vomiting; the management of emotional stress such as anxiety, tension, agitation, or itching caused by allergies.

General Information

Hydroxyzine Hydrochloride may be of value in relieving temporary anxiety such as stress of dental or other minor surgical procedures, acute emotional problems, and the management of anxiety associated with stomach and digestive disorders, skin problems, and behavior difficulties in children. This drug has also been used in the treatment of alcoholism.

Cautions and Warnings

Hydroxyzine Hydrochloride should not be used if you know you are sensitive or allergic to this drug.

Pregnancy/Breast-feeding

Antihistamines have not been proven to be a cause of birth defects or other problems in pregnant women, although studies in animals have shown that Hydroxyzine may cause birth defects during the first months of pregnancy. Do not take any antihistamine without your doctor's knowledge.

Small amounts of antihistamine medicines pass into breast milk and may affect a nursing infant. Nursing mothers should avoid antihistamines or use alternative feeding methods while taking the medicine.

Seniors

Seniors are more sensitive to antihistamine side effects. Confusion, difficult or painful urination, dizziness, drowsiness, a faint feeling, nightmares or excitement, nervousness, restlessness, irritability, or dry mouth, nose, or throat are more likely to occur among older adults.

Possible Side Effects

The primary side effect of Hydroxyzine Hydrochloride is drowsiness, but this disappears in a few days or when the dose is reduced. At higher doses, you may experience dry mouth and occasional tremors or convulsions.

Drug Interactions

Hydroxyzine Hydrochloride has a depressive effect on the nervous system, producing drowsiness and sleepiness. It should not be used with alcohol, sedatives, tranquilizers, antihistamines, or other depressants.

Usual Dose

Adult: 25 to 100 milligrams 3 to 4 times per day.

Child (age 6 and over): 5 to 25 milligrams 3 to 4 times per day.

Child (under age 6): 5 to 10 milligrams 3 to 4 times per day.

Special Information

Be aware of the depressive effect of Hydroxyzine Hydrochloride: Be careful when driving or operating heavy or dangerous machinery.

If you forget to take a dose of Hydroxyzine Hydrochloride, take it as soon as you remember. If it is almost time for your next regularly scheduled dose, skip the one you forgot and continue with your regular schedule. Do not take a double dose.

Generic Name

Ibuprofen

Brand Names

Children's Advil	PediaProfen
Ibuprohm (400 mg)	Rufen
Ibu-Tab (400-800 mg)	Saleto-400/-600/-800
Motrin	

The following products are available without a prescription:

Aches-N-Pain	Midol 200
Advil	Motrin IB
Genpril	Nuprin
Haltran	Pamprin-IB
Ibuprin	Saleto-200
Ibuprohm (200 mg)	Trendar
Medipren	

(Also available in generic form)

Type of Drug

Nonsteroidal anti-inflammatory.

Prescribed for

Relief of pain and inflammation of joints and muscles, fever, arthritis, mild to moderate pain of menstrual cramps, dental surgery and extractions, and athletic injuries such as sprains and strains.

General Information

Ibuprofen is one of several nonsteroidal anti-inflammatory drugs (NSAIDs) used to reduce inflammation, relieve pain, or reduce fever. All NSAIDs share the same side effects and may be used by patients who cannot tolerate Aspirin because of its stomach-upsetting effect. Choice of one of these drugs over another depends on disease response, side effects seen in a particular patient, convenience of times to be taken, and cost. Different drugs or different doses of the same drug may be tried until the greatest effectiveness is seen with the fewest side effects.

A reduced-strength (200-milligram) Ibuprofen first became available without a prescription in 1984. These products (Advil, Nuprin, and others) are intended for the relief of mild to moderate pain and fever reduction, much the same way Aspirin is used. Ibuprofen is now far and away the most widely purchased over-the-counter drug in America.

Cautions and Warnings

Do not take Ibuprofen if you are allergic to this drug, Aspirin, or other NSAIDs. Ibuprofen may cause stomach ulcers. This drug should not be used by patients with severe kidney disease.

Pregnancy/Breast-feeding

This drug crosses into the blood circulation of a developing baby. It has not been found to cause birth defects. Pregnant women, or those who might become pregnant while taking this drug, should not take it without their doctor's approval. When the drug is considered essential by your doctor, the potential risk of taking the medicine must be carefully weighed against the benefit it might produce. Ibuprofen may also make labor longer.

This drug passes into breast milk, but has caused no problems among breast-fed infants. You must consider the potential effect on the nursing infant if breast-feeding while taking this medicine.

Seniors

Older adults are more sensitive to the stomach, kidney, and liver effects of this drug. Some doctors recommend that persons 70 and older take half the usual dose. Follow your doctor's directions and report any side effects at once.

Possible Side Effects

The most frequent side effects are stomach upset, dizziness, headache, drowsiness, and ringing in the ears.

Other side effects include heartburn, nausea, vomiting, bloating, gas in the stomach, stomach pain, diarrhea, constipation, dark stool, nervousness, insomnia, depression, confusion, tremor, loss of appetite, fatigue, itching, rash, double vision, abnormal heart rhythm, anemia or other changes in the composition of the blood, changes in liver function, loss of hair, tingling in the hands and feet, fever, breast enlargement, lowered blood sugar, effects on the kidneys. If symptoms appear, stop taking the medicine and see your doctor immediately.

Drug Interactions

Ibuprofen increases the action of Phenytoin, sulfa drugs, antidiabetics, and anticoagulants. If you are taking any of these medicines, be sure to discuss it with your doctor, who will probably change the dose of the other drug.

An adjustment in the dose of Ibuprofen may be needed if you take Phenobarbital.

Food Interactions

Take with meals to reduce stomach upset.

Usual Dose

800 to 1600 or even 3200 milligrams per day.

Overdosage

Symptoms may include drowsiness, dizziness, confusion, disorientation, lethargy, tingling in the hands or feet, numbness, nausea, vomiting, upset stomach, stomach pains, headache, ringing or buzzing in the ears, sweating and blurred vision. Take the victim to a hospital emergency room at once for treatment. ALWAYS bring the medicine bottle with you.

Special Information

Avoid Aspirin and alcoholic beverages while taking this medication.

You may become dizzy or drowsy while taking this medicine. Be careful while driving or operating complex equipment.

Call your doctor if you develop a skin rash, itching, swelling, visual disturbances, black stools, or a persistent headache while taking this medication.

If you forget to take a dose of Ibuprofen, take it as soon as you remember. If it is almost time for your next regularly scheduled dose, skip the one you forgot and continue with your regular schedule. Do not take a double dose.

Generic Name

Imipramine

Brand Names

Janimine
Tofranil
Tofranil-PM

(Also available in generic form)

Type of Drug

Antidepressant.

Prescribed for

Depression with or without symptoms of anxiety.

General Information

Imipramine and other members of this group are effective in treating symptoms of depression. They can elevate your mood, increase physical activity and mental alertness, and improve appetite and sleep patterns. These drugs are mild sedatives and therefore useful in treating mild forms of depression associated with anxiety. You should not expect instant results with this medicine: Benefits are usually seen after 1 to 4 weeks. If symptoms are not affected after 6 to 8 weeks, contact your doctor. Occasionally this drug and other members of the group of drugs have been used in treating nighttime bed-wetting in young children, but they do not

produce long-lasting relief, and therapy with one of them
for nighttime bed-wetting is of questionable value.

Cautions and Warnings

Do not take Imipramine if you are allergic or sensitive to this
or other members of this class of drug: Doxepin, Nortriptyline, Amitriptyline, Desipramine, and Protriptyline. The drugs
should not be used if you are recovering from a heart attack.
Imipramine may be taken with caution if you have a history
of epilepsy or other convulsive disorders, difficulty in urination, glaucoma, heart disease, or thyroid disease. Do not
stop taking this medicine without first discussing it with your
doctor, since stopping may cause you to become nauseated,
weak, and headachy.

Pregnancy/Breast-feeding

This drug, like some other antidepressants, crosses into
your developing baby's circulation and may cause birth defects if taken during the first 3 months of pregnancy. There
have been reports of newborn infants suffering from heart,
breathing, and urinary problems after their mothers had
taken an antidepressant of this type immediately before delivery. You should avoid taking this medication while
pregnant.

Antidepressants of this type are known to pass into breast
milk and may affect a breast-feeding infant, although this
has not been proven. Nursing mothers should consider alternative feeding methods if taking this medicine.

Seniors

Older adults are more sensitive to the effects of this drug
and often require a lower dose than a younger adult to do
the same job. Follow your doctor's directions and report any
side effects at once.

Possible Side Effects

Changes in blood pressure (both high and low), abnormal
heart rates, heart attack, confusion, especially in elderly patients, hallucinations, disorientation, delusions, anxiety, restlessness, excitement, numbness and tingling in the

extremities, lack of coordination, muscle spasms or tremors, seizures and/or convulsions, dry mouth, blurred vision, constipation, inability to urinate, rash, itching, sensitivity to bright light or sunlight, retention of fluids, fever, allergy, changes in composition of blood, nausea, vomiting, loss of appetite, stomach upset, diarrhea, enlargement of the breasts in males and females, increased or decreased sex drive, increased or decreased blood sugar.

Less common side effects are agitation, inability to sleep, nightmares, feeling of panic, peculiar taste in the mouth, stomach cramps, black coloration of the tongue, yellowing eyes and/or skin, changes in liver function, increased or decreased weight, perspiration, flushing, frequent urination, drowsiness, dizziness, weakness, headache, loss of hair, nausea, not feeling well.

Drug Interactions

Interaction with monoamine oxidase (MAO) inhibitors can cause high fevers, convulsions, and occasionally death. Don't take MAO inhibitors until at least 2 weeks after Imipramine has been discontinued.

Imipramine interacts with Guanethidine and Clonidine, drugs used to treat high blood pressure: If your doctor prescribes Imipramine and you are taking medicine for high blood pressure, be sure to discuss this with him.

Imipramine increases the effects of barbiturates, tranquilizers, other depressive drugs, and alcohol. Don't drink alcoholic beverages if you take this medicine.

Taking Imipramine and thyroid medicine will enhance the effects of the thyroid medicine. The combination can cause abnormal heart rhythms. The combination of Imipramine and Reserpine may cause overstimulation.

Large doses of Vitamin C (Ascorbic Acid), oral contraceptives, or smoking can reduce the effect of Imipramine. Drugs such as Bicarbonate of Soda, Acetazolamide, Quinidine, or Procainamide will increase the effect of Imipramine. Ritalin and phenothiazine drugs such as Thorazine and Compazine block the metabolism of Imipramine, causing it to stay in the body longer. This can cause possible overdose.

The combination of Imipramine with large doses of the sleeping pill Ethchlorvynol has caused patients to experience passing delirium.

Food Interactions

This drug is best taken on an empty stomach but you can take it with food if it upsets your stomach.

Usual Dose

Adult: initial dose, about 75 milligrams per day in divided doses; then increased or decreased as judged necessary by your doctor. The individualized dose may be less than 75 or up to 200 milligrams. Long-term patients being treated for depression may be given extended-acting medicine daily at bedtime or several times per day.

Adolescent and senior: initial dose, 30 or 40 milligrams per day. These patients require less of the drug because of increased sensitivity. Maintenance dose is usually less than 100 milligrams per day.

Child: dose for nighttime bed-wetting is 25 milligrams per day (age 6 and over), an hour before bedtime. If relief of bed-wetting does not occur within 1 week, the dose is increased to a daily 50 to 75 milligrams, depending on age; often in midafternoon and at bedtime. (A dose greater than 75 milligrams will increase side effects without increasing effectiveness.) The medication should be gradually tapered off; this may reduce the probability that the bed-wetting will return.

Overdosage

Symptoms are confusion, inability to concentrate, hallucinations, drowsiness, lowered body temperature, abnormal heart rate, heart failure, large pupils of the eyes, convulsions, severely lowered blood pressure, stupor, and coma (as well as agitation, stiffening of body muscles, vomiting, and high fever). The patient should be taken to a hospital emergency room immediately. ALWAYS bring the medicine bottle.

Special Information

Do not stop taking this medicine unless your doctor has specifically told you to do so. Abruptly stopping this medicine may cause nausea, headache, and a sickly feeling.

This medicine can cause drowsiness, dizziness, and blurred

vision. Be careful when driving or operating complicated machinery.

Avoid exposure to the sun or sun lamps for long periods of time.

Call your doctor if dry mouth, difficulty urinating, or excessive sedation develops.

If you take Imipramine several times a day and forget a dose, take it as soon as you remember. If it is almost time for your next regularly scheduled dose, skip the one you forgot and continue with your regular schedule. If you take it once a day at bedtime and forget, don't take it when you get up; go back to your regular schedule. Call your doctor if you skip 2 or more days of medication. Never take a double dose.

Brand Name

Inderide

Ingredients

Hydrochlorothiazide
Propranolol

(Also available in generic form)

Type of Drug

Antihypertensive.

Prescribed for

High blood pressure.

General Information

Inderide is a combination of 2 proven antihypertensive drugs. One of these works by directly affecting the dilation of the blood vessels; the other works by affecting the nerves which control the dilating of the blood vessels. The more dilated (open) these vessels are, the lower the blood pressure. This combination is good as long as both ingredients are present in the right amounts. If you need more or less of one ingredient than the other, you must take the ingredients as separate pills. Often, doctors are able to lower your blood pressure most effectively by manipulating the dose of one drug or the other. Inderide is also available in a long-acting combination known as Inderide LA.

Cautions and Warnings

Do not take this drug if you are allergic to either of the active ingredients or to sulfa drugs. If you have a history of heart failure, asthma, or upper respiratory disease, Inderide may aggravate the situation.

Pregnancy/Breast-feeding

This drug may cause birth defects or interfere with your baby's development. Check with your doctor before taking it if you are, or might be, pregnant.

If this drug is considered essential for a nursing mother, she should change the method of feeding her infant.

Seniors

Older adults are more sensitive to the effects of this drug. Follow your doctor's directions and report any side effects at once.

Possible Side Effects

Decrease in heart rate, aggravation of heart failure or some other heart diseases, tingling in the hands or feet, lightheadedness, depression, sleeplessness, weakness, tiredness, feelings of apathy, hallucinations, visual disturbances, disorientation, loss of short-term memory, nausea, vomiting, upset stomach, cramps, diarrhea, constipation, allergic reactions (including sore throat, rash, and fever). Inderide can also cause adverse effects on the blood.

Inderide can cause hypokalemia (lowering of body potassium). The signs of this include dryness of the mouth, weakness, thirst, lethargy, drowsiness, restlessness, muscle pains or cramps, muscle tiredness, low blood pressure, decreased frequency of urination. To treat this, potassium supplements are given as tablets, liquids, or powders.

Less common side effects include loss of appetite, dizziness, headache, increased sensitivity to the sun, dizziness when rising quickly from a sitting or lying position, muscle spasms, and loss of hearing (it comes back after the drug has been stopped).

Drug Interactions

Inderide may interact with Reserpine and similar drugs to cause very low blood pressure, slowed heart rate, and dizziness.

Inderide may cause a need for the alteration of your daily dose of oral antidiabetic drug.

Inderide should not be taken with Lithium drugs since there is an increased possibility of Lithium toxicity.

This drug may interact with digitalis drugs to cause abnormal heart rhythms. This effect results from potassium loss and may be prevented by taking extra potassium.

Avoid any over-the-counter drugs containing stimulants. If you are unsure of which ones to avoid, ask your pharmacist.

Food Interactions

You may increase your natural consumption of potassium by eating more bananas, citrus fruits, melons, or tomatoes.

Usual Dose

4 tablets of either strength per day. The dose of this drug must be tailored to your needs for maximum benefit.

Overdosage

In case of overdosage contact your doctor or poison control center immediately. The patient may have to be taken to a hospital emergency room for treatment. ALWAYS bring the medicine bottle with you.

Special Information

Do not stop taking this medicine unless your doctor tells you to.

If you develop rash, severe muscle pains, or difficulty in breathing, call your doctor.

If you forget to take a dose of Inderide, take it as soon as possible. However, if it is within 4 hours of your next dose (8 hours for Inderide LA), skip the forgotten dose and go back to your regular schedule. Do not take a double dose.

Generic Name

Indomethacin

Brand Name

Indocin
Indocin SR

(Also available in generic form)

Type of Drug

Nonsteroidal anti-inflammatory.

Prescribed for

Arthritis and other forms of inflammation of joints and muscles.

General Information

Indomethacin has pain-relieving, fever-lowering, and in-flammation-reducing effects, but we do not know exactly how these effects are produced. Part of these actions may be due to Indomethacin's prostaglandin-inhibitory effects. It also can produce serious side effects at high doses. For this reason, the drug should be taken with caution. It is not a simple analgesic, like Aspirin or Ibuprofen.

Cautions and Warnings

Use Indomethacin with extra caution if you have a history of ulcers, bleeding diseases, or allergic reaction to Aspirin. It should be avoided by children under age 14 and patients with nasal polyps. This drug is not a simple pain reliever; it should be used only under the strict supervision of your doctor.

Pregnancy/Breast-feeding

This drug crosses into the blood circulation of a developing baby and may cause birth defects, especially during the last 3 months of your pregnancy. Pregnant women, or those who might become pregnant while taking this drug, should not take it without their doctors' approval. When the drug is considered essential by your doctor, the potential risk of taking the medicine must be carefully weighed against the benefit it might produce.

This drug passes into breast milk and has caused problems in at least one breast-fed infant. You must consider the potential effect on the nursing infant if breast-feeding while taking this medicine.

Seniors

Older adults are more sensitive to the side effects of this drug, especially those affecting your stomach, liver, kidneys, and nervous system. Some doctors recommend persons 70 and older take half the usual dose. Follow your doctor's directions and report any side effects at once.

Possible Side Effects

Indomethacin may produce severe stomach upset or other reactions. It has caused ulcers in all portions of the gastrointestinal tract, including the esophagus, stomach, small intestine, and large intestine. For this reason any unusual stomach upset, nausea, vomiting, loss of appetite, gas, gaseous feeling, or feeling of being bloated must be reported immediately to your doctor.

Indomethacin may cause blurred vision: This is an important side effect and must be reported to your doctor immediately. If you develop a persistent headache while taking Indomethacin, report this to your doctor immediately and stop taking the drug.

Indomethacin may aggravate preexisting psychiatric disturbances, epilepsy, or Parkinson's disease. It may cause reduction in mental alertness and coordination which can affect you particularly while driving, operating a machine or appliance, or engaging in any activity requiring alertness and concentration.

On rare occasions Indomethacin can cause effects on the liver and anemia or other effects on components of the blood. People who are allergic to the drug can develop reactions, including a rapid fall in blood pressure, difficulty in breathing, itching, and rashes. It has also caused ringing in the ears, retention of fluids in the body, elevation of blood pressure, passing of blood in the urine, loss of hair (occasional), vaginal bleeding, and increased blood sugar.

Drug Interactions

Avoid alcohol, which will aggravate any problem with drowsiness or lack of alertness.

Probenecid (Benemid) increases the amount of Indomethacin in your blood by reducing its elimination from the body. This interaction will reduce the amount of Indomethacin required.

If you are taking an anticoagulant (blood-thinning) drug and start taking Indomethacin, you probably will experience no serious interaction, but your doctor should know that you are taking both drugs so he can monitor the anticoagulant during the first week or two of Indomethacin therapy, in case dosage adjustment may be required.

Indomethacin increases the effect of antidiabetes drugs, digitalis drugs, Sulfinpyrazone, Lithium, and Verapamil. Indomethacin may reduce the effects of some blood-pressure-lowering drugs.

Food Interactions

Since Indomethacin causes stomach upset in many patients and can be a source of ulcers, it should be taken with food or antacids. Adrenal corticosteroids, Aspirin, or other drugs may aggravate this problem. Space Indomethacin and such drugs at least 2 to 3 hours apart to minimize irritating effects on the stomach.

Usual Dose

50 to 150 milligrams per day, individualized to patient's needs.

Overdosage

Symptoms may include drowsiness, dizziness, confusion, disorientation, lethargy, tingling in the hands or feet, numbness, nausea, vomiting, upset stomach, stomach pains, headache, ringing or buzzing in the ears, sweating, and blurred vision. Take the victim to the hospital emergency room at once for treatment. ALWAYS bring the medicine bottle with you.

Special Information

Avoid Aspirin and alcoholic beverages while taking this medication.

You may become dizzy or drowsy while taking this medicine. Be careful while driving or operating complex equipment.

Call your doctor if you develop a skin rash, itching, swelling, visual disturbances, black stools, or a persistent headache while taking this medication.

The sustained-release capsules should not be crushed or chewed.

If you forget to take a dose of Indomethacin and you remember within about an hour of your regular time, take it right away. If you do not remember until later, skip the forgotten dose and go back to your regular schedule. Do not take a double dose.

Generic Name

Insulin

Brand Names

Insulin for Injection

Beef Regular Iletin II	Pork Regular Iletin II
Humulin BR	Regular Iletin
Humulin R	Regular Insulin
Novolin R	Regular Purified Pork Insulin
Novoline R PenFill	Velosulin

Insulin Zinc Suspension

Humulin L	Lente Insulin
Lente Iletin	Lente Purified Pork Insulin
Lente Iletin II	Novolin L

Insulin Zinc Suspension, Extended

Ultralente Iletin
Ultralente Insulin
Ultralente Purified Beef

Insulin Zinc Suspension, Prompt

Semilente Iletin
Semilente Insulin
Semilente Purified Pork

Isophane Insulin Suspension and Insulin Injection

Mixtard
Novolin 70/30

Isophane Insulin Suspension (NPH)

Beef NPH Iletin II	NPH Iletin
Humulin N	NPH Insulin
Insulatard NPH	NPH Purified Pork
Novolin N	Pork NPH Iletin II

Protamine Zinc Insulin Suspension

Protamine Zinc and Iletin (Beef and Pork)	Protamine Zinc and Iletin II (Pork)
Protamine Zinc and Iletin II (Beef)	

Type of Drug

Antidiabetic.

Prescribed for

Diabetes mellitus that cannot be controlled by dietary restriction. Insulin may also be used in a hospital to treat hyperkalemia (high blood-potassium levels).

General Information

Insulin is a complex hormone normally produced by the pancreas. Diabetes develops when we do not make enough Insulin or when the Insulin we do make is not effective in our bodies. At one time, most of the Insulin we used as a drug was obtained from animals. Today, most of the Insulin used is human Insulin manufactured by biosynthetic techniques, although people whose diabetes is well controlled using Insulin derived from an animal source should not be automatically switched to a human Insulin product.

Insulin derived from pork is closer in chemical structure to our own Insulin than that derived from beef. It causes fewer reactions. So-called human Insulin products differ in slight, but significant, ways from animal-derived Insulin. Human Insulin is the choice product for people with allergies to other Insulin products, all pregnant diabetic women, and people who need Insulin only occasionally. It is associated with fewer allergic reactions than the older Insulins manufactured from pork and/or beef sources. Human Insulins may also be produced by semi-synthetic processes. These semi-synthetic Insulins, however, start with an animal product and may contain some of the same impurities. Animal Insulin used for injection is the unmodified material derived from an animal source, usually beef or pork.

All Insulin starts to work quickly and lasts only 6 to 8 hours. People using only Insulin injection must take several injections per day. Pharmaceutical scientists have been able to add other structures onto the Insulin molecule to extend the time over which the drug works. Insulin Zinc Suspension, like Insulin for injection, is considered rapid-acting. It starts to work in 30 to 60 minutes and lasts 12 to 16 hours.

Intermediate-acting Insulin starts working 1 to 1½ hours after injection and continues to work for 24 hours. Isophane Insulin Suspension and Insulin Zinc Suspension are intermediate-acting forms of Insulin. Long-acting Insulin begins working 4 to 8 hours after injection, and its effect lasts for 36 hours or more. Protamine Zinc Insulin Suspension and Insulin Zinc Suspension (Extended) are long-acting types of Insulin.

Other factors have a definite influence on patients' response to Insulin: diet, amount of regular exercise, and other medicines being used.

Insulin products derived from natural sources contain a number of normal contaminants. In the 1970s, processes were developed to remove many of these contaminants. The first process resulted in single-peak Insulin, with only one high point of drug effect, making the action of the drug more predictable and therefore safer than unpurified Insulin. Today, all Insulin sold in the United States is single-peak, and most of that is identical to natural human Insulin. The second refinement resulted in purified Insulin. Several purified Insulin products are available. The advantage of purified Insulin over single-peak is that it produces fewer reactions at the injection site.

Cautions and Warnings

Patients taking Insulin *must* follow the diet that the doctor has prescribed. Be sure to take exactly the dose of Insulin that was prescribed. Too much Insulin will cause excessive lowering of the blood sugar and too little will not control the diabetes. Avoid alcoholic beverages.

Pregnancy/Breast-feeding

This drug has been found to be safe for use during pregnancy and breast-feeding. Pregnant women who must take Insulin injections should be using human Insulin. Remember to check with your doctor before taking any drug if you are pregnant. Pregnant diabetic women must exactly follow their doctors' directions for Insulin use because Insulin requirements normally go down during the first half of pregnancy and then are increased over normal requirements during the second half.

Seniors

Older adults may use Insulin without special restriction. Be sure to follow your doctor's directions for medication and diet.

Possible Side Effects

Allergic reactions.

Drug Interactions

Insulin dosage may be affected by any medication that tends to increase blood-sugar levels. These medications include Acetazolamide, corticosteroids, amphetamines, Baclofen, oral contraceptives, Danazol, Dextrothyroxine, thiazide-type diuretics, estrogens, Ethacrynic Acid, Furosemide, Molindone, Phenytoin, thyroid hormones, Triamterene.

Some medicines can lower blood sugar and may require a downward dosage of your Insulin. These medicines include Alcohol, anabolic steroids, androgenic hormones, Phenylbutazone, Sulfinpyrazone, Tetracycline, Disopyramide, Guanethidine, monoamine oxidase (MAO) inhibitor antidepressants, and Aspirin (in large doses). Oral antidiabetes drugs also lower blood sugar and should be taken together with Insulin only if you are under the direct care of a doctor.

Nonsteroidal anti-inflammatory drugs (NSAIDS) may also increase the blood-sugar-lowering effect of Insulin, but by a different mechanism.

Beta-blocking drugs can mask the symptoms of low blood sugar and thus increase the risk of taking Insulin.

Stopping smoking cigarettes, chewing Nicotine gum, or taking other smoking deterrents can also lower blood sugar by increasing the amount of Insulin that is absorbed after injection under the skin. A downward adjustment of your Insulin dose may be necessary if you stop smoking.

Insulin may affect blood-potassium levels and can therefore affect Digitalis drugs.

Food Interactions

Follow your doctor's directions for diet restrictions. Diet is a key element in controlling your disease.

Usual Dose

The dose and kind of Insulin must be individualized to the patient's need. Insulin is generally injected half an hour before meals; the longer-acting forms are taken half an hour before breakfast. Since Insulin can only be given by injection, patients must learn to give themselves their Insulin subcutaneously (under the skin) or have a family member or friend give them injections. Hospitalized patients may receive Insulin injection directly into a vein.

One manufacturer has developed a device to aid in injecting Insulin. The device looks like a pen and is easily used. Another type of injection convenience device is the Insulin infusion pump. The infusion pump automatically administers a predetermined amount of regular Insulin. Consult your doctor or pharmacist for complete details on either of these devices.

Special Information

You may develop low blood sugar if you take too much Insulin, work or exercise more strenuously than usual, skip a meal, take Insulin too long before a meal, or vomit before a meal. Signs of low blood sugar may be fatigue, headache, drowsiness, nausea, tremulous feeling, sweating, or nervousness. If you develop any of these signs while taking Insulin, your blood sugar may be too low. The usual treatment for low blood sugar is eating a candy bar or lump of sugar, which diabetics should carry with them at all times.

If the signs of low blood sugar do not clear up within 30 minutes, call your doctor. You may need further treatment.

If your Insulin is in suspension form, you must evenly distribute the suspended particles throughout the liquid before taking the dose out. Do this by rotating the vial and turning it over several times. Do not shake the vial too strenuously.

Insulin products are generally stable at room temperatures for about 2 years. They must be kept away from direct sunlight and extreme temperatures. Most manufacturers, however, still recommend that Insulin be stored in a refrigerator or a cool place whenever possible. Insulin should not be put in a freezer or exposed to very high temperatures; this can affect its stability. Partly used vials of Insulin should be thrown away after several weeks if not used. Do not use any Insulin that looks lumpy, grainy or that sticks to the bottle. Do not use regular Insulin that has become thick or cloudy; use it only if it is clear and colorless.

Some Insulin products can be mixed. Mix 2 or more different Insulins only if you have been so directed by your doctor. Your pharmacist may also mix your Insulins for you to assure accuracy. Insulin for injection may be mixed with Isophane Insulin Suspension and Protamine Zinc Insulin in any proportion. Insulin Zinc Suspension, Insulin Zinc Suspension (Prompt), and Insulin Zinc Suspension (Extended) may also be mixed in any proportions. Insulin for injection and Insulin Zinc Suspension must be mixed immediately before using. You should consistently use the same type and brand of Insulin syringes to prevent measuring errors and possible dosing errors.

If you forget a dose Insulin, take it as soon as you remember. If you don't remember until it is almost time for your next dose, or if you completely forget one or more doses, call your doctor for exact instructions as to what to do.

Generic Name

Iodinated Glycerol

Brand Names

Iophen
Organidin

(Also available in generic form)

Type of Drug

Expectorant.

Prescribed for

Iodinated Glycerol is prescribed to help remove excess mucus that accumulates during a cold or other respiratory infection.

General Information

Iodinated Glycerol works by stimulating the production of normal respiratory fluids. This makes thick, accumulated mucus thinner and easier to remove by coughing. Expectorants do not suppress your cough.

Many experts in the field of upper-respiratory medicine are skeptical about the effectiveness of this medication, especially for removing mucus that accumulates in serious respiratory conditions like bronchitis, bronchial asthma, emphysema, cystic fibrosis, and chronic sinusitis.

Cautions and Warnings

People who are sensitive or allergic to Iodine or Iodine-containing products may also react to Iodinated Glycerol.

People with a history of thyroid disease should use this medication with care.

Children with cystic fibrosis are more likely than other children to develop an enlarged thyroid gland after taking Iodinated Glycerol. They should not use this product.

Iodinated Glycerol may worsen an existing case of acne.

Pregnancy/Breast-feeding

Iodinated Glycerol should not be taken by women who are or might become pregnant. It can interfere with the development of the baby's thyroid gland, resulting in an enlarged and possibly underactive thyroid.

Nursing mothers should not take Iodinated Glycerol. It passes into breast milk and may cause a rash and an underactive thyroid gland in the nursing infant.

Seniors

Older adults may use this medicine without restriction.

Possible Side Effects

Common side effects are diarrhea, nausea, vomiting, and stomach pains.

Prolonged use of Iodinated Glycerol may cause skin rash that can, rarely, become severe or fatal.

Prolonged use of Iodinated Glycerol may result in an underactive thyroid. Symptoms of this are dry skin, swelling around the eyes, unusual sensitivity to the cold, tiredness or weakness, and weight gain. Other side effects of long term use are burning of the mouth and throat, severe headache, increased salivation, runny nose, sneezing and cold symptoms, irritation of the eyes or swelling of the eyelids, a metallic taste in the mouth, and soreness of the teeth and gums. Swelling of the neck may indicate thyroid enlargement.

Drug Interactions

The combination of Iodinated Glycerol with Lithium or an antithyroid medicine may reduce thyroid function. These combinations should be used with caution.

Food Interactions

Iodinated Glycerol should be taken with a full glass of water or other fluid to get the best effect from it.

Usual Dose

Adult: 60 milligrams 4 times a day.
Child: Up to 30 milligrams 4 times a day.
This drug should not be given to newborns.

Overdosage

There are no reports of problems with Iodinated Glycerol overdose. Call your local poison control center or hospital emergency room for more information.

Special Information

Call your doctor at the first sign of nausea or vomiting, drug allergy (fever, joint pains, skin rash, hives, or swelling of the face or lips), chills, headache, loss of appetite, sore throat, swelling of the neck, tiredness, weakness, sensitivity to the cold, or weight gain. Other side effects should be reported if they are particularly bothersome or persistent.

   Drink a full glass of water with each dose of Iodinated Glycerol to help thin mucus secretions.

   If you take Iodinated Glycerol 3 or more times a day and forget a dose, take it as soon as you remember. If it is almost time for your next dose, take one dose as soon as you re- member and another in 3 or 4 hours, then go back to your regular schedule. Do not take a double dose.

Generic Name

Isosorbide Dinitrate

Brand Names

Dilatrate-SR	Isotrate Timecelles
Iso-Bid	Sorbitrate
Isordil Sublingual/Tembids/	Sorbitrate SA
Titradose	

(Also available in generic form)

Type of Drug

Antianginal agent.

Prescribed for

Relief of heart or chest pain associated with angina pectoris. It is also used to control or prevent the recurrence of chest or heart pain and to reduce heart work in congestive heart failure and other similar conditions.

General Information

Isosorbide Dinitrate belongs to the class of drugs known as nitrates, which are used to treat pain associated with heart problems. The exact nature of their action is not fully understood. However, they are believed to relax muscles of veins and arteries.

Cautions and Warnings

If you know that you are allergic or sensitive to this drug or other drugs for heart pain such as Nitroglycerin, do not use Isosorbide Dinitrate. Anyone who has a head injury or has recently had a head injury should use this drug with caution. Other conditions where the use of Isosorbide should be carefully weighed are severe anemia, glaucoma, severe liver disease, overactive thyroid, cardiomyopathy (disease of the heart muscle), low blood pressure, recent heart attack, severe kidney problems, and overactive gastrointestinal tract.

Pregnancy/Breast-feeding

This drug crosses into the blood circulation of a developing baby. It has not been found to cause birth defects. Pregnant women, or those who might become pregnant while taking this drug, should not take it without their doctors' approval. When the drug is considered essential by your doctor, the potential risk of taking the medicine must be carefully weighed against the benefit it might produce.

This drug passes into breast milk, but has caused no problems among bread-fed infants. You must consider the potential effect on the nursing infant if breast-feeding while taking this medicine.

Seniors

Older adults may take this medicine without restriction. Be sure to follow your doctor's directions for use.

Possible Side Effects

Flushing of the skin and headache are common, but should disappear after your body has had an opportunity to get used to the drug. You may experience dizziness and weakness in the process.

There is a possibility of blurred vision and dry mouth; if this happens stop taking the drug and call your physician.

Less common side effects include nausea, vomiting, weakness, sweating, rash with itching, redness, possible peeling. If these signs appear, discontinue the medication and consult your physician.

Drug Interactions

If you take Isosorbide Dinitrate, do not self-medicate with over-the-counter cough and cold remedies, since many of them contain ingredients which may aggravate heart disease.

Interaction with large amounts of whiskey, wine, or beer can cause rapid lowering of blood pressure, resulting in weakness, dizziness, and fainting.

Food Interactions

Take Isosorbide Dinitrate on an empty stomach unless you get a headache which cannot be controlled by the usual means. If this occurs, the medication can be taken with meals.

Usual Dose

Average daily dose, 10 to 20 milligrams 4 times per day. The drug may be given in doses from 5 milligrams to 40 milligrams 4 times per day.

Sustained-release: 40 to 80 milligrams every 8 to 12 hours.

Overdose

Isosorbide overdose can result in low blood pressure, very rapid heart beat flushing, perspiration (later on, your skin can become cold, bluish, and clammy), headache, heart palpitations, blurring and other visual disturbances, dizziness, nausea, vomiting, difficult, slow breathing, slow pulse, confusion, moderate and paralysis. Overdose victims should be taken to a hospital emergency room at once for treatment. ALWAYS remember to bring the medicine bottle with you.

Special Information

If you take this drug sublingually (under the tongue), be sure
the tablet is fully dissolved before you swallow the drug. Do
not crush or chew the sustained-release capsules or tablets.

Call your doctor if you develop a headache, dizziness, facial flushing, blurred vision, or dry mouth.

If you take regular Isosorbide and forget to take a dose,
take it as soon as you remember, unless it is within 2 hours
of your next scheduled dose. If that happens, skip the dose
you forgot and continue with your regular schedule.

If you take long-acting Isosorbide and forget to take a
dose, take it as soon as you remember, unless it is within 6
hours of your next scheduled dose. If that happens, skip the
dose you forgot and continue with your regular schedule.
Do not take a double dose.

Generic Name

Isotretinoin

Brand Name

Accutane

Type of Drug

Antiacne.

Prescribed for

Severe cystic acne that has not responded to other treatment,
including medicines applied to the skin and antibiotics.

Isotretinoin has been used experimentally to treat a variety of other skin disorders involving the process of keratinization, or hardening of skin cells, and a condition known as
mycosis fungoides that begins in the skin and can progress
to a form of leukemia. Isotretinoin treatment is usually successful for these conditions, but relatively high doses are
usually needed.

General Information

Isotretinoin was one of the first specialized products of vitamin research to be released for prescription by doctors. Researchers have long known that several vitamins, including A and D, have special properties that make them attractive treatments for specific conditions. However, the vitamins themselves are not appropriate treatments for these conditions because of the side effects that would develop if you took the quantities needed to produce the desired effects.

It is not known exactly how Isotretinoin works in cases of severe cystic acne. But its effect is to reduce the amount of sebum (the oily substance that serves as the skin's natural lubricant) in the skin, shrink the skin glands that produce sebum, and inhibit the process of keratinization, in which skin cells become hardened and block the flow of sebum onto the skin. Keratinization is key to the problem of severe acne because it leads to the buildup of sebum within skin follicles and causes the formation of closed comedones (whiteheads). Sebum production may be permanently reduced after Isotretinoin treatment, but no one knows why it has this effect.

Cautions and Warnings

People allergic or sensitive to Vitamin A, any Vitamin A product, or to Paraben preservatives used in Accutane should not use Isotretinoin.

Isotretinoin has been associated with several cases of increased fluid pressure inside the head. The symptoms of this condition, known as pseudotumor cerebri, are severe headaches, nausea, vomiting, and visual disturbances. Isotretinoin may cause temporary opaque spots on the cornea of your eye, causing visual disturbances. These generally go away by themselves within 2 months after the drug has been stopped. Several cases of severe bowel inflammation, indicated by abdominal discomfort and pain, severe diarrhea, or bleeding from the rectum, have developed in people taking Isotretinoin.

Pregnancy/Breast-feeding

This product should never be used by women who are pregnant or who might become pregnant while using it because it is known to cause harm to the developing baby when taken during pregnancy. Specifically, Isotretinoin can cause abnormalities of the head, brain, eye, ear, and hearing mechanisms. Several cases of spontaneous abortion have been linked to Isotretinoin.

Before taking this drug, women of childbearing age or potential should take a simple urinary pregnancy test to confirm that they are not pregnant. Also, you must be absolutely certain that effective birth control is used for 1 month before, during, and 1 month after Isotretinoin treatment. Accidental pregnancy during Isotretinoin therapy should be considered possible grounds for a therapeutic abortion. Discuss this with your doctor immediately.

Nursing mothers should not take Isotretinoin because of the possibility that it will affect the nursing infant. It is not known if Isotretinoin passes into breast milk.

Seniors

Older adults may take this medication without special restriction. Follow your doctor's directions and report any side effects at once.

Possible Side Effects

The frequency of side effects increases with your daily dose, the most severe effects occurring at daily doses above 0.45 milligrams per pound of body weight per day. The most common side effects are dry, chapped, and inflamed lips, dry mouth, dry nose, nosebleeds, eye irritation and conjunctivitis (red-eye), dry and flaky skin, rash, itching, peeling of skin from the face, palms of the hands, and soles of the feet, unusual sensitivity to sunlight, temporary skin discoloration, dry mucous membranes of the mouth and nose, brittle nails, inflammation of the nailbed or bone under the nail of either the hands or feet, temporary thinning of the hair, nausea, vomiting, and abdominal pains, tiredness, lethargy, sleeplessness, headache, tingling in the hands or feet, dizziness, protein, blood, and white blood cells in the urine, blurred vision, urinary difficulty, bone and joint aches and pains, muscle pains, and stiffness.

Isotretinoin causes extreme elevations of blood triglycerides and milder elevations of other blood fats, including cholesterol. It also can cause an increased blood-sugar and uric-acid level and an increase in liver-function-test values.

Less common side effects are crusting over wounds caused by an exaggerated healing response stimulated by the drug, hair problems (other than thinning), loss of appetite, upset stomach or intestinal discomfort, severe bowel inflammation, stomach or intestinal bleeding, weight loss, visual disturbances, pseudotumor cerebri (see "Cautions and Warnings" for symptoms), mild bleeding or easy bruising, fluid retention, infections of the lungs or respiratory system. Several people taking Isotretinoin have developed widespread herpes simplex infections.

Drug Interactions

Supplemental Vitamin A increases Isotretinoin side effects and must be avoided while you are taking this medicine.

Alcohol should be avoided while you are taking Isotretinoin since the combination can cause severe elevations of blood triglyceride levels.

People taking Isotretinoin who have developed pseudotumor cerebri have usually been taking a Tetracycline antibiotic. Although the link has not been definitely established, you should avoid Tetracycline antibiotics while taking this medicine.

Food Interactions

Isotretinoin should be taken with food or meals.

Avoid eating beef liver, calf's liver, or chicken liver while taking Isotretinoin. Liver contains extremely large amounts of Vitamin A. Foods with moderate amounts of Vitamin A that you need not avoid but should limit your intake of are apricots, broccoli, cantaloupe, carrots, endive, persimmon, pumpkin, spinach, and winter squash.

Usual Dose

0.22 to 0.9 milligrams per pound of body weight per day, in 2 divided doses for 15 to 20 weeks. Lower doses may be effective, but relapses are more common. Since Isotretinoin, like Vitamin A, dissolves in body fat, people weighing more than 155 pounds may need doses at the high end of the usual range.

If the total cyst count drops by 70 percent before 15 to 20 weeks, the drug may be stopped. Treatment should stop for

2 months after the 15-to-20 week treatment. A second course
of treatment may be given if the acne doesn't clear up.

Overdosage

Isotretinoin overdose is likely to cause nausea, vomiting,
lethargy, and other frequent side effects. Patients taking an
overdose of this drug must be made to vomit with Syrup of
Ipecac (available at any pharmacy) to remove any remaining
drug from the stomach. Call your doctor or a poison control
center before doing this. If you must go to a hospital emergency room, ALWAYS bring the medicine bottle.

Special Information

You may become unusually sensitive to sunlight while taking this drug. Use a sunscreen and wear protective clothing
until your doctor can determine if you are likely to develop
this effect.

Be sure your doctor knows if you are pregnant or plan to
become pregnant while taking Isotretinoin, if you are breast-
feeding, if you are a diabetic, if you are taking a Vitamin A
supplement (as a multivitamin or Vitamin A alone), or if you
or any family member has a history of high blood triglyceride levels.

Call your doctor if any severe side effects develop. Abdominal pain, bleeding from the rectum, severe diarrhea,
headache, nausea and vomiting, visual difficulty of any kind,
severe muscle or bone and joint aches or pains, and unusual
sensitivity to sunlight or to ultraviolet light are especially
important.

Sometimes, acne actually gets a little worse when Isotretinoin treatment begins, but subsequently it starts to improve.
Don't be alarmed if this happens, but be sure to tell your
doctor, who will want to know.

Do not donate blood during Isotretinoin treatment or for
up to 30 days after you have stopped because of risk to a
developing fetus of a pregnant woman who might receive
the blood.

If you forget to take a dose of Isotretinoin, take it as soon
as you remember. If it is almost time for your next regularly
scheduled dose, skip the one you forgot and continue with
your regular schedule. Do not take a double dose.

Generic Name

Isradipine

Brand Name

DynaCirc

Type of Drug

Calcium channel blocker.

Prescribed for

High blood pressure. It has also been prescribed to treat chronic stable angina pectoris.

General Information

Isradipine is one of a growing number of calcium channel blockers to be marketed in the United States. It works by blocking the passage of calcium into smooth muscle. Since calcium is an essential factor in muscle contraction, any drug that affects calcium in this way will interfere with the contraction of these muscles. When this happens, several things can result. Blood vessels will dilate (widen) because the muscles that normally keep them narrowed are not contracting, and the amount of oxygen used by heart muscle may also be reduced. Therefore, Isradipine dilates (opens) the arteries that carry blood and prevents spasm of these arteries. Isradipine is also used in the treatment of angina, a type of heart pain related to poor oxygen supply to the heart muscles. Isradipine affects the movement of calcium only into muscle cells. It does not have any affect on calcium in the blood.

Cautions and Warnings

Do not take this drug if you have had an allergic reaction to it. Use Isradipine with caution if you have heart failure, since the drug can worsen the condition. Abruptly stopping this medication can cause increased chest pain. If you must stop, the drug dose should be gradually reduced.

Pregnancy/Breast-feeding

This drug was found to affect the development of animal fetuses in laboratory studies. It has not been found to cause human birth defects. Pregnant women, or those who might become pregnant while taking this drug, should not take Isradipine without their doctors' approval. When the drug is considered essential by your doctor, the potential risk of taking the medicine must be carefully weighed against the benefit it might produce.

It is not known if Isradipine passes into breast milk. It has caused no problems among breast-fed infants. Women who must take Isradipine should consider the potential effect on their infants before breast-feeding while taking this medicine.

Seniors

Older adults may take Isradipine without special precautions. Follow your doctor's directions and report any side effects at once.

Possible Side Effects

Common side effects include light-headedness, flushing, heart palpitations, swelling of the arms or legs, a feeling of warmth, and headache.

Less common side effects are low blood pressure, dizziness, fainting, heart failure, heart attack, angina pains, rapid heartbeat, abnormal heart rhythms, stroke, numbness, drowsiness, nervousness, depression, paranoia, memory loss, hallucinations, psychoses, visual disturbances, fatigue, sleeplessness, tingling in the hands or feet, nausea, constipation, diarrhea, stomach upset and cramps, vomiting, dry mouth, itching, rash, flushing, changes in certain blood-cell components, frequent urination (especially at night), sweating, reduced sex drive or poor sexual performance, leg and foot cramps, muscle cramps and inflammation, joint pains, sore throat, and cough. Isradipine can cause increases in certain blood enzyme tests.

Drug Interactions

Isradipine may interact with beta-blocking drugs to cause heart failure, very low blood pressure, or an increased incidence of angina pain. However, in many cases these drugs have been taken together with no problem.

Isradipine may, in rare instances, increase the effects of anticoagulant (blood-thinning) drugs.

Additional drug interactions occur with other members of this class but have not been seen with Isradipine.

Food Interactions

Taking Isradipine with food has a minor effect on the absorption of the drug. You may take it with food if it upsets your stomach.

Usual Dose

5 to 20 milligrams per day in 2 doses.

Do not stop taking the drug abruptly. The dosage should be gradually reduced over a period of time.

Overdosage

Overdose of Isradipine can cause nausea, dizziness, weakness, drowsiness, confusion and slurred speech, very low blood pressure, reduced heart efficiency, and unusual heart rhythms. Victims of an Isradipine overdose should be taken to a hospital emergency room for treatment. ALWAYS bring the medicine bottle.

Special Information

Call your doctor if you develop swelling in the arms or legs, difficulty breathing, abnormal heartbeat, increased heart pains, dizziness, constipation, nausea, light-headedness, or very low blood pressure.

If you forget to take a dose of Isradipine, take it as soon as you remember. If it is almost time for your next regularly scheduled dose, skip the forgotten dose and continue with your regular schedule. Do not take a double dose.

Generic Name

Ketoconazole

Brand Names

Nizoral Cream/Tablets

Type of Drug

Antifungal.

Prescribed for

Thrush and other systemic fungus infections, including candidiasis, histoplasmosis, and blastomycosis. Ketoconazole may also be prescribed for fungus infections of the skin, fingernails, and vagina.

General Information

This medicine is effective against a wide variety of fungus organisms. It works by disrupting the fungus cell's membrane, ultimately destroying the cell.

Cautions and Warnings

Ketoconazole has been associated with liver inflammation and damage. At least 1 of every 10,000 people who take the drug will develop this condition. In most cases, the inflammation subsides when the drug is discontinued. Do not take Ketoconazole if you have had an allergic reaction to it. It should not be used to treat fungus infections of the nervous system because only small amounts of the drug will enter that part of the body.

Pregnancy/Breast-feeding

Animals given doses of Ketoconazole larger than the maximum human dose have shown some damage in their developing offspring. This drug should be avoided by pregnant women or women who may become pregnant while using it. In those situations where it is deemed essential, the potential risk of the drug must be carefully weighed against any benefit it might produce.

Nursing mothers who must take Ketoconazole should find an alternative method of feeding their infants because the drug passes into breast milk.

Seniors

Older adults may take this medication without special restriction. Follow your doctor's directions and report any side effects at once.

Possible Side Effects

Nausea, vomiting, upset stomach, abdominal pain or discomfort, itching, swelling of male breasts. Most of these side effects are mild, and only a small number of people (1.5 percent) have to stop taking the drug because of severe side effects.

Less common side effects include headache, dizziness, drowsiness or tiredness, fever, chills, unusual sensitivity to bright lights, diarrhea, reduced sperm count, male impotence, and reduced levels of blood platelets.

Drug Interactions

Antacids, histamine H_2 antagonists, and other drugs that reduce the amount of acid in the stomach will counteract the effects of Ketoconazole by preventing it from being absorbed. This drug requires an acid environment to pass into the blood.

When Ketoconazole is taken together with Rifampin, both drugs lose their effectiveness.

The combination of Isoniazid and Ketoconazole causes a neutralization of the Ketoconazole's effect. These interactions occur even when drug doses are separated by 12 hours.

Ketoconazole increases the amount of Cyclosporine in your blood and the chances for kidney damage caused by Cyclosporine. It also increases the effect of oral anticoagulant drugs.

Taking Ketoconazole and Phenytoin can affect the amount of either medicine in your blood, increasing or decreasing either drug's effect.

Food Interactions

Ketoconazole should be taken with food or meals to increase the amount absorbed into the blood. This happens because food stimulates acid release, and Ketoconazole is absorbed much more efficiently when there is acid in the stomach.

Usual Dose

Tablets:
Adult: 200 to 400 milligrams taken once per day. Dosage

may continue for several months, depending on the type of infection being treated.

Child (age 2 and up): 1.5 to 3 milligrams per pound of body weight once per day.

Child (under age 2): This drug should not be used.

Cream: Apply to affected and immediate surrounding areas 1 or 2 times a day for 14 days.

Overdosage

The most likely effects of Ketoconazole overdose are liver damage and exaggerated versions of the drug's side effects. Victims of Ketoconazole overdose should be immediately given Bicarbonate of Soda or any other antacid to reduce the amount of drug absorbed into the blood. Call your local poison control center for more information. If you take the victim to a hospital emergency room for treatment, ALWAYS bring the prescription bottle.

Special Information

If you must take antacids or other ulcer treatments, separate doses of those medicines from Ketoconazole doses by at least 2 hours. Anything that reduces your stomach-acid levels will reduce the amount of Ketoconazole absorbed into the blood.

This drug can cause headaches, dizziness, and drowsiness. Use caution while doing anything that requires intense concentration, like driving a car, or operating machinery.

Call your doctor if you develop pains in the stomach or abdomen, severe diarrhea, a high fever, unusual tiredness, loss of appetite, nausea, vomiting, yellow discoloration of the skin or whites of the eyes, pale stools, or dark urine.

If you forget to take a dose of Ketoconazole, take it as soon as you remember. If it is almost time for your next regularly scheduled dose, space the missed dose and the next dose 10 to 12 hours apart. Then go back to your regular schedule.

Generic Name

Ketoprofen

Brand Name
Orudis

Type of Drug
Nonsteroidal anti-inflammatory.

Prescribed for
Rheumatoid and osteoarthritis; pain associated with amenorrhea.

General Information
Ketoprofen is one of many nonsteroidal anti-inflammatory drugs (NSAIDs) sold in the United States to reduce inflammation, relieve pain and fever, and relieve menstrual cramps and discomfort. The choice of one member of this group over another often depends on your individual response to a specific drug. Because of this, it is common to try several of these drugs before you find the one that is right for you. Ketoprofen starts working in about a half hour and will last for about 3 hours.

Cautions and Warnings
Do not take this product if you are allergic to Aspirin or to any other NSAID. This drug can worsen stomach ulcers or cause a new ulcer to develop. It should be used with caution if you have kidney disease.

Pregnancy/Breast-feeding
This drug crosses into the blood circulation of a developing baby. It has not been found to cause birth defects. Pregnant women, or those who might become pregnant while taking this drug, should not take it without their doctors' approval. When the drug is considered essential by your doctor, the potential risk of taking the medicine must be carefully weighed against the benefit it might produce.

This drug passes into breast milk, but has caused no problems among breast-fed infants. You must consider the potential effect on the nursing infant if breast-feeding while taking this medicine.

Seniors

Older adults are more sensitive to the stomach, kidney, and liver effects of this drug. Some doctors recommend that persons 70 years of age and older take half the usual dose. Follow your doctor's directions and report any side effects at once.

Possible Side Effects

The most frequent side effects are upset stomach, dizziness, headache, drowsiness, and ringing in the ears.

Other side effects include heartburn, nausea, vomiting, bloating, stomach gas or pain, diarrhea, constipation, dark stools, nervousness, sleeplessness, depression, confusion, tremor, loss of appetite, fatigue, itching, rash, double or blurred vision, dry or irritated eyes, heart failure, palpitations, abnormal heart rhythms, anemia or other changes in the composition of your blood, changes in liver function, hair loss, tingling in the hands or feet, fever, enlarged breasts, blood in the urine, urinary irritation, thirst, frequent urination, kidney damage, low blood sugar, asthma, difficulty breathing, skin rash, itching, swelling, black-and-blue marks.

Drug Interactions

Aspirin causes this drug to be eliminated from the body more rapidly than normal.

Do not take this drug together with Methotrexate, used to treat cancers. One person died from the combination.

Ketoprofen may increase the effectiveness of anticoagulant (blood-thinning) drugs. It can increase blood-clotting time by 3 to 4 minutes.

Taking this drug together with a thiazide diuretic increases the chances for kidney failure.

Ketoprofen may increase the effects of sulfa drugs, antidiabetes drugs, and Phenytoin or other drugs for seizure disorders.

Food Interactions

You may take this drug with food if it upset your stomach.

Usual Dose

50 to 75 milligrams 3 or 4 times a day. No more than 300 milligrams per day.

Senior and patient with kidney problems: start with one-half to one-third the usual dose.

Overdosage

Symptoms may include drowsiness, dizziness, confusion, disorientation, lethargy, tingling in the hands or feet, numbness, nausea, vomiting, upset stomach, stomach pains, headache, ringing or buzzing in the ears, sweating, and blurred vision. Take the victim to a hospital emergency room at once for treatment. ALWAYS bring the medicine bottle with you.

Special Information

Avoid Aspirin and alcoholic beverages while taking this medication.

You may become dizzy or drowsy while taking this medicine. Be careful while driving or operating complex equipment.

Call your doctor if you develop a skin rash, itching, swelling, visual disturbances, black stools, or a persistent headache while taking this medication.

If you forget to take a dose of Ketoprofen, take it as soon as you remember. If it is almost time for your next regularly scheduled dose, skip the one you forgot and continue with your regular schedule. Do not take a double dose.

Generic Name

Labetalol Hydrochloride

Brand Names

Normodyne
Trandate

Type of Drug

Alpha-beta-adrenergic blocking agent.

Prescribed for

High blood pressure.

General Information

This drug, first studied for its effect as a beta blocker, is a unique approach to high-blood-pressure treatment because it selectively blocks both alpha and beta adrenergic impulses. This combination of actions contributes to its ability to reduce your blood pressure. It may be better than other beta-blocking drugs because it rarely affects heart rate. Other drugs can increase or decrease heart rate.

Cautions and Warnings

People with asthma, severe heart failure, reduced heart rate, and heart block should not take Labetalol Hydrochloride.

People with angina who take Labetalol Hydrochloride for high blood pressure should have their dose reduced gradually over a 1-to-2-week period, instead of having it discontinued suddenly, to avoid possible aggravation of the angina.

Labetalol Hydrochloride should be used with caution if you have liver disease because your ability to eliminate the drug from your body may be impaired.

Pregnancy/Breast-feeding

This drug crosses into the blood circulation of a developing baby. It has not been found to cause birth defects. Pregnant women, or those who might become pregnant while taking this drug, should not take it without their doctor's approval. When the drug is considered essential by your doctor, the potential risk of taking the medicine must be carefully weighed against the benefit it might produce.

This drug passes into breast milk, but has caused no problems among breast-fed infants. You must consider the potential effect on the nursing infant if breast-feeding while taking this medicine.

Seniors

Senior citizens may be more or less sensitive to the effects of this medicine. Your dosage of this drug must be adjusted to your individual needs by your doctor. Seniors may be more likely to suffer from cold hands and feet and reduced body temperature, chest pains, a general feeling of ill health, sudden difficulty breathing, sweating, or changes in heartbeat because of this medicine.

Possible Side Effects

Most Labetalol Hydrochloride side effects develop early in the course of treatment and increase with larger doses. Side effects include dizziness, tingling of the scalp, nausea, vomiting, upset stomach, taste distortion, fatigue, sweating, male impotence, urinary difficulty, diarrhea, bile-duct blockage, bronchial spasm, breathing difficulty, muscle weakness, cramps, dry eyes, blurred vision, rash, swelling of the face, and loss of hair.

Less frequent adverse effects of Labetalol Hydrochloride include aggravation of lupus erythematosus, a disease of body connective tissue, and stuffy nose. Because this drug is a beta blocker, it has the potential to cause mental depression, confusion and disorientation, loss of short-term memory, emotional instability, colitis, drug allergy (fever, sore throat, breathing difficulty), and reduction in the levels of white blood cells and blood platelets.

Drug Interactions

Labetalol Hydrochloride may prevent normal signs of low blood sugar from appearing and can also interfere with the action of oral antidiabetes drugs.

The combination of Labetalol Hydrochloride and a tricyclic antidepressant drug can cause tremor.

This drug may interfere with the effectiveness of some antiasthma drugs, especially Ephedrine, Isoproterenol, and other beta stimulants.

Cimetidine increases the amount of Labetalol Hydrochloride absorbed into the bloodstream from oral tablets.

Labetalol Hydrochloride may increase the blood-pressure-lowering effect of Nitroglycerin.

Food Interactions

This medicine may be taken with food if it upsets your stomach because it is unaffected by food in the stomach. In fact, food increases the amount of Labetalol Hydrochloride absorbed into your blood.

Usual Dose

The usual starting dose is 100 milligrams taken twice per day. The dosage may be increased gradually to as much as 1200 milligrams twice per day, but the usual maintenance dose is in the range of 200 to 400 milligrams twice daily.

Overdosage

Labetalol Hydrochloride overdose slows your heart rate and causes an excessive drop in blood pressure. The possible consequences of these effects can be treated only in a hospital emergency room. ALWAYS bring the medicine bottle with you.

Special Information

This medication is meant to be taken on a continuing basis. Do not stop it unless instructed to do so by your doctor. Weakness, breathing difficulty, or other side effects should be reported to your doctor as soon as possible. Most side effects are not serious, but a small number of people (about 7 in 100) have to switch to another medicine because of drug side effects.

If you forget to take a dose of Labetalol Hydrochloride, take it as soon as possible. However, if it is within 8 hours of your next dose, skip the forgotten dose and go back to your regular schedule. Do not take a double dose.

Generic Name

Levobunolol

Brand Name

Betagan Liquifilm

Type of Drug

Beta-adrenergic blocking agent.

Prescribed for

Open-angle glaucoma (increased fluid pressure inside the eye).

General Information

When applied to the eye, Levobunolol eyedrops work in the same way as the other beta-blocker eyedrops, Timolol and Betaxolol. It reduces fluid pressure inside the eye by reducing the production of eye fluids and slightly increasing the rate at which fluids flow through and leave the eye. Beta-blocking eyedrops produce a greater drop in eye pressure than either Pilocarpine or Epinephrine but may be combined with these or other drugs to produce a more pronounced drop in eye pressure.

Cautions and Warnings

Levobunolol should not be used if you have asthma or other severe lung disease, heart failure, heart block, or a very slow heart rate. Your doctor should give careful consideration to the use of Levobunolol if you have diabetes or overactive thyroid because Levobunolol may mask important signs of low blood sugar or overactive thyroid. Emphysema and other chronic (lung) diseases should be considered as a reason to avoid this drug because it can, if absorbed into your blood, cause spasm of the bronchial muscles and may counteract the effect of drugs used to treat these diseases.

Pregnancy/Breast-feeding

This drug may cross into the blood circulation of a developing baby. It has not been found to cause birth defects. Pregnant women, or those who might become pregnant while using these eyedrops, should not take them without their doctors' approval. When the drug is considered essential by your doctor, the potential risk of taking the medicine must be carefully weighed against the benefit it might produce.

It is not known if Levobunolol passes into breast milk. Levobunolol has caused no problems among breast-fed infants. You must consider the potential effect on the nursing infant if breast-feeding while taking this medicine.

Seniors

Senior citizens may be more or less sensitive to the effects of this medication. Your dosage of Levobunolol must be adjusted to your individual need by your doctor. Seniors are more likely to suffer from drug side effects.

Possible Side Effects

The more common side effects of Levobunolol include tearing, stinging of the eye, and redness or inflammation of the eye.

Less common side effects include headache, dizziness, poor muscle control, lethargy and, rarely, a skin rash. If Levobunolol is absorbed into your bloodstream, it can cause the same side effects as Timolol eyedrops.

Drug Interactions

Levobunolol should be used with caution if you are taking another beta-blocking drug by mouth. If Levobunolol is absorbed into your bloodstream it can increase the effects of that oral drug on your body and also increase the chance for drug side effects.

If Levobunolol is absorbed into the blood, it can mask the effects of antidiabetes medicine and can enhance the effects of Reserpine, producing very low blood pressure, dizziness, and possible fainting.

Usual Dose

One drop in the affected eye 1 or 2 times a day.

Overdosage

Possible symptoms are very slow heartbeat, heart failure, low blood pressure, and spasms of the bronchial muscles, making it hard to breathe. Take the victim to a hospital emergency room for treatment. ALWAYS bring the medicine container with you.

Special Information

To administer the eyedrop, lie down or tilt your head backward and look at the ceiling. Hold the dropper above your eye and drop the medicine inside your lower lid while looking up. To prevent possible infection, don't allow the dropper to touch your fingers, eyelid, or any surface. Release the lower lid and keep your eye open. Don't blink for about 30 seconds. Press gently on the bridge of your nose at the inside corner of your eye for about a minute. This will help circulate the medicine around your eye. Wait at least 5 minutes before using any other eyedrops.

If you forget to instill a dose of Levobunolol, do it as soon as you remember. If it is almost time for your next regularly scheduled dose, skip the one you forgot and continue with your regular schedule. Do not instill a double dose.

If you use Levobunolol once a day and forget to take it for an entire day, skip the forgotten dose and follow your regular schedule.

Generic Name

Levodopa (L-Dopa)

Brand Names

Dopar
Larodopa

(Also available in generic form)

Type of Drug

Anti-Parkinsonian.

Prescribed for

Parkinson's disease; relief of pain associated with shingles (herpes zoster).

General Information

Parkinson's disease can develop as a result of changes in the utilization of dopamine in the brain or damage to the central nervous system caused by carbon monoxide poisoning or manganese poisoning. It usually develops in older adults because of hardening of the arteries. In many cases, the cause of Parkinson's disease is not known. Levodopa works by entering into the brain, where it is converted to dopamine, a chemical found in the central nervous system. The new dopamine replaces what is deficient in people with Parkinson's disease. Another drug used to treat Parkinson's disease is Amantadine (Symmetrel). It has been shown to increase the amount of dopamine released in the brain.

Cautions and Warnings

Patients with severe heart or lung disease, asthma, or kidney, liver, or hormone diseases should be cautious about using this drug. Do not take it if you have a history of stomach ulcer. People with a history of psychosis must be treated with extreme care; this drug can cause depression with suicidal tendencies.

Pregnancy/Breast-feeding

Levodopa has not been studied in humans; however, studies show problems with the babies' growth in pregnant and nursing animals. Pregnant women should take this drug only if it is absolutely necessary. Women taking this drug must not breast-feed their infants.

High doses of Amantadine (Symmetrel), another drug used to treat Parkinson's disease, have been shown to cause birth defects and harm the unborn child. Nursing while using Amantadine is not recommended since it can cause skin rashes, vomiting, or urination problems in the baby.

Seniors

Older adults may require smaller doses of Levodopa than younger adults because they are less tolerant to the drug's effects. Also, the body enzyme that breaks the drug down decreases with age, so a large dose is not needed.

Seniors who respond to Levodopa treatments, especially those with osteoporosis, should resume activity gradually. Sudden increases in mobility lead to a greater possibility of broken bones than a gradual return to physical activity.

Seniors, especially those with heart disease, are more likely to develop abnormal heart rhythms and other cardiac side effects of Levodopa.

Possible Side Effects

Muscle spasms, inability to control arms, legs, or facial muscles, loss of appetite, nausea, vomiting (with or without stomach pain), dry mouth, difficulty eating, dribbling saliva from the corners of the mouth (due to poor muscle control), tiredness, hand tremors, headache, dizziness, numbness, weakness and a faint feeling, confusion, sleeplessness, grinding of the teeth, nightmares, euphoria, hallucinations, delusions, agitation and anxiousness, feeling of general ill health.

Less common side effects include heart irregularities or palpitations, dizziness when standing or arising in the morning, mental changes (depression, with or without suicidal tendencies; paranoia; loss of some intellectual function), difficulty urinating, muscle twitching, burning of the tongue, bitter taste, diarrhea, constipation, unusual breathing patterns, double or blurred vision, hot flashes, weight gain or loss, darkening of the urine, and sweat.

Rare adverse effects include stomach bleeding, development of an ulcer, high blood pressure, convulsions, adverse effects on the blood, difficulty controlling the eye muscles, feeling of being stimulated, hiccups, loss of hair, hoarseness, decreasing size of male genitalia, and retention of fluids.

Drug Interactions

The effect of Levodopa is increased when it is used together with an anticholinergic drug (such as Trihexyphenidyl). If one of these drugs is stopped, the change must be gradual to allow for adjustments in the other one.

Levodopa can interact with drugs for high blood pressure to cause further lowering of pressure. Dosage adjustments in the high blood pressure medication may be needed. Methyldopa (a drug for high blood pressure) may increase the effects of Levodopa.

The effects of Levodopa may be antagonized by Reserpine, benzodiazepine drugs, phenothiazine-type tranquilizing drugs, Phenytoin, Papaverine, and Vitamin BF.

Patients taking monoamine oxidase (MAO) inhibitor drugs should stop taking them 2 weeks before starting to take Levodopa.

Levodopa may increase the effects of stimulants such as amphetamines, Ephedrine, Epinephrine, Isoproterenol, and the tricyclic antidepressant drugs.

Levodopa will affect the blood sugar of diabetic patients. Adjustments in dosages of antidiabetic medicine may be needed.

Food Interactions

Do not take vitamin preparations which contain Vitamin B_6 (pyridoxine). Vitamin B_6 will decrease the effectiveness of Levodopa.

This drug can cause upset stomach; each dose should be taken with food.

Usual Dose

0.5 to 8 grams per day. Dosage must be individualized to the patient's need.

Overdosage

People taking an overdose of Levodopa must be treated in a hospital emergency room. ALWAYS bring the prescription bottle with you.

Special Information

Be careful while driving or operating any machinery.

Call your doctor *immediately* if any of the following occur: abnormal urine test for sugar (diabetics); uncontrollable movement of the face, eyelids, mouth, tongue, neck, arms, hands, or legs; mood changes; palpitations or irregular heartbeats; difficulty urinating; severe nausea or vomiting.

If you forget to take a dose of Levodopa, take it as soon as possible. However, if it is within 2 hours of your next dose, skip the forgotten dose and go back to your regular schedule. Do not take a double dose.

Generic Name

Levothyroxine Sodium

Brand Names

Levothroid
Synthroid

(Also available in generic form)

Type of Drug

Thyroid replacement.

Prescribed for

Replacement of thyroid hormone or low output of hormone from the thyroid gland.

General Information

Levothyroxine Sodium is one of several thyroid replacement products available. The major difference between these products is in effectiveness in treating certain phases of thyroid disease.

Although several different companies make generic versions of this drug, you should not switch between brands unless your doctor knows about it. This applies to all brands and generic versions of Levothyroxine tablets.

Cautions and Warnings

If you have hyperthyroid disease or high output of thyroid hormone you should not use Levothyroxine Sodium. Symptoms of hyperthyroid disease include headache, nervousness, sweating, rapid heartbeat, chest pains, and other signs of central-nervous-system stimulation. If you have heart disease or high blood pressure, thyroid therapy should not be used unless it is clearly indicated and supervised by your physician. If you develop chest pains or other signs of heart disease while you are taking thyroid medication, contact your doctor immediately.

Pregnancy/Breast-feeding

Small amounts of the thyroid hormones will find their way into the bloodstream of a developing fetus. However, they have not been associated with birth defects or other problems when used in the dosages required to maintain normal thyroid function in the mother.

Small amounts of the thyroid hormones pass into breast milk but have not been associated with problems in nursing infants.

Seniors

Older adults are more sensitive to the effects of the thyroid hormones. The usual dosage of thyroid hormones should be reduced by about 25 percent after age 60.

Possible Side Effects

The most common side effects are palpitations of the heart, rapid heartbeat, abnormal heart rhythms, weight loss, chest pains, shaking of the hands, headache, diarrhea, nervousness, menstrual irregularity, inability to sleep, sweating, inability to stand heat. These symptoms may be controlled by adjusting the dose of the medication. If you are suffering from one or more side effects, you must contact your doctor immediately so that the proper dose adjustment can be made.

Drug Interactions

Taking a thyroid hormone together with Colestipol or Cholestyramine can reduce the effect of the thyroid product by preventing its passage into your bloodstream. Separate doses of these medicines by 4 to 5 hours.

The combination of Maprotiline and a thyroid hormone may increase the chances for abnormal heart rhythms. Your doctor may have to adjust the dose of your thyroid hormone.

Aspirin and other salicylate products may increase the effectiveness of your thyroid hormone by releasing more drug into the blood from body storage sites.

Estrogen drugs may increase your need for thyroid hormones.

Avoid taking over-the-counter products containing stimulant drugs, such as many drugs used to treat coughs, colds, or allergies, which will affect your heart and may cause symptoms of overdosage.

Thyroid replacement therapy may increase the effect of anticoagulant (blood-thinning) drugs such as Warfarin or Bishydroxycoumarin. Be sure you report this to your physician as it will be necessary to reduce the dose of your anticoagulant drug by approximately one-third at the beginning of thyroid therapy (to avoid hemorrhage). Further adjustments may be made later after your doctor reviews your blood tests.

Diabetics may have to increase their dose of Insulin or oral antidiabetic drugs. Changes in dose must be made by a doctor.

Food Interactions

This drug is best taken on an empty stomach but may be taken with food.

Usual Dose

Initial dose, as little as 25 micrograms per day; then increased in steps of 25 micrograms once every 3 to 4 weeks, depending upon response, with final dose of 100 to 200 micrograms per day, or even 300 to 400 micrograms if needed to achieve normal function.

Overdosage

Symptoms are headache, irritability, nervousness, sweating, rapid heartbeat with unusual stomach rumbling and with or without cramps, chest pains, heart failure, and shock. The patient should be taken to a hospital emergency room immediately. ALWAYS bring the medicine bottle.

Special Information

Thyroid replacement therapy is usually lifelong treatment. Be sure you have a fresh supply of your medication and always remember to take it according to your doctor's directions. Don't stop taking the medicine unless instructed to do so by your doctor.

Call your doctor if you develop nervousness, diarrhea, excessive sweating, chest pains, increased pulse rate, heart palpitations, intolerance to heat, or any other unusual occurrence.

Children beginning on thyroid treatment may lose some hair during the first few months, but this is only temporary and the hair generally grows back.

If you forget to take a dose of Levothyroxine Sodium, take it as soon as you remember. If it is almost time for your next regularly scheduled dose, skip the one you for] got and continue with your regular schedule. Do not take a double dose. Call your doctor if you forget 2 or more doses in a row.

Brand Name

Limbitrol

Ingredients

Amitriptyline
Chlordiazepoxide

Type of Drug

Antianxiety-antidepressant combination.

Prescribed for

Moderate to severe anxiety and depression.

General Information

This combination contains 2 drugs often used by themselves. Some reports have stated that this combination takes effect sooner than other treatments. Symptoms that may respond to this treatment are sleeplessness, feelings of guilt or worthlessness, agitation, anxiety, suicidal thoughts, and appetite loss.

Cautions and Warnings

Do not take this drug if you are allergic to either of the ingredients or related drugs. It should be used with caution if you have a history of heart disease, epilepsy, or other convulsive disorder, difficulty urinating, glaucoma, or thyroid disease.

Pregnancy/Breast-feeding

This drug may cause birth defects or interfere with your baby's development. Check with your doctor before taking it if you are, or might be, pregnant.

If Limbitrol is used during breast-feeding the baby may be overtired, be short of breath, or have a low heartbeat.

Seniors

Older adults are more sensitive to the side effects of this drug, especially those people with cardiac problems, glaucoma, urinary and stomach problems. Follow your doctor's directions and report any side effects at once.

Possible Side Effects

Mild drowsiness, changes in blood pressure, abnormal heart rates, heart attacks, confusion (especially in older patients), hallucinations, disorientation, delusions, anxiety, restlessness, lethargy, depression, inactivity, slurred speech, stupor, dizziness, excitement, numbness and tingling in the extremities, blurred vision, constipation, difficult urination, lack of coordination, muscle spasms, seizures or convulsions, dry mouth, blurred vision, rash, itching, sensitivity to the sun or bright light, retention of fluids, fever, drug allergy, changes in blood composition, nausea, vomiting, loss of appetite, stomach upset, diarrhea, enlargement of the breasts, changes in sex drive, changes in blood sugar.

Less common side effects are headache, changes in menstrual cycle, blurred or double vision, inability to fall asleep, nightmares, feeling of panic, peculiar taste in the mouth, stomach cramps, black coloration of the tongue, yellowing of the eyes or skin, changes in liver function, changes in weight, sweating, flushing, loss of hair, feeling of ill health.

Drug Interactions

Avoid monoamine oxidase (MAO) inhibitors while taking this combination. The addition of MAO inhibitors can cause fever and convulsions.

Do not take this drug together with Guanethidine. If you

are taking high blood pressure medicine with this combination, consult your doctor.

Do not take this combination drug with alcohol, sleeping pills, or other depressive drugs.

Large doses of Vitamin C can reduce the effect of Amitriptyline, one ingredient of Limbitrol.

Food Interactions

This medication is best taken on an empty stomach but may be taken with food if it irritates your stomach.

Usual Dose

1 to 2 tablets 3 to 4 times per day.

Overdosage

Overdose may cause confusion, drowsiness, difficulty concentrating, abnormal heart rate, convulsions, and coma. Bring the patient to a hospital emergency room and ALWAYS bring the medicine bottle.

Special Information

Avoid alcoholic beverages while you are taking this medicine. Sleeping pills, narcotics, barbiturates, other tranquilizers, or other drugs causing nervous-system depression should be used with caution while you are taking the medication. Tell your doctor if you become pregnant or are breast-feeding.

This combination drug can cause drowsiness or dizziness. Drive and operate equipment with extreme caution.

If you forget to take a dose of Limbitrol, do not take the forgotten dose. Skip the dose and go back to your regular schedule. Do not take a double dose.

Generic Name

Lindane

Brand Names

G-Well Lotion/Shampoo   Lindane Lotion/Shampoo
Kwell Cream/Lotion/Shampoo   Scabene Lotion/Shampoo

(Also available in generic form)

Type of Drug

Parasiticide.

Prescribed for

Topical treatment of head lice, crab lice, and scabies.

General Information

Lindane is considered to be the most effective agent against lice and scabies by many authorities. It should be used only when prescribed by a physician because it cannot prevent infestation, it can only treat it. Also, this medication is extremely irritating, particularly when applied to the eyelids and genital areas. If allowed to remain in contact with the skin for too long, Lindane will be absorbed directly into the bloodstream, causing signs of drug overdose.

Cautions and Warnings

Lindane is poisonous. Don't let any of it get into your eyes or mouth or in any open cut or scratch. Use rubber gloves if applying Lindane to another person. Call your doctor if you develop a rash or irritation while using this medicine, become clumsy or unsteady, if you have an unexplained seizure, become nervous, restless, irritable, vomit, or develop a very fast heartbeat.

Pregnancy/Breast-feeding

Lindane is absorbed through the skin and may cause unwanted effects in both pregnant mother and unborn baby. It is not recommended for use during pregnancy.

Lindane passes into breast milk in small amounts. Use an alternative feeding method while using this medicine.

Seniors

Older adults should follow the same precautions as all others when using Lindane.

Possible Side Effects

Skin rash.

Drug Interactions

None known.

Usual Dose

For head lice: Pour 1 ounce of shampoo on the affected area; rub vigorously; be sure to wet all hairy areas. Wet hair with warm water and work into a full lather for at least 4 minutes. Rinse hair thoroughly and rub with a dry towel. Comb with a fine-tooth comb to remove any remaining nit shells. A second application is usually not needed, but may be made after 24 hours if necessary. The drug should not be used more than twice in 1 week. The shampoo may also be used for crab lice.

For crab lice: After a bath or shower, apply a thin layer of lotion to hairy areas and over the skin of adjacent areas. Leave on for 12 to 24 hours, then wash thoroughly and put on freshly laundered or dry-cleaned clothing. Repeat after 4 days if necessary.

For scabies: After a bath or shower, apply a thin layer of the lotion over the entire skin surface. Leave on for 24 hours, then wash thoroughly. If necessary, a second and third weekly application may be made.

Overdosage

Anyone who ingests this drug accidentally should be taken to a hospital emergency room immediately. When taken internally, Lindane is a stimulant; the patient may require Phenobarbital or a similar depressant to neutralize the effect.

If contact with your eyes occurs during shampoo or other use, flush the eyes and surrounding area with water. If irritation or sensitization occurs, discontinue use and call a doctor.

Special Instructions

Do not apply to face. Flush thoroughly with water if medication comes in contact with eyes. Do not exceed prescribed dose.

Generic Name

Liothyronine

Brand Name

Cytomel

(Also available in generic form)

Type of Drug

Thyroid replacement.

Prescribed for

Replacement of thyroid hormone or low output from the thyroid gland.

General Information

Liothyronine is one of several thyroid replacement products available in the United States. The major difference between these products is the fact that they are actually different thyroid hormones and may be better at treating different phases of thyroid disease.

Cautions and Warnings

Do not take this product if you have hyperthyroid disease or high output of thyroid hormone. Symptoms of hyperthyroidism are headache, nervousness, sweating, rapid heartbeat, chest pain, and stimulation of the nervous system. If you have heart disease or high blood pressure, thyroid-replacement therapy should not be used unless it is clearly needed and supervised by your doctor.

Pregnancy/Breast-feeding

Small amounts of the thyroid hormones will find their way into the bloodstream of a developing fetus. However, they have not been associated with birth defects or other problems when used in the dosages required to maintain normal thyroid function in the mother.

Small amounts of the thyroid hormones pass into breast milk but have not been associated with problems in nursing infants.

Seniors

Older adults are more sensitive to the effects of the thyroid hormones. The usual dosage of thyroid hormones should be reduced by about 25 percent after age 60.

Possible Side Effects

The most common side effects are heart palpitations, rapid

heartbeat, abnormal heart rhythms, weight loss, chest pains, shaking of the hands, headache, diarrhea, nervousness, menstrual irregularity, difficulty sleeping, excessive sweating, intolerance to heat. These symptoms may be controlled by adjusting the dose of your medication. If you are suffering from one or more side effects, contact your doctor so that the proper dosage adjustment can be made.

Drug Interactions

Avoid over-the-counter products containing stimulant drugs, including many products sold to treat symptoms of the common cold or allergies. The stimulant-thyroid combination can affect your heart and may cause symptoms of overdosage.

Thyroid-replacement therapy may increase the effect of anticoagulant (blood-thinning) drugs such as Warfarin or Bishydroxycoumarin. Be sure your doctor knows if you are taking both drugs because it will be necessary to reduce your anticoagulant dosage by one-third at the beginning of your thyroid therapy to avoid hemorrhage. Further adjustments may be needed later after your doctor reviews your blood tests.

Diabetics may have to increase their dose of Insulin or antidiabetic medicine. Dosage changes must be made by your doctor.

Taking a thyroid hormone together with Colestipol or Cholestyramine can reduce the effect of the thyroid product by preventing its passage into your bloodstream. Separate doses of these 2 medicines by 4 to 5 hours.

The combination of Maprotiline and a thyroid hormone may increase the chances for abnormal heart rhythms. Your doctor may have to adjust the dose of your thyroid hormone.

Aspirin and other salicylate products may increase the effectiveness of your thyroid hormone by releasing more drug into the blood from body storage sites.

Estrogen drugs may increase your need for thyroid hormones.

Food Interactions

This drug is best taken on an empty stomach but may be taken with food.

Usual Dose

Adult: 5 to 100 micrograms per day, depending on the condition being treated and your response to therapy.

Child and senior: Begin at the low end of the dosage range and increase slowly until the desired effect has been achieved.

Overdosage

Symptoms are headache, irritability, nervousness, sweating, rapid heartbeat, unusual stomach rumbling with or without cramps, chest pains, heart failure, shock. Take the victim to a hospital emergency room at once for treatment. ALWAYS bring the medicine bottle with you.

Special Information

Thyroid-replacement therapy is usually lifelong treatment. Be sure you have a fresh supply of your medication and always remember to take it according to your doctor's directions. Don't stop taking the medicine unless instructed to do so by your doctor.

Call your doctor if you develop nervousness, diarrhea, excessive sweating, chest pains, increased pulse rate, heart palpitations, intolerance to heat, or any other unusual occurrence.

Children beginning on thyroid treatment may lose some hair during the first few months, but this is only temporary and hair generally grows back.

If you forget to take a dose of Liothyronine, take it as soon as you remember. If it is almost time for your next regularly scheduled dose, skip the one you forgot and continue with your regular schedule. Do not take a double dose. Call your doctor if you forget to take 2 or more doses in a row.

Generic Name

Liotrix

Brand Names

Euthroid
Thyrolar

Type of Drug

Thyroid replacement.

Prescribed for

Replacement of thyroid hormone or low output from the thyroid gland.

General Information

Liotrix is one of several thyroid-replacement products available in the United States. It is unique in that it is a mixture of 2 synthetic thyroid hormones (Liothyronine and Levothyroxine). Some doctors feel that this mixture is superior to single-hormone or natural thyroid products.

Cautions and Warnings

Do not take this product if you have hyperthyroid disease or high output of thyroid hormone. Symptoms of hyperthyroidism are headache, nervousness, sweating, rapid heartbeat, chest pain, and stimulation of the nervous system. If you have heart disease or high blood pressure, thyroid-replacement therapy should not be used unless it is clearly needed and supervised by your doctor.

Pregnancy/Breast-feeding

Small amounts of the thyroid hormones will find their way into the bloodstream of a developing fetus. However, they have not been associated with birth defects or other problems when used in the dosages required to maintain normal thyroid function in the mother.

Small amounts of the thyroid hormones pass into breast milk but have not been associated with problems in nursing infants.

Seniors

Older adults are more sensitive to the effects of the thyroid hormones. The usual dosage of thyroid hormones should be reduced by about 25 percent after age 60.

Possible Side Effects

The most common side effects are heart palpitations, rapid

heartbeat, abnormal heart rhythms, weight loss, chest pains, shaking of the hands, headache, diarrhea, nervousness, menstrual irregularity, difficulty sleeping, excessive sweating, intolerance to heat. These symptoms may be controlled by adjusting the dose of your medication. If you are suffering from one or more side effects, contact your doctor so that the proper dosage adjustment can be made.

Drug Interactions

Avoid over-the-counter products containing stimulant drugs, including many products sold to treat symptoms of the common cold or allergies. The stimulant-thyroid combination can affect your heart and may cause symptoms of overdosage.

Thyroid-replacement therapy may increase the effect of anticoagulant (blood-thinning) drugs such as Warfarin or Bishydroxycoumarin. Be sure your doctor knows if you are taking both drugs because it will be necessary to reduce your anticoagulant dosage by one-third at the beginning of your thyroid therapy to avoid hemorrhage. Further adjustments may be needed later after your doctor reviews your blood tests.

Diabetics may have to increase their dose of Insulin or antidiabetic medicine. Dosage changes must be made by your doctor.

Taking a thyroid hormone together with Colestipol or Cholestyramine can reduce the effect of the thyroid product by preventing its passage into your bloodstream. Separate doses of these 2 medicines by 4 to 5 hours.

The combination of Maprotiline and a thyroid hormone may increase the chances for abnormal heart rhythms. Your doctor may have to adjust the dose of your thyroid hormone.

Aspirin and other salicylate products may increase the effectiveness of your thyroid hormone by releasing more drug into the blood from body storage sites.

Estrogen drugs may increase your need for thyroid hormones.

Food Interactions

This drug is best taken before breakfast but may be taken with food.

Usual Dose

Adult: a single "¼" to "2" tablet each day (see "Special Information" below for an explanation), depending on the condition being treated and your response to therapy.

Child and senior: Begin at the low end of the dosage range and increase slowly until the desired effect has been achieved.

Overdosage

Symptoms are headache, irritability, nervousness, sweating, rapid heartbeat, unusual stomach rumbling with or without cramps, chest pains, heart failure, shock. Take the victim to a hospital emergency room at once for treatment. ALWAYS bring the medicine bottle with you.

Special Information

Liotrix tablets are rated according to their approximate equivalent to thyroid hormone. A "½" tablet is roughly equal to 30 milligrams of thyroid hormone, a "1" tablet to 60 milligrams, a "2" tablet to 120 milligrams, and so on.

Thyroid-replacement therapy is usually lifelong treatment. Be sure you have a fresh supply of your medication and always remember to take it according to your doctor's directions. Don't stop taking the medicine unless instructed to do so by your doctor.

Call your doctor if you develop nervousness, diarrhea, excessive sweating, chest pains, increased pulse rate, heart palpitations, intolerance to heat, or any other unusual occurrence.

Children beginning on thyroid treatment may lose some hair during the first few months, but this is only temporary and the hair generally grows back.

If you forget to take a dose of Liotrix, take it as soon as you remember. If it is almost time for your next regularly scheduled dose, skip the one you forgot and continue with your regular schedule. Do not take a double dose. Call your doctor if you forget to take 2 or more doses in a row.

Generic Name

Lisinopril

Brand Names

Prinivil
Zestril

Type of Drug

Antihypertensive; ACE inhibitor.

Prescribed for

High blood pressure. Low doses may be used to treat mild to moderate blood pressure. This medicine may be taken alone or with a thiazide-type diuretic.

General Information

This medicine belongs to a class of drugs, ACE inhibitors, that work by preventing the conversion of a potent hormone called Angiotensin 1. This directly affects the production of other hormones and enzymes which participate in the regulation of blood pressure. Lisinopril starts lowering blood pressure within 1 hour after you take the medicine.

Cautions and Warnings

This drug can cause kidney problems, especially loss of protein in the urine. Patients taking Lisinopril should have the amount of protein in the urine measured during the first month of treatment and monthly for the next few months. The drug can also cause a reduction in white-blood-cell count, leading to a potential for increased susceptibility to infection. Lisinopril should be used with caution by people who have kidney disease or diseases of the immune/collagen system (particularly lupus erythematosus) or who have taken other drugs that affect the white-blood-cell count.

Pregnancy/Breast-feeding

The effect of Lisinopril on a developing fetus is not known. However, animal studies indicate that Lisinopril may affect a developing fetus. Women who are, or might become, preg-

nant while taking this drug should discuss the matter with
their doctor.

It is not known if Lisinopril passes into breast milk or if it will
affect a nursing infant.

Seniors

Older adults are as sensitive to the blood-pressure-lowering
effects of this drug as younger adults, but they absorb twice
as much of the drug. Dosage must be individualized to your
needs.

Possible Side Effects

Dizziness, tiredness, headache, diarrhea, nausea, low blood
pressure, cough, rash (usually mild), and cough are the most
common side effects.

Less common drug side effects are itching, fever, temporary loss of taste perception, stomach irritation, chest pain,
heart palpitations, difficulty sleeping, tingling in the hands or
feet, vomiting, jaundice and liver damage, excessive sweating, muscle cramps, joint and muscle pains, (male) impotence, and muscle weakness. Some people experience
unusual reactions after taking the first dose of the drug which
can include facial flushing and swelling, swelling of the arms
and legs, and closing of the throat.

Drug Interactions

The blood-pressure-lowering effect of Lisinopril is additive
with diuretic drugs and the beta blockers. Other drugs that
cause rapid drops in blood pressure should be used with extreme caution because of a possible severe drop when taken
together with Lisinopril.

Lisinopril may increase potassium levels in your blood, especially when given with potassium-sparing diuretics and/or
potassium supplements.

Avoid over-the-counter drugs such as decongestants, diet
pills, and stimulants that can raise your blood pressure.

Food Interactions

This drug is best taken on an empty stomach, usually 1 hour
before or 2 hours after a meal.

Usual Dose

10 to 40 milligrams once a day. Some people may take their total daily dosage in 2 divided doses.

People with poor kidney function have to take less medicine to achieve reduced blood pressure.

Overdosage

The primary effect of Lisinopril overdosage is a rapid drop in blood pressure, as evidenced by dizziness or fainting. Take the overdose victim to a hospital emergency room immediately. ALWAYS remember to bring the medicine bottle.

Special Information

Call your doctor if you develop fever, sore throat, mouth sores, abnormal heartbeat, or chest pain, or if you have persistent rash or loss of taste perception.

Lisinopril may cause dizziness when you quickly rise from a lying or sitting position.

Avoid strenuous exercise and/or very hot weather because heavy sweating and/or dehydration can cause a rapid drop in blood pressure.

Do not stop taking this medicine without your doctor's knowledge.

If you forget to take a dose of Lisinopril, take it as soon as you remember. If it is almost time for your next dose, skip the forgotten dose and go back to your regular schedule.

Generic Name
Lithium

Brand Names

Cibalith-S Syrup
Eskalith Capsules/Tablets
Eskalith-CR Controlled Release Tablets
Lithane Tablets
Lithium Carbonate Capsules/Tablets
Lithium Citrate Syrup
Lithobid Tablets
Lithonate Capsules
Lithotabs

(Also available in generic form)

Type of Drug

Antipsychotic; antimanic.

Prescribed for

Treatment of the manic phase of manic-depressive illness.
Lithium has also been used in cancer treatment; for migraine
headaches, premenstrual tension, bulimia, alcoholism, and
overactive thyroid; and as a lotion for genital herpes and
dandruff.

General Information

Lithium is the only medicine which is effective as an antimanic drug. It reduces the level of manic episodes and may
produce normal activity within the first 3 weeks of treatment.
Typical manic symptoms include rapid speech, elation, hyperactive movements, need for little sleep, grandiose ideas, poor
judgment, aggressiveness, and hostility.

Cautions and Warnings

This drug should not be given to patients with heart or kidney
disease, dehydration, low blood sodium, or to patients who
take diuretic drugs. If such patients require Lithium they must
be very closely monitored by their doctors.

Pregnancy/Breast-feeding

Lithium can cause heart and thyroid birth defects, especially
if taken during the first 3 months of pregnancy. It can affect
the newborn infant if present in your blood during your delivery. Talk with your doctor about the risk of taking this drug
during your pregnancy versus any benefit it will produce for
you.

Lithium passes readily into breast milk and can affect a
nursing infant. Signs of these effects are weak muscle tone,
low body temperature, bluish discoloration of the skin, and
abnormal heart rhythms in the nursing infant. Use an alternative feeding method while taking this medicine.

Seniors

Older adults are more sensitive to the effects of Lithium because they cannot clear it out of the body through their kidneys as rapidly as younger adults. Lithium is potentially toxic

to the central nervous system in older adults, even when Lithium blood levels are in the desired range. Also, older adults are more likely to develop an underactive thyroid because of Lithium treatment.

Possible Side Effects

Side effects of Lithium are directly associated with the amount of this drug in the blood. At usual doses, the patient may develop a fine hand tremor, thirst, and excessive urination. Mild nausea and discomfort may be present during the first few days of treatment. At higher levels, diarrhea, vomiting, drowsiness, muscle weakness and poor coordination, giddiness, ringing in the ears, and blurred vision may occur.

The following body systems can be affected by Lithium, producing symptoms which tend to become worse with more of this drug in the body: muscles, nerves, central nervous system (blackouts, seizures, dizziness, incontinence, slurred speech, coma), heart and blood vessels, stomach and intestines, kidney and urinary tract, skin, thyroid gland. Lithium can also cause changes in tests used to monitor heart-brain function and can cause dry mouth and blurred vision.

Drug Interactions

When combined with Haloperidol, Lithium may cause an unusual set of symptoms including weakness, tiredness, fever, and confusion. In a few patients these symptoms have been followed by permanent brain damage.

Lithium may reduce the effect of Chlorpromazine.

The drug is counteracted by Sodium Bicarbonate, Acetazolamide, Urea, Mannitol, and Aminophylline, which increase the rate at which Lithium is released from the body.

Long-term use of thiazide diuretic drugs may decrease the clearance of Lithium from the body. Salt (sodium chloride) is directly related to this drug in the body. You will retain more of the drug than normal if the salt level in your body is low and will hold less if you have a high salt level.

Food Interactions

It is essential to maintain a normal diet, including salt and fluid intake, while taking Lithium, since it can cause a natural reduction in body salt levels. Lithium should be taken immediately after meals or with food or milk.

Usual Dose

Must be individualized to each patient's need. Most patients will respond to 600 milligrams 3 times per day at first, then will require 300 milligrams 3 to 4 times per day.

Slow release: 900 milligrams twice a day.

Overdosage

Toxic blood levels of Lithium are only slightly above the levels required for treatment. If diarrhea, vomiting, tremors, drowsiness, or poor coordination occur, stop taking the medicine and call your doctor immediately.

Special Information

Lithium may cause drowsiness. Be cautious while driving or operating any machinery.

If you forget to take a dose of Lithium, take it as soon as possible. However, if it is within 2 hours of your next dose (6 hours if you take a long-acting form of Lithium), skip the forgotten dose and go back to your regular schedule. Do not take a double dose.

Brand Name

Lomotil Liquid/Tablets

Ingredients

Atropine Sulfate
Diphenoxylate

Other Brand Names

Lofene Tablets
Logen Tablets
Lomanate Liquid

Lonox Tablets
Low-Quel Tablets

(Also available in generic form)

Type of Drug

Antidiarrheal.

Prescribed for

Symptomatic treatment of diarrhea.

General Information

Lomotil and other antidiarrheal agents should be used only for short periods; they will relieve the diarrhea, but not its underlying causes. Sometimes these drugs should not be used even though there is diarrhea present: People with some kinds of bowel, stomach, or other disease may be harmed by taking antidiarrheal drugs. Obviously, the decision to use Lomotil must be made by your doctor. Do not use Lomotil without your doctor's advice advice.

Cautions and Warnings

Do not take Lomotil if you are allergic to this medication or any other medication containing Atropine Sulfate or if you are jaundiced (yellowing of the whites of the eyes and/or skin) or are suffering from diarrhea caused by antibiotics such as Clindamycin or Lincomycin.

Pregnancy/Breast-feeding

This drug crosses into the blood circulation of a developing baby. It has not been found to cause birth defects. Pregnant women, or those who might become pregnant while taking this drug, should not take it without their doctor's approval. When the drug is considered essential by your doctor, the potential risk of taking the medicine must be carefully weighed against the benefit it might produce.

This drug passes into breast milk, but has caused no problems among breast-fed infants. You must consider the potential effect on the nursing infant if breast-feeding while taking this medicine.

Seniors

Older adults are more sensitive to the side effects of this drug, especially breathing difficulty. Follow your doctor's directions and report any side effects at once.

Possible Side Effects

The most common side effects are dryness of the skin inside the nose or mouth, flushing or redness of the face, fever, unusual heart rates, inability to urinate.

Less commonly, people taking Lomotil for extended periods may experience abdominal discomforts, swelling of the gums, interference with normal breathing, feeling of numbness in the extremities, drowsiness, restlessness, rashes, nausea, sedation, vomiting, headache, dizziness, depression, feeling unwell, lethargy, loss of appetite, euphoria, itching, and coma.

Drug Interactions

Lomotil, a depressant on the central nervous system, may cause tiredness or inability to concentrate, and may thus increase the effect of sleeping pills, tranquilizers, and alcohol. Avoid drinking large amounts of alcoholic beverages while taking Lomotil.

Usual Dose

Adult: 4 tablets per day until diarrhea has stopped; then reduce to the lowest level that will control diarrhea (usually 2 tablets per day or less).

The liquid form, supplied with a dropper calibrated to deliver medication as desired in milliliters, is used for children age 2 to 12.

Child (age 8 to 12, or about 60 to 80 pounds): 4 milliliters 5 times per day.

Child (age 5 to 8, or about 45 to 60 pounds): 4 milliliters 4 times per day.

Child (age 2 to 5, or about 26 to 45 pounds): 4 milliliters 3 times per day.

Child (under age 2): not recommended.

Overdosage

Lomotil overdose is generally accidental: Patients, feeling that the prescribed amount has not cured their diarrhea, will take more medication on their own. Symptoms of overdosage (particularly effects on breathing) may not be evident until 12 to 30 hours after the medication has been taken. Symptoms are dryness of skin, mouth, and/or nose, flushing, fever and abnormal heart rates with possible lethargy, coma, or depression of breathing. The patient should be taken to a hospital emergency room immediately. ALWAYS bring the medicine bottle.

Special Information

Lomotil may cause drowsiness and difficulty concentrating: Be careful while driving or operating any appliance or equipment.

Notify your doctor if heart palpitations occur.

If you forget to take a dose of Lomotil, take it as soon as you remember. If it is almost time for your next regularly scheduled dose, skip the one you forgot and continue with your regular schedule. Do not take a double dose.

Generic Name

Loperamide

Brand Name

Imodium
Imodium-AD

Type of Drug

Antidiarrheal.

Prescribed for

Symptomatic treatment of diarrhea.

General Information

Loperamide and other antidiarrheal agents should be used only for short periods; they will relieve the diarrhea, but not its underlying causes. Sometimes these drugs should not be used even though there is diarrhea present: People with some kinds of bowel, stomach, or other disease may be harmed by taking antidiarrheal drugs. A low-dose version of Loperamide can be purchased without a prescription as Imodium-AD.

Cautions and Warnings

Do not use Loperamide if you are allergic or sensitive to it
or if you suffer from diarrhea associated with colitis. Also,
do not use when intestinal toxins from bacteria such as *E.
coli*, Salmonella, or *Shigella* are present (as in most forms
of traveler's diarrhea) or with certain drugs such as Clindamycin. Loperamide is not known to be addictive.

Pregnancy/Breast-feeding

This drug crosses into the blood circulation of a developing
baby. It has not been found to cause birth defects. Pregnant
women, or those who might become pregnant while taking
this drug, should not take it without their doctors' approval.
When the drug is considered essential by your doctor, the
potential risk of taking the medicine must be carefully
weighed against the benefit it might produce.

This drug passes into breast milk, but has caused no problems among breast-fed infants. You must consider the potential effect on the nursing infant if breast-feeding while
taking this medicine.

Seniors

Older adults are more sensitive to the constipating effects
of this drug. Follow your doctor's directions and report any
side effects at once.

Possible Side Effects

The incidence of side effects from Loperamide is low. Stomach and abdominal pain, bloating or other discomfort, constipation, dryness of the mouth, dizziness, tiredness, nausea
and vomiting, and rash are possible.

Drug Interactions

Loperamide, a depressant on the central nervous system,
may cause tiredness and inability to concentrate, and may
thus increase the effect of sleeping pills, tranquilizers, and
alcohol. Avoid drinking large amounts of alcoholic beverages while taking Loperamide.

Usual Dose

Adult and child (age 12 and over): 2 capsules to start,

followed by 1 capsule after each loose stool, up to 8 capsules per day maximum. Improvement should be seen in 2 days. People with long-term (chronic) diarrhea usually need 2 to 4 capsules per day. This drug usually is effective within 10 days or not at all.

Child (under age 12): not recommended.

Overdosage

Symptoms are constipation, irritation of the stomach, and tiredness. Large doses cause vomiting. The patient should be taken to the emergency room immediately. ALWAYS bring the medicine bottle.

Special Information

Loperamide may cause drowsiness and difficulty concentrating: Be careful while driving or operating any appliance or equipment.

If you forget to take a dose of Loperamide, do not take the forgotten dose. Skip the dose and go back to your regular schedule. Do not take a double dose.

Generic Name

Lorazepam

Brand Name

Ativan

(Also available in generic form)

Type of Drug

Minor tranquilizer.

Prescribed for

Relief of symptoms of anxiety, tension, fatigue, or agitation.

General Information

Lorazepam is a member of the group of drugs known as benzodiazepines. These drugs are used as antianxiety agents, anticonvulsants, or sedatives (sleeping pills). They exert their effects by relaxing the large skeletal muscles and by a direct effect on the brain. In doing so, they can relax you and make you either more tranquil or sleepier, depending on the drug and how much you use. Many doctors prefer Lorazepam and other members of this class to other drugs that can be used for the same effect. Their reason is that the benzodiazepines tend to be safer, have fewer side effects, and are usually as, if not more, effective.

These drugs are generally used in any situation where they can be a useful adjunct.

Cautions and Warnings

Benzodiazepine tranquilizing drugs can be abused if taken for long periods of time, and it is possible to develop withdrawal symptoms if you discontinue the therapy abruptly. Withdrawal symptoms include convulsions, tremor, muscle cramps, stomach cramps, vomiting, and sweating.

Do not take Lorazepam if you know you are sensitive or allergic to this drug or to other benzodiazepines such as Chlordiazepoxide, Oxazepam, Clorazepate, Diazepam, Prazepam, Flurazepam, Clonazepam, and Temazepam.

Lorazepam and other members of this drug group may aggravate narrow-angle glaucoma, but if you have open-angle glaucoma you may take the drugs. In any case, check this information with your doctor.

Pregnancy/Breast-feeding

Avoid taking this drug during the first 3 months of pregnancy except under strict supervision of your doctor. The baby may become dependent on Lorazepam if it is used continually during pregnancy. If used during the last weeks of pregnancy or during breast-feeding, the baby may be over-tired, be short of breath, or have a low heartbeat. Use during labor may cause weakness in the newborn.

Seniors

Older adults are more sensitive to the effects of this drug, especially dizziness and drowsiness. They should closely follow their doctor's directions and report any side effects at once.

Possible Side Effects

The most common side effect is mild drowsiness during the first few days of therapy, especially in older adults or the debilitated. If drowsiness persists, contact your doctor.

Less common side effects include confusion, depression, lethargy, disorientation, headache, lack of activity, slurred speech, stupor, dizziness, tremor, constipation, dry mouth, nausea, inability to control urination, changes in sex drive, irregular menstrual cycle, changes in heart rhythm, lowered blood pressure, retention of fluids, blurred or double vision, itching, rash, hiccups, nervousness, inability to fall asleep, (occasional) liver dysfunction. If you experience any of these reactions stop taking the medicine and contact your doctor immediately.

Drug Interactions

Lorazepam is a central-nervous-system depressant. Avoid alcohol, tranquilizers, narcotics, sleeping pills, barbiturates, monoamine oxidase (MAO) inhibitors, antihistamines, and other medicines used to relieve depression.

Food Interactions

Lorazepam is best taken on an empty stomach, but may be taken with food if it upsets your stomach.

Usual Dose

Adult: 2 to 10 milligrams per day as individualized for maximum benefit, depending on symptoms and response to treatment, which may call for a dose outside the range given. Most people require 2 to 6 milligrams per day. 2 to 4 milligrams may be taken at bedtime for sleep.

Senior: usually requires less of the drug to control anxiety and tension.

Child: not recommended.

Overdosage

Symptoms are confusion, sleep or sleepiness, lack of response to pain such as a pin stick, shallow breathing, lowered blood pressure, and coma. The patient should be taken to a hospital emergency room immediately. ALWAYS bring the medicine bottle.

Special Information

Lorazepam can cause tiredness, drowsiness, inability to concentrate, or similar symptoms. Be careful if you are driving, operating machinery, or performing other activities that require concentration.

Do not drink alcoholic beverages while taking Lorazepam. Sleeping pills, narcotics, other tranquilizers, or any other drug producing nervous-system depression should be used with caution while taking Lorazepam.

If you forget to take a dose of Lorazepam and you remember within about an hour of your regular time, take it right away. If you do not remember until later, skip the forgotten dose and go back to your regular schedule. Do not take a double dose.

Brand Name

Lotrisone Cream

Ingredients

Betamethasone
Clotrimazole

Type of Drug

Steroid-antifungal combination.

Prescribed for

Severe fungal infection or rash.

General Information

Lotrisone cream is used to relieve the symptoms of itching, rash, or skin inflammation associated with a severe fungus infection. It may treat the underlying cause of the skin problem by killing the fungus and relieves inflammation that may be associated with the infection. This combination product should be used only on your doctor's prescription. A combination such as this may be less effective than applying either Clotrimazole cream or Betamethasone cream to the skin.

Improvement usually occurs within the first week of treatment. If you don't get better after using Lotrisone for 4 weeks, your doctor should reevaluate your condition and prescribe a different medicine.

Cautions and Warnings

Do not use Lotrisone if you are sensitive or allergic to either of its active ingredients. Do not apply Lotrisone to the eye, or to the ear if the eardrum is perforated, unless specifically directed to do so by your doctor.

Check with your doctor before using the contents of an old tube of Lotrisone for a new skin problem.

Pregnancy/Breast-feeding

Pregnant women should not use this product, especially during the first 3 months, because it can affect the development of the fetus.

Seniors

Seniors may use Lotrisone without special precaution.

Possible Side Effects

Itching, stinging, burning, skin peeling, swelling.

Drug Interactions

None known.

Special Information

Apply a thin film of Lotrisone to affected area(s). Washing or soaking the skin before applying the medicine may increase the amount that penetrates your skin.

Stop using the medicine and call your doctor if Lotrisone causes itching, burning, or skin irritation.

Generic Name

Lovastatin

Brand Name

Mevacor

Type of Drug

Cholesterol-lowering agent.

Prescribed for

High blood-cholesterol levels, in conjunction with a low-cholesterol diet program.

General Information

The value of Lovastatin and other drugs that reduce blood cholesterol lies in the assumption that reducing levels of blood fats reduces the chance of heart disease. Studies conducted by the National Heart, Lung, and Blood Institute have identified high levels of blood fats (cholesterol and LDL) as a cause of heart and blood-vessel disease. Drugs that can reduce the amounts of either or both of these blood fats can reduce the risk of deaths and nonfatal heart attacks.

Lovastatin reduces both total cholesterol and LDL-cholesterol counts. A significant response is seen after 2 weeks of treatment. Blood-fat levels reach their lowest levels within 4 to 6 weeks after you start taking this medication and remain at or close to that level so long as you continue to take the medicine.

Cautions and Warnings

People with a history of liver disease should avoid this medication because of the possibility that the drug can aggravate or cause liver disease. Your doctor should take a blood sample to test your liver function every month or so during the first year of treatment to be sure that the drug is not adversely affecting you.

Lovastatin causes muscle aches in a small number of people that can be a sign of a more serious condition.

Pregnancy/Breast-feeding

Pregnant women should not take Lovastatin. Laboratory studies have shown that daily doses of Lovastatin 500 times the maximum recommended human dose cause malformations of the skeleton in fetal laboratory animals. Because hardening of the arteries is a chronic, long-term process, temporarily stopping this medication during pregnancy should cause no problem. If you become pregnant while taking Lovastatin, stop the drug immediately and call your doctor.

Lovastatin passes into breast milk. Women taking this medication should not breast-feed their infants.

Seniors

Lovastatin is only likely to be prescribed for an older adult with severely elevated blood cholesterol. However, the drug may be taken in the same doses as by a younger adult. Be sure to report any side effects to your doctor.

Possible Side Effects

Most people who take Lovastatin tolerate it very well. Studies of the drug revealed that only 2 out of every 100 had to stop taking it because of intolerable side effects.

The most common side effect of Lovastatin is headache. Other common side effects are constipation, diarrhea, stomach gas, abdominal pain or cramps, itching, and rash. Other side effects include upset stomach, nausea, and muscle aches.

Rare side effects include heartburn, muscle cramps, blurred vision, changes in taste perception, and changes in the lens of your eye.

Drug Interactions

The cholesterol-lowering effects of Lovastatin and Cholestyramine are additive when the 2 drugs are taken together.

Food Interactions

Take Lovastatin with meals to reduce the chance of upset stomach or intestinal side effects. Continue your low-cholesterol diet while taking Lovastatin.

Usual Dose

Adult: The usual dose of Lovastatin is 20 to 80 milligrams per day. Your daily dosage should be adjusted about once a month, based on your doctor's assessment of how well the drug is working to reduce your blood cholesterol.

Child: The effect of Lovastatin in children has not been studied.

Overdosage

Persons suspected of having taken an overdose of Lovastatin should be taken to a hospital emergency room for
evaluation and treatment. The effects of overdose are not
well known.

Special Information

Lovastatin causes muscle aches in a small number of people. Call your doctor if this happens to you.

Although the manufacturer of this drug recommends a
maximum daily dose of 80 milligrams, studies have shown
that the cholesterol-lowering effect of Lovastatin continues
to increase up to a daily dose of 120 milligrams.

If you forget to take a dose of Lovastatin, take it as soon
as you remember. If it is almost time for your next regularly
scheduled dose, skip the one you forgot and continue with
your regular schedule. Do not take a double dose.

Generic Name
Malathion

Brand Name
Ovide Lotion

Type of Drug
Scabacide.

Prescribed for
Head lice.

General Information

Ordinarily used as an agricultural insecticide, Malathion has
been tested and found to be effective against common lice
and the eggs they leave behind in the scalp. Malathion
works by interfering with the normal breakdown of acety-
choline, a common carrier of nervous system impulses. The
excess of acetylcholine produced by Malathion accounts for
its toxicity.

After it has been applied to the hair, Malathion binds slowly with the hair shaft, providing some protection against another infestation after the treatment has been completed. This binding process, and the protection it carries, takes about 6 hours to develop and reaches its maximum in 12 hours. Normally about 8 percent of the Malathion applied to your skin is absorbed into the bloodstream, but larger quantities may be absorbed if the lotion is applied to broken skin or open sores.

Cautions and Warnings:

Malathion is an extremely toxic substance if swallowed (see "Overdosage" for more information). People with proven Malathion sensitivity should not use this product.

Malathion is flammable. Do not expose the lotion or hair that is still wet with the lotion to an open flame or to an electric dryer because of the possibility of fire. Allow hair to dry naturally after application.

Malathion can severly damage your eyes. If some of it gets into your eyes, they must be flushed with water immediately.

People with any of the following conditions should be cautious when using Malathion because it can precipitate an attack or worsen the condition: asthma, very slow heartbeat and low blood pressure, stomach spasms or ulcer, recent heart attack, and Parkinson's disease.

Malathion can worsen the following conditions: severe anemia, dehydration, insecticide exposure effects, liver disease or cirrhosis, malnutrition, myasthenia or other neuromuscular diseases, and seizure disorders.

People with recent brain surgery should be concerned about using this product because it can initiate toxic nervous system effects, including seizures.

Pregnancy/Breast-feeding

Malathion may be absorbed and affect a developing fetus. Pregnant women or women who might be pregnant should not use it or apply it to others.

It is not known if Malathion passes into breast milk, but nursing mothers should temporarily use an alternative feeding method while using Malathion because of the chance that some of the insecticide will be absorbed into the blood.

Seniors

There is no known reason for seniors to take special precautions when using this product.

Possible Side Effects

The only known side effect is scalp irritation.

Drug Interactions

No drug interactions have been reported. However, unusually large amounts of Malathion could interact with some injectable antibiotics called aminoglycosides to cause breathing problems, with local anesthetics to interfere with their breakdown and cause systemic side effects, and with some eyedrops (Physostigmine, Echothiophate, Demercarium, and Isoflurophate) used in glaucoma to cause drug side effects. Consult your doctor or pharmacist for more information.

Usual Dose

Adult and child (age 2 and over): Apply to the hair and scalp and repeat after a week, if necessary.

Overdosage

Malathion is potentially deadly. People who swallow this product may not experience toxic effects for up to 12 hours but must be taken to a hospital emergency room for treatment AT ONCE. ALWAYS bring the medicine bottle with you.

The toxic symptoms of Malathion include abdominal cramps, anxiety, restlessness, clumsiness, unsteadiness, confusion, depression, diarrhea, dizziness, drowsiness, sweating, watery eyes or mouth, loss of bowel or bladder control, muscle twitching in the eyelids face or neck, pinpoint pupils, difficulty breathing, seizures, slow heartbeat, trembling, or weakness.

If any Malathion gets into your eyes, flush them with water IMMEDIATELY to remove the insecticide and avoid damage to your vision. DO NOT wait to get to a hospital.

Special Information

Do not use more medicine or use it more often than your

doctor has prescribed. Do not use it without your doctor's specific instruction to do so.

When using Malathion, follow this procedure: Sprinkle the lotion onto DRY hair and rub in until the hair and scalp are wet. Wash your hands immediately after applying the lotion to remove any remaining Malathion from your skin. Allow the treated hair to dry naturally; do not cover it or use an electric dryer or other heat source. Do not shampoo the hair and scalp for 8 to 12 hours to allow the medicine to work. After 8 to 12 hours have passed, shampoo with a plain shampoo and remove the dead lice and eggs from the scalp with a fine-toothed comb.

Avoid contact with the eyes.

Other household members may have caught the lice and require Malathion treatments. Call your doctor for information.

After head lice have been found, be sure to practice good hygiene to prevent spreading the lice and possible reinfestation of the treated scalp. Wash all clothing, bedding, towels, and washcloths in very hot water or dryclean them to kill any lice or eggs. Hairbrushes or combs used by people with head lice infestation must be washed in very hot, soapy water to remove any remaining lice or eggs. Do not share brushes and combs because they may spread the lice. Clean the entire living area with a vacuum cleaner to remove any remaining lice or eggs.

Be careful to avoid being exposed to other insecticides while being treated with Malathion.

Generic Name
Maprotiline

Brand Name

Ludiomil

Type of Drug

Antidepressant.

Prescribed for

Depression with or without symptoms of anxiety.

General Information

Maprotiline and other members of this group are effective
in treating symptoms of depression. They can elevate your
mood, increase physical activity and mental alertness, or improve appetite and sleep patterns. These drugs are mild
sedatives and therefore useful in treating mild forms of depression associated with anxiety. You should not expect instant results with this medicine: Benefits are usually seen
after 1 to 4 weeks. If symptoms are not affected after 6 to 8
weeks, contact your doctor. Occasionally, other members of
this group of drugs have been used in treating nighttime
bed-wetting in the young child, but they do not produce
long-lasting relief, and therapy with one of them for nighttime bed-wetting is of questionable value.

Cautions and Warnings

Do not take Maprotiline if you are allergic or sensitive to this
or other members of this class of drug: Doxepin, Nortriptyline, Imipramine, Desipramine, Protriptyline, and Amitriptyline. The drugs should not be used if you are recovering
from a heart attack. Maprotiline may be taken with caution if
you have a history of epilepsy or other convulsive disorders,
difficulty in urination, glaucoma, heart disease, or thyroid
disease.

Pregnancy/Breast-feeding

This drug, like other antidepressants, crosses into your developing baby's circulation and may cause birth defects if
taken during the first 3 months of pregnancy. There have
been reports of newborn infants suffering from heart,
breathing, and urinary problems after their mothers had
taken an antidepressant of this type immediately before delivery. You should avoid taking this medication while pregnant.

Antidepressants of this type are known to pass into breast
milk and may affect a breast-feeding infant, although this
has not been proven. Nursing mothers should consider alternative feeding methods if taking this medicine.

Seniors

Older adults are more sensitive to the effects of this drug
and often require a lower dose than a younger adult to do

the same job. Follow your doctor's directions and report any side effects at once.

Possible Side Effects

Changes in blood pressure (both high and low), abnormal heart rates, heart attack, confusion, especially in older patients, hallucinations, disorientation, delusions, anxiety, restlessness, excitement, numbness and tingling in the extremities, lack of coordination, muscle spasms or tremors, seizures and/or convulsions, dry mouth, blurred vision, constipation, inability to urinate, rash, itching, sensitivity to bright light or sunlight, retention of fluids, fever, allergy, changes in composition of blood, nausea, vomiting, loss of appetite, stomach upset, diarrhea, enlargement of the breasts in males and females, increased or decreased sex drive, increased or decreased blood sugar.

Less common side effects include agitation, inability to sleep, nightmares, feeling of panic, development of a peculiar taste in the mouth, stomach cramps, black coloration of the tongue, yellowing eyes and/or skin, changes in liver function, increased or decreased weight, increased perspiration, flushing, frequent urination, drowsiness, dizziness, weakness, headache, loss of hair, nausea, not feeling well.

Drug Interactions

Interaction with monoamine oxidase (MAO) inhibitors can cause high fevers, convulsions, and occasionally death. Don't take MAO inhibitors until at least 2 weeks after Maprotiline has been discontinued.

Maprotiline interacts with Guanethidine, a drug used to treat high blood pressure: If your doctor prescribes Maprotiline and you are taking medicine for high blood pressure, be sure to discuss this with him.

Maprotiline increases the effects of barbiturates, tranquilizers, other depressive drugs, and alcohol. Don't drink alcoholic beverages if you take this medicine.

Taking Maprotiline and thyroid medicine will enhance the effects of the thyroid medicine. The combination can cause abnormal heart rhythms.

Large doses of Vitamin C (Ascorbic Acid) can reduce the effect of Maprotiline. Drugs such as Bicarbonate of Soda or Acetazolamide will increase the effect of Maprotiline.

Food Interactions

This drug is best taken on an empty stomach but can be taken with food if it upsets your stomach.

Usual Dose

Adult: 75 to 225 milligrams per day. Hospitalized patients may need up to 300 milligrams per day. The dose of this drug must be tailored to patient's need.

Senior: Lower doses are recommended for people over 60 years of age, usually 50 to 75 milligrams per day.

Overdosage

Symptoms are confusion, inability to concentrate, hallucinations, drowsiness, lowered body temperature, abnormal heart rate, heart failure, large pupils of the eyes, convulsions, severely lowered blood pressure, stupor, and coma (as well as agitation, stiffening of body muscles, vomiting, and high fever). The patient should be taken to a hospital emergency room immediately. ALWAYS bring the medicine bottle.

Special Information

Do not stop taking this medicine unless your doctor has specifically told you to do so. Abruptly stopping this medicine may cause nausea, headache, and a sickly feeling.

This medicine can cause drowsiness, dizziness, and blurred vision. Be careful when driving or operating complicated machinery.

Avoid exposure to the sun or sun lamps for long periods of time.

Call your doctor if dry mouth, difficulty urinating, or excessive sedation develops.

If you forget to take a dose of Maprotiline, take it as soon as you remember. If it is almost time for your next regularly scheduled dose, skip the one you forgot and continue with your regular schedule. Do not take a double dose. If you take Maprotiline at bedtime and forget the dose, skip it and continue with your regular schedule.

Brand Name
Marax DF Syrup/Tablets

Ingredients

Ephedrine Sulfate
Hydroxyzine Hydrochloride
Theophylline

Other Brand Names

Hydrophed Tablets
Moxy Compound Tablets
T.E.H. Tablets

(Also available in generic form)

Type of Drug

Antiasthmatic combination product.

Prescribed for

Relief of asthma symptoms or other upper respiratory disorders.

The actions of this drug should be considered as "possibly effective." There is considerable doubt among medical experts that this drug produces the effects claimed for it.

General Information

Marax is one of several antiasthmatic combination products prescribed for the relief of asthmatic symptoms and other breathing problems. These products contain drugs to help relax the bronchial muscles, drugs to increase the diameter of the breathing passages, and mild tranquilizers to help relax the patient. Other products in this class may contain similar ingredients along with other medicine to help eliminate mucus from the breathing passages.

Cautions and Warnings

This drug should not be taken if you have severe kidney or liver disease.

Pregnancy/Breast-feeding

This drug crosses into the blood circulation of a developing baby. It has not been found to cause birth defects. Pregnant women, or those who might become pregnant while taking this drug, should not take it without their doctors' approval. When the drug is considered essential by your doctor, the potential risk of taking the medicine must be carefully weighed against the benefit it might produce.

This drug passes into breast milk, but has caused no problems among breast-fed infants. You must consider the potential effect on the nursing infant if breast-feeding while taking this medicine.

Seniors

Older adults may take longer to clear Theophylline, an ingredient in this combination, from their bodies than younger adults. Older adults with heart failure or other cardiac conditions, chronic lung disease, a virus infection with fever, or reduced liver function may require a lower dosage of this medication to account for the clearance effect.

Possible Side Effects

Large doses of Marax can produce excitation, shakiness, sleeplessness, nervousness, rapid heartbeat, chest pains, irregular heartbeat, dizziness, dryness of the nose and throat, headache, and sweating. Occasionally people have been known to develop hesitation or difficulty in urination. Marax may also cause stomach upset, diarrhea, and possible bleeding, so you are advised to take this drug with food.

Less frequent side effects are excessive urination, heart stimulation, drowsiness, muscle weakness, muscle twitching, unsteady walk. These effects can usually be controlled by having your doctor adjust the dose.

Drug Interactions

Marax may cause sleeplessness or drowsiness. Do not take this drug with alcoholic beverages.

Taking Marax or similar medicines with a monoamine oxidase (MAO) inhibitor can produce severe interaction. Consult your doctor first.

Marax or similar products taken together with Lithium Carbonate will increase the excretion of Lithium; they have neutralized the effect of Propranolol.

Erythromycin and similar antibiotics cause the body to hold Theophylline, leading to possible side effects.

Food Interactions

Take the drug with food to help prevent stomach upset.

Actions and side effects of Marax may be enhanced by ingestion of caffeine from sources including various teas, coffee, chocolate, and soft drinks.

Usual Dose

Tablet:
Adult: 1 tablet 2 to 4 times per day.
Child (over age 5): ½ tablet 2 to 4 times per day.
Syrup:
Child (over age 5): 1 teaspoon 3 to 4 times per day.
Child (age 2 to 5): ½ teaspoon 3 to 4 times per day.

Take doses at least 4 hours apart. The dose is adjusted to severity of disease and patient's ability to tolerate side effects.

Special Information

If you forget to take a dose of Marax, take it as soon as you remember. If it is almost time for your next regularly scheduled dose, skip the one you forgot and continue with your regular schedule. Do not take a double dose.

Generic Name

Mazindol

Brand Names

Mazanor
Sanorex

Type of Drug

Nonamphetamine appetite suppressant.

Prescribed for

Short-term (2 to 3 months) appetite suppression; treating obesity.

General Information

Although this medicine is not an amphetamine, it has many of the same effects as amphetamine drugs and suppresses appetite by working on specific areas in the brain. Each dose of Mazindol works for 8 to 15 hours.

Cautions and Warnings

Do not take Mazindol if you have heart disease, high blood pressure, thyroid disease, or glaucoma, or if you are sensitive or allergic to this or other appetite suppressants. Do not use this medicine if you are prone to emotional agitation or drug abuse.

Pregnancy/Breast-feeding

Studies have shown that large doses of Mazindol may damage an unborn baby. The use of this and other appetite suppressants should be avoided by women who are or could become pregnant, unless the potential benefit outweighs any possible drug hazard.

It is not known if Mazindol passes into breast milk. Nursing mothers should not take this or any other appetite suppressant.

Seniors

Older adults should not take this medicine unless prescribed by a doctor. It can aggravate diabetes or high blood pressure, conditions common to older adults.

Possible Side Effects

Common side effects are a false sense of well-being, nervousness, overstimulation, restlessness, and trouble sleeping. Other, less common, side effects are palpitations, high blood pressure, drowsiness, sedation, weakness, dizziness, tremor, headache, dry mouth, nausea, vomiting, diarrhea, other intestinal disturbances, rash, itching, changes in sex drive, hair loss, muscle pains, difficulty urinating, sweating, chills, blurred vision, and fever.

Drug Interactions

Taking other stimulants together with Mazindol may result in excessive stimulation. Taking this medicine within 14 days of any monoamine oxidase (MAO) inhibitor drug may result in severe high blood pressure.

Appetite suppressants may reduce the effects of some medicines used to treat high blood pressure.

One case of Lithium toxicity occurred in a person taking Mazindol.

Food Interactions

Do not crush or chew this product. Mazindol can be taken on a full stomach to reduce upset stomach caused by the drug.

Usual Dose

1 milligram 3 times a day, 1 hour before meals, or 2 milligrams once a day, before lunch.

Overdosage

Symptoms of overdose are restlessness, tremor, shallow breathing, confusion, hallucinations, and fever, followed by fatigue and depression. Additional symptoms are changes in blood pressure, cold and clammy skin, nausea, vomiting, diarrhea, and stomach cramps. Take the victim to a hospital emergency room immediately. ALWAYS bring the medicine bottle.

Special Information

Do not take this medicine for more than 12 weeks as part of a weight-control program, and take it only under a doctor's supervision. This medicine will not reduce body weight by itself. You must limit or modify your food intake.

This drug can cause dry mouth, which can be relieved by sugarless candy or gum or by ice chips.

If you forget to take a dose of Mazindol, do not take the forgotten dose. Skip the dose and go back to your regular schedule. Do not take a double dose.

Generic Name

Meclizine

Brand Names

Antivert	Dizmiss
Antrizine	Meni-D
Bonine	Ru Vert M

(Also available in generic form)

Type of Drug

Antiemetic; antivertigo agent.

Prescribed for

Relief of nausea, vomiting, and dizziness associated with motion sickness or disease affecting the middle ear.

General Information

Meclizine is an antihistamine used to treat or prevent nausea, vomiting, and motion sickness. It takes a little longer to start working than most other drugs of this type but its effects last much longer (1 to 2 days). The specific method by which Meclizine acts on the brain to prevent dizziness and the nausea associated with it is not fully understood. In general, Meclizine does a better job of preventing motion sickness than of treating the symptoms once they are present.

Use with caution in children as a treatment for vomiting or nausea. This drug may obscure symptoms important in reaching the diagnosis of underlying disease. Meclizine is one of several drugs prescribed for the relief of nausea, vomiting, or dizziness that do not cure any underlying problems.

Cautions and Warnings

Do not take this medication if you think you are allergic to it or other antihistamines.

Pregnancy/Breast-feeding

Meclizine may cause birth defects or other problems in pregnant women. Do not take this medicine without your doctor's knowledge.

Small amounts of antihistamine medicines pass into breast milk and may affect a nursing infant. Nursing mothers should avoid antihistamines or use alternative feeding methods while taking the medicine.

Seniors

Seniors are more sensitive to antihistamine side effects. Confusion, difficult or painful urination, dizziness, drowsiness, a faint feeling, dry mouth, nose, or throat, nightmares or excitement, nervousness, restlessness, or irritability are more likely to occur among older adults.

Possible Side Effects

The most common side effects are drowsiness, dry mouth, blurred vision.

Infrequent side effects include difficulty in urination, constipation. Adverse effects are usually not cause for great concern. If they become serious, discuss them with your doctor.

Drug Interactions

Meclizine may cause sleepiness, tiredness, or inability to concentrate. Avoid tranquilizers, sleeping pills, alcoholic beverages, barbiturates, narcotics, and antihistamines, which can add to these effects.

Usual Dose

Adult: 25 to 50 milligrams 1 hour before travel; repeat every 24 hours for duration of journey. For control of dizziness (diseases affecting middle ear, etc.), 25 to 100 milligrams per day in divided doses.

Child: This drug should not be used.

Overdosage

Symptoms are depression or stimulation (especially in children), dry mouth, fixed or dilated pupils, flushing of the skin, and stomach upset. Take the patient to a hospital emergency room immediately, if you cannot make him or her vomit. ALWAYS bring the medicine bottle.

Special Information

Meclizine may cause tiredness, sleepiness, and inability to concentrate. Be extremely careful while driving or operating any machinery, appliances, or delicate equipment.

If you forget to take a dose of Meclizine, take it as soon as you remember. If it is almost time for your next regularly scheduled dose, skip the one you forgot and continue with your regular schedule. Do not take a double dose.

Generic Name

Meclofenamate Sodium

Brand Name

Meclomen

(Also available in generic form)

Type of Drug

Nonsteroidal anti-inflammatory.

Prescribed for

Arthritis; mild to moderate pain from menstrual cramps, dental surgery and extractions, and athletic injuries such as sprains and strains.

General Information

Meclofenamate Sodium is one of many nonsteroidal anti-inflammatory drugs (NSAIDs) available in the United States for the treatment of pain and inflammation of arthritis and osteoarthritis. Many people find they must try several of these NSAIDs before they find the one that is right for their condition. Meclofenamate Sodium must be taken for several days before it exerts any effect, and takes 2 to 3 weeks for the maximum effect to develop.

As a group, these drugs reduce inflammation and ease pain via the same mechanism and share many side effects, the most common of which are stomach upset and irritation. In fact, the potential effect of Meclofenamate Sodium on the stomach and intestines is so severe that it is recommended for use only after other medications have proven ineffective for controlling a patient's symptoms.

Cautions and Warnings

Do not use Meclofenamate Sodium if you have had an allergic reaction to it or to any other NSAIDs. Also, people allergic to Aspirin should not take Meclofenamate Sodium.

People with reduced kidney function should receive lower than the usual dose because their ability to remove the drug from the body is impaired. Their kidney function should be monitored by periodic measurements of blood-creatinine levels.

Pregnancy/Breast-feeding

Meclofenamate Sodium should be avoided by pregnant women, women who may become pregnant while using it, and nursing mothers, since this drug may pass into breast milk. In those situations where the drug is deemed essential, the potential risk of taking it must be carefully weighed against any benefit it might produce.

Seniors

Older patients should be treated with a reduced daily dosage because they are more likely to be sensitive to the side effects. Report any side effects to your doctor at once.

Possible Side Effects

The most common side effects are nausea, vomiting, and diarrhea, which may be severe. Other possible side effects are heartburn, stomach pain and discomfort, stomach ulcer, bleeding in the stomach or intestines, liver inflammation and jaundice, dizziness, headache, and rashes.

Less common side effects include light-headedness, nervousness, tension, fainting, tingling in the hands or feet, muscle weakness and aches, tiredness, a feeling of ill health, difficulty sleeping, drowsiness, strange dreams, confusion, loss of the ability to concentrate, depression, personality changes, stuffy nose, changes in taste perception, heart failure, low blood pressure, fluid retention, cystitis, urinary infection, changes in kidney function, nosebleeds, hemorrhage, easy bruising, reduction in the count of some white blood cells, itching, hair loss, appetite and body-weight changes, increased sugar in the blood or urine, increased need for Insulin in diabetic patients, flushing or sweating, menstrual difficulty, and vaginal bleeding.

Drug Interactions

Meclofenamate Sodium may enhance the activity of oral anticoagulants (blood-thinning agents), Phenytoin and other antiseizure drugs, oral antidiabetes drugs, and sulfa drugs by increasing the amounts of these agents in the bloodstream. People taking Meclofenamate Sodium in combination with any of these medications may require a reduction in the dosage of the latter drugs.

Aspirin reduces the effectiveness of Meclofenamate Sodium. These drugs should never be taken together.

Probenecid may increase the action of Meclofenamate Sodium in your blood and cause side effects. People taking these drugs in combination should report any side effects or adverse effects to their doctor at once.

Food Interactions

Meclofenamate Sodium may be taken with food or meals if it upsets your stomach. If your stomach is still irritated, your dosage may have to be reduced, or you may have to change to another NSAID.

Usual Dose

200 to 400 milligrams per day.

Overdosage

The primary symptom of overdose is acute stomach and intestinal distress. Symptoms generally develop within an hour of the overdose and resolve on their own within another 24 hours. Patients taking an overdose of this drug must be made to vomit with Syrup of Ipecac (available at any pharmacy) to remove any remaining drug from the stomach if the overdose was taken within the past hour. Call your doctor or a poison control center before doing this. If more than an hour has passed, go to a hospital emergency room. ALWAYS bring the medicine bottle.

Accutane 20 mg p. 436	**Acetaminophen** w/ Codeine #3 p. 14	**Achromycin V** 250 mg p. 855	**Actigall** 300 mg p. 945
Adalat 10 mg p. 609	**Advil** 200 mg p. 412	**Aldactazide** 25/25 p. 30	**Aldomet** 250 mg p. 540
Allopurinol 300 mg p. 33	**Altace** 2.5 mg p. 790	**Alupent** 10 mg p. 526	**Amitriptyline** 25 mg p. 45
Amitriptyline 50 mg p. 45	**Amoxicillin** 250 mg p. 671	**Amoxicillin** 500 mg p. 671	**Amoxil** 250 mg p. 671
Amoxil 500 mg p. 671	**Amoxil Chewable** 125 mg p. 671	**Amoxil Chewable** 250 mg p. 671	**Ampicillin** 250 mg p. 671

A

Anafranil 25 mg p. 166	Anafranil 50 mg p. 166	Anaprox 275 mg p. 596	
Anaprox DS 550 mg p. 596		Ancobon 500 mg p. 352	Ansaid 50 mg p. 368
Antivert 12.5 mg p. 502	Antivert 25 mg p. 502	Antivert Chewable 25 mg p. 502	Armour Thyroid 1 1/2 gr p. 878
Armour Thyroid 4 gr p. 878	Asendin 25 mg p. 48	Asendin 50 mg p. 48	Atarax 25 mg p. 410
Atarax 50 mg p. 410	Ativan 0.5 mg p. 483	Ativan 1 mg p. 483	Atromid-S 500 mg p. 162

B

Augmentin 250 mg p. 671	**Augmentin** 500 mg p. 671

Augmentin Chewable 125 mg p. 671	**Azulfidine** 500 mg p. 820	**Bactrim DS** p. 806

Beepen VK 250 mg p. 672	**Blocadren** 10 mg p. 882	**Brethine** 2.5 mg p. 846	**Bricanyl** 2.5 mg p. 846

Bumex 1 mg p. 97	**BuSpar** 5 mg p. 104	**Butazolidin** 100 mg p. 708	**Butazolidin** 100 mg p. 708

Calan 40 mg p. 954	**Calan** 80 mg p. 954	**Calan** 120 mg p. 954	**Calan SR** 180 mg p. 954

C

Calan SR 240 mg p. 954	**Capoten** 12.5 mg p. 111	**Capoten** 25 mg p. 111
Capoten 50 mg p. 111	**Capoten** 100 mg p. 111	**Capozide** 25/15 p. 108
	Capozide 25/25 p. 108	
Carafate 1 g p. 818	**Cardene** 20 mg p. 601	**Cardizem** 30 mg p. 255
Cardizem 60 mg p. 255	**Cardizem** 90 mg p. 255	
Cardizem 120 mg p. 255	**Cardizem-SR** 60 mg p. 255	**Cardizem-SR** 90 mg p. 255

D

Cardizem-SR 120 mg p. 255	**Cardura** 2 mg p. 272	**Cardura** 4 mg p. 272	**Cartrol** 2.5 mg p. 120
Catapres 0.1 mg p. 173	**Catapres** 0.2 mg p. 173	**Ceclor** 250 mg p. 124	**Ceclor** 500 mg p. 124
Ceftin 125 mg p. 124	**Ceftin** 250 mg p. 124	**Ceftin** 500 mg p. 124	
Centrax 10 mg p. 738	**Cephalexin** 250 mg p. 124	**Cephalexin** 500 mg p. 124	**Chlor-Trimeton** 4 mg p. 134
Chlor-Trimeton Repetabs 8 mg p. 134	**Chlorpropamide** 250 mg p. 140		**Cinobac** 250 mg p. 151

E

Cipro 250 mg p. 153	Cipro 500 mg p. 153

Cipro 750 mg p. 153	Cleocin 150 mg p. 160	Clinoril 150 mg p. 824

Clozaril 25 mg p. 181	Cogentin 1 mg p. 82	Compazine 10 mg p. 755	Compazine Spansule 15 mg p. 755

Cordarone 200 mg p. 41	Corgard 40 mg p. 593	Corgard 160 mg p. 593

Cotrim DS p. 806	Coumadin 5 mg p. 959	Coumadin 7.5 mg p. 959

F

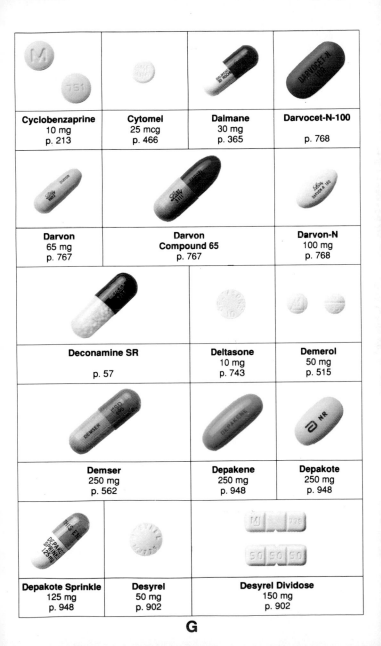

Cyclobenzaprine 10 mg p. 213	**Cytomel** 25 mcg p. 466	**Dalmane** 30 mg p. 365	**Darvocet-N-100** p. 768

Darvon 65 mg p. 767	**Darvon** **Compound 65** p. 767	**Darvon-N** 100 mg p. 768

Deconamine SR p. 57	**Deltasone** 10 mg p. 743	**Demerol** 50 mg p. 515

Demser 250 mg p. 562	**Depakene** 250 mg p. 948	**Depakote** 250 mg p. 948

Depakote Sprinkle 125 mg p. 948	**Desyrel** 50 mg p. 902	**Desyrel Dividose** 150 mg p. 902

G

DiaBeta 2.5 mg p. 385	**Diabinese** 250 mg p. 140	**Diflucan** 50 mg p. 349	**Dilantin** 100 mg p. 711
Ditropan 5 mg p. 651	**Diulo** 5 mg p. 864	**Diuril** 500 mg p. 863	
Dolobid 250 mg p. 248	**Donnatal** p. 269	**Donnatal** p. 269	**Dopar** 250 mg p.455
Doral 7.5 mg p. 780	**Doral** 15 mg p. 780	**Doxepin** 25 mg p. 275	**Doxycycline** 100 mg p. 279
Dramamine 50 mg p. 258	**Drixoral** p. 58	**Duricef** 500 mg p. 124	**Duricef** 1 g p. 124

H

Dyazide 50/25 p. 286	**DynaCirc** 2.5 mg p. 441	**E.E.S. 400** 400 mg p. 304	**E-Mycin** 250 mg p. 304
E-Mycin 333 mg p. 304	**Elavil** 10 mg p. 45	**Elavil** 25 mg p. 45	**Elavil** 75 mg p. 45
Elavil 150 mg p. 45	**Eldepryl** 5 mg p. 802	**Elixophyllin SR** 125 mg p. 859	**Empirin with Codeine #2** p. 65
Empirin with Codeine #3 p. 65	**Empirin with Codeine #4** p. 65	**Endep** 10 mg p. 45	**Endep** 50 mg p. 45
Enduron 2.5 mg p. 864	**Entex LA** p. 297	**Equagesic** p. 300	

I

ERYC 250 mg p. 304	**EryPed** 200 mg p. 304	**Ery-Tab** 250 mg p. 304	**Ery-Tab** 333 mg p. 304
Ery-Tab 500 mg p. 304	**Erythrocin Stearate** 250 mg p. 304	**Erythromycin Base** 250 mg p. 304	**Esgic** p. 341
Esidrix 25 mg p. 863	**Eskalith** 300 mg p. 475	**Estrace Oral** 1 mg p. 312	**Ethmozine** 250 mg p. 585
Etrafon 2/10 p. 910	**Etrafon** 4/10 p. 910	**Fastin** 30 mg p. 706	**Feldene** 10 mg p. 728
Feldene 20 mg p. 728	**Fioricet** p. 341		**Fiorinal** p. 340

J

Fiorinal with Codeine 30 mg p. 343	**Flagyl** 250 mg p. 559	**Flexeril** 10 mg p. 213	**Floxin** 200 mg p. 635
Furosemide 40 mg p. 374	**Glucotrol** 5 mg p. 381	**Halcion** 0.125 mg p. 913	**Halcion** 0.25 mg p. 913
Haldol 0.5 mg p. 404	**Haldol** 2 mg p. 404	**Haldol** 10 mg p. 404	**Halotestin** 5 mg p. 360
Hismanal 10 mg p. 68	**Hydro-Diuril** 25 mg p. 863	**Hydroxyzine** 25 mg p. 410	**Hygroton** 25 mg p. 863
Hytrin 1 mg p. 843	**Hytrin** 5 mg p. 843	**Ibuprofen** 400 mg p. 412	

K

Ibuprofen 600 mg p. 412	**Ibuprofen** 800 mg p. 412

Imodium 2 mg p. 481	**Inderal** 10 mg p. 770	**Inderal** 20 mg p. 770	**Inderal** 40 mg p. 770
Inderal 80 mg p. 770	**Inderal LA** 60 mg p. 770	**Inderal LA** 120 mg p. 770	**Inderide** 40/25 p. 419
Inderide LA 80/50 p. 420	**Indocin** 25 mg p. 422	**Indocin SR** 75 mg p. 422	**Ionamin** 15 mg p. 706

Ismelin 10 mg p. 395	**Isoptin** 40 mg p. 954	**Isoptin** 120 mg p. 954

L

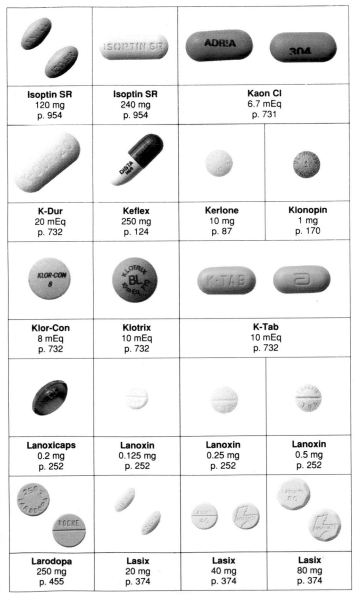

Isoptin SR 120 mg p. 954	**Isoptin SR** 240 mg p. 954	**Kaon Cl** 6.7 mEq p. 731	
K-Dur 20 mEq p. 732	**Keflex** 250 mg p. 124	**Kerlone** 10 mg p. 87	**Klonopin** 1 mg p. 170
Klor-Con 8 mEq p. 732	**Klotrix** 10 mEq p. 732	**K-Tab** 10 mEq p. 732	
Lanoxicaps 0.2 mg p. 252	**Lanoxin** 0.125 mg p. 252	**Lanoxin** 0.25 mg p. 252	**Lanoxin** 0.5 mg p. 252
Larodopa 250 mg p. 455	**Lasix** 20 mg p. 374	**Lasix** 40 mg p. 374	**Lasix** 80 mg p. 374

M

Ledercillin VK 250 mg p. 672	**Levatol** 20 mg p. 667	**Libritabs** 10 mg p. 128	
Librium 10 mg p. 128	**Limbitrol** p. 462	**Lithobid** 300 mg p. 475	**Lithonate** 300 mg p. 475
Lo/Ovral 28 p. 196	**Lodine** 200 mg p. 325	**Lomotil** p. 196	
		Lopid 600 mg p. 378	**Lopressor** 50 mg p. 555
Lopressor 100 mg p. 555	**Lorazepam** 0.5 mg p. 483	**Lorelco** 250 mg p. 750	**Lortab** 5 mg p. 956

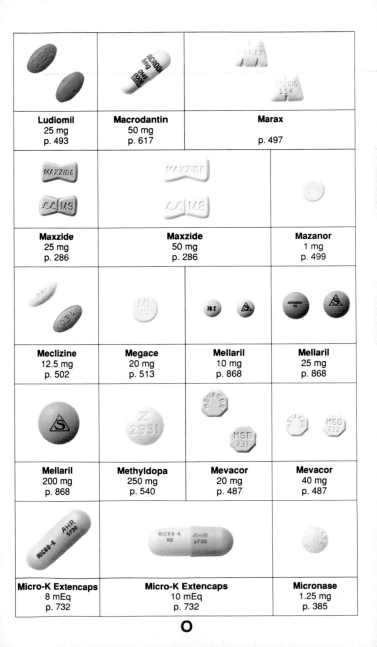

Ludiomil 25 mg p. 493	**Macrodantin** 50 mg p. 617	**Marax** p. 497
Maxzide 25 mg p. 286	**Maxzide** 50 mg p. 286	**Mazanor** 1 mg p. 499
Meclizine 12.5 mg p. 502	**Megace** 20 mg p. 513	**Mellaril** 10 mg p. 868
Mellaril 200 mg p. 868	**Methyldopa** 250 mg p. 540	**Mellaril** 25 mg p. 868
		Mevacor 20 mg p. 487
Micro-K Extencaps 8 mEq p. 732	**Micro-K Extencaps** 10 mEq p. 732	**Mevacor** 40 mg p. 487
		Micronase 1.25 mg p. 385

O

Micronor Dialpak

p. 197

Minipress
1 mg
p. 741

Minipress
2 mg
p. 741

Minizide
1 mg
p. 570

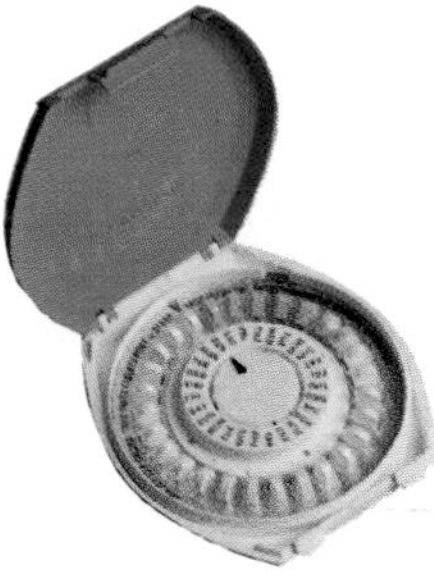

Modicon Dialpak

p. 196

Moduretic

p. 582

Motofen

p. 589

Motrin
400 mg
p. 412

Motrin
800 mg
p. 412

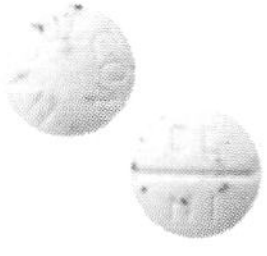

Naldecon

p. 58

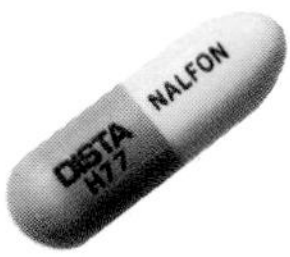

Nalfon
300 mg
p. 335

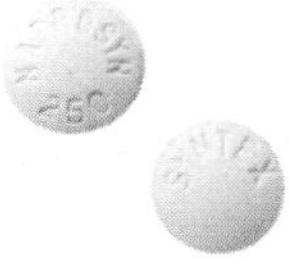

Naprosyn
250 mg
p. 596

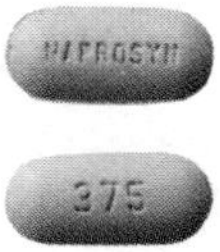

Naprosyn
375 mg
p. 596

P

Nicorette 2 mg p. 604	**Nifedipine** 10 mg p. 609	**Nifedipine** 20 mg p. 609	**Nitro-Bid** 2.5 mg p. 620

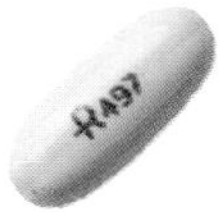

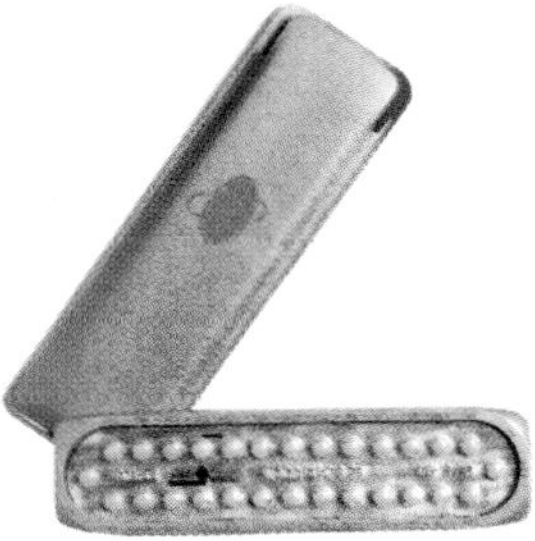

	Nizoral 200 mg p. 443	**Nolvadex** 10 mg p. 830

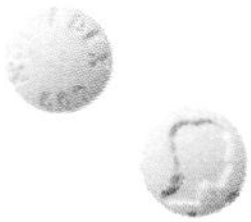

Nordette-28

p. 196

Norgesic Forte

p. 627

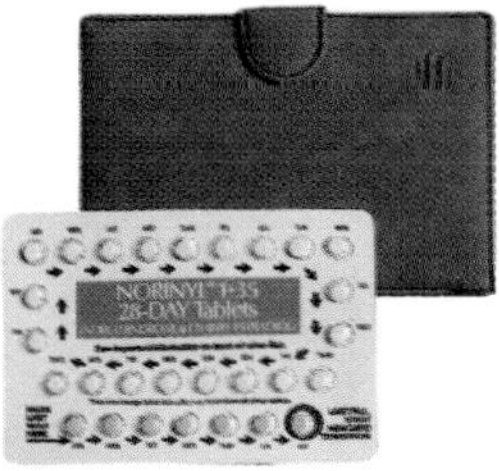

Norinyl
1-35
p. 196

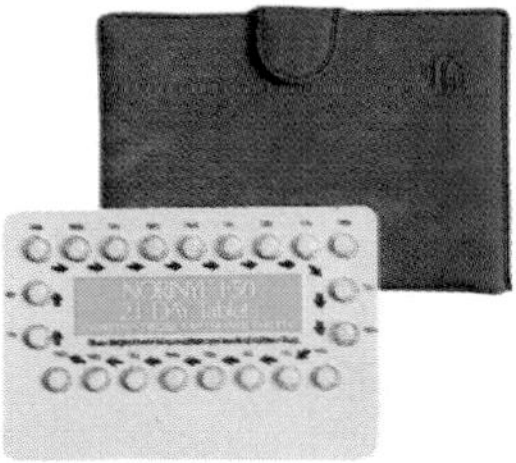

Norinyl
1-50
p. 196

Q

Normodyne 200 mg p. 449	**Noroxin** 400 mg p. 624	

Norpace 100 mg p. 266	**Norpace CR** 100 mg p. 266	**Norpramin** 10 mg p. 231	**Norpramin** 50 mg p. 231

Norpramin 100 mg p. 231	**Novafed A** p. 57	**Nuprin** 200 mg p. 412

Ogen 0.625 mg p. 312	**Ogen** 2.5 mg p. 312

Omnipen 250 mg p. 671	**Orap** 2 mg p. 717	**Organidin** 30 mg p. 431	**Orinase** 250 mg p. 896

R

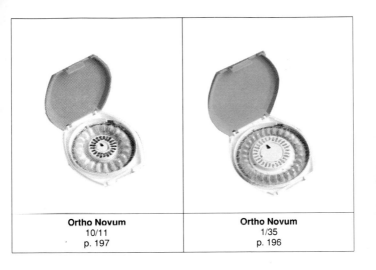

Ortho Novum
10/11
p. 197

Ortho Novum
1/35
p. 196

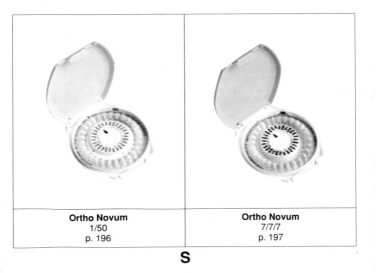

Ortho Novum
1/50
p. 196

Ortho Novum
7/7/7
p. 197

S

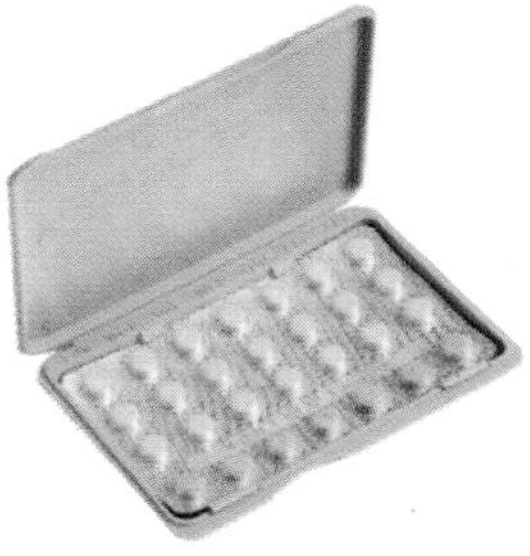

Ovcon-35

p. 196

Ovcon-50

p. 196

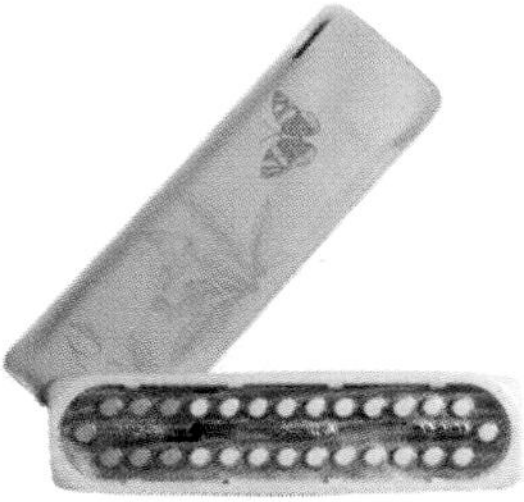

Ovral-28

p. 197

Oxycodone with Acetaminophen
p. 685

Oxycodone and Aspirin
p. 688

Pamelor
25 mg
p. 630

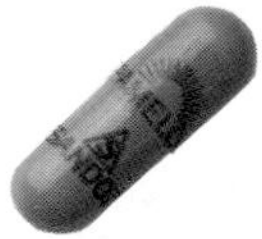

Pamelor
75 mg
p. 630

Parafon Forte DSC
500 mg
p. 143

PCE
333 mg
p. 305

PCE
500 mg
p. 305

T

Pen-Vee K 250 mg p. 672	**Pen-Vee K** 500 mg p. 672	**Penicillin G** 400,000 U p. 672	**Pentids** 400 mg p. 672
Pepcid 20 mg p. 329	**Pepcid** 40 mg p. 329	**Percocet** p. 685	
Percodan p. 688		**Permax** 0.05 mg p. 691	**Phenaphen with Codeine #2** p. 17
Phenaphen with Codeine #3 p. 17	**Phenaphen with Codeine #4** p. 17	**Phenergan** 25 mg p. 759	**Phenobarbital** 15 mg p. 699
Phenobarbital 30 mg p. 699	**Phenobarbital** 60 mg p. 699	**Plegine** 35 mg p. 694	**Polycillin** 250 mg p. 671

U

Ponstel 250 mg p. 509	**Premarin** 0.3 mg p. 312	**Premarin** 0.625 mg p. 312	**Premarin** 0.9 mg p. 312
Premarin 1.25 mg p. 312	**Premarin** 2.5 mg p. 312	**Prilosec** 20 mg p. 641	**Principen** 250 mg p. 671
Prinivil 5 mg p. 473	**Prinivil** 20 mg p. 473	**Procan SR** 250 mg p. 753	**Procan SR** 750 mg p. 753
Procardia 10 mg p. 609	**Procardia** 20 mg p. 609	**Procardia XL** 30 mg p. 609	**Procardia XL** 60 mg p. 609
Procardia XL 90 mg p. 609		**Prolixin** 5 mg p. 362	**Prolixin** 10 mg p. 362

Proloid 32 mg p. 875	**Proloid** 130 mg p. 875	**Proloid** 200 mg p. 875	**Pronestyl** 250 mg p. 753

Pronestyl 500 mg p. 753	**Pronestyl SR** 500 mg p. 753	**Propacet 100** p. 768

Propoxyphene Napsylate **w/Acetaminophen** p. 768	**Proventil Repetabs** 4 mg p. 26	**Provera** 2.5 mg p. 507

Provera 5 mg p. 507	**Provera** 10 mg p. 507	**Prozac** 20 mg p. 356

Quinaglute Dura-Tabs 324 mg p. 787	**Quinidex** **Extentabs** 300 mg p. 787	**Reglan** 5 mg p. 553

W

Restoril 30 mg p. 834	**Retrovir** 100 mg p. 964	**Rimactane** 300 mg p. 795	**Ritalin** 5 mg p. 544
Ritalin 20 mg p. 544	**Ritalin SR** 20 mg p. 544	**Rufen** 400 mg p. 412	**Rufen** 800 mg p. 412
Rythmol 150 mg p. 763	**Sansert** 2 mg p. 549	**Sectral** 200 mg p. 11	**Seldane** 60 mg p. 850
Septra 400/800 p. 805	**Septra DS** 800/160 p. 806	**Serax** 10 mg p. 644	**Serax** 30 mg p. 644
Sinemet 10-100 p. 808	**Sinemet** 25-100 p. 808	**Sinemet** 25-250 p. 808	

Sinequan 10 mg p. 275	**Sinequan** 50 mg p. 275	**Sinequan** 100 mg p. 275	**Sinequan** 150 mg p. 275
Skelaxin 400 mg p. 528		**Slo-Bid Gyrocaps** 50 mg p. 859	**Slo-Bid Gyrocaps** 100 mg p. 859
Slo-Bid Gyrocaps 300 mg p. 859	**Slo-Phyllin Gyrocaps** 125 mg p. 859	**Slo-Phyllin Gyrocaps** 250 mg p. 859	**Slow K** 600 mg p. 732
Sorbitrate 5 mg p. 433	**Sorbitrate** 10 mg p. 433	**Sorbitrate** 20 mg p. 433	**Sorbitrate** 40 mg p. 433
Sorbitrate SA 40 mg p. 433		**Spectrobid** 400 mg p. 671	

Y

Stelazine 2 mg p. 916	**Stelazine** 10 mg p. 916	**Sudafed** 30 mg p. 778	**Sumycin** 250 mg p. 855

Suprax 200 mg p. 124	**Suprax** 400 mg p. 124

Surmontil 25 mg p. 925	**Surmontil** 100 mg p. 925	**Symmetrel** 100 mg p. 456	**Synalgos DC** p. 827

Synthroid 0.025 mg p. 459	**Synthroid** 0.05 mg p. 459	**Synthroid** 0.075 mg p. 459	**Synthroid** 0.1 mg p. 459

Synthroid 0.125 mg p. 459	**Synthroid** 0.15 mg p. 459	**Synthroid** 0.2 mg p. 459	**Synthroid** 0.3 mg p. 459

Z

Tagamet 200 mg p. 148	**Tagamet** 300 mg p. 148	**Tagamet** 400 mg p. 148	**Tagamet** 800 mg p. 148
Talwin NX p. 677	**Tavist** 2.68 mg p. 158	**Tavist D** 75/1.34 p. 58	**Tedral SA** p. 832
Tegopen 250 mg p. 672	**Tegretol** 200 mg p. 114	**Tegretol Chewable** 100 mg p. 114	
Teldrin 12 mg p. 134	**Tenex** 1 mg p. 398	**Tenoretic-50** p. 838	**Tenoretic-100** p. 838
Tenormin 50 mg p. 70	**Tenormin** 100 mg p. 70	**Tenuate Dospan** 75 mg p. 246	**Tetracycline** 250 mg p. 855

AA

Theo-Dur 100 mg p. 859	**Theo-Dur** 200 mg p. 859	**Theo-Dur** 300 mg p. 859	**Theo-Dur** 450 mg p. 859
Theolair 125 mg p. 859	**Theolair SR** 250 mg p. 859	**Theolair SR** 500 mg p. 859	**Thorazine** 10 mg p. 137
Thorazine 50 mg p. 137	**Thorazine** 100 mg p. 137	**Thorazine Spansule** 75 mg p. 137	**Thorazine Spansule** 200 mg p. 137
Tigan 100 mg p. 922	**Tigan** 250 mg p. 922	**TMP/SMZ** p. 806	**Tofranil** 10 mg p. 415
Tofranil 25 mg p. 415	**Tofranil PM** 75 mg p. 415	**Tolectin DS** 400 mg p. 899	**Tolinase** 100 mg p. 893

BB

Tonocard 400 mg p. 890	**Tonocard** 600 mg p. 890	**Trandate** 100 mg p. 449	**Trandate** 300 mg p. 449
Tranxene T-Tab 3.75 mg p. 176	**Tranxene T-Tab** 15 mg p. 176	**Trental** 400 mg p. 682	
Triavil 2-10 p. 910	**Triavil** 2-25 p. 910	**Triavil** 4-10 p. 910	**Triavil** 4-25 p. 910

	Trimox 500 mg p. 671
Tri-Levlen 28 p. 197	**Trinalin Repetabs** p. 57

CC

Tri-Norinyl 28 p. 197	**TriPhasil-28** p. 197

Tuss-Ornade p. 943	**Tylenol with Codeine #1** p. 17	**Tylenol with Codeine #2** p. 17	**Tylenol with Codeine #3** p. 17
Tylenol with Codeine #4 p. 17	**Tylox** p. 685	**Ultracef** 500 mg p. 124	**V-Cillin K** 125 mg p. 672
V-Cillin K 500 mg p. 672	**Valium** 2 mg p. 240	**Valium** 5 mg p. 240	**Valium** 10 mg p. 240

DD

Valrelease 15 mg p. 240	**Vaseretic** 10-25 p. 950	**Vasotec** 2.5 mg p. 294	**Vasotec** 5 mg p. 294
Vasotec 10 mg p. 294	**Vasotec** 20 mg p. 294	**Veetids** 250 mg p. 672	**Veetids** 500 mg p. 672
Velosef 250 mg p. 125	**Velosef** 500 mg p. 125	**Ventolin** 2 mg p. 26	**Ventolin** 4 mg p. 26
Verelan 120 mg p. 954	**Vibra-Tabs** 100 mg p. 279	**Vibramycin** 50 mg p. 279	**Vicodin** 5-500 p. 956
Vicoden-ES 7.5-750 p. 956	**Visken** 5 mg p. 723	**Vivactil** 10 mg p. 774	**Voltaren** 25 mg p. 243

Voltaren 50 mg p. 243	**Voltaren** 75 mg p. 243	**Wellbutrin** 75 mg p. 100	**Wymox** 250 mg p. 671
Wytensin 4 mg p. 390	**Xanax** 0.25 mg p. 35	**Xanax** 0.5 mg p. 35	**Xanax** 1 mg p. 35
Xanax 2 mg p. 35	**Yutopar** 10 mg p. 797	**Zantac** 150 mg p. 792	**Zantac** 300 mg p. 792
Zaroxolyn 2.5 mg p. 864	**Zaroxolyn** 10 mg p. 864	**Zestril** 5 mg p. 473	**Zestril** 40 mg p. 473
ZORprin 800 mg p. 61		**Zovirax** 200 mg p. 22	**Zovirax** 800 mg p. 22

FF

Special Information

Meclofenamate Sodium may cause blurred vision or drowsiness. Because of this, you should be especially careful while driving or doing anything else that requires concentration.

Call your doctor if you develop severe stomach or intestinal irritation, sudden weight gain, rash, itching, swelling, black or tarry bowel movements, or intense headaches.

If you forget to take a dose of Meclofenamate Sodium, take it as soon as you remember. If it is almost time for your next regularly scheduled dose, skip the one you forgot and continue with your regular schedule. Do not take a double dose.

Generic Name

Medroxyprogesterone Acetate

Brand Names

Amen   Cycrin
Curretab   Provera

(Also available in generic form)

Type of Drug

Progestogen.

Prescribed for

Irregular menstrual bleeding.

General Information

Because of the potential development of secondary disease after a long period of taking Medroxyprogesterone Acetate, the decision to take this medication chronically should be made cautiously by you and your doctor. Your continued need for chronic therapy with Medroxyprogesterone Acetate should be evaluated at least every 6 months to be sure that this therapy is absolutely necessary.

Cautions and Warnings

Do not take this drug if you have a history of blood clots or similar disorders, a history of convulsions, liver disease, known or suspected breast cancer, undiagnosed vaginal bleeding, or miscarriage. Medroxyprogesterone Acetate use should be carefully considered if you have asthma, cardiac insufficiency, epilepsy, migraine headaches, kidney problems, diabetes, a history of ectopic pregnancy, high blood-fat levels, or depression.

Pregnancy/Breast-feeding

This drug is known to cause birth defects or interfere with your baby's development. It is not considered safe for use during pregnancy.

This drug passes into breast milk, but has caused no problems among breast-fed infants. You must consider the potential effect on the nursing infant if breast-feeding while taking this medicine.

Seniors

Older adults with severe liver disease are more sensitive to the effects of this drug. Follow your doctor's directions and report any side effects at once.

Possible Side Effects

Breakthrough bleeding, spotting, changes in or loss of menstrual flow, retention of water, increase or decrease in weight, jaundice, rash (with or without itching), mental depression.

A significant association has been demonstrated between the use of progestogen drugs and the development of blood clots in the veins, lungs, or brain. Other possible adverse effects include changes in libido or sex drive, changes in appetite and mood, headache, nervousness, dizziness, tiredness, backache, loss of scalp hair, growth of hair in unusual quantities or places, itching, symptoms similar to urinary infections, unusual rashes.

Drug Interactions

Medroxyprogesterone Acetate may interfere with the effects

of Bromocriptine and should not be used at the same time as that drug.

Food Interactions

This medicine is best taken on an empty stomach, but you may take it with food if it upsets your stomach.

Usual Dose

5 to 10 milligrams per day for 5 to 10 days beginning on what is assumed to be the 16th to 21st day of the menstrual cycle.

Overdose

Medroxyprogesterone Acetate overdose may result in exaggerated side effects. In may cases, small overdoses will result in no unusual symptoms. Call your local poison control center or hospital emergency room for more information.

Special Information

At the first sign of sudden, partial, or complete loss of vision, leg cramps, water retention, unusual vaginal bleeding, migraine headache, or depression, or if you think you have become pregnant, stop the drug immediately and call your doctor.

If you forget to take a dose of Medroxyprogesterone Acetate, take it as soon as you remember. If it is almost time for your next regularly scheduled dose, skip the one you forgot and continue with your regular schedule. Do not take a double dose.

Generic Name

Mefenamic Acid

Brand Name

Ponstel

Type of Drug

Nonsteroidal anti-inflammatory.

Prescribed for

Mild to moderate pain when anti-inflammatory effects are desirable and treatment will last a week or less; menstrual cramps; migraine headache; dental surgery and extractions; athletic injuries such as sprains and strains.

General Information

Mefenamic Acid is one of many nonsteroidal anti-inflammatory drugs (NSAIDs) available in the United States for the treatment of pain. Many people find they must try several of these NSAIDs before they find the one that is right for their condition.

As a group, these drugs reduce inflammation and ease pain via the same mechanism and share many side effects, the most common of which are stomach upset and irritation. In fact, the potential effect of Mefenamic Acid on the stomach and intestines is so severe that it is recommended for use only after other medications have proven ineffective for controlling a patient's symptoms.

Cautions and Warnings

Do not use Mefenamic Acid if you have had an allergic reaction to it or to any other NSAIDs. Also, people allergic to Aspirin should not take Mefenamic Acid.

Do not use Mefenamic Acid if you have ulcers or chronic inflammation of either the upper or lower GI tract. If diarrhea develops, call your doctor at once. Your dosage may be reduced or you may be switched to another NSAID.

People with reduced kidney function should receive lower than the usual dose because their ability to remove the drug from the body is impaired. Their kidney function should be monitored by periodic measurements of blood-creatinine levels.

Pregnancy/Breast-feeding

This drug should be avoided by pregnant women, women who may become pregnant while using it, and nursing mothers, since this drug may pass into breast milk. In those situations where the drug is deemed essential, the potential risk of taking it must be carefully weighed against any benefit it might produce.

Seniors

Older patients should be given a lower daily dosage of Mefenamic Acid than younger adults because they are more likely
to be sensitive to drug side effects. Report any side effects
to your doctor at once.

Possible Side Effects

The most common side effects are nausea, vomiting, and
diarrhea, which may be severe. Other possible side effects
are heartburn, stomach pain and discomfort, stomach ulcer,
bleeding in the stomach or intestines, liver inflammation and
jaundice, dizziness, headache, and rashes.

Less common side effects include light-headedness, nervousness, tension, fainting, tingling in the hands or feet,
muscle weakness and aches, tiredness, a feeling of ill health,
difficulty sleeping, drowsiness, strange dreams, confusion,
loss of the ability to concentrate, depression, personality
changes, stuffy nose, changes in taste perception, heart failure, low blood pressure, fluid retention, cystitis, urinary infection, changes in kidney function, nosebleeds, hemorrhage,
easy bruising, reduction in the count of some white blood
cells, itching, hair loss, appetite and body-weight changes,
increased sugar in the blood or urine, increased need for
Insulin in diabetic patients, flushing or sweating, menstrual
difficulty, and vaginal bleeding.

Drug Interactions

Mefenamic Acid may enhance the activity of oral anticoagulants (blood-thinning agents), Phenytoin and other antiseizure drugs, oral antidiabetes drugs, and sulfa drugs by
increasing the amounts of these agents in the bloodstream.
People taking Mefenamic Acid in combination with any of
these medications may require a reduction in the dosage of
the latter drugs.

Mefenamic Acid may interfere with the blood-pressure-
lowering effects of beta-blocking drugs.

Aspirin reduces the effectiveness of Mefenamic Acid.
These drugs should never be taken together.

Probenecid may increase the action of Mefenamic Acid in
your blood and cause side effects. People taking these drugs

in combination should report any side effects or adverse effects to their doctor at once.

Food Interactions

Mefenamic Acid should be taken with food or meals if it upsets your stomach. If your stomach still becomes irritated, your dosage may have to be reduced, or you may have to change to another NSAID.

Usual Dose

500 milligrams to start, then 250 milligrams every 6 hours.

Overdosage

The primary symptom of overdose is acute stomach and intestinal distress. Symptoms generally develop within an hour of the overdose and resolve on their own within another 24 hours. Patients taking an overdose of this drug must be made to vomit with Syrup of Ipecac (available at any pharmacy) to remove any remaining drug from the stomach if the overdose was taken within the past hour. Call your doctor or a poison control center before doing this. If more than an hour has passed, go to a hospital emergency room. ALWAYS bring the medicine bottle.

Special Information

Mefenamic Acid may cause blurred vision or drowsiness. Because of this, you should be especially careful while driving or doing anything else that requires concentration.

Call your doctor if you develop diarrhea, dizziness, drowsiness, vision problems, severe stomach or intestinal irritation, sudden weight gain, rash, itching, hives, swelling, black or tarry bowel movements, difficulty breathing, fever with or without chills, mouth sores or white spots, sore throat, unusual tiredness or weakness, or cystitis-like symptoms or if other symptoms become particularly bothersome or persistent.

It is important to maintain good dental hygiene while taking Mefenamic Acid and to use extra care when using your toothbrush or dental floss because of the chance that the drug will make you more susceptible to some infections.

If you forget to take a dose of Mefenamic Acid, take it as

soon as you remember. If it is almost time for your next regularly scheduled dose, skip the one you forgot and continue with your regular schedule. Do not take a double dose.

Generic Name

Megestrol Acetate

Brand Name

Megace

Type of Drug

Progestational hormone.

Prescribed for

Cancer of the breast or endometrium.

General Information

Megestrol Acetate has been used quite successfully in the treatment of the cancers cited above. It exerts its effect by acting as a hormonal counterbalance in areas rich in estrogen (breast and endometrium). Other progestational hormones, such as Norethindrone (Norlutin, Norlutate), may be used to treat cancer of the endometrium or uterus or to correct hormone imbalance.

Cautions and Warnings

This drug should be used only for its 2 specifically approved indications. The use of this drug should be accompanied by close, continued contact with your doctor. Megestrol use should be carefully considered if you have a history of blood clots or similar disorders, a history of convulsions, liver disease, undiagnosed vaginal bleeding, asthma, cardiac insufficiency, epilepsy, migraine headaches, kidney problems, diabetes, a history of ectopic pregnancy, high blood-fat levels, or depression.

Pregnancy/Breast-feeding

This drug is known to cause birth defects or interfere with

your baby's development. It is not considered safe for use
during pregnancy.

Megestrol passes into breast milk, but has caused no
problems among breast-fed infants. You must consider the
potential effect on the nursing infant if breast-feeding while
taking this medicine.

Seniors

Older adults with severe liver disease are more sensitive to
the effects of this drug. Follow your doctor's directions and
report any side effects at once.

Possible Side Effects

Back or stomach pain, headache, nausea, vomiting. If any of
these symptoms appear, contact your doctor immediately.
This drug should be used with caution if you have a history
of blood clots in the veins.

Drug Interactions

Megestrol may interfere with the effects of Bromocriptine
and should not be used at the same time as that drug.

Food Interactions

This medicine is best taken on an empty stomach, but you
may take it with food if it upsets your stomach.

Usual Dose

40 to 320 milligrams per day.

Overdose

Megestrol overdose may result in exaggerated side effects.
In may cases, small overdoses will result in no unusual
symptoms. Call your local poison control center or hospital
emergency room for more information.

Special Information

Continued treatment for 2 months is usually required to determine if Megestrol is effective treatment for your condition.

If you forget to take a dose of Megestrol Acetate, take it
as soon as you remember. If it is almost time for your next

regularly scheduled dose, skip the one you forgot and continue with your regular schedule. Do not take a double dose.

Generic Name

Meperidine

Brand Names

Demerol

(Also available in generic form)

Type of Drug

Narcotic analgesic.

Prescribed for

Moderate to severe pain.

General Information

Meperidine is a narcotic drug with potent pain-relieving effect. It is also used before surgery to reduce patient anxiety and help bring the patient into the early stages of anesthesia. Meperidine is probably the most commonly used narcotic analgesic in American hospitals. Its effects compare favorably with those of Morphine Sulfate, the standard against which other narcotics are judged.

Meperidine is a narcotic drug with pain-relieving and cough-suppressing activity. As an analgesic it is useful for mild to moderate pain. 25 to 50 milligrams of Meperidine are approximately equal in pain-relieving effect to 2 Aspirin tablets (650 milligrams). Meperidine may be less active than Aspirin for types of pain associated with inflammation, since Aspirin reduces inflammation and Meperidine does not. Meperidine suppresses the cough reflex but does not cure the underlying cause of the cough. In fact, sometimes it may not be desirable to overly suppress cough, because cough suppression reduces your ability to naturally eliminate excess mucus produced during a cold or allergy attack.

Cautions and Warnings

The side effects of narcotic drugs are exaggerated when the patient has a head injury, brain tumor, or other head problem. Narcotics can also hide the symptoms of head injury. They should be used with extreme caution in patients with head injuries.

Pregnancy/Breast-feeding

No studies of this medication have been done in women and no reports of human birth defects exist, but animal studies show that high doses of the drug can cause problems in a developing fetus. Pregnant women, or women who might become pregnant while using this drug, should talk to their doctor about the risk of taking this medicine versus the benefits it can provide.

This drug passes into breast milk, but no problems in nursing infants have been seen. Breast-feeding women should consider the possibility of adverse effects on their nursing infant. Choose another feeding method if you must take this medicine.

Seniors

Seniors are more likely to be sensitive to side effects of this drug and should be treated with smaller dosages than younger adults.

Possible Side Effects

The most frequent side effects are light-headedness, dizziness, sleepiness, nausea, vomiting, loss of appetite, sweating. If these occur, consider asking your doctor about lowering your present dose of Meperidine. Usually the side effects disappear if you simply lie down.

More serious side effects of Meperidine are shallow breathing or difficulty in breathing.

Less common side effects include euphoria (feeling high), weakness, sleepiness, headache, agitation, uncoordinated muscle movement, minor hallucinations, disorientation and visual disturbances, dry mouth, loss of appetite, constipation, flushing of the face, rapid heartbeat, palpitations, faintness, urinary difficulties or hesitancy, reduced sex drive and/ or potency, itching, skin rashes, anemia, lowered blood

sugar, and a yellowing of the skin and/or whites of the eyes.
Narcotic analgesics may aggravate convulsions in those
who have had convulsions in the past.

Drug Interactions

Because of its depressant effect and potential effect on
breathing, Meperidine should be taken with extreme care in
combination with alcohol, sleeping medicine, tranquilizers,
or other depressant drugs.

Food Interactions

This drug may be taken with food to reduce stomach upset.

Usual Dose

Adult: 50 to 150 milligrams every 3 to 4 hours as needed.
Child: 0.5 to 0.8 milligrams per pound every 3 to 4 hours
as needed, up to the adult dose.

Overdosage

Symptoms are depression of respiration (breathing), extreme tiredness progressing to stupor and then coma, pinpointed pupils of the eyes, no response to stimulation such
as a pin stick, cold and clammy skin, slowing down of the
heartbeat, lowering of blood pressure, convulsions, and cardiac arrest. The patient should be taken to a hospital emergency room immediately. ALWAYS bring the medicine
bottle.

Special Information

If you are taking Meperidine, be extremely careful while driving or operating machinery. Avoid alcoholic beverages.
   Call your doctor if this drug makes you very nauseated or
constipated or if you have trouble breathing.
   If you forget to take a dose of Meperidine, take it as soon
as you remember. If it is almost time for your next regularly
scheduled dose, skip the one you forgot and continue with
your regular schedule. Do not take a double dose.

Generic Name

Meprobamate

Brand Names

Equanil
Meprospan
Miltown
Neuramate

(Also available in generic form)

Type of Drug

Minor tranquilizer.

Prescribed for

Relief of anxiety and tension; promoting sleep in anxious or tense patients.

General Information

Meprobamate and the other drugs in its chemical group are used as antianxiety agents, anticonvulsants, or sedatives (sleeping pills). This drug exerts effects by relaxing the large skeletal muscles and by a direct effect on the brain. In doing so, it can relax you and make you either more tranquil or sleepier, depending on the drug and how much you use.

Meprobamate is generally used in any situation where it can be a useful adjunct.

Cautions and Warnings

You should not take Meprobamate if you are allergic to it or if you feel that you may be allergic to a related drug such as Carisoprodol, Mebutamate, or Carbromal.

Severe physical and psychological dependence has been experienced by people taking Meprobamate for long periods of time. The drug can produce chronic intoxication after prolonged use or if used in greater than recommended doses, leading to adverse effects such as slurred speech, dizziness, and general sleepiness or depression. Sudden withdrawal of Meprobamate after prolonged and excessive use may result

in drug withdrawal symptoms, including severe anxiety, loss
of appetite, sleeplessness, vomiting, tremors, muscle twitching, severe sleepiness, confusion, hallucinations, and possibly convulsions. Such withdrawal symptoms usually begin
12 to 48 hours after Meprobamate has been stopped and
may last 1 to 4 days. When someone has taken this medication in excessive quantities for weeks, months, or longer,
the medication must be gradually reduced over a period of
1 or 2 weeks in order to avoid these withdrawal symptoms.

Pregnancy/Breast-feeding

Use with extreme caution if you are in the first 3 months
of pregnancy or if you suspect that you may be pregnant;
Meprobamate has been shown to increase the chance of
birth defects and may cause tiredness in nursing infants. If
you are pregnant and are taking this medication, you should
discuss it with your doctor.

Meprobamate passes into breast milk. Its effect on nursing
infants is unknown.

Seniors

Older adults are more sensitive to the effects of this drug.
Follow your doctor's directions and report any side effects
at once.

Possible Side Effects

The most common side effects are drowsiness, sleepiness,
dizziness, slurred speech, headache, weakness, tingling in
the arms and legs, euphoria, and possibly excitement or par-
adoxical reactions such as overstimulation.

Infrequent side effects include nausea, vomiting, diarrhea,
abnormal heart rhythms, low blood pressure, itching, rash,
effects on various components of the blood. Quite rarely
there has been severe hypersensitivity or allergic reactions
producing high fever, chills, closing of the throat (bronchospasm), loss of urinary function, and other severe symptoms.

Drug Interactions

Interactions with other drugs that produce depression of the
central nervous system can cause sleepiness, tiredness, and
tranquilization. Interaction with other tranquilizers, alcoholic

beverages in excessive quantities, narcotics, barbiturates and other sleeping pills, or antihistamines can cause excessive depression, sleepiness, and fatigue.

Food Interactions

This medicine is best taken on an empty stomach, but you may take it with food if it upsets your stomach.

Usual Dose

Adult (when used as a tranquilizer): 1200 to 1600 milligrams per day in divided doses; maximum permissible, 2400 milligrams per day.

Child (age 6 to 12): 100 to 200 milligrams 2 to 3 times per day.

Child (under age 6): This drug should not be used.

Overdosage

In attempted suicide or accidental overdose, symptoms are extreme drowsiness, lethargy, stupor, and coma, with possible shock and respiratory collapse (breathing stops).

The overdosed patient must be taken to a hospital emergency room immediately. ALWAYS bring the medicine bottle. Some people have died after taking 30 tablets, others have survived after taking 100.

The overdose is much worse if there is interaction with alcohol or another depressant: A much smaller dose of Meprobamate can produce fatal results.

After a large overdose, the patient will go to sleep very quickly, and blood pressure, pulse, and breathing levels will be greatly reduced. After the patient is taken to the hospital his stomach should be pumped and respiratory assistance and other supportive therapy given.

Special Information

Be sure to take this medicine according to your doctor's direction. Do not change your dose without your doctor's approval.

This drug causes drowsiness, poor concentration, and makes it more difficult to drive a car, operate machinery, or perform complicated activities.

Call your doctor at once if you develop fever, sore throat,

nosebleeds, mouth sores, unexplained black-and-blue marks, easy bruising or bleeding.

If you forget to take a dose of Meprobamate and you remember within about an hour of your regular time, take it right away. If you do not remember until later, skip the forgotten dose and go back to your regular schedule. Do not take a double dose.

Generic Name
Mesalamine

Brand Name
Rowasa Suspension

Type of Drug
Anti-inflammatory.

Prescribed for
Ulcerative colitis, proctitis, or proctosigmoiditis.

General Information
Sulfasalazine, a widely used treatment for ulcerative colitis and other inflammatory conditions, is broken down in the colon to Mesalamine. It is thought that Mesalamine is the active agent in treating the symptoms of bowel inflammation. No one knows how Mesalamine produces its effect, but it is thought to be a direct effect in the bowel, not one involving the rest of the body.

Little of the drug is absorbed into the blood; 70 to 90 percent of the drug stays in the colon.

Cautions and Warnings
Mesalamine may cause cramping, sudden abdominal pain, and bloody diarrhea. Fever, headache, and a rash may also occur. The symptoms may occur suddenly and are reason to call your doctor and stop taking the drug at once.

People who are sensitive to Sulfasalazine have been able

to tolerate Mesalamine because so little of the drug is absorbed into the blood.

Pregnancy/Breast-feeding

Animal studies have revealed no indication that Mesalamine can harm a developing fetus. Pregnant women should consult with their doctor before using this medication.

It is not known if Mesalamine passes into breast milk.

Seniors

Seniors may use this drug without special precaution. Be sure to report any unusual side effects to your doctor.

Possible Side Effects

Mesalamine is generally well tolerated with few side effects. Among those that do occur, the most common are abdominal pain, cramps, and discomfort, headache, intestinal gas, nausea, flu, feeling tired or weak, not feeling well, fever, and rash.

Less common side effects are common cold, sore throat, diarrhea, joint and leg pains, dizziness, bloating, back pain, pain on inserting the enema tip, hemorrhoids, itching, rectal pain, soreness or burning, constipation, hair loss, swelling of the arms and legs, urinary burning, urinary infections, weakness, and sleeplessness.

Drug Interactions

None known.

Usual Dose

One rectal enema (1 bottle) at bedtime every night for 3 to 6 weeks. The enema liquid should be retained for about 8 hours.

Special Information

Shake the bottle well and remove the protective sheath from the applicator tip. Lie on your left side with your lower leg extended and the upper leg flexed to maintain balance. Gently insert the applicator tip in the rectum pointing toward your navel. Steadily squeezing the bottle will discharge most of the contents into your colon.

Call your doctor if you forget a dose of Mesalamine.

Generic Name

Mesoridazine

Brand Name

Serentil

Type of Drug

Phenothiazine antipsychotic.

Prescribed for

Psychotic disorders; moderate to severe depression with anxiety; control of agitation or aggressiveness of disturbed children; alcohol withdrawal symptoms; intractable pain; senility.

General Information

Mesoridazine and other members of the phenothiazine group act on a portion of the brain called the hypothalamus. They affect parts of the hypothalamus that control metabolism, body temperature, alertness, muscle tone, hormone balance, and vomiting and may be used to treat problems related to any of these functions.

Cautions and Warnings

Mesoridazine should not be taken if you are allergic to one of the drugs in the broad classification known as phenothiazine drugs. Do not take Mesoridazine if you have any blood, liver, kidney, or heart disease. This medication is a tranquilizer and can have a depressive effect, especially during the first few days of therapy.

This drug should be used with caution and under strict supervision of your doctor if you have glaucoma, epilepsy, ulcers, or difficulty passing urine.

Pregnancy/Breast-feeding

Infants born to women taking this medication have experienced drug side effects (liver jaundice, nervous-system effects) immediately after birth. Check with your doctor about taking this medicine if you are or might become pregnant.

This drug may pass into breast milk and affect a nursing infant. Consider alternative feeding methods if you take this medicine.

Seniors

Older adults are more sensitive to the effects of Mesoridazine than younger adults and usually require a lower dosage to achieve a desired effect. Also, older adults are more likely to develop drug side effects. Some experts feel that older patients should be treated with one-half to one-quarter the usual adult dose.

Possible Side Effects

The most common side effect is drowsiness, especially during the first or second week of therapy. If the drowsiness becomes troublesome, contact your doctor.

Mesoridazine can cause jaundice (yellowing of the whites of the eyes of skin), usually in 2 to 4 weeks. The jaundice usually goes away when the drug is discontinued, but there have been cases when it did not. If you notice this effect or if you develop symptoms such as fever and generally not feeling well, contact your doctor immediately. Less frequent side effects include changes in components of the blood, including anemias, raised or lowered blood pressure, abnormal heart rates, heart attack, feeling faint or dizzy.

Phenothiazines can produce extrapyramidal effects, such as spasm of the neck muscles, rolling back of the eyes, convulsions, difficulty in swallowing, and symptoms associated with Parkinson's disease. These effects look very serious but go away after the drug has been withdrawn; however, symptoms of the face, tongue, and jaw may persist for as long as several years, especially in older adults with a history of brain damage. If you experience extrapyramidal effects, contact your doctor immediately.

Mesoridazine may cause an unusual increase in psychotic symptoms or may cause paranoid reactions, tiredness, lethargy, restlessness, hyperactivity, confusion at night, bizarre dreams, inability to sleep, depression, and euphoria. Other reactions are itching, swelling, unusual sensitivity to bright lights, red skin (particularly in exposed areas), and rash. There have been cases of breast enlargement, false positive pregnancy tests, changes in menstrual flow in females and impotence and changes in sex drive in males, stuffy nose, headache, nausea, vomiting, loss of appetite, change in body temperature, loss of facial color, excessive salivation and perspiration, constipation, diarrhea, changes in urine and stool habits, worsening of glaucoma, blurred vision, weakening of eyelid muscles and spasms in bronchial and other muscles, increased appetite, and excessive thirst.

Drug Interactions

Mesoridazine should be avoided in combination with barbiturates, sleeping pills, narcotics, other tranquilizers, or any other medication which may produce a depressive effect. Avoid alcohol.

Usual Dose

30 to 400 milligrams per day, depending on the condition being treated.

Overdosage

Symptoms are depression, extreme weakness, tiredness, desire to go to sleep, coma, lowered blood pressure, uncontrolled muscle spasms, agitation, restlessness, convulsions, fever, dry mouth, and abnormal heart rhythms. The patient should be taken to a hospital emergency room immediately. ALWAYS bring the medicine bottle.

Special Information

This medication may cause drowsiness. Use caution when driving or operating complex equipment and avoid alcoholic beverages while taking the medicine.

The drug may also cause unusual sensitivity to the sun and can turn your urine reddish-brown to pink.

If dizziness occurs, avoid sudden changes in posture and avoid climbing stairs.

Use caution in hot weather. This medicine may make you more prone to heat stroke.

If you take Mesoridazine once a day and forget your dose, take it as soon as possible. If you don't remember until the next day, skip the forgotten dose and continue with your regular schedule.

If you take the medicine more than once a day and forget a dose, take the forgotten dose as soon as possible. If it is almost time for your next dose, skip the forgotten dose and go on with your regular schedule.

Generic Name

Metaproterenol

Brand Names

Alupent Inhalation Aerosol/Solution/Syrup/Tablets
Metaprel Inhalation Aerosol/Solution/Syrup/Tablets

(Also available in generic form)

Type of Drug

Bronchodilator.

Prescribed for

Asthma and spasm of the bronchial muscles.

General Information

Metaproterenol can be taken both by mouth as a tablet or syrup and by inhalation. This drug may be used together with other drugs to produce the desired relief from asthmatic symptoms. Oral Metaproterenol begins working 15 to 30 minutes after a dose and its effects may last for up to 4 hours. Metaproterenol inhalation begins working in 1 to 5 minutes and lasts for 3 to 4 hours.

Cautions and Warnings

This drug should be used with caution by patients who have angina, heart disease, high blood pressure, a history of stroke or seizures, diabetes, thyroid disease, prostate disease, or glaucoma. Excessive use of Metaproterenol inhalant could lead to worsening of your condition.

Pregnancy/Breast-feeding

This drug should be used by women who are pregnant or

breast-feeding only when absolutely necessary. The potential hazard to the unborn child or nursing infant is not known at this time. However, it has caused birth defects when given in large amounts to pregnant animals.

Seniors

Older adults are more sensitive to the effects of this drug. Closely follow your doctor's directions and report any side effects at once.

Possible Side Effects

Restlessness, anxiety, fear, tension, sleeplessness, tremors, convulsions, weakness, dizziness, headache, flushing, pallor, sweating, nausea; also vomiting, loss of appetite, muscle cramps, urinary difficulties.

Less commonly, Metaproterenol can cause some side effects on the heart and cardiovascular system, such as high blood pressure, abnormal heart rhythms, and angina. It is less likely to cause these effects than some of the older drugs.

Drug Interactions

The effect of this drug may be increased by antidepressant drugs, some antihistamines, Levothyroxine, and monoamine oxidase (MAO) inhibitor drugs.

This drug may antagonize the effects of Reserpine or Guanethidine.

Food Interactions

If the tablets cause an upset stomach, they may be taken with food.

Usual Dose

Oral:
Adult and child (over 60 pounds, or over age 9): 60 to 80 milligrams per day.
Child (under 60 pounds, or age 6 to 9): 30 to 40 milligrams per day.
Inhalation:
Adult and child (over age 12): 2 to 3 puffs every 3 to 4 hours.

Child (under age 12): not recommended.

Each canister contains about 300 inhalations. Do not use more than 12 puffs per day.

Overdosage

Symptoms of Metaproterenol overdose are palpitation, abnormal heart rhythms, rapid or slow heartbeat, chest pain, high blood pressure, fever, chills, cold sweat, blanching of the skin, nausea, vomiting, sleeplessness, delirium, tremor, pinpoint pupils, convulsions, coma, and collapse. If you or someone you know has taken an overdose of this drug call your doctor or bring the patient to a hospital emergency room. ALWAYS remember to bring the prescription bottle or inhaler with you.

Special Information

Be sure to follow your doctor's instructions for this drug. Using more of it than was prescribed can lead to drug tolerance and actually cause your condition to worsen.

Metaproterenol inhalation should be used during the second half of your inward breath, since this allows it to reach more deeply into your lungs.

Call your doctor immediately if you develop chest pain, palpitations, rapid heartbeat, muscle tremors, dizziness, headache, facial flushing, or urinary difficulty or if you still have trouble breathing after using this medicine.

If you miss a dose of Metaproterenol, take it as soon as possible. Take the rest of that day's dose at regularly spaced time intervals. Go back to your regular schedule the next day.

Generic Name

Metaxalone

Brand Name

Skelaxin

Type of Drug

Skeletal muscle relaxant.

Prescribed for

Painful muscle spasms.

General Information

Metaxalone is prescribed as a part of a coordinated program of rest, physical therapy, and other measures for the relief of acute, painful spasm conditions. It does not directly relax skeletal muscles; the exact way it produces its effect is unknown.

Cautions and Warnings

Metaxalone should be taken with caution if you have had a reaction to it in the past, if you have a tendency toward anemia, or if you have loss of kidney or liver function.

Pregnancy/Breast-feeding

As with all drug products, pregnant women or those who might become pregnant should not use Metaxalone unless the advantages of the drug have been carefully weighed against the possible dangers of taking it while pregnant.

It is not known if this drug passes into breast milk; no drug-related problems have been known to occur. Nursing mothers who use it should exercise caution.

Seniors

No problems have been reported in older adults. However, older adults are likely to have normal loss of some kidney and/or liver function. This factor should be be taken into account by your doctor when determining your Metaxalone dosage.

Possible Side Effects

The most common side effects of Metaxalone are nausea, vomiting, upset stomach or stomach cramps, drowsiness, dizziness, headache, nervousness, and irritability.

Other possible side effects include unusual tiredness, breathing difficulty, rash, hives, itching, redness, and yellowing of the eyes or skin.

Drug Interactions

Tranquilizers, alcohol, and other nervous-system depressants may increase the depressant effects of Metaxalone.

Food Interactions

Metaxalone may be taken with food or meals if it upsets your stomach.

Usual Dose

800 milligrams 3 to 4 times a day.

Overdosage

Overdose symptoms are likely to be exaggerated side effects, but may include some less common reactions. Overdose victims should be taken to a hospital emergency room for treatment. ALWAYS bring the medicine bottle with you.

Special Information

People taking Metaxalone for long-term treatment should have their liver functions monitored by their doctors, since Metaxolone can be toxic to the liver.

People taking Metaxalone must be careful when performing tasks reguiring concentration and coordination because of the chance that the drug will make them tired, dizzy, or light-headed.

Call your doctor if you develop trouble breathing, unusual tiredness or weakness, fever, chills, cough or hoarseness, lower back or side pain, painful urination, yellow skin or eyes, rash, hives, itching or redness. Other symptoms should be also brought to the doctor's attention if they are particularly bothersome or persistent.

If you forget a dose of Metaxalone, take it as soon as you remember. If it is almost time for your next dose, take one dose as soon as you remember and another in 3 or 4 hours, then go back to your regular schedule. Do not take a double dose.

Type of Drug
Methenamine

Brand Names

Generic Name: Methenamine Hippurate

Hiprex
Urex

Generic Name: Methenamine Mandelate

Mandameth
Mandelamine
Methenamine Mandelate

(Also available in generic form)

Type of Drug

Urinary anti-infective.

Prescribed for

Chronic urinary tract infections.

General Information

Methenamine drugs work by turning into formaldehyde and
ammonia when the urine is acidic. It is the formaldehyde
that kills the bacteria in the urinary tract. These drugs do
not break down in the blood. Acidification of the urine may
be necessary with 4 to 12 grams per day of Ascorbic Acid
(Vitamin C) or Ammonium Chloride tablets.

Cautions and Warnings

Patients with kidney disease, dehydration, or severe liver
disease should not use this drug.

Pregnancy/Breast-feeding

This drug crosses into the blood circulation of a developing
baby. It has not been found to cause birth defects. Pregnant
women, or those who might become pregnant while taking
this drug, should not take it without their doctors' approval.

When the drug is considered essential by your doctor, the potential risk of taking the medicine must be carefully weighed against the benefit it might produce.

This drug passes into breast milk, but has caused no problems among breast-fed infants. You must consider the potential effect on the nursing infant if breast-feeding while taking this medicine.

Seniors

Older adults may take this medication without special restriction. Follow your doctor's directions and report any side effects at once.

Possible Side Effects

Large doses for long periods of time may cause bladder irritation, painful and frequent urination, and protein or blood in the urine. This drug may cause elevation in liver enzymes.

Less common side effcts include upset stomach and rash.

Drug Interactions

Do not take this with sulfa drugs, since the sulfas can form a precipitate in the urine when mixed with Methenamine, which may lead to a kidney stone.

Sodium Bicarbonate and Acetazolamide will decrease the effect of Methenamine by making the drug less acidic.

Food Interactions

The action of Methenamine will be decreased by foods which reduce urine acidity, including milk and dairy products. Avoid these agents in large quantities when taking Methenamine.

Take Methenamine with food to minimize upset stomach.

Usual Dose

Adult: 1 gram 2 to 4 times a day.
Child (age 6 to 12): 0.5 to 1 gram 2 to 4 times per day.

Overdose

Typical side effects of Methenamine overdose are upset stomach and exaggerated drug side efects. Call your local poison control center or hospital emergency room for more information.

Special Information

Take each dose with at least 8 ounces of water. Call your doctor if you develop pain when urinating or severe upset stomach.

If you miss a dose of Methenamine, take it as soon as possible. Take the rest of that day's doses at regularly spaced time intervals. Go back to your regular schedule the next day.

Generic Name

Methotrexate

Brand Names

Methotrexate
Rheumatrex

(Also available in generic form)

Type of Drug

Antimetabolite; antiarthritis; anti-inflammatory.

Prescribed for

Cancer chemotherapy; psoriasis; rheumatoid arthritis; severe asthma.

General Information

Methotrexate and other antimetabolites were among the first drugs found to be effective against certain cancers in the late 1940s. More recent research applying smaller doses of this drug to other diseases has resulted in its acceptance as a treatment for psoriasis, rheumatoid arthritis, and severe asthma. Methotrexate doses differ dramatically for each use of the drug, but you should be aware that Methotrexate can be extremely toxic, even in the relatively low doses prescribed for rheumatoid arthritis.

Methotrexate should be considered last-resort therapy for rheumatoid arthritis, to be used only for severe cases that have not responded satisfactorily to any other form of therapy.

Methotrexate should be prescribed only by doctors who are familiar with the drug and its potential for producing toxic effects. It may be effective after 3 to 6 weeks of treatment, and improvement in the condition may continue for another 12 weeks or more. Although the drug clearly reduces arthritis symptoms, it does not alter the basic course of the disease. Arthritis improvements have been maintained for 2 years or more by people who continued their Methotrexate therapy. Unfortunately, the benefits of Methotrexate are lost after use of the drug is discontinued.

Cautions and Warnings

Methotrexate can trigger a unique and dangerous form of lung disease any time during your course of therapy. This reaction can occur at doses as low as 7.5 milligrams a week, which is the antiarthritis dose of Methotrexate. Symptoms of this condition are cough, respiratory infection, difficulty breathing, abnormal chest x-ray, and low blood concentration oxygen. Any change in your breathing or lung status while taking Methotrexate should be reported to your doctor.

Methotrexate can cause severe liver damage, but this usually occurs only after taking the drug for a long period of time. Changes in liver enzyme values (measured by a blood test) are common.

Methotrexate should be used with caution, and the dosage should be reduced for people with kidney disease and those who have lost some kidney function.

Methotrexate can cause severe reduction in red and white blood cell and blood platelet counts.

Your doctor should test your blood periodically for cell counts and liver enzyme measurements while you are taking Methotrexate. Kidney function should also be tested.

Methotrexate can cause severe diarrhea, stomach irritation, and mouth or gum sores. Death can result from intestinal perforation caused by Methotrexate.

Pregnancy/Breast-feeding

Methotrexate can cause the death of a developing fetus or

severe birth defects in a surviving fetus. This drug should not be taken by pregnant women. Women who might become pregnant and who must take Methotrexate should be careful to use effective birth control during their treatment. Women should not attempt to become pregnant during their Methotrexate treatment or for at least one menstrual cycle after the treatment is completed.

Nursing mothers who must take Methotrexate should use an alternative feeding method because of the possibility of serious Methotrexate reactions in the nursing infant.

Methotrexate can also affect sperm. Men should not attempt to father a child during Methotrexate treatment or for 3 months after treatment has been completed to avoid possible birth defects.

Seniors

Not much is known about the specific reaction of Methotrexate in the bodies of older adults, who may be more susceptible to drug side effects. People with kidney and/or liver disease require smaller doses than those with normal kidneys and livers to obtain the same effect.

The relatively low doses of Methotrexate prescribed for rheumatoid arthritis may be well tolerated by seniors, but they should be closely monitored by their doctor while taking Methotrexate.

Possible Side Effects

The most common side effects of Methotrexate are liver irritation, loss of some kidney function, reduction in blood cell counts, nausea, vomiting, diarrhea, stomach upset and irritation, itching, rash, hair loss, dizziness, and increased susceptibility to infection.

Less common side effects include reduced blood hematocrit (a measure of red blood cell count), unusual sensitivity to the sun, acne, headache, drowsiness, blurred vision, respiratory infection and breathing problems, loss of appetite, muscle aches, chest pain, coughing, painful urination, eye discomfort, nose bleeds, fever, infections, blood in the urine, sweating, ringing or buzzing in the ears, defective sperm production, reduced sperm count, menstrual dysfunction and vaginal discharge, convulsions, and slight paralysis.

Drug Interactions

Fatal reactions have developed in people taking Methotrexate together with some NSAIDs (Ketoprofen, Naproxen, Indomethacin, and Phenylbutazone). Do not take any other anti-inflammatory or antiarthritis drug (even Ibuprofen, which can be bought without a prescription) together with Methotrexate unless specifically directed to do so by your doctor.

Aspirin and other salicylates, Probenecid, and sulfa drugs can increase the therapeutic and toxic effects of Methotrexate. Avoid these combinations.

Food Interactions

Food slows the rate at which Methotrexate is absorbed into the blood from your stomach. It is best taken on an empty stomach or 2 hours after meals, but you may take it with food if it upsets your stomach.

Usual Dose

Methotrexate dosage varies with the condition being treated. Some cancers can be treated with 10 to 30 milligrams per day, while others are treated with hundreds or thousands of milligrams given by intravenous injection in the hospital.

The starting Methotrexate dose for rheumatoid arthritis is 7.5 milligrams a week by mouth, either as a single dose or in 3 separate doses of 2.5 milligrams taken every 12 hours. Weekly dosage may be increased gradually up to 20 milligrams. Doses above 20 milligrams a week are more likely to cause severe side effects.

Overdosage

Methotrexate overdose can be serious and life-threatening. Every Methotrexate overdose victim should be taken at once to a hospital emergency room for treatment. A specific antidote to the effects of Methotrexate, Calcium Leucovorin, is available in every hospital. ALWAYS remember to bring the prescription container with you.

Special Information

If you vomit after taking a dose of Methotrexate, do not take a replacement dose unless instructed to do so by your doctor.

Call your doctor immediately if you develop diarrhea, fever or chills, reddening of the skin, mouth or lip sores, stomach pain, unusual bleeding or bruising, blurred vision, seizures, cough, difficulty breathing.

These symptoms are less severe but should stilll be reported to the doctor: back pain, darkened urine, dizziness, drowsiness, headache, unusual tiredness or sickness, yellowing of the eyes or skin.

If you forget to take a dose of Methotrexate, skip the forgotten dose and continue with your regular schedule. Tell your doctor about the dose you forgot to take. Do not take a double dose of Methotrexate.

Generic Name

Methsuximide

Brand Name

Celontin

Type of Drug

Anticonvulsant.

Prescribed for

Control of petit mal seizures.

General Information

Methsuximide and the other succinimide-type anticonvulsants control petit mal seizures by slowing the transmission of impulses through certain areas of the brain. The succinimides are first choice of treatment for this type of seizure, although Methsuximide is used only after Ethosuximide has been tried. If Methsuximide doesn't work, the condition may be treated with Clonazepam.

Cautions and Warnings

Methsuximide may be associated with severe reductions in white-blood-cell and platelet counts. Your doctor should perform periodic blood counts while you are taking this medicine.

In patients with grand mal and petit mal, succinimide-type anticonvulsants, when used alone, may increase the number of grand mal seizures and necessitate more medicine to control those seizures.

Abrupt withdrawal of any anticonvulsant may lead to severe seizures. It is important that your dosage be gradually reduced by your doctor.

Pregnancy/Breast-feeding

This drug should be avoided by women who may become pregnant while using it and by pregnant and nursing mothers, since it will cross into the developing infant's circulation, and possible adverse effects on the infant are not known. In those situations where it is deemed essential, the potential risk of the drug must be carefully weighed against any benefit it might produce.

Recent reports suggest a strong association between the use of anticonvulsant drugs and birth defects. Although most of the information pertains to Phenytoin and Phenobarbital, not Methsuximide, other reports indicate a general association between all anticonvulsant drug treatments and birth defects. It is possible that the epileptic condition itself or genetic factors common to people with seizure disorders may also be a factor in the higher incidence of birth defects.

Mothers taking Methsuximide should not breast-feed because of the possibility that the drug will pass into their breast milk and affect the baby. Use an alternative feeding method.

Seniors

Older adults may take this medication without special restriction. Follow your doctor's directions and report any side effects at once.

Possible Side Effects

Nausea, vomiting, upset stomach, stomach cramps and pain, loss of appetite, diarrhea, constipation, weight loss, drowsiness, dizziness, and poor muscle control.

Less common side effects include reductions in white-blood-cell and platelet counts, nervousness, hyperactivity, sleeplessness, irritability, headache, blurred vision, unusual sensitivity to bright lights, hiccups, a euphoric feeling, a dreamlike state, lack of energy, fatigue, confusion, mental instability, mental slowness, depression, sleep disturbances, nightmares, loss of the ability to concentrate, aggressiveness, constant concern with well-being and health, paranoid psychosis, suicidal tendencies, increased sex drive, itching, frequent urination, kidney damage, blood in the urine, swelling around the eyes, hair loss, hairiness, muscle weakness, nearsightedness, vaginal bleeding, and swelling of the tongue and/or gums.

Drug Interactions

The depressant effects of Methsuximide are increased by alcohol, tranquilizers, sleeping pills, narcotic pain relievers, antihistamines, monoamine oxidase (MAO) inhibitors, antidepressants, and other anticonvulsants.

Methsuximide may increase the action of Phenytoin by increasing the blood levels of that drug. Your doctor should be sure that your dosages of the 2 drugs are appropriate to your condition.

Carbamazepine, another medicine prescribed to treat seizure disorders, may interfere with Methsuximide action by increasing the rate at which it is removed from the body.

The action of Methsuximide may be increased by Isoniazid, prescribed to prevent tuberculosis, and by Valporic Acid, another anticonvulsant drug, possibly leading to an increase in drug side effects when both drugs are taken together.

Food Interactions

Methsuximide is best taken on an empty stomach but may be taken with food if it upsets your stomach.

Usual Dose

300 milligrams per day to start. If needed, the dose may be increased in steps of 300 milligrams every 7 days until seizures are controlled or side effects develop. The maximum daily dose is 1200 milligrams.

Dosage adjustments may be required for people with reduced kidney or liver function.

Overdosage

Methsuximide overdose will cause exaggerated side effects. If the overdose is discovered immediately, it may be helpful to induce vomiting with Syrup of Ipecac to remove any remaining medicine from the stomach. But all victims of Methsuximide overdose must be taken to a hospital emergency room for treatment. ALWAYS bring the prescription bottle with you.

Special Information

Call your doctor if side effects become intolerable. Especially important are sore throat, joint pains, unexplained fever, rashes, unusual bleeding or bruising, drowsiness, dizziness, and blurred vision. Be sure to tell your doctor if you become pregnant while taking this medicine.

Methsuximide may interfere with your ability to drive a car or perform other complex tasks because it can cause drowsiness and difficulty concentrating.

Your doctor should perform periodic blood counts while you are taking this drug to check for possible adverse drug effects.

Do not suddenly stop taking the medicine, since to do so can result in severe seizures. The dosage must be discontinued gradually by your doctor.

Carry identification or wear a bracelet indicating that you suffer from a seizure disorder for which you take Methsuximide.

If you forget to take a dose of Methsuximide, take it as soon as possible, unless it is within 4 hours of your next dose. If that is the case, skip the forgotten dose and go back to your regular schedule. Do not take a double dose.

Generic Name

Methyldopa

Brand Names

Aldomet
Amodopa

(Also available in generic form)

Type of Drug

Antihypertensive.

Prescribed for

High blood pressure.

General Information

Methyldopa's mechanism of action in the body is quite complicated and not well understood. It takes about 2 days of treatment to reach Methyldopa's maximal antihypertensive effect.

Methyldopa is usually prescribed with one or more of the other high blood pressure medications or a diuretic.

This does not cure high blood pressure, but helps to control it.

Cautions and Warnings

You should not take Methyldopa if you have hepatitis or active cirrhosis or if you have ever developed a reaction to Methyldopa.

Pregnancy/Breast-feeding

This drug crosses into the blood circulation of a developing baby. It has not been found to cause birth defects. Pregnant women, or those who might become pregnant while taking this drug, should not take it without their doctors' approval. When the drug is considered essential by your doctor, the potential risk of taking the medicine must be carefully weighed against the benefit it might produce.

This drug passes into breast milk, but has caused no problems among breast-fed infants. You must consider the potential effect on the nursing infant if breast-feeding while taking this medicine.

Seniors

Older adults are more sensitive to the sedative and blood-pressure-lowering effects of this drug. Follow your doctor's directions and report any side effects at once.

Possible Side Effects

Most people have little trouble with Methyldopa, but it can

cause transient sedation during the first few weeks of therapy or when the dose is increased. Transient headache or weakness are other possible early symptoms.

Less common side effects include dizziness, light-headedness, tingling in the extremities, unusual muscle spasms, decreased mental acuity, and psychic disturbances, including nightmares, mild psychosis, or depression. Other effects are changes in heart rate, increase of pain associated with angina pectoris, retention of water, resulting weight gain, orthostatic hypotension (dizziness when rising suddenly from a sitting or lying position), nausea, vomiting, constipation, diarrhea, mild dryness of the mouth, and sore and/or black tongue.

The drug may cause liver disorders: You may develop jaundice (yellowing of the skin and/or whites of the eyes), with or without fever, in the first 2 to 3 months of therapy. If you are taking Methyldopa for the first time, be sure your doctor checks your liver function, especially during the first 6 to 12 weeks of therapy. If you develop fever or jaundice, stop taking the drug and contact your physician immediately; if the reactions are due to Methyldopa, your temperature and/or liver abnormalities will reverse toward normal as soon as the drug is discontinued.

Still other adverse effects are stuffy nose, breast enlargement, lactation (in females), impotence or decreased sex drive, mild symptoms of arthritis, and skin reactions.

Drug Interactions

Methyldopa will increase the effect of other blood-pressure-lowering drugs. This is a desirable interaction which benefits patients with high blood pressure.

Avoid over-the-counter cough, cold and allergy preparations containing stimulant drugs that can aggravate your high blood pressure. Information on over-the-counter drugs that are safe for you can be obtained from your pharmacist.

Methyldopa may increase the blood sugar, lowering effect of Tolbutamine or other oral antidiabetic drugs.

If Methyldopa is given together with Phenoxybenzamine, inability to control one's bladder (urinary incontinence) may result.

The combination of Methyldopa and Lithium may cause

symptoms of Lithium overdose, even though blood levels of Lithium do not change.

Methyldopa when given together with Haloperidol may produce irritability, aggressiveness, assaultive behavior, or other psychiatric symptoms.

Food Interactions

This medicine is best taken on an empty stomach, but you may take it with food if it upsets your stomach.

Usual Dose

Adult: starting dose, 250-milligram tablet 2 to 3 times per day for first 2 days. Dosage may be increased or decreased until blood-pressure control is achieved. Maintenance dose, 500 milligrams to 3000 milligrams per day in 2 to 4 divided doses, per patient's needs.

Child: 5 milligrams per pound of body weight per day in 2 to 4 divided doses per patient's needs. Maximum dose, 30 milligrams per pound of body weight per day, up to 3 grams per day.

Special Information

Take this drug exactly as prescribed by your doctor so you can maintain maximum control over your high blood pressure.

A mild sedative effect is to be expected from Methyldopa and will resolve within several days.

Do not stop taking this medicine unless you are told to by your doctor. Call your doctor if you develop fever, prolonged general tiredness, or unusual dizziness.

If you forget to take a dose of Methyldopa, take it as soon as you remember. If it is almost time for your next regularly scheduled dose, skip the one you forgot and continue with your regular schedule. Do not take a double dose.

Generic Name

Methylphenidate

Brand Name

Ritalin
Ritalin-SR

(Also available in generic form)

Type of Drug

Central-nervous-system stimulant.

Prescribed for

Attention deficit syndrome in children; psychological, educational, or social disorders; narcolepsy and mild depression.

General Information

The primary use for Methylphenidate is the treatment of minimal brain dysfunction or attention deficit disorders in children. Common signs of this disease are short attention span, easy distractibility, emotional instability, impulsiveness, and moderate to severe hyperactivity. Children who suffer from this disorder will find it difficult to learn. There are many who feel that Methylphenidate is only a temporary solution because it does not permanently change patterns of behavior. When Methylphenidate is used, it must be used with other special measures.

Cautions and Warnings

Chronic or abusive use of Methylphenidate can cause the development of drug dependence or addiction. The drug can also cause severe psychotic episodes.

   Do not take Methylphenidate if you are extremely tense or agitated, have glaucoma, are allergic to this drug, have high blood pressure, or have a history of epilepsy or other seizures.

Pregnancy/Breast-feeding

This drug crosses into the blood circulation of a developing baby. It has not been found to cause birth defects. Pregnant women, or those who might become pregnant while taking this drug, should not take it without their doctors' approval. When the drug is considered essential by your doctor, the potential risk of taking the medicine must be carefully weighed against the benefit it might produce.

This drug passes into breast milk, but has caused no problems among breast-fed infants. You must consider the potential effect on the nursing infant if breast-feeding while taking this medicine.

Seniors

Older adults may take this medication without special restriction. Follow your doctor's directions and report any side effects at once.

Possible Side Effects

The most common side effects in adults are nervousness and inability to sleep, which are generally controlled by reducing or eliminating the afternoon or evening dose. The most common in children are loss of appetite, stomach pains, weight loss (especially during prolonged periods of therapy), difficulty sleeping, and abnormal heart rhythms.

Infrequent side effects in adults are skin rash, itching, fever, symptoms similar to arthritis, loss of appetite, nausea, dizziness, abnormal heart rhythms, headache, drowsiness, changes in blood pressure or pulse, chest pains, stomach pains, psychotic reactions, effects on components of the blood, loss of some scalp hair.

Drug Interactions

Methylphenidate will decrease the effectiveness of Guanethidine, a drug used to treat high blood pressure.

Interaction with monoamine oxidase (MAO) inhibitors may vastly increase the effect of Methylphenidate and cause problems.

If you take Methylphenidate regularly, avoid alcoholic beverages; they will add to the drowsiness problem.

Interaction with anticoagulants (blood-thinning drugs), some drugs used to treat epilepsy or other kinds of convulsions, Phenylbutazone and Oxyphenbutazone, and antidepressant drugs will slow the rate at which these drugs are broken down by the body, making more of them available in the bloodstream. Thus it may be necessary to lower their dose.

Food Interactions

This medicine is best taken on an empty stomach, but you may take it with food if it upsets your stomach.

Usual Dose

Doses should be tailored to individual needs; the doses listed here are only guidelines.

Adult: 10 or 20 to 30 or even 60 milligrams per day in divided doses 2 to 3 times per day, preferably 30 to 45 minutes before meals.

Child (over age 6): initial dose, 5 milligrams before breakfast and lunch; then increase in steps of 5 to 10 milligrams each week as required, but not to exceed 60 milligrams per day.

Overdosage

Symptoms are stimulation of the nervous system such as vomiting, agitation, tremors (uncontrollable twitching of the muscles), convulsions followed by coma, euphoria, confusion, hallucinations, delirium, sweating, flushing (face, hands, and extremities will be red), headache, high fever, abnormal heart rate, high blood pressure, and dryness of the mouth and nose. The patient should be taken to a hospital emergency room. ALWAYS bring the medicine bottle.

Special Information

Methylphenidate can mask the signs of temporary drowsiness or fatigue: Be careful while driving or operating machinery.

You should take the last daily dose of Methylphenidate by 6 P.M., to avoid sleeping problems.

If you miss a dose of Methylphenidate, take it as soon as possible. Take the rest of that day's doses at regularly spaced time intervals. Go back to your regular schedule the next day.

Generic Name

Methyltestosterone

Brand Names

Android   Testred
Metandren   Virilon
Oreton Methyl

(Also available in generic form)

Type of Drug

Androgenic (male) hormone.

Prescribed for

Diseases in which male hormone replacement or augmentation is needed; male menopause.

General Information

This is a member of the androgenic, or male, hormone group, which includes Testosterone, Calusterone, and Dromostanolone Propionate. (The last 2 are used primarily to treat breast cancer in women.)

Cautions and Warnings

Females taking any androgenic drug should watch for deepening of the voice, oily skin, acne, hairiness, increased libido, and menstrual irregularities, which may be related to the so-called virilizing effects of these hormones. Virilization is a sign that the drug is starting to produce changes in secondary sex characteristics. The drugs should be avoided if possible by boys who have not gone through puberty.

Men who have an unusually high blood level of calcium, known or suspected cancer of the prostate, prostate destruction or disease, cancer of the breast, liver, heart, or kidney disease should not use this medication.

Pregnancy/Breast-feeding

Women who are pregnant or breast-feeding should not use Methyltestosterone, since it may cause unwanted problems in babies, such as the development of male features in female babies.

Seniors

Older men treated with this drug run an increased risk of developing prostate enlargement or prostate cancer.

Possible Side Effects

In males: inhibition of testicle function, impotence, chronic erection of the penis, enlargement of the breast.

In females: unusual hairiness, baldness in a pattern similar to that seen in men, deepening of the voice, enlargement of the clitoris. These changes are usually irreversible once they have occurred. Females also experience menstrual irregularities and increases in blood calcium.

In both sexes: changes in libido, flushing of the skin, acne, mild dependence on the drug, excitation, chills, sleeplessness, water retention, nausea, vomiting, diarrhea. Symptoms resembling stomach ulcer may develop. Methyltestosterone may affect level of blood cholesterol.

Drug Interactions

Methyltestosterone may increase the effect of oral anticoagulants; dosage of the anticoagulant may have to be decreased.

The drug may have an effect on the glucose tolerance test, a blood test used to screen people for diabetes mellitus.

Usual Dose

5 to 200 milligrams per day, depending upon the disease being treated and patient's response.

Special Information

Methyltestosterone and other androgens are potent drugs. They must be taken only under the close supervision of your doctor and never used casually. The dosage and clinical effects of the drug vary widely and require constant monitoring.

Buccal tablets are intended to be dissolved between the cheek and gum. While buccal tablets are in your mouth you should refrain from eating, smoking, or drinking.

If you take Methyltestosterone once a day and forget your dose, take it as soon as possible. If you don't remember until the next day, skip the forgotten dose and continue with your regular schedule.

If you take the medicine more than once a day and forget a dose, take the forgotten dose as soon as possible. If it is almost time for your next dose, skip the forgotten dose and go on with your regular schedule.

Generic Name
Methysergide Maleate

Brand Name
Sansert

Type of Drug
Migraine headache preventive.

Prescribed for
Severe or frequent migraine headaches.

General Information
Methysergide is prescribed to prevent or reduce the number of migraine headache attacks in people who regularly suffer at least one migraine a week or for people whose headaches are severe, regardless of how often they occur.

Methysergide is derived from ergot, a natural plant fungus. The exact mechanism by which Methysergide produces its effects is not known, but it does block the effects of serotonin, a hormone that is active in many portions of the brain and central nervous system and in blood vessels that carry blood to the brain. Serotonin inhibition may be the key to Methysergide's action.

Methysergide must be taken for 1 to 2 days before you will feel the effects of the drug. Similarly, Methysergide's effects will persist for 1 to 2 days after you stop taking it.

Cautions and Warnings

People who are sensitive or allergic to Methysergide or any other ergot-derived medicine should not take this drug.

People with vascular (blood vessel) disease, severe hardening of the arteries, very high blood pressure, angina or other signs of coronary artery disease, disease of the heart valves, phlebitis, pulmonary disease, connective tissue disease (lupus and others), liver or kidney disease, or serious infections and those who are severely ill should be cautious about taking this medication.

People taking Methysergide for long periods of time may develop thickening of tissues surrounding the lung, making it more difficult to breathe; thickening of the heart valves, which may interfere with heart function; and fibrous tissues in the abdomen. To prevent these from occurring, you should take a drug holiday (a drug-free period) of 3 to 4 weeks after each 6 months of continuous Methysergide therapy. Then you may go back to taking the drug for another 6 months.

Methysergide tablets contain tartrazine dye for coloring, which should be avoided by asthmatics and other individuals allergic to tartrazine. Your pharmacist can contact the manufacturer to ask about obtaining tartrazine-free lots of Methysergide.

Pregnancy/Breast-feeding

Methysergide must not be used by pregnant women or women who might become pregnant because the drug will cause miscarriages.

Methysergide passes into breast milk and may cause the nursing baby to develop vomiting, diarrhea, and seizures. Nursing mothers who must take Methysergide should bottle-feed their infants.

Seniors

Older adults taking Methysergide may develop hypothermia (low body temperature) and other drug complications. This is because older people are more likely to have restricted blood flow to vessels supplying the arms, legs, and trunk before Methysergide treatment is started. Older adults are likely to need less Methysergide than younger adults because of natural, age-related losses of kidney function.

Possible Side Effects

Forty percent of people who take Methysergide are likely to experience a drug side effect. Nausea, vomiting, constipation, diarrhea, heartburn, and abdominal pain usually develop early in drug treatment; these adverse effects are generally avoided by a gradual increase of drug dose and by taking the drug with food or meals.

Other side effects include sleeplessness, drowsiness, a mild "high," dizziness, weakness, light-headedness, feelings of disassociation or hallucinations, flushing, raised red spots appearing in the skin, temporary hair loss, swelling, alterations in some components of the blood, muscle and joint aches, and weight gain.

In addition to the possibility of developing fibrosis (experienced as chest or abdominal pain or cold, numb, painful hands or feet with possible tingling and loss of pulse in the arms or legs), other rare side effects of Methysergide include visual changes, clumsiness, rash, and depression.

Drug Interactions

Nicotine, drug products containing another ergot derivative, and blood-vessel constrictors like Cocaine, Epinephrine, Metaraminol, Methoxamine, and Norepinephrine will increase the vasoconstrictor effect of Methysergide. Methysergide dose reduction may be needed if any of these other medications is used on a regular basis.

Alcohol, tranquilizers, and other nervous-system depressants will increase the depressant effects of this drug. Also, alcohol worsens migraine headaches.

Food Interactions

Methysergide should be taken with food or meals to relieve or avoid upset stomach.

Usual Dose

4 to 8 milligrams daily, taken with food or meals.

Overdosage

Overdose symptoms include cold and pale hands or feet, severe dizziness, excitement, and convulsions. Overdose victims should be taken to a hospital emergency room for treatment. ALWAYS bring the medicine bottle with you.

Special Information

Do not take Methysergide for more than 6 months at a time without a 3 to 4 week drug-free period.

Do not stop taking Methysergide without your doctor's knowledge and approval. Withdrawal headaches can occur if the drug is stopped suddenly. It should be gradually stopped over a 2 to 3 week period.

If Methysergide does not produce an improvement within the first 3 weeks of treatment, it is unlikely that the drug is going to be effective for you. Other treatments may be needed.

Heavy smokers experience increased blood-vessel constriction while taking Methysergide, leading to cold hands or feet, chest and abdominal pains, itching, numbness, and tingling of the toes, fingers, or face. Call your doctor if any of these symptoms develop (especially if you don't smoke) or if you develop visual changes, clumsiness, nervous system stimulation, swelling, changes in heart rate, fever, chills, cough, hoarseness, lower back or side pain, urinary difficulty, depression, skin rash, redness or darkening of the face, red spots on the skin, leg cramps, loss of appetite, difficulty breathing, or swelling of the hands, legs, ankles or feet.

People taking Methysergide must be careful when performing tasks requiring concentration and coordination because of the chance that the drug will make them tired, dizzy, or light-headed.

Excessive cold may worsen feelings of coldness, tingling, or pain caused by Methysergide. Take care during the winter to protect yourself from the cold weather.

Call your doctor if any kind of infection develops, because infections can increase your sensitivity to the effects of Methysergide.

If you take Methysergide twice a day and forget a dose, take it as soon as you remember. If it is almost time for your next dose, take one dose as soon as you remember and another in 5 or 6 hours, then go back to your regular schedule. Do not take a double dose.

If you take Methysergide 3 times a day and forget a dose, take it as soon as you remember. If it is almost time for your next dose, take one dose as soon as you remember and another in 3 or 4 hours, then go back to your regular schedule. Do not take a double dose.

Generic Name

Metoclopramide

Brand Names

Clopra   Reclomide
Maxolon   Reglan
Octamide

(Also available in generic form)

Type of Drug

Gastrointestinal stimulant.

Prescribed for

Symptoms of diabetic gastroparesis (stomach paralysis), including nausea, vomiting, fullness after meals, and loss of appetite. It is used to facilitate certain X-ray diagnostic procedures, to relieve nausea and vomiting, and to treat certain cases of stomach ulcers and anorexia nervosa. Metoclopramide is also used by nursing mothers to improve lactation.

General Information

This drug stimulates movement of the upper gastrointestinal tract but does not stimulate excess stomach acids or other secretions. It has been investigated in the United States as an antinauseant for patients receiving anticancer drugs. It has been used extensively for this purpose in Europe and South America. Although it is not known exactly how the drug works, its results may be caused by the direct effect of Metoclopramide on special receptors in the brain. Its value as an antiemetic is about the same as that of other currently available drugs.

Cautions and Warnings

This drug should not be used where stimulation of the gastrointestinal tract could be dangerous (bleeding ulcers, etc.) and should not be used if you are allergic to the drug.

This drug can cause extrapyramidal side effects similar to those caused by phenothiazine drugs. Do not take the 2 classes of drugs together. Extrapyramidal effects occur in only about 0.2 percent of the people taking the drug and usually include restlessness and involuntary movements of arms and legs, face, tongue, lips, or other parts of the body.

Pregnancy/Breast-feeding

This drug crosses into the blood circulation of a developing baby. It has not been found to cause birth defects. Pregnant women, or those who might become pregnant while taking this drug, should not take it without their doctors' approval. When the drug is considered essential by your doctor, the potential risk of taking the medicine must be carefully weighed against the benefit it might produce.

This drug passes into breast milk, but has caused no problems among breast-fed infants. You must consider the potential effect on the nursing infant if breast-feeding while taking this medicine.

Seniors

Older adults are more sensitive to the extrapyramidal effects of this drug (see "Cautions and Warnings"). Follow your doctor's directions and report any side effects at once.

Possible Side Effects

Restlessness, drowsiness, tiredness.

Less common side effects are sleeplessness, headache, dizziness, nausea, upset stomach.

Drug Interactions

The effects of Metoclopramide on the stomach are antagonized by narcotics and anticholinergic drugs.

Metoclopramide may interact with alcohol, sedatives, or other depressant drugs to produce excessive sleepiness or tiredness.

Because of its effects on the gastrointestinal tract, this drug may affect the passage of drugs through the stomach or intestines into the bloodstream.

Food Interactions

When taking this drug for nausea, be sure to take it 30 minutes before meals and at bedtime.

Usual Dose

Adult: 1 to 2 tablets before meals and at bedtime. Single doses of 1 to 2 tablets are used before X-ray diagnostic procedures.

Child (age 6 to 14): $\frac{1}{2}$ to $\frac{1}{4}$ the adult dose.

Child (under age 6): 0.05 milligrams per pound of body weight per dose.

Overdosage

Symptoms are drowsiness, disorientation, restlessness, or uncontrollable muscle movements. Symptoms usually disappear within 24 hours after the drug has been stopped. Anticholinergic drugs will antagonize these symptoms.

Special Information

If you forget to take a dose of Metoclopramide, take it as soon as you remember. If it is almost time for your next regularly scheduled dose, skip the forgotten dose and continue with your regular schedule. Do not take a double dose.

Generic Name

Metoprolol

Brand Names

Lopressor
Toprol XL

Type of Drug

Beta-adrenergic blocking agent.

Prescribed for

High blood pressure; angina pains; abnormal heart rhythms; prevention of a second heart attack; headache; tremors; anxiety pheochromocytoma; overactive thyroid symptoms; mitral valve prolapse.

General Information

This drug is very much like Propranolol but it has a more specific effect on the heart and a less specific effect on receptors in the blood vessels and respiratory tract. This means that the drug is safer for asthmatics and has a more specific effect on heart functions. The long-acting form of Metoprolol may cause fewer side effects than the regular tablet because it provides a steady flow of the drug into the bloodstream over a 24-hour period, avoiding drug peaks that can be associated with side effects.

Cautions and Warnings

All beta-blocking drugs should be used with care if you have a history of asthma, upper respiratory disease, or seasonal allergy, which may be worsened if you take this drug.

Pregnancy/Breast-feeding

Animal studies have shown that drugs similar to Metoprolol cause problems during pregnancy when used in very high amounts. Pregnant and breast-feeding women should use this drug only if it is essential.

Seniors

Older adults may be more or less sensitive to the effects of Metoprolol than younger adults. Your dosage must be adjusted to your individual needs by your doctor. Seniors may be more likely to suffer from cold hands and feet, reduced body temperature, chest pains, a general feeling of ill health, sudden breathing difficulties, sweating, or changes in heartbeat because of this medicine.

Possible Side Effects

Metoprolol may decrease heart rate; worsen congestive heart failure; and cause very low blood pressure, tingling in the extremities, light-headedness, mental depression (including sleeping difficulties), weakness, and tiredness. The depression may reverse itself when you stop taking the drug. Visual disturbances, hallucinations, disorientation, and short-term memory loss may occur. People taking Metoprolol may experience nausea, vomiting, stomach upset, abdominal cramps and diarrhea, or constipation. If you are allergic to Metoprolol, you may show typical signs of drug allergy, including sore throat, fever, breathing difficulty, and changes in the elements of your blood. Metoprolol may cause bronchospasms (spasms of the bronchial muscles), which will worsen any existing asthmatic or upper respiratory condition.

Occasionally, people taking Metoprolol experience emotional instability, a feeling of detachment, or personality changes. The drug may also cause changes in the blood system.

Drug Interactions

Metoprolol will interact with any psychotropic, or psychoactive, drug—including monoamine oxidase (MAO) inhibitors—that stimulates one of the adrenergic segments of the nervous system. Since most people taking a psychotropic drug don't have this information, discuss this possible problem with your doctor.

Metoprolol may increase the effectiveness of Insulin or oral antidiabetic drugs. If you are diabetic, discuss the situation with your doctor; a reduction in the dose of antidiabetic medication will probably be made.

Metoprolol may interact with certain other drugs to lower blood pressure. This interaction often has positive results in patients who need to take medicines to lower their blood pressure.

Do not self-medicate with over-the-counter cold, cough, or allergy remedies that may contain stimulant drugs that will aggravate your heart disease or high blood pressure or other ingredients that can antagonize the effects of Metoprolol. Check with your doctor or pharmacist before taking any over-the-counter medication.

Food Interactions

Take this medicine with food if it upsets your stomach. The long-acting form of Metoprolol is unaffected by food and may be taken at any time.

Usual Dose

100 to 450 milligrams per day. Metoprolol dosage must be tailored to your specific needs.

Overdosage

Symptoms of Metoprolol overdose are slowed heart rate, heart failure, low blood pressure, and spasms of the bronchial muscles, making it difficult to breathe. The overdose victim should be taken to a hospital emergency room for treatment. ALWAYS bring the medicine bottle with you.

Special Information

Metoprolol can make you tired, so take care when driving or operating machinery.

Call your doctor if you become depressed or confused or if you develop a skin rash, difficulty breathing, chest pains, yellow skin or eyes, cold hands or feet, unusual bleeding or bruising, fever or sore throat, hallucinations, slow heartbeat, or back or joint pains. Other side effects need to be reported only if they become bothersome or unusually persistent.

Do not stop taking this medicine abruptly unless your doctor tells you to do so, or serious angina (heart pain) may develop.

If you forget to take a dose of Metoprolol, take it as soon as possible. However, if it is within 8 hours of your next dose, skip the forgotten dose and go back to your regular schedule. Do not take a double dose.

Generic Name

Metronidazole

Brand Names

Femazole   Protostat
Flagyl

(Also available in generic form)

Type of Drug

Amoebicide and antibiotic.

Prescribed for

Acute amoebic dysentery; infections of the vagina, bone, brain, nervous system, urinary tract, abdomen, and skin caused by bacteria or other microorganisms that are sensitve to the drug's effects. Metronidazole may also be prescribed for pneumonia, inflammatory bowel disease, colitis caused by other antibiotics, periodontal infections.

General Information

Metronidazole may be prescribed for symptomless disease when the doctor feels that the use of this drug is indicated; specifically, asymptomatic females may be treated with this drug when vaginal examination shows evidence of trichomonas. Because trichomonas infection of the vaginal area is a venereal disease, asymptomatic sexual partners of treated patients should be treated simultaneously if the organism has been found to be present in the woman's genital tract, to prevent reinfection of the partner. The decision to treat an asymptomatic male partner who does not have the organism present is an individual one and must be made by the doctor. Metronidazole kills microorganisms by disrupting the DNA of the organism after it enters the cell.

Cautions and Warnings

If you have a history of blood disease or if you know that you are sensitive or allergic to Metronidazole you should not use this drug. It should not be taken if you have active nervous system disease, including epilepsy, or if you have severe heart or liver problems.

Metronidazole has been shown to be carcinogenic (cancer-inducing) in mice and possibly in rats. This effect has not been found in humans.

Pregnancy/Breast-feeding

Metronidazole enters the blood circulation of the developing fetus soon after you take it. It is not recommended for use during the first 3 months of pregnancy and should be taken with care during the last 6 months of pregnancy. If you are pregnant or might become pregnant, Metronidazole should be used with caution.

Metronidazole passes into breast milk in about the same concentration as it is present in your blood. Because of this, breast-feeding while taking Metronidazole may cause unwanted side effects in your infant. If you must take Metronidazole, you should temporarily bottle-feed your baby and discard any pumped breast milk you might have saved. Nursing can be resumed 1 or 2 days after stopping Metronidazole.

Seniors

Older adults with severe liver disease are more sensitive to the effects of this drug. Follow your doctor's directions and report any side effects at once.

Possible Side Effects

The most common side effects are symptoms in the gastro-intestinal tract, including nausea (sometimes accompanied by headache), loss of appetite, occasional vomiting, diarrhea, stomach upset, abdominal cramping, and constipation. A sharp, unpleasant metallic taste is also associated with the use of this drug. Dizziness and, rarely, incoordination have been reported. Numbness or tingling in the extremities and occasional joint pains have been associated with Metronidazole therapy, as have confusion, irritability, depression, inability to sleep, and weakness. Itching and a sense of pelvic pressure have been reported.

Rare side effects include fever, increased urination, incontinence, decrease of libido.

Drug Interactions

Avoid alcoholic beverages: Interaction with Metronidazole may cause abdominal cramps, nausea, vomiting, headaches, and flushing. Modification of the taste of alcoholic beverages has also been reported.

People taking oral anticoagulant (blood-thinning) drugs such as Warfarin will have to have the dose changed because Metronidazole increases the effect of anticoagulants.

Cimetidine can interfere with the liver's ability to break down Metronidazole, causing increased amounts of drug in your blood. Your doctor may have to reduce your Metronidazole dosage while you are taking Cimetidine.

Phenobarbital can increase the rate at which Metronidazole is broken down, reducing the amount of the antibiotic in your blood.

Metronidazole should not be used if you are taking Disulfiram, used to maintain abstinence from alcohol, because the combination can cause confusion and psychotic reactions.

Drugs that cause nervous system toxicity, including Mexiletine, Ethambutol, Isoniazid, Lindane, Lincomycin, Lithium, Pemoline, Quinacrine, and long-term high-dose Vitamin B6 (Pyridoxine), should not be taken with Metronidazole because of the chance that nervous system effects may be increased.

Metronidazole may increase blood levels of Phenytoin by interfering with its breakdown in the liver. This could result in Phenytoin side effects and may result in your doctor having to adjust your Phenytoin dosage.

Food Interactions

This medicine is best taken with food or meals to avoid upset stomach.

Usual Dose

Adult: for the treatment of amoebic dysentery, 500 to 750 milligrams 3 times per day for 5 to 10 days. For trichomonal infections, 250 milligrams 3 times per day for 7 days, or 2 grams in 1 dose.

Child: for amoebic dysentery, 16 to 23 milligrams per pound of body weight daily divided in 3 equal doses, for 10 days.

Overdosage

Single doses as large as 15 grams (15,000 milligrams) have been taken in suicide attempts and accidental doses. Overdose symptoms include nausea, clumsiness and unsteadiness, seizures, pain or tingling in the hands or feet. Call your local poison control center or hospital emergency room for more information.

Special Information

Call your doctor if you become dizzy or light-headed while taking this drug or if you develop numbness, tingling, pain, or weakness in your hands or feet, or seizures (with high doses of Metronidazole). Rare side effects that demand your doctor's attention include clumsiness or unsteadiness; mood changes; unusual vaginal irritation, discharge, or dryness; skin rash, hives, or itching; or severe pain of the abdomen or back accompanied by vomiting, appetite loss, or nausea. Call your doctor if other side effects become particularly bothersome or persistent.

Follow your doctor's dosage instructions faithfully and don't stop until the full course of therapy has been taken.

The occasional darkening of urine of patients taking Metronidazole is of uncertain clinical significance and is probably not important.

Metronidazole may cause dry mouth that can be relieved with ice, hard candy, or gum. Call your dentist if dry mouth persists for more than 2 weeks.

If you forget to take a dose of Metronidazole, take it as soon as you remember. If it is almost time for your next regularly scheduled dose, skip the forgotten dose and continue with your regular schedule. Do not take a double dose.

Generic Name

Metyrosine

Brand Name

Demser

Type of Drug

Antihypertensive.

Prescribed for

Controlling high blood pressure caused by a pheochromocytoma.

General Information

Pheochromocytoma is the term applied to a particular tumor
of the adrenal gland. It causes very high blood pressure because it produces vast quantities of 2 hormones called norepinephrine and epinephrine. Metyrosine is prescribed only
to prepare someone for surgery to remove the tumor, to
control blood pressure when surgery cannot be performed,
or for chronic treatment of a malignant pheochromocytoma.
It works by blocking the natural body processes that manufacture the 2 hormones in question.

Metyrosine is not intended to control the garden-variety-
type of high blood pressure normally treated with other antihypertensive drugs.

Cautions and Warnings

This drug is intended for short-term use. Prolonged Metyrosine treatment should be carried out with caution in people
with a history of liver or kidney problems.

Pregnancy/Breast-feeding

Little is known about the safety of taking this drug during
pregnancy. It should be taken only after the potential benefits have been weighed against the potential dangers.

It is not known if this drug passes into breast milk. Nursing
mothers who must take Metyrosine should consider bottle-
feeding their babies.

Seniors

There are no special precautions for seniors. However, the
caution against long-term use is especially important because of the gradual loss of kidney function that is a normal
part of the aging process.

Possible Side Effects

The most common side effects of Metyrosine are sedation, drooling, speech difficulty and tremor, and diarrhea.

Other side effects include sleeplessness, feelings of increased alertness and ambition, headache, depression, hallucinations, disorientation and confusion, decreased salivation, dry mouth, nausea, vomiting, abdominal pain, male impotence, drug crystal formation in the kidney or urine, slight breast swelling, stuffed nose, changes in blood composition and swelling in the hands and feet. Drug reactions such as fever, itching, and difficulty breathing are rare.

Drug Interactions

Some of the side effects (tremors, parkinsonism, drooling, muscle spasms, jerky movements) of Haloperidol and the phenothiazine antipsychotic drugs may be enhanced by Metyrosine.

Alcohol, tranquilizers, and other nervous-system depressants will increase the depressant effects of Metyrosine.

Food Interactions

Metyrosine may be taken without regard to food or meals.

Usual Dose

Adult and child (over age 12): 1000 milligrams a day to start, gradually increased to 2000 or 3000 milligrams a day, as needed. Maximum daily dose is 4000 milligrams. For best results, each dose of Metyrosine should be taken at the same time every day.

Child (age 12 and under): The safety of Metyrosine in children of this age has not been established.

Overdosage

Metyrosine overdose is likely to produce normally expected drug side effects. Call your local poison control center or hospital emergency room for more information. ALWAYS remember to bring the medicine bottle with you.

Special Information

Metyrosine crystals may form in the kidney. To prevent this, you should drink at least 2 quarts of fluid every day while taking this drug, especially if your daily dose is more than 2000 milligrams a day.

Sedation, a common side effect of Metyrosine, begins within the first day of treatment, peaks in 2 or 3 days, and then slowly subsides. By the end of 1 week, the sedative effect is usually gone, unless the dosage has reached 2000 milligrams a day. Several other side effects are dose-related and will subside if your daily dosage is reduced.

Call your doctor if you start to drool or to develop speech problems, tremors, unusual muscle spasms, disorientation, diarrhea, or pain on urination. Also contact the doctor if other symptoms become particularly bothersome or interfere with daily functioning.

People taking Metyrosine must be careful when performing tasks requiring concentration and coordination because of the chance that the drug will make them tired, dizzy, or light-headed.

If you forget a dose of Metyrosine, take it as soon as you remember. If it is almost time for your next dose, take one dose as soon as you remember and another in 3 or 4 hours, then go back to your regular schedule. Do not take a double dose.

Generic Name

Mexiletine

Brand Name

Mexitil

Type of Drug

Antiarrhythmic.

Prescribed for

Abnormal heart rhythms.

General Information

Mexiletine is generally prescribed only after other drugs have been tried. When Mexiletine is replacing other drug treatments, it may be given 6 to 12 hours after the last dose of Quinidine or Disopyramide, 3 to 6 hours after the last dose of Procainamide, or 12 hours after the last dose of Tocainide.

Cautions and Warnings

Since this drug is broken down by your liver and it can cause some liver problems of its own, people with severe liver disease must be cautious while taking this medicine. Other conditions for which special considerations must be taken into account if you are to take Mexiletine are heart block, heart failure, heart attack, low blood pressure, and seizure disorders (Mexiletine causes seizures in a small number of people who take it).

Pregnancy/Breast-feeding

This drug crosses into the blood circulation of a developing baby. It has not been found to cause human birth defects, but it does affect animal fetuses. Pregnant women, or those who might become pregnant while taking this drug, should not take it without their doctors' approval. When the drug is considered essential by your doctor, the potential risk of taking the medicine must be carefully weighed against the benefit it might produce.

This drug passes into breast milk, but has caused no problems among breast-fed infants. The possible side effects of this drug make it necessary to bottle-feed if you must take this medicine.

Seniors

Older adults with severe liver disease are more sensitive to the effects of this drug. Follow your doctor's directions and report any side effects at once.

Possible Side Effects

The most common side effects are nausea, vomiting, diarrhea, constipation, tremors, dizziness, light-headedness, nervousness, and poor coordination. These side effects can be reversed if the drug dose is reduced, the medicine is taken with food or antacids, or the drug is stopped.

Other common side effects include heart palpitations,

chest pains, angina, changes in appetite, abdominal pains or cramps, stomach ulcers and bleeding, difficulty swallowing, dry mouth, altered taste, changes in the saliva and mucous membranes of your mouth, tingling or numbness in the hands or feet, weakness, fatigue, ringing or buzzing in the ears, depression, speech difficulties, rash, difficulty breathing, swelling.

Less common or rare side effects include abnormal heart rhythms, memory loss, hallucinations and other psychological problems, fainting, low blood pressure, slow heartbeat, swelling, hot flashes, high blood pressure, shock, joint pains, fever, sweating, hair loss, impotence, decreased sex drive, feeling sickly, difficulty urinating, hiccups, and dry skin.

Drug Interactions

The effects of Mexiletine are reduced by Ammonium Chloride and Vitamin C. Phenytoin, Rifampin, Phenobarbital, and other drugs that stimulate the liver to break down drugs more rapidly also reduce this drug's effect. Tobacco smoking, which also stimulates drug breakdown in the liver, reduces the effectiveness of this drug.

Antacids, bicarbonates, and Acetazolamide decrease the clearance of this drug through the kidney and therefore increase its effects.

Cimetidine raises blood levels of this drug, leading to a possible increase in Mexiletine side effects.

Other drugs for abnormal heart rhythms may produce an additive effect on the heart, although drug combinations are sometimes the only way to control an abnormal rhythm.

Food Interactions

Taking this drug with food reduces the rate at which it is absorbed into your blood and can reduce the incidence of some very common side effects, especially those related to your stomach and intestines.

Usual Dose

600 to 1200 milligrams per day in 3 divided doses.

Overdosage

Symptoms of overdose are generally expressed as drug side

effects. The most dangerous are those that affect the heart or nervous system. Take the overdose victim to a hospital emergency room at once for treatment. ALWAYS bring the medicine bottle with you.

Special Information

Call your doctor if you develop chest pain, a fast or irregular heartbeat, breathing problems, seizures, tiredness, yellow skin or eyes, sore throat, fever or chills, or unexplained bruising or bleeding, or if any side effect becomes bothersome or intolerable. .

Avoid diets that can change the acidity of your urine. A high-acid diet will increase the rate at which Mexiletine is removed from your body, and a basic diet will cause the drug to be retained in your body. Your doctor or pharmacist can give you more information on this.

If you miss a dose of Mexiletine, take it as soon as you can. If it is more than 4 hours past your dose time, skip the missed dose and go back to your usual dose schedule.

Generic Name

Miconazole Nitrate

Brand Names

Micatin Cream/Liquid Spray/   Monistat 7 Cream/
  Powder   Suppositories
Monistat 3 Suppositories   Monistat-Derm Cream

(Also available in generic form)

Type of Drug

Antifungal.

Prescribed for

Treatment of fungus infections in the vagina, on the skin, and in the blood.

General Information

Miconazole Nitrate is used as a vaginal cream, vaginal sup-

positories, or topical cream, powder, or lotion or by intravenous injection. When given as an injection to hospitalized
patients, it is effective against serious fungal infections.
When used for vaginal or topical infections, it is effective
against several nonfungus types of organisms, as well as
fungus-type infections. On the skin, it is used for common
fungus infections such as athlete's foot or jock itch.

Cautions and Warnings

Do not use Miconazole Nitrate if you know you are allergic
to it.

Pregnancy/Breast-feeding

Pregnant women should avoid using the vaginal cream during the first 3 months of pregnancy. They should use it during the next 6 months only if it is absolutely necessary.

Miconazole Nitrate has not been shown to cause problems
in breast-fed infants.

Seniors

Older adults may take this medication without special restriction. Follow your doctor's directions and report any side
effects at once.

Possible Side Effects

After intravenous injection: vein irritation, itching, rash, nausea, vomiting, fever, drowsiness, diarrhea, loss of appetite,
flushing.

After vaginal administration: itching, burning or irritation,
pelvic cramps, hives, rash, headache.

After application to the skin: irritation, burning.

Drug Interactions

None known.

Usual Dose

Intravenous: 200 to 3600 milligrams per day.

Vaginal suppository or cream: One applicatorful or suppository into the vagina at bedtime for 3 to 7 days.

Topical: Apply to affected areas of skin twice a day for up
to 1 month.

Special Information

When using the vaginal cream, insert the whole applicatorful of cream high into the vagina and be sure to complete the full course of treatment prescribed for you. Call your doctor if you develop burning or itching.

If you forget to take a dose of Miconazole Nitrate, take it as soon as you remember. If it is almost time for your next regularly scheduled dose, skip the forgotten dose and continue with your regular schedule. Do not take a double dose.

Brand Name

Minizide

Ingredients

Polythiazide
Prazosin Hydrochloride

Type of Drug

Antihypertensive combination.

Prescribed for

High blood pressure.

General Information

This is one of many fixed-dose combinations available to treat high blood pressure. It is a combination of 2 popular medicines often prescribed individually; it offers the advantage of allowing the patient to take only one capsule per dose. These combinations are useful only when you require the exact dosage of each ingredient contained in the product. Minizide is available in 3 different strength combinations to allow proper dosage adjustment.

Cautions and Warnings

Prazosin Hydrochloride, an ingredient in this combination, can cause dizziness and fainting, usually because of an effect called postural hypotension, where blood supply to the brain is reduced when you rise suddenly from a sitting or lying position. This usually occurs after taking the first dose of Prazosin.

Pregnancy/Breast-feeding

Polythiazide, an ingredient in this combination, may cross into the blood circulation of a developing baby. The combination has not been found to cause birth defects, but may cause other problems in the newborn. Pregnant women, or those who might become pregnant while taking this drug, should not take it without their doctors' approval. When the drug is considered essential by your doctor, the potential risk of taking the medicine must be carefully weighed against the benefit it might produce.

Polythiazide may pass into breast milk. The combination has caused no problems among breast-fed infants, but you must consider the potential effect on the nursing infant if breast-feeding while taking this medicine.

Seniors

Older adults should use this combination with caution because of greater sensitivity to drug side effects. Also, older adults are more likely to develop hypothermia (low body temperature) caused by the Prazosin ingredient.

Possible Side Effects

The most common side effects of this combination are dizziness, headache, drowsiness, lack of energy, weakness, heart palpitations, and nausea.

Less common side effects are loss of appetite, vomiting, diarrhea, constipation, upset stomach, stomach pains, swelling of the arms or legs, shortness of breath, fainting, rapid heartbeat, chest pains (angina), muscle spasms, nervousness, depression, tingling in the hands or feet, unusual sensitivity to the sun, rash, itching, frequent urination, loss of urinary control, impotence (men), blurred vision, eye redness, ringing or buzzing in the ears, stuffed nose, sweating, dry mouth.

Drug Interactions

Minizide's effectiveness may be lessened when it is taken

together with anti-inflammatory pain relievers, especially In-domethacin, or with estrogen-containing drugs.

Avoid over-the-counter diet pills, decongestants, and products for the common cold that contain stimulants and can raise your blood pressure. Ask your pharmacist to suggest a product you can safely take.

Minizide's effectiveness is increased when it is combined with other antihypertensive medicines.

Food Interactions

Take this medicine with food if it upsets your stomach.

Usual Dose

1 capsule 2 to 3 times per day.

Overdosage

Symptoms can be very low blood pressure, drowsiness, slow reflexes, weakness, tingling in the arms or legs, changes in heartbeat, dry mouth, a sickly feeling, restless-ness, muscle pains or cramps, urinary difficulty, nausea, or vomiting. Take the victim to a hospital emergency room at once for treatment. ALWAYS remember to bring the medicine bottle with you.

Special Information

Take this medication exactly as prescribed and don't stop taking it without your doctor's permission, even if you feel perfectly well. High blood pressure has few symptoms, and most people with high blood pressure feel fine.

This product can cause dizziness, drowsiness, and head-ache. Avoid driving or operating complex equipment if this happens to you. You may want to take the first dose of medicine before you go to bed. If you get extremely dizzy, lie down and let the episode pass.

If you forget to take a dose of Minizide, take it as soon as you remember. If it is almost time for your next regularly scheduled dose, skip the forgotten dose and continue with your regular schedule. Do not take a double dose.

Generic Name

Minocycline

Brand Name

Minocin

Type of Drug

Broad-spectrum tetracycline-type antibiotic.

Prescribed for

Sexually transmitted diseases such as gonorrhea, syphilis, and chlamydia; infections of the mouth, gums, teeth; Rocky Mountain spotted fever and other fevers caused by ticks and lice from a variety of carriers; urinary tract infections; respiratory system infections such as pneumonia and bronchitis.

These diseases are produced by gram-positive and gram-negative organisms such as diplococci, staphylococci, streptococci, gonococci, *E. coli*, and *Shigella*.

Minocycline has also been successfully used to treat some skin infections, but it is not considered the first-choice antibiotic for the treatment of general skin infections or wounds.

General Information

Minocycline works by interfering with the normal growth cycle of the invading bacteria, preventing them from reproducing and thus allowing the body's normal defenses to fight off the infection. This process is referred to as bacteriostatic action. Minocycline has also been used along with other medicines to treat amoebic infections of the intestinal tract, known as amoebic dysentery. It is also prescribed for diseases caused by ticks, fleas, and lice.

Minocycline has been successfully used for the treatment of adolescent acne, in small doses over a long period of time. Adverse effects or toxicity in this type of therapy are almost unheard of.

Since the action of this antibiotic depends on its concentration within the invading bacteria, it is imperative that you completely follow your doctor's directions.

Cautions and Warnings

Minocycline should not be given to people with known liver
disease or kidney or urine excretion problems. You should
avoid taking high doses of Minocycline or undergoing extended Minocycline therapy if you will be exposed to sunlight for a long period because this antibiotic can interfere
with your body's normal sun-screening mechanism, possibly causing a severe sunburn. If you have a known history
of allergy to Minocycline you should avoid taking this drug
or other drugs within this category, such as Aureomycin,
Terramycin, Rondomycin, Vibramycin, Demeclocycline, and
Tetracycline.

Pregnancy/Breast-feeding

You should not use Minocycline if you are pregnant, especially during the last half of pregnancy, or during breast-
feeding when bones and teeth are being formed. Minocycline when used in children has been shown to interfere
with the development of the long bones and may retard
growth. Exceptions would be when Minocycline is the only
effective antibiotic available and all risk factors have been
made known to the patient.

Seniors

Older adults may take this drug without special precaution.

Possible Side Effects

As with other antibiotics, the common side effects of Minocycline are stomach upset, nausea, vomiting, diarrhea, and
skin rash. Less common side effects include hairy tongue and
itching and irritation of the anal and/or vaginal region. If
these symptoms appear, consult your physician immediately. Periodic physical examinations and laboratory tests
should be given to patients who are on long-term
Minocycline.

Other uncommon side effects include loss of appetite,
peeling of the skin, sensitivity to the sun, fever, chills, anemia, possible brown spotting of the skin, decrease in kidney
function, damage to the liver.

Drug Interactions

Minocycline (a bacteriostatic drug) may interfere with the action of bactericidal agents such as Penicillin. It is not advisable to take both during the same course of therapy.

Don't take multivitamin products containing minerals at the same time as Minocycline, or you may reduce the antibiotic's effectiveness. You may take these 2 medicines at least 2 hours apart.

People receiving anticoagulation therapy (blood-thinning agents) should consult their doctor, since Minocycline will interfere with this form of therapy. An adjustment in the anticoagulant dosage may be required.

This drug can increase the level of Digoxin in the blood and lead to digoxin toxicity. This effect can persist for months after Minocycline has been discontinued.

Minocycline can reduce the amount of Insulin needed to maintain a diabetic patient. Your doctor should closely monitor your Insulin need and blood sugar while you are taking this drug.

Minocycline can affect blood Lithium levels. Your doctor should closely monitor your blood Lithium while you are taking this drug.

Minocycline and other Tetracycline antibiotics can interfere with the effects of oral contraceptive drugs. Use extra contraceptive precautions if you are taking this combination.

Food Interactions

Minocycline, unlike most other Tetracycline antibiotics, may be taken with food or milk if it upsets your stomach.

Usual Dose

Adult: first dose, 200 milligrams, followed by 100 milligrams every 12 hours. Or, 100 to 200 milligrams may be given to start, followed by 50 milligrams 4 times per day.

Child (age 9 and over): approximately 2 milligrams per pound of body weight initially, followed by 1 milligram per pound every 12 hours.

Child (up to age 8): This drug is not recommended because it has been shown to produce serious discoloration of the permanent teeth.

Overdose

Symptoms of overdose are generally exaggerated drug side effects. Call your local poison control center or hospital emergency room for more information.

Special Information

Minocycline can be stored at room temperature. DO NOT take this drug if the expiration date has passed. The decomposition of Minocycline produces a highly toxic substance which can cause serious kidney damage. Call your doctor if your side effects become intolerable, especially if you become dizzy or unsteady.

If you miss a dose of Minocycline, take it as soon as possible. If it is almost time for your next dose and you take the medication once a day, space the next 2 doses 10 to 12 hours apart, then go back to your regular daily schedule. If it is almost time for your next dose and you take the medicine twice a day, space the next 2 doses 5 to 6 hours apart, then go back to your regular schedule.

Generic Name

Minoxidil

Brand Names

Loniten Tablets   Rogaine Lotion
Minodyl Tablets

(Also available in generic form)

Type of Drug

Antihypertensive; hair growth stimulant.

Prescribed for

Severe high blood pressure not controllable with other drugs; early baldness in men and women.

General Information

The oral form of this drug can cause severe adverse effects on the heart. It is usually given together with a beta-blocking antihypertensive drug (Propranolol, Metoprolol, Nadolol, etc.) to prevent rapid heartbeat and a diuretic to prevent fluid accumulation. Some patients may have to be hospitalized when treatment with this drug is started, to avoid too rapid a drop in blood pressure.

Minoxidil works by dilating peripheral blood vessels and allowing more blood to flow through arms and legs. This increased blood flow reduces the resistance levels in central vessels (heart, lungs, kidneys, etc.) and therefore reduces blood pressure. Its effect on blood pressure can be seen a half hour after a dose is taken and lasts up to 3 days. Patients usually take the medicine once or twice a day. Maximum drug effect occurs as early as 3 days after the drug is started, if the dose is large enough (40 milligrams per day).

The ideal strength of Minoxidil in lotion form for application to the scalp to treat baldness is 2%. Applying this solution does not work for all people who try it, and it is necessary to continue Minoxidil applications to maintain new hair growth stimulated by the drug. Minoxidil lotion was approved by the FDA in mid-1988.

The ideal candidate for Minoxidil's hair-restoring effect is a man just starting to lose his hair. Women may also be helped by Minoxidil lotion. The drug won't help unless hair in the balding area is at least a half-inch long. It takes 4 to 6 months of application before an effect can be expected. Stopping the medication will nullify any benefit you have gained, and any hair you have grown will fall out. For men, Rogaine only slows the rate of hair loss.

Cautions and Warnings

This drug should not be used by people with pheochromocytoma, a rare tumor in which extra body stimulants (catecholamines) are made. Minoxidil may cause the accumulation of water and sodium in the body, leading to heart failure. It also increases heart rate. To protect you from these side effects, Minoxidil must be given with other drugs, a diuretic and a beta-adrenergic blocker.

Minoxidil has not been carefully studied in patients who have suffered a heart attack within the past month.

Pregnancy/Breast-feeding

This drug crosses into the blood circulation of a developing baby. It has not been found to cause birth defects. Pregnant women, or those who might become pregnant while taking this drug, should not take it without their doctors' approval. When the drug is considered essential by your doctor, the potential risk of taking the medicine must be carefully weighed against the benefit it might produce.

This drug passes into breast milk, but has caused no problems among breast-fed infants. You must consider the potential effect on the nursing infant if breast-feeding while taking this medicine.

Seniors

Older adults are more sensitive to the blood-pressure-lowering effects of this drug because of a normal loss of some kidney capacity to clear the drug from your body. Follow your doctor's directions and report any side effects at once.

Possible Side Effects

Water and sodium retention can develop, leading to heart failure. Also, some patients taking this drug may develop fluid in the sacs surrounding the heart. This is treated with diuretic drugs.

Eighty percent of people taking this drug experience thickening, elongation, and darkening of body hair within 3 to 6 weeks after starting Minoxidil. This is usually first noticed on the temples, between the eyebrows, between the eyebrows and hairline, or on the upper cheek. Later on it will extend to the back, arms, legs, and scalp. This effect stops when the drug is stopped and symptoms will disappear in 1 to 6 months. Electrocardiogram changes occur in 60 percent of patients but are usually not associated with any symptoms. Some other laboratory tests (blood, liver, kidney) may be affected by Minoxidil. Local irritation has occurred when Minoxidil has been used topically.

People using 2% Minoxidil lotion may experience irritation or itching. The amount of Minoxidil absorbed into the scalp is too small to affect blood pressure or cause other serious side effects.

Drug Interactions

Minoxidil may interact with Guanethidine to produce dizziness when rising from a sitting or lying position.

Do not take over-the-counter drugs containing stimulants.
If you are unsure which drugs to avoid, ask your pharmacist.

Food Interactions

This drug may be taken at any time. It is not affected by
food or liquid intake.

Usual Dose

Adult and child (age 12 and over): 5 milligrams to start;
may be increased to 40 milligrams per day. Do not take
more than 100 milligrams per day. The daily dose of Minoxidil must be tailored to each patient's needs.

Child (under age 12): 0.1 milligrams per pound per day to
start; may be increased to 0.5 milligrams per pound per day.
Do not use more than 50 milligrams per day. The daily dose
of Minoxidil must be tailored to each patient's needs.

Minoxidil is usually given together with a diuretic (Hydrochlorothiazide, 100 milligrams per day; Chlorthalidone, 50 to
100 milligrams per day; or Furosemide, 80 milligrams per
day) and a beta-adrenergic blocker (Propranolol, 80 to 160
milligrams per day, or the equivalent dose of another drug).
People who cannot take a beta-adrenergic blocker may take
Methyldopa, 500 to 1500 milligrams per day, instead. 0.2 to
0.4 milligrams per day of Clonidine may also be used.

Minoxidil lotion: Apply to scalp twice a day.

Overdosage

Symptoms may be those associated with too-low blood
pressure. Contact your doctor or poison control center if an
overdose of Minoxidil occurs.

Special Information

Since Minoxidil is usually given with 2 other medications, a
beta-adrenergic blocker and a diuretic, do not discontinue
any of these drugs unless told to do so by your doctor. Take
all medication exactly as prescribed.

The effect of this drug on body hair (see "Possible Side
Effects") is a nuisance but not dangerous. Do not stop taking
Minoxidil because of it.

Call your doctor if you experience an increase in your
pulse of 20 or more beats per minute, weight gain of more

than 5 pounds, unusual swelling of your arms and/or legs, face, or stomach, chest pain, difficulty in breathing, dizziness, or fainting spells.

If you forget to take a dose of Minoxidil, take it as soon as you remember. If it is almost time for your next regularly scheduled dose, skip the forgotten dose and continue with your regular schedule. Do not take a double dose.

Generic Name

Misoprostol

Brand Name

Cytotec

Type of Drug

Antiulcer.

Prescribed for

Prevention of stomach ulcers associated with taking nonsteroidal anti-inflammatory drugs (for arthritis).

General Information

Misoprostol is intended to prevent severe stomach irritation or ulcers in people taking a nonsteroidal anti-inflammatory drug (NSAID) for arthritis. It does not prevent duodenal ulcers. Like Cimetidine and some other antiulcer drugs, Misoprostol supresses stomach acid. It has shown an ability to protect the stomach lining from damage, although the exact way that the drug produces this effect is not known. Misoprostol may stimulate the body to produce more stomach lining; increase the thickness of the protective gel layer that lines the stomach; increase blood flow in the stomach lining, making it repair itself more quickly; or increase the production of bicarbonate, a "natural antacid," in the stomach.

Misoprostol is likely to be an effective ulcer treatment for people who have not responded to Cimetidine, Ranitidine, or Lisinopril, or who cannot take one of these drugs because of interaction with another drug or side effects.

Cautions and Warnings

This drug may make men and women less fertile.

Pregnancy/Breast-feeding

Misoprostol can cause spontaneous miscarriage. Women who are, or might become, pregnant while taking Misoprostol should not take this medicine. The chances of a woman of childbearing age taking this medicine are rather small, since it is generally intended for older adults who take anti-arthritis medicine on a regular basis. Nevertheless, this caution should be kept in mind.

Do not take Misoprostol if you are nursing.

Seniors

Older adults absorb more Misoprostol than younger people do, although adverse effects usually do not accompany this phenomenon. The dosage of Misoprostol should be reduced if intolerable side effects develop. This drug is intended for seniors and others with a history of ulcer or stomach disease or those who have been unable to tolerate anti-arthritis drugs in the past.

Possible Side Effects

The most common side effects of Misoprostol are diarrhea, nausea, vomiting, upset stomach, stomach pain, and stomach gas. Most cases of diarrhea are mild and last a maximum of 2 to 3 days.

Drug Interactions

Misoprostol reduces stomach acid and may interfere with the absorption of drugs such as Diazepam and Theophylline, which may depend upon the presence of stomach acid for their absorption.

Food Interactions

Misoprostol should be taken with food.

Usual Dose

800 micrograms per day.

Overdosage

The toxic dose of Misoprostol in humans is not known. Up to 1600 micrograms per day have been taken with only minor discomfort. Overdose symptoms are sedation, tremor, convulsions, breathing difficulty, stomach pain, diarrhea, fever, changes in heart rate (very fast or very slow), and low blood pressure. Animals given much larger doses have developed liver, kidney, heart, and testicular damage. Overdose victims should be taken to a hospital emergency room for treatment. ALWAYS remember to bring the prescription bottle with you.

Special Information

Do not stop taking Misoprostol without your doctor's knowledge.

Do not share this drug with anyone else, especially a woman of childbearing age.

If you forget to take a dose of Misoprostol, take it as soon as you remember. If you don't remember until it is almost time to take your next dose, skip the forgotten dose and continue with your regular schedule.

Brand Name

Moduretic

Ingredients

Amiloride
Hydrochlorothiazide

Type of Drug

Diuretic.

Prescribed for

High blood pressure or any condition where it is desirable to eliminate excess water from the body.

General Information

Moduretic is a combination of 2 diuretics. It is a convenient, effective approach for the treatment of diseases where the elimination of excess water is required. One of the ingredients in Moduretic, Amiloride, holds potassium in the body while producing a diuretic effect. This balances the Hydrochlorothiazide, which often causes a loss of body potassium.

Combination drugs such as Moduretic should be used only when you need the exact amount of ingredients contained in the product and when your doctor feels you would benefit from taking fewer pills per day.

Cautions and Warnings

This drug should not be used by people with diabetes or severe kidney disease or those who are allergic to either of these ingredients or to sulfa drugs. This drug may cause abnormally high blood-potassium levels. Since too much potassium in your blood can be fatal, your doctor should test blood-potassium levels periodically.

Pregnancy/Breast-feeding

This drug should be used by pregnant women or nursing mothers only if absolutely necessary. It may cause birth defects or interfere with your baby's development. Check with your doctor before taking it if you are, or might be, pregnant.

Seniors

Older adults are more sensitive to the effects of this drug. They should closely follow their doctor's directions and report any side effects at once.

Possible Side Effects

Headache, weakness, tiredness, dizziness, difficulty in breathing, abnormal heart rhythms, nausea, loss of appetite, diarrhea, stomach and abdominal pains, decrease in blood potassium, rash, itching, leg pains.

Less common side effects are feeling sick, chest and back pain, heart palpitations, dizziness when rising from a sitting or lying position, angina pain, constipation, stomach bleeding, stomach upset, appetite changes, feeling of being bloated, hiccups, thirst, vomiting, stomach gas, gout, dehydration, flushing, muscle cramps or spasms, joint pain, tingling in the arms or legs, feeling of numbness, stupor,

sleeplessness, nervousness, depression, sleepiness, confusion, visual disturbances, bad taste in the mouth, stuffy
nose, sexual impotence, urinary difficulties, dry mouth, adverse effects on the blood system, fever, shock, allergic reactions, jaundice, liver damage, sugar in the blood or urine,
unusual sensitivity to the sun, restlessness.

Drug Interactions

Moduretic will add to the action of other bloodpressure-lowering drugs. Since this is beneficial, it is frequently used to
help lower blood pressure in patients with hypertension.

The possibility of developing imbalances in body fluids
(electrolytes) is increased if you take other medications such
as Digitalis and adrenal corticosteroids while you are taking
Moduretic.

If you are taking an oral antidiabetic drug and begin taking
Moduretic, the antidiabetic dose may have to be altered.

Lithium Carbonate should not be taken with Moduretic because the combination may increase the risk of Lithium
toxicity.

Avoid over-the-counter cough, cold, or allergy remedies
containing stimulant drugs which can aggravate your condition.

Moduretic may interfere with the oral blood-thinning drugs
such as Warfarin by making the blood more concentrated
(thicker).

Food Interactions

Take Moduretic with food if it upsets your stomach.

Usual Dose

1 to 2 tablets per day.

Overdosage

Signs are tingling in the arms or legs, weakness, fatigue, slow
heartbeat, a sickly feeling, dryness of the mouth, lethargy, restlessness, muscle pains or cramps, low blood pressure, rapid
heartbeat, urinary difficulty, nausea, or vomiting. A patient
who has taken a Moduretic overdose should be taken to a
hospital emergency room. ALWAYS bring the medicine bottle.

Special Information

This drug can affect your concentration. Do not drive or operate machinery while taking it.

Call your doctor if you develop muscle or stomach cramps, nausea, diarrhea, unusual thirst, headache, or rash.

Moduretic should be taken in the morning, no later than 10 A.M.

If you forget to take a dose of Moduretic, take it as soon as you remember. If it is almost time for your next regularly scheduled dose, skip the forgotten dose and continue with your regular schedule. Do not take a double dose.

Generic Name

Moricizine

Brand Name

Ethmozine

Type of Drug

Antiarrhythmic.

Prescribed for

Life-threatening ventricular arrhythmias.

General Information

Moricizine treatment should always be started in a hospital because of the close cardiac monitoring that is required during the first phase of drug treatment. It should not be prescribed for minor arrhythmias or those that do not cause symptoms of their own. Moricizine works by stabilizing heart tissues and making them less sensitive to excessive stimulation. People with heart failure are usually able to tolerate this drug, but should be closely monitored for any sign of worsening of the condition.

Cautions and Warnings

Ironically, Moricizine can cause abnormal rhythms of its own or worsen existing rhythm problems. This property calls for close monitoring by a doctor of patients taking Moricizine. It is often not possible to distinguish between a drug-induced arrhythmia and one that occurs naturally, except when the arrhythmia occurs soon after drug treatment has been started and the patient is on continuous heart monitoring. Any arrhythmia can produce serious, life-threatening consequences. Moricizine should be used with caution in patients with a form of heart disease called "sick sinus syndrome," in which the part of the heart that initiates heart contractions is not working properly.

Moricizine causes changes in electrocardiograms and may cause changes in the actual conduction of electrical impulses throughout the heart.

People with electronic pacemakers who start taking this drug may need their pacemakers reset because of changes in the sensitivity of heart tissue to electrical impulses caused by Moricizine.

This drug should be used with care by people with liver or kidney disease. Because Moricizine is broken down by the liver and passes out of the body through the kidneys, these organs are essential to the efficient removal of the drug from the body. People with kidney and/or liver disease should receive lower than usual doses of the drug and be monitored more closely for unwanted drug effects.

In animal studies, Moricizine caused various tumors in animals given very large doses of the drug in their food. It is not known to cause tumors of any kind in people.

A small number of people taking Moricizine may develop drug fevers or other drug sensitivity reactions. If fever develops, it should subside within 2 days after stopping the medicine.

Pregnancy/Breast-feeding

In studies with pregnant animals, Moricizine affected the size and weight of the offspring or development of the fetuses. There is no information on the effect of Moricizine on pregnant women. The drug should only be taken by a pregnant woman after the possible benefits of taking it have been weighed against the potential harm it might cause.

Moricizine passes into breast milk. Nursing mothers who must take this medicine should bottle-feed their babies.

Seniors

Older adults generally experience the same side effects as younger adults, although studies of the drug showed that stopping drug treatment because of newly discovered arrhythmias was more common among older adults. Older adults are also more likely to have some degree of kidney and/or liver problem. Those conditions call for starting Moricizine at a lower dose and increasing the dosage more cautiously.

Possible Side Effects

The most common side effects are dizziness, nausea, vomiting, headache, pain, breathing difficulties, fatigue, and drug-induced abnormal heart rhythms; this last side effect is the most dangerous.

Other side effects are heart palpitations, chest pain, heart failure, heart attack, cardiac death, changes in blood pressure, fainting, very slow heart rate, blood clots in the lungs, stroke, muscle weakness, nervousness, tingling in the hands or feet, sleep difficulties, tremors, anxiety, depression, euphoria, confusion, agitation, seizure, coma, difficulty walking, hallucinations, blurred or double vision, speech difficulties, memory loss, coordination difficulties, and ringing or buzzing in the ears.

Moricizine may cause urinary difficulty, loss of urinary control, kidney pain, loss of sex drive, male impotence, hyperventilation, asthma, breathing difficulty, sore throat, cough, sinus irritation, abdominal pain, upset stomach, diarrhea, loss of appetite, a bitter taste, stomach gas and cramps, difficulty swallowing, sweating, dry mouth, muscle pain, drug fever, low body temperature, intolerance to heat or cold, eye pains, rash, itching, dry skin, swelling of the lips or tongue, or swelling around the eyes.

On rare occasions, people taking Moricizine experience hepatitis or jaundice (yellowing of the skin or eyes).

Drug Interactions

Cimetidine, Propranolol, and Digoxin may increase the amount of Moricizine in the blood, increasing the possibility of drug side effects.

Moricizine may drastically decrease the amount of The-

ophylline in the blood by increasing the rate at which it is
cleared from the body. Theophylline dosage adjustment
may be needed.

Many other drugs have been reported to interact with
Moricizine, but their interaction does not produce any serious consequences.

Food Interactions

Moricizine may be taken without regard to food or meals,
although taking the drug a half hour after eating delays the
absorption of the drug into the blood. You may take Moricizine with food if it upsets your stomach.

Usual Dose

600 to 900 milligrams a day.

Senior: older adults should be started at a dose below 600
milligrams; the dose should be gradually increased until the
maximum effect is achieved.

Overdosage

Overdose symptoms are vomiting, lethargy, fainting, coma,
low blood pressure, abnormal heart rhythms, worsening of
heart failure, heart attack, and breathing difficulty. Death has
occurred after doses of 2,250 milligrams (17 tablets of the
250-milligram strength) and 10,000 milligrams. Victims of a
Moricizine overdose should be taken to a hospital for treatment at once. ALWAYS bring the medicine bottle with you.

Special Information

People switching to Moricizine from another antiarrhythmic
should not take their first dose of Moricizine until several
hours after their last dose of the old medicine. This is necessary to allow most of the old medicine to clear from the
body. The waiting period varies from 3 to 12 hours, depending on which antiarrhythmic is being discontinued.

Some side effects may be related to the size of an individual dose. Therefore, it is usually better to divide the total
daily dose into 3 separate doses, rather than taking it once
or twice a day.

Call your doctor if you develop any cardiac problems; dizziness; anxiety; drug fever; swelling of the tongue, lips, or

the area around the eyes; visual or urinary difficulties; yellow discoloration of the skin or eyes; severe nausea; diarrhea; or vomiting. Other side effects should also be reported if they are persistent or bothersome.

If you take Moricizine twice a day and forget a dose, take it as soon as you remember. If it is almost time for your next dose, take one dose as soon as you remember and another in 5 or 6 hours, then go back to your regular schedule. Do not take a double dose.

If you take Moricizine 3 times a day and forget a dose, take it as soon as you remember. If it is almost time for your next dose, take one dose as soon as you remember and another in 3 or 4 hours, then go back to your regular schedule. Do not take a double dose.

Brand Name
Motofen

Ingredients
Atropine Sulfate
Difenoxin

Type of Drug
Antidiarrheal.

Prescribed for
Acute and chronic diarrhea that does not respond to other treatments.

General Information
Difenoxin is an antidiarrheal agent chemically related to Meperidine (Demerol), a narcotic pain reliever. Atropine is added to prevent overdose and product abuse. Atropine causes undesirable effects at doses that are far smaller than those that would be linked with narcotic abuse. Difenoxin works by slowing the rate at which intestinal-wall muscle contracts. It is a chemical byproduct of Diphenoxylate, a popular antidiarrheal product.

Motofen and other antidiarrheals should be used only for short periods; they will relieve diarrhea, but not its underlying cause. Some people should not use this drug even if diarrhea is present: People with some types of stomach, bowel, or other conditions may be harmed by antidiarrheal drugs. Obviously, the decision to take Motofen must be made by your doctor. Do not use Motofen without his or her advice.

Cautions and Warnings

Do not use Motofen if you are allergic to either of the ingredients, to Lomotil, or to any other medicine containing Atropine; if you have advanced liver disease or are jaundiced (yellow discoloration of the skin or eyes); or if you are suffering from diarrhea caused by taking Clindamycin or another antibiotic.

Your doctor may prescribe fluid and salt mixtures to replace the body fluids you lose while taking Motofen.

Pregnancy/Breast-feeding

As with all drug products, pregnant women, or those who might become pregnant, should not use Motofen unless the advantages of the product have been carefully weighed against the possible dangers of taking it while pregnant.

Do not breast-feed while taking Motofen. Nursing mothers who must take it should bottle-feed their babies until the need for the drug has passed.

Seniors

No problems have been reported in older adults. However, older adults with severe kidney and/or liver disease should be given lower dosages by their doctors.

Possible Side Effects

The most common side effects are nausea, vomiting, dry mouth, dizziness, light-headedness, drowsiness, and headache.

Other side effects are constipation, upset stomach, confusion, tiredness, or sleeplessness. The least frequent side effects are burning of the eyes, blurred vision, dry skin, temperature, rapid heartbeat, and urinary difficulty.

Drug Interactions

Motofen may increase the effects of alcoholic beverages, tranquilizers, pain relievers, and other nervous-system depressants, and these nervous-system depressants may in turn increase the depressant effects of Motofen. Avoid these combinations, if possible.

Monoamine oxidase (MAO) inhibitor antidepressants may, in theory, produce a high-blood-pressure crisis in combination with Motofen. Do not use Motofen if you take an MAO inhibitor drug unless you are under a doctor's care.

Usual Dose

Adult and child (over age 12): 2 tablets to start, then 1 after each loose stool or every 3 to 4 hours, as needed; up to 8 tablets in any day. Treatment for more than 2 consecutive days is usually not needed.

Overdosage

Motofen overdose is usually accidental. Overdose symptoms are dry skin, mouth, and nose; flushing, fever; and rapid heartbeat. This may be followed by lethargy or coma, loss of natural reflexes, pinpoint pupils, droopy eyelids, and breathing difficulty. Take the victim to a hospital emergency room at once for treatment. ALWAYS bring the medicine bottle.

Special Information

People taking Motofen must be careful when performing tasks requiring concentration and coordination because of the chance that the drug will make them tired, dizzy, or light-headed.

Alcohol, tranquilizers, or other nervous-system depressants will increase the depressant effects of this drug.

Call your doctor if you develop heart palpitations while taking Motofen or if your symptoms don't clear up in 2 days. You may need a different dose or a different medicine for your problem.

If you forget a dose of Motofen, take it as soon as you remember. If it is almost time for your next dose, skip the one you forgot and continue with your regular schedule. Do not take a double dose.

Generic Name

Mupirocin

Brand Name

Bactroban

Type of Drug

Topical antibiotic.

Prescribed for

Impetigo; eczema; inflammation of the hair follicles; minor
bacterial skin infections.

General Information

This is a unique, non-penicillin product that is effective
against the common microorganisms that cause impetigo in
children. It is used to supplement other treatments for impetigo, although many doctors prefer to prescribe oral medicine for the condition. It is not known how Mupirocin works,
but it kills bacteria in high concentrations and stops them
from growing in the lower concentrations.

Cautions and Warnings

Mupirocin ointment is not for use in the eye. Do not use this
product if you are allergic to any of its components.

Pregnancy/Breast-feeding

Animal studies have revealed no potential for damage to
the developing fetus. Nevertheless, this drug should be used
by women who are or might become pregnant only if
necessary.

It is unlikely that Mupirocin will enter breast milk because
very little of it is absorbed into the blood.

Seniors

Seniors may use Mupirocin without restriction.

Possible Side Effects

Common side effects are burning, stinging or pain where

the ointment is applied, itching, rash, nausea, redness, dry skin, tenderness, swelling, and increased oozing from impetigo lesions.

Drug Interactions

None known.

Usual Dose

Apply a small amount to the affected areas 3 times a day. Cover with gauze, if desired.

Special Information

If the Mupirocin does not work within several days or a week, call your doctor for an alternative treatment.

Call your doctor if any of the following symptoms develop: dry skin, rash, itching, redness, stinging, or pain.

If you forget to apply a dose of Mupirocin, do it as soon as you remember. If it is almost time for your next dose, skip the one you forgot and continue with your regular schedule.

Generic Name

Nadolol

Brand Name

Corgard

Type of Drug

Beta-adrenergic blocking agent.

Prescribed for

High blood pressure; angina pectoris (a specific type of chest pain).

General Information

This drug is quite similar to Propranolol, another beta-blocking agent. It has not been studied in as many kinds of problems as Propranolol, but it is very useful because it can

be taken once a day. When used for high blood pressure, it
is usually given with a diuretic such as Hydrochlorothiazide.

Cautions and Warnings

Nadolol should be used with care if you have a history of
asthma or other upper respiratory disease or of heart failure.
You should stop taking the drug several days before major
surgery, if possible. Do not do this without telling your doctor. Nadolol can hide some symptoms of diabetes or thyroid
disease.

Pregnancy/Breast-feeding

This drug crosses into the blood circulation of a developing
baby. It has not been found to cause birth defects. Pregnant
women, or those who might become pregnant while taking
this drug, should not take it without their doctors' approval.
When the drug is considered essential by your doctor, the
potential risk of taking the medicine must be carefully
weighed against the benefit it might produce.
   This drug passes into breast milk, but has caused no problems among breast-fed infants. You must consider the potential effect on the nursing infant if breast-feeding while
taking this medicine.

Seniors

Senior citizens may be more or less sensitive to the effects
of this medication. Your dosage of this drug must be adjusted to your individual needs by your doctor. Seniors may
be more likely to suffer from cold hands and feet and reduced body temperature, chest pains, a general feeling of ill
health, sudden difficulty breathing, sweating, or changes in
heartbeat because of this medicine.

Possible Side Effects

Nadolol may decrease the heart rate, aggravate a condition
of congestive heart failure, and produce lowered blood pressure, tingling in the extremities, light-headedness, mental
depression including inability to sleep, weakness, and tiredness. It may also produce a mental depression which is reversible when the drug is withdrawn, visual disturbances,

hallucinations, disorientation, and short-term memory loss. Patients taking Nadolol may experience nausea, vomiting, stomach upset, abdominal cramps and diarrhea, or constipation. If you are allergic to this drug, you may show typical reactions associated with drug allergies, including sore throat, fever, difficulty in breathing, and various effects on the blood system. Nadolol may induce bronchospasms (spasms of muscles in the bronchi), which will make any existing asthmatic condition or any severe upper respiratory disease worse.

Occasionally, patients taking Nadolol may experience emotional instability, or a feeling of detachment or personality change, or the drug may produce unusual effects on the blood system.

Drug Interactions

This drug will interact with any psychotropic drug, including any monoamine oxidase (MAO) inhibitor, that stimulates one of the adrenergic segments of the nervous system. Since this information is not generally known, you should discuss the potential problem of using Nadolol with your doctor if you are taking any psychotropic or psychiatric drug.

Nadolol may cause increased effectiveness of Insulin or oral antidiabetic drugs. If you are diabetic, discuss the situation with your doctor; a reduction in dose of antidiabetic medication will probably be made.

Nadolol may reduce the effectiveness of Digitalis on your heart. Any dose of Digitalis medication will have to be altered. If you are taking Digitalis for a purpose other than congestive heart failure, the effectiveness of the Digitalis may be increased by Nadolol, and the dose of Digitalis may have to be reduced.

Nadolol may interact with certain other drugs to lower blood pressure. This interaction often has positive results in the treatment of patients with high blood pressure.

Do not self-medicate with over-the-counter cold, cough, or allergy remedies which may contain stimulant drugs that will aggravate certain types of heart disease and high blood pressure or other ingredients that may antagonize the effects of Nadolol. Double-check with your doctor or pharmacist before taking any over-the-counter medication.

Food Interactions

Take this medicine with food if it upsets your stomach.

Usual Dose

40 to 240 milligrams per day.

Patients with bad kidneys may take their medication dosage as infrequently as once every 60 hours.

Overdosage

Symptoms are slowed heart rate, heart failure, lowered blood pressure, and spasms of the bronchial muscles which make it difficult to breathe. The patient should be taken to a hospital emergency room where proper therapy can be given. ALWAYS bring the medicine bottle with you.

Special Information

Since this drug is taken only once a day, be sure to take it at the same time every day.

Do not stop taking the drug abruptly unless your doctor tells you to, or serious heart pain and other effects can occur.

Call your doctor if you have trouble breathing when you exert yourself or are lying down, have a nighttime cough, or develop swollen ankles, arms, or legs.

If you forget to take a dose of Nadolol, take it as soon as possible. However, if it is within 8 hours of your next dose, skip the forgotten dose and go back to your regular schedule. Do not take a double dose.

Generic Name

Naproxen

Brand Names

Anaprox
Anaprox DS
Naprosyn

(Also available in generic form)

Type of Drug

Nonsteroidal anti-inflammatory.

Prescribed for

Relief of pain and inflammation of joints and muscles; mild to moderate pain of menstrual cramps, dental surgery and extractions, rheumatoid arthritis and osteoarthritis, ankylosing spondylitis, tendonitis, bursitis, and acute gout. Naproxen has also been prescribed for the fever that occurs in pediatric cancer patients.

General Information

Naproxen is one of several nonsteroidal anti-inflammatory drugs (NSAIDs) used to reduce inflammation, relieve pain, or reduce fever. All NSAIDs share the same side effects and may be used by patients who cannot tolerate Aspirin. Choice of one of these drugs over another depends on disease response, side effects seen in a particular patient, convenience of times to take it, and cost. Different drugs or different doses of the same drug may be tried until the greatest effectiveness is seen with the fewest side effects.

Cautions and Warnings

Do not take Naproxen if you are allergic or sensitive to this drug, Aspirin, or other NSAIDs. Naproxen may cause stomach ulcers. This drug should not be used by patients with severe kidney or liver disease.

Pregnancy/Breast-feeding

This drug crosses into the blood circulation of a developing baby. It has not been found to cause birth defects, but it may cause unwanted effects on the heart or blood flow of the newborn. It may also prolong labor or cause other problems during delivery. Pregnant women, or those who might become pregnant while taking this drug, should not take it without their doctors' approval. When the drug is considered essential by your doctor, the potential risk of taking the medicine must be carefully weighed against the benefit it might produce.

This drug passes into breast milk, but has caused no problems among breast-fed infants. You must consider the po-

tential effect on the nursing infant if breast-feeding while
taking this medicine.

Seniors

Older adults are more sensitive to the stomach, kidney, and
liver effects of this drug. Some doctors recommend that persons 70 and older take half the usual dose. Follow your doctor's directions and report any side effects at once.

Possible Side Effects

The most frequent side effects are stomach upset, dizziness,
headache, drowsiness, ringing in the ears.

Others side effects include heartburn, nausea, vomiting,
bloating, gas in the stomach, stomach pain, diarrhea, constipation, dark stool, nervousness, insomnia, depression, confusion, tremor, loss of appetite, fatigue, itching, rash, double
vision, abnormal heart rhythm, anemia or other changes in
the composition of the blood, changes in liver function, loss
of hair, tingling in the hands and feet, fever, breast enlargement, lowered blood sugar, effects on the kidneys. If symptoms appear, stop taking the medicine and see your doctor
immediately.

Drug Interactions

Naproxen increases the action of Phenytoin, sulfa drugs,
antidiabetic drugs, and anticoagulants (blood-thinning drugs).
If you are taking any of these medicines, be sure to discuss
it with your doctor, who will probably change the dose of
the other drug.

An adjustment in the dose of Naproxen may be needed if
you take Phenobarbital.

Do not take Aspirin while you are taking Naproxen. This
combination offers no advantages and may be detrimental.

Food Interactions

Take this medicine with food or an antacid if it upsets your
stomach.

Usual Dose

Adult: 250 milligrams to 375 milligrams morning and
night, to start. Dose may be adjusted up to 1250 milligrams

per day, if needed. Mild to moderate pain: 250 milligrams every 6 to 8 hours.

Child: 4.5 milligrams per pound of body weight divided into 2 doses per day.

Overdosage

Symptoms may include drowsiness, dizziness, confusion, disorientation, lethargy, tingling in the hands or feet, numbness, nausea, vomiting, upset stomach, stomach pains, headache, ringing or buzzing in the ears, sweating, and blurred vision. Take the victim to a hospital emergency room at once for treatment. ALWAYS bring the medicine bottle with you.

Special Information

Avoid Aspirin and alcoholic beverages while taking this medication.

You may become dizzy or drowsy taking this medicine. Be careful while driving or operating complex equipment.

Call your doctor if you develop a skin rash, itching, swelling, visual disturbances, black stools, or a persistent headache while taking this medication.

If you forget to take a dose of Naproxen, take it as soon as you remember. If it is almost time for your next regularly scheduled dose, skip the forgotten dose and continue with your regular schedule. Do not take a double dose.

Brand Name

Neosporin Ophthalmic Solution

Ingredients

Gramicidin
Neomycin Sulfate
Polymyxin-B Sulfate

(Also available in generic form)

Type of Drug

Topical antibiotic for use in the eye.

Prescribed for

Superficial infections of the eye.

General Information

Neosporin Ophthalmic Solution is a combination of antibiotics which are effective against the most common eye infections. It is most useful when the infecting organism is one known to be sensitive to one of the 3 antibiotics contained in Neosporin Ophthalmic Solution. It is also useful when the infecting organism is not known because of the drug's broad range of coverage.

Prolonged use of any antibiotic product in the eye should be avoided because of the possibility of developing sensitivity to the antibiotic. Frequent or prolonged use of antibiotics in the eye may result in the growth of other organisms such as fungi. If the infection does not clear up within a few days, contact your doctor.

Neosporin (or its generic equivalent) is also available as an eye ointment with a minor formula change. Both the eyedrops and eye ointment are used for the same things.

Cautions and Warnings

Neosporin Ophthalmic Solution should not be used if you know you are sensitive to or have an allergy to this product or to any of the ingredients in it.

Pregnancy/Breast-feeding

This drug has been found to be safe for use during pregnancy or breast-feeding. Remember, you should check with your doctor before taking any drug if you are pregnant.

Seniors

Older adults may take this medication without special restriction. Follow your doctor's directions and report any side effects at once.

Possible Side Effects

Occasional local irritation after application to the eye.

Drug Interactions

None known.

Usual Dose

1 to 2 drops in the affected eye or eyes 2 to 4 times per day; more frequently if the infection is severe.

Special Information

Tilt the head backward when applying the eyedrops. Pull the lower eyelid away from the eye to form a pouch. After applying the drop, keep the eye closed for a minute or so. This allows the medication to come in contact with the infection.

If you forget to take a dose of Neosporin, take it as soon as you remember. If it is almost time for your next regularly scheduled dose, skip the forgotten dose and continue with your regular schedule. Do not take a double dose.

Generic Name

Nicardipine

Brand Name

Cardene

Type of Drug

Calcium channel blocker.

Prescribed for

Angina pectoris; high blood pressure.

General Information

Nicardipine is one of several calcium channel blockers available in the United States; some others are Diltiazem, Nifedipine, and Verapamil. These drugs work by slowing the passage of calcium into muscle cells. This causes the muscles in the blood vessels that supply your heart with blood to open wider, allowing more blood to reach heart tissues. They also decrease muscle spasm in those blood vessels. Nicardipine also reduces the speed at which electrical impulses are carried through heart tissue, adding to its ability to slow the heart and prevent the pain of angina. It can help to reduce high blood pressure by causing blood vessels throughout the body to widen, allowing blood to flow more easily through them, especially when combined with a diuretic, beta blocker, or other blood-pressure-lowering drug.

Cautions and Warnings

Nicardipine can slow your heart rate and interfere with normal electrical conduction in heart muscle. For some people, this can result in temporary heart stoppage; people whose hearts are otherwise healthy will not develop this effect.

Pregnancy/Breast-feeding

Large doses of calcium channel blockers may cause prolonged pregnancy and harm to the fetus, including poor bone development and stillbirths. Nicardipine should be avoided by pregnant women or women who may become pregnant while using it. In situations where it is deemed essential, the potential risk of the drug must be carefully weighed against any benefit it might produce.

Nursing mothers should watch their babies for any possible drug effect. It is not known if Nicardipine passes into breast milk.

Seniors

Older adults may be more sensitive to the side effects of Nicardipine. Because of the possibility of reduced kidney and/or liver function in older adults, they should receive smaller doses than younger adults, beginning with 20 milligrams 2 to 3 times a day and continuing with carefully increased doses.

Possible Side Effects

The most common side effects of Nicardipine are abnormal heart rhythms, fluid accumulation in the hands, legs, or feet, headache, fatigue, nausea, and skin rash.

Less common side effects include low blood pressure, dizziness, fainting, changes in heart rate (increase or decrease), heart failure, light-headedness, nervousness, tingling in the hands or feet, hallucinations, temporary memory loss, difficulty sleeping, weakness, diarrhea, vomiting, constipation, upset stomach, itching, unusual sensitivity to the sun, painful or stiff joints, liver inflammation, and increased urination, especially at night.

Drug Interactions

Taking Nicardipine with a beta-blocking drug to treat high blood pressure is usually well tolerated but may lead to heart failure in susceptible people.

Calcium channel blockers, including Nicardipine, may add to the effects of Digoxin, although this is not observed with any consistency and occurs only in people with a large amount of Digoxin already in their systems.

Blood levels of Cyclosporine may be increased by Nicardipine, increasing the chance for Cyclosporine-related kidney damage.

The effect of Quinidine may be altered by Nicardipine.

Food Interactions

Nicardipine is best taken on an empty stomach, at least 1 hour before or 2 hours after meals, but it may be taken with food or milk if it upsets your stomach.

Usual Dose

60 to 120 milligrams per day.

Overdosage

The 2 major symptoms of Nicardipine overdose are very low blood pressure and reduced heart rate. Nicardipine can be removed from the stomach by giving the victim Syrup of Ipecac to induce vomiting, but this must be done within 30 minutes of the actual overdose, before the drug can be absorbed into the blood. Once symptoms develop or if more than 30 minutes have passed since the overdose, the victim must be taken to a hospital emergency room for treatment.

Special Information

Call your doctor if you develop any of the following symptoms: swelling of the hands, legs, or feet, severe dizziness, constipation or nausea, or very low blood pressure.

Some people may experience a slight increase in blood pressure just before their next dose is due. You will be able to see this effect only if you use a home blood pressure monitoring device. If this happens, contact your doctor at once.

If you forget to take a dose of Nicardipine, take it as soon as you remember. If it is almost time for your next dose, skip the forgotten dose and continue with your regular schedule.

Generic Name
Nicotine

Brand Name
Nicorette Chewing Gum

Type of Drug
Smoking deterrent.

Prescribed for
People addicted to cigarettes who need another source of their drug (Nicotine) to help break the smoking habit.

General Information
Nicotine is known to affect many brain functions, including improving memory, increasing one's ability to perform a number of different tasks, reducing hunger, and increasing tolerance to pain. This chewing gum, a source of noninhaled Nicotine, makes cigarette withdrawal much easier for many people. Although this product is designed to fulfill a specific need in those trying to quit smoking, there are a great many other social and psychological needs filled by smoking. These must be dealt with through counseling or other psychological support in order for a program to be successful.

You may be addicted to Nicotine if you smoke more than 15 cigarettes per day; prefer unfiltered cigarettes or those with a high nicotine content; usually inhale the smoke; have your first cigarette within 30 minutes of getting up in the morning; find the first morning cigarette the hardest to give up; smoke most frequently in the morning hours; find it hard to obey "no smoking signs or rules; smoke even when you are sick in bed.

Cautions and Warnings

Nicotine chewing gum should not be used by nonsmokers or others who are not addicted to the effects of this drug. It should not be used during the period immediately following a heart attack or if severe abnormal heart rhythms, angina pains, or severe temperomandibular joint (TMJ) disease are present. People with other heart conditions must be evaluated by a cardiologist (heart doctor) before starting treatment with Nicotine chewing gum.

This product should be used with caution by diabetics being treated with Insulin or people with an overactive thyroid, pheochromocytoma, high blood pressure, stomach ulcers, and chronic dental problems that might be worsened by Nicotine chewing gum.

It is possible for Nicotine addiction to be transferred from cigarettes to the gum or for the addiction actually to worsen while using the product.

Pregnancy/Breast-feeding

This product should not be used by women who are pregnant or who might become pregnant because Nicotine is known to harm the developing baby when taken during the last 3 months of pregnancy. Nicotine, whether from cigarettes or chewing gum, interferes with the newborn baby's ability to breathe properly. Additionally, one miscarriage has occurred in a woman using Nicotine chewing gum.

Mothers should not breast-feed while using this product because Nicotine passes into breast milk and can be harmful to a growing infant.

Seniors

Older adults with severe liver damage may be more sensitive to the effects of this drug. Follow your doctor's directions and report any side effects at once.

Possible Side Effects

Injury to gums, jaw, or teeth; stomach growling due to swallowing air. Other common systemic side effects are nausea, vomiting, hiccups, and upset stomach.

Less common side effects are excessive salivation, dizziness, light-headedness, irritability, headache, increased bowel movement, diarrhea, constipation, gas pains, dry mouth, hoarseness, facial flushing, sneezing, coughing, feeling high, and sleeplessness.

Drug Interactions

Heavy smokers who suddenly stop smoking may experience an increase in the effects of a variety of drugs whose breakdowns are known to be stimulated by cigarettes. If you are taking any of the following medications, your dosage may have to be reduced to account for this effect: Theophylline, Imipramine, Pentazocine, Furosemide, Propranolol, Propoxyphene Hydrochloride.

Smoking increases the rate at which your body breaks down caffeine. Stopping Nicotine may make you more sensitive to the effects of the caffeine in coffee or tea.

Usual Dose

1 piece of gum whenever you feel the urge for a cigarette, not more than 30 per day. Each piece contains 2 milligrams of Nicotine.

Overdosage

Nicotine overdosage can be deadly. Symptoms include salivation, nausea, vomiting, diarrhea, abdominal pains, headache, cold sweats, dizziness, hearing and visual disturbances, weakness, and confusion. If untreated, these symptoms will be followed by fainting, very low blood pressure, a pulse that is weak, rapid, and irregular, convulsions, and death by paralysis of the muscles that control breathing. The lethal dose of Nicotine is about 50 milligrams.

Nicotine stimulates the brain's vomiting center, making this reaction common, but not automatic. Spontaneous vomiting may be sufficient to remove the poison from the victim's system. If this has not occurred, call your doctor or poison control center for instructions on how to make the victim vomit by giving Syrup of Ipecac. If the victim must be treated in a hospital emergency room, ALWAYS bring the chewing gum package with you.

Special Information

Follow the instructions on the patient-information sheet included in each package of the gum.

Chew each piece of the gum slowly and intermittently for about 30 minutes to promote slow and even absorption of the Nicotine through the tissues in your mouth. Too-rapid chewing releases the Nicotine too quickly and can lead to side effects of nausea, hiccups, or throat irritation.

You will learn to control your daily dose of Nicotine chewing gum so that your smoking habit is broken and side effects are minimized. Do not chew more than 30 pieces of gum per day. The amount of gum chewed each day should be gradually reduced after 3 months of successful treatment.

Nicotine chewing gum is not recommended for more than 6 months at a time.

Generic Name

Nicotinic Acid (Niacin)

Brand Names

Nia-Bid	Nico-400
Niac	Nicolar
Niacels	Nicotinex
Niacor	Slo-Niacin
Nicobid	

(Also available in generic form)

Type of Drug

Vitamin.

Prescribed for

Treatment of Nicotinic Acid deficiency (pellagra). This drug is also prescribed to help lower blood-fat levels and to help dilate or widen certain blood vessels.

General Information

Nicotinic Acid or Niacin, also known as Vitamin B3, is essential to normal body function through the part it plays in enzyme activity. It is effective in lowering blood levels of fats and can help enlarge or dilate certain blood vessels, but we do not know exactly how it does these things. Normally, individual requirements of Nicotinic Acid are easily supplied in a well-rounded diet.

Cautions and Warnings

Do not take this drug if you are sensitive or allergic to it or to any related drugs or if you have liver disease, stomach ulcer, severely low blood pressure, gout, or hemorrhage (bleeding).

Pregnancy/Breast-feeding

When used in normal doses Nicotinic Acid can be taken by pregnant women, but if it is used in high doses (to help lower blood levels of fats) there may be some problems. Although this drug has not been shown to cause birth defects or problems in breast-fed infants, if you are pregnant or nursing consult with your doctor.

Seniors

Older adults may take this medication without special restriction. Follow your doctor's directions and report any side effects at once.

Possible Side Effects

The most common side effect is flushing (redness and a warm sensation in the face and hands).

Less common side effects are decreased sugar tolerance in diabetics, activation of stomach ulcers, jaundice (yellowing of the whites of the eyes and skin), stomach upset, oily skin, dry skin, possible aggravation of skin conditions such as acne, itching, high blood levels of uric acid, low blood pressure, temporary headache, tingling feeling, skin rash, abnormal heartbeats, dizziness.

Drug Interactions

Nicotinic Acid can intensify the effect of antihypertensive (blood-pressure-lowering) drugs, causing postural hypotension (getting dizzy when you rise quickly from a sitting or lying position).

If you are diabetic, large doses of Nicotinic Acid can throw your blood sugar slightly out of control; your doctor may have to adjust either your diet or your drug therapy.

Usual Dose

As a supplementary vitamin product: 25 milligrams per day.

For treatment of high blood-fat levels: initial dose, 500 milligrams to 3 grams per day with or after meals (take with cold water to assist in swallowing). If 3 grams does not prove effective the dose may be increased slowly to a maximum of 6 grams per day.

The dose should be built up slowly so you can watch carefully for common side effects: flushing or redness of the face and extremities, itching, and stomach upset.

Overdosage

Overdose victims experience drug side effects. Take the victim to an emergency room for treatment. Bring the medicine bottle with you.

Special Information

If you forget to take a dose of Nicotinic Acid, take it as soon as you remember. If it is almost time for your next regularly scheduled dose, skip the forgotten dose and continue with your regular schedule. Do not take a double dose.

Generic Name
Nifedipine

Brand Names

Adalat
Procardia
Procardia XL

(Also available in generic form)

Type of Drug
Calcium channel blocker.

Prescribed for

Angina pectoris; Prinzmetal's angina; high blood pressure.

Nifedipine has also been prescribed to prevent migraine headaches and to treat asthma, heart failure, Raynaud's disease, disorders of the esophagus, gall bladder and kidney stone attacks, and severe high blood pressure associated with pregnancy (preterm labor).

General Information

Nifedipine is one of a growing number of calcium channel blockers to be marketed in the United States. Calcium channel blockers work by blocking the passage of calcium into heart and smooth muscle. Since calcium is an essential factor in muscle contraction, any drug that affects calcium in this way will interfere with the contraction of these muscles. When this happens the amount of oxygen used by the muscles is also reduced. Therefore, Nifedipine is used in the treatment of angina, a type of heart pain related to poor oxygen supply to the heart muscles. Also, Nifedipine dilates (opens) the vessels that supply blood to the heart muscles and prevents spasm of these arteries. Nifedipine affects the movement of calcium only into muscle cells; it does not have any affect on calcium in the blood.

Nifedipine capsules contain liquid medicine. In cases where the drug is needed in the blood as rapidly as possible, the capsules may be punctured and their contents squeezed under the tongue; medicine is rapidly absorbed into the blood in this manner. Thus, Nifedipine capsules are useful in situations where extremely high blood pressure must be rapidly lowered. Some researchers feel that biting the capsule in your mouth and swallowing the contents gets the medicine into your blood even faster than keeping it under the tongue.

Cautions and Warnings

Nifedipine may cause unwanted low blood pressure in some people taking it for reasons other than hypertension.

Patients taking a beta-blocking drug who begin taking Nifedipine may develop heart failure or increased angina pain. Angina pain may also increase when your Nifedipine dosage is increased.

Do not take this drug if you have had an allergic reaction to it in the past.

Nifedipine may interfere with one of the mechanisms by which blood clots form, especially if you are also taking Aspirin. Call your doctor if you develop unusual bruises, bleeding, or black-and-blue marks.

People with severe liver disease break down Nifedipine much more slowly than people with less severe disease or normal livers. Your doctor should take this into account when determining your Nifedipine dosage.

Pregnancy/Breast-feeding

Nifedipine crosses into the blood circulation of a developing baby. It has been used to treat severe high blood pressure associated with pregnancy and not caused any unusual effect on the baby. Nevertheless, pregnant women, or those who might become pregnant while taking this drug, should not take it without their doctors' approval. When the drug is considered essential by your doctor, the potential risk of taking the medicine must be carefully weighed against the benefit it might produce.

Small amounts of Nifedipine may pass into breast milk, but the drug has caused no problems among breast-fed infants. You must consider the potential effect on the nursing infant if breast-feeding while taking this medicine.

Seniors

Older adults are more sensitive to the effects of this drug because it takes longer to pass out of their bodies. Follow your doctor's directions and report any side effects at once.

Possible Side Effects

Common side effects are dizziness; light-headedness; flushing; a feeling of warmth; headache; weakness; nausea; muscle cramps, inflammation, and pains; swelling of the arms or legs; nervousness; mood changes; heart palpitations; heart failure; heart attack; difficulty breathing; coughs; fluid in the lungs; wheezing; stuffy nose; and sore throat.

Less common side effects include low blood pressure, unusual heart rhythms, angina pains, fainting, shortness of breath, diarrhea, cramps, constipation, stomach gas, dry mouth, taste changes, frequent urination (especially at night), stiffness and inflammation of the joints, arthritis, shakiness, jitteriness, psychotic reaction, anxiety, memory loss, paranoia, hallucinations, tingling in the hands or feet, tiredness, muscle weakness, liver inflammation, blurred vision, ringing or buzzing in the ears, difficulty sleeping, unusual dreams, respiratory infections, anemia, bleeding, bruising, nosebleeds, swollen gums, weight gain, reduced white-blood-cell counts, difficulty maintaining balance, itching, rash, hair loss, painful breast inflammation, unusual sensitivity to the sun, severe skin reactions, fever, sweating, chills, and sexual difficulties. Nifedipine can cause increases in certain blood-sugar and some enzyme tests.

Drug Interactions

Nifedipine may interact with beta-blocking drugs to cause heart failure, very low blood pressure, or an increased incidence of angina pain. However, in many cases these drugs have been taken together with no problem.

Nifedipine may cause unexpected blood pressure reduction in patients already taking medicine to control their high blood pressure through interaction with other antihypertensive drugs.

Cimetidine and Ranitidine increase the amount of Nifedipine in the blood and may account for a slight increase in Nifedipine's effect.

The combination of Quinidine (for abnormal heart rhythm) and Nifedipine must be used with caution because it can produce low blood pressure, very slow heart rate, abnormal heart rhythms, and swelling in the arms or legs.

Nifedipine can, rarely, increase the effects of oral anticoagulant (blood-thinning) drugs.

Nifedipine can increase the effects of Theophylline products (for asthma and other respiratory problems).

Food Interactions

Nifedipine can be taken without regard to food or meals.

Usual Dose

30 to 120 milligrams per day of regular Nifedipine. No patient should take more than 180 milligrams per day.

The usual dose for the sustained-release version of Nifedipine (Procardia XL) is 30 to 60 milligrams taken once a day.

Do not stop taking Nifedipine abruptly. The dosage should be gradually reduced over a period of time.

Overdosage

Overdose of Nifedipine can cause low blood pressure. If you think you have taken an overdose of Nifedipine, call your doctor or go to a hospital emergency room. ALWAYS bring the medicine bottle.

Special Information

Call your doctor if you develop constipation, nausea, very low blood pressure, swelling in the hands or feet, difficulty breathing, increased heart pains, or dizziness or light-headedness or if other side effects are particulary bothersome or persistent.

If you are taking Nifedipine for high blood pressure, be sure to continue taking your medicine and follow any instructions for diet restriction or other treatments. High blood pressure is a condition with few recognizable symptoms; it may seem to you that you are taking medicine for no good reason. Call your doctor or pharmacist if you have any questions.

If you take Procardia XL be sure not to break or crush the tablets. You may notice an empty tablet in your stool. This is not cause for alarm, because the medicine is normally released from the sustained-release tablet without actually destroying it.

It is important to maintain good dental hygiene while taking Nifedipine and to use extra care when using your toothbrush or dental floss because of the chance that the drug will make you more susceptible to some infections.

If you forget a dose of Nifedipine, take it as soon as you remember. If it is almost time for your next regularly scheduled dose, skip the forgotten dose and continue with your regular schedule. Do not take a double dose.

Generic Name

Nimodipine

Brand Name

Nimotop

Type of Drug

Calcium channel blocker.

Prescribed for

Functional losses following a stroke. Nimodipine may also be prescribed for migraine and cluster headaches.

General Information

Nimodipine is one of several calcium channel blockers available in the United States. Unlike the other members of this group, Nimodipine has a negligible effect on the heart. It is unique because it is the only calcium channel blocker proven effective as a drug to help improve neurological function after a stroke. Calcium channel blockers work by slowing the passage of calcium into cells. This causes muscles in the blood vessels that supply your heart and other tissues to open wider, allowing more blood to flow through them. They also decrease muscle spasm in those blood vessels.

Nimodipine readily dissolves in fatty tissues and reaches very high concentrations in the brain and spinal fluid. Because of this, it has a greater effect on blood vessels in the brain than on those in other parts of the body. Nimodipine relieves stroke symptoms but does not reduce spasms in brain blood vessels. A great deal of research still needs to be done to discover exactly how this drug works.

Cautions and Warnings

Nimodipine should not be taken if you are sensitive or allergic to it or if you have a condition called aortic stenosis, in which the aorta becomes stiffer and less flexible than normal. Animals given Nimodipine developed a high rate of testicular and uterine cancer. It is not known if the drug has this effect on humans.

Liver disease, including cirrhosis, may slow the breakdown of Nimodipine by the body. This can produce a need
to take a lower than normal dose of the drug.

Pregnancy/Breast-feeding

Animal studies have shown that Nimodipine can cause mal-
formation of a fetus. Very high doses can cause poor fetal
growth, death of the fetus, and fetal bone problems. Nimodipine should be avoided by pregnant women or women who
may become pregnant while using it. In situations where the
drug is deemed essential by your doctor, the potential risk
of the drug must be carefully weighed against any benefit
it might produce.

Nimodipine has been shown, in animal studies, to pass
into breast milk. Women who must use Nimodipine should
use an alternative feeding method.

Seniors

Older adults, especially those with severe liver disease, may
be more sensitive to the side effects of Nimodipine.

Possible Side Effects

The most common side effects of Nimodipine are diarrhea
and headache.

Less common side effects include swelling of the arms or
legs, changes in blood pressure (low or high), heart failure,
rapid heartbeat, changes in the electrocardiogram, depression, memory loss, psychosis, paranoid feelings, hallucinations, nausea, itching, acne, rash, anemia, bleeding or
bruising, abnormal blood clotting, flushing, breathing difficulty, stomach bleeding, and muscle cramps.

Rare side effects include dizziness, heart attack, liver inflammation or jaundice, vomiting, and sexual difficulties.

Drug Interactions

Calcium channel blockers may cause bleeding when taken
alone or together with Aspirin.

Cimetidine may increase the effects of Nimodipine by decreasing the rate at which Nimodipine is broken down by
the liver.

Taking Nimodipine together with a beta-blocking drug is

usually well-tolerated but may lead to heart failure in susceptible people.

Calcium channel blockers, including Nimodipine, may add to the effects of Digoxin, although this effect is not observed with any consistency and only affects people with a large amount of Digoxin already in their system.

Food Interactions

Nimodipine is best taken on an empty stomach—at least 1 hour before or 2 hours after meals—but may be taken with food or milk if it upsets your stomach.

Usual Dose

60 milligrams 4 times a day beginning within 96 hours after the stroke and continuing for 21 days.

Overdosage

The major symptoms of Nimodipine overdose are nausea, weakness, dizziness, drowsiness, confusion, and slurred speech. Blood pressure and heart rate may also be affected. Nimodipine can be removed from a victim's stomach by giving Syrup of Ipecac to induce vomiting, but this should be done only under a doctor's supervision or direction. Once symptoms develop, the victim must be taken to a hospital emergency room for treatment.

Special Information

Call your doctor if you develop any of the following symptoms: swelling of the arms or legs, breathing difficulty, severe dizziness, constipation, or nausea.

Patients who are unable to swallow Nimodipine capsules because of their condition may have the liquid withdrawn from the capsule with a syringe and mixed with other liquids to be given orally or through a feeding tube.

If you forget to take a dose of Nimodipine, take it as soon as you remember. If it is almost time for your next dose, skip the forgotten dose and continue with your regular schedule. Call your doctor if you miss more than 2 doses.

Generic Name

Nitrofurantoin

Brand Names

Furadantin
Furalan
Furan
Furanite

Macrodantin (Macro
   Crystals)
Nitrofan

(Also available in generic form)

Type of Drug

Urinary anti-infective.

Prescribed for

Preventing and treating urinary tract infections—such as pyelonephritis, pyelitis, and cystitis—caused by organisms susceptible to Nitrofurantoin.

General Information

Nitrofurantoin, like several other drugs (including Nalidixic Acid [NegGram]), is of value in treating urinary tract infections because it appears in large amounts in the urine. It should not be used to treat infections in other parts of the body.

Cautions and Warnings

Do not take Nitrofurantoin if you have kidney disease, or if you are allergic to this agent.

Rarely, severe chest pain, difficulty breathing, cough, fever and chills may develop within hours to weeks after taking Nitrofurantoin. These symptoms usually go away within 1 to 2 days after you stop taking the drug. People who take Nitrofurantoin for prolonged periods of time may develop cough, breathing problems and feelings of ill health after 1 to 6 months or more of treatment. Respiratory failure and death have occurred in a few cases.

Nitrofurantoin may cause a rare reaction called hemolytic anemia. People with a deficiency of the enzyme G-6-PD are most susceptible to this reaction and should not take Nitrofurantoin.

Rarely, Nitrofurantoin causes hepatitis, which may lead to death. This appears to be a rare drug sensitivity reaction and is most likely to develop if you are taking long-term Nitrofurantoin treatments.

Pregnancy/Breast-feeding

Nitrofurantoin should be taken by pregnant women only if the risk outweighs any possible benefits of the drug. It should never be taken by pregnant women with G-6-PD deficiency and those who are near term because it can interfere with the developing baby's immature enzyme systems and cause a blood problem called hemolytic anemia.

This medicine passes into breast milk and may affect some nursing infants, especially those who are G-6-PD deficient. Check with your doctor about the need for using an alternative feeding method while taking this medication.

Seniors

Older adults with kidney disease may be more sensitive to some nervous system and lung effects of this drug. Follow your doctor's directions and report any side effects at once. Also, older adults are likely to have some reduction of kidney function and might require a dosage reduction to account for that loss.

Possible Side Effects

The most common side effects are loss of appetite, nausea, vomiting, stomach pain, diarrhea. Some people develop hepatitis symptoms.

Side effects are less prominent when Macrodantin (the large-crystal form of Nitrofurantoin) is used rather than Furadantin (the regular-crystal form).

Less common side effects include fever, chills, cough, chest pain, difficulty in breathing, development of fluid in the lungs; if these occur in the first week of therapy they can generally be resolved by stopping the medication. Side effects that take a longer time to develop may be more difficult for your doctor to associate with Nitrofurantoin. Other adverse effects include rashes, itching, asthmatic attacks in patients with history of asthma, drug fever, symptoms similar to arthritis, jaundice (yellowing of the whites of the eyes and/or skin), effects on components of the blood, headache, dizziness, drowsiness, temporary loss of hair.

This drug is known to cause changes in the blood. Therefore, it should be used only under strict supervision by your doctor.

Drug Interactions

Nitrofurantoin may increase the toxic effects of other drugs on the liver and can increase the chances of hemolytic anemia if you are taking another drug associated with that problem, such as the oral antidiabetes drugs, Methyldopa, Primaquine, Procainamide, Quinidine, Quinine, and the sulfa drugs.

Nitrofurantoin interferes with the effect of Nalidixic Acid. Don't take these drugs together.

Sulfinpyrazone or Probenecid may interfere with the passage of Nitrofurantoin through the kidneys, increasing blood levels of the drug. The reduces the drug's effectiveness because Nitrofurantoin depends on being present in the urine in very large quantities for its effect. Some drug side effects may also be increased by this interaction.

Drugs that cause nervous system toxicity, including Metronidazole, Mexiletine, Ethambutol, Isoniazid, Lindane, Lincomycin, Lithium, Pemoline, Quinacrine, and long-term high-dose Vitamin B6 (Pyridoxine), should not be taken with Nitrofurantoin because of the chance that nervous system effects may be increased.

Food Interactions

Nitrofurantoin may be taken with food to help decrease stomach upset, loss of appetite, nausea, or other gastrointestinal symptoms. Avoid eating citrus fruits or milk products while taking Nitrofurantoin. These can change the acidity of your urine and affect the drug's action.

Usual Dose

Adult: 50 to 100 milligrams 4 times per day.

Child (over age 3 months): 2 to 3 milligrams per pound of body weight in 4 divided doses.

Child (age 3 months and under): not recommended.

Nitrofurantoin may be used in lower doses over a long period by people with chronic urinary infections.

Continue to take this medicine at least 3 days after you stop experiencing symptoms of urinary tract infection.

Special Information

Call your doctor if you develop chest pains or trouble breathing, sore throat, pale skin, unusual tiredness or weakness, dizziness, drowsiness, headache, skin rash and itching, yellow skin, achy joints, fever and chills, or numbness, tingling, or burning of the face or mouth, or if other side effects are especially persistent or bothersome.

Nitrofurantoin may give your urine a brownish color: This is usual and not dangerous. The oral liquid form of Nitrofurantoin can stain your teeth if you don't swallow the medicine rapidly.

If you miss a dose of Nitrofurantoin, take it as soon as possible. If it is almost time for your next dose and you take the medicine 3 or more times a day, space the missed dose and your next dose by 2 to 4 hours or double your next dose and then continue with your regular schedule.

Generic Name

Nitroglycerin

Brand Names

Nitro-Bid Ointment/Plateau Caps
Nitrocine Timecaps
Nitrodisc Patches
Nitro-Dur Patches
Nitrogard Tablets
Nitroglyn Capsules
Nitrolingual Spray
Nitrol Ointment
Nitrong Tablets
Nitrostat Sublingual Tablets
Transderm Nitro Patches

(Also available in generic form)

Type of Drug

Antianginal agent.

Prescribed for

Prevention and treatment of chest pains associated with angina pectoris. Nitroglycerin injection also used as a treatment after a heart attack, for heart failure and high blood pressure.

General Information

Nitroglycerin is available in several dosage forms, including sublingual tablets (which are taken under the tongue and are allowed to dissolve), capsules (which are swallowed), transmucosal tablets (which are placed between lip or cheek and gum and allowed to dissolve), oral sprays (sprayed directly on the inside of the cheek), patches (which deliver Nitroglycerin through the skin over a 24-hour period), and ointment (which is usually spread over the chest wall, although it can be spread on any area of the body). Frequently patients may take one or more dosage forms of Nitroglycerin to prevent and/or treat the attack of chest pain associated with angina.

Cautions and Warnings

You should not take Nitroglycerin if you are known to be allergic to it. Also, because Nitroglycerin will increase the pressure of fluid inside your head, it should be taken with great caution if head trauma or bleeding in the head is present. Other conditions where the use of nitroglycerin should be carefully weighed are severe anemia, glaucoma, severe liver disease, overactive thyroid, cardiomyopathy (disease of the heart muscle), low blood pressure, recent heart attack, severe kidney problems, and overactive gastrointestinal tract.

Pregnancy/Breast-feeding

This drug crosses into the blood circulation of a developing baby. It has not been found to cause birth defects. Pregnant women, or those who might become pregnant while taking this drug, should not take it without their doctors' approval. When the drug is considered essential by your doctor, the potential risk of taking the medicine must be carefully weighed against the benefit it might produce.

This drug passes into breast milk but has caused no problems among breast-fed infants. You must consider the potential effect on the nursing infant if breast-feeding while taking this medicine.

Seniors

Older adults may take Nitroglycerin without restriction. Be sure to follow your doctor's directions for use.

Possible Side Effects

The most frequent side effect of Nitroglycerin is flushing of the skin. Headache is common and may be severe or persistent. Once in a while, episodes of dizziness and weakness have been associated with the use of Nitroglycerin. There is a possibility that you will experience blurred vision. If this occurs, stop taking the drug and call your physician.

Occasionally an individual exhibits a marked sensitivity to the blood-pressure-lowering effect of Nitroglycerin, causing severe responses of nausea, vomiting, weakness, restlessness, loss of facial color or pallor, perspiration, and collapse even with the usual therapeutic dose. Drug rash occasionally occurs.

Drug Interactions

If you are taking Nitroglycerin continuously, avoid excessive alcohol intake, which may cause lowering of blood pressure and resulting faintness and dizziness.

Avoid over-the-counter drugs containing stimulants, which may aggravate your heart disease. Such drugs are used to treat coughs, colds, and allergies and as appetite suppressants.

Food Interactions

Do not use any oral form of Nitroglycerin with food or gum in your mouth. Nitroglycerin pills intended for swallowing (most are *not*) are best taken on an empty stomach.

Usual Dose

Only as much as is necessary to control chest pains. Since the sublingual dosage form acts within 10 to 15 seconds of being taken, the drug is taken only when necessary.

Long-acting (sustained-release) capsules or tablets: generally used to prevent chest pains associated with angina, with the dose being 1 capsule or tablet every 8 to 12 hours.

Ointment: 1 to 2 inches of ointment are squeezed from the tube onto a prepared piece of paper with markings on it (some patients may require as much as 4 to 5 inches). The ointment is spread on the skin every 3 to 4 hours as needed for control of chest pains. The drug is absorbed through the skin. Application sites should be rotated to prevent skin inflammation and rash.

Patches: placed on the chest once a day and left on for 24 hours.

Aerosol: delivers a premeasured dose. Spray 1 or 2 doses under or on your tongue and repeat as needed to relieve an angina attack.

Overdose

Nitroglycerin overdose can result in low blood pressure, very rapid heartbeat, flushing, perspiration (later on, your skin can become cold, bluish, and clammy), headache, heart palpitations, blurring and other visual disturbances, dizziness, nausea, vomiting, difficult and slow breathing, slow pulse, confusion, moderate fever, and paralysis. Overdose victims should be taken to a hospital emergency room at once for treatment. ALWAYS remember to bring the medicine bottle with you.

Special Information

The sublingual form should be acquired from your pharmacist only in the original, unopened bottle, and the tablets must not be transferred to a secondary bottle or container; otherwise the tablets may lose potency. Close the bottle tightly after each use or the drug may evaporate from the tablets.

The sublingual form should produce a burning sensation under the tongue, which indicates that the drug is potent and will produce the desired effect. If there is no such sensation you must have the tablets replaced immediately.

When applying Nitroglycerin ointment, do not rub or massage into the skin. Any excess ointment should be washed from hands after application.

Orthostatic hypotension, where more blood stays in the

extremities and less becomes available to the brain, resulting in light-headedness or faintness if you stand up suddenly, can be a problem if you take Nitroglycerin over a long period of time. Avoid prolonged standing and be careful to stand up slowly.

If you take Nitroglycerin on a regular schedule and forget a dose take it as soon as you remember. If you use regular Nitroglycerin tablets and it is within 2 hours of your next dose, skip the forgotten dose and continue with your regular schedule. If you take extended-release Nitroglycerin tablets or capsules and it is within 6 hours of your next dose, skip the forgotten dose and continue with your regular schedule.

Generic Name

Norfloxacin

Brand Name

Noroxin

Type of Drug

Urinary anti-infective.

Prescribed for

Treating and preventing urinary infections, prostate infection, and gonorrhea. Norfloxacin may also be useful in treating bronchitis, pneumonia, bone infections, and traveler's diarrhea. This medicine does not work against the common cold, flu, or other virus infections.

General Information

Norfloxacin was the first of a new class of antibacterial drugs, called fluoroquinolones, to be marketed in the United States. This drug works against many organisms that traditional treatments like antibiotics have trouble killing. It is chemically related to an older antibacterial called Nalidixic Acid, but works better than that drug against urinary infections. Research conducted after the drug was approved for marketing has shown that it can be used to treat gonorrhea.

Cautions and Warnings

Do not take Norfloxacin if you have had an allergic reaction to it in the past, or if you have had a reaction to a related medication like Nalidixic Acid. Severe, possibly fatal allergic reactions can occur as soon as after the first dose of medicine. Norfloxacin is eliminated by the kidneys; the drug dose must be adjusted in the presence of kidney failure.

This drug may cause increased pressure on parts of the brain, leading to convulsions and psychotic reactions. This can also cause restlessness, light-headedness, confusion, and hallucinations. Norfloxacin should be used with caution by people with seizure disorder or other conditions of the nervous system.

Prolonged use of Norfloxacin, as with any other anti-infective, can lead to fungal overgrowth.

Pregnancy/Breast-feeding

Pregnant women or women who might become pregnant should not take this medication unless the risks have been weighed against the possible benefits of its use. Studies with monkeys have shown that this drug can reduce your chances for a successful pregnancy, and that doses 10 times greater than the maximum human dose can cause spontaneous abortion. The drug has not caused birth defects in animals given up to 50 times the human dose.

In studies, low doses of Norfloxacin did not pass into breast milk, but nursing mothers should avoid taking it unless it is absolutely necessary because of the chance that the drug might pass into breast milk. Be sure your doctor knows if you are breast-feeding.

Seniors

Studies with healthy older adults showed that Norfloxacin is released from their bodies more slowly than from the bodies of younger adults because of decreased kidney function. Since most seniors have lost some kidney function, your doctor will take this factor into account by giving you a lower daily dosage of Norfloxacin.

Possible Side Effects

The most common side effects are nausea, headache, dizziness, and light-headedness.

Other side effects are rash, fatigue, drowsiness, depression, difficulty sleeping, upset stomach, abdominal pains, stomach gas, constipation, and heartburn.

Rare side effects include seizures, confusion, psychotic reactions, tingling in the hands or feet, itching, skin peeling, severe skin reactions, dry mouth, diarrhea, colitis, fever, and vomiting. Hearing and visual disturbances (such as blurred or double vision, changes in color perception, halos around lights, and sensitivity to bright lights) are rare but should be reported to your doctor.

Drug Interactions

Antacids will decrease the amount of Norfloxacin absorbed into the blood. If you must take them, separate your antacid dose from your Norfloxacin dose by at least 2 hours.

Probenecid and Azlocillin will decrease the amount of Norfloxacin released through your kidneys and may increase the chance of drug side effects.

Anticancer drugs may decrease the amount of Norfloxacin in your blood.

Nitrofurantoin may antagonize Norfloxacin's antibacterial effects. Do not take these drugs together.

Norfloxacin may increase the amount of Theophylline in the blood, leading to increased drug side effects and possible drug toxicity. Norfloxacin may increase the effects of anticoagulant (blood-thinning) drugs and can increase the kidney toxicity of Cyclosporine, which is used to prevent rejection in kidney and other organ transplants.

This drug increases the effects of caffeine on your body.

Food Interactions

Take this medicine with a full glass of water either 1 hour before or 2 hours after meals. Food interferes with the absorption of this drug into the bloodstream.

Usual Dose

400 to 800 milligrams per day. Daily dosage is adjusted in the presence of kidney failure.

Overdosage

The symptoms of Norfloxacin overdose are the same as

those found under "Possible Side Effects." Overdose victims should be taken to a hospital emergency room for treatment of those symptoms. However, you may induce vomiting with Syrup of Ipecac to remove excess medicine from the victim's stomach. Consult your local poison control center or hospital emergency room for specific instructions.

Special Information

Take each dose with a full glass of water and be sure to drink at least 8 glasses of water a day while taking Norfloxacin. This will promote removal of the drug from your system and help to avoid side effects.

Call your doctor if you faint or if you develop facial swelling, itching, rash, difficulty breathing, convulsions, depression, visual disturbances, dizziness, headache, light-headedness, or any intolerable side effects.

It is essential that you take this medicine according to your doctor's directions. Do not stop taking it if you begin to feel better a few days after you start treatment unless directed to do so by your doctor.

Since Norfloxacin can cause visual changes, dizziness, drowsiness, or light-headedness, it can affect your ability to drive a car or do other things requiring full concentration and attention.

If you forget to take a dose of Norfloxacin, take it as soon as you remember. If it is almost time for your next regularly scheduled dose, skip the forgotten dose and continue with your regular schedule. Do not take a double dose.

Brand Name

Norgesic Forte

Ingredients

Aspirin
Caffeine
Orphenadrine Citrate

Other Brand Name

Orphengesic Forte

Type of Drug

Muscle relaxant combination.

Prescribed for

Muscle spasms.

General Information

The primary ingredient in Norgesic Forte is Orphenadrine Citrate, a derivative of the antihistamine Diphenhydramine Hydrochloride (Benadryl). It is a moderately effective muscle relaxant which works by exerting a general sedative effect. The Aspirin in Norgesic Forte is there only for pain relief.

Norgesic Forte cannot solve the problems of pain due to muscle spasm: It can only temporarily relieve the pain. You must follow any additional advice given regarding exercise, diet, or immobilization to help solve the underlying problem.

Cautions and Warnings

Norgesic Forte should not be used if you have a history of glaucoma, stomach ulcer, intestinal obstruction, difficulty in passing urine, or known sensitivity or allergy to this drug or any of its ingredients. It should not be used by children.

Pregnancy/Breast-feeding

This product has not been studied for its effect on a developing baby. However, too much Aspirin late in a pregnancy can decrease a newborn's weight and cause other problems. Pregnant women, or those who might become pregnant while taking this drug, should not do so without their doctors' approval. When the drug is considered essential by your doctor, the potential risk of taking the medicine must be carefully weighed against the benefit it might produce.

It is not known if this drug passes into breast milk, but you must consider the potential effect on the nursing infant if breast-feeding while taking this medicine.

Seniors

Older adults may be more sensitive to the side effects of this medication.

Possible Side Effects

Dryness of the mouth is usually the first side effect to appear. As the daily dose increases, other possible side effects include rapid heartbeat, palpitations, difficulty in urination, blurred vision, enlarged pupils, weakness, nausea, vomiting, headache, dizziness, constipation, drowsiness, rash, itching, runny or stuffy nose, hallucinations, agitation, tremor, and stomach upset. Older patients taking this drug may occasionally experience some degree of mental confusion. Large doses or prolonged therapy may result in Aspirin intoxication with symptoms of ringing in the ears, headache, dizziness, fever, confusion, sweating, thirst, drowsiness, dimness of vision, rapid breathing, increased pulse rate, or diarrhea.

Drug Interactions

One of the ingredients in Norgesic Forte is Aspirin, which may significantly affect the effectiveness of oral anticoagulant (blood-thinning) drugs, increase the effect of Probenecid, and increase the blood-sugar-lowering effects of oral antidiabetic drugs such as Chlorpropamide and Tolbutamide.

Interaction with Propoxyphene (Darvon) may cause confusion, anxiety, tremors, or shaking.

Long-term users should avoid excessive alcohol intake, which may aggravate stomach upset and bleeding.

Food Interactions

Take with food or at least half a glass of water to prevent stomach upset.

Usual Dose

½ to 1 tablet 3 to 4 times per day.

Overdosage

2 to 3 grams of Orphenadrine (40 to 60 Norgesic Forte tablets) is lethal to adults. Large overdoses can be rapidly fatal. The victim must be taken to a hospital emergency room as quickly as possible for treatment. ALWAYS bring the medicine bottle with you.

Special Information

Norgesic Forte may make you drowsy. Take care while driving or operating complex equipment.

Avoid alcoholic beverages, which can enhance the irritating effect of this product on your stomach and its depressive effect.

If you forget to take a dose of Norgesic Forte and you remember within about an hour of your regular time, take the dose right away. If you do not remember until later, skip the forgotten dose and go back to your regular schedule. Do not take a double dose.

Generic Name

Nortriptyline

Brand Names

Aventyl
Pamelor

Type of Drug

Antidepressant.

Prescribed for

Depression with or without symptoms of anxiety.

General Information

Nortriptyline and other members of this group are effective in treating symptoms of depression. They can elevate your mood, increase physical activity and mental alertness, and improve appetite and sleep patterns. These drugs are mild sedatives and therefore useful in treating mild forms of depression associated with anxiety. You should not expect instant results with this medicine: Benefits are usually seen after 1 to 4 weeks. If symptoms are not affected after 6 to 8 weeks, contact your doctor. Occasionally this drug and other members of the group of drugs have been used in treating nighttime bed-wetting in young children, but they do not produce long-lasting relief, and therapy with one of them for nighttime bed-wetting is of questionable value.

Cautions and Warnings

Do not take Nortriptyline if you are allergic or sensitive to this or other members of this class of drug: Doxepin, Protriptyline, Imipramine, Desipramine, and Amitriptyline. The drugs should not be used if you are recovering from a heart attack. Nortriptyline may be taken with caution if you have a history of epilepsy or other convulsive disorders, difficulty in urination, glaucoma, heart disease, or thyroid disease.

Pregnancy/Breast-feeding

This drug, like other antidepressants, crosses into your developing baby's circulation and may cause birth defects if taken during the first 3 months of pregnancy. There have been reports of newborn infants suffering from heart, breathing, and urinary problems after their mothers had taken an antidepressant of this type immediately before delivery. You should avoid taking this medication while pregnant.

Antidepressants of this type are known to pass into breast milk and may affect a breast-feeding infant, although this has not been proven. Nursing mothers should consider alternative feeding methods if taking this medicine.

Seniors

Older adults are more sensitive to the effects of this drug and often require a lower dose than a younger adult to do the same job. Follow your doctor's directions and report any side effects at once.

Possible Side Effects

Changes in blood pressure (both high and low), abnormal heart rates, heart attack, confusion (especially in older patients), hallucinations, disorientation, delusions, anxiety, restlessness, excitement, numbness and tingling in the extremities, lack of coordination, muscle spasms or tremors, seizures and/or convulsions, dry mouth, blurred vision, constipation, inability to urinate, rash, itching, sensitivity to bright light or sunlight, retention of fluids, fever, allergy, changes in composition of blood, nausea, vomiting, loss of appetite, stomach upset, diarrhea, enlargement of the breasts in males and females, increased or decreased sex drive, increased or decreased blood sugar.

Less common side effects include agitation, inability to sleep, nightmares, feeling of panic, development of a pecu-

liar taste in the mouth, stomach cramps, black coloration
of the tongue, yellowing eyes and/or skin, changes in liver
function, increased or decreased weight, perspiration, flushing, frequent urination, drowsiness, dizziness, weakness,
headache, loss of hair, nausea, not feeling well.

Drug Interactions

Interaction with monoamine oxidase (MAO) inhibitors can
cause high fevers, convulsions, and occasionally death.
Don't take any MAO inhibitors until at least 2 weeks after
Nortriptyline has been discontinued.

In patients who require concomitant use of Nortriptyline and
an MAO inhibitor, close medical observation is warranted.

Nortriptyline interacts with Guanethidine and Clonidine,
drugs used to treat high blood pressure: If your doctor prescribes Nortriptyline and you are taking medicine for high
blood pressure, be sure to discuss this with him.

Nortriptyline increases the effects of barbiturates, tranquilizers, other sedative drugs, and alcohol. Don't drink alcoholic
beverages if you take this medicine.

Taking Nortriptyline and thyroid medicine will enhance the
effects of the thyroid medicine. The combination can cause
abnormal heart rhythms. The combination of Nortriptyline
and Reserpine may cause overstimulation.

Large doses of Vitamin C (Ascorbic Acid), oral contraceptives, or smoking can reduce the effect of Nortriptyline.
Drugs such as Bicarbonate of Soda, Acetazolamide, Quinidine, or Procainamide will increase the effect of Nortriptyline. Ritalin and phenothiazine drugs such as Thorazine and
Compazine block the metabolism of Nortriptyline, causing it
to stay in the body longer. This can cause possible overdose.

The combination of Nortriptyline with large doses of the
sleeping pill Ethchlorvynol has caused patients to experience passing delirium.

Food Interactions

Take this drug on an empty stomach. If it upsets your stomach you may take it with food.

Usual Dose

Adult: 25 milligrams 3 times per day, which may be increased to 150 milligrams per day if necessary. The medication must be tailored to the needs of the patient.

Adolescent and senior: Lower doses are recommended—generally, 30 to 50 milligrams per day.

Overdosage

Symptoms are confusion, inability to concentrate, hallucinations, drowsiness, lowered body temperature, abnormal heart rate, heart failure, enlarged pupils of the eyes, convulsions, severely lowered blood pressure, stupor, and coma (as well as agitation, stiffening of body muscles, vomiting, and high fever). The patient should be taken to a hospital emergency room immediately. ALWAYS bring the medicine bottle.

Special Information

Do not stop taking this medicine unless your doctor has specifically told you to do so. Abruptly stopping this medicine may cause nausea, headache, and a sickly feeling.

This medicine can cause drowsiness, dizziness, and blurred vision. Be careful when driving or operating complicated machinery.

Avoid exposure to the sun or sun lamps for long periods of time.

Call your doctor if dry mouth, difficulty urinating, or excessive sedation develops.

If you take Nortriptyline several times a day and forget a dose, take it as soon as you remember. If it is almost time for your next regularly scheduled dose, skip the forgotten dose and continue with your regular schedule.

If you take it once a day at bedtime and forget, don't take it when you get up; go back to your regular schedule. Call your doctor if you skip 2 or more days of medication. Never take a double dose.

Generic Name

Nystatin

Brand Names

Mycostatin Vaginal Tablets
Nilstat Vaginal Tablets
O-V Statin Oral/Vaginal Therapy Pack

(Also available in generic form)

Type of Drug

Vaginal anti-infective.

Prescribed for

Fungal infection of the vagina.

General Information

Generally you will have relief of symptoms in 1 to 3 days. Nystatin vaginal tablets effectively control troublesome and unpleasant symptoms such as itching, inflammation, and discharge. In most cases, 2 weeks of therapy is sufficient for treatment, but prolonged treatment may be necessary. It is important that you continue using this medicine during menstruation. This drug has been used to prevent thrush or candida infection in the newborn infant by treating the mother for 3 to 6 weeks before her due date. At times the vaginal tablet has been used to treat candida infections of the mouth: The vaginal tablet is used as a lozenge and is allowed to be dissolved in the mouth and then swallowed.

O-V Statin is packaged in a "therapy pack." This package contains both vaginal and oral tablets for dual treatment when required.

Cautions and Warnings

Do not take this drug if you know you may be sensitive or allergic to Nystatin vaginal tablets.

Pregnancy/Breast-feeding

Pregnant and breast-feeding women may use this product with no restriction.

Seniors

Older adults may use this product with no restriction.

Possible Side Effects

Nystatin vaginal tablets are virtually nontoxic and are generally well tolerated. The only side effect reported has been intravaginal irritation: If this occurs, discontinue the drug and contact your doctor.

Drug Interactions

None known.

Usual Dose

1 tablet inserted high in the vagina daily for 2 weeks.

Special Information

Do not stop taking the medication just because you begin to feel better. All the medication prescribed must be taken for at least 2 days after the relief of symptoms.

Some of the brands of Nystatin vaginal tablets require storage in the refrigerator. Ask your pharmacist for specific instructions.

If you forget a dose of Nystatin, take it as soon as you remember. If it is almost time for your next regularly scheduled dose, skip the one you forgot and continue with your regular schedule. Do not take a double dose.

Generic Name

Ofloxacin

Brand Name

Floxin

Type of Drug

Urinary anti-infective.

Prescribed for

Treating and preventing lower-respiratory-tract infections,

sexually transmitted diseases (except syphilis), urinary infections, prostate infection, and skin and other infections. Ofloxacin may also be useful in treating bronchitis, pneumonia, bone infections, and traveler's diarrhea. This medicine does not work against the common cold, flu, or other virus infections.

General Information

Ofloxacin is one of the class of antibacterial drugs called fluoroquinolones. It is effective against a wide variety of microorganisms and may be used to treat infections in almost any part of the body. Ofloxacin works against many organisms that traditional treatments like antibiotics have trouble killing. It is chemically related to an older antibacterial called Nalidixic Acid, but works better than that drug against urinary infections. Research conducted after the drug was approved for marketing has shown that it can be used to treat a wide variety of infections.

Cautions and Warnings

Do not take Ofloxacin if you have had an allergic reaction to it in the past, or if you have had a reaction to a related medication like Nalidixic Acid. Severe, possibly fatal allergic reactions can occur as soon as after the first dose of medicine. Ofloxacin is eliminated by the kidneys; the drug dose must be adjusted in the presence of kidney failure.

This drug may cause increased pressure on parts of the brain, leading to convulsions and psychotic reactions. This can also cause restlessness, light-headedness, confusion, and hallucinations. Ofloxacin should be used with caution by people with seizure disorders or other conditions of the nervous system.

Prolonged use of Ofloxacin, as with any other anti-infective, can lead to fungal overgrowth.

Pregnancy/Breast-feeding

Pregnant women or women who might become pregnant should not take this medication unless the risks have been weighed against the possible benefits of its use. Animal studies have shown that this drug can reduce your chances for a successful pregnancy, and that doses 10 to 50 times greater than the maximum human dose can cause spontaneous abortion. The drug has not caused birth defects in animals given up to 50 times the human dose.

Usual doses of Ofloxacin produced drug levels in breast milk that were similar to those found in the blood. Nursing mothers should avoid taking Ofloxacin unless it is absolutely necessary because of the chance that the drug will affect the nursing infant. Be sure your doctor knows if you are breast-feeding.

Seniors

Studies with healthy older adults showed that Ofloxacin is released from their bodies more slowly than from the bodies of younger adults because of decreased kidney function. Since most seniors have lost some kidney function, your doctor will take this factor into account by giving you a lower daily dosage of Ofloxacin.

Possible Side Effects

The most common side effects are nausea, abdominal pains, diarrhea, vomiting, dry mouth, headache, dizziness and light-headedness, fatigue, feelings of ill health, sleeplessness, drowsiness, visual disturbances (including blurred or double vision, changes in color perception, halos around lights, and sensitivity to bright lights), vaginal irritation, and fever.

Other side effects are rash, itching, depression, upset stomach, stomach gas, constipation, heartburn, high blood pressure, heart palpitations, fainting, chills, and swelling.

Rare side effects include seizures, tingling in the hands or feet, itching, colitis, and hearing disturbances.

Drug Interactions

Antacids will decrease the amount of Ofloxacin absorbed into the blood. If you must take them, separate your antacid dose from your Ofloxacin dose by at least 2 hours.

Probenecid and Azlocillin will decrease the amount of Ofloxacin released through your kidneys and may increase the chance of drug side effects.

Anticancer drugs may decrease the amount of Ofloxacin in your blood.

Nitrofurantoin may antagonize Ofloxacin's antibacterial effects. Do not take these drugs together.

Ofloxacin may increase the amount of Theophylline in the blood, leading to increased drug side effects and possible drug toxicity.

Ofloxacin may increase the effects of anticoagulant (bloodthinning) drugs and can increase the kidney toxicity of Cyclosporine, which is used to prevent rejection in kidney and other organ transplants.

Food Interactions

Take this medicine with a full glass of water either 1 hour before or 2 hours after meals. Food may interfere with the absorption of this drug into the bloodstream.

Usual Dose

400 to 800 milligrams per day. Daily dosage is adjusted in the presence of kidney failure.

Overdosage

The symptoms of Ofloxacin overdose are the same as those found under "Possible Side Effects." Overdose victims should be taken to a hospital emergency room for treatment of those symptoms. However, you may induce vomiting with Syrup of Ipecac to remove excess medicine from the victim's stomach. Consult your local poison control center or hospital emergency room for specific instructions.

Special Information

Take each dose with a full glass of water and be sure to drink at least 8 glasses of water a day while taking Ofloxacin. This will promote removal of the drug from your system and help to avoid side effects.

Call your doctor if you faint or develop facial swelling, itching, rash, difficulty breathing, convulsions, depression, visual disturbances, dizziness, headache, light-headedness, or any intolerable side effects.

It is essential that you take this medicine according to your doctor's directions. Do not stop taking it if you begin to feel better a few days after you start treatment unless directed to do so by your doctor.

Since Ofloxacin can cause visual changes, dizziness, drowsiness, or light-headedness, it can affect your ability to drive a car or do other things requiring full concentration and attention.

If you forget to take a dose of Ofloxacin, take it as soon as you remember. If it is almost time for your next regularly scheduled dose, skip the forgotten dose and continue with your regular schedule. Do not take a double dose.

Generic Name

Olsalazine

Brand Name

Dipentum

Type of Drug

Anti-colitis treatment.

Prescribed for

Treatment and maintenance of ulcerative colitis.

General Information

This drug is broken down to the anti-inflammatory compound Mesalamine after it enters the colon. Mesalamine acts as an anti-inflammatory agent inside the bowel and is effective for ulcerative colitis. Little of Mesalamine is absorbed into the bloodstream; 70 to 90 percent of it remains in the colon, where it works.

Cautions and Warnings

Do not take this product if you are allergic to Aspirin or Aspirin-related compounds because the active metabolic product of Olsalazine is closely related to Aspirin.

Pregnancy/Breast-feeding

Olsalazine has caused birth defects in lab animals, but no such effect is known in humans. This drug should not be used

unless the possible benefits have been weighed against all
the possible risks of taking it.

It is not known if Olsalazine or Mesalamine passes into
breast milk, although it has been shown to affect nursing rat
offspring. Nursing mothers should take this drug only after
completely reviewing the possibilities with their doctors.

Seniors

This drug may be used without any special precautions by
older adults.

Possible Side Effects

The most common side effects are diarrhea, stomach cramps
or pain, and muscle aches.

Other side effects of Olsalazine include headache, fatigue
or drowsiness, nausea, vomiting, upset stomach, bloating,
yellowing of the skin or eyes, depression, dizziness, fainting,
loss of appetite, skin rash and itching.

Many other side effects have been reported, but their link
to Olsalazine is not well established.

Drug Interactions

None known.

Food Interactions

Take this drug with food or meals to reduce upset stomach.

Usual Dose

1000 milligrams a day in divided doses.

Overdosage

Overdose symptoms are diarrhea, vomiting, and lethargy.
Take the victim to a hospital emergency room for treatment.
ALWAYS bring the medicine bottle with you.

Special Information

Call your doctor if you develop fever, pale skin, sore throat,
unusual bruising or bleeding, unusual tiredness or weakness, or yellow eyes or skin or if your colitis gets worse
while taking Olsalazine. Other symptoms, such as diarrhea,
andominal pains, upset stomach, loss of appetite, nausea,

and vomiting, should be reported if they become particularly bothersome or severe.

If you forget a dose of Olsalazine, take it as soon as you remember. If it is almost time for your next dose, take one dose as soon as you remember and another in 5 or 6 hours, then go back to your regular schedule. Do not take a double dose.

Generic Name

Omeprazole

Brand Name

Prilosec

Type of Drug

Stomach-acid inhibitor; antiulcer.

Prescribed for

Gastroesophageal disease, stomach and duodenal ulcers, and conditions in which there is an excess of stomach acid.

General Information

Omeprazole is officially accepted in the United States for gastroesophageal reflux disease, a condition in which some stomach contents flow backward into the esophagus, the pipe that connects the throat to the stomach. This can result in erosion of the esophagus caused by the stomach acid. Omeprazole actually stops the production of stomach acid by a method that is different from that of Cimetidine, Ranitidine, and the other H2 antagonists. Omeprazole is also officially approved for several other conditions in which stomach acid plays a key role or in which excess stomach acid is produced as a part of the condition.

Omeprazole has not yet been officially accepted for ulcers (stomach and duodenal), although it is widely prescribed for that purpose.

Cautions and Warnings

Do not take Omeprazole if you have had an allergic reaction to it in the past.

In laboratory animal studies conducted over a 2-year period, Omeprazole was found to increase the numbers of some tumors. These studies have raised questions about the long-term safety of Omeprazole and the possible relationship between Omeprazole's effects and human tumors, although there is no currently available information that shows a human-tumor risk with Omeprazole.

Pregnancy/Breast-feeding

Animal studies with Omeprazole have shown toxic effects to developing fetuses, but no problems have been reported in women taking the medication. As with all drug products, pregnant women or those who might become pregnant should not use Omeprazole unless its advantages have been carefully weighed against the possible dangers of taking it while pregnant.

It is not known if Omeprazole passes into breast milk; no drug-related problems have been known to occur. Nursing mothers who use it should exercise caution.

Seniors

Studies of Omeprazole have shown a similar rate of side effects in older and younger adults. However, older adults are likely to have age-related reduction in kidney and/or liver function, which could account for increased amounts of drug in the bloodstream.

Possible Side Effects

Generally, Omeprazole causes few side effects. Those that may occur include headache, diarrhea, abdominal pain, nausea, sore throat, fever, vomiting, dizziness, rash, constipation, muscle pain, unusual tiredness, cough, back pain, and urinary infection.

Rare reactions include abdominal swelling, a feeling of ill health, angina pain, appetite loss, stool discoloration, irritable bowel, fungus infection in the esophagus, dry mouth, low blood sugar, weight gain, muscle cramps, joint and leg pains, dizziness, fainting, nervousness, sleeplessness, apathy, anxiety, unusual dreams, tingling in the hands or feet, nosebleeds, itching and inflammation of the skin, dry skin, hair loss, sweating, frequent urination, and testicle pain.

Drug Interactions

Omeprazole may increase the effects of Diazepam, Phenytoin, and Warfarin by slowing the breakdown of these drugs by the liver. It may also interact with other drugs broken down by the liver.

Omeprazole may interfere with the absorption from the stomach of drugs that require stomach acid as part of the process (e.g., Iron, Ampicillin, Ketoconazole).

The use of Omeprazole together with drugs that reduce the production of blood cells by the bone marrow may further reduce the numbers of those cells.

Food Interactions

Omeprazole should be taken immediately before a meal, preferably in the morning.

Usual Dose

20 to 80 milligrams a day.

Overdosage

There is limited experience with Omeprazole overdose, although people with a disorder called Zollinger-Ellison syndrome have taken 360 milligrams per day without a problem. Overdose symptoms are likely to be similar to drug side effects. Call your local poison control center or hospital emergency room for more information.

Special Information

Omeprazole should be taken immediately before a meal or with an antacid if it upsets your stomach.

Call your doctor if you develop unusual tiredness or weakness, sore throat, fever, sores in the mouth that don't heal, unusual bleeding or bruising, bloody or cloudy urine, or urinary difficulties, or if side effects are unusually persistent or bothersome.

Continue taking the medication until your doctor tells you

to stop, even though your symptoms may improve after a week or 2.

If you forget to take a dose of Omeprazole, take it as soon as you remember. If it is almost time for your next dose, skip the one you forgot and continue with your regular schedule. Do not take a double dose.

Generic Name

Oxazepam

Brand Name

Serax

(Also available in generic form)

Type of Drug

Tranquilizer.

Prescribed for

Relief of symptoms of anxiety, tension, fatigue, or agitation.

General Information

Oxazepam is a member of the group of drugs known as benzodiazepines. These drugs are used as antianxiety agents, anticonvulsants, or sedatives (sleeping pills). They exert their effects by relaxing the large skeletal muscles and by a direct effect on the brain. In doing so, they can relax you and make you either more tranquil or sleepier, depending on the drug and how much you use. Many doctors prefer Oxazepam and the other members of this class to other drugs that can be used for the same effect. Their reason is that the benzodiazepines tend to be safer, have fewer side effects, and are usually as, if not more, effective.

These drugs are generally used in any situation where they can be a useful adjunct.

Cautions and Warnings

Benzodiazepine tranquilizing drugs can be abused if taken

for long periods of time, and it is possible to develop withdrawal symptoms if you discontinue the therapy abruptly. Withdrawal symptoms include convulsions, tremor, muscle cramps, stomach cramps, vomiting, and sweating.

Do not take Oxazepam if you know you are sensitive or allergic to this drug or other benzodiazepines such as Chlordiazepoxide, Prazepam, Clorazepate, Diazepam, Lorazepam, Flurazepam, and Clonazepam.

Oxazepam and other members of this drug group may aggravate narrow-angle glaucoma, but if you have open-angle glaucoma you may take the drugs. In any case, check this information with your doctor.

Pregnancy/Breast-feeding

Do not take Oxazepam if you are planning to become pregnant or are pregnant or nursing. An increased chance of birth defects has not been seen; however, there is a risk factor to be considered. Other drugs similar to Oxazepam have been shown to cause birth defects.

The baby may become dependent on Oxazepam if it is used continually during pregnancy. If used during the last weeks of pregnancy or during breast-feeding, the baby may be over-tired, be short of breath, or have a low heartbeat.

Use during labor may cause weakness in the newborn.

Seniors

Older adults are more sensitive to the effects of this drug, especially dizziness and drowsiness. Follow your doctor's directions closely and report any side effects at once.

Possible Side Effects

The most common side effect is mild drowsiness during the first few days of therapy, especially in older adults or the debilitated. If drowsiness persists, contact your doctor.

Less common side effects include confusion, depression, lethargy, disorientation, headache, lack of activity, slurred speech, stupor, dizziness, tremor, constipation, dry mouth, nausea, inability to control urination, changes in sex drive, irregular menstrual cycle, changes in heart rhythm, lowered blood pressure, retention of fluids, blurred or double vision, itching, rash, hiccups, nervousness, inability to fall asleep, (occasional) liver dysfunction. If you experience any of these reactions stop taking the medicine and contact your doctor immediately.

Drug Interactions

Oxazepam is a central-nervous-system depressant. Avoid alcohol, tranquilizers, narcotics, sleeping pills, barbiturates, monoamine oxidase (MAO) inhibitors, antihistamines, and other medicines used to relieve depression.

Food Interactions

Oxazepam is best taken on an empty stomach, but may be taken with food.

Usual Dose

Adult: 10 to 120 milligrams per day as individualized for maximum benefit, depending on symptoms and response to treatment, which may require a dose outside the range given.

Senior: usually requires less of the drug to control anxiety and tension.

Overdosage

Symptoms are confusion, sleep or sleepiness, lack of response to pain such as a pin stick, shallow breathing, lowered blood pressure, and coma. The patient should be taken to a hospital emergency room immediately. ALWAYS bring the medicine bottle.

Special Information

Oxazepam can cause tiredness, drowsiness, inability to concentrate, or similar symptoms. Be careful if you are driving, operating machinery, or performing other activities that require concentration.

If you forget to take a dose of Oxazepam and you remember within about an hour of your regular time, take it right away. If you do not remember until later, skip the forgotten dose and go back to your regular schedule. Do not take a double dose.

Generic Name

Oxiconazole

Brand Name

Oxistat Cream

Type of Drug

Antifungal.

Prescribed for

Fungus infections of the skin.

General Information

Oxiconazole is a general purpose antifungal product. It works by interfering with the cell membrane of the fungal organism. Oxiconazole penetrates the skin after application, but little is absorbed into the bloodstream.

Cautions and Warnings

Do not take this product if you are allergic to Oxiconazole or any other ingredient in Oxistat Cream.

Large doses of Oxiconazole have caused reduced fertility in lab animals. This should be taken into account when considering the use of this product, although there is no evidence that Oxiconazole reduces fertility in women.

Pregnancy/Breast-feeding

Pregnant animals fed doses of approximately 1 milligram per pound of body weight per day showed no damage to the developing fetus. However, Oxiconazole has not been tested on pregnant women and should be used by pregnant women only if it is absolutely necessary.

Nursing mothers should avoid using this drug because significant amounts of Oxiconazole may pass into breast milk.

Seniors

Seniors may use Oxiconazole without special precautions.

Possible Side Effects

The most common side effect of Oxiconazole is itching and irritation of the skin after application.

Other side effects include burning, irritation, swelling, cracking, and redness of the skin.

Drug Interactions

None known.

Usual Dose

Oxiconazole should be applied to affected areas every evening for 2 weeks to a month, depending on the type of fungus present.

Overdosage

Oxiconazole is not intended to be taken internally. People who swallow Oxiconazole should be taken to a hospital emergency room for evaluation and treatment.

Special Information

Oxiconazole is meant only for application to the skin. Do not put this product into the eyes or swallow it.

If redness or irritation develops, stop using the product at once and notify your doctor.

If you forget to apply a dose of Oxiconazole, apply it as soon as you remember. If it is almost time for your next dose, skip the forgotten dose and continue with your regular schedule.

Generic Name

Oxtriphylline

Brand Name

Choledyl
Choledyl SA

(Also available in generic form)

Type of Drug

Xanthine bronchodilator.

Prescribed for

Relief of bronchial asthma and spasms of bronchial muscles associated with emphysema, bronchitis, and other diseases.

General Information

Oxtriphylline is one of several drugs, known as xanthine derivatives, which are the mainstay of therapy for bronchial asthma and similar diseases. Other members of this group include Aminophylline, Dyphylline, and Theophylline. Although the dosage for each of these drugs is different, they all work by relaxing bronchial muscles and helping reverse spasms in these muscles.

Cautions and Warnings

Do not use this drug if you are allergic or sensitive to it or to any related drug, such as Aminophylline. If you have a stomach ulcer or heart disease, you should use this drug with caution.

Pregnancy/Breast-feeding

This drug passes into the circulation of the developing baby. It does not cause birth defects but may result in dangerous drug levels in the infant's bloodstream. Babies born of mothers taking this medication may be nervous, jittery, and irritable and may gag and vomit when fed. Women who must use this medication to control asthma or other conditions should talk with their doctors about the relative risks of using this medication and the benefits it will produce for them.

This medication passes into breast milk and may cause a nursing infant to have difficulty sleeping and be nervous or irritable.

Seniors

Older adults may take longer to clear this drug from their bodies than younger adults. Older adults with heart failure or other cardiac conditions, chronic lung disease, a virus infection with fever, or reduced liver function may require a lower dosage of this medication to account for the clearance effect.

Possible Side Effects

Possible side effects from Oxtriphylline or other xanthine derivatives are nausea, vomiting, stomach pain, diarrhea, ir- ritability, restlessness, difficulty sleeping, excitability, muscle twitching or spasms, heart palpitations, other unusual heart rates, low blood pressure, and rapid breathing.

Infrequent side effects are vomiting blood, fever, head- ache, dehydration.

Drug Interactions

Taking Oxtriphylline at the same time as another xanthine derivative may increase side effects. Don't do it except under the direct care of a doctor.

Oxtriphylline is often given in combination with a stimu- lant drug such as Ephedrine. Such combinations can cause excessive stimulation and should be used only as specifi- cally directed by your doctor.

Some reports have indicated that combining Erythromycin and Oxtriphylline will give you higher blood levels of Oxtri- phylline. Remember that higher blood levels mean the possi- bility of more side effects. Other drugs that may increase blood levels are Cimetidine Allopurinol.

Cigarette smoking may decrease this drug's effectiveness.

Food Interactions

Take on an empty stomach, at least 1 hour before or 2 hours after meals. Occasional mild stomach upset can be mini- mized by taking the dose with some food (note if you do this, a reduced amount of drug will be absorbed into your bloodstream).

The way Oxtriphylline acts in your body may be influ- enced by your diet. Charcoal-broiled beef, for example, may cause a greater amount of Oxtriphylline to be eliminated in the urine. Therefore you may experience a decreased effect of the drug. This effect also occurs in people whose diet is low in carbohydrates and high in protein or in people who smoke. Caffeine (also a xanthine derivative) may add to the side effects of Oxtriphylline. It is recommended that you avoid large amounts of caffeine-containing foods such as coffee, tea, cocoa, cola, or chocolate.

Usual Dose

Adult: 200 milligrams 4 times per day. SA (sustained action): 400 to 600 milligrams every 12 hours.

Child (age 2 to 12): 100 milligrams for every 60 pounds of body weight taken 4 times a day.

Note: Each 100 milligrams of Oxtriphylline is equal to 64 milligrams of Theophylline in potency.

Overdosage

The first symptoms are loss of appetite, nausea, vomiting, difficulty sleeping, and restlessness, followed by unusual behavior patterns, frequent vomiting, and extreme thirst, with delirium, convulsions, very high temperature, and collapse. These serious toxic symptoms are rarely experienced after overdose by mouth, which produces loss of appetite, nausea, vomiting, and stimulation. The overdosed patient should be taken to a hospital emergency room where proper treatment can be given. ALWAYS bring the medicine bottle.

Special Information

Oxtriphylline and the other xanthine drugs are intended to be taken around the clock to maintain constant levels in your body. If you miss a dose, take it as soon as you can. If it is almost time for your next dose, skip the missed dose and go back to your usual dose schedule.

Generic Name

Oxybutynin

Brand Name

Ditropan

Type of Drug

Antispasmodic; anticholinergic.

Prescribed for

Excessive urination in people with bladder conditions.

General Information

Oxybutynin directly affects the smooth muscle that controls
the opening and closing of the bladder. It is 4 to 10 times
more potent an antispasmodic than Atropine, but has only
one-fifth the anticholinergic effect of that drug. This is important because the anticholinergic properties are most responsible for the drug's side effects.

Cautions and Warnings

Do not take Oxybutynin if you are allergic to it or if you have
developed itching or rash while taking it in the past, since
these symptoms may be mild signs of drug allergy.

Oxybutynin should be used with caution if you have glaucoma, intestinal obstruction, poor intestinal function, mega-
colon, severe or ulcerative colitis, myasthenia, or an unstable
cardiovascular status.

Oxybutynin should be used with caution if you have liver
or kidney disease. It may worsen symptoms of an overactive thyroid gland, coronary heart disease, abnormal heart
rhythm, rapid heartbeat, high blood pressure, prostate disease, and hiatus hernia.

Pregnancy/Breast-feeding

The safety of Oxybutynin use by pregnant women is not
known. It should only be used when the benefits outweigh
the possible damage the drug might do.

It is not known if Oxybutynin passes into breast milk.
Nursing mothers should use another feeding method if they
must take this drug.

Seniors

Older adults may be more susceptible to the side effects of
Oxybutynin and should take it with caution. Report anything
unusual to your doctor at once.

Possible Side Effects

The most common side effects are dry mouth, decreased
sweating, and constipation.

Other side effects include difficulty urinating, blurred vision, widening of the pupils of the eyes, worsening of glaucoma, palpitations, drowsiness, sleeplessness, weakness, nausea, vomiting, constipation, a bloated feeling, impotence (male), reduced production of breast milk (women), itching, and rash.

Drug Interactions

Oxybutynin may interact with other anticholinergic drugs, including some antihistamines, to produce excessive dry mouth or blurred vision.

It may increase the effects of nervous-system depressants such as tranquilizers, antihistamines, barbiturates, pain medicines, and anticonvulsants.

Food Interactions

This drug is best taken on an empty stomach, but may be taken with food or milk if it upsets your stomach.

Usual Dose

10 to 20 milligrams per day in divided doses.

Overdosage

The result of Oxybutynin overdose is exaggerated side effects. Overdose victims should be taken to a hospital emergency room at once. ALWAYS remember to bring the prescription bottle with you.

Special Information

Oxybutynin may interfere with your ability to concentrate. Take care while doing anything that requires a lot of concentration, including driving a car. Blurred vision, another effect of Oxybutynin, may also make it difficult for you to drive.

Your eyes may become more sensitive to bright light while taking Oxybutynin. You may compensate for this by wearing sunglasses or protective lenses.

Dry mouth may be treated with sugarless gum or candy or with ice chips. Excessive dryness of the mouth can lead to tooth decay and should be brought to your dentist's attention if it lasts for more than 2 weeks.

If you forget to take a dose of Oxybutynin, take it as soon

as you remember. If it is almost time for your next dose, skip the forgotten dose and continue with your regular schedule.

Generic Name

Oxymetazoline Hydrochloride

Brand Names

Nose Drops and Sprays

Afrin Drops/Spray
Allerest 12 Hour Nasal
  Spray
Coricidin Nasal Mist Spray
Dristan Long Lasting Spray
Duramist Plus Spray
Duration Spray
4-Way Long Acting Nasal
  Spray

Genasal Drops
Neo-Synephrine 12 Hour
  Drops/Spray
Nostrilla Spray
NTZ Long Acting Nasal
  Drops/Spray
Sinarest 12-Hour Spray
Sinex Long-Acting Spray
Twice-A-Day Drops

(Also available in generic form)

Eyedrops

Ocu-Clear

Type of Drug

Decongestant.

Prescribed for

The nose drops are prescribed for relieving stuffy noses due to allergy, the common cold, or any other cause. The eyedrops are prescribed for red eyes caused by minor irritation.

Cautions and Warnings

Do not use Oxymetazoline Hydrochloride nose drops, spray, or eyedrops if you are taking a monoamine oxidase (MAO) inhibitor or antidepressant, if you are allergic to Oxymetazoline or any other decongestant eyedrops, or if you have glaucoma, high blood pressure, heart disease, chest pains, thyroid disease, or diabetes.

The eyedrops should be stopped before any surgery requiring general anesthesia.

Pregnancy/Breast-feeding

Oxymetazoline crosses into the blood circulation of a developing baby. It has not been found to cause birth defects. Pregnant women, or those who might become pregnant while taking this drug, should not take it without their doctors' approval. When the drug is considered essential by your doctor, the potential risk of taking the medicine must be carefully weighed against the benefit it might produce.

Oxymetazoline passes into breast milk, but has caused no problems among breast-fed infants. You must consider the potential effect on the nursing infant if breast-feeding while taking this medicine.

Seniors

Older adults are more sensitive to the effects of this drug. Follow your doctor's directions and report any side effects at once.

Possible Side Effects

Common side effects of Oxymetazoline nose drops and spray are burning, stinging, dryness of the mucosa inside the nose, and sneezing. Oxymetazoline eyedrops may cause temporary stinging in the eye and blurred vision. These symptoms generally go away if you stop using the medication.

Less commonly, Oxymetazoline in any form may produce abnormal heart rhythms, increase in blood pressure, headache, feeling of light-headedness, nervousness, difficulty sleeping, blurred vision, some drowsiness or lethargy, headache, tremors, sweating and faintness.

Drug Interactions

Oxymetazoline is a stimulant drug that will increase the effect of any other stimulant.

Oxymetazoline may block some of the effect of depressant

drugs such as tranquilizers or sleeping medications, but this is unusual if recommended doses are observed.

Interaction with MAO inhibitor drugs may cause severe stimulation.

Beta-blocking drugs may increase the chances of Oxymetazoline side effects.

Usual Dose

Nose drops:
Adult and child (age 6 and over): 2 to 3 drops or sprays of the (generally 0.05 percent) solution in each nostril no more than twice a day.

Child (age 2 to 5): 2 to 3 drops of half-strength (0.025 percent) solution in each nostril no more than twice a day.

Eyedrops: 1 or 2 drops in the affected eye every 6 hours.

Overdosage

Symptoms are sedation; desire to go to sleep; possible coma or—with extreme overdosage—high blood pressure; low heart rate; other effects on the heart, including possible collapse of the cardiovascular system; and depressed breathing. The patient should be taken to a hospital emergency room immediately, where proper care can be provided. ALWAYS bring the medicine bottle.

Special Information

Use this drug exactly as directed. If Oxymetazoline is used more than twice a day or in excessive quantities, "rebound congestion" will occur. The eye can become excessively red and congested and your nose will produce excessive amounts of mucus in reaction to the medication, which may lead to overdosage and possible toxicity.

Do not use Oxymetazoline eyedrops for more than 3 days or the nose drops or spray for more than 1 week without first consulting your doctor.

Stop using the medicine and call your doctor if your eyes become excessively red and congested or if you develop severe eye pain (with or without looking at light), headache, OR vision changes.

If you forget to take a dose of Oxymetazoline, take it as

soon as you remember. If it is almost time for your next regularly scheduled dose, skip the forgotten dose and continue with your regular schedule. Do not take a double dose.

Generic Name

Oxyphenbutazone

Brand Name

Oxalid

(Also available in generic form)

Type of Drug

Anti-inflammatory agent.

Prescribed for

Local inflammation related to gout, rheumatoid arthritis, osteoarthritis, painful shoulder such as bursitis or arthritis of a joint, or other inflammatory diseases which cause pain that cannot be controlled by Aspirin, and when severe disability, because of the inflammation, is not relieved by usual treatment.

General Information

This drug should never be taken without strict medical supervision. Oxyphenbutazone should be used only for the short-term relief of pain due to inflammation of muscles, tendons, and joint area.

Oxyphenbutazone and its sister drug Phenylbutazone are toxic and dangerous and should be used only when absolutely necessary. The list of potential side effects is long. Therefore, any change in habits or unusual effect which may be even remotely connected with the use of these drugs should be reported immediately to your doctor.

Cautions and Warnings

You should not take Oxyphenbutazone if you have a history of symptoms associated with gastrointestinal inflammation or ulcer, including severe, recurrent, or persistent upset stomach. This drug is not a simple pain reliever and should never be taken casually. It should not be prescribed before a careful and detailed history, plus physical and laboratory tests, have been completed by the doctor. If your problem can be treated by a less toxic drug such as Aspirin, use that first and try to stay away from Oxyphenbutazone. Never take more than the recommended dosage: This would lead to toxic effects. If you have blurred vision, fever, rash, sore throat, sores in the mouth, upset stomach or pain in the stomach, feeling of weakness, bloody, black, or tarry stool, water retention, or a significant or sudden weight gain, report this to the doctor immediately. In addition, stop taking the drug. If the drug is not effective after 1 week, stop taking it. Use Oxyphenbutazone with caution and in consultation with a doctor if you are a pregnant or lactating woman.

Pregnancy/Breast-feeding

This drug crosses into the blood circulation of a developing baby. It is not recommended for use late in pregnancy because of the possibility that the drug will affect your developing baby's heart. It may delay or prolong your labor. Studies in laboratory animals have shown that this medication produces birth defects. Pregnant women, or those who might become pregnant while taking this drug, should not take it without their doctors' approval. When the drug is considered essential by your doctor, the potential risk of taking the medicine must be carefully weighed against the benefit it might produce.

This drug passes into breast milk and should not be taken if you are nursing an infant. The drug can cause severe blood problems in a nursing infant. Use an alternative feeding method if you must take this medicine.

Seniors

Seniors are more likely to develop the blood, stomach, kidney, and liver side effects of this drug because of a general reduction in kidney function. People 60 years of age and older should be limited to short periods of treatment (no more than 1 week, if possible) because of the possibility of severe, possibly fatal reactions.

Some doctors recommend that drug dosage be reduced by half in people age 60 and older.

Possible Side Effects

The most common side effects are stomach upset, drowsiness, water retention.

Infrequent side effects include acute gastric or duodenal ulcer, ulceration or perforation of the large bowel, bleeding from the stomach, anemia, stomach pain, vomiting, vomiting of blood, nausea, diarrhea, changes in the components of the blood, water retention, disruption of normal chemical balance of the body. This drug can cause fatal or nonfatal hepatitis, black-and-blue marks on the skin, serum sickness, drug allergy serious enough to cause shock, itching, serious rashes, fever, and signs of arthritis. It has been known to cause kidney effects, including bleeding and kidney stones. Oxyphenbutazone may be a cause of heart disease, high blood pressure, blurred vision, bleeding in the back of the eye, detachment of a retina, hearing loss, high blood sugar, thyroid disease, agitation, confusion, or lethargy.

Drug Interactions

Oxyphenbutazone increases the effects of anticoagulant (blood-thinning) drugs, Phenytoin, Insulin, and oral antidiabetic agents. If you are taking any of these drugs, discuss this matter with your doctor immediately.

Food Interactions

Oxyphenbutazone causes stomach upset in many patients; take your dose with food or antacids, and if stomach pain continues, notify your doctor.

Usual Dose

Adult and child (age 14 years or over): Depending upon the condition being treated, 300 to 600 milligrams per day in 3 to 4 equal doses for 7 days. If dose is effective it can then be reduced to 100 to 400 milligrams per day, depending on the condition being treated.

Senior: to be given for only 7 days because of high risk of severe reactions. Not to be given to senile patients.

Child (under age 14): not recommended.

Overdosage

Symptoms are upper stomach pain, nausea, vomiting, convulsions, euphoria, depression, headache, hallucinations, giddiness, dizziness, coma, rapid breathing rate, and insomnia or sleeplessness. Contact your doctor immediately. If you must go to a hospital emergency room, ALWAYS bring the medicine bottle.

Special Information

Oxyphenbutazone is a central-nervous-system depressant that can cause drowsiness and tiredness: Be careful when driving or operating other equipment, and avoid large quantities of alcoholic beverages, which will aggravate the situation.

If you take Oxyphenbutazone once or twice a day and forget to take a dose, take it as soon as you remember. If it is almost time for your next regularly scheduled dose, skip the one you forgot and continue with your regular schedule. Do not take a double dose.

If you take Oxyphenbutazone 3 or 4 times a day and forget to take a dose, and you remember within about an hour of your regular time, take it right away. If you do not remember until later, skip the forgotten dose and go back to your regular schedule. Do not take a double dose.

Generic Name
Paregoric

Brand Name

Paregoric

(Also available in generic form)

Type of Drug

Antidiarrheal.

Prescribed for

Symptomatic treatment of diarrhea.

General Information

Paregoric is only a symptomatic treatment: It should be accompanied by fluids and other therapy prescribed by your doctor.

Paregoric and other antidiarrheal agents should be used only for short periods: They will relieve the diarrhea, but not its underlying causes. Sometimes these drugs should not be used even though there is diarrhea present: People with some kinds of bowel, stomach, or other disease may be harmed by taking antidiarrheal drugs. Obviously, the decision to use Paregoric must be made by your doctor. Do not use Paregoric without his or her advice.

Cautions and Warnings

Paregoric is a derivative of Morphine; the cautions and warnings that go with the use of narcotics also go with the use of Paregoric. When taken in the prescribed dose, however, there should be no serious problems.

Pregnancy/Breast-feeding

This drug crosses into the blood circulation of a developing baby. It has not been found to cause birth defects. If used continuously for long periods, however, both the mother and child may become addicted and undergo withdrawal when the drug is stopped. Pregnant women or those who might become pregnant while taking this drug should not take it without their doctors' approval. When the drug is considered essential by your doctor, the potential risk of taking the medicine must be carefully weighed against the benefit it might produce.

This drug passes into breast milk, but has caused no problems among breast-fed infants. Some physicians recommend waiting 4 to 6 hours after taking the drug before beginning a breast-feeding session. You must consider the potential effect on the nursing infant if breast-feeding while taking this medicine.

Seniors

Older adults are more sensitive to the effects of this drug, and may especially have difficulty breathing. Follow your doctor's directions and report any side effects at once.

Possible Side Effects

Most people do not experience side effects from Paregoric but some may experience nausea, upset stomach, and other forms of gastrointestinal disturbance.

Rarely, prolonged use of Paregoric may produce some of the narcotic effects such as difficulty in breathing, lightheadedness, dizziness, sedation, nausea, and vomiting.

Drug Interactions

Paregoric, a depressant on the central nervous system, may cause tiredness or inability to concentrate and may thus increase the effect of sleeping pills, tranquilizers, and alcohol. Avoid large amounts of alcoholic beverages.

Food Interactions

To help mask the taste, Paregoric can be mixed with a small amount of water or juice immediately before it is taken. The milky color of the mixture is of no consequence.

Usual Dose

Adult: for diarrhea, 1 to 2 teaspoons 4 times per day.
Infant: for diarrhea, 2 to 10 drops up to 4 times per day.

Overdosage

A patient with Paregoric overdose should be taken to a hospital emergency room immediately. ALWAYS bring the medicine bottle.

Special Information

Take care while driving, or operating any appliance or machine.

If you forget to take a dose of Paregoric, take it as soon as you remember. If it is almost time for your next regularly scheduled dose, skip the forgotten dose and continue with your regular schedule. Do not take a double dose.

Brand Name

Pediazole

Ingredients

Erythromycin Ethylsuccinate
Sulfisoxazole Acetyl

Other Brand Name

Eryzole

(Also available in generic form)

Type of Drug

Antibiotic anti-infective.

Prescribed for

Middle-ear and sinus infections in children.

General Information

This combination of an antibiotic and a sulfa drug has been specifically formulated for its effect against Hemophilus influenza, an organism responsible for many cases of difficult-to-treat middle-ear infection in children. At present, Pediazole is approved by the Food and Drug Administration only for this specific use, although the combination is also useful for a variety of other infections against which both drugs are effective.

Each teaspoonful of the medicine contains 200 milligrams of Erythromycin and 600 milligrams of Sulfisoxazole. The 2 drugs work by completely different mechanisms; they complement each other, each working against organisms that the other is unable to affect. Pediazole is especially valuable in cases of Hemophilus influenza middle-ear infection that do not respond to Ampicillin, a widely used and generally effective antibiotic.

Cautions and Warnings

This combination should not be given to infants under 2 months of age because their body systems are not yet suffi-

ciently developed to break down sulfa drugs. Children who
are allergic to any sulfa drug or to any form of Erythromycin
should not be given this product.

Possible Side Effects

It is possible for children given this combination to develop
any side effect known to be caused by either Erythromycin
or Sulfisoxazole. The most common side effects are upset
stomach, cramps, drug allergy, and rashes.

Less common side effects are nausea, vomiting, and diarrhea. Sulfa drugs may make your child more sensitive to
sunlight, an effect that can last for many months after the
medicine has been discontinued.

Drug Interactions

Pediazole may increase the effects of Digoxin (a heart medicine), Tolbutamide and Chlorpropamide (antidiabetes drugs),
Methotrexate (an immunosuppressant), Theophylline (for
asthma), Warfarin (an anticoagulant), Phenylbutazone (a potent anti-inflammatory agent), Aspirin or other salicylates,
Carbamazepine and Phenytoin (for control of seizures), and
Probenecid (for gout). The potential results of such an interaction are an increase in drug side effects and a possible
need for dosage adjustment of the interacting drug.

Food Interactions

This combination is best taken on an empty stomach, at
least 1 hour before or 2 hours after meals. However, if it
causes upset stomach, have your child take each dose with
food or meals. Be sure your child drinks lots of water while
using Pediazole.

Usual Dose

The dosage of Pediazole depends on your child's body
weight and varies from half a teaspoonful to 2 teaspoonsful
every 6 hours, usually for 10 days. Each dose of Pediazole
should be followed by a full glass of water.

Overdosage

The strawberry-banana flavoring of this product makes it a
good candidate for accidental overdose, so be sure it is

stored in the area of your refrigerator that is least accessible to your child. Overdosage with Pediazole is most likely to result in blood in the urine, nausea, vomiting, stomach upset and cramps, dizziness, headache, and drowsiness. Sulfisoxazole overdosage is more dangerous than Erythromycin overdosage. Patients taking an overdose of this drug must be made to vomit with Syrup of Ipecac (available at any pharmacy) to remove any remaining drug from the stomach. Call your doctor or a poison control center before doing this. If you must go to a hospital emergency room, ALWAYS bring the medicine bottle.

Special Information

This product must be stored under refrigeration and discarded after 2 weeks. Be sure it is labeled with an expiration date when you leave the pharmacy.

Do not stop giving your child this medicine when the symptoms disappear. It must be taken for the complete course of treatment prescribed by your doctor.

Call your doctor if nausea, vomiting, diarrhea, stomach cramps, discomfort, or other symptoms persist, especially after giving the dosage with meals or food. Your child may be unable to tolerate the antibiotic and will have to receive different therapy.

Severe or unusual side effects should be reported to your doctor at once. Especially important are yellow discoloration of the eyes or skin, darkening of the urine, pale stools, or unusual tiredness, which can be signs of liver irritation.

If your child misses a dose of Pediazole, he or she should take it as soon as possible. If it is almost time for the next dose, space the missed dose and the next dose by 2 to 4 hours and then continue with your child's regular schedule.

Generic Name
Pemoline

Brand Name

Cylert
Cylert Chewable

Type of Drug

Psychotherapeutic.

Prescribed for

Children with attention deficit syndrome who are also in a program that includes social, psychological, and educational counseling. Pemoline may also be prescribed to treat daytime sleepiness.

General Information

This drug stimulates the central nervous system, although its mechanism of action is not known in children with attention deficit disorder (formerly called hyperactivity). It should always be used as part of a total therapeutic program and only when prescribed by a qualified pediatrician.

Cautions and Warnings

Do not use if the patient is allergic or sensitive to Pemoline. Children under age 6 should not receive this medication. Psychotic children may experience worsening of symptoms while taking Pemoline. Patients taking this drug should have periodic blood tests for the liver.

Pregnancy/Breast-feeding

This drug crosses into the blood circulation of a developing baby. It has not been found to cause human birth defects, but animal studies have shown that large doses can cause stillbirths and decreased newborn survival. Pregnant women, or those who might become pregnant while taking this drug, should not take it without their doctors' approval. When the drug is considered essential by your doctor, the potential risk of taking the medicine must be carefully weighed against the benefit it might produce.

This drug passes into breast milk, but has caused no problems among breast-fed infants. You must consider the potential effect on the nursing infant if breast-feeding while taking this medicine.

Possible Side Effects

Sleeplessness, appetite loss, stomachache, rash, irritability, depression, nausea, dizziness, headache, drowsiness, hallucination. Drug hypersensitivity may occur. Uncontrolled movements of lips, face, tongue, and the extremities and wandering eye may also occur.

Food Interactions

This medicine is best taken on an empty stomach, but you may take it with food if it upsets your stomach.

Usual Dose

37.5 to 75 milligrams per day. Do not take more than 112.5 milligrams per day.

Overdosage

Symptoms are rapid heartbeat, hallucinations, agitation, uncontrolled muscle movements, and restlessness. Patients suspected of taking an overdose of Pemoline must be taken to a hospital. ALWAYS bring the medicine bottle with you.

Special Information

Take the daily dose at the same time each morning. If Pemoline is taken too late in the day, you may have trouble sleeping. Call your doctor if sleeplessness develops.

If you forget to take a dose of Pemoline, take it as soon as you remember. If it is almost time for your next regularly scheduled dose, skip the forgotten dose and continue with your regular schedule. Do not take a double dose.

Generic Name
Penbutolol

Brand Name
Levatol

Type of Drug
Beta-adrenergic blocking agent.

Prescribed for

High blood pressure; angina pectoris (a specific type of chest pain).

General Information

This drug is quite similar to Propranolol, the original beta-blocking agent, although it has not been studied under as many kinds of conditions as Propranolol and most of the other beta-blocking drugs. Penbutolol is very useful because it can be taken once a day. When used for high blood pressure, it is often given with a diuretic such as Hydrochlorothiazide, but may be taken by itself.

Cautions and Warnings

Penbutolol should be used with care if you have a history of asthma or other upper respiratory disease or of heart failure. It should not be used if your heart rate is consistently very slow. You should stop taking the drug several days before major surgery, if possible; do not do this without telling your doctor. Penbutolol can hide some symptoms of diabetes or thyroid disease.

Pregnancy/Breast-feeding

This drug crosses into the blood circulation of a developing baby. It has not been found to cause birth defects. Pregnant women, or those who might become pregnant while taking this drug, should not take it without their doctors' approval. When the drug is considered essential by your doctor, the potential risk of taking the medicine must be carefully weighed against the benefit it might produce.

It is not known if Penbutolol passes into breast milk. In general, women taking beta blockers are strongly urged to not breast-feed their babies because of possible drug side effects.

Seniors

A variety of possible different factors may make older adults more or less sensitive to the effects of this medication. Your dosage of this drug must be adjusted to your individual needs by your doctor. Seniors may be more likely to suffer from cold hands and feet and reduced body temperature, chest pains, a general feeling of ill health, sudden difficulty breathing, sweating, or changes in heartbeat because of this medicine.

Possible Side Effects

Penbutolol may decrease the heart rate; worsen congestive heart failure; or produce lowered blood pressure, tingling in the extremities, light-headedness, difficulty sleeping, vivid dreams, dizziness, fainting, or weakness. It may also produce visual disturbances, disorientation, and short-term memory loss. Patients taking Penbutolol may experience, dry eyes, nausea, vomiting, stomach upset, abdominal cramps and diarrhea, or reduced sex drive. If you are allergic to this drug, you may show typical reactions associated with drug allergies, including difficulty breathing and various effects on the blood system. Penbutolol may induce bronchospasms (spasms of muscles in the bronchi), which will make any existing asthmatic condition or any severe upper respiratory disease worse.

Occasionally, patients taking Penbutolol may experience emotional instability or a feeling of detachment or of personality change, or the drug may produce unusual effects on the blood system.

Drug Interactions

Penbutolol's effectiveness in lowering blood pressure may be reduced by nonsteroidal anti-inflammatory drugs (NSAIDs), estrogens, Theophylline, and Aminophylline.

The drug's effectiveness may be increased by Cimetidine, Molindone, Nicotine chewing gum, and phenothiazine antipsychotic medicines and by stopping cigarette smoking.

It is not recommended that beta blockers be taken together with monoamine oxidase (MAO) inhibitor drugs because of a possible sudden increase in blood pressure.

Penbutolol may increase the effectiveness of Insulin or oral antidiabetes drugs. If you are diabetic, discuss the situation with your doctor; a reduction in dose of antidiabetic medication will probably be made.

Penbutolol may reduce the effectiveness of Digitalis and related drugs (Digoxin, Digitoxin) for congestive heart failure. Your Digitalis dose will have to be altered. If you are taking Digitalis for a purpose other than congestive heart failure, Digitalis's effect may be increased by Penbutolol, and the dose of Digitalis may have to be reduced.

Penbutolol may interact with certain other drugs to lower blood pressure. This interaction often has positive results in the treatment of patients with high blood pressure.

Do not self-medicate with over-the-counter cold, cough, or allergy remedies that may contain stimulant drugs that will aggravate certain types of heart disease and high blood pressure or other ingredients that may antagonize the effects of Penbutolol. Double-check with your doctor or pharmacist before taking any over-the-counter medication.

Food Interactions

Take this medicine with food if it upsets your stomach.

Usual Dose

20 milligrams once a day. Older adults may require more or less medication than younger adults and must be carefully monitored by their doctors.

Patients with liver problems may require dosage reduction of this drug.

Overdosage

Symptoms of overdose are slowed heart rate, heart failure, lowered blood pressure, and spasms of the bronchial muscles, which make it difficult to breathe. The patient should be taken to a hospital emergency room where proper therapy can be given. ALWAYS bring the medicine bottle with you.

Special Information

Since this drug is taken only once a day, be sure to take it at the same time every day.

Do not stop taking the drug abruptly unless your doctor tells you to, or serious heart pain and other effects can occur.

Call your doctor if you have trouble breathing when you exert yourself or are lying down; have a nighttime cough; or develop chest pains or swollen ankles, arms, or legs or if your side effects are particularly persistent or intolerable.

If you forget to take a dose of Penbutolol, take it as soon as possible. However, if it is within 8 hours of your next dose, skip the forgotten dose and go back to your regular schedule. Do not take a double dose.

Type of Drug
Penicillin Antibiotics

Brand Names

Generic Name: Amoxicillin

Amoxil	Trimox
Biomox	Wymox
Polymox	

(Also available in generic form)

Generic Name: Amoxicillin and Potassium Clavulanate

Augmentin

Generic Name: Ampicillin

D-Amp	Principen
Omnipen	Totacillin
Polycillin	

(Also available in generic form)

Generic Name: Ampicillin with Probenecid

Polycillin-PRB
Probampacin

Generic Name: Bacampicillin

Spectrobid

Generic Name: Carbenicillin Indanyl Sodium

Geocillin

Generic Name: Cloxacillin Sodium

Cloxapen
Tegopen

(Also available in generic form)

Generic Name: Dicloxacillin Sodium

Dycill
Dynapen
Pathocil

(Also available in generic form)

Generic Name: Nafcillin

Unipen

Generic Name: Oxacillin

Bactocill
Prostaphlin

(Also available in generic form)

Generic Name: Penicillin G

Penicillin GK
Pentids

(Also available in generic form)

Generic Name: Penicillin V (Phenoxymethyl Penicillin)

Beepen-VK   Pen-Vee K
Betapen-VK   Robicillin VK
Ledercillin VK   V-Cillin K
Penicillin VK   Veetids
Pen-V

(Also available in generic form)

Type of Drug

Antibiotic.

Prescribed for

Bacterial infections susceptible to the antibiotic.

General Information

Penicillin-type antibiotics fight infection by killing bacteria and other microorganisms. They do this by destroying the cell walls of the invading organisms. Other antibiotics simply prevent the invading organisms from reproducing. Many infections can be treated by almost any kind of Penicillin, but some infections can be treated only by a specific Penicillin antibiotic.

Penicillin cannot treat a cold, flu, or any virus infection and should never be taken unless prescribed by a doctor for a specific illness. Always take your antibiotic exactly according to your doctor's directions, including the number of pills to take every day and the number of days to take the medicine. If you do not follow directions, you will not get the antibiotic's full benefit.

Cautions and Warnings

Serious and occasionally fatal allergic reactions have occurred with Penicillin. Although this is more common following injection of the drug, it has occurred with oral use and is more common among people with a history of sensitivity to this or another Penicillin antibiotic or who suffer from multiple allergies.

Some penicillin drug reactions can be treated with antihistamines and other medicines. In a small number of cases where the infection is life threatening and can only be treated with Penicillin, minor reactions may be treated with other medicines while the Penicillin is continued. Generally, though, other drugs can be substituted to treat the infection.

Cystic fibrosis patients are more likely to suffer from drug side effects to some Penicillins.

Pregnancy/Breast-feeding

Penicillin has not caused birth defects and is often prescribed for pregnant women. Make sure your doctor knows you are taking it if you are or might be pregnant.

Penicillin is generally safe during breast-feeding; however, it is possible for the baby to receive enough of this drug to cause upset stomach, diarrhea, allergic reactions, or other problems.

Seniors

Seniors may take Penicillin without special precautions.

Possible Side Effects

The most important Penicillin side effect, seen in up to 10 percent of people who take these antibiotics, is drug allergy. These reactions are more common among people who have had a previous reaction to Penicillin and those who have had asthma, hay fever or other allergies. Some of the allergic symptoms include itching, rash, swelling, breathing difficulty, very low blood pressure, blood vessel collapse, skin peeling and other severe reactions, chills, fever, muscle aches, arthritis-like pains, and feelings of ill health. Severe reactions can lead to death.

Other side effects of oral Penicillin include stomach upset, abdominal pains, nausea, vomiting, diarrhea, colitis, sore mouth, coating of the tongue, rash, itching, various types of anemia, other effects on the blood system, and oral or rectal infestation with fungal diseases.

Less common side effects of Penicillin include vaginitis, loss of appetite, itchy eyes, body warmth, and, rarely, yellowing of the skin or eyes.

People who receive injectable Penicillin may become dizzy or tired or experience hallucinations, seizures, anxiety, depression, confusion, agitation, or hyperactivity.

Drug Interactions

Penicillin should not be given together with a bacteriostatic antibiotic such as Chloramphenicol, Erythromycin, Tetracycline, or Neomycin, which may diminish the effectiveness of Penicillin.

Penicillin may interfere with the effectiveness of oral contraceptive drugs.

Penicillin reactions may be increased by beta-blocking drugs.

Injectable Penicillin can increase the effect of anticoagulant (blood-thinning) drugs.

Food Interactions

Do not take Penicillin with fruit juice or carbonated beverages because the acid in these beverages can destroy the Penicillin.

Most of the penicillins, including Bacampicillin suspension, are best absorbed on an empty stomach. It can be taken 1 hour before or 2 hours after meals, or first thing in the morning and last thing at night with the other doses spaced evenly through the day. Amoxicillin, Amoxicillin and Potassium Clavulanate, and Bacampicillin tablets can be taken without regard to food or meals.

Usual Dose

Amoxicillin:
Adult: 250 to 500 milligrams every 8 hours.
Child: 10 to 20 milligrams per pound per day, divided into 3 doses.

Amoxicillin and Potassium Clavulanate:
Adult: a "250" or "500" tablet every 8 hours.
Child: 10 to 20 milligrams per pound per day divided into 3 doses.

Ampicillin:
Adult: 1 to 12 grams daily, divided into 4 to 6 doses.
Child: 25 to 100 milligrams per pound per day, divided into 4 to 6 doses.

Ampicillin with Probenecid: 3.5 grams of Ampicillin and 1 gram of Probenicid as a single dose for gonorrhea.

Bacampicillin:
Adult: 400 to 800 milligrams every 12 hours; 1,600 milligrams Bacampacillin plus 1 gram of Probenecid for gonorrhea.
Child: 12 to 25 milligrams per pound per day, divided into 2 doses.

Carbenicillin Indanyl Sodium: 382 to 764 milligrams 4 times a day.

Cloxacillin Sodium:
Adult: 250 milligrams every 6 hours.
Child: 25 milligrams per pound per day, divided into 4 doses.

Dicloxacillin Sodium:
Adult: 125 to 250 milligrams every 6 hours.
Child: 6 to 12 milligrams per pound per day, divided into 4 doses.

Nafcillin:
Adult: 250 to 1,000 milligrams every 4 to 6 hours.
Child: 5 to 25 milligrams per pound every 6 to 8 hours.

Oxacillin:
Adult: 500 to 1,000 milligrams every 4 to 6 hours.
Child: 25 to 50 milligrams per pound per day, divided into 4 or 6 doses.

Penicillin G:
Adult: 200,000 to 800,000 units (125 to 500 milligrams) every 6 to 8 hours for 10 days.
Child (under age 12): 12,000 to 40,000 units per pound per day, divided into 3 to 6 doses.

Penicillin V:
Adult: 125 to 500 milligrams 4 times a day. Patients with severe kidney disease should not take more than 250 milligrams every 6 hours.
Child (under age 12): 12 to 25 milligrams per pound per day, divided into 3 or 4 doses.

Overdosage

Penicillin overdose is unlikely but may result in diarrhea or upset stomach. Massive overdose can result in seizures or excitability. Call your local poison control center or hopital emergency room for more information.

Special Information

Oral Penicillin liquids should be stored in a refrigerator. The bottle should be labeled to that effect and must be discarded after 14 days in the refrigerator or 7 days at room temperature.

Call your doctor if you develop black tongue, skin rash, itching, hives, diarrhea, wheezing, breathing difficulty, sore throat, nausea, vomiting, fever, swollen joints, unusual bleeding or bruising, or feelings of ill health.

It takes 7 to 10 days for Penicillin to be effective against most susceptible organisms; be sure to take all the medicine prescribed for the full period prescribed. It is best taken at evenly spaced intervals throughout the entire day.

If you miss a dose of a penicillin antibiotic, take it as soon as possible. If it is almost time for your next dose, space the missed dose and your next dose by 2 to 4 hours and then continue with your regular schedule.

Generic Name

Pentazocine

Brand Names

Talacen (Pentazocine with Acetaminophen)
Talwin Compound (Pentazocine with Aspirin)
Talwin NX (Pentazocine with Naloxone)

Type of Drug

Nonnarcotic analgesic.

Prescribed for

Relief of moderate to severe pain.

General Information

Pentazocine is used for mild to moderate pain. Fifty to 100 milligrams of Pentazocine is approximately equal in pain-relieving effect to 2 Aspirin tablets (650 milligrams). Pentazocine may be less active than Aspirin for types of pain associated with inflammation, since Aspirin reduces inflammation but Pentazocine does not. Talwin NX was formulated to prevent drug abuse.

Cautions and Warnings

Do not use Pentazocine if you believe that you are allergic to it. It is possible to develop addiction to or dependence on Pentazocine but addiction is much more likely to occur with people who have a history of abusing narcotics or other drugs. Abrupt stoppage of Pentazocine after extended periods of therapy has produced withdrawal symptoms such as stomach cramps, fever, stuffy or runny nose, restlessness, anxiety, and tearing of the eyes. The drug may cause visual hallucinations or make you disoriented and confused; if this happens, stop taking the drug immediately and contact your physician. Never give this drug or any other potent painkillers to a patient with a head injury.

Pregnancy/Breast-feeding

No studies of this medication have been done in women and no reports of human birth defects exist, but animal studies show that high doses of the drug can cause problems in a developing fetus. Pregnant women, or women who might become pregnant while using this drug, should talk to their doctors about the risk of taking this medicine versus the benefits it can provide.

This drug passes into breast milk, but no problems in nursing infants have been seen. Breast-feeding women should consider the possibility of adverse effects on their nursing infant. Choose another feeding method if you must take this medicine.

Seniors

Seniors are more likely to be sensitive to the side effects of this drug and should be treated with smaller dosages than younger adults.

Possible Side Effects

Nausea, vomiting, constipation, cramps, stomach upset, loss of appetite, diarrhea, dry mouth, alteration of taste, dizziness, light-headedness, sedation, euphoria, headache, difficulty sleeping, disturbed dreams, hallucinations, muscle spasms, irritability, excitement, nervousness, apprehension and depression, feeling of being disoriented and detached from your body.

Less common side effects include blurred vision, difficulty in focusing the eyes, double vision, sweating, flushing chills, rash, itching, swelling of the face, flushing and reddening of the skin, changes in blood pressure, abnormal heart rate, difficulty in breathing, effects on components of the blood, difficult urination, tingling in the arms and legs.

Drug Interactions

Avoid interaction with drugs that have a sedative or depressive effect, such as alcohol, barbiturates, sleeping pills, and some pain-relieving medications. The combination will produce extreme sedation, sleepiness, and difficulty concentrating.

Pentazocine has the unusual effect of being a mild narcotic antagonist. If you must take narcotics for pain relief, do not take Pentazocine at the same time, because it will reverse the effect of the narcotic drug. This can be a special problem for patients in Methadone treatment programs. If one of these patients takes Pentazocine, he or she will experience narcotic withdrawal effects.

Food Interactions

This product is best taken on an empty stomach but can be taken with food.

Usual Dose

Adult: 50 milligrams every 3 to 4 hours. Maximum dose, 600 milligrams per day to control pain.
Child: not recommended.

Overdosage

Symptoms resemble those of narcotic overdose: decreased breathing, sleepiness, lassitude, low blood pressure, and even coma. The patient should be taken to a hospital emergency room immediately. ALWAYS bring the medicine bottle.

If you forget to take a dose of Pentazocine, take it as soon as you remember. If it is almost time for your next regularly scheduled dose, skip the forgotten dose and continue with your regular schedule. Do not take a double dose.

Generic Name

Pentobarbital

Brand Name

Nembutal

(Also available in generic form)

Type of Drug

Hypnotic; sedative.

Prescribed for

Daytime sedation; sleeping medication.

General Information

Pentobarbital, like the other barbiturates, appears to act by interfering with nerve impulses to the brain.

Cautions and Warnings

Pentobarbital may slow down your physical and mental reflexes, so you must be extremely careful when operating machinery, driving an automobile, or performing other potentially dangerous tasks. Pentobarbital is classified as a barbiturate; long-term or unsupervised use may cause addiction. Older adults taking Pentobarbital may exhibit nervousness and confusion at times. Barbiturates are neutralized in the liver and eliminated from the body through the kidneys; consequently, people who have liver or kidney disorders—namely, difficulty in forming or excreting urine-should be carefully monitored by their doctor when taking Pentobarbital.

If you have known sensitivities or allergies to barbiturates, if you have previously been addicted to sedatives or hypnotics, or if you have a disease affecting the respiratory system, you should not take Pentobarbital.

Pregnancy/Breast-feeding

Regular use of any barbiturate during the last 3 months of pregnancy can cause the baby to be born dependent on the medicine. Also, barbiturate use increases the chance of bleeding problems, brain tumors, and breathing difficulties in the newborn.

Barbiturates pass into breast milk and can cause drowsiness, slow heartbeat, and breathing difficulty in nursing infants.

Seniors

Older adults are more sensitive to the effects of barbiturates, especially nervousness and confusion, and often require a lower dose than a younger adult to do the same job. Follow your doctor's directions and report any side effects at once.

Possible Side Effects

Drowsiness, lethargy, dizziness, hangover, difficulty in breathing, rash, and general allergic reaction such as runny nose, watering eyes, and scratchy throat.

Less common side effects are nausea, vomiting, diarrhea. More severe adverse reactions may include anemia and yellowing of the skin and eyes.

Drug Interactions

Interaction with alcohol, tranquilizers, or other sedatives increases the effect of Pentobarbital.

Interaction with anticoagulants (blood-thinning agents) can reduce their effect. This is also true of muscle relaxants, painkillers, anticonvulsants, Quinidine, Theophylline, Metronidazole, Phenmetrazine, birth control pills, and Acetaminophen.

Food Interactions

This medicine is best taken on an empty stomach, but may be taken with food if it upsets your stomach.

Usual Dose

As a daytime sedative: 30 milligrams 3 to 4 times per day.

As a hypnotic for sleep: 100 milligrams at bedtime; this may be repeated once if necessary (occasionally) to induce sleep.

Overdosage

Symptoms are difficulty in breathing, decrease in size of the pupils of the eyes, lowered body temperature progressing to fever as time passes, fluid in the lungs, and eventually coma.

Anyone suspected of having taken an overdose must be taken to the hospital for immediate care. ALWAYS bring the medicine bottle to the emergency room physician so he or she can quickly and correctly identify the medicine and start treatment. Severe overdosage of this medication can kill; the drug has been used many times in suicide attempts.

Special Information

Avoid alcohol and other drugs that depress the nervous system while taking this barbiturate.

Be sure to take this medicine according to your doctor's direction. Do not change your dose without your doctor's approval.

This drug causes drowsiness and poor concentration and makes it more difficult to drive a car, operate machinery, or perform complicated activities.

Call your doctor at once if you develop fever, sore throat, nosebleeds, mouth sores, unexplained black-and-blue marks, easy bruising or bleeding.

If you forget to take a dose of Pentobarbital, take it as soon as you remember. If it is almost time for your next regularly scheduled dose, skip the one you forgot and continue with your regular schedule. Do not take a double dose.

Generic Name

Pentoxifylline

Brand Name

Trental

Type of Drug

Blood viscosity reducer.

Prescribed for

Relief of intermittent claudication, or blood vessel spasms and painful leg cramps, caused by poor blood supply associated with arteriosclerotic disease. It has also been used to treat cases of inadequate blood flow to the brain.

General Information

This medicine, available in Europe since 1972, is the first true "blood thinner." It reduces the blood's viscosity, or thickness, and improves the ability of red blood cells to modify their shape. In doing so, this medication may help people who experience severe leg pains when they walk by improving blood flow to their leg muscles. Leg cramps occur when muscles are deprived of oxygen. When blood flow is improved, the cramps are less severe or do not occur at all. Studies of Pentoxifylline's effectiveness have yielded mixed results, but it may be helpful for people who do not respond to other treatments.

It should be noted that physical training is probably a more effective treatment for intermittent claudication than is Pentoxifylline. However, the medicine may be helpful for people who cannot follow a training program and who are not candidates for surgery, which is another treatment for this condition.

Cautions and Warnings

People who cannot tolerate Caffeine, Theophylline, or Theobromine should not use this medicine, since Pentoxifylline is chemically related to those products.

Pregnancy/Breast-feeding

This drug crosses into the blood circulation of a developing baby. It has not been found to cause birth defects. Pregnant women, or those who might become pregnant while taking this drug, should not take it without their doctors' approval. When the drug is considered essential by your doctor, the potential risk of taking the medicine must be carefully weighed against the benefit it might produce.

This drug passes into breast milk, but has caused no problems among breast-fed infants. You must consider the potential effect on the nursing infant if breast-feeding while taking this medicine.

Seniors

Older adults are more sensitive to the effects of this drug because they absorb more and eliminate it more slowly than younger adults. Follow your doctor's directions and report any side effects at once.

Possible Side Effects

The most common side effects are mild nausea, upset stomach, dizziness, and headache.

Less frequently encountered reactions to Pentoxifylline include chest pains, difficulty breathing, swelling of the arms or legs, low blood pressure, stomach gas, loss of appetite, constipation, dry mouth, excessive thirst, tremors, anxiety, confusion, stuffy nose, nosebleeds, flu symptoms, sore throat, laryngitis, swollen glands, itching, rash, brittle fingernails,

blurred vision, conjunctivitis (red-eye), earache, a bad taste in
the mouth, a general feeling of ill health, and changes in body
weight.

The rarest side effects of Pentoxifylline are rapid or abnormal heart rhythms, hepatitis, yellow discoloration of the skin,
reduction in white-blood-cell count, and small hemorrhages
under the skin.

Drug Interactions

Pentoxifylline may add to the blood-pressure-lowering effects
of other medicines. Your doctor may have to change the dosage of your blood-pressure medicines.

Food Interactions

It is preferable to take each dose of Pentoxifylline on an empty
stomach. However, if it causes stomach upset or gas, the medicine may be taken with food.

Usual Dose

400 milligrams 2 to 3 times per day.

Overdosage

The severity of symptoms is directly related to the amount of
drug taken. Symptoms of overdosage usually appear 4 to 5
hours after the medicine was taken and can last for about 12
hours. Some of the reported effects of Pentoxifylline overdose
are flushing, low blood pressure, fainting, depression of the
nervous system, and convulsions. Patients taking an overdose
of this drug must be made to vomit with Syrup of Ipecac
(available at any pharmacy) to remove any remaining drug
from the stomach. Call your doctor or a poison control center
before doing this. If you must go to a hospital emergency
room, ALWAYS bring the medicine bottle.

Special Information

Call your doctor if any side effects develop. Some people may
have to stop using this medicine if side effects become intolerable. You may feel better within 2 weeks after starting to take

Pentoxifylline, but the treatments should be continued for at least 2 months to gain maximum benefit.

If you forget to take a dose of Pentoxifylline, take it as soon as you remember. If it is almost time for your next regularly scheduled dose, skip the one you forgot and continue with your regular schedule. Do not take a double dose.

Brand Name

Percocet

Ingredients

Acetaminophen
Oxycodone Hydrochloride

Other Brand Names

Oxycodone with   Roxicet
  Acetaminophen   Tylox

(Also available in generic form)

Type of Drug

Narcotic analgesic combination.

Prescribed for

Relief of mild to moderate pain.

General Information

Percocet is generally prescribed for the patient who is in pain but is allergic to or intolerant of Aspirin. Percocet is probably not effective for arthritis or other pain associated with inflammation because Acetaminophen does not reduce inflammation; Aspirin does.

Cautions and Warnings

Do not take Percocet if you know you are allergic or sensitive to any of its components. Use this drug with extreme caution if you suffer from asthma or other breathing problems. Long-term use of this drug may cause drug dependence or addiction. The Oxycodone Hydrochloride component of Percocet is a respiratory depressant, and affects the central nervous system, producing sleepiness, tiredness, and/or inability to concentrate.

Pregnancy/Breast-feeding

Neither Acetaminophen nor Oxycodone has been associated with birth defects, but taking too much of any narcotic, including Oxycodone, during pregnancy can lead to the birth of a drug-dependent infant and drug-withdrawal symptoms in the baby. All narcotics, including Oxycodone, can cause breathing problems in the newborn if taken just before delivery.

Percocet has not caused any problems among nursing mothers or their infants.

Seniors

The Oxycodone in this combination product may have more of a depressant effect on seniors than younger adults. Other effects that may be more prominent are dizziness, light-headedness, or fainting when rising suddenly from a sitting or lying position.

Possible Side Effects

The most frequent side effects are light-headedness, dizziness, sleepiness, nausea, vomiting, loss of appetite, and sweating. If these effects occur, consider asking your doctor about lowering your dose of Percocet. Usually the side effects disappear if you simply lie down.

More serious side effects of Percocet are shallow breathing or difficulty breathing.

Less common side effects are euphoria (feeling high), weakness, sleepiness, headache, agitation, uncoordinated muscle movement, minor hallucinations, disorientation, visual disturbances, dry mouth, loss of appetite, constipation, flushing of the face, rapid heartbeat, palpitations, faintness, urinary difficulties or hesitancy, reduced sex drive and/or potency, itching, rashes, anemia, lowered blood sugar, and a yellowing of the skin and/or whites of the eyes. Narcotic analgesics may aggravate convulsions in those who have had convulsions in the past.

Drug Interactions

Because of its depressant effect and potential effect on breathing, Percocet should be taken with extreme care in combination with alcohol, sleeping medicine, tranquilizers, or other depressant drugs.

Food Interactions

Percocet is best taken with food or at least half a glass of water to prevent stomach upset.

Usual Dose

Adult: 1 to 2 tablets every 4 hours.
Child: not recommended.

Overdosage

Symptoms of overdose are depression of respiration (breathing), extreme tiredness progressing to stupor and then coma, pinpointed pupils of the eyes, no response to stimulation such as a pin stick, cold and clammy skin, slowing down of the heart rate, lowering of blood pressure, yellowing of the skin and/or whites of the eyes, bluish color of skin of hands and feet, fever, excitement, delirium, convulsions, cardiac arrest, and liver toxicity (shown by nausea, vomiting, pain in the abdomen, and diarrhea). The patient should be taken to a hospital emergency room immediately. ALWAYS bring the medicine bottle.

Special Information

The Oxycodone Hydrochloride component of Percocet is a respiratory depressant and affects the central nervous system, producing sleepiness, tiredness, and/or inability to concentrate. Be careful if you are driving, operating machinery, or performing other functions requiring concentration.

If you forget to take a dose of Percocet, take it as soon as you remember. If it is almost time for your next regularly scheduled dose, skip the one you forgot and continue with your regular schedule. Do not take a double dose.

Brand Name

Percodan

Ingredients

Aspirin
Oxycodone Hydrochloride
Oxycodone Terephthalate

Other Brand Names

Oxycodone and Aspirin
Percodan-Demi
Roxiprin

(Also available in generic form)

Type of Drug

Narcotic analgesic combination.

Prescribed for

Relief of mild to moderate pain.

General Information

Percodan is one of many combination products containing narcotics and analgesics. These products often also contain barbiturates or tranquilizers, and Acetaminophen may be substituted for Aspirin.

Cautions and Warnings

Do not take Percodan if you know you are allergic or sensitive to any of its components. Use this drug with extreme caution if you suffer from asthma or other breathing problems. Long-term use of this drug may cause drug dependence or addiction. The Oxycodone component of Percodan is a respiratory depressant and affects the central nervous system, producing sleepiness, tiredness, and/or inability to concentrate.

Pregnancy/Breast-feeding

Check with your doctor before taking any Aspirin-containing product during pregnancy. Aspirin can cause bleeding problems in the developing fetus during the last 2 weeks of a pregnancy. Taking Aspirin during the last 3 months of pregnancy may lead to a low-birth-weight infant, prolong labor, extend the length of pregnancy, and cause bleeding in the mother before, during, or after delivery.

Oxycodone has not been associated with birth defects, but taking too much of it, or any other narcotic, during pregnancy can lead to the birth of a drug-dependent infant and drug-withdrawal symptoms in the baby. All narcotics, including Oxycodone, can cause breathing problems in the newborn if taken just before delivery.

Percodan has not caused any problems among nursing mothers or their infants.

Seniors

The Oxycodone in this combination product may have more of a depressant effect on seniors than younger adults. Other effects that may be more prominent are dizziness, light-headedness, or fainting when rising suddenly from a sitting or lying position.

Possible Side Effects

The most frequent side effects are light-headedness, dizziness, sleepiness, nausea, vomiting, loss of appetite, sweating. If these effects occur, consider asking your doctor about lowering the dose of Percodan you are taking. Usually the side effects disappear if you simply lie down.

More serious side effects of Percodan are shallow breathing or difficulty in breathing.

Less common side effects include euphoria (feeling high), weakness, sleepiness, headache, agitation, uncoordinated muscle movement, minor hallucinations, disorientation and visual disturbances, dry mouth, loss of appetite, constipation, flushing of the face, rapid heartbeat, palpitations, faintness, urinary difficulties or hesitancy, reduced sex drive and/or potency, itching, skin rashes, anemia, lowered blood sugar, yellowing of the skin and/or whites of the eyes. Nar-

cotic analgesics may aggravate convulsions in those who
have had convulsions in the past.

Drug Interactions

Interaction with alcohol, tranquilizers, barbiturates, or sleeping pills produces tiredness, sleepiness, or inability to concentrate and seriously increases the depressive effect of
Percodan.

The Aspirin component of Percodan can affect anticoagulant (blood-thinning) therapy. Be sure to discuss this with
your doctor so that the proper dosage adjustment can be
made.

Interaction with adrenal corticosteroids, Phenylbutazone,
or alcohol can cause severe stomach irritation with possible
bleeding.

Food Interactions

Take with food or half a glass of water to prevent stomach
upset.

Usual Dose

1 tablet every 6 hours as needed for relief of pain.

Overdosage

Symptoms are depression of respiration (breathing), extreme tiredness progressing to stupor and then coma, pinpointed pupils of the eyes, no response to stimulation such
as a pin stick, cold and clammy skin, slowing down of the
heartbeat, lowering of blood pressure, convulsions, and cardiac arrest. The patient should be taken to a hospital emergency room immediately. ALWAYS bring the medicine
bottle.

Special Information

Drowsiness may occur. Be careful when driving or operating
hazardous machinery.

If you forget to take a dose of Percodan, take it as soon
as you remember. If it is almost time for your next regularly
scheduled dose, skip the one you forgot and continue with
your regular schedule. Do not take a double dose.

Generic Name

Pergolide Mesylate

Brand Name

Permax

Type of Drug

Anti-Parkinsonian.

Prescribed for

Parkinson's disease.

General Information

Pergolide is often used together with Levodopa or Carbidopa to control Parkinson's disease. It works by stimulating a specific kind of nerve ending in the central nervous system that is normally stimulated by the hormone dopamine. Pergolide also inhibits the production of a hormone called prolactin, involved in the production of breast milk; affects growth-hormone levels; and affects a reproductive hormone called luteinizing hormone (LH).

Cautions and Warnings

People who have had a reaction to Pergolide or other drugs derived from the fungus ergot should be cautious about using this product.

Pergolide may cause hallucinations in a large number of people. This side effect should be reported to your doctor at once.

People who are prone to abnormal heart rhythms should be cautious when taking Pergolide because of possiblity of cardiac side effects.

Animal studies have shown that Pergolide-treated female animals develop tumors of the uterus, but there is no information on this effect in humans.

Pregnancy/Breast-feeding

Pregnant women or those who might become pregnant should not use Pergolide unless the advantages of the product have been carefully weighed against the possible dangers of taking this drug while pregnant.

Nursing mothers may not use Pergolide because it interferes with milk production. Women who must take Pergolide should bottle-feed their babies.

Seniors

Older adults may take Pergolide without special consideration.

Possible Side Effects

Pergolide can affect virtually any body part or system because of its effect on basic body hormones.

The most common side effects of Pergolide are hallucinations, confusion, twisting, abnormal body movements, tiredness, sleeplessness, nausea, constipation, diarrhea, upset stomach, and runny nose. In studies of the drug, about 1 in 4 people who started to take Pergolide stopped because of drug side effects.

Some of the other, less common, side effects are generalized pain, abdominal pain, neck or back pain, migraine headaches, muscle weakness, chest pain, flu-like illness, chills, facial swelling, infections, dizziness when rising from a sitting or lying position, fainting, heart palpitations, blood pressure changes, abnormal heart rhythms, heart attack, heart failure, appetite changes, dry mouth, vomiting, stomach gas, yellow discoloration of the skin or eyes, enlarged saliva glands, stomach irritation, intestinal ulcer or obstruction, gum irritation, tooth cavities, colitis, loss of bowel control, blood in the stool, vomiting blood, muscle bone and joint pains, bursitis, muscle twitching, anxiety, tremors, depression, unusual dreams, personality changes, psychosis, changes in how you walk, loss of coordination, tingling in the hands or feet, speech problems, muscle stiffness, difficulty breathing, hiccups, pneumonia, coughing, sinus irritation, bronchitis, asthma, nosebleeds, rash, skin discoloration, skin ulcers, acne, fungus infection of the skin, eczema, hair growth, hair loss, cold sores, sweating, vision changes, double vision, conjunctivitis, cataracts, retinal detachment, blindness, eye or ear pain, middle ear infection, ringing or buzzing in the ears, deafness, taste changes, frequent or painful urination, urinary infection, blood in the urine, swelling of the arms or legs, weight gain, anemia, breast pain, painful menstruation, breast oozing, underactive thyroid, thyroid tumor, and diabetes.

Drug Interactions

Many psychoactive drugs—including the phenothiazines, the thioxanthenes, Haloperidol, Droperidol, Loxapine, Methyldopa, Molindone, Papaverine, Reserpine, and Metoclopramide—will counter the effect of Pergolide because they antagonize the effects of dopamine in the body.

Alcohol, tranquilizers, and other nervous-system depressants will increase the depressant effects of this drug.

Drugs that cause low blood pressure will exaggerate the blood-pressure-lowering effect of Pergolide.

Food Interactions

Take Pergolide with food or meals if it upsets your stomach.

Usual Dose

Start at 50 micrograms a day and gradually increase by 100 to 250 micrograms every third day until an effect is achieved. Maximum dose is 5 milligrams (5000 micrograms) a day.

Overdosage

Symptoms of a Pergolide overdose may include nausea, vomiting, agitation, low blood pressure, hallucinations, involuntary body and muscle movements, tingling in the arms or legs, heart palpitation, abnormal heart rhythms, and nervous-system stimulation. Overdose victims should be taken to a hospital emergency room for treatment. ALWAYS bring the medicine bottle with you.

Special Information

Many people taking Pergolide for the first time experience dizziness and fainting caused by low blood pressure. Your doctor will gradually increase your Pergolide dose to avoid this effect. However, any dizziness or fainting should be reported to your doctor at once. Do not stop taking Pergolide or change your dose without your doctor's knowledge.

Other side effects to report to the doctor include any nervous-system effects of Pergolide (confusion, uncontrolled body movements, hallucinations), pain or burning on urination, high blood pressure, severe headache, seizures, sudden vision changes, sudden weakness, severe chest pain, fainting, rapid heartbeat, severe nausea, excessive sweating, nervousness, unexplained shortness of breath, and weakness. In addition, make sure your doctor knows about any side effect that is particularly bothersome or persistent.

It is important to maintain regular contact with your doctor while taking Pergolide to allow for observation of drug effects and side effects.

People taking Pergolide must be careful when performing tasks requiring concentration and coordination because of the chance that the drug will make them tired, dizzy, or lightheaded.

Dry mouth can be avoided by using sugarless gum, candy, ice, or a saliva substitute.

If you take Pergolide once a day and forget to take a dose, take it as soon as you remember. If it is almost time for your next dose, skip the one you forgot and continue with your regular schedule. Do not take a double dose.

If you take it twice a day and forget a dose, take it as soon as you remember. If it is almost time for your next dose, take one dose as soon as you remember and another in 5 or 6 hours, then go back to your regular schedule. Do not take a double dose.

If you take Pergolide 3 times a day and forget a dose, take it as soon as you remember. If it is almost time for your next dose, take one dose as soon as you remember and another in 3 or 4 hours, then go back to your regular schedule. Do not take a double dose.

Generic Name

Phendimetrazine Tartrate

Brand Names

Anorex	Plegine
Bacarate	Trimstat
Bontril PDM	Trimtabs
Melfiat	Weh-less
Metra	Weightrol
Obalan	

Sustained-Release Products

Adipost	Prelu-2
Bontril Slow-Release	Slyn-LL
Dyrexan-OD	Trimcaps
Melfiat-105	Weh-less Timecelles

(Also available in generic form)

Type of Drug

Nonamphetamine appetite suppressant.

Prescribed for

Suppression of appetite and treatment of obesity.

General Information

Although Phendimetrazine Tartrate is not an amphetamine, it can produce the same adverse effects as the amphetamine appetite suppressants. There are several other nonamphetamine appetite suppressants, including Phenmetrazine Tartrate (Preludin), which is closely related to Phendimetrazine Tartrate and has similar actions and effects.

Cautions and Warnings

Do not use Phendimetrazine Tartrate if you have heart disease, high blood pressure, thyroid disease, or glaucoma, or if you are sensitive or allergic to this or similar drugs. Prolonged use of this drug may be habit-forming.

Pregnancy/Breast-feeding

This drug may cause birth defects or interfere with your baby's development. Check with your doctor before taking it if you are, or might be, pregnant.
   This drug may pass into breast milk and should be avoided if you are nursing.

Seniors

Older adults should not take this medicine unless it is prescribed by a doctor. It can aggravate diabetes and high blood pressure, conditions common to older adults.

Possible Side Effects

Common side effects are a false sense of well-being, nervousness, overstimulation, restlessness, and trouble sleeping. Other side effects are palpitations, high blood pressure, drowsiness, sedation, weakness, dizziness, tremor, headache, dry mouth, nausea, vomiting, diarrhea and other intestinal disturbances, rash, itching, changes in sex drive, hair loss, muscle pain, difficulty in passing urine, sweating, chills, blurred vision, fever.

Drug Interactions

Do not take Phendimetrazine Tartrate if you take other stimulants or antidepressants.

This drug may reduce the effectiveness of antihypertensive drugs.

Food Interactions

Take this drug before meals.

Usual Dose

Tablets: 35 milligram tablet 1 hour before meals 2 to 3 times per day.

Sustained-release capsules: 105 milligrams once per day in the morning.

Overdosage

Symptoms are restlessness, tremor, shallow breathing, confusion, hallucinations, and fever, followed by fatigue and depression, with additional symptoms such as high or possibly low blood pressure, cold and clammy skin, nausea, vomiting, diarrhea, and stomach cramps. The patient should be taken to a hospital emergency room immediately. ALWAYS bring the medicine bottle.

Special Information

Use for no more than 12 weeks as an adjunct to diet, under strict supervision of your doctor.

Medicine alone will not take off weight. You must limit and modify your food intake, preferably under medical supervision.

This drug can cause dry mouth, which may be relieved by sugarless gum, candy, or ice chips.

If you take Phendimetrazine Tartrate once a day and forget to take a dose, take it as soon as you remember. If it is almost time for your next regularly scheduled dose, skip the one you forgot and continue with your regular schedule. Do not take a double dose.

If you take it 2 to 3 times a day and forget to take a dose, and you remember within about an hour of your regular time, take it right away. If you do not remember until later, skip the forgotten dose and go back to your regular schedule. Do not take a double dose.

Generic Name

Phenmetrazine

Brand Name

Preludin

Type of Drug

Nonamphetamine appetite suppressant.

Prescribed for

Short-term (2 to 3 months) appetite suppression; treating obesity.

General Information

Although this medicine is not an amphetamine, it has many of the same effects as amphetamine drugs and suppresses appetite by working on specific areas in the brain. The effects of a single dose of Phenmetrazine can last from 4 to 6 hours (non-sustained release).

Cautions and Warnings

Do not take Phenmetrazine if you have heart disease, high blood pressure, thyroid disease, or glaucoma, or if you are sensitive or allergic to this or other appetite suppressants.

Do not use this medicine if you are prone to emotional agitation or drug abuse.

Pregnancy/Breast-feeding

Studies have shown that Phenmetrazine can affect an unborn baby. The use of this and other appetite suppressants should be avoided by women who are or could become pregnant, unless the potential benefit outweighs any possible drug hazard.

It is not known if Phenmetrazine passes into breast milk. Nursing mothers should not take this or any other appetite suppressant.

Seniors

Older adults should not take this medicine unless it is prescribed by a doctor. It can aggravate diabetes or high blood pressure, conditions common to older adults.

Possible Side Effects

Common side effects are a false sense of well-being, nervousness, overstimulation, restlessness, and trouble sleeping. Other, less common, side effects are palpitations, high blood pressure, drowsiness, sedation, weakness, dizziness, tremor, headache, dry mouth, nausea, vomiting, diarrhea and other intestinal disturbances, rash, itching, changes in sex drive, hair loss, muscle pains, difficulty urinating, sweating, chills, blurred vision and fever.

Drug Interactions

Taking other stimulants together with Phenmetrazine may result in excessive stimulation. Taking this medicine within 14 days of any monoamine oxidase (MAO) inhibitor drug may result in severe high blood pressure.

Appetite suppressants may reduce the effects on some medicines used to treat high blood pressure.

Food Interactions

This medicine is best taken on an empty stomach; it should be taken 1 hour before meals.

Usual Dose

25 milligrams (1 tablet) 2 to 3 times per day, 1 hour before meals.

Sustained-release: 75 milligrams (1 capsule) once a day.

Overdosage

Symptoms of overdose are restlessness, tremor, shallow breathing, confusion, hallucinations, and fever, followed by fatigue and depression. Additional symptoms are changes in blood pressure, cold and clammy skin, nausea, vomiting, diarrhea, and stomach cramps. Take the victim to a hospital emergency room immediately. ALWAYS bring the medicine bottle.

Special Information

Do not take this medicine for more than 12 weeks as part of a weight control program, and take it only under a doctor's supervision. This medicine will not reduce body weight by itself. You must limit or modify your food intake.

This drug can cause dry mouth, which can be relieved by sugarless candy, gum, or ice chips.

If you forget to take a dose of Phenmetrazine, take it as soon as you remember. If it is almost time for your next regularly scheduled dose, skip the one you forgot and continue with your regular schedule. Do not take a double dose.

Generic Name

Phenobarbital

Brand Names

Barbita
Solfoton

(Also available in generic form)

Type of Drug

Hypnotic; sedative; anticonvulsive.

Prescribed for

Epileptic seizures; convulsions; as an anticonvulsive; as a daytime sedative; as a mild hypnotic (sleeping medication); for eclampsia (toxemia in pregnancy).

General Information

Phenobarbital, like the other barbiturates, appears to act by interfering with nerve impulses to the brain. When used as an anticonvulsive, Phenobarbital is not very effective by itself, but when used with anticonvulsive agents such as Phenytoin, the combined action of Phenobarbital and Phenytoin is dramatic. This combination has been used very successfully to control epileptic seizures.

Cautions and Warnings

Phenobarbital may slow down your physical and mental reflexes, so you must be extremely careful when operating machinery, driving an automobile, or performing other potentially dangerous tasks. Phenobarbital is classified as a barbiturate; long-term or unsupervised use may cause addiction. Barbiturates are neutralized in the liver and eliminated from the body through the kidneys: consequently, people who have liver or kidney disorders—namely, difficulty in forming or excreting urine—should be carefully monitored by their doctors when taking Phenobarbital.

If you have known sensitivities or allergies to barbiturates, if you have previously been addicted to sedatives or hypnotics, or if you have a disease affecting the respiratory system, you should not take Phenobarbital.

Pregnancy/Breast-feeding

There is an increased chance of birth defects when women use Phenobarbital during pregnancy. Phenobarbital may be required to be used if a serious situation arises which threatens the mother's life.

Regular use of any barbiturate during the last 3 months of pregnancy can cause the baby to be born dependent on the medicine. Also, barbiturate use increases the chance of bleeding problems, brain tumors, and breathing difficulties in the newborn.

Barbiturates pass into breast milk and can cause drowsiness, slow heartbeat, and breathing difficulty in nursing infants.

Seniors

Older adults are more sensitive to the effects of barbiturates, especially nervousness and confusion, and often require a lower dose than a younger adult to do the same job. Follow your doctor's directions and report any side effects at once.

Possible Side Effects

Drowsiness, lethargy, dizziness, hangover, difficulty in breathing, skin rash, and general allergic reaction such as runny nose, watering eyes, and scratchy throat.

Less common side effects are nausea, vomiting, diarrhea. More severe adverse reactions may include anemia and yellowing of the skin and eyes.

Drug Interactions

Interaction with alcohol, tranquilizers, the antibiotic Chloramphenicol, or other sedatives increases the sedative effect of Phenobarbital.

Interaction with anticoagulants (blood-thinning agents) can reduce their effect. This is also true of muscle relaxants, other anticonvulsants, Quinidine, Theophylline, Metronidazole, Phenmetrazine, birth control pills, and Acetaminophen. Phenobarbital has been shown to reduce the potency of the antibiotic Doxycycline.

Food Interactions

This medicine is best taken on an empty stomach, but may be taken with food if it upsets your stomach.

Usual Dose

As an anticonvulsant: 50 to 100 milligrams 2 to 3 times per day.

As a hypnotic (for sleep): 100 to 320 milligrams at bedtime.

As a sedative: 15 to 120 milligrams in 2 to 3 divided doses.

Specific dose is determined by patient's size, weight, and physical condition.

Overdosage

Symptoms are difficulty in breathing, decrease in size of the
pupils of the eyes, lowered body temperature progressing to
fever as time passes, fluid in the lungs, and eventually coma.

Anyone suspected of having taken an overdose must be
taken to the hospital for immediate care. ALWAYS bring the
medicine bottle to the emergency room physician so he can
quickly and correctly identify the medicine and start treatment.
Severe overdosage of this medication can kill; the drug has
been used many times in suicide attempts.

Special Information

Avoid alcohol and other drugs that depress the nervous system while taking this barbiturate.

Be sure to take this medicine according to your doctor's
direction. Do not change your dose without your doctor's
approval.

This drug causes drowsiness and poor concentration and
makes it more difficult to drive a car, operate machinery, or
perform complicated activities.

Call your doctor at once if you develop fever, sore throat,
nosebleeds, mouth sores, unexplained black-and-blue marks,
easy bruising or bleeding.

If you forget to take a dose of Phenobarbital, take it as
soon as you remember. If it is almost time for your next
regularly scheduled dose, skip the one you forgot and continue with your regular schedule. Do not take a double dose.

Generic Name

Phensuximide

Brand Name

Milontin

Type of Drug

Anticonvulsant.

Prescribed for

Control of petit mal seizures.

General Information

Phensuximide and the other succinimide-type anticonvulsants control petit mal seizures by slowing the transmission
of impulses through certain areas of the brain. Generally,
Ethosuximide is prescribed first for this type of seizure. Phensuximide may be prescribed if Ethosuximide does not
work. If the succinimides are ineffective, the condition may
then be treated with Clonazepam.

Cautions and Warnings

Phensuximide may be associated with severe reductions in
white-blood-cell and platelet counts. Your doctor should
perform periodic blood counts while you are taking this
medicine.

In patients with grand mal and petit mal, succinimide-type
anticonvulsants, when used alone, may increase the number
of grand mal seizures and necessitate more medicine to control those seizures.

Abrupt withdrawal of any anticonvulsant may lead to severe seizures. It is important that your dosage be reduced
gradually by your doctor.

Pregnancy/Breast-feeding

This drug should be avoided by women who may become
pregnant while using it and by pregnant and nursing mothers, since it will cross into the developing baby, and possible
adverse effects on the infant are not known. In those situations where it is deemed essential, the potential risk of the
drug must be carefully weighed against any benefit it might
produce.

Recent reports suggest a strong association between the
use of anticonvulsant drugs and birth defects. Although
most of the information pertains to Phenytoin and Phenobarbital, not Phensuximide, other reports indicate a general
association between all anticonvulsant drug treatments and
birth defects. It is possible that the epileptic condition itself
or genetic factors common to people with seizure disorders
may also figure in the higher incidence of birth defects.

Mothers taking Phensuximide should not breast-feed because of the possibility that the drug will pass into their breast milk and affect the baby. Use an alternative feeding method.

Seniors

Older adults may take this medication without special restriction. Follow your doctor's directions and report any side effects at once.

Possible Side Effects

Nausea, vomiting, upset stomach, stomach cramps and pain, loss of appetite, diarrhea, constipation, weight loss, drowsiness, dizziness, and poor muscle control.

Less common side effects include reductions in white-blood-cell and platelet counts, nervousness, hyperactivity, sleeplessness, irritability, headache, blurred vision, unusual sensitivity to bright lights, hiccups, a euphoric feeling, a dreamlike state, lack of energy, fatigue, confusion, mental instability, mental slowness, depression, sleep disturbances, nightmares, loss of the ability to concentrate, aggressiveness, constant concern with well-being and health, paranoid psychosis, suicidal tendencies, increased sex drive, rash, itching, frequent urination, kidney damage, blood in the urine, swelling around the eyes, hair loss, hairiness, muscle weakness, nearsightedness, vaginal bleeding, and swelling of the tongue and/or gums.

Drug Interactions

The depressant effects of Phensuximide are increased by tranquilizers, sleeping pills, narcotic pain relievers, antihistamines, alcohol, monoamine oxidase (MAO) inhibitors, antidepressants, and other anticonvulsants.

Phensuximide may increase the action of Phenytoin by increasing the blood levels of that drug. Your doctor should be sure that your dosages of the 2 drugs are appropriate to your condition.

Carbamazepine, another medicine prescribed to treat seizure disorders, may interfere with Phensuximide action by increasing the rate at which it is removed from the body.

The action of Phensuximide may be increased by Isoniazid, prescribed for tuberculosis prevention, and by Valproic Acid, another anticonvulsant drug, possibly leading to an increase in drug side effects when both drugs are taken together.

Food Interactions

Phensuximide is best taken on an empty stomach but may be taken with food if it upsets your stomach.

Usual Dose

500 to 1000 milligrams 2 or 3 times per day, with weekly adjustments to meet your individual needs.

Dosage adjustments may be required for people with reduced kidney or liver function.

Overdosage

Phensuximide overdose will cause exaggerated side effects. If the overdose is discovered immediately, it may be helpful to make the victim vomit. All victims of Phensuximide overdose must be taken to a hospital emergency room for treatment. ALWAYS bring the prescription bottle with you.

Special Information

Phensuximide will color your urine pink or red-brown. This is harmless and should be ignored.

Call your doctor if side effects become intolerable. Especially important are sore throat, joint pains, unexplained fever, rashes, unusual bleeding or bruising, drowsiness, dizziness, and blurred vision. Be sure to tell your doctor if you become pregnant while taking this medicine.

Phensuximide may interfere with your ability to drive a car or perform other complex tasks because it can cause drowsiness and difficulty concentrating.

Your doctor should perform periodic blood counts while you are taking this drug to check for possible adverse drug effects.

Do not suddenly stop taking this medicine, since to do so can result in severe seizures. The dosage must be discontinued gradually by your doctor.

Carry identification or wear a bracelet indicating that you suffer from a seizure disorder for which you take Phensuximide.

If you forget to take a dose of Phensuximide, take it as soon as possible. However, if it is within 4 hours of your next dose, skip the forgotten dose and go back to your regular schedule. Do not take a double dose.

Generic Name

Phentermine Hydrochloride

Brand Names

Adipex-P
Dapex 37.5
Fastin
Ionamin
Obe-Nix

Obephen
Obermin
Obestin-30
Phentrol

(Also available in generic form)

Type of Drug

Nonamphetamine appetite suppressant.

Prescribed for

Suppression of appetite and treatment of obesity.

General Information

Although Phentermine Hydrochloride is not an amphetamine, it can produce the same adverse effects as the amphetamine appetite suppressants.

The effects of a single dose of Phentermine Hydrochloride can last from 4 to 6 hours. The sustained-release lasts all day.

Cautions and Warnings

Do not use Phentermine Hydrochloride if you have heart disease, high blood pressure, thyroid disease, or glaucoma, or if you are sensitive or allergic to this or similar drugs. Prolonged use of this drug may be habit-forming.

Pregnancy/Breast-feeding

This drug may cause birth defects or interfere with your baby's development. Check with your doctor before taking it if you are, or might be, pregnant.

This drug may pass into breast milk and should be avoided if you are nursing.

Seniors

Older adults should not take this medicine unless it is prescribed by a doctor. It can aggravate diabetes and high blood pressure, conditions common to older adults.

Possible Side Effects

Common side effects are a false sense of well-being, nervousness, overstimulation, restlessness, and trouble sleeping.

Other side effects are palpitations, high blood pressure, drowsiness, sedation, weakness, dizziness, tremor, headache, dry mouth, nausea, vomiting, diarrhea and other intestinal disturbances, rash, itching, changes in sex drive, hair loss, muscle pain, difficulty in passing urine, sweating, chills, blurred vision, and fever.

Drug Interactions

Do not take Phentermine Hydrochloride if you take other stimulants or antidepressants.

Phentermine Hydrochloride may reduce the effectiveness of antihypertensive drugs.

Food Interactions

Take this drug before meals.

Usual Dose

Adult: 8 milligrams ½ hour before meals, or 15 to 37.5 milligrams once a day before breakfast.

Child: not recommended.

Overdosage

Symptoms are restlessness, tremor, shallow breathing, confusion, hallucinations, and fever followed by fatigue and depression, with additional symptoms such as high or possibly low blood pressure, cold and clammy skin, nausea, vomiting, diarrhea, and stomach cramps. The patient should be taken to a hospital emergency room immediately. ALWAYS bring the medicine bottle.

Special Information

Use only for a few weeks as an adjunct to diet, under strict supervision of your doctor.

Medicine alone will not take off weight. You must limit and modify your food intake, preferably under medical supervision.

This drug can cause dry mouth, which can be relieved by sugarless gum, candy, or ice chips.

If you forget to take a dose of Phentermine Hydrochloride, and you remember within about an hour of your regular time, take it right away. If you do not remember until later, skip the forgotten dose and go back to your regular schedule. Do not take a double dose.

Generic Name

Phenylbutazone

Brand Name

Butazolidin

(Also available in generic form)

Type of Drug

Anti-inflammatory agent.

Prescribed for

Local inflammation of bone joints that cannot be controlled by Aspirin or other anti-inflammatory drugs. Some examples are gout, rheumatoid arthritis, osteoarthritis, and bursitis.

General Information

This drug should never be taken without strict medical supervision. Phenylbutazone should be used only for the short-term relief of pain due to inflammation of muscles, tendons, and joint area. It has anti-inflammatory, analgesic, and fever-reducing properties. This drug is quite useful but is limited by its side effects and adverse drug reactions.

Phenylbutazone and its sister drug Oxyphenbutazone are toxic and dangerous and should be used only when absolutely necessary. The list of potential side effects is long. Therefore, any change in habits or unusual effect which may be even remotely connected with the use of these drugs should be reported immediately to your doctor.

Cautions and Warnings

You should not take Phenylbutazone if you have a history of symptoms associated with gastrointestinal inflammation or ulcer, including severe, recurrent, or persistent upset stomach. This drug is not a simple pain reliever and should never be taken casually. It should not be prescribed before a careful and detailed history, plus physical and laboratory tests, have been completed by the doctor. Always discuss your state of health and medical history with your doctor completely before taking this medicine. If your problem can be treated by a less toxic drug such as Aspirin, use that first and try to avoid taking Phenylbutazone. Never take more than the recommended dosage: This would lead to toxic effects. If you have blurred vision, fever, rash, sore throat, sores in the mouth, upset stomach or pain in the stomach, feeling of weakness, bloody, black, or tarry stool, water retention, or a significant or sudden weight gain, report this to the doctor immediately. In addition, stop taking the drug. If the drug is not effective after 1 week, stop taking it.

Pregnancy/Breast-feeding

This drug crosses into the blood circulation of a developing baby. It is not recommended for use late in pregnancy because of the possibility that the drug will affect your developing baby's heart. It may delay or prolong your labor. Studies in laboratory animals have shown that this medication produces birth defects. Pregnant women, or those who might become pregnant while taking this drug, should not take it without their doctors' approval. When the drug is considered essential by your doctor, the potential risk of taking the medicine must be carefully weighed against the benefit it might produce.

This drug passes into breast milk and should not be taken if you are nursing an infant. The drug can cause severe blood problems in a nursing infant. Use an alternative feeding method if you must take this medicine.

Seniors

Seniors are more likely to develop the blood, stomach, kidney, and liver side effects of this drug because of a general reduction in kidney function. People 60 years of age and older should be limited to short periods of treatment (no more than 1 week, if possible) because of the possibility of severe, possibly fatal, reactions.

Some doctors recommend that drug dosage be reduced by half in people age 60 and older.

Possible Side Effects

The most common side effects are stomach upset, drowsiness, water retention.

Less common side effects include gastric or duodenal ulcer, ulceration or perforation of the large bowel, bleeding from the stomach, anemia, stomach pain, vomiting, vomiting of blood, nausea, diarrhea, changes in the components of the blood, water retention, disruption of normal chemical balance of the body. This drug can cause fatal or nonfatal hepatitis, black-and-blue marks on the skin, serum sickness, drug allergy serious enough to cause shock, itching, serious rashes, fever, and signs of arthritis. It has been known to cause kidney effects including bleeding and kidney stones. Phenylbutazone may be a cause of heart disease, high blood pressure, blurred vision, bleeding in the back of the eye, detachment of a retina, hearing loss, high blood sugar, thyroid disease, agitation, confusion, or lethargy.

Drug Interactions

Phenylbutazone increases the effects of anticoagulant (blood-thinning) drugs, Phenytoin, Insulin, and oral antidiabetic agents. If you are taking any of these drugs, discuss this matter with your doctor immediately.

Food Interactions

Avoid alcoholic beverages. Phenylbutazone causes stomach

upset in many patients; take your dose with food or antacids, and if stomach pain continues, notify your doctor.

Usual Dose

Adult and child (age 14 or over): 300 to 600 milligrams per day in 3 to 4 equal doses for 7 days. If dose is effective it can then be reduced to 100 to 400 milligrams per day, depending on the condition being treated.

Senior: to be given for 7 days because of high risk of severe reactions. Not to be given to senile patients.

Child (under age 14): not recommended.

Overdosage

If symptoms of nausea, vomiting, convulsions, euphoria, depression, headache, hallucinations, giddiness, dizziness, coma, rapid breathing rate, continued stomach pain, and insomnia or sleeplessness appear, contact your doctor immediately.

Special Information

This drug can make you drowsy and/or tired: Be careful when driving or operating equipment.

If you take Phenylbutazone once or twice a day and forget to take a dose, take it as soon as you remember. If it is almost time for your next regularly scheduled dose, skip the one you forgot and continue with your regular schedule. Do not take a double dose.

If you take it 3 to 4 times a day and forget to take a dose, and you remember within about an hour of your regular time, take it right away. If you do not remember until later, skip the forgotten dose and go back to your regular schedule. Do not take a double dose.

Generic Name

Phenytoin

Brand Names

Extended-Action Products

Dilantin Kapseals
Phenytoin Sodium Extended

Prompt-Acting Products

Dilantin Infatab
Dilantin-30 Pediatric
Dilantin-125 Suspension

Diphenylan Sodium
Phenytoin Sodium

(Also available in generic form)

Type of Drug

Anticonvulsant.

Prescribed for

Control of epileptic seizures.

General Information

Phenytoin is one of several drugs of the same chemical group used to control convulsions. All these drugs act by the same mechanism, although some patients may respond to some and not others.

There are 2 kinds of Phenytoin: prompt, which must be taken several times a day, and extended, which can be taken either once a day or several times a day. Many people find the extended action more convenient, but the shorter-acting product gives the doctor more flexibility in designing a daily dose schedule.

Phenytoin may or may not be used in combination with other anticonvulsants, like Phenobarbital.

Cautions and Warnings

If you have been taking Phenytoin for a long time and no longer need it, the dosage should be reduced gradually over a period of about a week. Stopping abruptly may bring on severe epileptic seizures.

Pregnancy/Breast-feeding

Phenytoin crosses into the blood circulation of a developing baby. Most mothers who take this medicine deliver healthy, normal babies, but some babies are born with cleft lip, cleft palate, and heart malformations. Also, there is a recognized group of deformities, known as "fetal hydantoin syndrome," that affects children of mothers taking this medicine (although the medicine has not been definitely implicated as the cause of these deformities). These deformities consist of abnormalities in the skull and face, small brain, growth deficiency, deformed fingernails, and mental deficiency.

Children born of mothers taking Phenytoin are more likely to have a Vitamin K deficiency, leading to serious, life-threatening hemorrhage during the first 24 hours of life. Also, the mother may be deficient in Vitamin K because of Phenytoin, leading to increased bleeding during delivery.

Phenytoin passes into breast milk and may affect a nursing infant. Use an alternative feeding method if you are taking this medication.

Seniors

Older adults break down this drug more slowly than younger adults and are more sensitive to the effects of this drug. Follow your doctor's directions and report any side effects at once.

Possible Side Effects

The most common side effects are slurred speech, mental confusion, nystagmus (a rhythmic, uncontrolled movement of the eyeballs), dizziness, insomnia, nervousness, uncontrollable twitching, double vision, tiredness, irritability, depression, tremors, headaches. These side effects will generally disappear as therapy continues and the dosage is reduced.

Less common side effects include nausea, vomiting, diarrhea, constipation, fever, rashes, balding, weight gain, numbness of the hands and feet, chest pains, retention of water, sensitivity to bright lights, especially sunlight, conjunctivitis, changes of the blood system including anemia, swollen glands. Phenytoin can cause an abnormal growth of the gums surrounding the teeth, so good oral hygiene including gum massage, frequent brushing, and appropriate dental care is very important. Occasionally Phenytoin produces unusual hair growth over the body and liver damage, including hepatitis.

Drug Interactions

A barbiturate taken with Phenytoin may increase the rate at which Phenytoin is excreted from the body; then if the barbiturate is discontinued the patient may show an in-

creased response to Phenytoin, and the dose may have to
be reduced slightly.

Warfarin, Isoniazid, Chloramphenicol, Disulfiram, Phenylbutazone, and Oxyphenbutazone can cause Phenytoin to remain in the body for a longer time, increasing the incidence
of Phenytoin side effects.

Folic acid or high doses of tricyclic antidepressant drugs
may increase seizures. The dose of Phenytoin may have to
be adjusted by your doctor.

Food Interactions

The amount of Phenytoin that is absorbed from the small
intestine can be decreased if you eat foods high in calcium
or take calcium supplements. This may result in less
Phenytoin available for action in the body.

If you get upset stomach after taking Phenytoin, take the
medicine with meals.

Usual Dose

Adult: initial dose, 300 milligrams per day. If this does
not result in satisfactory control, gradually increase to 600
milligrams per day. (The most frequent maintenance dose
is 300 to 400 milligrams per day.) Only Dilantin may be taken
once daily. The other brands of Phenytoin must be taken
throughout the day, as convenient.

Child: initial dose, 2.5 milligrams per pound of body
weight per day in 2 to 3 equally divided doses; then adjust
according to needs and response of child (normal maintenance dose, 2 to 4 milligrams per pound of body weight per
day). Children over age 6 may require the same dose as an
adult, but no child should be given more than 300 milligrams
per day.

Overdosage

Symptoms are listed in "Possible Side Effects" above. The
patient should be taken to a hospital emergency room immediately. ALWAYS bring the medicine bottle.

Special Information

If you develop a rash, sore throat, fever, unusual bleeding,
or bruising, contact your doctor immediately.

Phenytoin sometimes produces a pink-brown color in the urine; don't worry about it.

Do not change brands of Phenytoin without notifying your doctor. Dosage adjustment may be required.

If you take Phenytoin once a day and forget to take a dose, take it as soon as you remember. If it is almost time for your next regularly scheduled dose, skip the one you forgot and continue with your regular schedule. Do not take a double dose.

If you take it several times a day and forget to take a dose, and you remember within 4 hours of your regular time, take it right away. If you do not remember until later, skip the forgotten dose and go back to your regular schedule. Do not take a double dose.

Generic Name

Pilocarpine

Brand Names

Adsorbocarpine Solution
Akarpine Solution
I-Pilopine Solution
Isopto Carpine Solution

Ocusert Pilo Ocular
　Therapeutic System
Pilocar Solution
Pilopine HS Gel

(Also available in generic form)

Type of Drug

Miotic agent.

Prescribed for

Management of glaucoma (increased pressure in the eye).

General Information

Pilocarpine ophthalmic solution is the drug of choice in the treatment of open-angle glaucoma. It works on muscles in the eye to open passages so that fluid can normally flow out of the eye chamber, reducing fluid pressure inside the eye. Pilocarpine may also help reduce the amount of fluid produced within the eye.

Although used as eyedrops, the drug can affect other parts of the body, especially after long use. When this drug is prescribed, it is usually given for long periods of time, as long as eye pressure does not increase or eyesight does not worsen. The concentration of Pilocarpine is determined by the physician and is based on the severity of the disease. The usual concentration of the eyedrops is 0.5 to 4 percent. Concentrations above 4 percent are used less often. The most frequently used concentrations are 1 and 2 percent.

This drug is also marketed in a special form called Ocusert Pilo, a thin football-shaped wafer designed to continuously release the drug for 1 week. This eliminates the need for putting drops in your eyes 3 to 4 times a day. The wafer is placed under the eyelid similarly to the way contact lenses are placed. Pilopine HS is a gel rather than eyedrops. Pilocarpine is also available in many combination products. These may be useful in special circumstances.

If you use the conventional eyedrops, be very careful not to touch the eyelids or surrounding area with the dropper tip; otherwise you will contaminate the dropper and cause the medicine to become unsterile. Be sure you recap the bottle tightly in order to preserve the sterility of the medicine.

Cautions and Warnings

Pilocarpine should be used only when prescribed by an ophthalmologist. This drug should not be used if you are allergic to it.

Pregnancy/Breast-feeding

This drug has been found to be safe for use during pregnancy and breast-feeding. Remember, you should check with your doctor before taking any drug if you are pregnant, since it may be absorbed into the bloodstream.

Seniors

Older adults may take this medication without special restriction. Follow your doctor's directions and report any side effects at once.

Possible Side Effects

This drug may produce spasms of the eye muscles resulting in an aching feeling over the brow. You may also find it hard to focus your eyes. These effects are seen in younger people and will disappear with continued use. Some people may complain of decreased vision in low light.

Less commonly, allergy or itching and tearing of the eye may develop after prolonged use.

Usual Dose

Initial dose, 1 to 2 drops in the affected eye up to 6 times per day. Maintenance dose is based on severity of disease.

Ocusert Pilo: Insert into eye sac and replace weekly.

At first Pilocarpine is also placed in the healthy eye to keep it from becoming diseased.

Overdosage

After long-term use, small amounts of Pilocarpine may be absorbed by the drainage systems of the eye. If symptoms of stomach upset, nausea, vomiting, diarrhea, and cramps appear, contact your doctor immediately.

Special Information

After placing drops in your eye you may feel a stinging sensation; this is normal in the Pilocarpine solutions. You should not close your eyes tightly or blink more than normally, which removes the drops from the eye.

If you forget to take a dose of Pilocarpine, take it as soon as you remember. If it is almost time for your next regularly scheduled dose, skip the one you forgot and continue with your regular schedule. Do not take a double dose.

Generic Name

Pimozide

Brand Name

Orap

Type of Drug

Antipsychotic.

Prescribed for

Verbal and physical expressions of Gilles de la Tourette's syndrome; some cases of chronic schizophrenia.

General Information

Pimozide works on very specific brain cells, those which are stimulated by the hormone dopamine. This very specific activity allows Pimozide to be effective in reducing the verbal and physical expressions of Gilles de la Tourette's syndrome, a condition characterized by inappropriate noise, physical movement, and verbal statements. It should be used only by people with severe symptoms who are unable to tolerate Haloperidol, the usual first-line treatment for Tourette's syndrome, or for whom Haloperidol does not work.

Pimozide may be prescribed for some cases of chronic schizophrenia, but it should be used only for people without symptoms of agitation, excitement, or hyperactivity.

Cautions and Warnings

Pimozide should not be used to treat conditions other than those listed above or conditions that respond to other drugs because of Pimozide's risk for cardiac and nervous-system side effects. It should not be used for acute schizophrenia or other psychiatric disorders that may be treated with other drug therapies.

People who are sensitive or allergic to Pimozide or to other antipsychotic drugs should avoid Pimozide. People who are sensitive to Haloperidol, Loxapine, Molindone, and phenothiazine-type or thioxanthene-type antipsychotics may also be sensitive to Pimozide.

People with a history of heart disease or severe toxic depression should use this drug with caution because of the possibility that Pimozide-related side effects will worsen those situations.

Sudden cardiac death has occured in Tourette's patients taking Pimozide at doses of about 0.5 milligram per pound of body weight. Sudden death and seizures have occured at doses above 20 milligrams per day. Your doctor should do an electrocardiogram (ECG) before you start on Pimozide and periodically thereafter to monitor for signs that might lead to sudden cardiac problems. Dosage reduction at the first sign of ECG problems can avoid serious problems.

Pimozide has caused tumors in laboratory animals. Although this effect has not been seen in humans, the tendency should be taken into account in cases where the drug may have to be taken regularly for many years, especially by children with Tourette's syndrome.

Liver and kidney function are very important because Pimozide is removed from the body by these organs. Any loss of organ function must be compensated for by a smaller drug dose.

Pregnancy/Breast-feeding

Animal studies have shown that Pimozide may affect fertility (the ability to become pregnant) and the development of the fetus. As with all drug products, pregnant women or those who might become pregnant should not use this drug unless the advantages of Pimozide have been carefully weighed against the possible dangers of taking it while pregnant.

It is not known if Pimozide passes into breast milk. However, the chance of cardiac or other side effects in the nursing infant is a good enough reason for a woman who must take Pimozide to bottle-feed her baby.

Seniors

Older adults should be treated with a lower dose of Pimozide than younger patients because of the tendency to develop higher blood levels of the drug and increased sensitivity to drug side effects. In addition, older adults, especially women, are more likely to develop tardive dyskinesia (see "Possible Side Effects") and Parkinson's Disease while taking Pimozide.

Possible Side Effects

Extrapyramidal effects (unusual body movements, twisting, unusual postures, restlessness, etc.) often develop during the first few days of Pimozide treatment and generally go away if you stop taking the drug. The chance of developing these effects and their severity increase with the dosage of the drug; your doctor may prescribe additional medicines to counteract these side effects.

A potentially fatal group of symptoms called neuroleptic malignant syndrome (NMS) has been associated with antipsychotic drugs. Signs of NMS are fever, muscle stiffness, changed mental status, blood pressure changes, sweating, and abnormal heart rhythms. NMS demands that Pimozide treatment be stopped at once and that your doctor treat the individual symptoms. If you have experienced NMS in the past, you should be aware of a possible relapse when taking Pimozide and report any symptoms to your doctor immediately.

Persistent rhythmic movements of the tongue, face, mouth, or jaw, sometimes accompanied by involuntary movements of the arms or legs, may develop after relatively brief treatment with low doses of Pimozide or as the drug is being withdrawn after long-term treatment. Known as tardive dyskinesia, these symptoms may worsen as treatment is continued and the dose is increased, and they may become permanent after a time. Tardive dyskinesia is especially likely to develop in older women taking Pimozide. If the drug is stopped at the earliest sign of tardive dyskinesia (unusual tongue movements), the syndrome may not develop.

Pimozide may also cause dry mouth, constipation or diarrhea, thirst, appetite changes, belching, salivation, nausea, vomiting, upset stomach, muscle tightness, cramps and posture changes, headache, drowsiness, sedation, sleeplessness, rigidity, speech and/or handwriting changes, dizziness, tremors, fainting, depression, excitement, nervousness, behavioral changes, visual and taste disturbances, unusual sensitivity to bright lights, cataracts, spots before the eyes, swelling around the eyes, changes in urinary habits, male impotence, loss of sex drive, dizziness or fainting when rising suddenly from a sitting or lying position, blood-pressure changes, heart palpitations, chest pains, rash, sweating, skin irritations, body weight changes, menstrual disorders, and breast secretions.

Drug Interactions

Antipsychotic drugs should be used with caution in people

taking Pimozide because of the possibility of aggravating or bringing on tardive dyskinesia (see "Possible Side Effects").

Pimozide may increase the sensitivity of people with seizure disorders and their need for anticonvulsant medicine. Your doctor may have to increase your anticonvulsant dose.

Alcohol, tranquilizers, and other nervous-system depressants should be used with caution by people taking Pimozide because of the chance of increasing Pimozide-related drowsiness or sedation.

Amphetamines, Methylphenidate, and Pemoline should be discontinued before starting Pimozide because they can cause abnormal muscle movements that may be confused with Tourette's syndrome.

Antihistamines and other medicines with an anticholinergic (drying) effect should not be taken with Pimozide because of the chance that such a combination will produce more severe side effects (dry mouth, visual disturbances, urinary difficulty, etc.).

Tricyclic antidepressants, Disopyromide, Maprotiline, Quinidine, phenothiazines, and Procainamide may increase the chance for cardiac side effects of Pimozide. The combination of any of these drugs and Pimozide should be used only under a direct doctor's care. Phenothiazines may also increase the depressive and anticholinergic effects of Pimozide.

Food Interactions

Low blood-potassium levels may increase the chance of cardiac side effects associated with Pimozide. Be sure to include a sufficient supply of potassium-rich foods (bananas, tomatoes, etc.) in your diet.

Usual Dose

Adult and child (age 12 and over): 1 to 2 milligrams a day to start, increasing gradually to a maximum of 10 to 20 milligrams per day.

Child (under age 12): There is limited experience in children under 12 years, but the general recommendation is for very low doses and gradual increases because children are particularly sensitive to the effects of this drug.

Overdosage

Overdose symptoms are cardiac abnormalities, severe extra-pyramidal effects (see "Possible Side Effects"), low blood pressure, coma, and breathing difficulty. Pimozide overdose victims must be taken to a hospital emergency room at once. ALWAYS bring the medicine bottle with you.

Special Information

Pimozide can make you drowsy. Avoid alcohol, tranquilizers, and other drugs that can worsen that effect. Take care while driving or doing anything else that requires intense concentration.

Take care when rising rapidly from a sitting or lying position.

Dry mouth caused by Pimozide may increase the chance for dental cavities, oral infections, and gum disease. Dry mouth can be avoided with sugarless gum, candy, ice, or a saliva substitute. Blood disorders associated with Pimozide may delay healing and cause oral bleeding.

Do not take more Pimozide than your doctor has prescribed. People taking more than 20 milligrams a day have experienced sudden and unexpected death.

Regular visits to your doctor are important while taking this drug because of the need to monitor for cardiac or other developing side effects.

Call your doctor if dry mouth lasts 2 weeks or more or if you develop any unusual side effect, including fever, dehydration, cardiac pains or abnormal rhythms, muscle rigidity, restlessness, involuntary movements, posture changes, restlessness, or mood changes. Other symptoms should be reported if they are bothersome or unusually persistent.

If you forget to take a dose of Pimozide, take the forgotten dose as soon as you remember and divide the remaining doses equally throughout the rest of the day. Do not take a double dose.

Generic Name
Pindolol

Brand Name
Visken

Type of Drug
Beta-adrenergic blocking agent.

Prescribed for
High blood pressure.

General Information
Pindolol is a unique beta-adrenergic blocker. It is similar to Propanolol, Nadolol, and Timolol Maleate in that it works on both beta receptors in the heart and those in blood vessels. But it differs from those medications in its ability to increase the heart's activity. As a result, this drug causes less of a reduction in heart rate than the other beta blockers, making it useful for people with heart failure, who cannot take other beta blockers. Pindolol can be taken with a diuretic drug or by itself to treat high blood pressure.

Unlike other beta blockers, which can be used to treat a variety of heart conditions, migraine headaches, schizophrenia, tremors, panic, and other symptoms, Pindolol should not be taken for any purpose other than treating high blood pressure.

Cautions and Warnings
Heart failure, although far less likely with Pindolol than with the other beta blockers, is the most important caution for people taking this drug. Pindolol should not be discontinued abruptly because of the possibility of developing tremors, sweating, heart pain, palpitations, headache, and a feeling of ill health. The drug should be discontinued gradually over a period of several weeks.

Pindolol must be used with extreme caution by asthmatics and others with respiratory disease, since this and other beta blockers can worsen bronchial spasms. This effect is less prominent with Pindolol than some other drugs, but is still possible.

This drug should be stopped several days or weeks before major surgery to prevent the risk of its affecting the ability of your heart to respond during the surgical procedure.

All beta blockers can mask the signs or symptoms of diabetes and low blood sugar and an overactive thyroid. Be sure the doctor prescribing Pindolol knows your complete medical history.

This drug must be used with caution by people with severe liver disease.

Pregnancy/Breast-feeding

There are no adequate studies undertaken on the effects of Pindolol during pregnancy. This drug should be avoided by pregnant women or women who may become pregnant while using it. In those situations where it is deemed essential, the potential risk of the drug must be carefully weighed against any benefit it might produce.

Nursing mothers who must take Pindolol should use an alternative method of feeding their infants since the drug definitely passes into breast milk.

Seniors

Older adults may be more or less sensitive to the effects of this medication. Your dosage of this drug must be adjusted to your individual needs by your doctor. Seniors may be more likely to suffer from cold hands and feet and reduced body temperature, chest pains, a general feeling of ill health, sudden difficulty breathing, sweating, or changes in heartbeat because of this medicine.

Possible Side Effects

Most side effects are mild and will pass on their own. The most common are anxiety, bizarre dreams, hallucinations, dizziness, fatigue or tiredness, lethargy, difficulty sleeping, nervousness, weakness, visual disturbances, tingling in the hands or feet, breathing difficulty, retention of fluid, heart failure, heart palpitations, weight gain (when the drug is taken alone), chest and joint pains, muscle cramps and pain, nausea, abdominal discomfort and pain, itching, and rash.

Less common side effects include sore throat, fever, slowing of the heart, coldness of the arms or legs, leg pains, stroke, fainting, low blood pressure, rapid heartbeat, abnormal heart rhythms, depression, loss of the ability to concentrate, sedation, odd behavior and disorientation (especially in older adults), memory loss, emotional upset, slurred speech, ringing or buzzing in the ears, light-headedness, changes in blood-sugar level (up or down), stomach gas and pain, constipation, diarrhea, dry mouth, vomiting, loss of appetite, bloating, loss of sexual potency and/or drive, difficulty urinating, skin discoloration, sweating, hair loss, dry skin, eye irritation or discomfort, and dry or burning eyes.

Drug Interactions

Chlorpromazine, Cimetidine, Furosemide, Hydralazine Hydrochloride, oral contraceptive pills, and Reserpine increase Pindolol's effect on the body.

Indomethacin and Aspirin or Aspirin-containing drugs may counteract the blood-pressure-reducing effect of Pindolol.

Beta blockers, such as Pindolol, can antagonize the effects of Theophylline. They can increase the effects of Insulin and can worsen the body's reaction to the sudden discontinuation of Clonidine (taken for high blood pressure) and the usual "first dose" reaction to Prazosin Hydrochloride.

Food Interactions

Take this medicine with food if it upsets your stomach.

Usual Dose

Up to 60 milligrams per day has been used successfully.

Overdosage

The symptoms of Pindolol overdose can include a drastic reduction in heart rate, heart failure, very low blood pressure, breathing difficulty because of bronchial muscle spasm, seizures, delirium, coma, and possible loss of consciousness. Very large Pindolol overdoses can cause your heart to beat faster and blood pressure to increase. Patients taking an overdose of this drug must be made to vomit with Syrup of Ipecac (available at any pharmacy) to remove any remaining drug from the stomach. Call your doctor or a poison control center before doing this. If you must go to a hospital emergency room, ALWAYS bring the medicine bottle.

Special Information

Don't stop taking this medicine without your doctor's specific knowledge and approval. Sudden discontinuation could result in heart pains or other symptoms.

Call your doctor if it becomes gradually more difficult to breathe while you are taking Pindolol, especially when you are lying down, when you cough at night, or when you retain fluid in your legs. These may be signs of heart failure. Other symptoms to tell your doctor about are slow pulse, dizziness, light-headedness, depression, confusion, rash, fever, sore throat, and unusual bleeding or bruising.

Since Pindolol can cause loss of concentration and visual disturbances, be careful while driving or operating machinery.

If you forget to take a dose of Pindolol, take it as soon as possible. However, if it is within 8 hours of your next dose, skip the forgotten dose and go back to your regular schedule. Do not take a double dose.

Generic Name

Pirbuterol Acetate

Brand Name

Maxair Inhaler

Type of Drug

Bronchodilator.

Prescribed for

Asthma and bronchospasm.

General Information

Pirbuterol is currently available only as an inhalation. It may be taken in combination with other medicines to control your asthma. The drug starts working 3 to 4 minutes after it is taken and continues to work for 5 to 8 hours. It can be used only when necessary to treat an asthmatic attack or on a regular basis to prevent an attack.

Cautions and Warnings

Pirbuterol should be used with caution if you have had angina, heart disease, high blood pressure, a history of stroke or seizures, diabetes, prostate disease, or glaucoma.

Pregnancy/Breast-feeding

Pirbuterol should be used by a pregnant or breast-feeding woman only when it is absolutely necessary. The potential benefit of using this medicine must be weighed against the potential, but unknown, hazard it can pose to your baby.

Seniors

Older adults are more sensitive to the effects of this drug. Follow your doctor's directions closely and report any side effects at once.

Possible Side Effects

Pirbuterol's side effects are similar to those associated with other bronchodilator drugs. The most common side effects are restlessness, weakness, anxiety, fear, tension, sleeplessness, tremors, convulsions, dizziness, headache, flushing, loss of appetite, pallor, sweating, nausea, vomiting, and muscle cramps.

Less common side effects include angina, abnormal heart rhythms, heart palpitations, high blood pressure, and urinary difficulty. Pirbuterol has been associated with abnormalities in blood tests for the liver and white blood cells and with tests for urine protein, but the true importance of this reaction is not known.

Drug Interactions

Pirbuterol's effects may be enhanced by monoamine (MAO) inhibitor drugs, antidepressants, thyroid drugs, other bronchodilators, and some antihistamines. It is antagonized by the beta-blocking drugs (Propranolol and others).

Pirbuterol may antagonize the effects of blood-pressure-lowering drugs, especially Reserpine, Methyldopa, and Guanethidine.

Food Interactions

Pirbuterol does not interact with food, since it is taken only
by inhalation into the lungs.

Usual Dose

Adult and child (over age 12): 1 or 2 inhalations every 4
to 6 hours. Do not take more than 12 inhalations per day.

Overdosage

Pirbuterol overdosage can result in exaggerated side effects,
including heart pains and high blood pressure, although the
pressure can drop after a short period of elevation. People
who inhale too much Pirbuterol should see a doctor, who
may prescribe a beta-blocking drug like Atenolol or Metoprolol to counter the bronchodilator's effects.

Special Information

Be sure to follow your doctor's directions for using Pirbuterol, and do not take more than 12 inhalations of Pirbuterol
each day. Using more than is prescribed can lead to drug
tolerance and can actually cause your condition to worsen.

The drug should be inhaled during the second half of your
breath. This allows the medicine to reach more deeply into
your lungs.

Call your doctor at once if you develop chest pains, rapid
heartbeat or heart palpitations, muscle tremors, dizziness,
headache, facial flushing, or urinary difficulty, or if you still
have trouble breathing after using the medicine.

If you forget a dose of Pirbuterol, take it as soon as you
remember and then continue with your regular schedule. Do
not take a double dose or take more than your doctor has
prescribed.

Generic Name

Piroxicam

Brand Name

Feldene

Type of Drug

Nonsteroidal anti-inflammatory.

Prescribed for

Arthritis and other forms of bone and joint inflammation.

General Information

This nonsteroidal anti-inflammatory drug (NSAID) represents an entirely different chemical class than any of its predecessors. It is long-acting and usually given only once a day, characteristics that have made Piroxicam one of the most widely prescribed NSAIDs in America. Like other NSAIDs, it is thought to work by preventing the body from manufacturing hormones called prostaglandins, thus reducing pain, inflammation, and fever.

Cautions and Warnings

Piroxicam should not be used by infants or children.

Do not take this drug if you are allergic to it, to Aspirin, or to other NSAIDs. It may cause stomach ulcers.

All patients taking this drug should have regular eye examinations since it may cause blurred vision or other problems.

Pregnancy/Breast-feeding

This drug may cause birth defects or interfere with your baby's development. Check with your doctor before taking it if you are, or might be, pregnant.

Piroxicam has not been shown to cause problems during breast-feeding. It may reduce the amount of milk you make.

Seniors

Older adults are more sensitive to the stomach, liver, and kidney side effects of this drug. Some doctors recommend that people age 70 and older take half the usual dose. Follow your doctor's directions and report any side effects at once.

Possible Side Effects

The most common side effects are upset stomach, nausea, iron deficiency, and blood loss through the gastrointestinal tract.

Piroxicam may also cause loss of appetite, abdominal discomfort, constipation, diarrhea, stomach gas or pains, indigestion, adverse effects on the blood system, reduced kidney function, dizziness, sleepiness, ringing or buzzing in the ears, headache, a sickly feeling, fluid in the arms or legs, itching, and rash. Older adults are more likely to experience side effects.

Less common side effects include reduced liver function, vomiting with or without blood, blood in the urine or stool, bleeding from the stomach, dry mouth, sweating, unusual bruising, loss of patches of skin, swollen eyes, blurred vision, eye irritations, high blood pressure, lowered blood sugar, body weight changes (either up or down), depression, nervousness, sleeplessness, heart palpitations, difficulty breathing, and difficulty in urination.

Drug Interactions

Avoid alcohol because it may increase upset stomach associated with Piroxicam or aggravate any problems with drowsiness or lack of alertness.

Piroxicam may interact with anticoagulant (blood-thinning) drugs. Although you will probably not experience a serious interaction, your doctor should monitor your anticoagulant therapy during the first few weeks of Piroxicam therapy in case any adjustment is needed.

Aspirin, in doses of 12 tablets per day or more, will reduce the effect of Piroxicam by reducing its level in the blood. These drugs should not be taken together since there is no special benefit from the combination and it may cause unwanted side effects.

Since Piroxicam may cause lowered blood-sugar levels, diabetics taking Piroxicam may need to have the dose of their antidiabetic drug reduced.

Food Interactions

If you get an upset stomach after taking Piroxicam, take it with meals.

Usual Dose

10 to 20 milligrams per day.

Overdosage

Overdose effects include drowsiness, dizziness, confusion, disorientation, tingling or numbness in the hands or feet, nausea, vomiting, upset stomach, abdominal pain, severe headache, sweating, ringing or buzzing in the ears, blurred vision, seizures, and coma. Take the overdose victim to a hospital emergency room for treatment.

Special Information

You will not feel the maximum effects of Piroxicam until you have taken the drug for 2 to 3 months, although you may begin to experience some relief as early as 2 weeks after beginning treatment.

If you develop swollen hands or feet, itching, rash, black tarry stools, vomiting, blurred vision or other visual disturbances, or unusual bruises, contact your doctor immediately.

If you forget to take a dose of Piroxicam, take it as soon as you remember. If it is almost time for your next regularly scheduled dose, skip the one you forgot and continue with your regular schedule. Do not take a double dose.

Generic Name

Potassium Replacement Products

Brand Names

Potassium Chloride Liquids

Cena-K	Klorvess
Kaochlor	Potachlor
Kaochlor S-F	Potasalan
Kaon-Cl	Rum-K
Kay Ciel	

Potassium Gluconate Liquids

Kaon	K-G Elixir
Kaylixir	My-K Elixir

Potassium Salt Liquid Combinations

Duo-K	Tri-K
Kolyum	Twin-K

Potassium Chloride Powders

Gen-K	K-Lor
Kato	Klor-Con
Kay Ciel	K-Lyte/Cl

Potassium Salt Powder Combinations

Klorvess
Kolyum

Potassium Effervescent Tablets

Effer-K	K-Lyte
Klor-Con/EF	K-Lyte/Cl
Klorvess	K-Lyte DS

Potassium Chloride Controlled Release

Kaon-Cl	K-Tab
K-Dur	Micro-K
Klor-Con	Slow-K
Klotrix	Ten-K
K-Norm	

Potassium Gluconate Chewable Product

Osto-K

(Potassium Chloride and Gluconate are also available in generic form)

Type of Drug

Potassium supplement.

Prescribed for

Replacement of potassium in the body.

General Information

Potassium is a very important component of the body and

has a major effect in maintaining the proper tone of all body cells. Potassium is also important for the maintenance of normal kidney function; it is required for the passage of electrical impulses in the nervous system; and it has a major effect on the heart and all other muscles of the body. Potassium also plays a role in the metabolism of proteins and carbohydrates.

Potassium supplements are available in a wide variety of dosage forms to meet your individual needs. Potassium Chloride is most often used in these formulations because it contains the most potassium per unit weight. Potassium Gluconate provides about one-third as much potassium as the chloride.

Foods rich in potassium can provide a natural potassium source; they include apricots, avocados, bananas, beans, beef, broccoli, brussels sprouts, cantaloupes, chicken, dates, fish, ham, lentils, milk, potatoes, prunes, raisins, shellfish, spinach, turkey, veal, and watermelon.

Cautions and Warnings

Potassium replacement should always be monitored and controlled by your physician. Potassium tablets have produced ulceration in some patients with compression of the esophagus. Potassium supplements for these patients should be given in liquid form. Potassium tablets have been reported to cause ulcers of the small bowel, leading to hemorrhage, obstruction, and/or perforation.

Do not take Potassium supplements if you are dehydrated or experiencing muscle cramps due to excessive sun exposure. The drug should be used with caution in patients who have kidney and/or heart disease.

Pregnancy/Breast-feeding

This drug has been found to be safe for use during pregnancy. Remember, you should check with your doctor before taking any drug if you are pregnant.

Breast-feeding while taking Potassium may cause unwanted side effects in your infant. If you must take Potassium, you should temporarily stop nursing and discard pumped breast milk. Nursing can resume 1 to 2 days after stopping Potassium.

Seniors

Older adults may take this medication without special restriction. Follow your doctor's directions and report any side effects at once.

Possible Side Effects

Potassium toxicity, or overdose, is extremely rare. Toxicity can occur when high doses of Potassium supplements are taken in combination with foods high in Potassium. Common side effects are nausea, vomiting, diarrhea, and abdominal discomfort.

Less common side effects are tingling of hands and feet, listlessness, mental confusion, weakness and heaviness of legs, decreased blood pressure, and/or heart rhythm changes.

Drug Interactions

Potassium supplements should not be taken with Spironolactone, Triamterene, or combinations of these drugs because Potassium toxicity may occur.

Food Interactions

Salt substitutes may contain large amounts of Potassium. You should discuss their use with your doctor.

If stomach upset occurs, take after meals or with food.

Usual Dose

As regulated by physician; generally 20 to 60 milliequivalents per day.

Overdosage

Large overdoses of Potassium supplements may cause muscle weakness, breathing difficulty, and abnormal heart rhythms. Call a poison control center or hospital emergency room for more information.

Special Information

Directions for taking and using Potassium supplements should be followed closely. Effervescent tablets, powders, and liquids should be properly and completely dissolved or diluted in a glass of cold water or juice and drunk slowly.

Oral tablets or capsules should not be chewed or crushed and are intended to be swallowed whole.

Notify your physician if you have continued abdominal pain or black stool.

If you forget to take a dose of Potassium, and you remember within about 2 hours of your regular time, take it right away. If you do not remember until later, skip the forgotten dose and go back to your regular schedule. Do not take a double dose.

Generic Name

Pravastatin

Brand Name

Pravachol

Type of Drug

Cholesterol-lowering agent.

Prescribed for

High blood-cholesterol levels, in conjunction with a low-cholesterol diet program.

General Information

The value of Pravastatin and other drugs that reduce blood cholesterol lies in the assumption that reducing levels of blood fats reduces the chance of heart disease. Studies conducted by the National Heart, Lung, and Blood Institute have identified high levels of blood fats (cholesterol and LDL) as a cause of heart and blood-vessel disease. Drugs that can reduce the amounts of either or both of these blood fats can reduce the risk of deaths and nonfatal heart attacks.

Pravastatin reduces both total cholesterol and LDL-cholesterol counts. It also reduces levels of VLDL blood fats and triglycerides while increasing levels of HDL cholesterol and apolipoprotein B, the so-called good blood fats. A significant response is seen after 2 weeks of treatment. Blood-fat levels reach their lowest levels within 4 to 6 weeks after you start

taking this medication and remain at or close to that level
as long as you continue to take the medicine.

Cautions and Warnings

Pravastatin can aggravate existing liver disease. People with
a history of liver disease should avoid this medication. Your
doctor should take a blood sample to test your liver function
every month or so during the first year of treatment to be
sure that the drug is not adversely affecting you.

Pravastatin causes, in a small number of people, muscle
aches that can be an indication of a more serious condition.

Pregnancy/Breast-feeding

Pregnant women should not take Pravastatin. Laboratory
studies have not demonstrated a specific effect with Pravastatin. However, any drug that interferes with the natural formation of cholesterol is likely to cause birth defects because
of the essential role of cholesterol in the developing baby.
Since hardening of the arteries is a chronic, long-term condition, temporarily stopping this medication during your pregnancy should cause no problem. If you become pregnant
while taking Pravastatin, stop taking the drug immediately
and call your doctor.

Small amounts of Pravastatin pass into breast milk. Because of the chance for severe side effects in the nursing
baby, women taking this medication must use an alternative
feeding method.

Seniors

Special precautions are not necessary for older adults taking
Pravastatin. Most seniors can achieve the maximum effects
of Pravastatin with 10 to 20 milligrams a day. Be sure to
report any side effects to your doctor.

Possible Side Effects

Most people who take Pravastatin tolerate it very well. Studies of the drug revealed that less than 2 out of every 100
had to stop taking it because of intolerable side effects, virtually the same number of people who stopped taking a placebo (inactive product) for the same reason.

The most common side effect of Pravastatin is headache.

Other side effects include nausea, vomiting, diarrhea, constipation, stomach gas and pains, heartburn, skin rash, dizziness, fatigue, and localized pain.

Rare side effects include chest pain, muscle aches, urinary difficulties, cough, and runny nose.

Lovastatin, a chemically similar cholesterol-lowering drug has been associated with a number of other side effects not yet seen with Pravastatin, including drug sensitivity, liver problems, and cataracts. Be sure to report anything unusual to your doctor.

Drug Interactions

The cholesterol-lowering effects of Pravastatin and Cholestyramine or Colestipol are additive when the drugs are taken together.

Gemfibrozil may interfere with the body's handling of Pravastatin. This combination is generally not recommended.

The risk of muscle problems with Pravastatin is increased if you are taking Cyclosporine, Gemfibrozil, Erythromycin, or Niacin.

Lab studies indicate that Pravastatin is not expected to increase the breakdown of other drugs metabolized by the liver, but this information has not been tested in patients. Take Pravastatin with caution if you are also taking any seizure medicine, Warfarin, Cimetidine, Digoxin, or any other drug broken down by the liver. Check with your doctor or pharmacist for more information on this potential problem.

Food Interactions

Food reduces the amount of Pravastatin absorbed into the bloodstream, but taking it with food or meals does not affect its ability to lower blood-fat levels. You may take it with food if needed to reduce the chance of upset stomach or intestinal side effects. Continue your low-cholesterol diet while taking Pravastatin.

Usual Dose

Adult: The usual dose of Pravastatin is 10 to 20 milligrams at bedtime. Your daily dosage should be adjusted about once a month and can be increased up to 40 milligrams a

day, based on your doctor's assessment of how well the
drug is working to reduce your blood cholesterol.

Child: The effect of Pravastatin in children has not been
studied.

Overdosage

Persons suspected of having taken an overdose of Pravastatin should be taken to a hospital emergency room for evaluation and treatment. ALWAYS bring the medicine bottle
with you. The effects of overdose are not well known.

Special Information

Pravastatin causes muscle aches in a small number of people. Call your doctor if this happens to you.

If you forget to take a dose of Pravastatin, take it as soon
as you remember. If it is almost time for your next regular
dose, skip the one you forgot and continue with your regular
schedule. Do not take a double dose.

Generic Name

Prazepam

Brand Name

Centrax

Type of Drug

Tranquilizer.

Prescribed for

Relief of symptoms of anxiety, tension, fatigue, or agitation.

General Information

Prazepam is a member of the group of drugs known as benzodiazepines. These drugs are used as antianxiety agents,
anticonvulsants, or sedatives (sleeping pills). They exert
their effects by relaxing the large skeletal muscles and by a
direct effect on the brain. In doing so, they can relax you
and make you either more tranquil or sleepier, depending

on the drug and how much you use. Many doctors prefer Prazepam and the other members of this class to other drugs that can be used for the same effect. Their reason is that the benzodiazepines tend to be safer, have fewer side effects, and are usually as, if not more, effective.

These drugs are generally used in any situation where they can be a useful adjunct.

Cautions and Warnings

Benzodiazepine tranquilizing drugs can be abused if taken for long periods of time and it is possible to develop withdrawal symptoms if you discontinue the therapy abruptly. Withdrawal symptoms include convulsions, tremor, muscle cramps, stomach cramps, vomiting, and sweating.

Do not take Prazepam if you know you are sensitive or allergic to this drug or other benzodiazepines such as Chlordiazepoxide, Oxazepam, Clorazepate, Diazepam, Lorazepam, Flurazepam, and Clonazepam.

Prazepam and other members of this drug group may aggravate narrow-angle glaucoma, but if you have open-angle glaucoma you may take the drugs. In any case, check this information with your doctor.

Pregnancy/Breast-feeding

This drug, like all members of the benzodiazepine family, crosses into your developing baby's circulation and may cause birth defects if taken during the first 3 months of pregnancy. You should avoid taking this medication while pregnant.

Members of the benzodiazepine family pass into breast milk. Since infants break the drug down more slowly than adults, it is possible for the medicine to accumulate and have an undesired effect on the baby.

Seniors

Older adults are more sensitive to the effects of this drug, especially dizziness and drowsiness. Follow your doctor's directions and report any side effects at once.

Possible Side Effects

The most common side effect is mild drowsiness during the

first few days of therapy, especially in older adults or the debilitated. If drowsiness persists, contact your doctor.

Less common side effects include confusion, depression, lethargy, disorientation, headache, lack of activity, slurred speech, stupor, dizziness, tremor, constipation, dry mouth, nausea, inability to control urination, changes in sex drive, irregular menstrual cycle, changes in heart rhythm, lowered blood pressure, retention of fluids, blurred or double vision, itching, rash, hiccups, nervousness, inability to fall asleep, (occasional) liver dysfunction. If you experience any of these reactions stop taking the medicine and contact your doctor immediately.

Drug Interactions

Prazepam is a central-nervous-system depressant. Avoid alcohol, tranquilizers, narcotics, sleeping pills, barbiturates, monoamine oxidase (MAO) inhibitors, antihistamines, and other medicines used to relieve depression.

Food Interactions

Prazepam is best taken on an empty stomach but may be taken with food.

Usual Dose

Adult: 20 to 60 milligrams per day as individualized for maximum benefit, depending on symptoms and response to treatment, which may require a dose outside the range given. 20 milligrams may be taken at bedtime for sleep.

Senior: usually requires less of the drug to control anxiety and tension: about 10 to 15 milligrams per day.

Overdosage

Symptoms are confusion, sleep or sleepiness, lack of response to pain such as a pin stick, shallow breathing, lowered blood pressure, and coma. The patient should be taken to a hospital emergency room immediately. ALWAYS bring the medicine bottle.

Special Information

Prazepam can cause tiredness, drowsiness, inability to concentrate, or similar symptoms. Be careful if you are driving, operating machinery, or performing other activities that require concentration.

If you forget to take a dose of Prazepam, and you remember within about an hour of your regular time, take it right away. If you do not remember until later, skip the forgotten dose and go back to your regular schedule. Do not take a double dose.

Generic Name

Prazosin Hydrochloride

Brand Name

Minipress

Type of Drug

Antihypertensive.

Prescribed for

High blood pressure. It is also prescribed for heart failure and for Raynaud's disease.

General Information

Prazosin Hydrochloride works by dilating and reducing pressure in blood vessels. It is quite effective when used in combination with a thiazide diuretic and/or beta-adrenergic blocker. It is much safer than the other drugs which work in the same way because it does not directly affect the heart.

Cautions and Warnings

This drug can cause dizziness and fainting, most often due to an effect called "postural hypotension," where blood supply to the brain is reduced when you rise suddenly from a sitting or lying-down position. This often occurs after taking the first dose of 2 milligrams or more of Prazosin Hydrochloride.

Pregnancy/Breast-feeding

This drug has not been found to cause birth defects. Pregnant women, or those who might become pregnant while taking this drug, should not take it without their doctors' approval. When the drug is considered essential by your doctor, the potential risk of taking the medicine must be carefully weighed against the benefit it might produce.

This drug has caused no problems among breast-fed infants. You must consider the potential effect on the nursing infant if breast-feeding while taking this medicine.

Seniors

Older adults should use this product with caution because of greater sensitivity to the drug's effects and side effects. Older adults are more likely to develop Prazosin-caused low body temperature (hypothermia).

Possible Side Effects

The most common side effects of Prazosin Hydrochloride are dizziness, headache, drowsiness, lack of energy, weakness, heart palpitations, and nausea. Usually these side effects subside and people become more tolerant of the drug.

Less common side effects include vomiting, diarrhea, constipation, stomach upset or pain, unusual swelling in the arms or legs, shortness of breath, passing out, rapid heart rate, increased chest pain (angina), nervousness, depression, tingling in the hands or feet, rash, itching, frequent urination, poor urinary control, sexual impotence, blurred vision, redness of the eyes, ringing or buzzing in the ears, dry mouth, stuffy nose, sweating.

Drug Interactions

Prazosin Hydrochloride's effectiveness may be lessened when it is taken together with anti-inflammatory pain relievers, especially Indomethacin; estrogen-containing drugs; or drugs with stimulant properties, such as decongestants and diet pills.

Do not take over-the-counter drugs containing stimulants. If you are unsure which ones to avoid, ask your pharmacist.

Prazosin Hydrochloride's effectiveness is increased when combined with other antihypertensive medicines.

Food Interactions

Take this medicine with food if it upsets your stomach.

Usual Dose

1 milligram 2 to 3 times per day to start; the dose may be increased to 20 milligrams a day, and 40 milligrams has been used in some cases. The daily dose of Prazosin Hydrochloride must be tailored to the patient's needs.

Overdosage

Overdosage may lead to very slow blood pressure. Call your doctor or a poison control center for advice. If you go to a hospital emergency room, remember, ALWAYS bring the medicine bottle.

Special Information

Take this drug exactly as prescribed. Do not stop taking Prazosin Hydrochloride unless directed to do so by your doctor.

Prazosin Hydrochloride can cause dizziness, drowsiness, or headache, especially when you begin taking the drug. Avoid driving or operating any equipment 4 hours after the first dose and take care for the first few days. You may want to take the first dose before you go to bed. If you experience severe dizziness, lie down and wait for the episode to pass.

If you forget to take a dose of Prazosin Hydrochloride, take it as soon as you remember. If it is almost time for your next regularly scheduled dose, skip the one you forgot and continue with your regular schedule. Do not take a double dose.

Generic Name

Prednisone

Brand Names

Deltasone	Prednicen-M
Liquid Pred	Prednisone Intensol
Meticorten	Concentrate
Orasone	Sterapred
Panasol-S	Sterapred DS

(Also available in generic form)

Type of Drug

Adrenal corticosteroid.

Prescribed for

The variety of disorders for which Prednisone is prescribed is almost endless, from skin rash to cancer. The drug may be used as a treatment for adrenal gland disease, since one of the hormones produced by the adrenal gland is very similar to Prednisone. If patients are not producing sufficient adrenal hormones, Prednisone may be used as replacement therapy. It may also be prescribed for the treatment of bursitis; arthritis; severe skin reactions, such as psoriasis or other rashes; severe allergic conditions; asthma; drug or serum sickness; severe, acute, or chronic allergic inflammation of the eye and surrounding areas, such as conjunctivitis; respiratory diseases, including pneumonitis; blood disorders; gastrointestinal diseases, including ulcerative colitis; and inflammation of the nerves, heart, or other organs.

General Information

Prednisone is one of many adrenal corticosteroids used in medical practice today. The major differences between Prednisone and other adrenal corticosteroids are potency of medication and variation in some secondary effects. Choice of an adrenal corticosteroid to be used for a specific disease is usually a matter of doctor preference and past experience. Other adrenal corticosteroids include Cortisone, Hydrocortisone, Prednisolone, Triamcinolone, Methylprednisolone, Meprednisone, Paramethasone, Fluprednisolone, Dexamethasone, Betamethasone, and Fludrocortisone.

Cautions and Warnings

Because of the effect of Prednisone on your adrenal gland, it is essential that the dose be tapered from a large dose down to a small dose over a period of time. Do not stop taking this medication suddenly or without the advice of your doctor. If you do, you may cause a failure of the adrenal gland with extremely serious consequences.

Prednisone has a strong anti-inflammatory effect and may mask some signs of infections. If new infections appear during the use of Prednisone therapy, they may be difficult to discover and may grow more rapidly due to your decreased resistance. If you think you are getting an infection during the time that you are taking Prednisone, you should contact your doctor, who will prescribe appropriate therapy.

If you are taking Prednisone, you should not be vaccinated against any infectious diseases, because Prednisone interferes with the body's normal reaction to vaccination. Discuss this with your doctor before he or she administers any vaccination.

Pregnancy/Breast-feeding

Studies have shown that corticosteroids taken in large amounts or over long periods of time can be the cause of birth defects. Pregnant women or those who might become pregnant while using this medicine should not do so unless they are under a doctor's care.

Corticosteroid drugs taken by mouth pass into breast milk and large drug doses may interfere with the growth of a nursing infant. Do not use the medicine unless under a doctor's care.

Seniors

Older adults are more likely to develop high blood pressure while taking this medicine (by mouth). Also, older women are more susceptible to osteoporosis (bone degeneration) associated with large doses of medicines in this class.

Possible Side Effects

Stomach upset is one of the more common side effects of Prednisone, which may in some cases cause gastric or duodenal ulcers. Other side effects include retention of water, heart failure, potassium loss, muscle weakness, loss of muscle mass, loss of calcium which may result in bone fractures and a condition known as aseptic necrosis of the femoral and humoral heads (the ends of the large bones in the hip degenerate from loss of calcium), slowing down of wound healing, black-and-blue marks on the skin, increased sweating, allergic skin rash, itching, convulsions, dizziness, headache.

Less common side effects are irregular menstrual cycles, slow growth in children, particularly after the medication has

been taken for long periods of time, depression of the adrenal and/or pituitary glands, development of diabetes, increased pressure of the fluid inside the eye, hypersen]
sitivity or allergic reactions, blood clots, insomnia, weight gain, increased appetite, nausea, and feeling of ill health. Psychic derangements may appear which range from euphoria to mood swings, personality changes, and severe depression. Prednisone may also aggravate existing emotional instability.

Drug Interactions

Prednisone and other adrenal corticosteroids may interact with Insulin and oral antidiabetic drugs, causing an increased requirement of the antidiabetic drugs.

Interaction with Phenobarbital, Ephedrine, and Phenytoin may reduce the effect of Prednisone by increasing its removal from the body.

If a doctor prescribes Prednisone you should discuss any oral anticoagulant (blood-thinning) drugs you are taking: The dose of them may have to be changed.

Interaction with diuretics such as Hydrochlorothiazide may cause you to lose blood potassium. Be aware of signs of lowered potassium level such as weakness, muscle cramps, and tiredness, and report them to your physician. Eat high-potassium foods such as bananas, citrus fruits, melons, and tomatoes.

Prednisone and other steroids can interfere with laboratory tests. You should notify your physician that you are taking these drugs so that the tests can be properly analyzed.

Food Interactions

If you notice a slight stomach upset when you take your dose of Prednisone, take this medication with food or a small amount of antacid. If stomach upset continues or bothers you, notify your doctor.

Usual Dose

Initial dose, 5 to 60 or more milligrams. Maintenance dose, 5 to 60 milligrams depending on patient's response.

Dose also varies according to disease being treated. The

lowest effective dose is desirable. Stressful situations may cause a need for a temporary increase in your Prednisone dose.

This drug must be tapered off slowly, not stopped abruptly. Prednisone may be given in alternate-day therapy; twice the usual daily dose is given every other day.

Overdosage

There is no specific treatment for overdosage of adrenal corticosteroids. Symptoms are anxiety, depression and/or stimulation, stomach bleeding, increased blood sugar, high blood pressure, and retention of fluid. The patient should be taken to a hospital emergency room immediately, where stomach pumping, oxygen, intravenous fluids, and other supportive treatments are available. ALWAYS bring the medicine bottle.

Special Information

Do not stop taking this medicine on your own. Suddenly stopping this or any other corticosteroid drug can have severe consequences; the dosage will be gradually reduced by your doctor.

If you miss a dose of Prednisone and you take several doses per day, take the missed dose as soon as you can. If it is almost time for your next dose, skip the missed dose and double the next dose.

If you take one dose per day, and you do not remember the missed dose until the next day, skip the missed dose and take your usual dose. Do not double up your dose.

If you take Prednisone every other day, take the missed dose if you remember it that morning. If it is much later in the day, skip the missed dose and take it the following morning, then go back to your usual dose schedule.

Generic Name

Primidone

Brand Name

Mysoline

(Also available in generic form)

Type of Drug

Anticonvulsant.

Prescribed for

Control of epileptic and other seizures.

General Information

Although this drug is not a barbiturate, it is a close chemical cousin to the barbiturates and possesses many of their characteristics. It acts on a portion of the brain that inhibits the usual nerve transmissions that are present in seizure disorders.

Primidone may be used in combination with other anticonvulsant drugs to achieve the best results.

Cautions and Warnings

If you have been taking Primidone for a long time and no longer need it, do not stop abruptly, but reduce the dosage gradually over a period of about a week. Stopping abruptly may bring on severe epileptic seizures.

Pregnancy/Breast-feeding

Primidone crosses into the blood circulation of a developing baby. Most mothers who take this medicine deliver healthy, normal babies, but some are born with cleft lip, cleft palate, and heart malformations. Also, there is a recognized group of deformities, known as "fetal hydantoin syndrome," that affects children of mothers taking this medicine (although the medicine has not been definitely implicated as the cause of these deformities). These deformities consist of abnormalities in the skull and face, small brain, growth deficiency, deformed fingernails, and mental deficiency.

Children born of mothers taking Primidone are more likely to have a Vitamin K deficiency, leading to serious, life-threatening hemorrhage during the first 24 hours of life. Also, the mother may be deficient in Vitamin K because of Primidone, leading to increased bleeding during delivery.

Primidone passes into breast milk and may affect a nursing infant. Use an alternative feeding method if you are taking this medication.

Seniors

Older adults sometimes become restless and excited while taking Primidone, the opposite of what you might expect from this medicine.

Possible Side Effects

Dizziness and some loss of muscle coordination. Side effects tend to disappear with time.

Less common side effects include fatigue, loss of appetite, nystagmus (a rhythmic, uncontrolled movement of the eyeballs), irritability, emotional upset, sexual impotence, double vision, rash. If side effects are persistent or severe, your doctor may have to discontinue treatment or use a different medication.

Drug Interactions

This drug, because of its relation to barbiturates, may affect oral anticoagulants, Doxycycline, corticosteroids, or Griseofulvin.

Special care should be taken if you need any sedative, sleeping pill, antidepressant, or strong analgesic because of the possibility of drug interaction. Consult your physician or pharmacist for more information.

Avoid alcoholic beverages, which may enhance the side effects of fatigue and dizziness normally experienced with Primidone.

Food Interactions

If you get an upset stomach after taking Primidone, take the medicine with meals.

Usual Dose

Adult and child (age 8 and over): 250 milligrams per day to start. Dose may be increased in steps of 250 milligrams per day up to 1500 milligrams per day, according to patient's need.

Child (under age 8): 125 milligrams per day to start. Dose may be increased in steps of 125 milligrams per day up to 750 milligrams per day, according to patient's need. Doses may be divided 3 to 6 times per day.

Overdosage

Symptoms are listed in "Possible Side Effects" above. The patient should be taken to a hospital emergency room immediately. ALWAYS bring the medicine bottle.

Special Information

If you develop a rash, sore throat, fever, or unusual bleeding or bruising, contact your doctor immediately.

Primidone sometimes produces a pink-brown color in the urine; this is normal and not a cause for worry.

If you forget to take a dose of Primidone, take it as soon as you remember. If it is almost time for your next regularly scheduled dose, skip the one you forgot and continue with your regular schedule. Do not take a double dose.

Generic Name

Probucol

Brand Name

Lorelco

Type of Drug

Antihyperlipidemic (blood-fat reducer).

Prescribed for

People with excessively high levels of cholesterol.

General Information

Probucol consistently reduces blood-cholesterol levels, but is prescribed only for people who have not responded to diet changes or other therapies. Probucol has little effect on blood triglycerides.

Probucol increases the body's breakdown of cholesterol, reduces the amount of cholesterol manufactured by the liver, and reduces the amount of cholesterol absorbed from foods.

Cautions and Warnings

Probucol should not be taken by people who have had allergic reactions to the drug. Probucol users may have an increased chance of developing abnormal heart rhythms and should realize that this drug, like other blood-fat reducers, including Clofibrate and Gemfibrozil, have not been proven to reduce the chances of fatal heart attacks.

Pregnancy/Breast-feeding

Animal studies of this drug have revealed no harmful effects on the developing fetus. However, because there have been no controlled studies of pregnant women, Probucol should be avoided by pregnant women or women who may become pregnant while using it. Women who are trying to become pregnant should discontinue the drug and use birth control for at least 6 months before they want to conceive, because the drug remains in the body for extended periods.

It is not known if Probucol passes into human breast milk, but this has been observed in animal studies. Nursing mothers should not breast-feed while taking this drug.

Seniors

Older adults may take this medication without special restriction. Follow your doctor's directions and report any side effects at once.

Possible Side Effects

Most side effects are mild and last for only short periods of time. The most common are diarrhea or loose stools, headaches, dizziness, and reduction in some white-blood-cell counts.

Less common side effects include abnormal heart rhythms, heart palpitations, chest pains, stomach and abdominal pains or gas, nausea, vomiting, anemia, itching, rash, male impotence, sleeplessness, conjunctivitis (red-eye), tearing, blurred vision, ringing or buzzing in the ears, loss of appetite, reduced senses of taste and/or smell, heartburn, indigestion, stomach or intestinal bleeding, easy bruising, goiter, nighttime waking to urinate, and excessive and possibly malodorous sweat.

Drug Interactions

None known.

Food Interactions

Take each dose with food or a meal to ensure better drug absorption.

Usual Dose

500 milligrams twice per day with breakfast and evening meal.

Overdosage

There are no reports of Probucol overdosage, but victims might be expected to develop exaggerated versions of the drug's side effects. Less than 10 percent of each dose of Probucol is absorbed from the stomach and intestines. Because of this, the chances are that few symptoms other than those affecting the stomach and intestines will develop. Patients taking an overdose of this drug must be made to vomit with Syrup of Ipecac (available at any pharmacy) to remove any remaining drug from the stomach. Call your doctor or a poison control center before doing this. If you must go to a hospital emergency room, ALWAYS bring the medicine bottle.

Special Information

Follow your doctor's dietary guidelines.

Probucol occasionally causes dizziness and blurred vision. Use caution while driving or doing anything else that requires concentration and alertness.

Call your doctor if any drug side effects become severe or intolerable, especially diarrhea, nausea, vomiting, or stomach pains and/or gas. These may be resolved with a reduction in drug dose.

If you forget to take a dose of Probucol, take it as soon as you remember. If it is almost time for your next regularly scheduled dose, skip the one you forgot and continue with your regular schedule. Do not take a double dose.

Generic Name

Procainamide Hydrochloride

Brand Names

Promine
Pronestyl

Sustained-Release Products

Procan SR   Rhythmin
Pronestyl SR

(Also available in generic form)

Type of Drug

Antiarrhythmic.

Prescribed for

Abnormal heart rhythms.

General Information

Procainamide Hydrochloride is frequently used as the primary treatment for arrhythmia (abnormal heart rhythms), which it controls by affecting the response of heart muscle to nervous system stimulation. It also slows the rate at which nervous system impulses are carried through the heart. It may be given to patients who do not respond to or cannot tolerate other antiarrhythmic drugs.

Cautions and Warnings

Tell your doctor if you have the disease myasthenia gravis. If you do, you should be taking a drug other than Procainamide Hydrochloride. Tell your doctor if you are allergic to Procainamide Hydrochloride or to the local anesthetic Procaine. Patients taking this drug should be under strict medical supervision.

This drug is eliminated from the body through the kidney and liver. If you have either kidney or liver disease your dose of Procainamide Hydrochloride may have to be adjusted.

Pregnancy/Breast-feeding

This drug crosses into the blood circulation of a developing baby. It has not been found to cause birth defects. Pregnant women, or those who might become pregnant while taking this drug, should not take it without their doctors' approval. When the drug is considered essential by your doctor, the potential risk of taking the medicine must be carefully weighed against the benefit it might produce.

This drug passes into breast milk, but has caused no problems among breast-fed infants. You must consider the potential effect on the nursing infant if breast-feeding while taking this medicine.

Seniors

Older adults are more sensitive to the effects of this drug, especially low blood pressure and dizziness. Follow your doctor's directions and report any side effects at once.

Possible Side Effects

Large oral doses of Procainamide Hydrochloride may produce loss of appetite, nausea, or itching. A group of symptoms resembling the disease lupus erythematosus has been reported in patients taking the drug: fever and chills, nausea, vomiting, and abdominal pains. Your doctor may detect enlargement of your liver and changes in blood tests indicating a change in the liver. Soreness of the mouth or throat, unusual bleeding, rash, or fever may occur. If any of these symptoms occur while you are taking Procainamide Hydrochloride, tell your doctor immediately.

Less common side effects are bitter taste in the mouth, diarrhea, weakness, mental depression, giddiness, hallucinations, drug allergy (such as rash and drug fever).

Drug Interactions

Avoid over-the-counter cough, cold, or allergy remedies containing drugs which have a direct stimulating effect on your heart. Ask your pharmacist to tell you about the ingredients in over-the-counter remedies.

Food Interactions

This medicine is best taken on an empty stomach, but you may take it with food if it upsets your stomach.

Usual Dose

Initial dose, 1000 milligrams. Maintenance dose, 25 milligrams per pound per day in divided doses every 3 hours, around the clock, adjusted according to individual needs.

The sustained-release products allow spacing doses 6 hours apart.

Special Information

If you forget to take a dose of Procainamide Hydrochloride, and remember within 2 hours (4 hours for long-acting Procainamide Hydrochloride), take it right away. If it is almost time for your next regularly scheduled dose, skip the one you forgot and continue with your regular schedule. Do not take a double dose.

Generic Name

Prochlorperazine

Brand Name

Compazine

(Also available in generic form)

Type of Drug

Phenothiazine antipsychotic; antinauseant.

Prescribed for

Severe nausea; vomiting; psychotic disorders; excessive anxiety; tension; agitation.

General Information

Prochlorperazine and other members of the phenothiazine group act on a portion of the brain called the hypothalamus. They affect parts of the hypothalamus that control metabolism, body temperature, alertness, muscle tone, hormone balance, and vomiting and may be used to treat problems related to any of these functions.

Cautions and Warnings

Sudden death has occurred in patients who have taken this drug because of its effect on the cough reflex. In some cases the patients choked to death because of failure of the cough reflex to protect them. Prochlorperazine, because of its effect in reducing vomiting, can obscure signs of toxicity due to overdose of other drugs or symptoms of disease.

Prochlorperazine should not be taken if you are allergic to one of the drugs in the broad classification known as phenothiazine drugs. Do not take Prochlorperazine if you have any blood, liver, kidney, or heart disease, very low blood pressure, or Parkinson's disease.

This drug should be used with caution and under strict supervision of your doctor if you have glaucoma, epilepsy, ulcers, or difficulty passing urine.

Avoid exposure to extreme heat, since this drug can affect your body's normal temperature mechanism.

Pregnancy/Breast-feeding

Infants born to women taking this medication have experienced drug side effects (liver jaundice, nervous system effects) immediately after birth. Check with your doctor about taking this medicine if you are, or might become, pregnant.

This drug may pass into breast milk and affect a nursing infant. Consider alternative feeding methods if you must take this medicine.

Seniors

Older adults are more sensitive to the effects of this medication than younger adults and usually require a lower dosage to achieve a desired effect. Also, older adults are more likely to develop drug side effects. Some experts feel that older patients should be treated with $\frac{1}{2}$ to $\frac{1}{4}$ the usual adult dose of Prochlorperazine.

Possible Side Effects

The most common side effect is drowsiness, especially during the first or second week of therapy. If the drowsiness becomes troublesome, contact your doctor.

Prochlorperazine can cause jaundice (yellowing of the

whites of the eyes or skin), usually in 2 to 4 weeks. The jaundice usually goes away when the drug is discontinued, but there have been cases when it did not. If you notice this effect or if you develop symptoms such as fever and generally not feeling well, contact your doctor immediately.

Less frequent side effects include changes in components of the blood including anemias, raised or lowered blood pressure, abnormal heart rates, heart attack, feeling faint or dizzy.

Phenothiazines can produce extrapyramidal effects, such as spasm of the neck muscles, rolling back of the eyes, convulsions, difficulty in swallowing, and symptoms associated with Parkinson's disease. These effects look very serious but disappear after the drug has been withdrawn; however, symptoms of the face, tongue, and jaw may persist for as long as several years, especially in older adults with a history of brain damage. If you experience extrapyramidal effects, contact your doctor immediately.

Prochlorperazine may cause an unusual increase in psychotic symptoms or may cause paranoid reactions, tiredness, lethargy, restlessness, hyperactivity, confusion at night, bizarre dreams, inability to sleep, depression, and euphoria. Other reactions are itching, swelling, unusual sensitivity to bright lights, red skin, and rash. There have been cases of breast enlargement, false positive pregnancy tests, changes in menstrual flow, impotence and changes in sex drive in males, as well as stuffy nose, headache, nausea, vomiting, loss of appetite, change in body temperature, pallor, excessive salivation, excessive perspiration, constipation, diarrhea, changes in urine and stool habits, worsening of glaucoma, blurred vision, weakening of eyelid muscles, and spasms in bronchial and other muscles, increased appetite, fatigue, excessive thirst, and changes in the coloration of skin, particularly in exposed areas.

Drug Interactions

Prochlorperazine should be taken with caution in combination with barbiturates, sleeping pills, narcotics, other tranquilizers, or any other medication which may produce a depressive effect.

Alcoholic beverages should be avoided. They can increase the depressant effects of Prochlorperazine.

Food Interactions

Antipsychotic effectiveness of Prochlorperazine or other members of the phenothiazine drug group may be counteracted by caffeine-containing food, such as coffee, tea, cola drinks, or chocolate.

Usual Dose

Adult: 15 to 150 milligrams per day, depending on disease and patient's response. For nausea and vomiting, 15 to 40 milligrams per day by mouth, 25 milligrams twice per day in rectal suppositories.

Child: 40 to 85 pounds, 10 to 15 milligrams per day; 30 to 40 pounds, 2.5 milligrams 2 to 3 times per day; 20 to 30 pounds, 2.5 milligrams 1 to 2 times per day; not recommended for children under age 2 or weight 20 pounds, except to save life. Usually only 1 to 2 days of therapy is needed for nausea and vomiting. For psychosis, doses of 25 milligrams or more per day may be required.

Overdosage

Symptoms are depression, extreme weakness, tiredness, desire to go to sleep, coma, lowered blood pressure, uncontrolled muscle spasms, agitation, restlessness, convulsions, fever, dry mouth, and abnormal heart rhythms. The patient should be taken to a hospital emergency room immediately. ALWAYS bring the medicine bottle.

Special Information

This medication is a tranquilizer and can have a depressive effect, especially during the first few days of therapy. Care should be taken when performing activities requiring a high degree of concentration, such as driving.

The drug may cause unusual sensitivity to the sun and can turn your urine reddish-brown to pink.

If dizziness occurs, avoid sudden changes in posture and avoid climbing stairs.

Use caution in hot weather. This medicine may make you more prone to heat stroke.

The liquid form of Prochlorperazine can cause skin irritations or rashes. Do not get it on your skin.

If you miss a dose of Prochlorperazine, take it as soon as

you can. If it is almost time for your next dose, skip the missed dose and go back to your usual dose schedule. Do not double any doses.

Generic Name

Promethazine Hydrochloride

Brand Name

Phenergan Tablets
Phenergan Plain Syrup

(Also available in generic form)

Combination products with alcohol and Codeine Phosphate:
Phenergan with Codeine Syrup
Pherazine with Codeine Syrup

(Also available in generic form)

Combination products with alcohol and Dextromethorphan Hydrobromide:
Phenergan with Dextromethorphan Liquid
Pherazine DM
Prometh with Dextromethorphan Syrup

(Also available in generic form)

Combination products with alcohol and Phenylephrine Hydrochloride:
Phenergan VC Syrup
Pherazine VC Syrup
Prometh VC Plain Liquid

(Also available in generic form)

Combination products with alcohol, Codeine Phosphate, and Phenylephrine Hydrochloride:
Mallergan VC with Codeine Syrup
Phenergan VC with Codeine Syrup
Pherazine VC with Codeine Syrup

(Also available in generic form)

Type of Drug

Antihistamine.

Prescribed for

Relief of allergy symptoms, motion sickness, nausea, and vomiting; sedation.

General Information

Promethazine is a member of the phenothiazine class of anti-histamines. It is one of the older members of the group and has been used by millions of people as an individual product and in combination with cough suppressants and deconges-tants. Many of the newer antihistamines have replaced Pro-methazine as a routine antihistamine, but it is still widely used for its other effects.

Cautions and Warnings

Promethazine should be used with caution if you are allergic to or cannot tolerate any of the other phenothiazine drugs including Chlorpromazine and Prochlorperazine. Prometha-zine should be used with care if you have heart, blood, liver, or kidney disease; very low blood pressure; or Parkinson's disease. This drug should be used with caution and under your doctor's strict supervision if you have ulcers, epilepsy, glaucoma, or urinary dificulty.

Children with a history of intermittent breathing while sleeping (sleep apnea), a family history of sudden infant death syndrome, liver disease, or Reye's syndrome should not take Promethazine.

Pregnancy/Breast-feeding

Some babies born to women who have taken other pheno-thiazines have suffered drug side effects at birth (yellow skin, nervous-system effects). Promethazine taken within 2 weeks before delivery may affect the baby's blood-clotting system. As with all drug products, pregnant women or those who might become pregnant should not use Promethazine unless its advantages have been carefully weighed against the pos-sible dangers of taking it while pregnant.

Antihistamines should not be used by nursing mothers, especially those with premature or newborn babies, because of the chance that the drugs will effect the nursing infants. Women who must take Promethazine should bottle-feed their babies.

Seniors

Seniors are more sensitive to dizziness, sedation, confusion, and low blood pressure when taking Promethazine than younger adults and should be careful when taking the drug. Nervous-system side effects, including parkinsonism and unusual or uncoordinated movements, are also more likely to develop in older adults.

Possible Side Effects

The most common side effects of Promethazine are drowsiness, mucus thickening, and sedation.

Less common side effects include sore throat and fever; unusual bleeding or bruising; tiredness or weakness; dizziness; feeling faint; clumsiness and unsteadiness; dry mouth, nose, and throat; facial redness; trouble breathing; hallucinations; seizures; muscle spasms (especially in the back and neck); restlessness; a shuffling walk; jerky movements of the head and face; shaking and trembling of the hands; blurring and other visual changes; confusion; urinary difficulties; rapid heartbeat; sensitivity to the sun; sweating; and loss of appetite.

Promethazine suppositories can cause rectal burning or stinging.

Difficulty sleeping, excitement, nervousness, restlessness, and irritability are more likely to develop in children and older adults than younger adults.

Drug Interactions

The sedative effects of Promethazine are amplified by any nervous-system depressants, including tranquilizers, alcohol, hypnotics, sedatives, antianxiety drugs, and narcotics. These combinations should be used with extreme caution.

Use of a monoamine oxidase (MAO) inhibitor drug together with Promethazine may cause low blood pressure and unusual, uncoordinated movements.

Promethazine will antagonize the effects of amphetamines and other appetite suppressants (diet pills).

The combination of Promethazine with an oral antithyroid drug may increase the chances for agranulocytosis (severe reductions in white-blood-cell count).

The combination of Quinidine and Promethazine may produce an additive cardiac effect contributed to by both drugs.

Promethazine may increase the need for anticonvulsant medicine, Bromocriptine, Guanadrel, Guanethidine, and Levodopa. Dosage adjustments may be needed.

Riboflavin requirements are increased in people taking Promethazine.

Promethazine may interfere with some blood sugar tests and some home pregnancy tests.

Food Interactions

Take Promethazine with food if it upsets your stomach.

Usual Dose

Allergy: 6.25 to 12.5 milligrams several times a day and 25 milligrams at bedtime.

Motion sickness: 25 milligrams twice a day.

Nausea and vomiting: 25 milligrams when needed, up to 6 times a day.

Sedation: 12.5 to 50 milligrams at bedtime.

Overdosage

Symptoms are likely to be drowsiness; confusion; clumsiness; dry mouth, nose, or throat; hallucinations; seizures; and other known Promethazine side effects. Overdose victims should be taken to a hospital emergency room for treatment. ALWAYS remember to bring the medicine bottle with you.

Special Information

People taking Promethazine must be careful when performing tasks requiring concentration and coordination because of the chance that the drug will make them tired, dizzy, or light-headed.

Call your doctor if you develop sore throat; fever or chills; unusual bleeding or bruising; unusual tiredness or weakness; clumsiness; unsteadiness; very dry mouth, nose, or throat; hallucinations; seizures; sleeping problems; faintness; facial flushing; or breathing difficulty or if other side effects are persistent or very bothersome.

Check with your doctor or dentist if dry mouth caused by Promethazine is not taken care of by gum or hard candies or lasts more than 2 weeks.

It is important to maintain good dental hygiene while taking this drug and to use extra care when using your toothbrush or dental floss because of the chance that the dry mouth it can cause will make you more susceptible to some infections. Dental work should be completed prior to starting on this drug.

If you take Promethazine twice a day and forget a dose, take it as soon as you remember. If it is almost time for your next dose, take one dose as soon as you remember and another in 5 or 6 hours, then go back to your regular schedule. Do not take a double dose.

If you take Promethazine 3 or more times a day and forget a dose, take it as soon as you remember. If it is almost time for your next dose, take one dose as soon as you remember and another in 3 or 4 hours, then go back to your regular schedule. Do not take a double dose.

Generic Name

Propafenone

Brand Name

Rythmol

Type of Drug

Antiarrhythmic.

Prescribed for

Life-threatening cardiac arrhythmias (abnormal heart rhythms).

General Information

Propafenone slows nerve conduction in the heart and reduces the sensitivity of nerves that are present in heart muscle. It also stabilizes the membranes of heart muscle, making them less sensitive to stimulation by cardiac nerves. Propafenone also has a very mild beta-blocking effect, which helps in stabilizing abnormal rhythms. However, this drug can cause abnormal rhythms of its own and, for that reason, is usually recommended only after other drug treatments have not worked. It is in the same class of antiarrhythmic drugs as Encainide and Flecainide.

Cautions and Warnings

Propafenone should not be used by people with severe heart failure, very low blood pressure, or a very slow heart rate. In some cases, Propafenone is not recommended unless an artificial pacemaker has been implanted to control basic heart function. People with a pacemaker may have to have some adjustments made in the programming of the device because of changes brought about by the drug in the sensitivity of heart muscle to the device.

Propafenone, like some other antiarrhythmic drugs, can worsen some abnormal rhythms or create abnormalities of its own, including some severe arrhythmias of the ventricle. Overall, about 5 percent of people who take this drug will develop abnormal rhythms because of the drug itself.

Most people's bodies break down Propafenone relatively quickly and efficiently, but others handle Propafenone very differently and eliminate the drug much more slowly. People in the latter group (less than 10 percent of all users) have 1.5 to 2 times as much Propafenone in their blood for a given dose and must be treated carefully by their doctors to avoid drug side effects.

People with heart failure, chronic bronchitis, or emphysema should probably not use Propafenone because the drug's beta-blocking effect may worsen their condition.

Recent heart attack victims should be treated with other agents before Propafenone because the benefits of the drug may not prove positive in those cases.

Pregnancy/Breast-feeding

Animal studies with Propafenone have shown that the drug can be toxic to developing embryos. As with all drug products, pregnant women or those who might become pregnant should not use this drug unless the advantages of the product

have been carefully weighed against the possible dangers of
taking it while pregnant.

It is not known if this drug passes into breast milk. Nursing
mothers who must take Propafenone should bottle-feed their
babies.

Seniors

Older adults are likely to have age-related reduction in kidney
and/or liver function. Because Propafenone is broken down
almost completely by the liver and its byproducts eliminated
by the kidneys, this factor should be be taken into account by
your doctor when determining your dosage of Propafenone.
Older adults may resond to a lower dosage of Propafenone
than younger adults.

Possible Side Effects

Generally, side effects increase as drug dosage is increased.
The most common side effects of the drug are angina pains;
heart failure; heart palpitations; abnormal heart rhythms, including rhythm changes in the ventricles; dizziness; headache;
nausea and vomiting; constipation; taste and smell changes;
upset stomach; blurred vision; and breathing difficulty.

Less common side effects include weakness, tremor, rash,
joint pain, swelling, sweating, stomach gas, upset stomach,
dry mouth, diarrhea, constipation, cramps, tiredness, headache, sleeplessness, drowsiness, dizziness, fainting, muscle
weakness, loss of appetite, anxiety, low blood pressure, low
heart rate, and chest pain.

Propafenone is also associated with a large number of rare
side effects, including hair loss, impotence, increased blood
sugar, low blood potassium, kidney failure, pain, itching,
lupus, unusual dreams, flushing, hot flashes, psychosis, seizures, ringing or buzzing in the ears, gall bladder problems,
anemia, bruising, bleeding, and changes to blood
components.

Drug Interactions

The combination of Propafenone and some beta blockers
(such as Metoprolol and Propranolol) has been shown to increase blood concentration of the beta blocker and decrease
its rate of release from the body, increasing the beta blocker's

effects. Beta-blocker dosage reduction is likely to be required
if you are taking this combination.

Alcohol, tranquilizers, and other nervous-system depressants will increase the depressant effects of this drug.

Cimetidine reduces the rate at which Propafenone is broken
down by the liver and may increase blood concentrations of
Propaphenone by 20 percent. Dosage adjustment may be
necessary.

Propafenone increases Digoxin levels between 35 and 80
percent, depending on the drug dosage; the higher the Propafenone dose, the greater the effect. Your doctor will balance
your Digoxin dose if you must take this combination.

Propafenone may increase the nervous-system side effects
of local anesthetics that are likely to be used during minor
surgery or dental work.

Quinidine, even in small doses, interferes completely with
one of the major pathways by which Propafenone is broken
down by the liver. This makes any patient taking Quinidine
a slow metabolizer of Propafenone. Appropriate Propafenone
dosage adjustment will be necessary.

Propafenone will increase the amount of Warfarin, an anticoagulant (blood-thinner), in the blood by about 40 percent. Warfarin dosage adjustment will solve the problem.

Food Interactions

Food may increase the amount of drug absorbed but does not
affect the total amount absorbed over time. Propafenone may
be taken without regard to food or meals.

Usual Dose

150 milligrams every 8 hours to start. Dosage adjustments can
be made in steps up to 900 milligrams per day, but may also
be reduced from the starting dose. Older adults may require
a lower dose than younger adults.

Overdosage

Overdose symptoms are usually the worst within 3 hours of
swallowing the pills. Symptoms may include weakness, tiredness, low blood pressure and slow heart rate. Fever is possible. Overdose victims should be taken to a hospital emergency

room at once for treatment. ALWAYS bring the medicine bottle with you.

Special Information

See your doctor regularly while you are taking Propafenone and call the doctor if you feel that your rhythm problem is worsening or not improving, an effect you are most likely to experience at higher drug doses. Other important symptoms to report to your doctor are chest pain, breathing difficulty, swelling, trembling or shaking, dizziness or fainting, joint pains, a slow heart rate, fever, or chills. Other side effects should be reported if they are particularly persistent or bothersome.

People taking Propafenone must be careful when performing tasks requiring concentration and coordination because of the chance that the drug will make them tired, dizzy, or light-headed.

It is very important to take your Propanefone regularly every day and at evenly spaced times around the clock because maintaining the drug's effect depends on a steady amount of the drug in your body. If you forget a dose, take it as soon as you remember. If it is almost time for your next dose, take one dose as soon as you remember. If 4 hours have passed since the forgotten dose should have been taken, skip the it and continue with your regular schedule. Do not take a double dose.

Type of Drug

Propoxyphene

Brand Names

Generic Name: Propoxyphene Hydrochloride

Darvon
Dolene

Combination Products with Aspirin and Caffeine:
Darvon Compound-65

Combination Products with Acetaminophen:
Dolene AP-65
Genagesic
Wygesic

Generic Name: Propoxyphene Napsylate

Darvon-N

Combination Products with Acetaminophen:
Darvocet-N 100
Propacet 100

(Also available in generic form)

Type of Drug

Analgesic.

Prescribed for

Relief of pain.

General Information

Propoxyphene is a chemical derivative of Methadone, a narcotic used for pain relief. It is estimated that Propoxyphene is about ½ to ⅔ as strong a pain reliever as Codeine and about as effective as Aspirin. Propoxyphene is widely used for mild pain; it can produce drug dependence when used for extended periods of time.

Propoxyphene is more effective when used in combination products with Aspirin or Acetaminophen than when used alone. The Propoxyphene used in these combinations is either the Hydrochloride or Napsylate salt. The Hydrochloride salt is about 30 percent more potent.

Cautions and Warnings

Never take more medicine than is prescribed by your doctor. Do not take Propoxyphene if you are allergic to this or similar drugs. This drug can produce psychological or physical drug dependence (addiction). The major sign of dependence is anxiety when the drug is suddenly stopped. Propoxyphene can be abused to the same degree as Codeine.

Pregnancy/Breast-feeding

No studies of this medication have been done in women and no reports of human birth defects exist, but animal studies show that high doses of the drug can cause problems in a developing fetus. Pregnant women, or women who might become pregnant while using this drug, should talk to their doctors about the risk of taking this medicine versus the benefits it can provide.

This drug passes into breast milk, but no problems in nursing infants have been seen. Breast-feeding women should consider the possibility of adverse effects on their nursing infant. Choose another feeding method if you must take this medicine.

Seniors

Seniors are more likely to be sensitive to the side effects of this drug and should be treated with smaller dosages than younger adults.

Possible Side Effects

Dizziness, sedation, nausea, vomiting. These effects usually disappear if you lie down and relax for a few moments.

Infrequent side effects are constipation, stomach pain, skin rashes, light-headedness, headache, weakness, euphoria, minor visual disturbances. Taking Propoxyphene over long periods of time and in very high doses has caused psychotic reactions and convulsions.

Drug Interactions

Propoxyphene may cause drowsiness. Therefore, avoid other drugs which also cause drowsiness, such as tranquilizers, sedatives, hypnotics, narcotics, alcohol, and possibly antihistamines.

There may be an interaction between Propoxyphene and Orphenadrine. However, this reaction is only a probability and only for patients who have a tendency toward low-blood sugar.

Food Interactions

Take with a full glass of water or with food to reduce the possibility of stomach upset.

Usual Dose

Propoxyphene Hydrochloride: 65 milligrams every 4 hours as needed.

Propoxyphene Napsylate: 100 milligrams every 4 hours as needed.

Overdosage

Symptoms resemble those of a narcotic overdose: decrease in rate of breathing (in some people breathing rate is so low that the heart stops), changes in breathing pattern, extreme sleepiness leading to stupor or coma, pinpointed pupils, convulsions, abnormal heart rhythms, and development of fluid in the lungs. The patient should be taken to a hospital emergency room immediately. ALWAYS bring the medicine bottle.

Special Information

Use caution while performing any tasks that require you to be alert, such as driving or operating machinery.

If you forget to take a dose of Propoxyphene, take it as soon as you remember. If it is almost time for your next regularly scheduled dose, skip the one you forgot and continue with your regular schedule. Do not take a double dose.

Generic Name

Propranolol Hydrochloride

Brand Names

Inderal Tablets
Inderal LA Capsules
Ipran Tablets
Propanolol Hydrochloride Oral Solution/Tablets
Propranolol Intensol Oral Solution

(Also available in generic form)

Type of Drug

Beta-adrenergic blocking agent.

Prescribed for

High blood pressure; angina pectoris (a specific type of chest pain); abnormal heart rhythm; reducing the possibility of a second heart attack; thyroid disease; pheochromocytoma (a tumor associated with hypertension). In addition, Propranolol Hydrochloride has been studied for its effect on migraine headaches, diarrhea, stagefright, and schizophrenia.

General Information

Propranolol Hydrochloride was the first beta-adrenergic blocking agent available in the United States. The drug acts to block a major chemical reaction of the nervous system in our bodies. For this reason, it can exert a broad range of effects, as is evident from the wide variety of diseases in which it can be used effectively. Because of this spectrum of effects, it is impossible to say specifically what you will be taking this drug for. Therefore, this information must be discussed with your doctor. This drug has been used, for example, in low (5 to 10 milligrams) doses by musicians and others to treat nervousness experienced before going on stage.

Cautions and Warnings

Propranolol Hydrochloride should be used with care if you have a history of asthma, upper respiratory disease, or seasonal allergy, which may be made worse by the effects of this drug.

Pregnancy/Breast-feeding

This drug crosses into the blood circulation of a developing baby. It has not been found to cause birth defects, but there has been some association between Propranolol Hydrochloride and breathing problems or lower heart rates in newborns. Pregnant women, or those who might become pregnant while taking this drug, should not take it without their doctors' approval. When the drug is considered essential by your doctor, the potential risk of taking the medicine must be carefully weighed against the benefit it might produce.

This drug passes into breast milk, but has caused no problems among breast-fed infants. You must consider the po-

tential effect on the nursing infant if breast-feeding while
taking this medicine.

Seniors

Seniors may be more or less sensitive to the effects of this
medication. Your dosage of this drug must be adjusted to
your individual needs by your doctor. Seniors may be more
likely to suffer from cold hands and feet and reduced body
temperature, chest pains, a general feeling of ill health, sudden difficulty breathing, sweating, or changes in heartbeat
because of this medicine.

Possible Side Effects

Propranolol Hydrochloride may decrease the heart rate; may
aggravate congestive heart failure; and may produce lowered blood pressure, tingling in the extremities, light-headedness, mental depression including inability to sleep,
weakness, and tiredness. It may also produce a mental depression which is reversible when the drug is withdrawn,
visual disturbances, hallucinations, disorientation, and short-
term memory loss. Patients taking Propranolol Hydrochloride may experience nausea, vomiting, stomach upset, abdominal cramps and diarrhea, or constipation. If you are
allergic to this drug, you may show typical reactions associated with drug allergies, including sore throat, fever, difficulty in breathing, and various effects on the blood system.
Propranolol Hydrochloride may induce bronchospasms
(spasms of muscles in the bronchi), which will aggravate
any existing asthmatic condition or any severe upper respiratory disease.

Occasionally, patients taking Propranolol Hydrochloride
may experience emotional instability or appear to be somewhat detached or show other unusual personality changes,
or the drug may produce unusual effects on the blood
system.

Drug Interactions

This drug will interact with any psychotropic drug, including
the monoamine oxidase (MAO) inhibitors, that stimulates
one of the adrenergic segments of the nervous system.
Since this information is not generally known, you should

discuss the potential problem of using Propranolol Hydrochloride with your doctor if you are taking any psychotropic or psychiatric drug.

Propranolol Hydrochloride may cause increased effectiveness of Insulin or oral antidiabetic drugs. If you are diabetic, discuss the situation with your doctor, who will probably reduce the dose of antidiabetic medication.

Propranolol Hydrochloride may reduce the effectiveness of Digitalis on your heart. Any dose of Digitalis medication will have to be altered. If you are taking Digitalis for a purpose other than congestive heart failure, the effectiveness of the Digitalis may be increased by Propranolol Hydrochloride, and the dose of Digitalis may have to be reduced.

Propranolol Hydrochloride may interact with certain other drugs to produce lowering of blood pressure. This interaction often has positive results in the treatment of patients with high blood pressure.

Do not self-medicate with over-the-counter cold, cough, or allergy remedies which may contain stimulant drugs that will aggravate certain types of heart disease and high blood pressure or other ingredients that may antagonize the effects of Propranolol Hydrochloride. Double-check with your doctor or pharmacist before taking any over-the-counter medication.

Food Interactions

Take Propranolol Hydrochloride before meals for maximum effectiveness.

Usual Dose

30 to 700 milligrams per day, depending on disease treated and patient's response. The drug is given in the smallest effective dose, that is, the smallest dose that will produce the desired therapeutic effect.

Overdosage

Symptoms are slowed heart rate, heart failure, lowered blood pressure, and spasms of the bronchial muscles which make it difficult to breathe. The patient should be taken to a hospital emergency room where proper therapy can be given. ALWAYS bring the medicine bottle with you.

Special Information

There have been reports of serious effects on the heart when this drug is stopped abruptly. The dose should be lowered gradually over a period of 2 weeks.

If you forget to take a dose of Propranolol Hydrochloride, take it as soon as possible. However, if it is within 4 hours of your next dose (8 hours if you take long-acting Propranolol Hydrochloride), skip the forgotten dose and go back to your regular schedule. Do not take a double dose.

Generic Name
Protriptyline Hydrochloride

Brand Name
Vivactil

Type of Drug
Antidepressant.

Prescribed for
Depression with or without symptoms of anxiety.

General Information

Protriptyline Hydrochloride and other members of this group are effective in treating symptoms of depression. They can elevate your mood, increase physical activity and mental alertness, improve appetite and sleep patterns. These drugs are mild sedatives and therefore useful in treating mild forms of depression associated with anxiety. You should not expect instant results with this medicine: Benefits are usually seen after 1 to 4 weeks. If symptoms are not affected after 6 to 8 weeks, contact your doctor. Occasionally other members of this group of drugs have been used in treating nighttime bed-wetting in young children, but they do not produce long-lasting relief, and therapy with one of them for nighttime bed-wetting is of questionable value.

Cautions and Warnings

Do not take Protriptyline Hydrochloride if you are allergic or sensitive to this or other members of this class of drug: Doxepin, Nortriptyline, Imipramine, Desipramine, and Amitriptyline. The drugs should not be used if you are recovering from a heart attack. Protriptyline Hydrochloride may be taken with caution if you have a history of epilepsy or other convulsive disorders, difficulty in urination, glaucoma, heart disease, or thyroid disease.

Pregnancy/Breast-feeding

This drug, like other tricyclic antidepressants, crosses into your developing baby's circulation and may cause birth defects if taken during the first 3 months of pregnancy. There have been reports of newborn infants suffering from heart, breathing, and urinary problems after their mothers had taken an antidepressant of this type immediately before delivery. You should avoid taking this medication while pregnant.

Antidepressants of this type are known to pass into breast milk and may affect a breast-feeding infant, although this has not been proven. Nursing mothers should consider alternative feeding methods if taking this medicine.

Seniors

Older adults are more sensitive to the effects of this drug and often require a lower dose than a younger adult to do the same job. Follow your doctor's directions and report any side effects at once.

Possible Side Effects

Changes in blood pressure (both high and low), abnormal heart rates, heart attack, confusion, especially in elderly patients, hallucinations, disorientation, delusions, anxiety, restlessness, excitement, numbness and tingling in the extremities, lack of coordination, muscle spasms or tremors, seizures and/or convulsions, dry mouth, blurred vision, constipation, inability to urinate, rash, itching, sensitivity to bright light or sunlight, retention of fluids, fever, allergy, changes in composition of blood, nausea, vomiting, loss of appetite, stomach upset, diarrhea, enlargement of the breasts in males and females, increased or decreased sex drive, increased or decreased blood sugar.

Infrequent side effects include agitation, inability to sleep, nightmares, feeling of panic, a peculiar taste in the mouth, stomach cramps, black coloration of the tongue, yellowing eyes and/or skin, changes in liver function, increased or decreased weight, perspiration, flushing, frequent urination, drowsiness, dizziness, weakness, headache, loss of hair, nausea, not feeling well.

Drug Interactions

Interaction with monoamine oxidase (MAO) inhibitors can cause high fevers, convulsions, and occasionally death. Don't take MAO inhibitors until at least 2 weeks after Protriptyline Hydrochloride has been discontinued.

Protriptyline Hydrochloride interacts with Guanethidine, a drug used to treat high blood pressure: If you are prescribed Protriptyline Hydrochloride and you are taking medicine for high blood pressure, be sure to discuss this with your doctor.

Protriptyline Hydrochloride increases the effects of barbiturates, tranquilizers, other depressive drugs, and alcohol. Don't drink alcoholic beverages if you take this medicine.

Taking Protriptyline Hydrochloride and thyroid medicine will enhance the effects of the thyroid medicine. The combination can cause abnormal heart rhythms.

Large doses of Vitamin C (Ascorbic Acid) can reduce the effect of Protriptyline Hydrochloride. Drugs such as Bicarbonate of Soda or Acetazolamide will increase the effect of Protriptyline Hydrochloride.

Food Interactions

This drug is best taken on an empty stomach but you can take it with food if it upsets your stomach.

Usual Dose

Adult: 15 to 60 milligrams per day in 3 or 4 divided doses.
Adolescent and senior: Lower doses are recommended, usually up to 20 milligrams per day. A senior taking more

than 20 milligrams per day should have regular heart examinations.

The dose of this drug must be tailored to the patient's need.

Overdosage

Symptoms are confusion, inability to concentrate, hallucinations, drowsiness, lowered body temperature, abnormal heart rate, heart failure, large pupils of the eyes, convulsions, severely lowered blood pressure, stupor, and coma (as well as agitation, stiffening of body muscles, vomiting, and high fever). The patient should be taken to a hospital emergency room immediately. ALWAYS bring the medicine bottle.

Special Information

Do not stop taking this medicine unless your doctor has specifically told you to do so. Abruptly stopping this medicine may cause nausea, headache, and a sickly feeling.

This medicine can cause drowsiness, dizziness, and blurred vision. Be careful when driving or operating complicated machinery.

Avoid exposure to the sun or sun lamps for long periods of time.

Call your doctor if dry mouth, difficulty urinating, or excessive sedation develops.

If you take Protriptyline Hydrochloride several times a day and forget a dose, take it as soon as you remember. If it is almost time for your next regularly scheduled dose, skip the one you forgot and continue with your regular schedule. If you take it once a day at bedtime and forget, don't take it when you get up; go back to your regular schedule. Call your doctor if you skip 2 or more days of medication. Never take a double dose.

Generic Name

Pseudoephedrine

Brand Names

Cenafed Syrup/Tablets

Children's Sudafed Liquid

Decofed Syrup

DeFed-60 Tablets

Dorcal Children's Decongestant Liquid

Halofed Syrup/Tablets

Myfedrine Liquid

PediaCare Infants' Decongestant Drops

Pseudogest Tablets

Pseudo Syrup

Sudafed Tablets

Sudrin Tablets

Timed-Release or Repeat-Action

Afrinol Tablets

Novafed Capsules

Sudafed 12 Hour Capsules

(Also available in generic form)

Type of Drug

Bronchodilator-decongestant.

Prescribed for

Symptomatic relief of stuffy nose, upper respiratory congestion, or bronchospasms associated with asthma, asthmatic bronchitis, or a similar disorder.

General Information

There are almost 200 products available that contain Pseudoephedrine. These combinations range from pain relievers to antihistamines to cough suppressants; some can be obtained only with a prescription while others are available over the counter. These products provide symptomatic relief of respiratory conditions, but do not treat the underlying disease. If you are taking an over-the-counter (available without a prescription) Pseudoephedrine medication, you should always inform your doctor.

Cautions and Warnings

Pseudoephedrine produces central-nervous-system stimulation, and it should not be taken by people with heart disease or high blood pressure. Do not take Pseudoephedrine if you are allergic or sensitive to this or similar drugs or if you have severe high blood pressure, coronary artery disease (angina pectoris), abnormal heart rhythms, or close-angle glaucoma. This drug should be used with caution and only under medical supervision if you have chest pain, stroke, diabetes, overactive thyroid, or history of convulsions.

Pregnancy/Breast-feeding

This drug crosses into the blood circulation of a developing baby. It has not been found to cause birth defects. Pregnant women, or those who might become pregnant while taking this drug, should not take it without their doctors' approval. When the drug is considered essential by your doctor, the potential risk of taking the medicine must be carefully weighed against the benefit it might produce.

This drug passes into breast milk, but has caused no problems among breast-fed infants. You must consider the potential effect on the nursing infant if breast-feeding while taking this medicine.

Seniors

Older adults are more likely to experience adverse effects from this and other stimulant drugs; overdosage of stimulants in this age group may cause hallucinations, convulsions, depression, and even death.

Older adults with severe kidney problems may be more sensitive to the effects of this drug. Follow your doctor's directions and report any side effects at once.

Possible Side Effects

Excessive tiredness or drowsiness, restlessness, nervousness with an inability to sleep.

Less frequent side effects include tremor, headache, palpitations, elevation of blood pressure, sweating, sleeplessness, loss of appetite, nausea, vomiting, dizziness, constipation.

Drug Interactions

Pseudoephedrine may increase the effect of antidepressant drugs and antihistamines and reduce the effect of some high blood pressure medicines like Reserpine or Guanethidine.

Do not self-medicate with additional over-the-counter drugs for the relief of cold symptoms: Taking Pseudoephedrine with such drugs may result in aggravation of high blood pressure, heart disease, diabetes, or thyroid disease.

Do not take Pseudoephedrine if you are taking or suspect you may be taking a monoamine oxidase (MAO) inhibitor: Severe elevation in blood pressure may result.

Interaction with alcoholic beverages may produce excessive drowsiness, sleepiness, and/or inability to concentrate.

Food Interactions

Take this medicine with food if it upsets your stomach.

Usual Dose

Adult: 60 milligrams every 6 hours.
Child (age 6 to 12): 30 milligrams every 6 hours.
Child (age 2 to 5): 15 milligrams every 6 hours.

Combination products provide a fixed amount of drug per dose and should be taken according to recommendations.

Special Information

If you forget to take a dose of Pseudoephedrine, take it as soon as you remember. If it is almost time for your next regularly scheduled dose, skip the one you forgot and continue with your regular schedule. Do not take a double dose.

Generic Name

Quazepam

Brand Name

Doral

Type of Drug

Sedative; hypnotic.

Prescribed for

Insomnia or sleeplessness, frequent nighttime awakening, or waking up too early in the morning.

General Information

Quazepam, used only for its effect as a sleep inducer, is a member of the group of drugs known as benzodiazepines. Characterized by Diazepam (Valium), other benzodiazepine drugs are used as antianxiety agents, anticonvulsants, and sedatives (sleeping pills). They exert their effects by relaxing large skeletal muscles and by increasing the effect, in the brain, of an amino acid known as GABA, which slows nerve transmission. Benzodiazepines make it easier to go to sleep and decrease the number of times you wake up during the night.

Quazepam takes about 2 hours to reach its highest blood levels, but breakdown products of the drug are likely to remain in the bloodstream for days. Quazepam produces more daytime drowsiness (hangover) than most other benzodiazepine sleeping pills. However, some people who use it on a regular basis may find that they become tolerant to the drug and may still arise early in the morning after taking it continuously for several months. This happens because the body's mechanisms for breaking down the drug build up very quickly in an attempt to get it out of the blood as quickly as possible.

Benzodiazepines can be abused if taken for long periods of time, and sudden discontinuation of a benzodiazepine can cause drug withdrawal symptoms. Withdrawal symptoms include convulsions, tremors, muscle cramps, insomnia, agitation, diarrhea, vomiting, sweating, and convulsions.

Cautions and Warnings

Do not take Quazepam if you know you are sensitive or allergic to this drug or other benzodiazepines, such as Chlordiazepoxide, Oxazepam, Chlorazepate, Diazepam, Lorazepam, Prazepam, and Clonazepam.

Quazepam and other members of this drug group may aggravate narrow-angle glaucoma, but if you have open-angle glaucoma you may take these drugs. In any case, check this information with your doctor.

Pregnancy/Breast-feeding

This drug may cause birth defects or interfere with your baby's development. Check with your doctor before taking Quazepam if you are, or might be, pregnant. Your baby may become dependent on Quazepam if the drug is used continually during pregnancy. If used during the last weeks of pregnancy or during breast-feeding, the baby may be overtired, be short of breath, or have a low heartbeat. Use during labor may cause weakness in the newborn.

Seniors

Older adults are more sensitive to the effects of this drug, especially daytime drowsiness. Follow your doctor's directions and report any side effects at once.

Possible Side Effects

The most common side effects are mild drowsiness during the first few days of therapy, especially in older adults or the debilitated. If drowsiness persists, contact your doctor.

Less common side effects include confusion, depression, lethargy, disorientation, headache, tiredness, slurred speech, stupor, dizziness, tremor, constipation, dry mouth, nausea, inability to control urination, changes in sex drive, irregular menstrual cycle, changes in heart rhythm, lowered blood pressure, fluid retention, blurred or double vision, itching, rash, hiccups, nervousness, inability to fall asleep, and, occasionally, liver dysfunction. If you experience any of these reactions, stop taking the medicine and contact your doctor immediately.

Drug Interactions

Quazepam is a central-nervous-system depressant. Avoid alcohol, tranquilizers, narcotics, sleeping pills, barbiturates, antihistamines, monoamine oxidase (MAO) inhibitors, and other medicines used to relieve depression, which may increase Quazepam's depressant effects.

The effects of Quazepam may be increased if you are taking Cimetidine, an oral contraceptive, Disulfiram, Isoniazid, or Probenecid.

Quazepam's effects may be decreased if you are also taking Theophylline or if you smoke cigarettes regularly.

Benzodiazepines may increase the amount of Digoxin or Phenytoin in your blood.

Food Interactions

Quazepam is best taken on an empty stomach but may be taken with food if it upsets your stomach.

Usual Dose

7.5 to 15 milligrams at bedtime. The dose must be individualized for maximum benefit.

Overdosage

Symptoms are confusion, sleepiness, lack of response to pain such as a pin stick, shallow breathing, lowered blood pressure, and coma. The overdose victim should be taken to a hospital emergency room immediately. ALWAYS bring the medicine bottle.

Special Information

Quazepam can cause tiredness, drowsiness, inability to concentrate, and similar symptoms. Be careful if you are driving, operating machinery, or performing activities that require concentration.

Avoid alcoholic beverages while taking Quazepam. Use with caution other sleeping pills, narcotics, tranquilizers, and other drugs that depress the nervous system and/or may interfere with breathing while taking Quazepam.

If you have been taking this drug for a long time, you may experience drug withdrawal symptoms (drug craving, disturbed sleep) if you stop taking it abruptly. Talk to your doctor about gradually reducing the dosage and stopping the medicine.

If you forget to take a dose of Quazepam and you remember within about an hour of your regular time, take it right away. If you do not remember until later, skip the forgotten dose and go back to your regular schedule. Do not take a double dose.

Brand Name

Quibron Capsules/Liquid

Ingredients

Guaifenesin
Theophylline

Other Brand Names

Bronchial Capsules   Theo-G Capsules
Glyceryl T Capsules/Liquid   Theolate Liquid
Lanophyllin GG Capsules   Theophylline-Guaifenesin
Slo-Phyllin GG Capsules/   Liquid
  Syrup

The following products contain the same ingredients in different concentrations:

Asbron G Inlay-Tabs/Elixir
Elixophyllin-GG Liquid
Quibron-300 Capsules

(Also available in generic form)

Type of Drug

Antiasthmatic combination product.

Prescribed for

Relief of asthma symptoms or other upper respiratory disorders.

General Information

Quibron, a xanthine combination, is one of several antiasthmatic combination products prescribed for the relief of asthmatic symptoms and other breathing problems. These products contain drugs which help relax the bronchial muscles, drugs which increase the diameter of the breathing passages, and a mild tranquilizer to help relax the patient. Other products in this class may contain similar ingredients along with other medicine to help eliminate mucus from the breathing passages.

Cautions and Warnings

Do not use this drug if you are allergic or sensitive to it or to any related drug, such as Aminophylline. If you have stomach ulcer or heart disease, you should use this drug with caution. This drug should not be taken if you have severe kidney or liver disease.

Pregnancy/Breast-feeding

If you are pregnant or think that you may be pregnant you should carefully discuss the use of this drug with your doctor. Quibron may be required by a woman during pregnancy. However, there is an increased chance of birth defects while using Quibron during pregnancy. Regularly using Quibron during the last 3 months of pregnancy may cause drug dependency of the newborn. Labor may be prolonged and delivery may be delayed, and there may be breathing problems in the newborn if Quibron is used.

Breast-feeding while using Quibron may cause increased tiredness, shortness of breath, or a slow heartbeat in the baby.

Theophylline, an ingredient in Quibron, may cause a fast heartbeat, irritability, or breathing problems in the unborn or nursing child if too much is used by the mother.

Seniors

Older adults may take longer to clear this drug from their bodies than younger adults. Those with heart failure or other cardiac conditions, chronic lung disease, a virus infection with fever, or reduced liver function may require a lower dosage of this medication to account for the clearance effect.

Possible Side Effects

Large doses of Quibron can produce excitation, shakiness, sleeplessness, nervousness, rapid heartbeat, chest pains, or irregular heartbeat. Occasionally people have been known to develop hesitation or difficulty in urination.

Less common side effects include excessive urination, heart stimulation, drowsiness, muscle weakness, muscle twitching, unsteady walk. These effects can usually be controlled by having your doctor adjust the dose.

Drug Interactions

Quibron may cause sleeplessness and/or drowsiness.

Taking Quibron with a monoamine oxidase (MAO) inhibitor can produce severe interaction. Consult your doctor first.

Quibron or similar products taken together with Lithium Carbonate will increase the excretion of Lithium.

Quibron and similar products have neutralized the effect of Propranalol.

Erythromycin and similar antibiotics cause the body to hold Theophylline, leading to possible side effects.

Do not take this drug with alcoholic beverages.

Food Interactions

The way Quibron acts in your body may be influenced by your diet. Charcoal-broiled beef, for example, may cause the amount of Quibron that is being eliminated in the urine to increase. Therefore you may experience a decreased effect of the drug. This is also true for people whose diet is low in carbohydrates and high in protein or for people who smoke.

Caffeine (also a xanthine derivative) may add to the side effects of Quibron. It is recommended that you avoid large amounts of caffeine-containing foods, such as coffee, tea, cocoa, colas, or chocolate.

Take this drug with food to avoid upset stomach.

Usual Dose

Capsules: 1 to 2 every 6 to 8 hours.
Liquid: 1 to 2 tablespoons every 6 to 8 hours.

Special Information

If you forget to take a dose of Quibron, take it as soon as you remember. If it is almost time for your next regularly scheduled dose, skip the one you forgot and continue with your regular schedule. Do not take a double dose.

Type of Drug

Quinidine

Brand Names

Generic Name: Quinidine Sulfate

Cin-Quin
Quinora

Sustained-release product:
Quinidex Extentabs

Generic Name: Quinidine Gluconate

Sustained-release products:
Duraquin   Quinatime
Quinaglute Dura-Tabs   Quin-Release

Generic Name: Quinidine Polygalacturonate

Cardioquin

(Also available in generic forms)

Type of Drug

Antiarrhythmic.

Prescribed for

Abnormal heart rhythms.

General Information

Derived from the bark of the cinchona tree (which gives us
Quinine), this drug works by affecting the flow of potassium
into and out of cells of the myocardium (heart muscle). Its
basic action is to slow down the pulse. Its action allows
normal control mechanisms in the heart to take over and
keep the heart beating at a normal rate of rhythm.

The 3 kinds of Quinidine provide different amounts of active drug. Quinidine Sulfate provides the most active drug.

Some of the different brands come in sustained-release
form so that fewer pills are required throughout the day.

Cautions and Warnings

Do not take Quinidine Sulfate if you are allergic to it or a related drug.

Pregnancy/Breast-feeding

This drug may cause birth defects or interfere with your baby's development. Check with your doctor before taking it if you are, or might be, pregnant.

Quinidine Sulfate does not cause problems while breast-feeding and may be used by nursing mothers.

Seniors

Older adults may take this medication without special restriction. Follow your doctor's directions and report any side effects at once.

Possible Side Effects

High doses of Quinidine Sulfate can give you rash, changes in hearing, dizziness, ringing in the ears, headache, nausea, or disturbed vision: This group of symptoms, called cinchonism, is due to ingestion of large amounts of Quinidine Sulfate and is not necessarily a toxic reaction. However, report signs of cinchonism to your doctor immediately. Do not stop taking this drug unless instructed to do so by your doctor.

Less commonly, Quinidine Sulfate may cause unusual heart rhythms, but such effects are generally found by your doctor during routine examination or electrocardiogram. It can cause nausea, vomiting, stomach pain, and diarrhea. It may affect components of the blood system and can cause headache, fever, dizziness, feeling of apprehension or excitement, confusion, delirium, disturbed hearing, blurred vision, changes in color perception, sensitivity to bright lights, double vision, difficulty seeing at night, flushing of the skin, itching, cramps, unusual urge to defecate or urinate, and cold sweat.

Drug Interactions

If you are taking an oral anticoagulant (blood-thinning medicine) and have been given a new prescription for Quinidine Sulfate, be sure your doctor knows about the blood-thinning medication, because Quinidine Sulfate may affect the ability

of the anticoagulant to do its job. The anticoagulant dose
may have to be adjusted for the effect of Quinidine Sulfate.

Either Phenobarbital or Phenytoin may reduce the time
that Quinidine Sulfate is effective in your body and may
increase your need for it. Quinidine Sulfate in combination
with Digoxin can increase the effects of the Digoxin causing
possible Digoxin toxicity. This combination should be monitored closely by your doctor.

Avoid over-the-counter cough, cold, allergy, or diet preparations. These medications may contain drugs which will
stimulate your heart; this can be dangerous while you are
taking Quinidine Sulfate. Ask your pharmacist if you have
any questions about the contents of a particular cough, cold,
or allergy remedy.

Food Interactions

If Quinidine Sulfate gives you stomach upset, take it with
food. Quinidine is also available in forms that are supposed
to be less irritating to the stomach; contact your doctor if
upset stomach persists.

Usual Dose

Extremely variable, depending on disease and patient's response. Most doses are 800 to 1200 milligrams per day.

Sustained-release: Most doses are 600 to 1800 milligrams
per day.

Overdosage

Overdose produces abnormal effects on the heart and symptoms of cinchonism. The patient should be taken to a hospital emergency room where proper therapy can be given.
ALWAYS bring the medicine bottle.

Special Information

Do not crush or chew the sustained-release products.

If you forget to take a dose of Quinidine Sulfate, and you
remember within about 2 hours of your regular time, take it
right away. If you do not remember until later, skip the forgotten dose and go back to your regular schedule. Do not
take a double dose.

Generic Name

Ramipril

Brand Name

Altace

Type of Drug

Antihypertensive.

Prescribed for

High blood pressure. This medicine may be taken alone or with a thiazide-type diuretic.

General Information

This medicine belongs to a class of drugs, the ACE inhibitors, that work by preventing the conversion of a potent hormone called Angiotensin 1. This directly affects the production of other hormones and enzymes that are a part of the system that regulates blood pressure. The drug begins working about an hour after you take it. Some people taking Ramipril with a diuretic experience a rapid blood pressure drop. To prevent this from happening, your doctor may tell you to stop the diuretic 2 or 3 days before starting Ramipril and start the diuretic again if your blood pressure is not controlled by Ramipril alone.

Cautions and Warnings

Ramipril can affect your kidneys. It is advisable for your doctor to check your urine for abnormalities during the first few months of treatment. It can also affect your white-blood-cell count, possibly increasing your susceptibility to infection. The drug should be used with caution if you have kidney disease or a disease of the immune/collagen system (particularly lupus erythematosus) or if you have taken other drugs that can affect white-blood-cell count.

Pregnancy/Breast-feeding

The affect of Ramipril on the developing fetus is not known.

This product should be used with caution by women who are or might become pregnant.

It is not known if Ramipril passes into breast milk or affects nursing infants.

Seniors

Older adults may be less sensitive to the blood-pressure-lowering effects of this drug than younger adults but more sensitive to the drug's side effects. Your Ramipril dosage must be individualized to your needs.

Possible Side Effects

Dizziness, tiredness, headache, mild rash, and cough are most common.

Less common side effects include itching, fever, temporary loss of taste perception, chest pain, stomach pain, low blood pressure, heart palpitations, sleeping difficulty, tingling in the hands or feet, nausea, vomiting, liver damage and jaundice (yellow discoloration of the skin or whites of the eyes), muscle cramps or weakness, and male impotence.

Drug Interactions

The blood-pressure-lowering effect of Ramipril is additive with diuretic drugs and beta blockers. Any other drug that causes a rapid blood pressure drop should be used with caution if you are taking Ramipril.

Ramipril may increase potassium levels in your blood, especially when taken together with Dyazide or another potassium-sparing diuretic.

Food Interactions

Ramipril is best taken on an empty stomach, 1 hour before or 2 hours after a meal.

Usual Dose

2.5 to 20 milligrams once or twice a day. People with poor kidney function may need less medicine to lower blood pressure.

Overdosage

The principal effect of Ramipril overdose is a rapid drop in blood pressure, as evidenced by dizziness or fainting. Take the overdose victim to a hospital emergency room immediately. ALWAYS remember to bring the medicine bottle.

Special Information

Call your doctor if you develop a sore throat, mouth sores, abnormal heartbeat, chest pain, a persistent rash, or loss of taste perception. You may get dizzy if you rise to your feet quickly from a sitting or lying position.

Avoid strenuous exercise and/or going out in very hot weather because heavy sweating or dehydration can cause a rapid blood pressure drop.

Avoid non-prescription diet pills, decongestants, or stimulants that can raise blood pressure.

If you take Ramipril once a day and forget to take a dose, take it as soon as you remember. If it is almost time for your next dose, skip the one your forgot and continue with your regular schedule. Do not take a double dose.

If you take Ramipril twice a day and forget a dose take it as soon as you remember. If it is almost time for your next dose, take one dose as soon as you remember and another in 5 or 6 hours, then go back to your regular schedule.

Generic Name

Ranitidine

Brand Name

Zantac

Type of Drug

Antiulcer; histamine H_2 antagonist.

Prescribed for

Short-term treatment of duodenal (intestinal) and gastric (stomach) ulcers. It is also prescribed for other conditions characterized by the secretions of large amounts of gastric fluids. A surgeon may prescribe Ranitidine for a patient

under anesthesia when it is desirable for the production of
stomach acid to be stopped completely.

General Information

Ranitidine was the second histamine H_2 antagonist to be
released in the United States. It is more potent than Cimetidine, the original histamine H_2 antagonist, and has less potential for causing drug interactions than Cimetidine.

Cautions and Warnings

Do not take Ranitidine if you have had an allergic reaction
to it in the past.

Pregnancy/Breast-feeding

Although studies with laboratory animals have revealed no
damage to a developing fetus, it is recommended that Ranitidine be avoided by pregnant women or women who might
become pregnant while using it. In those situations where it
is deemed essential, Ranitidine's potential risk must be carefully weighed against any benefit it might produce.

Ranitidine is known to pass into breast milk. No problems
among nursing infants have been reported, but nursing
mothers must consider the possibility of a drug effect while
nursing their infants.

Seniors

Older adults respond well to Ranitidine but may need less
medication than a younger adult to achieve the desired response, since the drug is eliminated through the kidneys
and kidney function tends to decline with age. Older adults
may be more susceptible to some side effects of this drug,
especially confusion.

Possible Side Effects

The most common side effects are headache, dizziness, constipation, abdominal discomfort, rash, and a feeling of ill
health.

Ranitidine may rarely cause a reduction in the levels of
either white blood cells or blood platelets. Hepatitis is another rare consequence of Ranitidine treatment.

Drug Interactions

The effects of Ranitidine may be reduced if it is taken together with antacids. This minor interaction may be avoided
by separating doses of Ranitidine and antacid by about 3
hours.

Ranitidine may interfere with the absorption of Diazepam
tablets into the blood. This interaction is considered of only
minor importance and is unlikely to affect many people.

Ranitidine may decrease the effect of Theophylline, prescribed for asthma and other respiratory conditions, while
the 2 drugs are being taken together and for several days
after the Ranitidine has been discontinued. This interaction
is far less severe than the Cimetidine-Theophylline interaction, which may require temporary dosage adjustments.

Cigarettes are known to be associated with stomach ulcers
and will reverse the effect of Ranitidine on stomach acid.

Food Interactions

You may take each dose with food or meals if Ranitidine
upsets your stomach.

Usual Dose

150 to 300 milligrams per day. People with severe conditions
may require more than the average dose.

Overdosage

Overdose victims may be expected to show exaggerated
side-effect symptoms, but little else is known about Ranitidine overdose. Patients taking an overdose of this drug must
be made to vomit with Syrup of Ipecac (available at any
pharmacy) to remove any remaining drug from the stomach.
Call your doctor or a poison control center before doing this.
If you must go to a hospital emergency room, ALWAYS
bring the medicine bottle.

Special Information

It may take several days for Ranitidine to begin to relieve
stomach pains.

You must take this medicine exactly as directed and follow
your doctor's instructions for diet and other treatments in
order to get the maximum benefit from it.

Call your doctor at once if any unusual side effects develop. Especially important are unusual bleeding or bruising, unusual tiredness, diarrhea, dizziness, rash, or hallucinations. Black, tarry stools or vomiting "coffee-ground" material may indicate your ulcer is bleeding.

If you forget to take a dose of Ranitidine, take it as soon as you remember. If it is almost time for your next regularly scheduled dose, skip the one you forgot and continue with your regular schedule. Do not take a double dose.

Generic Name

Rifampin

Brand Names

Rifadin
Rimactane

Type of Drug

Antitubercular.

Prescribed for

Tuberculosis; leoprosy; Legionnaires' disease; meningitis; staph infections.

General Information

This is an important drug for the treatment of tuberculosis. It is always used together with Isoniazid or another antitubercular drug because it is not effective by itself. It is also used to eradicate an organism which causes meningitis in people who are carriers: Although they are not infected, they carry the organism and spread it to others.

Rifampin may also be prescribed for staph infections of the skin, bones, or prostate; for Legionnaires' disease (when Erythromycin doesn't work); for leprosy; and for the prevention of meningitis caused by *H. influenzae*, especially common among children in day-care centers.

Cautions and Warnings

Do not take this drug if you are allergic to it. It may cause liver damage and should not be used by people with liver disease or those taking other drugs which may cause liver damage.

Pregnancy/Breast-feeding

This drug should be used only by pregnant women or nursing mothers if absolutely necessary. Animal studies indicate that Rifampin may cause backbone problems (spina bifida) in the fetus.

Rifampin has not been shown to cause problems to the infant while the mother is breast-feeding.

Seniors

Older adults with severe liver disease may be more sensitive to the effects of this drug. Follow your doctor's directions and report any side effects at once.

Possible Side Effects

Flulike symptoms, heartburn, upset stomach, loss of appetite, nausea, vomiting, stomach gas cramps, diarrhea, headache, drowsiness, tiredness, menstrual disturbances, dizziness, fever, pains in the arms and legs, confusion, visual disturbances, numbness, hypersensitivity to the drug.

Less commonly, Rifampin has an adverse effect on the blood, kidneys, or liver.

Drug Interactions

When this is taken with other drugs that cause liver toxicity, severe liver damage may develop.

Rifampin will increase patient requirements for oral anticoagulant (blood-thinning) drugs and may affect Methadone, oral antidiabetic drugs, digitalis drugs, or adrenal corticosteroids.

Women taking oral contraceptives and Rifampin should supplement with other contraceptive methods.

Food Interactions

Take this medicine 1 hour before or 2 hours after a meal, at the same time every day.

Usual Dose

Adult: 600 milligrams once daily.

Child: 4.5 to 9 milligrams per pound, or up to 600 milligrams per day.

Overdosage

Signs are nausea, vomiting, and tiredness. Unconsciousness may develop, with severe liver damage. A brown-red or orange discoloration of the skin may develop. Patients suspected of taking Rifampin overdose must be taken to the hospital at once. ALWAYS take the medicine bottle with you.

Special Information

This drug may cause a red-brown or orange coloration of the urine, stool, saliva, sweat, and tears.

Soft contact lenses may become permanently stained.

Call your doctor if you develop the flu, fever, chills, muscle pains, headache, tiredness or weakness, loss of appetite, nausea, vomiting, sore throat, unusual bleeding or bruising, or yellow discoloration of the skin or eyes, rash, or itching.

If you take daily doses of Rifampin and you miss a dose, consult your doctor. Reactions may occur if you start again.

Side effects may be more common and more severe if the drug is taken on an irregular basis.

If you forget to take a dose of Rifampin, take it as soon as you remember. If it is almost time for your next regularly scheduled dose, skip the one you forgot and continue with your regular schedule. Do not take a double dose.

Generic Name

Ritodrine Hydrochloride

Brand Name

Yutopar

Type of Drug

Uterine relaxant.

Prescribed for

Controlling preterm labor to prevent premature delivery.

General Information

This drug stimulates the beta nerve receptors in muscles in the uterus and prevents them from contracting. This drug must be used only under the direction of your doctor and only after the fifth month of pregnancy. It should be started with intravenous dosage and then continued as oral tablets.

Cautions and Warnings

This drug should not be used until after the twentieth week of pregnancy or if the mother has any complicating factors.

Possible Side Effects

Increased heart rate and blood pressure in both mother and child, palpitations, tremor, nausea, vomiting, headache, swelling of the extremities.

Less common side effects are nervousness, jitteriness, restlessness, emotional anxiety, upset, feeling of ill health, chest pains, abnormal heart rates, rash, heart murmur, upset stomach, bloating, constipation, diarrhea, sweating, chills, drowsiness, weakness, difficulty breathing, sugar in the urine.

Drug Interactions

Adrenal corticosteroids may lead to fluid in the lungs when given together with Ritodrine Hydrochloride.

All beta-adrenergic blocking drugs will directly inhibit the effect of Ritodrine Hydrochloride.

Usual Dose

30 minutes before intravenous therapy is to end, tablets are taken in a dose of 10 milligrams and every 2 hours for the first day; then 10 to 20 milligrams every 4 to 6 hours. The drug may be used as long as it is desirable to prolong the pregnancy.

Overdosage

Signs are rapid heart rate, palpitation, abnormal heartbeats, low blood pressure, nervousness, tremor, nausea, and vomiting. Take the patient to a hospital emergency room. ALWAYS bring the medicine bottle.

Special Information

Take only as directed by your doctor. Report any unusual effect immediately.

If you forget to take a dose of Ritodrine Hydrochloride, and you remember within about an hour of your regular time, take it right away. If you do not remember until later, skip the forgotten dose and go back to your regular schedule. Do not take a double dose.

Generic Name

Secobarbital

Brand Name

Seconal

(Also available in generic form)

Type of Drug

Hypnotic; sedative.

Prescribed for

Daytime sedation; sleeplessness; sedation before surgery.

General Information

Secobarbital, like the other barbiturates, works by interfering with the passage of certain nerve impulses to the brain. It is useful in any situation where a fast-acting sedative or hypnotic (sleep-producing) effect is needed. This drug can be addicting if taken for a period of time in large enough doses, especially if more than 400 milligrams a day is taken for 3 months. Larger doses will produce barbiturate addiction in a shorter time.

Cautions and Warnings

Secobarbital is classified as a barbiturate; long-term or un-supervised use may cause addiction. Barbiturates are neu-tralized in the liver and eliminated from the body through the kidneys; consequently, people who have liver or kidney disorders—namely, difficulty in forming or excreting urine—should be carefully monitored by their doctor when taking Secobarbital.

If you have known sensitivities or allergies to barbiturates, if you have previously been addicted to sedatives or hypno-tics, or if you have a disease affecting the respiratory sys-tem, you should not take Secobarbital.

Pregnancy/Breast-feeding

Regular use of any barbiturate during the last 3 months of pregnancy can cause the baby to be born dependent on the medicine. Also, barbiturate use increases the chance of bleeding problems, brain tumors, and breathing difficulties in the newborn.

Barbiturates pass into breast milk and can cause drowsi-ness, slow heartbeat, and breathing difficulty in nursing infants.

Seniors

Older adults are more sensitive to the effects of barbiturates, especially nervousness and confusion, and often require a lower dose than a younger adult to do the same job. Follow your doctor's directions and report any side effects at once.

Possible Side Effects

Drowsiness, lethargy, dizziness, hangover, difficulty in breath-ing, rash, and general allergic reaction such as runny nose, watery eyes, and scratchy throat.

Less common side effects are nausea, vomiting, diarrhea. More severe adverse reactions may include anemia and yel-lowing of the skin and eyes.

Drug Interactions

Interaction with alcohol, tranquilizers, or other sedatives in-creases the effect of Secobarbital.

Interaction with anticoagulants (blood-thinning agents) can

reduce their effect. This is also true of muscle relaxants, pain killers, anticonvulsants, Quinidine, Theophylline, Metronidazole, Phenmetrazine, birth control pills, and Acetaminophen.

Food Interactions

This medicine is best taken on an empty stomach, but may be taken with food if it upsets your stomach.

Usual Dose

As a daytime sedative: 30 to 50 milligrams.
As a hypnotic for sleep: 100 to 200 milligrams.
For sedation before surgery: 200 to 500 milligrams 1 to 2 hours before surgery.
Child: sedative, 2.7 milligrams per pound per day; sedation before surgery, 50 to 100 milligrams.

Overdosage

Symptoms are difficulty in breathing, decrease in size of the pupils of the eyes, lowered body temperature progressing to fever as time passes, fluid in the lungs, and eventually coma. Anyone suspected of having taken an overdose must be taken to the hospital for immediate care. ALWAYS bring the medicine bottle so the emergency room physician can quickly and correctly identify the medicine and start treatment. Severe overdosage of this medication can kill; the drug has been used many times in suicide attempts.

Special Information

Avoid alcohol and other drugs that depress the nervous system while taking this barbiturate.

Be sure to take this medicine according to your doctor's direction. Do not change your dose without your doctor's approval.

This drug causes drowsiness and poor concentration, and makes it more difficult to drive a car, operate machinery, or perform complicated activities.

Call your doctor at once if you develop fever, sore throat, nosebleeds, mouth sores, unexplained black-and-blue marks, easy bruising or bleeding.

If you forget to take a dose of Secobarbital, and you remember within about an hour of your regular time, take it right away. If you do not remember until later, skip the forgotten dose and go back to your regular schedule. Do not take a double dose.

Generic Name
Selegiline

Brand Name
Eldepryl

Type of Drug
Anti-Parkinsonian; selective MAO inhibitor.

Prescribed for
Parkinson's disease.

General Information
Selegiline is often used together with Levodopa or Carbidopa to control Parkinson's disease. Most people who begin taking Selegiline find that their doctors can reduce their Levodopa or Carbidopa doses within a few days.

The exact way that Selegiline works is not known. It is a very strong inhibitor of one form of the enzyme monoamine oxidase (MAO), found almost exclusively in the brain. Other, older, MAO inhibitor antidepressants work on both forms of MAO and affect the entire body. Selegiline also produces increased stimulation of dopamine receptors in the brain, possibly by making the dopamine that is available in the brain last longer by interfering with its being reabsorbed into brain nerve endings. In order for any drug to work in Parkinson's disease, it must somehow increase the activity of dopamine in the brain.

Some of Selegilene's side effects may be caused by 2 products of the body's metabolism of the drug: Methamphetamine and Amphetamine, extremely potent stimulants.

Cautions and Warnings
People who have had a reaction to Selegiline in the past should be cautious about using this product again.

Selegiline should not be taken in doses larger than 10 milligrams a day because of the possibility that large doses (20 milligrams and more) will affect both types of MAO and cause unexpected reactions, including very high, possibly fatal, blood pressure.

Pregnancy/Breast-feeding

Pregnant women or those who might become pregnant should not use Selegiline unless the advantages of the product have been carefully weighed against the possible dangers of taking it while pregnant.

It is not known if Selegiline passes into breast milk, and the effect of this drug in young children is not known. Nursing mothers who must use this drug should watch their children for any reaction.

Seniors

Older adults may take Selegiline without special consideration. The lowest effective dose should be used to minimize the possibility of drug side effects.

Possible Side Effects

When Selegiline dosage is limited to under 10 milligrams a day, most of the drug's side effects are not caused by the drug itself; rather, Selegiline increases the side effects of Levodopa. That is why it is important for your doctor to reduce your Levodopa dosage to as low an amount as possible.

The most common side effects experienced by people taking Selegiline are nausea, vomiting, dizziness, lightheadedness or fainting, and abdominal pains.

Other possible drug side effects are tremors; uncontrolled muscle movements; loss of balance; inability to move; increased slowness of movement (associated with Parkinson's disease); facial grimacing; falling down; stiff neck; muscle cramps; hallucinations; over-stimulation; dizziness; confusion; anxiety; depression; drowsiness; changes in mood or behavior; nightmares or unusual dreams; tiredness; delusions; disorientation; feelings of ill health; apathy; sleep disturbances; restlessness; weakness and irritability; generalized aches and pains; migraine or regular headache; back, leg, or muscle pains; ringing or buzzing in the ears; eye pain; finger or toe numbness; taste alterations; dizziness whem rising from a sitting or lying position; blood pressure changes; abnormal heart rhythms; heart palpitations; chest pains; rapid heartbeat; swelling in the arms or legs; constipation; appetite loss; weight loss; difficulty swallowing; diarrhea; heartburn; rectal bleeding; urinary difficulties; (male) impotence; prostate swelling; sweating; increased facial hair; hair loss; rash; unusual sensitivity to the sun; broken-blood accumulation under the skin; asthma; double or blurred vision; shortness of breath; speech problems; and dry mouth.

At doses above 10 milligrams a day, Selegiline may cause muscle twitching or spasms, memory loss, increased energy, a transient high, grinding of the teeth, decreased feeling in the penis, and (male) inability to achieve orgasm.

Drug Interactions

Selegiline should not be used with Meperidine or other narcotics because of the possibility of severe, possibly fatal, reactions similar to those with other MAO inhibitor drugs.

Alcohol taken with Selegiline can cause headache, high blood pressure, and fever.

Food Interactions

Take Selegiline with food or meals to avoid nausea.

Avoid Chianti and red wine; vermouth; unpasteurized and imported beer; beef or chicken liver; fermented sausages; tenderizer-prepared meats; caviar; dried fish; pickled herring; American, Brie, Cheddar, Camembert, Emmentaler, Boursault, Stilton, and other cheeses; avocados, yeast extracts, bananas, figs, raisins, soy sauce, miso soup, bean curd, fava beans, caffeine, and chocolate. These foods and others can cause severe, sudden high blood pressure to occur with Selegiline.

Usual Dose

5 milligrams taken with breakfast and lunch.

Overdosage

Symptoms of a Selegiline overdose may include excitement,

irritability, anxiety, low blood pressure, sleeplessness, restlessness, dizziness, weakness, drowsiness, flushing, sweating, heart palpitations, and unusual movements, including
grimacing and muscle twitching. Serious overdoses may
lead to coma, convulsions, incoherence, confusion, severe
headache, high fever, heart attack, and shock. Victims of a
Selegiline overdose should be taken to a hospital emergency
room for treatment. ALWAYS bring the medicine bottle with
you.

Special Information

After you have taken Selegiline for 2 or 3 days, your doctor
will probably reduce your Carbidopa or Levodopa dose by
10 to 30 percent. If the disease is still under control, your
dose may be further reduced to find the lowest effective
dose of medication to control your Parkinson's disease.

Headache, unusual body movements or muscle spasms,
mood changes, or other unusual, persistent side effects
should be reported to your doctor at once. Do not stop taking Selegiline or change your dose without your doctor's
knowledge.

It is important to maintain regular contact with your doctor
while taking Selegiline to allow for observation of drug effects and side effects.

Selegiline may increase the chance for cavities, gum disease, and oral infections because it reduces saliva flow in
the mouth. Dry mouth can be avoided by using sugarless
gum, candy, ice, or a saliva substitute.

If you forget a dose of Selegiline, take it as soon as you
remember. If it is almost time for your next dose, take one
dose as soon as you remember and another in 5 or 6 hours,
then go back to your regular schedule. Do not take a double
dose.

Brand Name

Septra

Ingredients

Sulfamethoxazole
Trimethoprim

Other Brand Names

Bactrim/Bactrim DS   Septra DS
Cotrim/Cotrim DS/Cotrim   Sulfatrim/Sulfatrim DS
  Pediatric   TMP-SMZ
Co-Trimoxazole

(Also available in generic form)

Type of Drug

Anti-infective.

Prescribed for

Urinary tract infections. Septra can also be used to treat bronchitis or ear infections in children caused by susceptible organisms and as prevention against traveler's diarrhea and pneumocystis carinii infections in AIDS and leukemia patients.

General Information

Septra is one of many combination products used to treat infections. This is a unique combination because it attacks the infecting organism in 2 ways; it is effective in many situations where other drugs are not. Bacterial resistance to the effects of Septra develops more slowly than resistance to the effects of Sulfamethoxazole and Trimethoprim used alone.

Cautions and Warnings

Do not take this medication if you have a folic acid deficiency or are allergic to either ingredient or to any sulfa drug.

Infants under age 2 months should not be given this combination product. Symptoms such as unusual bleeding or bruising, extreme tiredness, rash, sore throat, fever, pallor, or yellowing of the skin or whites of the eyes may be early indications of serious blood disorders. If any of these effects occur, contact your doctor immediately and stop taking the drug.

Pregnancy/Breast-feeding

This drug crossed into the drug circulation of a developing baby. Although it can affect the newborn infant, this rarely happens because of the mother's ability to protect her developing infant. Pregnant women, or those who might become pregnant while taking this drug, should not take it without their doctors' approval. When the drug is considered essential by your doctor, the potential risk of taking the medicine must be carefully weighed against the benefit it might produce.

Small amounts of this drug pass into breast milk, but it rarely causes problems among breast-fed infants. The notable exception to this are infants who are deficient in the enzyme known as G-6PD. Children deficient in this enzyme can develop a severe form of anemia. Talk to your doctor about the possible effect of this drug on your baby if you take it while nursing.

Seniors

Older adults may take this medication without special restriction. Follow your doctor's directions and report any side effects at once.

Possible Side Effects

Effects on components of the blood system; allergic reactions, including itching; rash; drug fever; swelling around the eyes; arthritislike pains.

Septra can also cause nausea, stomach upset, vomiting, abdominal pain, diarrhea, coating on the tongue, headache, tingling in the arms and/or legs, depression, convulsions, hallucinations, ringing in the ears, dizziness, difficulty sleeping, feeling of apathy, tiredness, weakness, and nervousness. Septra may affect your kidneys and cause you to produce less urine.

Drug Interactions

This drug may prolong the effects of blood-thinning agents (such as Warfarin) and antidiabetic oral drugs.

Food Interactions

Take each dose with a full glass of water and continue to drink fluids throughout the day. This is to decrease the chances of a stone forming in your kidneys.

Usual Dose

Tablets: 1 to 2 tablets every 12 hours for 10 to 14 days.

Oral suspension: 2 to 4 teaspoons every 12 hours for 10 to 14 days.

For pneumocystis carinii: 4 double-strength tablets every 6 hours.

Overdosage

Small overdoses are not likely to cause harm. Larger overdoses can cause exaggerated drug side effects. Call a poison control center or hospital emergency room for more information.

Special Information

Take Septra in the exact dosage and for the exact period of time prescribed. Do not stop taking it just because you are beginning to feel better.

You may develop unusual sensitivity to sun or bright light. If you have a history of light sensitivity or if you have sensitive skin, avoid prolonged exposure to sunlight while using Septra.

If you miss a dose of Septra, take it as soon as possible. If it is almost time for your next dose and you take the medicine twice a day, space the next 2 doses 5 to 6 hours apart, then go back to your regular schedule.

If it is almost time for your next dose and you take the medicine 3 or more times a day, space the missed dose and your next dose by 2 to 4 hours, then continue with your regular schedule.

Brand Name

Sinemet

Ingredients

Carbidopa
Levodopa

Type of Drug

Anti-Parkinsonian.

Prescribed for

Parkinson's disease.

General Information

The 2 ingredients in Sinemet interact for a beneficial drug interaction. Levodopa is the active ingredient that aids treatment of Parkinson's disease. Vitamin B_6 (Pyridoxine) destroys Levodopa, but Carbidopa prevents this. This allows more Levodopa to get into the brain, where it works.

This combination is so effective that the amount of Levodopa can be reduced by about 75 percent, which results in fewer side effects and, generally, safer drug treatment.

Cautions and Warnings

Do not take this drug if you are allergic to either of the ingredients. Patients being switched from Levodopa to Sinemet should stop taking Levodopa 8 hours before their first dose of Sinemet. It can be increased gradually, as needed. Side effects with Sinemet can occur at much lower dosages than with Levodopa, because of the effect of Carbidopa.

Pregnancy/Breast-feeding

These drugs are known to cause birth defects in laboratory animals. The effect in humans is not known. However, women who are pregnant or breast-feeding should use this drug only if it is absolutely necessary.

Seniors

Older adults may require smaller doses of this drug than younger adults because they are less tolerant of the drug's effects. Also, the body enzyme that breaks down Levodopa (and against which Carbidopa protects) decreases with age, reducing the overall dosage requirement. Seniors, especially those with heart disease, are more likely to develop abnormal heart rhythms and other cardiac side effects of this drug.

Seniors who respond to this treatment, especially those with osteoporosis, should resume activity gradually. Sudden

increases in activity and mobility lead to a greater possibility
of broken bones than a gradual return to physical activity.

Possible Side Effects

Uncontrolled muscle movements, loss of appetite, nausea,
vomiting, stomach pain, dry mouth, difficulty swallowing,
dribbling saliva from the side of the mouth, shaking of the
hands, headache, dizziness, numbness, weakness, feeling
faint, grinding of the teeth, confusion, sleeplessness, nightmares, hallucinations, anxiety, agitation, tiredness, feeling of
ill health, feeling of euphoria (high).

Less common side effects are heart palpitations; dizziness
when rising quickly from a sitting or lying position; sudden
extreme slowness of movement (on-off phenomenon); mental changes, including paranoia, psychosis, and depression;
and slowdown of mental functioning. Other side effects include difficult urination, muscle twitching, spasms of the
eyelids, lockjaw, burning sensation on the tongue, bitter
taste, diarrhea, constipation, stomach gas, flushing of the
skin, rash, sweating, unusual breathing, double or blurred
vision, dilation of the pupils of the eyes, hot flashes, changes
in body weight, darkening of the urine or sweat.

Occasionally Sinemet may cause bleeding of the stomach
or development of an ulcer, high blood pressure, adverse
effects on components of the blood, irritation of blood vessels, convulsions, inability to control movements of the eye
muscles, hiccups, feeling of being stimulated, retention of
body fluid, hair loss, hoarseness of the voice, or persistent
penile erection. The drug may affect blood tests for kidney
and liver function.

Drug Interactions

The effectiveness of Sinemet may be increased by taking drugs
with an anticholinergic effect, such as Trihexyphenidyl.

Methyldopa, an antihypertensive drug, has the same effect
on Levodopa as Carbidopa. It can increase the amount of
Levodopa available in the central nervous system, and it
may have a slight effect on Sinemet as well.

Patients taking Guanethidine or a diuretic to treat high
blood pressure may find they need less medication to control their pressure.

Reserpine, benzodiazepine tranquilizers, major tranquilizers, Phenytoin, and Papaverine may interfere with the effects of Sinemet. Vitamin B$_6$ will interfere with Levodopa but not with Sinemet.

Diabetics who start taking Sinemet may need adjustments in their antidiabetic drugs.

Patients taking Sinemet together with a monoamine oxidase (MAO) inhibitor drug may experience a rapid increase in blood pressure. MAO inhibitors should be stopped 2 weeks before Sinemet.

Sinemet may increase the effects of Ephedrine, amphetamines, Epinephrine, and Isoproterenol. This interaction can result in adverse effects on the heart. This reaction may also occur with some of the antidepressants.

Food Interactions

This drug may be taken with food to reduce upset stomach.

Usual Dose

Dose must be tailored to individual need and based on previous drug treatment. Three different Sinemet strengths are available to allow for individual variation: Sinemet 10/100, 25/100, and 25/250. The first number represents the milligrams of Carbidopa and the second number the Levodopa content. Dosage adjustments are made by adding or omitting ½ to 1 tablet per day. Maximum dose is 8 of the 25/250 tablets per day.

Overdosage

Overdose symptoms are exaggerated side effects. Take the victim to a hospital emergency room for treatment. ALWAYS bring the medicine bottle with you.

Special Information

Sinemet can cause tiredness or lack of concentration: Take care while driving or operating machinery.

Call your doctor if you experience dizziness, lightheadedness, or fainting spells, uncontrollable movements of the face, eyelids, mouth, tongue, neck, arms, hands, or legs, mood changes, mental changes, abnormal heartbeats or heart palpitations, difficult urination, or persistent nausea or vomiting or other stomach complaints.

This drug may cause darkening of the urine or sweat. This effect is not harmful, but may interfere with urine tests for diabetes.

Call your doctor before making any adjustments in your treatment.

If you forget to take a dose of Sinemet, take it as soon as you remember. If it is within 2 hours of your next regularly scheduled dose, skip the one you forgot and continue with your regular schedule. Do not take a double dose.

Brand Name
Singlet Tablets

Ingredients

Acetaminophen
Chlorpheniramine Maleate
Pseudoephedrine Hydrochloride

Other Brand Names

Simplet Tablets
Tricom Caplets

The following products contain the same ingredients in different concentrations:

Allergy-Sinus Comtrex Caplets/Tablets
Children's Tylenol Cold Liquid
Codimal Capsules/Tablets
Kolephrin Caplets
PhenAPAP Tablets
Sine-Off Maximum Strength A/S Caplets
Sinus Relief Tablets
Sinutab Maximum Strength Caplets

Type of Drug

Decongestant-antihistamine-analgesic combination.

Prescribed for

Relief of congestion, runny nose, and other general symptoms associated with the common cold, influenza, or other upper respiratory diseases.

General Information

Singlet is one of many products marketed to alleviate the symptoms of the common cold. These products contain medicine to relieve nasal congestion, dry up runny noses, or soothe scratchy throats; several of them may also contain ingredients to suppress cough or to help eliminate unwanted mucus. All of these products are only for the relief of symptoms and will not treat the underlying problem, such as a cold virus or other infections.

Cautions and Warnings

Singlet can cause excessive tiredness or drowsiness. People with glaucoma or difficulty in urinating should avoid this drug and other drugs containing antihistamines.

Pregnancy/Breast-feeding

The ingredients in this drug cross into the blood circulation of a developing baby, but have not been found to cause birth defects. Pregnant women, or those who might become pregnant, should not take it without their doctors' approval. When the drug is considered essential by your doctor, the potential risk of taking the medicine must be carefully weighed against the benefit it might produce.

The ingredients in this drug may pass into breast milk. You must consider the potential effect on the nursing infant if breast-feeding while taking this medicine.

Seniors

Older adults are more sensitive to the effects of this drug. Follow your doctor's directions and report any side effects at once.

Possible Side Effects

Excessive tiredness or drowsiness, restlessness, tension, nervousness, tremor, weakness, inability to sleep, headache, palpitations, elevation of blood pressure, sweating, sleeplessness, loss of appetite, nausea, vomiting, dizziness, constipation.

Drug Interactions

Interaction with alcoholic beverages may produce excessive drowsiness and/or sleepiness or inability to concentrate. Also avoid sedatives, tranquilizers, antihistamines, and sleeping pills.

Do not self-medicate with additional over-the-counter drugs for the relief of cold symptoms: Taking Singlet with such drugs may result in aggravation of high blood pressure, heart disease, diabetes, or thyroid disease.

Do not take Singlet if you are taking or suspect you may be taking a monoamine oxidase (MAO) inhibitor: Severe elevation in blood pressure may result.

Food Interactions

Take this medicine with food it it upsets your stomach.

Usual Dose

1 tablet 3 times per day.

Overdosage

The effects of overdose are generally exaggerated drug side effects. Call a poison control center or hospital emergency room for more information.

Special Information

Since drowsiness may occur during use of Singlet, be cautious while performing mechanical tasks requiring alertness.

If you forget to take a dose of Singlet, take it as soon as you remember. If it is almost time for your next regularly scheduled dose, skip the one you forgot and continue with your regular schedule. Do not take a double dose.

Brand Name

Sinubid Tablets

Ingredients

Acetaminophen
Phenyltoloxamine Citrate
Phenylpropanolamine Hydrochloride

Type of Drug

Decongestant-antihistamine-analgesic combination.

Prescribed for

Relief of congestion, runny nose, and other general symptoms associated with the common cold, influenza, or other upper respiratory diseases.

General Information

Sinubid is one of many products marketed to relieve the symptoms of the common cold. These products contain medicine to relieve nasal congestion, dry up runny noses, or relieve scratchy throats; several of them may contain ingredients to suppress cough or to help eliminate unwanted mucus. All these products are good only for the relief of symptoms and will not treat the underlying problem, such as cold virus or other infections.

Cautions and Warnings

This drug can cause excessive tiredness or drowsiness. Sinubid should not be used for newborn infants. People with glaucoma or difficulty in urinating should avoid this drug and other drugs containing antihistamines.

Pregnancy/Breast-feeding

This drug crosses into the blood circulation of a developing baby. It has not been found to cause birth defects. Pregnant women, or those who might become pregnant while taking this drug, should not take it without their doctors' approval. When the drug is considered essential by your doctor, the potential risk of taking the medicine must be carefully weighed against the benefit it might produce.

The ingredients in this drug may pass into breast milk. You must consider the potential effect on the nursing infant if breast-feeding while taking this medicine.

Seniors

Older adults are more sensitive to the effects of this drug. Follow your doctor's directions and report any side effects at once.

Possible Side Effects

Excessive tiredness or drowsiness, restlessness, tension, nervousness, tremor, weakness, inability to sleep, headache, palpitations, elevation of blood pressure, sweating, loss of appetite, nausea, vomiting, dizziness, constipation.

Drug Interactions

Interaction with alcoholic beverages may produce excessive drowsiness and/or sleepiness or inability to concentrate. Also avoid sedatives, tranquilizers, other antihistamines, and sleeping pills.

Do not self-medicate with over-the-counter drugs for the relief of cold symptoms: Taking Sinubid with such drugs may result in aggravation of high blood pressure, heart disease, diabetes, or thyroid disease.

Do not take Sinubid if you are taking or suspect you may be taking a monoamine oxidase (MAO) inhibitor: Severe elevation in blood pressure may result.

Food Interactions

Take this medicine with food if it upsets your stomach.

Usual Dose

1 tablet morning and night.

Overdosage

The effects of overdose are generally exaggerated drug side effects. Call a poison control center or hospital emergency room for more information.

Special Information

Since drowsiness may occur during use of Sinubid, be cautious while performing mechanical tasks requiring alertness.

If you forget to take a dose of Sinubid, take it as soon as you remember. If it is almost time for your next regularly scheduled dose, skip the one you forgot and continue with your regular schedule. Do not take a double dose.

Generic Name

Sucralfate

Brand Name
Carafate

Type of Drug
Local antiulcer therapy.

Prescribed for
Duodenal ulcer.

General Information
Sucralfate is minimally absorbed into the body from the gastrointestinal (GI) tract; it instead works within the GI tract by exerting a soothing local effect. After the drug binds to proteins in the damaged mucous tissue within the ulcer, it forms a barrier to acids and enzymes normally found in the gastrointestinal tract, protecting the ulcerated tissue from further damage and allowing it to begin to heal naturally. Although Sucralfate does not have any pronounced acid neutralizing effects, and its mechanism of action is completely different from that of Cimetidine, Sucralfate is equally effective in treating duodenal ulcer disease.

Cautions and Warnings
The use of Sucralfate in children is not recommended because the drug has been studied only in adults.

Pregnancy/Breast-feeding
This drug has not been found to cause birth defects. Pregnant women, or those who might become pregnant while taking this drug, should not take it without their doctors' approval. When the drug is considered essential by your doctor, the potential risk of taking the medicine must be carefully weighed against the benefit it might produce.

This drug passes into breast milk, but has caused no problems among breast-fed infants. You must consider the po-

tential effect on the nursing infant if breast-feeding while taking this medicine.

Seniors

Older adults may take this medication without special restriction. Follow your doctor's directions and report any side effects at once.

Possible Side Effects

The most frequent side effect is constipation. Others are diarrhea, nausea, upset stomach, indigestion, dry mouth, rash, itching, back pain, dizziness, sleepiness. The incidence of reported side effects of Sucralfate is only about 5 percent.

Drug Interactions

Sucralfate may decrease the action of Tetracycline, Phenytoin, or Cimetidine. To avoid this, separate doses by 2 hours.

Do not take antacids within a half hour of taking Sucralfate.

Usual Dose

One tablet 4 times per day on an empty stomach.

Overdosage

There have been no reports of human overdoses of Sucralfate. Animals given the equivalent of 5.5 grams per pound of body weight did not experience any unusual effects, and therefore the risk associated with Sucralfate overdose is thought to be minimal.

Special Information

Each dose may be taken 1 hour before meals or 2 hours after meals and before bedtime.

Be sure to take the medicine for a full 6- to 8-week course of treatment.

Notify your doctor if you develop constipation, diarrhea, or other gastrointestinal side effects.

If you forget to take a dose of Sucralfate, take it as soon as you remember. If it is almost time for your next regularly scheduled dose, skip the one you forgot and continue with your regular schedule. Do not take a double dose.

Type of Drug
Sulfa Drugs

Brand Names

Generic Name: Sulfacytine

Renoquid

Generic Name: Sulfadiazine

Microsulfon

(Also available in generic form)

Generic Name: Sulfisoxazole

Gantrisin

(Also available in generic form)

Generic Name: Sulfamethoxazole

Gantanol
Urobak

(Also available in generic form)

Generic Name: Sulfamethizole

Thiosulfil Forte

Generic Name: Sulfasalazine

Azulfidine
Azulfidine EN-Tabs
SAS-500

(Also available in generic form)

Generic Name: Trisulfapyrimidines (Multiple Sulfonamides)

Triple Sulfas No. 2

Prescribed for

Infections. Sulfasalazine may be prescribed for rheumatoid

arthritis, colitis, or Crohn's disease of the intestines. Sulfi-soxazole has been used to prevent middle ear infection.

General Information

Sulfa drugs are prescribed for infections in various parts of the body. They are particularly helpful for urinary tract infections because they tend to be concentrated in the urine when they pass out of the body. They kill bacteria by interfering with the organism's metabolic process. Some organisms may become resistant to the effects of sulfa drugs. Your doctor will test infected urine, blood, or tissue, if possible, against the drugs that may be used to pick the best one. Sulfas are usually a part of this screening process.

Sulfasalazine is different from the other sulfa drugs in that only about ⅓ of the drug is absorbed into the bloodstream. The rest of the dose stays in the intestines and has been found to be effective against colitis and other intestinal irritation.

Cautions and Warnings

Do not take any sulfa drug if you know you are allergic to any member of this group or to a drug chemically related to the sulfas (thiazide-type diuretic, oral antidiabetes medicines).

Sulfasalazine should not be used by people with Aspirin allergy or by children less than 2 years old.

Sulfas should not be taken by people with severe kidney or liver disease.

Pregnancy/Breast-feeding

Sulfa drugs pass into the circulation of a developing fetus. Although this can affect the growing infant, this rarely happens because of the mother's ability to protect her unborn child. Nevertheless, pregnant women and those who might become pregnant should not take a sulfa drug unless directed to do so by their doctors. When the drug is considered essential, the potential benefit of the drug should be weighed against the possible harm it might cause.

Small amounts of sulfa drugs pass into breast milk, but this rarely causes problems. The notable exception are infants deficient in the enzyme known as G-6PD. Infants with this deficiency can develop a severe form of anemia. A nursing infant may also develop diarrhea, rashes, and other problems. Talk to your doctor about the possible effect of taking a sulfa drug while nursing.

Seniors

Seniors with kidney or liver problems should take these drugs with caution. Other seniors may take sulfa drugs without special precaution. Follow your doctor's directions and report any side effects at once.

Possible Side Effects

Headache, itching, rash, sensitivity to strong sunlight, nausea, vomiting, cramps or pains in the abdomen or stomach, a tired or sick feeling, hallucinations, dizziness, ringing or buzzing in the ears, or chills.

Less common side effects are blood diseases or changes in blood composition, arthritic pain, itchy eyes, diarrhea, appetite loss, drowsiness, hearing loss, fever, hair loss, yellow eyes or skin. Sulfasalazine may cause a reduced sperm count.

Drug Interactions

Sulfa drugs may interact with oral antidiabetes drugs, Methotrexate, Warfarin, Phenylbutazone, nonsteroidal anti-inflammatory drugs, Thiazide diuretics, Aspirin drugs, Probenecid, and Phenytoin. In these interactions, amounts of either the sulfa or the other drug in the blood may increase. Contact your doctor or pharmacist for advice if you are taking a sulfa with one of these drugs.

Erythromycin increases the effect of sulfa drugs against infections caused by *H. influenza*, a common cause of middle ear infections.

Sulfa drugs may reduce the effectiveness of oral contraceptives. Women taking this combination may experience breakthrough bleeding.

Sulfasalazine may decrease the effectiveness of Digoxin.

The effects of folic acid may be antagonized by Sulfasalazine.

Food Interactions

Sulfa drugs should be taken on an empty stomach with a

full glass of water. Sulfasalazine may be taken with food if it upsets your stomach.

Usual Dose

Sulfacytine:
Adult: 500 to 1000 milligrams per day for 10 days.
Child (under 14 years of age): not recommended.

Sulfadiazine:
Adult: 2 to 6 grams per day.
Child (over 2 months of age): 34 to 68 milligrams per pound of body weight every day.

Sulfisoxazole:
Adult: 2 to 8 grams a day.
Child (over 2 months of age): 34 to 68 milligrams per pound of body weight every day.

Sulfamethoxazole:
Adult: 2 to 3 grams a day.
Child (over 2 months of age): 23 to 27 milligrams per pound of body weight every day.

Sulfamethizole:
Adult: 1.5 to 4 grams per day.
Child (over 2 months of age): 13 to 20 milligrams per pound of body weight every day.

Sulfasalazine:
Adult: 2 to 4 grams a day.
Child: 13 to 26 milligrams per pound of body weight every day.

Trisulfapyrimidines:
Adult: 2 to 4 grams a day.
Child (over 2 months of age): 34 to 68 milligrams per pound of body weight every day.

Overdosage

Overdose symptoms include appetite loss, nausea, vomiting and colic, dizziness, headache, drowsiness, unconsciousness, high fever. Individuals suspected of having taken a sulfa drug overdose should be taken to a hospital emergency room at once. ALWAYS remember to take the medicine bottle with you.

Special Information

Sulfa drugs often cause unusual sensitivity to the sun. Be sure to use a sunscreen or wear protective clothing until you see how sulfas affect you.

Sore throat, fever, chills, unusual bleeding or bruising, rash, and drowsiness are signs of serious blood disorders and should be reported to your doctor at once. Also call your doctor if you experience ringing in the ears, blood in the urine, difficulty breathing.

Be sure to take the full course of medicine your doctor has prescribed, even if you begin to feel a little better.

Sulfa drugs may interfere with the test for sugar in the urine.

If you forget to take a dose of sulfa medicine take it as soon as you remember. If it is almost time for your next dose and you take the medicine 2 times a day, space the missed dose and your next dose 5 to 6 hours apart, then go back to your regular schedule. If it is almost time for your next dose and you take the medicine 3 or more times a day, take the forgotten dose and the next dose 2 to 4 hours apart, then go back to your regular schedule.

Generic Name

Sulindac

Brand Name

Clinoril

Type of Drug

Nonsteroidal anti-inflammatory.

Prescribed for

Arthritis, bursitis, and other forms of inflammatory diseases.

General Information

Sulindac is one of 10 drugs available in the United States

for arthritis and joint pain. As with the other members of this group, patient response to Sulindac is individual. For some, this drug will work wonders; for others, it will do nothing.

Sulindac and several other nonsteroidal anti-inflammatory drugs (NSAIDs) reduce inflammation, relieve pain, or reduce fever. NSAIDs share the same side effects and may be used by patients who cannot tolerate Aspirin. Choice of one of these drugs over another depends on disease response, side effects seen in a particular patient, convenience of times to be taken, and cost. Different drugs or different doses of the same drug may be tried until the greatest effectiveness is achieved with the fewest side effects.

Treatment of some indications is required for only 7 to 14 days.

Cautions and Warnings

Use Sulindac with extra caution if you have a history of ulcers, bleeding diseases, or allergic reaction to Aspirin. Sulindac should be avoided by children under age 14 and those who have nasal polyps. It is not a simple pain reliever; it should be used only under the strict supervision of your doctor.

Pregnancy/Breast-feeding

Sulindac should be avoided by pregnant women and nursing mothers. When used by a pregnant woman, this drug may have unwanted effects on the heart and blood of the unborn child. If this drug is taken late in the pregnancy, the length of the pregnancy may be increased.

Seniors

Older adults are more sensitive to the effects of this drug. Follow your doctor's directions and report any side effects at once.

Possible Side Effects

Upset stomach, nausea, vomiting, constipation, loss of appetite, gas, stomach cramps and pain, itching and rash, dizziness, headache, nervousness, buzzing or ringing in the ears, swelling of the feet, legs, hands, or arms.

Less common side effects are stomach bleeding, irritation, and ulcer, as well as abnormal liver function, jaundice, and hepatitis. Heart failure in patients with already weak hearts, palpitations, blurred vision, and allergic reactions have occurred.

Drug Interactions

Sulindac may increase the effect of anticoagulant (blood-thinning) drugs.

Probenecid (Benemid) or Aspirin may increase the amount of Sulindac in your blood by reducing its elimination from the body.

Avoid taking Aspirin or alcoholic beverages.

DMSO may reduce the effectiveness of Sulindac.

Sulindac may increase the effects of sulfa drugs, antidiabetes drugs, and Phenytoin or other drugs for severe disorders.

Food Interactions

Since this drug can irritate the stomach, take each dose with food.

Usual Dose

Up to 200 milligrams twice per day.

Overdosage

Patients taking an overdose of Sulindac must be made to vomit to remove any remaining drug from the stomach. Call your doctor or poison control center before doing this. If you must go to a hospital emergency room, ALWAYS bring the medicine bottle.

Special Information

If you are allergic to Aspirin, you may be allergic to Sulindac.

Sulindac may cause blurred vision or dizziness. Take care while driving or performing any task requiring alertness.

Call your doctor if you develop rash, itching, hives, yellowing of the skin or whites of the eyes, black or tarry stools, swelling of hands or feet, sore throat, mouth sores, unusual bleeding or bruising, or shortness of breath.

If you forget to take a dose of Sulindac, take it as soon as

you remember. If it is almost time for your next regularly
scheduled dose, skip the one you forgot and continue with
your regular schedule. Do not take a double dose.

Brand Name

Synalgos-DC Capsules

Ingredients

Aspirin
Caffeine
Dihydrocodeine Bitartrate

(Also available in generic form)

Type of Drug

Narcotic analgesic combination.

Prescribed for

Relief of mild to moderate pain.

General Information

Synalgos-DC is one of many combination products containing a narcotic and an analgesic. These products often
also contain a barbiturate or a tranquilizer. Acetaminophen
may be substituted for Aspirin, or Caffeine may be omitted.
  Caffeine may be of benefit in treating vascular headaches.

Cautions and Warnings

Do not take Synalgos-DC if you know you are allergic or
sensitive to it. Use this drug with extreme caution if you
suffer from asthma or other breathing problems. Long-term
use of Synalgos-DC may cause drug dependence or addiction. Synalgos-DC is a respiratory depressant and affects the
central nervous system, producing sleepiness, tiredness,
and/or inability to concentrate.

Pregnancy/Breast-feeding

Synalgos-DC may cause birth defects or interfere with your

baby's development. Check with your doctor before taking it if you are, or might be, pregnant.

Aspirin used regularly may affect the heart of the newborn and if taken within the last 2 weeks of pregnancy may cause bleeding in the child. Problems may also be seen in the mother herself, such as bleeding or increasing the length of pregnancy or labor.

Caffeine can cause birth defects in animals but has not been shown to cause problems in humans.

Dihydrocodeine can cause addiction in the unborn child if used regularly during pregnancy. It may cause the unborn infant to become dependent on it and cause unwanted side effects. If taken at the time of delivery, Dihydrocodeine may cause breathing problems in the newborn.

Nursing infants may be affected by the narcotic ingredient in this product. Nursing mothers who must take this medicine should use alternative feeding methods.

Seniors

The Dihydrocodeine in this combination product may have more of a depressant effect on seniors than younger adults. Other effects that may be more prominent are dizziness, light-headedness, or fainting when rising suddenly from a sitting or lying position.

Possible Side Effects

The most frequent side effects are light-headedness, dizziness, sleepiness, nausea, vomiting, loss of appetite, sweating. If these effects occur, consider asking your doctor about lowering your dose. Usually the side effects disappear if you simply lie down.

More serious side effects of Synalgos-DC are shallow breathing or difficulty in breathing.

Less common side effects are euphoria (feeling high), weakness, sleepiness, headache, agitation, uncoordinated muscle movement, minor hallucinations, disorientation and visual disturbances, dry mouth, loss of appetite, constipation, flushing of the face, rapid heartbeat, palpitations, faintness, urinary difficulties or hesitancy, reduced sex drive and/or potency, itching, rashes, anemia, lowered blood sugar, yellowing of the skin and/or whites of the eyes. Narcotic analgesics may aggravate convulsions in those who have had convulsions in the past.

Drug Interactions

Interaction with alcohol, tranquilizers, barbiturates, or sleeping pills produces tiredness, sleepiness, or inability to concentrate and seriously increases the depressive effect of Synalgos-DC.

The Aspirin component of Synalgos-DC can affect anticoagulant (blood-thinning) therapy. Be sure to discuss this with your doctor so that the proper dosage adjustment can be made.

Interaction with adrenal corticosteroids, Phenylbutazone, or alcohol can cause severe stomach irritation with possible bleeding.

Food Interactions

Take with food or half a glass of water to prevent stomach upset.

Usual Dose

2 capsules every 4 hours.

Overdosage

Symptoms are depression of respiration (breathing), extreme tiredness progressing to stupor and then coma, pinpointed pupils of the eyes, no response to stimulation such as a pin stick, cold and clammy skin, slowing down of heartbeat, lowering of blood pressure, convulsions, and cardiac arrest. The patient should be taken to a hospital emergency room immediately. ALWAYS bring the medicine bottle.

Special Information

Drowsiness may occur: Be careful when driving or operating hazardous machinery.

If you forget to take a dose of Synalgos-DC, take it as soon as you remember. If it is almost time for your next regularly scheduled dose, skip the one you forgot and continue with your regular schedule. Do not take a double dose.

Generic Name

Tamoxifen Citrate

Brand Name

Nolvadex

Type of Drug

Antiestrogen.

Prescribed for

Breast cancer in women. When used together with chemotherapy after mastectomy surgery, Tamoxifen is effective in
delaying the recurrence of surgically curable cancers in post-
menopausal women or women over age 50. Tamoxifen has
also been prescribed to treat painful breasts and to decrease
swollen painful breasts in men.

General Information

Tamoxifen is effective against breast cancer in women
whose tumors are tested and found to be estrogen-positive.
It works by competing with the sites in tissues to which
estrogens attach. Once Tamoxifen binds to an estrogen receptor, it disrupts the cell in the same way that an estrogen
would and prevents the cancer cell from dividing. Of women
whose breast cancer has spread to other parts of their bodies, 50 to 60 percent may benefit from taking Tamoxifen.

Cautions and Warnings

Eye side effects have occurred in patients taking Tamoxifen
for a year or more in doses at least 4 times above the maximum recommended dosage. A few cases of decreased visual clarity and other eye side effects have been reported at
normal doses.

   Animal studies have shown that very high doses of Tamoxifen (15 milligrams per pound of body weight) may
cause liver cancer.

Pregnancy/Breast-feeding

Because of the antiestrogen effects of this drug, Tamoxifen

may cause harm to a developing baby. Although there are no studies of the effects of Tamoxifen in pregnant women, this drug should be avoided by women who are or might become pregnant. Women who must take Tamoxifen should use an effective contraceptive method since Tamoxifen can actually make you more fertile than normal.

It is not known if Tamoxifen passes into breast milk. Nursing mothers should use an alternative feeding method if they must take Tamoxifen.

Seniors

Seniors may take Tamoxifen without special precaution.

Possible Side Effects

The most common side effects are hot flashes, nausea, and vomiting.

Less common are vaginal bleeding or discharge, irregular periods, skin rash.

Infrequent side effects include high blood calcium levels, swelling of the arms or legs, taste changes, vaginal itch, depression, dizziness, light-headedness, headache, visual difficulty, reduced white-blood-cell count or reduced platelet count. Increases in tumor pain and local disease sometimes follow a good response with Tamoxifen.

Drug Interactions

Tamoxifen may raise blood calcium.

Food Interactions

Tamoxifen is best taken on an empty stomach, but may be taken with food or milk if it upsets your stomach.

Usual Dose

10 to 20 milligrams twice a day (morning and evening).

Overdosage

Overdose may lead to difficulty breathing and convulsions. Overdose victims should be taken to a hospital emergency room for treatment. ALWAYS remember to bring the prescription bottle with you.

Special Information

Be sure to tell your doctor if you become very weak or sleepy, or if you experience confusion, pain, or swelling of your legs, difficulty breathing, or blurred vision.

Tell your doctor if you experience bone pain, hot flashes, nausea, vomiting, weight gain, irregular periods, dizziness, headache, loss of appetite (all drug side effects) while taking Tamoxifen.

Tell your doctor if you vomit shortly after taking a dose of Tamoxifen. Your doctor may tell you to take another dose or wait until the next dose.

If you forget to take a dose of Tamoxifen, skip the forgotten dose, call your doctor, and continue your regular dosing schedule. Do not take a double dose of Tamoxifen.

Brand Name

Tedral Suspension/Tablets

Ingredients

Ephedrine Hydrochloride
Phenobarbital
Theophylline

The following products contain the same ingredients in different concentrations:

Tedral SA Tablets
Tedrigen Tablets

Theodrine Tablets
Theotal Tablets

(Also available in generic form)

Type of Drug

Antiasthmatic combination product.

Prescribed for

Relief of asthma symptoms or other upper respiratory disorders. The actions of this drug should be considered "possibly effective." There is considerable doubt among medical experts that this drug produces the effects claimed for it.

General Information

Tedral is one of several antiasthmatic combination products prescribed for the relief of asthmatic symptoms and other breathing problems. These products contain a drug to help relax the bronchial muscles, a drug to increase the diameter of the breathing passages, and a mild tranquilizer to help relax the patient. Other products in this class may contain similar ingredients along with other medicine to help eliminate mucus from the breathing passages.

Cautions and Warnings

This drug should not be taken if you have severe kidney or liver disease.

Pregnancy/Breast-feeding

Tedral may be required for a woman during pregnancy or nursing. However, there is an increased chance of birth defects while using Tedral during pregnancy. Regularly using Tedral during the last 3 months of pregnancy may cause drug dependency of the newborn. Labor may be prolonged, delivery may be delayed, and there may be breathing problems in the newborn if Tedral is used.

Breast-feeding while using Tedral may cause increased tiredness, shortness of breath, or a slow heartbeat in the baby.

Seniors

Older adults are more sensitive to the effects of this drug. Follow your doctor's directions and report any side effects at once.

Possible Side Effects

Large doses of Tedral can produce excitation, shakiness, sleeplessness, nervousness, rapid heartbeat, chest pains, irregular heartbeat, dizziness, dryness of the nose and throat, headache, and sweating. Occasionally people have been known to develop hesitation or difficulty in urination.

Less common side effects are excessive urination, heart stimulation, drowsiness, muscle weakness, muscle twitching, unsteady walk. These effects can usually be controlled by having your doctor adjust the dose.

Drug Interactions

Tedral may cause sleeplessness and/or drowsiness. Do not take this drug with alcoholic beverages.

Taking Tedral or similar medicines with a monoamine oxidase (MAO) inhibitor can produce severe interaction. Consult your doctor first.

Tedral or similar products taken together with Lithium Carbonate will increase the excretion of Lithium.

Tedral or similar products may neutralize the effect of Propranolol.

Food Interactions

Take the drug with food to help prevent stomach upset.

Usual Dose

Tablet: 1 to 2 tablets every 4 hours.
Sustained-action tablet: 1 tablet every 12 hours.
Elixir or suspension: 1 teaspoon per 60 pounds of body weight every 4 hours.

Overdosage

Symptoms of overdose can include stimulation, nausea, vomiting, nervousness, loss of appetite, irritability, headache, abnormal heart rhythms, convulsions, and seizures. Overdose victims should be taken to a hospital emergency room at once. ALWAYS bring the medicine bottle with you.

Special Information

If you forget to take a dose of Tedral take it as soon as you remember. If it is almost time for your next regularly scheduled dose, skip the one you forgot and continue with your regular schedule. Do not take a double dose.

Generic Name

Temazepam

Brand Name

Restoril

(Also available in generic form)

Type of Drug

Sedative; hypnotic.

Prescribed for

Insomnia or sleeplessness, frequent nighttime awakening, or waking up too early in the morning.

General Information

Temazepam, used only for its effect as a sleep inducer, is a member of the group of drugs known as benzodiazepines. Characterized by Diazepam (Valium), other benzodiazepine drugs are used as antianxiety agents, anticonvulsants, and sedatives (sleeping pills). They exert their effects by relaxing large skeletal muscles and by increasing the effect, in the brain, of an amino acid known as GABA, which slows nerve transmission. Benzodiazepines make it easier to go to sleep and decrease the number of times you wake up during the night.

Temazepam takes about 3 hours to reach its highest blood levels. Its effects last for about 12 hours. Temazepam produces less hangover than some benzodiazepine sleeping pills and more than others. Some people who use Temazepam on a regular basis may find that they get up too early in the morning after taking it for several months.

Benzodiazepines can be abused if taken for long periods of time, and sudden discontinuation of a benzodiazepine can cause drug withdrawal symptoms. Withdrawal symptoms include convulsions, tremors, muscle cramps, insomnia, agitation, diarrhea, vomiting, sweating, and convulsions.

Cautions and Warnings

Do not take Temazepam if you know you are sensitive or allergic to this drug or other benzodiazepines, such as Chlordiazepoxide, Oxazepam, Chlorazepate, Diazepam, Lorazepam, Prazepam, and Clonazepam.

Temazepam and other members of this drug group may aggravate narrow-angle glaucoma, but if you have open-angle glaucoma you may take the drugs. In any case, check this information with your doctor.

Pregnancy/Breast-feeding

This drug may cause birth defects or interfere with your baby's development. Check with your doctor before taking it if you are, or might be, pregnant. Your baby may become dependent on Temazepam if it is used continually during pregnancy. If used during the last weeks of pregnancy or during breast-feeding, the baby may be overtired or short of breath or have a low heartbeat. Use during labor may cause weakness in the newborn.

Seniors

Older adults are more sensitive to the effects of this drug, especially daytime drowsiness. Follow your doctor's directions and report any side effects at once.

Possible Side Effects

The most common side effects are mild drowsiness during the first few days of therapy, especially in older adults or the debilitated. If drowsiness persists, contact your doctor.

Less common side effects include confusion, depression, lethargy, disorientation, headache, tiredness, slurred speech, stupor, dizziness, tremor, constipation, dry mouth, nausea, inability to control urination, changes in sex drive, irregular menstrual cycle, changes in heart rhythm, lowered blood pressure, fluid retention, blurred or double vision, itching, rash, hiccups, nervousness, inability to fall asleep, and, occasionally, liver dysfunction. If you experience any of these reactions, stop taking the medicine and contact your doctor immediately.

Drug Interactions

Temazepam is a central-nervous-system depressant. Avoid alcohol, tranquilizers, narcotics, sleeping pills, barbiturates, monoamine oxidase (MAO) inhibitors, antihistamines, and other medicines used to relieve depression, which may increase Temazepam's depressant effects.

The effects of Temazepam may be increased if you are taking Cimetidine, an oral contraceptive, Disulfiram, Isoniazid, or Probenecid.

Temazepam's effects may be decreased if you are also taking Theophylline or if you smoke cigarettes regularly.

Benzodiazepines may increase the amounts of Digoxin or Phenytoin in your blood.

Food Interactions

Temazepam is best taken on an empty stomach but may be taken with food if it upsets your stomach.

Usual Dose

15 to 30 milligrams at bedtime. The dose must be individualized for maximum benefit.

Overdosage

Symptoms are confusion, sleepiness, lack of response to pain such as a pin stick, shallow breathing, lowered blood pressure, and coma. The patient should be taken to a hospital emergency room immediately. ALWAYS bring the medicine bottle.

Special Information

Temazepam can cause tiredness, drowsiness, inability to concentrate, and similar symptoms. Be careful if you are driving, operating machinery, or performing other activities that require concentration.

Avoid alcoholic beverages while taking Temazepam. Use with caution other sleeping pills, narcotics, tranquilizers, and other drugs that depress the nervous system and/or may interfere with breathing while taking Temazepam.

If you have been taking this drug for a long time, you may experience drug withdrawal symptoms (drug craving, disturbed sleep) if you stop taking it abruptly. Talk to your doctor about gradually reducing the dosage and stopping the medicine.

If you forget to take a dose of Temazepam and you remember within about an hour of your regular time, take it right away. If you do not remember until later, skip the forgotten dose and go back to your regular schedule. Do not take a double dose.

Brand Name

Tenoretic

Ingredients

Atenolol
Chlorthalidone

Type of Drug

Antihypertensive.

Prescribed for

High blood pressure.

General Information

This combination drug product takes advantage of 2 different drug types that are effective in treating high blood pressure: Atenolol is a beta blocker and Chlorthalidone is a diuretic. It is thought that beta blockers lower blood pressure by affecting body hormone systems and the heart, but the exact mechanism is not known. Diuretics lower blood pressure by affecting the amount of potassium in the muscles of blood vessels, helping them to open wider, reducing blood pressure.

Cautions and Warnings

You should be cautious about taking this Atenolol-containing combination if you have asthma, severe heart failure, very slow heart rate, or heart block because the drug can aggravate these conditions. Compared with the other beta blockers, Atenolol has less of an effect on your pulse and bronchial muscles and less of a rebound effect when the drug is discontinued; it produces less tiredness, depression, and intolerance to exercise than other beta-blocking drugs.

People with angina who take Atenolol for high blood pressure should have their drug dosage reduced gradually over 1 to 2 weeks rather than suddenly discontinued. This will avoid possible aggravation of the angina.

Atenolol should be used with caution if you have liver

disease because your ability to eliminate the drug from your body will be impaired.

Do not take Tenoretic if you are allergic or sensitive to it or any other thiazide drug or to any sulfa drug. If you have a history of allergy or bronchial asthma, you may also have a sensitivity or allergy to Tenoretic. It should be avoided if you have kidney or liver disease.

Pregnancy/Breast-feeding

Tenoretic should be avoided by pregnant women or women who might become pregnant while taking it. If the drug is considered essential by your doctor, the potential risk of taking the medicine must be carefully weighed against the benefit it might produce.

Small amounts of Tenoretic may pass into your breast milk. Nursing mothers taking this drug should observe their infants for possible drug-related side effects.

Seniors

Seniors may be more sensitive to the effects of Tenoretic than young adults. Your dosage of this drug must be adjusted to your individual needs by your doctor. Seniors may be more likely to suffer from cold hands and feet and reduced body temperature, chest pains, a general feeling of ill health, sudden difficulty breathing, sweating, or changes in heartbeat because of this medicine.

Possible Side Effects

Atenolol side effects are relatively uncommon, usually develop early in the course of treatment, are relatively mild, and are rarely a reason to stop taking the medication. Side effects increase with increasing dosage and include dizziness, tingling of the scalp, nausea, vomiting, upset stomach, taste distortion, fatigue, sweating, male impotence, urinary difficulty, diarrhea, bile duct blockage, breathing difficulty, bronchial spasms, muscle weakness, cramps, dry eyes, blurred vision, skin rash, hair loss, and facial swelling. Like other beta blockers, Atenolol can cause mental depression, disorientation, short-term memory loss, and emotional instability.

Common Chlorthalidone side effects are loss of body potassium, leading to dry mouth, thirst, weakness, drowsiness, restlessness, muscle pains, cramps, or tiredness, low blood pressure, decreased frequency of urination, abnormal heart rhythm, and upset stomach. Other side effects are loss of appetite, nausea, vomiting, stomach bloating or cramps, diarrhea, constipation, yellowing of the skin or whites of the eyes, pancreas inflammation, liver inflammation (hepatitis), frequent urination (especially at night), headache, dizziness, fatigue, loss of energy, tiredness, a feeling of ill health, numbness in the hands or feet, nervousness, tension, anxiety, irritability, and agitation.

Less common side effects are kidney inflammation, impotence, reduced sex drive, light-headedness, drowsiness, fainting, difficulty sleeping, depression, tingling in the hands or feet, blurred vision, reduced levels of white blood cells and platelets, dizziness when rising quickly from a sitting or lying position, heart palpitations, chest pain, gout attacks, chills, stuffed nose, facial flushing, weight loss, aggravation of lupus erythematosus (a disease of the body's connective tissues), colitis, drug allergy (fever, sore throat), and unusual bleeding or bruising.

Drug Interactions

Beta-blocking drugs may interact with surgical anesthetics to increase the risk of heart problems during surgery. Some anesthesiologists recommend stopping your beta blocker gradually 2 days before surgery.

Atenolol may interfere with the normal signs of low blood sugar and can interfere with the action of insulin or oral antidiabetes medicines.

Taking Atenolol together with Aspirin-containing drugs, Indomethacin, or Sulfinpyrazone can interfere with its blood-pressure-lowering effect.

The effects of Atenolol may be increased by taking phenothiazine antipsychotic medicines with other antihypertensives, like Clonidine, Diazoxide, Nifedipine, Reserpine, or with other drugs that can reduce blood pressure, like Nitroglycerin.

Atenolol may interfere with the effectiveness of some antiasthma drugs, especially Ephedrine and Isoproterenol, and with Theophylline or Aminophylline.

The combination of Atenolol and Phenytoin or Atenolol

and Digitalis drugs can result in excessive slowing of the heart and possible heart block.

Estrogen drugs can interfere with the blood-pressure-lowering effect of Atenolol.

The chances of losing body potassium are increased if you take Chlorthalidone with Digoxin or with a corticosteroid anti-inflammatory drug. If you are taking medicine to treat diabetes and begin taking Chlorthalidone, the dose of your diabetes medicine may have to be adjusted.

Chlorthalidone will increase the effects of Lithium and the chances of developing Lithium toxicity by preventing it from passing out of your body.

People taking Chlorthalidone for high blood pressure or heart failure should take care to avoid nonprescription medicines that might aggravate your condition, such as decongestants, cold and allergy treatments, and diet pills, all of which can contain stimulants. If you are unsure about which medicine to choose, ask your pharmacist.

Dizziness when rising from a sitting or lying position may be worsened by taking Chlorthalidone with alcoholic beverages, barbiturate-type sleeping pills, or narcotic pain relievers.

The effects of Chlorthalidone may be counteracted by Indomethacin because of its effect on the kidneys.

Taking Colestipol or Cholestyramine at the same time as Chlorthalidone will reduce the drug's effect by preventing it from being absorbed into the bloodstream.

Taking Chlorthalidone and other thiazide-type diuretics with calcium or Vitamin D could result in excessive levels of calcium in the blood.

Sulfa drugs may increase the effects of Chlorthalidone by increasing the amount of diuretic drug in the bloodstream.

Chlorthalidone may increase the effect of Quinidine, prescribed for abnormal heart rhythms, by interfering with its release from the body via your kidneys.

Food Interactions

Take this medicine with food if it upsets your stomach. Chlorthalidone may cause loss of hypokalemia (body potassium), a complication that can be avoided by adding foods rich in potassium to your diet. Some potassium-rich foods are tomatoes, citrus fruits, melons, and bananas. It can also be prevented by taking a potassium supplement in pill, powder, or liquid form.

Usual Dose

Adult: 1 to 2 tablets a day.

Senior: Older adults may respond to lower doses of this drug than younger adults and should be treated more cautiously.

Overdosage

Symptoms are changes in heartbeat (unusually slow, unusually fast, or irregular), severe dizziness or fainting, difficulty breathing, bluish-colored fingernails or palms of the hands and seizures, potassium deficiency, dehydration, confusion, dizziness, muscle weakness, upset stomach, excessive thirst, loss of appetite, lethargy (rare), drowsiness, restlessness (rare), tingling in the hands or feet, rapid heartbeat, nausea, and vomiting. The drug may be successfully removed from the stomach by giving Syrup of Ipecac within an hour of the overdose. After an hour has passed, much of the drug will have been absorbed into the blood and symptoms can develop. Take the victim to a hospital emergency room for treatment, and ALWAYS remember to bring the prescription bottle with you.

Special Information

Tenoretic is meant to be taken on a continuous basis. Do not stop taking it unless directed do so by your doctor. Possible side effects of abrupt withdrawal of Atenolol are chest pain, difficulty breathing, sweating, and unusually fast or irregular heartbeat.

Call your doctor at once if any of the following symptoms develop: back or joint pains, difficulty breathing, cold hands or feet, depression, skin rash, changes in heartbeat.

Call your doctor only if the following side effects persist or are bothersome anxiety, diarrhea, constipation, sexual impotence, mild dizziness, headache, itching, nausea or vomiting, nightmares or vivid dreams, upset stomach, trouble sleeping, stuffed nose, frequent urination, unusual tiredness or weakness.

Always take your daily dose of Tenoretic by 10:00 A.M.

Taking it later in the day will increase your chances of being kept awake at night by the need to urinate frequently.

Call your doctor if muscle weakness, cramps, nausea, dizziness, or other severe side effects develop.

If you forget to take a dose of Tenoretic and remember later in the same day, take it as soon as you remember. If you don't remember until the next day, or if it is almost time for your next dose, skip the forgotten dose and continue with your regular schedule. Do not take a double dose of Tenoretic.

Generic Name

Terazosin

Brand Name

Hytrin

Type of Drug

Antihypertensive.

Prescribed for

High blood pressure.

General Information

Terazosin works by opening blood vessels and reducing pressure in them. The tendency of Terazosin to cause water retention limits the usefulness of Terazosin by itself. Thus, Terazosin is generally used together with a diuretic and/or beta-blocking drug.

Cautions and Warnings

Terazosin can cause dizziness and fainting, especially after the first dose in Terazosin therapy is taken. This effect is called "postural hypotension." This effect can be minimized by limiting the first dose of Terazosin to 1 milligram at bedtime. Postural hypotension occurs in about 1 percent of people taking Terazosin and can occur at any time while you are taking the drug; it is rarely severe.

Some people taking Terazosin experience a small but important increase in blood-cholesterol levels. Individuals with an already high blood-cholesterol level should discuss the potential of this problem with their doctor.

Pregnancy/Breast-feeding

There are no studies of Terazosin in pregnant women, and the safety of Terazosin use during pregnancy is not known. Terazosin should be used only when the drug's potential benefits outweigh its potential dangers.

It is not known if Terazosin passes into breast milk. Nursing mothers should use an alternative feeding method if they must take this medication.

Seniors

Older adults may be more sensitive to the effects of Terazosin. Report any unusual side effects to your doctor.

Possible Side Effects

The most common side effects are dizziness, weakness, tiredness, headache.

Other common side effects are palpitations, nausea, stuffed nose, difficulty breathing, sinus irritation, pain in the arms or legs, back pain, nervousness, tingling in the hands or feet, sleepiness, bloating.

Less common side effects include dizziness when rising quickly from a sitting or lying position, rapid heartbeat, abnormal heart rhythms, chest pain, flushing, vomiting, dry mouth, diarrhea, constipation, abdominal pain or discomfort, weight gain, intestinal gas, symptoms of the common cold, flu, or bronchitis, nosebleeds, coughing, runny nose, sore throat, neck or shoulder pains, arthritis or joint pains, symptoms of gout, muscle aches, visual disturbances, reddened eyes, ringing or buzzing in the ears, anxiety and sleeplessness, urinary tract infection, frequent urination, itching, rash, sweating, swelling of the face, and fever.

Rare side effects include depression, reduced sex drive, swelling of the arms or legs, and weight gain.

Drug Interactions

Terazosin may interact with Nitroglycerin or calcium-

channel-blocking drugs to increase the chances of dizziness
and fainting. The blood-pressure-lowering effect of Terazosin may be reduced by Indomethacin.

Other blood-pressure-lowering drugs (diuretics, calcium
channel blockers, beta blockers, etc.) increase the blood-
pressure-lowering effect of Terazosin.

Avoid nonprescription drugs that contain stimulants because they can increase your blood pressure. Your pharmacist will be able to tell what you can and cannot take.

Food Interactions

Terazosin may be taken without regard to food or meals.

Usual Dose

The usual starting dose of Terazosin is 1 milligram at bedtime. The dosage may be increased to a total of 5 milligrams
a day. Terazosin may be taken once or twice a day.

Overdosage

Terazosin overdose may produce drowsiness, poor reflexes,
and reduced blood pressure. Overdose victims should be
taken to a hospital emergency room at once. ALWAYS remember to bring the prescription bottle with you.

Special Information

Take this drug exactly as prescribed. Do not stop taking Terazosin unless directed to do so by your doctor.

Terazosin can cause dizziness, headache, and drowsiness,
especially after you take your drug dose. Before driving or
doing anything that requires intense concentration, wait several hours after taking this medicine. Take your Terazosin at
bedtime to avoid this problem.

If you forget a dose of Terazosin, take it as soon as you
remember and continue with your regular schedule. If you
forget a bedtime dose and don't remember until the next
day, skip the forgotten dose. Do not take a double dose.

Generic Name

Terbutaline Sulfate

Brand Names

Brethaire Inhaler
Brethine Tablets
Bricanyl Tablets

Type of Drug

Bronchodilator.

Prescribed for

Asthma and spasm of the bronchial muscles. This drug has
been used experimentally to prevent or slow down premature labor in pregnant women.

General Information

Terbutaline has a more specific effect than some of the other
bronchodilator drugs and can cause a somewhat lower incidence of side effects on the heart. Often Terbutaline Sulfate
is used with other drugs to enhance beneficial effects. The
tablet takes effect 30 minutes after it has been taken and
continues working for 4 to 8 hours. Therefore it is not used
for an acute asthma attack, but rather to prevent one. Terbutaline inhalation starts working within 5 to 30 minutes and
lasts for 3 to 6 hours.

Cautions and Warnings

This drug should be used with caution by patients who have
angina, heart disease, high blood pressure, a history of
stroke or seizures, diabetes, thyroid disease, prostate disease, or glaucoma.

Pregnancy/Breast-feeding

This drug should be used by women who are pregnant or
breast-feeding only when absolutely necessary. The potential hazard to the unborn child or nursing infant is not known
at this time.

Seniors

Older adults are more sensitive to the effects of this drug. Follow your doctor's directions and report any side effects at once.

Possible Side Effects

Restlessness, anxiety, fear, tension, sleeplessness, tremors, convulsions, weakness, dizziness, headache, flushing, pallor, sweating, nausea and vomiting, loss of appetite, muscle cramps, urinary difficulties.

Less commonly, Terbutaline Sulfate can affect the heart and cardiovascular system, causing high blood pressure, abnormal heart rhythms, and angina. It is less likely to cause these effects than some of the older drugs.

Drug Interactions

The effect of this drug may be increased by antidepressant drugs, some antihistamines, and Levothyroxine. It may antagonize the effects of Reserpine or Guanethidine.

Food Interactions

If the drug causes upset stomach, each dose may be taken with food.

Usual Dose

Tablets:

Adult: 5 milligrams 3 times per day, every 6 hours. No more than 15 milligrams per day.

Child (age 12 to 15): 2.5 milligrams 3 times per day every 6 hours. No more than 7.5 milligrams per day.

Child (under age 12): not recommended.

Inhaler: 2 inhalations taken 1 minute apart every 4 to 6 hours.

Overdosage

Symptoms include palpitation, abnormal heart rhythms, rapid heartbeat, slow heartbeat, chest pain, high blood pressure, fever, chills, cold sweat, blanching of the skin, nausea, vomiting, sleeplessness, delirium, tremor, pinpoint pupils, convulsions, coma, and collapse. If you or someone you know has taken an overdose of this drug call your doctor or bring the patient to a hospital emergency room. ALWAYS remember to bring the prescription bottle with you.

Special Information

Be sure to follow your doctor's instructions for this drug. Using more of it than was prescribed can lead to drug tolerance and actually cause your condition to worsen.

Terbutaline inhalations should be used during the second half of your breath. This allows the medicine to reach more deeply into your lungs.

Call your doctor at once if you develop chest pains, palpitation, rapid heartbeat, muscle tremors, dizziness, headache, facial flushing, or urinary difficulty, or if you still have trouble breathing after using this medicine.

If you miss a dose of Terbutaline, take it as soon as possible. Take the rest of that day's doses at regularly spaced intervals. Go back to your regular schedule the next day.

Generic Name

Terconazole

Brand Names

Terazol 3 Vaginal Suppositories
Terazol 7 Vaginal Cream 0.4%
Terazol 3 Vaginal Cream 0.8%

Type of Drug

Antifungal.

Prescribed for

Treatment of fungus infections in the vagina.

General Information

Terconazole is used as a vaginal cream and as vaginal suppositories. It may also be applied to the skin to treat common fungal infections. It is effective against common fungus infections, but the exact mechanism by which Terconazole exerts its effect is not known.

Cautions and Warnings

Do not use Terconazole if you know you are allergic to it.

Pregnancy/Breast-feeding

Pregnant women should avoid using the vaginal cream during the first 3 months of pregnancy. They should use it during the next 6 months only if it is absolutely necessary.

Terconazole may cause problems in breast-fed infants. Women who must use this product should temporarily bottle-feed their babies or talk with their doctors about using a different product.

Seniors

Older adults may take this medication without special restriction. Follow your doctor's directions and report any side effects at once.

Possible Side Effects

Headache is the most common side effect of Terconazole, affecting 1 in 4 women who use it. Other side effects include body pain, vaginal burning or irritation, and itching. Application of Terconazole cream to the skin can cause unusual sensitivity to the sun.

Drug Interactions

None.

Usual Dose

Vaginal suppository or cream: one applicatorful or suppository into the vagina at bedtime for 3 to 7 days.

Topical: apply to affected areas of skin twice a day for up to 1 month.

Special Information

When using the vaginal cream, insert the whole applicatorful of cream high into the vagina and be sure to complete the full course of treatment prescribed for you. Call your doctor if you develop burning or itching.

Refrain from intercourse or use a condom while using this

product to avoid reinfection. Sanitary napkins may prevent staining of your clothing by Terconazole.

If you forget to take a dose of Terconazole, take it as soon as you remember. If it is almost time for your next regularly scheduled dose, skip the forgotten dose and continue with your regular schedule. Do not take a double dose.

Generic Name

Terfenadine

Brand Name

Seldane

Type of Drug

Antihistamine.

Prescribed for

Seasonal allergy, stuffy and runny nose, itching of the eyes, scratchy throat caused by allergies, and other allergic symptoms such as rash, itching, or hives.

General Information

Terfenadine causes less sedation than almost any other sedating antihistamine used in the United States. It has been widely used and accepted by people who find other antihistamines unacceptable because of the drowsiness and tiredness they cause. Terfenadine appears to work in exactly the same way as Chlorpheniramine and other widely used antihistamines.

Cautions and Warnings

Do not take Terfenadine if you have had an allergic reaction to it in the past. People with asthma or other deep-breathing problems, glaucoma (pressure in the eye), stomach ulcer, or other stomach problems should avoid Terfenadine because its side effects may aggravate these problems.

Pregnancy/Breast-feeding

Do not take any antihistamine without your doctor's knowledge. Animal studies of Terfenadine have shown that doses several times larger than the human dose lower the baby's weight and increase the risk of the baby's death.

Small amounts of antihistamine medicines pass into breast milk and may affect a nursing infant. Nursing mothers should avoid antihistamines or use alternative feeding methods while taking the medicine.

Seniors

Seniors may be more sensitive than younger adults to Terfenadine's side effects. Follow your doctor's directions and report any unusual side effects.

Possible Side Effects

Occasional side effects are headache, nervousness, weakness, upset stomach, nausea, vomiting, dry mouth, nose or throat, sore throat, nosebleeds, cough, stuffy nose, change in bowel habits. In scientific studies, Terfenadine was found to cause the same amount of drowsiness as a placebo (inactive pill) and about half that caused by other antihistamines. It is considered safe for use by people who cannot tolerate the sedating effects of other antihistamine drugs.

Less common side effects include rapid heartbeat, palpitations and other cardiac abnormalities, hair loss, allergic reactions, depression, sleeplessness, menstrual irregularities, muscle aches, sweating, tingling in the hands or feet, frequent urination, visual disturbances. A few people taking this drug have developed liver damage.

Drug Interactions

No interactions between Terfenadine and other drugs have been found. Unlike other antihistamines, Terfenadine does not interact with alcohol or other nervous-system depressants to produce drowsiness or loss of coordination.

Food Interactions

Terfenadine should be taken on an empty stomach, 1 hour before or 2 hours after food or meals, although it may be taken with food or milk if it upsets your stomach.

Usual Dose

Adult and child (over age 12): 60 milligrams twice a day.
Child (age 6 to 12): 30 to 60 milligrams twice a day.
Child (age 3 to 5): 15 milligrams twice a day.

Overdosage

Terfenadine overdose is likely to cause exaggerated side effects. Overdose victims should be given Syrup of Ipecac to make them vomit and be taken to a hospital emergency room for treatment. ALWAYS bring the prescription bottle with you.

Special Information

Report sore throat, unusual bleeding, bruising, tiredness or weakness or any other unusual side effects to your doctor. Terfenadine's only disadvantage is its cost. Equally effective antihistamines with a greater sedative effect are sold over-the-counter without a prescription and can be purchased for relatively little money.

If you forget to take a dose of Terfenadine, take it as soon as you remember. If it is almost time for your next regularly scheduled dose, skip the one you forgot and continue with your regular schedule. Do not take a double dose.

Generic Name

Terpin Hydrate with Codeine

(Available only in generic form)

Type of Drug

Cough suppressant and expectorant combination.

Prescribed for

Relief of coughs due to colds or other respiratory infections.

General Information

Terpin Hydrate decreases the production of mucus and other bronchial secretions which can cause coughs. The cough suppressant effect of Terpin Hydrate with Codeine is primarily due to the Codeine.

Cautions and Warnings

Do not take Codeine if you know you are allergic or sensitive to it. Use this drug with extreme caution if you suffer from asthma or other breathing problems. Long-term use of Codeine may cause drug dependence or addiction. Codeine is a respiratory depressant and affects the central nervous system, producing sleepiness, tiredness, and/or inability to concentrate.

Pregnancy/Breast-feeding

Terpin Hydrate with Codeine is 80 proof (40 percent alcohol). Too much alcohol taken by the mother during pregnancy and lactation may cause birth defects and unwanted problems during breast-feeding.

Terpin Hydrate has not been shown to cause birth defects. Too much (large amounts taken for a long time) narcotic used during pregnancy and breast-feeding may cause the baby to become dependent on the narcotic. Narcotics may also cause breathing problems in the infant during delivery.

Seniors

Older adults are more sensitive to the effects of this drug. Follow your doctor's directions and report any side effects at once.

Possible Side Effects

The most frequent side effects are light-headedness, dizziness, sedation or sleepiness, nausea, vomiting, sweating.

Less common side effects include euphoria (feeling high), weakness, sleepiness, headache, agitation, uncoordinated muscle movement, minor hallucinations, disorientation and visual disturbances, dry mouth, loss of appetite, constipation, flushing of the face, rapid heartbeat, palpitations, faintness, urinary difficulties or hesitancy, reduced sex drive and/or potency, itching, rashes, anemia, lowered blood sugar, yellowing of the skin and/or whites of the eyes. Narcotic analgesics may aggravate convulsions in those who have had convulsions in the past.

Drug Interactions

Codeine has a depressant effect and can affect your breathing. It should be taken with extreme care in combination with alcohol, sedatives, tranquilizers, antihistamines, or other depressant drugs.

Usual Dose

1 to 2 teaspoons every 3 or 4 hours as needed for relief of cough.

Overdosage

Overdose effects can include sleepiness, dizziness, or breathing difficulty. Overdose victims should be taken to a hospital emergency room for treatment. ALWAYS bring the medicine bottle with you.

Special Information

Terpin Hydrate with Codeine elixir contains 40 percent alcohol (80 proof), and it is an easily abused drug product.

Codeine can cause sleepiness, tiredness, or inability to concentrate. Be careful if you are driving, operating machinery, or performing other functions requiring concentration.

To help reduce the cough, try to cough up as much mucus as possible while taking this medication.

If you forget to take a dose of Terpin Hydrate with Codeine, take it as soon as you remember. If it is almost time for your next regularly scheduled dose, skip the one you forgot and continue with your regular schedule. Do not take a double dose.

Generic Name

Tetracycline Hydrochloride

Brand Names

Achromycin V	Sumycin
Ala-Tet	Teline
Nor-Tet	Tetracap
Panmycin	Tetralan
Robitet Robicaps	Tetram

Eye Ointment and Drops

Achromycin

Topical Solution

Topicycline

(Also available in generic form)

Type of Drug

Broad-spectrum antibiotic effective against gram-positive and gram-negative organisms.

Prescribed for

Bacterial infections such as gonorrhea, infections of the mouth, gums and teeth, Rocky Mountain spotted fever and other fevers caused by ticks and lice from a variety of carriers, urinary tract infections, and respiratory system infections such as pneumonia and bronchitis.

These diseases are produced by gram-positive and gram-negative organisms such as diplococci, staphylococci, streptococci, gonococci, *E. coli*, and *Shigella*.

Tetracycline has also been successfully used to treat some skin infections, but it is not considered the first-choice antibiotic for the treatment of general skin infections or wounds. It may be applied to the skin to treat acne.

General Information

Tetracycline Hydrochloride works by interfering with the normal growth cycle of the invading bacteria, preventing them from reproducing and thus allowing the body's normal defenses to fight off the infection. This process is referred to as bacteriostatic action. Tetracycline Hydrochloride has also been used along with other medicines to treat amoebic infections of the intestinal tract, known as amoebic dysentery. It is also prescribed for diseases caused by ticks, fleas, and lice, such as Lyme disease.

Tetracycline Hydrochloride has been successfully used for the treatment of adolescent acne, in small doses over a long period of time. Adverse effects or toxicity in this type of therapy are almost unheard of.

Since the action of this antibiotic depends on its concentration within the invading bacteria, it is imperative that you completely follow the doctor's directions. Another form of Tetracycline Hydrochloride is Oxytetracycline (Terramycin), which is given in the same dose and has the same effects as Tetracycline Hydrochloride.

Cautions and Warnings

Tetracycline Hydrochloride should not be given to people with known liver disease or kidney or urine excretion problems. You should avoid taking high doses of Tetracycline Hydrochloride or undergoing extended Tetracycline Hydrochloride therapy if you will be exposed to sunlight for a long period because this antibiotic can interfere with your body's normal sun-screening mechanism, possibly causing a severe sunburn. If you have a known history of allergy to Tetracycline Hydrochloride you should avoid taking this drug or other drugs within this category such as Aureomycin, Terramycin, Rondomycin, Doxycycline, Demeclocycline, and Minocycline.

Pregnancy/Breast-feeding

You should not use Tetracycline Hydrochloride if you are pregnant, especially during the last half of pregnancy, or when breast-feeding, when the child's bones and teeth are being formed. Tetracycline Hydrochloride when used in children has been shown to interfere with the development of the long bones and may retard growth. Exceptions would be when Tetracycline Hydrochloride is the only effective antibiotic available and all risk factors have been made known to the patient.

Seniors

Older adults, especially those with poor kidney function, may be more susceptible to long-term side effects from Tetracycline.

Possible Side Effects

As with other antibiotics, the common side effects of Tetracycline Hydrochloride are stomach upset, nausea, vomiting, diarrhea, and rash. Less common side effects include hairy tongue and itching and irritation of the anal and/or vaginal region. If these symptoms appear, consult your physician immediately. Periodic physical examinations and laboratory tests should be given to patients who are on long-term Tetracycline Hydrochloride.

Less common side effects include loss of appetite, peeling of the skin, sensitivity to the sun, fever, chills, anemia, possible brown spotting of the skin, decrease in kidney function, damage to the liver.

Drug Interactions

Tetracycline Hydrochloride (a bacteriostatic drug) may interfere with the action of bactericidal agents such as Penicillin. It is not advisable to take both during the same course of therapy.

Don't take multivitamin products containing minerals at the same time as Tetracycline Hydrochloride, or you may reduce the antibiotic's effectiveness. Space the taking of these medicines at least 2 hours apart.

People receiving anticoagulation therapy (blood-thinning agents) should consult their doctor, since Tetracycline Hydrochloride will interfere with this form of therapy. An adjustment in the anticoagulant dosage may be required.

Food Interactions

Take on an empty stomach 1 hour before or 2 hours after meals and with 8 ounces of water. The antibacterial effect of Tetracycline Hydrochloride may be neutralized when taken with food, some dairy products (such as milk or cheese), or antacids.

Usual Dose

Adult: 250 to 500 milligrams 4 times per day.

Child (age 9 and over): 50 to 100 milligrams 4 times per day.

Child (up to age of 8): should avoid Tetracycline Hydrochloride, as it has been shown to produce serious discoloration of the permanent teeth.

Overdosage

Overdose is most likely to affect the stomach and digestive system. Call a poison control center or hospital emergency room for more information.

Special Information

Do not take after the expiration date on the label. The decomposition of Tetracycline Hydrochloride produces a highly toxic substance that can cause serious kidney damage.

If you miss a dose of Tetracycline Hydrochloride, take it as soon as possible. If it is almost time for your next dose and you take the medication once a day, space the missed dose and your next dose 10 to 12 hours apart, then go back to your regular schedule.

If it is almost time for your next dose and you take the medicine twice a day, space the missed dose and your next dose by 5 to 6 hours, then go back to your regular schedule.

If it is almost time for your next dose and you take the medicine 3 or more times a day, space the missed dose and your next dose by 2 to 4 hours, then go back to your regular schedule.

Generic Name

Theophylline

Brand Names

Accurbron Syrup
Aerolate Oral Solution
Aquaphyllin Syrup
Asmalix Elixir
Bronkodyl Capsules
Elixomin Elixir
Elixophyllin Capsules/Elixir
Lanophyllin Elixir

Quibron-T Tablets
Slo-Phyllin Syrup/Tablets
Theoclear-80 Syrup

Theolair Solution/Tablets
Theostat 80 Syrup

Timed-Release Products

Aerolate Capsules
Constant-T Tablets
Elixophyllin SR Capsules
Quibron-T/SR Dividose
  Tablets
Respbid Tablets
Slo-Bid Gyrocaps
Slo-Phyllin Gyrocaps
Sustaire Tablets
Theobid Duracaps
Theobid Jr. Duracaps
Theochron Tablets

Theoclear L.A. Cenules
Theo-Dur Tablets
Theo-Dur Sprinkle Capsules
Theolair-SR Tablets
Theophylline S.R. Tablets
Theo-Sav Tablets
Theospan-SR Capsules
Theo-24 Capsules
Theovent Capsules
T-Phyl Tablets
Uniphyl Tablets

(Also available in generic form)

Type of Drug

Xanthine bronchodilator.

Prescribed for

Relief of bronchial asthma and spasms of bronchial muscles associated with emphysema, bronchitis, and other diseases.

General Information

Theophylline is one of several drugs known as xanthine derivatives, which are the mainstay of therapy for bronchial asthma and similar diseases. Other members of this group are Aminophylline, Dyphylline, and Oxtriphylline. Although the dosage for each of these drugs is different, they all work by relaxing bronchial muscles and helping reverse spasms in these muscles.

Timed-release products allow Theophylline to act continually throughout the day. This usually allows you to decrease the total number of different doses to be taken during a 24-hour period.

Initial Theophylline treatment requires your doctor to take

blood samples to assess how much Theophylline is in your blood. Usually a level of between 10 and 20 micrograms per milliliter (quantity per blood volume) is considered normal. Dosage adjustments may be required based on these blood tests and your response to the therapy.

Theophylline, or another xanthine, can be found combined in almost 100 prescription or nonprescription drugs.

Cautions and Warnings

Do not take Theophylline if you are allergic or sensitive to it or to any related drug, such as Aminophylline. If you have a stomach ulcer or heart disease, you should use this drug with caution.

Pregnancy/Breast-feeding

This drug passes into the circulation of the developing baby. It does not cause birth defects, but may result in dangerous drug levels in the infant's bloodstream. Babies born of mothers taking Theophylline may be nervous, jittery, and irritable, and may gag and vomit when fed. Women who must use this medication to control asthma or other conditions should talk with their doctor about the relative risks of using this medication and the benefits it will produce for them.

This medication passes into breast milk and may cause a nursing infant to have difficulty sleeping and be nervous or irritable.

Seniors

Older adults may take longer to clear this drug from their bodies than younger adults. Older adults with heart failure or other cardiac conditions, chronic lung disease, a virus infection with fever, or reduced liver function may require a lower dosage of this medication to account for the clearance effect.

Possible Side Effects

Possible side effects from Theophylline or other xanthine derivatives are nausea, vomiting, stomach pain, diarrhea, irritability, restlessness, difficulty sleeping, excitability, muscle twitching or spasms, heart palpitations, other unusual heart rates, low blood pressure, rapid breathing, and local irritation (particularly if a suppository is used).

Infrequent side effects include vomiting blood, fever, headache, dehydration.

Drug Interactions

Taking Theophylline at the same time as another xanthine derivative may increase side effects. Don't do it except under the direct care of a doctor.

Theophylline is often given in combination with a stimulant drug such as Ephedrine. Such combinations can cause excessive stimulation and should be used only as specifically directed by your doctor.

Reports have indicated that combining Erythromycin, flu vaccine, Allopurinol, or Cimetidine with Theophylline will give you higher blood levels of Theophylline. Remember that higher blood levels mean the possibility of more side effects.

Smoking cigarettes or marijuana makes Theophylline less effective.

Food Interactions

Take on an empty stomach, at least 1 hour before or 2 hours after meals. Occasional mild stomach upset can be minimized by taking the dose with some food (note that if you do this, a reduced amount of drug will be absorbed into your bloodstream).

The way Theophylline acts in your body may be influenced by your diet. Charcoal-broiled beef, for example, may cause the amount of Theophylline that is being eliminated in the urine to increase. Therefore you may experience a decreased effect of the drug. This is also true for people with a diet low in carbohydrates and high in protein or for people who smoke.

Caffeine (also a xanthine derivative) may add to the side effects of Theophylline. It is recommended that you avoid large amounts of caffeine-containing foods such as coffee, tea, cocoa, cola, or chocolate.

Usual Dose

These dosage guidelines may seem backwards because children require more drug per pound of body weight than adults. This is because children metabolize (chemically change) Theophylline faster than adults do.

Adult: 6 to 7.5 milligrams per pound of body weight per day, up to 900 or 1,100 milligrams.

Adolescent (age 12 to 16): 8.1 to 10.4 milligrams per pound of body weight per day.

Child (age 9 to 11): 9 to 11.5 milligrams per pound of body weight per day.

Child (under age 9): 10.9 to 13.8 milligrams per pound of body weight per day.

Timed-released products are usually taken 1 to 3 times per day at the same doses, depending on your response.

The best dose of Theophylline is tailored to your needs and the severity of your disease: It is the lowest dose that will produce maximum control of your symptoms.

Overdosage

The first symptoms are loss of appetite, nausea, vomiting, difficulty sleeping, and restlessness, followed by unusual behavior patterns, frequent vomiting, and extreme thirst, with delirium, convulsions, very high temperature, and collapse. These serious toxic symptoms are rarely experienced after overdose by mouth, which produces loss of appetite, nausea, vomiting, and stimulation. The overdosed patient should be taken to a hospital emergency room where proper treatment can be given. ALWAYS bring the medicine bottle.

Special Information

If you forget to take a dose of Theophylline, take it as soon as you remember. If it is almost time for your next regularly scheduled dose, skip the one you forgot and continue with your regular schedule. Do not take a double dose.

Type of Drug
Thiazide Diuretics

Brand Names

Generic Name: Bendroflumethiazide

Naturetin

Generic Name: Benzthiazide

Exna
Hydrex

Generic Name: Chlorothiazide

Diachlor
Diurigen
Diuril
(Also available in generic form)

Generic Name: Chlorthalidone

Hygroton
Hylidone
Thalitone

(Also available in generic form)

Generic Name: Hydrochlorothiazide

Diaqua	Hydro-T
Esidrix	Hydro-Z-50
Hydro-Chlor	Mictrin
HydroDIURIL	Oretic
Hydromal	Thiuretic

(Also available in generic form)

Generic Name: Hydroflumethiazide

Diucardin
Saluron

(Also available in generic form)

Generic Name: Indapamide

Lozol

Generic Name: Metolazone

Diulo
Microx
Zaroxolyn

Generic Name: Methyclothiazide

Aquatensen
Enduron
Ethon

(Also available in generic form)

Generic Name: Polythiazide

Renese

Generic Name: Quincthazone

Hydromox

Generic Name: Trichlormethiazide

Diurese   Niazide
Metahydrin   Trichlorex
Naqua

(Also available in generic form)

Prescribed for

Congestive heart failure, cirrhosis of the liver, kidney mal-
function, high blood pressure, and other conditions where it
is necessary to rid the body of excess water.

General Information

Thiazide diuretics act on the kidneys to stimulate the production of large amounts of urine. They also cause you to lose
bicarbonate, chloride, and potassium ions from the body.
They are used as part of the treatment of any disease where
it is desirable to eliminate large quantities of body water.
These diseases include heart failure, some kidney diseases,

and liver disease. Thiazide drugs are often taken together with other medicines to treat high blood pressure.

Cautions and Warnings

Do not take a thiazide diuretic if you are allergic or sensitive to any drugs of this group or to sulfa drugs. If you have a history of allergy or bronchial asthma, you may also have a sensitivity or allergy to thiazide diuretics.

Pregnancy/Breast-feeding

Although these drugs have been used to treat specific conditions in pregnancy, unsupervised use by pregnant patients should be avoided. Thiazide diuretics cross the placenta and can cause side effects in the newborn infant, such as jaundice, blood problems, and low potassium. Birth defects have not been seen in animal studies.

Thiazide diuretics pass into breast milk. No problems have been reported in nursing infants, but nursing mothers should consider an alternative feeding method.

Seniors

Older adults are more sensitive to the effects of these drugs, especially dizziness. They should closely follow their doctor's directions and report any side effects at once.

Possible Side Effects

Thiazide diuretics cause loss of body potassium. Signs of low potassium are dryness of the mouth, thirst, weakness, lethargy, drowsiness, restlessness, muscle pains or cramps, muscular tiredness, low blood pressure, decreased frequency of urination and decreased amount of urine produced, abnormal heart rate, stomach upset including nausea and vomiting. To treat this, potassium supplements are given in the form of tablets, liquids, or powders or by consumption of foods such as bananas, citrus fruits, melons, and tomatoes is increased.

Less common side effects are loss of appetite, stomach upset, nausea, vomiting, cramping, diarrhea, constipation, dizziness, headache, tingling of the toes and fingers, restlessness, changes in blood composition, sensitivity to sunlight, rash, itching, fever, difficulty in breathing, allergic reactions, dizziness when rising quickly from a sitting or lying position, muscle spasms, weakness, and blurred vision.

Drug Interactions

Thiazide diuretics increase the action of other blood-pressure-lowering drugs. This is good and is the reason why people with high blood pressure often take more than one medicine.

The possibility of developing imbalances in body fluids (electrolytes) is increased if you take medications such as Digitalis and adrenal corticosteroids while you take a thiazide diuretic.

If you are taking an oral antidiabetic drug and begin taking a thiazide diuretic, the antidiabetic dose may have to be altered.

Lithium Carbonate taken with a thiazide diuretic should be monitored carefully by a doctor because there may be an increased risk of Lithium toxicity.

If you are taking a thiazide diuretic for the treatment of high blood pressure or congestive heart failure, avoid over-the-counter medicines for the treatment of coughs, colds, and allergies: Such medicines may contain stimulants. If you are unsure about them, ask your pharmacist.

Usual Dose

Bendroflumethiazide: Initial dose, up to 20 milligrams 1 to 2 times per day. Maintenance dose, 2.5 to 5 milligrams per day. It is recommended that you take this drug in the morning to avoid the possibility of your sleep being disturbed by the need to urinate.

Benzthiazide: Initial dose, 50 to 200 milligrams per day. Daily dosages over 100 milligrams should be divided into 2 doses, to be taken after morning and evening meals. Maintenance dose, 50 to 150 milligrams per day.

Chlorothiazide:
Adult: 0.5 to 1 gram 1 to 2 times per day. Often people respond to intermittent therapy, that is, taking the drug on alternate days or 3 to 5 days per week. This reduces side effects.

Child: 10 milligrams per pound of body weight each day in 2 equal doses.

Infant (under age 6 months): up to 15 milligrams per pound of body weight per day in 2 equal doses.

Chlorthalidone: 50 to 100 milligrams per day, or 100 milligrams on alternate days or 3 days per week. Some patients may require 150 or 200 milligrams per day; doses of more than 200 milligrams per day generally do not produce greater response. A single dose is taken with food in the morning.

Hydrochlorothiazide:
Adult: 25 to 200 milligrams per day, depending on condition treated. Maintenance dose, 25 to 100 milligrams per day; some patients may require up to 200 milligrams per day. It is recommended that you take this drug early in the morning to avoid the possibility of your sleep being disturbed by the need to urinate.
Child (age 6 months and over): 1 milligram per pound of body we weight per day in 2 doses.
Infant (under age 6 months): 1.5 milligrams per pound per day in 2 doses.

Hydroflumethiazide: Initial dose, 50 milligrams 1 or 2 times per day. Maintenance dose, 25 to 200 milligrams per day. Daily dosages over 100 milligrams should be divided into separate doses.

Indapamide: 2.5 milligrams per day, taken in the morning. Dosage may be increased to 5 milligrams per day.

Metolazone: Dosage is individualized. Diulo and Zaroxolyn: 2.5 to 20 milligrams once per day, depending on condition treated. Microx: 0.5 milligrams once per day, taken in the morning. Dosage may be increased to 1 milligram per day.

Methyclothiazide: 2.5 to 10 milligrams per day, in the morning.

Polythiazide: 1 to 4 milligrams per day.

Quinethazone: 50 to 100 milligrams per day. Occasionally dosages of 100 milligrams are divided into 2 doses. Some patients may require 150 to 200 milligrams per day.

Trichlormethiazide: 1 to 4 milligrams per day.

Thiazide diuretic doses must be adjusted until maximum therapeutic response at minimum effective dose is reached.

Overdosage

Signs can be tingling in the arms or legs, weakness, fatigue, changes in your heartbeat, a sickly feeling, dry mouth, restlessness, muscle pains or cramps, urinary difficulty, nausea, or vomiting. Take the overdose victim to a hospital emergency room for treatment at once. ALWAYS bring the prescription bottle and any remaining medicine.

Special Information

If you forget to take a dose of a thiazide diuretic, take it as soon as you remember. If it is almost time for your next regularly scheduled dose, skip the one you forgot and continue with your regular schedule. Do not take a double dose.

Generic Name

Thioridazine Hydrochloride

Brand Name

Mellaril
Mellaril-S

(Also available in generic form)

Type of Drug

Phenothiazine antipsychotic.

Prescribed for

Psychotic disorders; moderate to severe depression with anxiety; control of agitation or aggressiveness in disturbed children; alcohol withdrawal symptoms; intractable pain; senility.

General Information

Thioridazine Hydrochloride and other members of the phenothiazine group act on a portion of the brain called the hypothalamus. They affect parts of the hypothalamus that control metabolism, body temperature, alertness, muscle tone, hormone balance, and vomiting and may be used to treat problems related to any of these functions.

Cautions and Warnings

Thioridazine Hydrochloride should not be taken if you are allergic to one of the drugs in the broad classification known as phenothiazine drugs. Do not take Thioridazine Hydrochloride if you have any blood, liver, kidney, or heart disease, very low blood pressure, or Parkinson's disease. This medication is a tranquilizer and can have a depressive effect, especially during the first few days of therapy.

This drug should be used with caution and under strict supervision of your doctor if you have glaucoma, epilepsy, ulcer, or difficulty passing urine.

Pregnancy/Breast-feeding

Infants born to women taking this medication have experienced drug side effects (liver jaundice, nervous system effects) immediately after birth. Check with your doctor about taking this medication if you are, or might become, pregnant.

This drug may pass into breast milk and affect a nursing infant. Consider alternative feeding methods if you must take this medicine.

Seniors

Older adults are more sensitive to the effects of this medication than younger adults and usually require a lower dosage to achieve a desired effect. Also, older adults are more likely to develop drug side effects. Some experts feel that seniors should be treated with $\frac{1}{2}$ to $\frac{1}{4}$ the usual adult dose.

Possible Side Effects

The most common side effect is drowsiness, especially during the first or second week of therapy. If the drowsiness becomes troublesome, contact your doctor.

Thioridazine Hydrochloride can cause jaundice (yellowing of the whites of the eyes or skin), usually in 2 to 4 weeks. The jaundice usually goes away when the drug is discontinued, but there have been cases when it did not. If you notice this effect or if you develop symptoms such as fever and generally not feeling well, contact your doctor immediately.

Less frequent side effects include changes in components of the blood including anemias, raised or lowered blood pressure, abnormal heart rates, heart attack, feeling faint or dizzy.

Phenothiazines can produce extrapyramidal effects, such as spasms of the neck muscles, rolling back of the eyes, convulsions, difficulty in swallowing, and symptoms associated with Parkinson's disease. These effects look very serious but disappear after the drug has been withdrawn; however, symptoms of the face, tongue, and jaw may persist for as long as several years, especially in older adults with a history of brain damage. If you experience extrapyramidal effects contact your doctor immediately.

Thioridazine Hydrochloride may cause an unusual increase in psychotic symptoms or may cause paranoid reactions, tiredness, lethargy, restlessness, hyperactivity, confusion at night, bizarre dreams, inability to sleep, depression and euphoria. Other reactions are itching, swelling, unusual sensitivity to bright lights, red skin, and rash. There have been cases of breast enlargement, false positive pregnancy tests, changes in menstrual flow in females, and impotence and changes in sex drive in males, as well as stuffy nose, headache, nausea, vomiting, loss of appetite, change in body temperature, loss of facial color, excessive salivation, excessive perspiration, constipation, diarrhea, changes in urine and stool habits, worsening of glaucoma, blurred vision, weakening of eyelid muscles, spasms in bronchial and other muscles, increased appetite, fatigue, excessive thirst, and changes in the coloration of skin, particularly in exposed areas.

Drug Interactions

Thioridazine Hydrochloride should be taken with caution in combination with barbiturates, sleeping pills, narcotics, other tranquilizers, or any other medication which may produce a depressive effect. Avoid alcohol.

Food Interactions

Caffeine-containing foods such as coffee, tea, cola drinks, or

chocolate may counteract the effects of Thioridazine Hydrochloride.

Usual Dose

Adult: for treatment of psychosis, 50 to 100 milligrams per
day at first, then 50 to 800 milligrams per day as required
to control symptoms effectively without overly sedating the
patient.
Child: 20 to 75 milligrams per day.

Overdosage

Symptoms are depression, extreme weakness, tiredness, desire to go to sleep, coma, lowered blood pressure, uncontrolled muscle spasms, agitation, restlessness, convulsions,
fever, dry mouth, and abnormal heart rhythms. The patient
should be taken to a hospital emergency room immediately.
ALWAYS bring the medicine bottle.

Special Information

This medication may cause drowsiness. Use caution when
driving or operating complex equipment and avoid alcoholic
beverages while taking the medicine.

The drug may also cause unusual sensitivity to the sun
and turn your urine reddish-brown to pink.

If dizziness occurs, avoid sudden changes in posture and
avoid climbing stairs.

Avoid insecticides. Also avoid exposure to extreme heat
because this drug can affect your body's temperature control center and make you more prone to heat stroke.

Liquid Thioridazine concentrate can cause local reactions;
avoid skin contact. You should dilute the concentrate just
before you take it by adding it to about 4 ounces of juice or
water.

If you take Thioridazine once a day and forget your dose,
take it as soon as possible. If you don't remember until the
next day, skip the forgotten dose and continue with your
regular schedule.

If you take the medicine more than once a day and forget
a dose, take the forgotten dose as soon as possible. If it is
almost time for your next dose, skip the forgotten dose and
go on with your regular schedule.

Generic Name

Thiothixene

Brand Name

Navane

(Also available in generic form)

Type of Drug

Thioxanthene antipsychotic.

Prescribed for

Psychotic disorders.

General Information

Thiothixene is one of many nonphenothiazine agents used in the treatment of psychosis. The drugs in this group are usually about equally effective when given in therapeutically equivalent doses. The major differences are in type and severity of side effects. Some patients may respond well to one and not at all to another: This variability is not easily explained and is thought to relate to inborn biochemical differences.

Cautions and Warnings

Thiothixene should not be used by patients who are allergic to it. Patients with blood, liver, kidney, or heart disease, very low blood pressure, or Parkinson's disease should avoid this drug.

Pregnancy/Breast-feeding

Infants born to women taking this medication have experienced drug side effects (liver jaundice, nervous system effects) immediately after birth. Check with your doctor about taking this medicine if you are, or might become, pregnant.

This drug may pass into breast milk and affect a nursing infant. Consider alternative feeding methods if you must take this medicine.

Seniors

Older adults are more sensitive to the effects of this medication than younger adults and usually require a lower dosage to achieve a desired effect. Also, older adults are more likely to develop drug side effects. Some experts feel that seniors should be treated with ½ to ¼ the usual adult dose.

Possible Side Effects

The most common side effect is drowsiness, especially during the first or second week of therapy. If the drowsiness becomes troublesome, contact your doctor.

Thiothixene can cause jaundice (yellowing of the whites of the eyes or skin), usually in 2 to 4 weeks. The jaundice usually goes away when the drug is discontinued, but there have been cases when it did not. If you notice this effect or if you develop symptoms such as fever and generally do not feel well, contact your doctor immediately.

Less frequent side effects include changes in components of the blood including anemias, raised or lowered blood pressure, abnormal heartbeat, heart attack, feeling faint or dizzy

Thioxanthene drugs can produce extrapyramidal effects, such as spasms of the neck muscles, severe stiffness of the back muscles, rolling back of the eyes, convulsions, difficulty in swallowing, and symptoms associated with Parkinson's disease. These effects look very serious but disappear after the drug has been withdrawn; however, symptoms of the face, tongue, and jaw may persist for several years, especially in the elderly with a long history of brain damage. If you experience extrapyramidal effects contact your doctor immediately.

Thiothixene may cause an unusual increase in psychotic symptoms or may cause paranoid reactions, tiredness, lethargy, restlessness, hyperactivity, confusion at night, bizarre dreams, inability to sleep, depression, or euphoria. Other reactions are itching, swelling, unusual sensitivity to bright lights, red skin, and rash. There have been cases of breast enlargement, false positive pregnancy tests, changes in menstrual flow in females, and impotence and changes in sex drive in males.

Thiothixene may also cause dry mouth, stuffy nose, head-

ache, nausea, vomiting, loss of appetite, change in body
temperature, loss of facial color, excessive salivation, excessive perspiration, constipation, diarrhea, changes in urine
and stool habits, worsening of glaucoma, blurred vision,
weakening of eyelid muscles, and spasms in bronchial and
other muscles, as well as increased appetite, fatigue, excessive thirst, and changes in the coloration of skin, particularly
in exposed areas.

Drug Interactions

Thiothixene should be taken with caution in combination
with barbiturates, sleeping pills, narcotics, other tranquilizers, or any other medication which produces a depressive
effect. Avoid alcohol.

Usual Dose

Adult and child (age 12 and over): 2 milligrams 3 times
per day, to start. Dose is increased according to patient's
need and may go to 60 milligrams per day.
   Child (under age 12): not recommended.

Overdosage

Symptoms are depression, extreme weakness, tiredness, desire to go to sleep, coma, lowered blood pressure, uncontrolled muscle spasms, agitation, restlessness, convulsions,
fever, dry mouth, and abnormal heart rhythms. The patient
should be taken to a hospital emergency room immediately.
ALWAYS bring the medicine bottle.

Special Information

This medication may cause drowsiness. Use caution when
driving or operating complex equipment and avoid alcoholic
beverages while taking the medicine.
   The drug may also cause unusual sensitivity to the sun
and can turn your urine reddish-brown to pink.
   If dizziness occurs, avoid sudden changes in posture and
avoid climbing stairs.
   Use caution in hot weather. This medicine may make you
more prone to heat stroke.
   Liquid Thiothixene concentrate can cause local reactions;
avoid skin contact. You should dilute the concentrate just

before you take it by adding it to about 4 ounces of juice or water.

If you forget to take a dose of Thiothixene, take it as soon as you remember. If it is within 2 hours of your next regularly scheduled dose, skip the one you forgot and continue with your regular schedule. Do not take a double dose.

Generic Name

Thyroglobulin

Brand Name

Proloid

Type of Drug

Thyroid replacement.

Prescribed for

Replacement of thyroid hormone or low output of hormone from the thyroid gland.

General Information

Thyroglobulin is used to replace the normal output of the thyroid gland when it is unusually low. The drug is obtained from purified extract of frozen hog thyroid and is chemically standardized according to its iodine content. Thyroglobulin, or other forms of thyroid therapy, may be used for short periods in some people or for long periods in others. Some people take a thyroid replacement drug for their entire lives. It is important for your doctor to check periodically that you are receiving the correct dose. Occasionally a person's need for thyroid replacement changes, in which case the dose should also be changed: Your doctor can do this only by checking certain blood tests.

Thyroglobulin is one of several thyroid replacement products available. The major difference between these products is in effectiveness in treating certain phases of thyroid disease.

Cautions and Warnings

If you have hyperthyroid disease or high output of thyroid hormone you should not use Thyroglobulin. Symptoms of hyperthyroid disease include headache, nervousness, sweating, rapid heartbeat, chest pains, and other signs of central-nervous-system stimulation. If you have heart disease or high blood pressure, thyroid replacement therapy should not be used unless it is clearly indicated and supervised by your doctor. If you develop chest pains or other signs of heart disease while you are taking thyroid medication, contact your doctor immediately.

Pregnancy/Breast-feeding

The amount of thyroid replacement hormone you take may have to be adjusted during pregnancy. Small amounts of the thyroid hormones will find their way into the bloodstream of a developing fetus. However, they have not been associated with birth defects or other problems when used in the dosages required to maintain normal thyroid function in the mother.

Small amounts of the thyroid hormones pass into breast milk but have not been associated with problems in nursing infants.

Seniors

Older adults are more sensitive to the effects of the thyroid hormones. The usual dosage of thyroid hormones should be reduced by about 25 percent after age 60.

Possible Side Effects

The most common side effects are palpitations of the heart, rapid heartbeat, abnormal heart rhythms, weight loss, chest pains, menstrual irregularity, shaking hands, headache, diarrhea, nervousness, inability to sleep, heat discomfort, and sweating. These symptoms may be controlled by adjusting the dose of the medication. If you are suffering from one or more side effects, you must contact your physician immediately so that the proper dose adjustment can be made.

Drug Interactions

Avoid over-the-counter coughs, cold, or allergy remedies

that contain stimulant drugs, which will affect your heart and may cause symptoms of overdosage.

Thyroid replacement therapy may increase the effect of anticoagulant (blood-thinning) drugs such as Warfarin or Bishydroxycoumarin. Be sure you report this to your physician because it will be necessary to reduce the dose of your anticoagulant drug by approximately ⅓ at the beginning of thyroid therapy (to avoid hemorrhage). Further adjustments may be made later, after your doctor reviews your blood tests.

Diabetics may have to increase their dose of Insulin or oral antidiabetic drugs. Changes in dose must be made by a physician.

Taking a thyroid hormone together with Colestipol or Cholestyramine can reduce the effect of the thyroid product by preventing its passage into your bloodstream. Separate doses of these 2 medicines by 4 to 5 hours.

The combination of Maprotiline and a thyroid hormone may increase the chances for abnormal heart rhythms. Your doctor may have to adjust the dose of your thyroid hormone.

Aspirin and other salicylate products may increase the effectiveness of your thyroid hormone by releasing more drug into the blood from body storage sites.

Estrogen drugs may increase your need for thyroid hormones.

Food Interactions

This drug is best taken on an empty stomach, but may be taken with food.

Usual Dose

Initial dose, 16 milligrams (¼ grain) per day, then increase at intervals of 1 to 2 weeks until response is satisfactory. Maintenance dose, 32 to 190 milligrams per day or even higher.

Overdosage

Symptoms are headache, irritability, nervousness, sweating, rapid heartbeat with unusual stomach rumbling (with or without cramps), chest pains, heart failure, and shock. The patient should be taken to a hospital emergency room immediately. ALWAYS bring the medicine bottle.

Special Information

Thyroid replacement therapy is usually lifelong treatment. Be sure you have a fresh supply of your medication, and always remember to take it according to your doctor's directions. Don't stop taking the medicine unless instructed to do so by your doctor.

Call your doctor if you develop nervousness, diarrhea, excessive sweating, chest pains, increased pulse rate, heart palpitations, intolerance to heat, or any other unusual occurrence.

Children beginning on thyroid treatment may lose some hair during the first few months, but this is only temporary and the hair generally grows back.

If you forget to take a dose of Thyroglobulin, take it as soon as you remember. If it is almost time for your next regularly scheduled dose, skip the one you forgot and continue with your regular schedule. Do not take a double dose. Call your doctor if you forget 2 or more doses in a row.

Generic Name

Thyroid Hormone

Brand Names

Armour Thyroid   Thyrar
S-P-T   Thyroid Strong

(Also available in generic form)

Type of Drug

Thyroid replacement.

Prescribed for

Replacement of thyroid hormone or low output of hormone from the thyroid gland.

General Information

Thyroid hormone is one of several thyroid replacement products available. The major difference between them is in effectiveness in treating certain phases of thyroid disease.

Other drugs, such as Methimazole (Tapazole) and Propyl-thiouracil (PTU), are given to people whose thyroid gland is overactive. Their effect on the thyroid gland is exactly the opposite of thyroid hormones. Check with your doctor if you are uncertain about why you have been given drugs which affect the thyroid gland.

If thyroid replacement therapy is required for a child, sleeping pulse rates or morning temperatures may have to be taken. These are good guides to treatment.

Cautions and Warnings

If you have hyperthyroid disease or high output of thyroid hormone you should not use thyroid hormone. Symptoms of hyperthyroid disease include headache, nervousness, sweating, rapid heartbeat, chest pains, and other signs of central-nervous-system stimulation. If you have heart disease or high blood pressure, thyroid therapy should not be used unless it is clearly indicated and supervised by your physician. If you develop chest pains or other signs of heart disease while you are taking thyroid medication, contact your doctor immediately.

Pregnancy/Breast-feeding

The amount of thyroid replacement hormone you take may have to be adjusted during pregnancy. Small amounts of the thyroid hormones will find their way into the bloodstream of a developing fetus. However, they have not been associated with birth defects or other problems when used in the dosages required to maintain normal thyroid function in the mother.

Small amounts of the thyroid hormones pass into breast milk, but they have not been associated with problems in nursing infants.

Seniors

Older adults are more sensitive to the effects of the thyroid hormones. The usual dosage of thyroid hormones should be reduced by about 25 percent after age 60.

Possible Side Effects

The most common side effects are palpitations of the heart, rapid heartbeat, abnormal heart rhythms, weight loss, chest pains, shaking hands, headache, diarrhea, nervousness, menstrual irregularity, inability to sleep, sweating, inability to stand heat. These symptoms may be controlled by adjusting the dose of the medication. If you are suffering from one or more side effects, you must contact your doctor immediately so that the proper dose adjustment can be made.

Drug Interactions

Avoid over-the-counter cough, cold, and allergy remedies containing stimulant drugs, which will affect your heart and may cause symptoms of overdosage.

Thyroid replacement therapy may increase the effect of anticoagulant (blood-thinning) drugs such as Warfarin or Bishydroxycoumarin. Be sure you report this to your physician because it will be necessary to reduce the dose of your anticoagulant drug by approximately one-third at the beginning of thyroid therapy (to avoid hemorrhage). Further adjustments may be made later, after your doctor reviews your blood tests.

Diabetics may have to increase their dose of Insulin or oral antidiabetic drugs. Changes in dose must be made by a doctor.

Taking a thyroid hormone together with Colestipol or Cholestyramine can reduce the effect of the thyroid product by preventing its passage into your bloodstream. Separate doses of these 2 medicines by 4 to 5 hours.

The combination of Maprotiline and a thyroid hormone may increase the chances for abnormal heart rhythms. Your doctor may have to adjust the dose of your thyroid hormone.

Aspirin and other salicylate products may increase the effectiveness of your thyroid hormone by releasing more drug into the blood from body storage sites.

Estrogen drugs may increase your need for thyroid hormones.

Food Interactions

This drug is best taken on an empty stomach, but may be taken with food.

Usual Dose

The dose is tailored to the individual.

Adult: initial dose, 15 to 30 milligrams per day, depending on severity of disease; may be increased gradually to 195 milligrams per day.

Child: initial dose, same as adult; but children may require greater maintenance doses because they are growing.

Take in 1 dose before breakfast.

Overdosage

Symptoms are headache, irritability, nervousness, sweating, rapid heartbeat with unusual stomach rumbling (with or without cramps), chest pains, heart failure, and shock. The patient should be taken to a hospital emergency room immediately. ALWAYS bring the medicine bottle.

Special Information

Thyroid replacement therapy is usually lifelong treatment. Be sure you have a fresh supply of your medication, and always remember to take it according to your doctor's directions. Don't stop taking the medicine unless instructed to do so by your doctor.

Call your doctor if you develop nervousness, diarrhea, excessive sweating, chest pains, increased pulse rate, heart palpitations, intolerance to heat, or any other unusual occurrence.

Children beginning on thyroid treatment may lose some hair during the first few months, but this is only temporary and the hair generally grows back.

If you forget to take a dose of thyroid hormone, take it as soon as you remember. If it is almost time for your next regularly scheduled dose, skip the one you forgot and continue with your regular schedule. Do not take a double dose. Call your doctor if you forget to take 2 or more doses in a row.

Generic Name

Timolol Maleate

Brand Names

Blocadren Tablets
Timoptic Eyedrops

Type of Drug

Beta-adrenergic blocking agent.

Prescribed for

Tablets: high blood pressure; reducing the possibility of a
second heart attack; migraine headaches. Eyedrops: glaucoma (increased fluid pressure inside the eye).

General Information

When applied directly to the eye, Timolol Maleate reduces
fluid pressure inside the eye by reducing the production of
eye fluids and increasing slightly the rate at which eye fluids
leave the eye. Studies have shown Timolol Maleate to produce a greater reduction in eye fluid pressure than either
Pilocarpine or Epinephrine.

Timolol Maleate eyedrops should not be used by people
who cannot take oral beta-blocking drugs, such as Propranolol. Studies have shown Timolol Maleate tablets to be very
effective for treating heart pain called angina. It has also
been used to treat high blood pressure.

The most famous Timolol Maleate study was published in
April 1981 in the prestigious New England Journal of Medicine. This study showed that people who had a heart attack
and took 20 milligrams of Timolol Maleate per day by mouth
had fewer additional heart attacks and additional heart problems and survived longer. The death rate in non-Timolol
Maleate patients was 1.6 times that in the Timolol Maleate
group. Other beta-adrenergic blockers currently available—
Propranolol, Metoprolol, Atenolol, Nadolol, and Pindolol—
also have this effect on heart attack patients.

Cautions and Warnings

Timolol Maleate should be used with care if you have a

history of asthma, upper respiratory disease, or seasonal allergy, which may become worsened by the effects of this drug. Do not use Timolol Maleate if you are allergic to it.

Pregnancy/Breast-feeding

This drug crosses into the blood circulation of a developing baby. It has not been found to cause birth defects. Pregnant women, or those who might become pregnant while taking this drug, should not take it without their doctors' approval. When the drug is considered essential by your doctor, the potential risk of taking the medicine must be carefully weighed against the benefit it might produce.

This drug passes into breast milk but has caused no problems among breast-fed infants. You must consider the potential effect on the nursing infant if breast-feeding while taking this medicine.

Seniors

Senior citizens may be more or less sensitive to the effects of this medication. Your dosage of this drug must be adjusted to your individual needs by your doctor. Seniors may be more likely to suffer from cold hands and feet and reduced body temperature, chest pains, a general feeling of ill health, sudden difficulty breathing, sweating, or changes in heartbeat because of this medicine.

Possible Side Effects

Timolol Maleate may decrease the heart rate, aggravate or worsen a condition of congestive heart failure, and may produce lowered blood pressure, tingling in the extremities, light-headedness, mental depression, inability to sleep, weakness, and tiredness. It can also produce visual disturbances, hallucinations, disorientation, and loss of short-term memory. People taking Timolol Maleate may experience nausea, vomiting, upset stomach, abdominal cramps and diarrhea, or constipation. If you are allergic to Timolol Maleate, you may show typical reactions associated with drug allergies including sore throat, fever, difficulty breathing, and various effects on the blood system. Timolol Maleate may induce spasm of muscles in the bronchi, which will aggravate any existing asthma or respiratory disease.

Occasionally, people taking Timolol Maleate may experience emotional instability, become detached, or show unusual personality change. Timolol Maleate may cause adverse effects on the blood system.

Drug Interactions

Timolol Maleate will interact with any psychotropic drug, including the monoamine oxidase (MAO) inhibitors, that stimulates one of the segments of the central nervous system. You should discuss this potential problem with your doctor if you are taking any psychotropic or psychiatric drug.

Timolol Maleate may cause increased effectiveness of Insulin or oral antidiabetic drugs. If you are diabetic, discuss the situation with your doctor. A reduction in dosage of your antidiabetic drug may be required.

Timolol Maleate may reduce the effectiveness of Digitalis on your heart. Any dose of Digitalis will have to be altered if you are taking Timolol Maleate. If you are taking Digitalis for a purpose other than heart failure, the effectiveness of the Digitalis may be increased by Timolol Maleate and the dose of Digitalis reduced.

Timolol Maleate may interact with other drugs to cause lowering of blood pressure. This interaction often has positive effects in the treatment of patients with high blood pressure.

Do not self-medicate with over-the-counter drugs for colds, coughs, or allergy which may contain either stimulants that will aggravate certain types of heart disease and high blood pressure or other ingredients that may antagonize the effects of Timolol Maleate. Check with your doctor or pharmacist before taking any over-the-counter medication.

Food Interactions

Take Timolol Maleate tablets before meals for maximum effect. The eyedrops may be used at any time.

Usual Dose

Eyedrops: 1 drop twice a day.
Tablets: 10 to 60 milligrams per day divided into 2 doses.

Overdosage

Symptoms are slowed heart rate, heart failure, lowered
blood pressure, and spasms of the bronchial muscles which
make it difficult to breathe. The patient should be taken to
a hospital emergency room where proper therapy can be
given. ALWAYS bring the medicine bottle with you.

Special Information

There have been reports of serious effects when Timolol
Maleate is stopped abruptly. The dose should be lowered
gradually over a period of 2 weeks.

If you are using Timolol Maleate eyedrops, press your
finger lightly just below the eye for one minute following
the instillation of the eyedrops.

If you forget to take a dose of Timolol Maleate tablets,
take it as soon as possible. However, if it is within 4 hours
of your next dose, skip the forgotten dose and go back to
your regular schedule. Do not take a double dose.

If you forget to take a dose of Timolol Maleate eyedrops,
take it as soon as you remember. If it is almost time for your
next regularly scheduled dose, skip the one you forgot and
continue with your regular schedule. Do not take a double
dose.

Generic Name

Tiopronin

Brand Name

Thiola

Type of Drug

Kidney stone preventive.

Prescribed for

Preventing kidney stones.

General Information

Tiopronin prevents the formation of kidney stones by forming a chemical complex with cysteine, an amino acid that is a key component of kidney stones. People with kidney stones normally have very high levels of cysteine in their urine. Each dose of Tiopronin causes a long-lasting reduction in the patient's urine cysteine level; the reduction lasts until he or she stops taking the drug.

Cautions and Warnings

Do not take Tiopronin if you are allergic to the active ingredient or to any component of the tablet.

People with a history of severe drops in white-blood-cell levels (agranulocytosis or thrombocytopenia) caused by drug treatment should avoid Tiopronin. Agranulocytosis or thrombocytopenia caused by Triopronin has the potential to bring about severe illness or death, although this has never actually happened to someone taking the drug.

Tiopronin can cause the loss of excessive amounts of protein through the urine.

Pregnancy/Breast-feeding

This drug can be expected to cause birth defects in laboratory animals and should be avoided by women who are, or might become, pregnant.

Tiopronin may pass into breast milk and should be avoided by nursing mothers. Mothers who must use Tiopronin should use an alternative feeding method.

Seniors

Seniors may be more sensitive to the side effects of this drug and should report any changes to the doctor at once.

Possible Side Effects

Drug fever may develop, especially during the first month of Tiopronin treatment. The drug may be restarted once the fever has gone down and gradually increased to the usual dose.

Other side effects include loss of taste sensation, Vitamin B_6 (Pyridoxine) deficiency, skin rash, and itching (the itching can be controlled with antihistamines and clears up when the drug is stopped). Because of the drug's effect on the skin's connective tissue, skin becomes thin and wrinkled after long-term Tiopronin treatment.

Fever, joint pain and swelling, and swollen lymph glands may be signs of serious drug side effects.

Drug Interactions

None yet known. Do not take Penicillamine, another drug that reduces urine levels of cysteine, and Tiopronin at the same time.

Food Interactions

You may take this drug with food if it upsets your stomach. Initial treatment to prevent kidney stones is typically based around diet and fluid intake. Be sure to follow your doctor's advice about diet restriction.

Usual Dose

800 to 1000 milligrams per day. Some people may require less.

Overdosage

Tiopronin overdose results in exaggerated side effects. Victims of Tiopronin overdose should be taken to a hospital emergency room for treatment. ALWAYS remember to bring the medicine bottle with you.

Special Information

Stop taking Tiopronin and call your doctor at once if you develop fever, joint pain, swelling, swollen lymph glands, changes in urinary function, unusual skin reactions, or muscle weakness, or if you begin to vomit blood or have difficulty breathing. These can be signs of severe side effects.

If you forget a dose of Tiopronin, take it as soon as you remember. If it is almost time for your next dose, skip the forgotten dose and continue with your regular schedule.

Generic Name

Tobramycin

Brand Name

Tobrex Ophthalmic Ointment/Solution

Type of Drug

Topical antibiotic for use in the eye.

Prescribed for

Superficial infections of the eye caused by bacteria that are susceptible to this antibiotic.

General Information

Tobramycin is a potent antibiotic that has been used for many years in an injectable form. It works against a wide variety of bacteria and is quite effective for eye infections.

For all but very superficial infections, your doctor will probably give you an antibiotic prescription to take by mouth in addition to the eye antibiotic. The purpose of this is to prevent the spread of the organism from your eye to the rest of your body.

Cautions and Warnings

Prolonged use of any antibiotic in the eye should be avoided because of the possibility of becoming sensitive to the antibiotic and because the bacteria could develop a form that is resistant to that particular treatment. Frequent use of an antibiotic could also lead to the overgrowth of a different bacteria or fungus in the eye. Call your doctor if the infection doesn't clear up in a few days.

Your doctor should take a bacterial culture of your eye fluid before starting treatment to be sure that the most effective antibiotic is being selected for your use.

Pregnancy/Breast-feeding

As with all drug products, pregnant women, or those who might become pregnant, should not use Tobramycin eyedrops unless the advantages of the product have been carefully weighed against the possible dangers of taking it while pregnant.

If you are nursing, you should not use Tobramycin; there is a chance that some of the drug could find its way into your breast milk and affect your baby. Nursing mothers who must use this product should temporarily bottle-feed their babies.

Seniors

Older adults may generally use these eyedrops without special precautions. However, those with substantial loss of kidney function could have a long-term reaction to Tobramycin (dizziness, ringing or buzzing in the ears, hearing loss) and should be carefully monitored for any effect if they must use this drug. Some older adults may have weaker eyelid muscles. This creates a small reservoir for the eyedrops and may actually increase the drug's effect by keeping it in contact with the eye for a longer period. Your doctor may take this into account when determining the proper drug dosage.

Possible Side Effects

Common side effects are itching and swelling of the eyelid and swelling of the eye.

Drug Interactions

None.

Usual Dose

Adult and child: 1 or 2 drops several times a day in the affected eye.

Overdosage

Tobramycin is generally not absorbed into the blood from the stomach and will not have any effect if swallowed. An overdose of the drops or ointment in the eye could produce exaggerated side effects, tearing, and irritation of the eye. Call your local poison control center or hospital emergency room for more information.

Special Information

To administer the eyedrops, lie down or tilt your head back-

ward and look at the ceiling. Hold the dropper above your
eye, hold out your lower lid to make a small pouch, and
drop the medicine inside while looking up. Release the lower
lid and keep your eye open. Don't blink for about 40 seconds. Press gently on the bridge of your nose at the inside
corner of your eye for about a minute to help circulate the
medicine around your eye.To prevent infection, don't touch
the dropper tip to your finger or eyelid. Wait 5 minutes before using any other eyedrop or ointment.

Call your doctor at once if your stinging, itching or burning, redness, irritation, swelling, or pain gets worse or if you
start having trouble seeing.

If you forget a dose of Tobramycin eyedrops, take it as
soon as you remember. If it is almost time for your next
dose, take one dose as soon as you remember, then go back
to your regular schedule. Do not take a double dose.

Generic Name

Tocainide Hydrochloride

Brand Name

Tonocard

Type of Drug

Antiarrhythmic.

Prescribed for

Abnormal heart rhythms.

General Information

Tocainide Hydrochloride affects the speed with which nerve
impulses are carried through the heart's ventricle. Tocainide
Hydrochloride affects different areas of your heart than do
other widely used oral antiarrhythmic drugs like Quinidine
Sulfate, Procainamide Hydrochloride, and Disopyramide.
Unlike those drugs, it does not interact negatively with Digoxin. Tocainide Hydrochloride is usually prescribed for

people who have been given Lidocaine in the hospital and who require some form of oral follow-up treatment.

Cautions and Warnings

This drug should not be used by people who are allergic to Tocainide Hydrochloride, Lidocaine, or to local anesthetics. Some people using Tocainide Hydrochloride may develop respiratory difficulties, including fluid buildup in the lungs, pneumonia, and irritation of the lungs. Report any cough or difficulty breathing to your doctor immediately. Tocainide Hydrochloride should not be used by people with heart failure, since the drug can actually worsen that condition.

Pregnancy/Breast-feeding

Animal studies employing doses 1 to 4 times larger than the human equivalent have revealed no adverse effects on developing fetuses, but have resulted in an unusually high rate of stillbirth and spontaneous abortion. This drug should be avoided by pregnant women or women who may become pregnant while using it. In those situations where its use is essential, the potential risks must be carefully weighed against any benefits.

Nursing mothers must be aware of any possible drug effect on their infants while taking this medicine, since it is not known if the active ingredients in it pass into breast milk. Consider an alternative infant feeding method if you must take Tocainide Hydrochloride to control an abnormal heart rhythm.

Seniors

Older adults are more sensitive to the side effects of this drug, especially dizziness and low blood pressure. Follow your doctor's directions and report any side effects at once.

Possible Side Effects

Nausea, vomiting, tingling in the hands or feet, light-headedness, dizziness, fainting, giddiness, tremors, confusion, disorientation, hallucinations, restlessness, blurred or double vision, visual disturbances, poor muscle coordination, anxiety, low blood pressure, slowing of the heart rate, heart palpitations, chest pains, cold sweats, headache, drowsiness, and lethargy.

Less common side effects are ringing or buzzing in the ears, rolling of the eyes, loss of appetite, diarrhea, rash, unusual feelings of heat or cold, joint inflammation and pain, and muscle aches. Other uncommon reactions may include seizures, depression, psychosis, mental changes, alterations of taste (including a metallic taste) and/or smell, agitation, difficulty concentrating, memory loss, slurred speech, difficulty sleeping, nightmares, unusual thirst, weakness, upset stomach or abdominal pains and discomfort, difficulty swallowing, breathing difficulty (see "Cautions and Warnings"), changes in white-blood-cell counts, anemia, urinary difficulty, hair loss, cold hands or feet, leg pains after minor exercise, dry mouth, earache, fever, hiccups, aching, a feeling of ill health, muscle twitches or spasms, neck or shoulder pains, facial flushing or pallor, and yawning.

Drug Interactions

The combination of Tocainide Hydrochloride and Metoprolol, prescribed for high blood pressure, can cause too rapid a drop in blood pressure and slowing of the heart.

If taken with other oral antiarrhythmic drugs, Tocainide Hydrochloride may produce an additive cardiac effect.

Tocainide Hydrochloride may increase the effects of other drugs that depress bone marrow function. This can result in reduced levels of white blood cells and blood platelets.

Food Interactions

You may take Tocainide Hydrochloride with food or meals if it causes upset stomach, nausea, or vomiting when taken alone.

Usual Dose

Adult: 1200 to 1800 milligrams per day, in divided doses.
Senior and patient with kidney or liver disease: less than 1200 milligrams per day.

Overdosage

There are no reports of overdosage. However, the symptoms can be expected to be exaggerated versions of Tocainide Hydrochloride side effects. Patients taking an overdose of this drug must be made to vomit with Syrup of Ipecac (available at any pharmacy) to remove any remaining drug from the stomach. Call your doctor or a poison control center before doing this. If you must go to a hospital emergency room, ALWAYS bring the medicine bottle.

Special Information

Be sure to report any side effects to your doctor. Most of them are minor or will respond to minor dosage adjustments. Especially important symptoms are difficulty breathing, coughing, unusual or easy bruising, and frequent infections.

Do not take more or less of this drug than prescribed.

If you forget to take a dose of Tocainide Hydrochloride and you remember within about 4 hours of your regular time, take it as soon as you remember. If you do not remember until later, skip the forgotten dose and go back to your regular schedule. Do not take a double dose.

Generic Name

Tolazamide

Brand Names

Tolamide
Tolinase

(Also available in generic form)

Type of Drug

Oral antidiabetic.

Prescribed for

Diabetes mellitus (sugar in the urine).

General Information

Tolazamide is one of several oral antidiabetic drugs that work by stimulating the production and release of Insulin from the pancreas. The primary difference between the oral antidiabetic drugs lies in their duration of action. Because these drugs do not lower blood sugar directly, they require some working pancreas cells.

Cautions and Warnings

Mild stress such as infection, minor surgery, or emotional upset reduces the effectiveness of Tolazamide. Remember that while you are taking this drug you should be under your doctor's continuous care.

Tolazamide and similar drugs are not oral Insulin, nor are they a substitute for Insulin. They do not lower blood sugar by themselves.

The treatment of diabetes is your responsibility. You should follow all instructions about diet, body weight, exercise, and personal hygiene and all measures to avoid infection. If you are not feeling well, or if you have symptoms such as itching, rash, yellowing of the skin or eyes, abnormally light-colored stools, a low-grade fever, sore throat, or diarrhea, contact your doctor immediately.

This drug should not be used if you have serious liver, kidney, or endocrine disease.

Pregnancy/Breast-feeding

This drug may cause birth defects or interfere with your baby's development. Check with your doctor before taking it if you are, or might be, pregnant.

If you take Tolazamide while nursing, the baby's sugar level may be adversely affected. Nursing mothers should use an alternative feeding method.

Seniors

Older adults with reduced kidney function may be more sensitive to drug side effects because of a reduced ability to eliminate the drug from the body. Low blood sugar, the major sign of drug overdose, may be more difficult to identify in an older adult than in a younger adult. Also, low blood sugar is more likely to be a cause of nervous system side effects in older adults.

Older adults taking antidiabetes drugs must keep in close touch with their doctors and closely follow their directions.

Possible Side Effects

The most common side effects are loss of appetite, nausea, vomiting, stomach upset. At times you may experience weakness or tingling in the hands and feet. These effects can be eliminated by reducing the daily dose of Tolazamide or, if necessary, by switching to a different oral antidiabetic drug. This decision must be made by your doctor.

Less commonly, Tolazamide may produce abnormally low levels of blood sugar when too much is taken for your immediate requirements. (Other factors which may cause lowering of blood sugar are liver or kidney disease, malnutrition, age, drinking alcohol, and diseases of the glands.)

Tolazamide may cause a yellowing of the whites of the eyes or skin, itching, rash, or changes in the results of laboratory tests made by your doctor. Usually these reactions will disappear in time. If they persist, you should contact your doctor.

Drug Interactions

Thiazide diuretics may call for a higher dose of Tolazamide, while Insulin, sulfa drugs, Oxyphenbutazone, Phenylbutazone, Aspirin and other salicylates, Probenecid, Dicumarol, Bishydroxycoumarin, Warfarin, Phenyramidol, and monoamine oxidase (MAO) inhibitor drugs prolong and enhance the action of Tolazamide, possibly requiring dose reduction.

Interaction with alcoholic beverages will cause flushing of the face and body, throbbing pain in the head and neck, difficult breathing, nausea, vomiting, sweating, thirst, chest pains, palpitations, lowered blood pressure, weakness, dizziness, blurred vision, and confusion. If you experience these reactions, contact your doctor immediately.

Because of the stimulant ingredients in many over-the-counter drug products for the relief of coughs, colds, and allergies, avoid them unless your doctor advises otherwise.

Food Interactions

This medicine is best taken on an empty stomach, but may be taken with food. Dietary management is an important part of the treatment of diabetes. Be sure to follow your doctor's directions about the foods you should avoid.

Usual Dose

Moderate diabetes: 100 to 250 milligrams daily.
Severe diabetes: 500 to 1000 milligrams daily.

Overdosage

A mild overdose of Tolazamide lowers the blood sugar, which can be treated by consuming sugar in such forms as candy, orange juice, or glucose tablets. A patient with a more serious overdose should be taken to a hospital emergency room immediately. ALWAYS bring the medicine bottle.

Special Information

Diet remains of primary importance in the treatment of your diabetes. Follow the diet plan your doctor has prescribed for you.

If you forget to take a dose of Tolazamide, take it as soon as you remember. If it is almost time for your next regularly scheduled dose, skip the one you forgot and continue with your regular schedule. Do not take a double dose.

Generic Name

Tolbutamide

Brand Names

Oramide
Orinase

(Also available in generic form)

Type of Drug

Oral antidiabetic.

Prescribed for

Diabetes mellitus (sugar in the urine).

General Information

Tolbutamide is one of several oral antidiabetic drugs that

work by stimulating the production and release of Insulin
from the pancreas. The primary difference between the oral
antidiabetic drugs lies in their duration of action. Because
they do not lower blood sugar directly, they require some
function of pancreas cells.

Cautions and Warnings

Mild stress such as infection, minor surgery, or emotional
upset reduces the effectiveness of Tolbutamide. Remember
that while taking this drug you should be under your doctor's continuous care.

Tolbutamide is an aid to, not a substitute for, a diet. Diet
remains of primary importance in the treatment of your diabetes. Follow the diet plan your doctor has prescribed for
you.

Tolbutamide and similar drugs are not oral Insulin, nor
are they a substitute for Insulin. They do not lower blood
sugar by themselves.

The treatment of diabetes is your responsibility. You
should follow all instructions about diet, body weight, exercise, and personal hygiene and all measures to avoid infection. If you are not feeling well, or if you have symptoms
such as itching, rash, yellowing of the skin or eyes, abnormally light-colored stools, a low-grade fever, sore throat, or
diarrhea, contact your doctor immediately.

This drug should be used with caution and under strict
supervision of your doctor if you have glaucoma, epilepsy,
ulcers, or difficulty passing urine. Avoid insecticides and extreme exposure to heat.

Pregnancy/Breast-feeding

This drug may cause birth defects or interfere with your
baby's development. Check with your doctor before taking
it if you are, or might be, pregnant.

If you take Tolbutamide while nursing, your baby's sugar
level may be adversely affected. Nursing mothers should
use an alternative feeding method.

Seniors

Older adults with reduced kidney function may be more sensitive to drug side effects because of a reduced ability to

eliminate it from the body. Low blood sugar, the major sign
of drug overdose, may be more difficult to identify in an
older adult than in a younger adult. Also, low blood sugar
is more likely to be a cause of nervous system side effects
in older adults.

Older adults taking antidiabetes drugs must keep in close
touch with their doctors and closely follow their directions.

Possible Side Effects

The most common side effcts are loss of appetite, nausea,
vomiting, stomach upset. At times you may experience
weakness or tingling in the hands and feet. These effects
can be eliminated by reducing the daily dose of Tolbutamide
or, if necessary, by switching to a different oral antidiabetic
drug. This decision must be made by your doctor.

Less commonly, Tolbutamide may produce abnormally
low levels of blood sugar when too much is taken for your
immediate requirements. (Other factors which may cause
lowering of blood sugar are liver or kidney disease, malnutrition, age, drinking alcohol, and diseases of the glands.)

Tolbutamide may cause a yellowing of the whites of the
eyes or skin, itching, rash, or changes in the results of laboratory tests made by your doctor. Usually these reactions
will disappear in time. If they persist you should contact
your doctor.

Drug Interactions

Thiazide diuretics may call for a higher dose of Tolbutamide,
while Insulin, sulfa drugs, Oxyphenbutazone, Phenylbutazone, Aspirin and other salicylates, Probenecid, Dicumarol,
Bishydroxycoumarin, Warfarin, Phenyramidol, and monoamine oxidase (MAO) inhibitor drugs prolong and enhance the
action of Tolbutamide, possibly requiring dose reduction.

Interaction with alcoholic beverages will cause flushing of
the face and body, throbbing pain in the head and neck,
difficult breathing, nausea, vomiting, sweating, thirst, chest
pains, palpitations, lowered blood pressure, weakness, dizziness, blurred vision, and confusion. If you experience these
reactions contact your doctor immediately.

Because of the stimulant ingredients in many over-the-
counter drug products for the relief of coughs, colds, and
allergies, avoid them unless your doctor advises otherwise.

Food Interactions

This medicine is best taken on an empty stomach, but may be taken with food. Dietary management is an important part of the treatment of diabetes. Be sure to follow your doctor's directions about the foods you should avoid.

Usual Dose

Begin with 1 to 2 grams per day; then increase or decrease according to patient's response. Maintenance dose, 250 milligrams to 2 (or, rarely, 3) grams per day.

Overdosage

A mild overdose of Tolbutamide lowers the blood sugar, which can be treated by consuming sugar in such forms as candy, orange juice, or glucose tablets. A patient with a more serious overdose should be taken to a hospital emergency room immediately. ALWAYS bring the medicine bottle.

Special Information

If you forget to take a dose of Tolbutamide, take it as soon as you remember. If it is almost time for your next regularly scheduled dose, skip the one you forgot and continue with your regular schedule. Do not take a double dose.

Generic Name

Tolmetin Sodium

Brand Name

Tolectin/Tolectin DS

Type of Drug

Nonsteroidal anti-inflammatory.

Prescribed for

Relief of pain and inflammation of joints and muscles; arthritis.

General Information

Tolmetin Sodium is one of several nonsteroidal anti-inflammatory drugs (NSAIDs) used to treat various types of arthritis. These drugs reduce inflammation and share side effects, the most common of which is possible formation of ulcers and upset stomach. The drugs are roughly comparable to Aspirin in controlling the symptoms of arthritis and are used by some people who cannot tolerate Aspirin.

Cautions and Warnings

Do not take Tolmetin Sodium if you are allergic or sensitive to this drug, Aspirin, or other NSAIDs. Tolmetin Sodium may cause stomach ulcers.

Pregnancy/Breast-feeding

This drug crosses into the blood circulation of a developing baby. If taken regularly during the last few months of pregnancy, Tolmetin Sodium may cause unwanted effects on the baby's heart or blood flow. Also, labor or the pregnancy itself may be prolonged. Pregnant women, or those who might become pregnant while taking this drug, should not take it without their doctors' approval. When the drug is considered essential by your doctor, the potential risk of taking the medicine must be carefully weighed against the benefit it might produce.

This drug passes into breast milk, but has caused no problems among breast-fed infants. You must consider the potential effect on the nursing infant if breast-feeding while taking this medicine.

Seniors

Older adults are more sensitive to the stomach, kidney, and liver effects of this drug. Some doctors believe that persons age 70 or older should take half the usual dose of Tolmetin. Follow your doctor's directions and report any side effects at once.

Possible Side Effects

The most frequent side effects are stomach upset, dizziness, headache, drowsiness, ringing in the ears.

Other side effects include heartburn, nausea, vomiting,

bloating, gas in the stomach, stomach pain, diarrhea, constipation, dark stool, nervousness, insomnia, depression, confusion, tremor, lack of appetite, fatigue, itching, rash, double
vision, abnormal heart rhythm, anemia or other changes in
the composition of the blood, changes in liver function, loss
of hair, tingling in the hands and feet, fever, breast enlargement, lowered blood sugar, occasional effects on the kidneys. If symptoms appear, stop taking the medicine and see
your doctor immediately.

Drug Interactions

Tolmetin Sodium increases the action of Phenytoin, sulfa
drugs, drugs used to control diabetes, and drugs used to
thin the blood. If you are taking one of these drugs, be sure
you discuss it with your doctor, who will probably change
the dose of the drug whose action is increased.

Avoid taking Aspirin while taking Tolmetin Sodium.

Food Interactions

If upset stomach occurs, take with food or milk.

Usual Dose

Adult: 400 milligrams 3 times per day, to start. Dosage
must then be adjusted to individual need. Do not take more
than 2000 milligrams per day.

Child (age 2 and over): 9 milligrams per pound of body
weight given in divided doses 3 to 4 times per day, to start.
Adjust dose to individual need. Do not give more than 13.5
milligrams per pound of body weight to a child.

Child (under age 2): not recommended.

Overdosage

Symptoms may include drowsiness, dizziness, confusion,
disorientation, lethargy, tingling in the hands or feet, numbness, nausea, vomiting, upset stomach, stomach pains,
headache, ringing or buzzing in the ears, sweating, and
blurred vision. Take the victim to a hospital emergency room
at once for treatment. ALWAYS bring the medicine bottle
with you.

Special Information

Avoid Aspirin and alcoholic beverages while taking this medication.

You may become dizzy or drowsy while taking this medicine. Be careful while driving or operating complex equipment.

Call your doctor if you develop a skin rash, itching, swelling, visual disturbances, black stools, or a persistent headache while taking this medication.

If you forget to take a dose of Tolmetin Sodium, take it as soon as you remember. If it is almost time for your next regularly scheduled dose, skip the one you forgot and continue with your regular schedule. Do not take a double dose.

Generic Name

Trazodone

Brand Name

Desyrel

(Also available in generic form)

Type of Drug

Antidepressant.

Prescribed for

Depression with or without anxiety. It may also be used for treating Cocaine withdrawal and aggressive behaviors.

General Information

Trazodone is as effective in treating the symptoms of depression as are other antidepressant tablets. However, it is chemically different from the other antidepressants and may be less likely to cause side effects.

For many people, symptoms will be relieved as early as 2 weeks after starting the medicine, but 4 weeks or more may be required to achieve maximum benefit.

Cautions and Warnings

Do not use Trazodone if you are allergic to it. It is not recommended during the initial stages of recovery from a heart attack. People with a previous history of heart disease should not use Trazodone because it may cause abnormal heart rhythms.

Pregnancy/Breast-feeding

This drug should not be taken by women who may become pregnant while using it or by pregnant or nursing mothers, since this drug may pass into breast milk. In situations where it is deemed essential, the potential risk of the drug must be carefully weighed against any benefit it might produce.

Seniors

Older adults are likely to be more sensitive to the effects and side effects of usual doses of Trazodone than younger adults. Medical experts recommend that older adults be started out with lower doses that are increased more carefully and slowly by their doctors.

Possible Side Effects

The most common side effects are upset stomach, constipation, abdominal pains, a bad taste in your mouth, nausea, vomiting, diarrhea, palpitations, rapid heartbeat, rashes, swelling of the extremities, elevated or depressed blood pressure, difficulty breathing, dizziness, anger, hostility, nightmares and/or vivid dreams, confusion, disorientation, loss of memory or concentration, drowsiness, fatigue, light-headedness, difficulty sleeping, nervousness, excitement, headache, loss of coordination, tingling in the hands or feet, tremor of the hands or arms, ringing or buzzing in the ears, blurred vision, red, tired, and itchy eyes, stuffy nose or sinuses, loss of sex drive, muscle aches and pains, loss of appetite, changes in body weight (up or down), sweating, clamminess, a feeling of ill health.

Less frequent reactions to Trazodone include drug allergy, chest pain, heart attack, delusions, hallucinations, agitation, difficulty speaking, restlessness, numbness, weakness, seizures, increased sex drive, a sustained and painful male erection, reverse ejaculation, impotence, missed or early

menstrual periods, stomach gas, increased salivation, anemia, reduced levels of some white blood cells, muscle
twitches, blood in the urine, reduced urine flow, increased
urinary frequency, increased appetite. Trazodone may cause
elevations in levels of body enzymes used to measure liver
function.

In rare instances, males taking Trazodone may notice prolonged or inappropriate erections. They should immediately
discontinue taking Trazodone and contact their physician.

Drug Interactions

Trazodone, when taken together with Digoxin or Phenytoin,
may increase the amount of those drugs in your blood, leading to a greater possibility of drug side effects.

Trazodone may make you more sensitive to drugs that
work by depressing the nervous system, including sedatives,
tranquilizers, and alcohol.

This medicine may cause a slight reduction in blood pressure. If you are taking medicine for high blood pressure and
begin to take Trazodone, you may find that a minor reduction in the dosage of your blood-pressure medicine is required. On the other hand, the action of Clonidine, a high-
blood-pressure medicine, can be inhibited by Trazodone.
These interactions must be evaluated by your doctor. Do not
change any blood-pressure medicines on your own.

Little is known about the potential interaction between
Trazodone and the monoamine oxidase (MAO) inhibitor
drugs. With most antidepressants, it is suggested that one
drug be discontinued for 2 weeks before the other is begun.
If these drugs are used together, they should be used
cautiously.

Food Interactions

Take each dose of Trazodone with a meal or snack to increase the amount of drug absorbed into your bloodstream
and to minimize the possibility of upset stomach, dizziness,
or light-headedness.

Usual Dose

150 milligrams per day with food, to start. This dose may
be increased by 50 milligrams per day every 3 to 4 days, to

a maximum of 400 milligrams per day. Severely depressed people may be given as much as 600 milligrams per day.

Overdosage

Drowsiness and vomiting are the most frequent signs of Trazodone overdose. The other signs are simply more severe side effects, especially those affecting the heart and mood. Fever may develop at first, but body temperature will drop below normal as time passes. ALL victims of antidepressant overdosage, especially children, must be taken to a hospital for treatment as quickly as possible. ALWAYS bring the medicine bottle with you.

Special Information

Use care while driving or doing anything else requiring concentration or alertness, and avoid alcohol or any other depressant while taking Trazodone.

Call your doctor if any side effects develop, especially blood in the urine, dizziness, or light-headedness. Trazodone may cause dry mouth, irregular heartbeat, nausea, vomiting, or difficulty breathing. Call your doctor if these symptoms become severe.

If you forget to take a dose of Trazodone, take it as soon as possible. However, if it is within 4 hours of your next dose, skip the forgotten dose and go back to your regular schedule. Do not take a double dose.

Generic Name

Tretinoin

Other Names

Retinoic Acid
Vitamin A Acid

Brand Name

Retin-A Cream/Gel/Liquid

Type of Drug

Antiacne.

Prescribed for

The early stages of acne. This drug is usually not effective in treating severe acne. It may also be prescribed for wrinkling, psoriasis, cancer, or other skin conditions.

General Information

This drug works by decreasing the cohesiveness of skin cells, causing the skin to peel, which is helpful in acne treatment. Because it is an irritant, any other skin irritant, such as extreme weather or wind, cosmetics, and some soaps, can cause severe irritation. Excessive application of Tretinoin will cause more peeling and irritation but will not give better results.

Medical research published in the *Journal of the American Medical Association* during January 1988 revealed that regular application of Tretinoin cream to aging skin prevented wrinkling and suggested that it could even reverse the wrinkling process for some people! As you might expect, this treatment, promoted in the media as "the closest thing we have to the fountain of youth," became instantly popular among older people who want younger skin and younger people who are concerned about future wrinkling and aging. The anti-wrinkling effect of Tretinoin remains controversial, and the drug manufacturer has been restricted by the federal government from promoting this effect of the drug.

Cautions and Warnings

Do not use this drug if you are allergic to it or any of its components. This drug may increase the skin-cancer-causing effects of ultraviolet light. Therefore, people using this drug must avoid exposure to the sun. If you can't avoid exposure to the sun, use sunscreen products and protective covering. Do not apply to areas around the eyes, corner of the mouth, or sides of the nose.

Pregnancy/Breast-feeding

Tretinoin has been shown to cause abnormal skull formation in animal fetuses. Birth defects in animals have also been caused by Tretinoin, but studies with humans have not been conducted. Pregnant women should avoid this drug.

Tretinoin has not caused problems in breast-fed infants.

Seniors

Older adults may use this product with no restriction.

Possible Side Effects

Redness, swelling, blistering, or formation of crusts on the skin near the areas to which the drug has been applied. Overcoloration of the skin, greater sensitivity to the sun.

All side effects disappear after the drug has been stopped.

Drug Interactions

Other skin irritants will cause excessive sensitivity, irritation, and side effects. Among the substances that cause this interaction are medications that contain Sulfur (topical), Resorcinol, Benzoyl Peroxide, or Salicylic Acid; abrasive soaps or skin cleansers; cosmetics or other creams, ointments, etc., with a severe drying effect; and products with a high alcohol, astringent, spice, or lime content.

Usual Dose

Apply a small amount to the affected area when you go to bed, after thoroughly cleansing the area.

Special Information

You may experience an increase in acne lesions during the first couple of weeks of treatment, because the drug is acting on deeper lesions which you had not seen before. This is beneficial and is not a reason to stop using the drug.

Results should be seen in 2 to 6 weeks.

Keep this drug away from your eyes, nose, mouth, and mucous membranes.

Avoid exposure to sunlight or sunlamp.

You may feel warmth and slight stinging when you apply Tretinoin. If you develop an excessive skin reaction or are uncomfortable, stop using this product for a short time.

If you forget a dose of Tretinoin, do not take the forgotten dose. Skip the dose and go back to your regular schedule. Do not take a double dose.

Generic Name

Triamcinolone

Brand Name

Azmacort Inhaler

Type of Drug

Adrenal corticosteroid.

Prescribed for

Chronic asthma or other respiratory condition.

General Information

The Triamcinolone used in this product is the same drug
applied to the skin as an ointment or other topical preparation. It can also be taken by mouth as a tablet. The Triamcinolone inhaler relieves the symptoms of asthma for people
who require regular steroid treatment by mouth. Using the
aerosol generally allows a reduction in the oral dose or elimination of oral steroids all together. It works by reducing
the inflammation of the mucosal lining within the bronchi,
making it easier to breathe. This product should be used
only as part of a preventive therapy program. It will not treat
an asthma attack.

Cautions and Warnings

This drug should not be used if your asthma can be controlled by other nonsteroid medicines. It is meant only for
people taking Prednisone or another steroid by mouth and
other asthma medicines but who are still not under control.
Do not use a Triamcinolone inhaler if you are allergic to this
drug or to any other steroid drug. During stressful periods,
you may have to go back to taking steroids by mouth if your
asthma is not controlled.

Pregnancy/Breast-feeding

Large amounts of Triamcinolone used during pregnancy
may slow the growth of a developing baby. Steroids can

cause birth defects or interfere with the developing fetus. Check with your doctor if you are, or might be, pregnant.

Triamcinolone may pass into breast milk and cause unwanted effects in a nursing infant.

Seniors

Older adults may use this medicine without special precaution. However, me sure your doctor knows if you have any bone disease, colitis, diabetes, bowel disease, glaucoma, fungus infection, heart disease, herpes infection, high blood pressure, high blood cholesterol, kidney disease, or underactive thyroid.

Possible Side Effects

The most common side effects are dry mouth and hoarseness. Less common are fungus infections of the mouth or throat.

Rarely, deaths due to failure of the adrenal gland have occurred during the process of switching from an oral product. Aerosol Triamcinolone is given in a much smaller dose than the oral tablets, reducing the chance for side effects. However, if the drug is used in very large amounts for a long period of time, you may develop a variety of other side effects. Information on those can be found in the entry for Prednisone.

Food Interactions

Do not use this product if you have any food in your mouth.

Usual Dose

Adult: 2 inhalations (0.2 milligrams) 3 or 4 times a day. Do not take more than 16 inhalations a day. Allow at least 1 minute between inhalations. People with more severe asthma may start out with a higher dose.

Child (age 6 to 12): 1 or 2 inhalations 3 or 4 times a day. Do not exceed 12 inhalations a day.

Child (under age 6): not recommended.

Special Information

Follow the instructions that come with your inhaler.

If you use a bronchodilator inhaler (Isoproterenol, Metaproterenol, etc.) at the same time as your Triamcinolone inhaler, use the bronchodilator first to open your bronchial tree and increase the amount of Triamcinolone that gets into your lungs.

If you forget to take a dose of Triamcinolone, take it as soon as you remember. If it is almost time for your next regularly scheduled dose, skip the one you forgot and continue with your regular schedule. Do not take a double dose.

Brand Name
Triavil

Ingredients

Amitriptyline Hydrochloride
Perphenazine

Other Brand Name

Etrafon

(Also available in generic form)

Type of Drug

Antidepressant tranquilizer combination.

Prescribed for

Relief of symptoms of anxiety or agitation and/or depression associated with chronic physical or psychiatric disease.

General Information

Triavil and other psychotherapeutic agents are effective in treating various symptoms of psychological or psychiatric disorders, which may result from organic disease or may be signs of psychiatric illness. Triavil must be used only under the supervision of a doctor. It will take a minimum of 2 weeks to 1 month for this medication to show beneficial effect, so don't expect instant results. If you feel there has been no change in symptoms after 6 to 8 weeks, discuss it with your doctor. Your doctor may tell you to continue taking the medicine and give it more time, or he or she may give you another drug that will possibly be more effective.

Cautions and Warnings

Do not take Triavil if you are allergic to it or to any related compound. For more information on drugs related to the ingredients found in Triavil, consult the entries for Amitriptyline and Chlorpromazine. Do not take Triavil if you have glaucoma or difficulty passing urine, unless you are specifically directed to by your physician. This drug is usually not recommended for patients who are recovering from heart attacks.

Pregnancy/Breast-feeding

Both ingredients in this drug cross into your developing baby's circulation and may cause birth defects if taken during the first 3 months of pregnancy. Newborn infants may suffer from drug side effects or heart, breathing, and urinary problems after their mothers take drugs of this type immediately before delivery. You should avoid taking this medication while pregnant.

Both the antidepressant and tranquilizer in Triavil are known to pass into breast milk and may affect a breast-feeding infant. Nursing mothers should consider alternative feeding methods if taking this medicine.

Seniors

Older adults are more sensitive to the effects of this drug and often require lower doses than younger adults to do the same job. Also, older adults are more likely to develop drug side effects. Follow your doctor's directions and report any side effects at once.

Possible Side Effects

The most frequent side effects are dry mouth, difficulty in urination, constipation, blurred vision, rapid heartbeat, numbness and tingling sensation in the arms and legs, yellowing of the skin and/or whites of the eyes, unusually low blood pressure, drowsiness, sleepiness.

Infrequent side effects include dizziness, nausea, excitement, fainting, slight twitching of the muscles, jittery feeling, weakness, headache, heartburn, loss of appetite, stomach cramps, increased perspiration, loss of coordination, skin rash with unusual sensitivity to bright lights, itching, redness, peeling away of large sections of skin. You may experience an allergic reaction: difficulty in breathing, retention of fluids in arms and legs, drug fever, swelling of the face and tongue.

Other infrequent side effects are effects on the hormone and blood system, convulsions, development of unusual skin colorations and spots, effect on sex drive and sexual performance.

Drug Interactions

Quinidine or Procainamide, drugs which are used to control heart rhythm, will strongly increase the effects of this drug.

Avoid depressive drugs such as other tranquilizers, sleeping pills, antihistamines, barbiturates, or alcohol. Interaction will cause excessive drowsiness, inability to concentrate, and/or sleepiness.

Some patients may experience changes in heart rhythm when taking this drug along with thyroid medication.

One of the ingredients in Triavil may increase your response to common stimulant drugs found in over-the-counter cough and cold preparations, causing stimulation, nervousness, and difficulty in sleeping.

Avoid large amounts of Vitamin C, which may cause you to release larger-than-normal amounts of Triavil from your body.

Both of the ingredients in Triavil may neutralize drugs used to treat high blood pressure. If you have high blood pressure and are taking Triavil, discuss this potential difficulty with your doctor or pharmacist to be sure that you are taking adequate doses of blood-pressure medicine.

If you are taking a monoamine oxidase (MAO) inhibitor drug, discuss this matter with your doctor, because there have been severe interactions.

Food Interactions

This medicine is best taken on an empty stomach, but you may take it with food if it upsets your stomach.

Usual Dose

1 or 2 tablets 3 to 4 times per day.

Overdosage

Symptoms are central-nervous-system depression to the point of possible coma, low blood pressure, agitation, restlessness, convulsions, fever, dry mouth, abnormal heart rhythms, confusion, hallucinations, drowsiness, unusually low body temperature, dilated eye pupils, and abnormally rigid muscles. The patient should be taken to a hospital emergency room immediately. ALWAYS bring the medicine bottle.

Special Information

Triavil may make you sleepy or tired, and it may also cause difficulty in concentration. Be extremely careful when driving a car or operating machinery while taking this drug, especially during the first couple of weeks of therapy.

If you forget to take a dose of Triavil take it as soon as possible. However, if it is within 2 hours of your next dose, skip the forgotten dose and go back to your regular schedule. Do not take a double dose.

Generic Name

Triazolam

Brand Name

Halcion

Type of Drug

Sedative.

Prescribed for

Short-term treatment of insomnia or sleeplessness, frequent nighttime awakening, waking too early in the morning.

General Information

Triazolam, used only as a sleep inducer, is a member of the group of drugs known as benzodiazepines. Characterized by Diazepam (Valium), other benzodiazepine drugs are used as antianxiety agents, anticonvulsants, and sedatives (sleeping pills). They exert their effects by relaxing large skeletal muscles and through a direct effect on the brain. In doing so, they can relax you and make you either more tranquil or sleepier, depending on the specific drug taken and how much of it has been prescribed. Many doctors prefer Triazolam and the other members of this class to other drugs that can be used for the same effect because the benzodiazepines tend to be safer, have fewer side effects, and are usually as, if not more, effective.

Triazolam is distinguished from other benzodiazepines by the fact that it has a very short duration of action and produces less hangover than other sleeping pills. However, some people who use it on a regular basis find that, because of the drug's short duration of effect, they still get up early in the morning or become anxious during the day.

Benzodiazepines, including Triazolam, can be abused if taken for long periods of time, and it is possible to develop drug-withdrawal symptoms if therapy is suddenly discontinued. Withdrawal symptoms include convulsions, tremors, muscle cramps, insomnia, agitation, diarrhea, vomiting, sweating, and convulsions. This problem has led to the removal of Triazolam from the British market and may lead to similar restrictions in the United States.

Cautions and Warnings

Triazolam is not intended for children under age 18.

Triazolam may interfere with daily tasks by producing some daytime drowsiness, although this is less of a problem than with other sedatives. Clinical depression may be increased by Triazolam or any other drug that has an ability to depress the nervous system. Intentional overdosage is more common among depressed people who take sleeping pills.

Pregnancy/Breast-feeding

This drug should not be used by pregnant women or women who may become pregnant while using it. Animal studies have shown that it passes easily into the blood system of a developing baby.

Triazolam and the products of its metabolism pass into mother's milk and the drug is not recommended for nursing mothers.

Seniors

Older adults are more susceptible to drug side effects than are younger adults and should take the lowest possible dosage of Triazolam.

Possible Side Effects

Drowsiness, headache, dizziness, nervousness, poor muscle coordination, light-headedness, nausea, and vomiting.

Less common side effects include a "high" feeling, rapid heartbeat, tiredness, confusion, temporary memory loss, cramps and pain, depression, blurred or double vision. The least often experienced adverse effects of Triazolam are constipation, changes in taste perception, stuffy nose, diarrhea, dry mouth, allergic reactions, rash, nightmares or strange dreams, difficulty sleeping, tingling in the hands or feet, temporary loss of normal sensation, and ringing or buzzing in the ears.

Drug Interactions

As for all other benzodiazepines, the effects of Triazolam may be enhanced if it is taken together with alcoholic beverages, antihistamines, tranquilizers, barbiturates, anticonvulsant medicines, antidepressants, and monoamine oxidase (MAO) inhibitor drugs (most often prescribed for severe depression).

Oral contraceptives, Cimetidine (for ulcers), and Disulfiram (for alcoholism) may increase the effect of Triazolam by interfering with the drug's breakdown in the liver.

Cigarette smoking may reduce the effect of Triazolam on your body, as it does with the other benzodiazepines.

The effectiveness of Levodopa (for Parkinson's disease) may be increased by benzodiazepine drugs, including Triazolam.

Food Interactions

Triazolam may be taken with food if it upsets your stomach.

Usual Dose

Adult: 0.25 to 0.5 milligrams about 30 minutes before you want to go to sleep.

Senior: 0.125 milligrams to start, then increase in 0.125-milligram increments until the desired effect is achieved.

Overdosage

The most common symptoms of Triazolam overdose are confusion, sleepiness, depression, loss of muscle coordination, and slurred speech. Coma may develop if the overdose was particularly large. Overdose symptoms can develop if a single dose of 2 milligrams (4 times the maximum daily dose) is taken. Patients taking an overdose of this drug must be made to vomit with Syrup of Ipecac (available at any pharmacy) to remove any remaining drug from the stomach. Call your doctor or a poison control center before doing this. If 30 minutes have passed since the overdose was taken or symptoms have begun to develop, the victim must be immediately transported to a hospital emergency room for treatment. ALWAYS bring the medicine bottle.

Special Information

Never take more of this medication than your doctor has prescribed. If you have been taking Triazolam for several months and decide to stop using it, your daily dosage should be gradually reduced rather than stopped all at once to avoid drug-withdrawal symptoms.

If you forget to take a dose of Triazolam and you remember within about an hour of your regular time, take it as soon as you remember. If you do not remember until later, skip the forgotten dose and go back to your regular schedule. Do not take a double dose.

Generic Name

Trifluoperazine

Brand Name

Stelazine

(Also available in generic form)

Type of Drug

Phenothiazine antipsychotic.

Prescribed for

Psychotic disorders; moderate to severe depression with anxiety; control of agitation or aggressiveness in disturbed children; alcohol withdrawal symptoms; intractable pain; senility.

General Information

Trifluoperazine and other members of the phenothiazine group act on a portion of the brain called the hypothalamus. They affect parts of the hypothalamus that control metabolism, body temperature, alertness, muscle tone, hormone balance, and vomiting and may be used to treat problems related to any of these functions.

Cautions and Warnings

Trifluoperazine should not be taken if you are allergic to one of the drugs in the broad classification known as phenothiazine drugs. Do not take Trifluoperazine if you have any blood, liver, kidney, or heart disease, very low blood pressure, or Parkinson's disease. This medication is a tranquilizer and can have a depressive effect, especially during the first few days of therapy.

This drug should be used with caution and under strict supervision of your doctor if you have glaucoma, epilepsy, ulcers, or difficulty passing urine.

Pregnancy/Breast-feeding

Infants born to women taking this medication have experienced drug side effects (liver jaundice, nervous system effects) immediately after birth. Check with your doctor about taking this medicine if you are, or might become, pregnant.

This drug may pass into breast milk and affect a nursing infant. Consider alternative feeding methods if you must take this medicine.

Seniors

Older adults are more sensitive to the effects of this medication than younger adults and usually require a lower dosage to achieve a desired effect. Also, older adults are more likely to develop drug side effects. Some experts feel that older patients should be treated with one-half to one-quarter the usual adult dose.

Possible Side Effects

The most common side effect is drowsiness, especially during the first or second week of therapy. If the drowsiness becomes troublesome, contact your doctor.

Trifluoperazine can cause jaundice (yellowing of the whites of the eyes or skin), usually in 2 to 4 weeks. The jaundice usually goes away when the drug is discontinued, but there have been cases when it did not. If you notice this effect or if you develop symptoms such as fever and generally not feeling well, contact your doctor immediately. Less frequent side effects include changes in components of the blood including anemias, raised or lowered blood pressure, abnormal heart rates, heart attack, feeling faint or dizzy.

Phenothiazines can produce extrapyramidal effects, such as spasm of the neck muscles, rolling back of the eyes, convulsions, difficulty in swallowing, and symptoms associated with Parkinson's disease. These effects look very serious but disappear after the drug has been withdrawn; however, symptoms of the face, tongue, and jaw may persist for as long as several years, especially in older adults with a history of brain damage. If you experience extrapyramidal effects contact your doctor immediately.

Trifluoperazine may cause an unusual increase in psychotic symptoms or may cause paranoid reactions, tiredness, lethargy, restlessness, hyperactivity, confusion at night, bizarre dreams, inability to sleep, depression, and euphoria. Other reactions are itching, swelling, unusual sensitivity to bright lights, red skin, and rash. There have been cases of breast enlargement, false positive pregnancy tests, changes in menstrual flow in females, and impotence and changes in sex drive in males, as well as stuffy nose, headache, nausea, vomiting, loss of appetite, change in body temperature, loss of facial color, excessive salivation, excessive perspiration, constipation, diarrhea, changes in urine and stool habits, worsening of glaucoma, blurred vision, weakening of eyelid muscles, spasms in bronchial and other muscles, increased appetite, fatigue, excessive thirst, and changes in the coloration of skin, particularly in exposed areas.

Drug Interactions

Trifluoperazine should be taken with caution in combination with barbiturates, sleeping pills, narcotics, other tranquilizers, or any other medication which may produce a depressive effect. Avoid alcohol.

Usual Dose

Adult: 2 to 40 milligrams per day (the lowest effective dose should be used). This long-acting drug will then be taken once or twice per day.

Senior: lower dose, because of greater sensitivity to phenothiazines.

Child (age 6 to 12): 1 to 15 milligrams per day, slowly increased until satisfactory control is achieved.

Overdosage

Symptoms are depression, extreme weakness, tiredness, desire to go to sleep, coma, lowered blood pressure, uncontrolled muscle spasms, agitation, restlessness, convulsions, fever, dry mouth, and abnormal heart rhythms. The patient should be taken to a hospital emergency room immediately. ALWAYS bring the medicine bottle.

Special Information

This medication may cause drowsiness. Use caution when driving or operating complex equipment and avoid alcoholic beverages while taking the medicine.

The drug may also cause unusual sensitivity to the sun and can turn your urine reddish-brown to pink.

Avoid insecticides.

If dizziness occurs, avoid sudden changes in posture and avoid climbing stairs.

Use caution in hot weather. This medicine may make you more prone to heat stroke.

If you take Trifluoperazine once a day and forget your dose, take it as soon as possible. If you don't remember until the next day, skip the forgotten dose and continue with your regular schedule.

If you take the medicine more than once a day and forget a dose, take the forgotten dose as soon as possible. If it is almost time for your next dose, skip the forgotten dose and go on with your regular schedule.

Generic Name

Trihexyphenidyl Hydrochloride

Brand Names

Artane/Artane Sequels
Trihexy

(Also available in generic form)

Type of Drug

Anticholinergic.

Prescribed for

Treatment of Parkinson's disease or prevention or control of muscle spasms caused by other drugs, particularly the phenothiazine drugs.

General Information

The drug has an action on the body similar to that of Atropine Sulfate. As an anticholinergic it has the ability to reduce muscle spasm, which makes the drug useful in treating Parkinson's disease and other diseases associated with spasm of skeletal muscles.

Cautions and Warnings

Trihexyphenidyl Hydrochloride should be used with caution if you have narrow-angle glaucoma, heart disease, stomach ulcers, obstructions in the gastrointestinal tract, prostatitis, or myasthenia gravis.

Pregnancy/Breast-feeding

Drugs of this type have not been proven to be a cause of birth defects or of other problems in pregnant women. However, women who are, or may become, pregnant while taking this medication should discuss the possibility of birth defects with their doctor and other therapies that may be substituted for this medicine.

This medication may reduce the amount of breast milk produced by a nursing mother.

Seniors

Seniors taking this medication on a regular basis may be more sensitive to drug side effects, including a predisposition to developing glaucoma, confusion, disorientation, agitation, and hallucinations with normal drug doses.

Possible Side Effects

Dry mouth, difficulty in urination, constipation, blurred vision, rapid or pounding heartbeat, possible mental confusion, and increased sensitivity to strong light. The effects may increase if Trihexyphenidyl Hydrochloride is taken with antihistamines, phenothiazines, antidepressants, or other anticholinergic drugs.

Side effects are less frequent and severe than those seen with Atropine Sulfate, to which this drug is therapeutically similar.

Drug Interactions

Interaction with other anticholinergic drugs, including tricyclic antidepressants, may cause severe stomach upset or unusual abdominal pain. If this happens, contact your doctor.

Avoid over-the-counter remedies which contain Atropine Sulfate or similar drugs. Your pharmacist can tell you the ingredients of over-the-counter drugs.

This drug should not be taken with alcohol.

Food Interactions

This medicine is best taken on an empty stomach, but may be taken with food if it upsets your stomach.

Usual Dose

1 to 15 milligrams per day, depending on the disease and the patient's response.

Overdosage

Signs of drug overdose include clumsiness or unsteadiness,

severe drowsiness, severely dry mouth, nose, or throat, hallucinations, mood changes, difficulty breathing, rapid heartbeat, and unusually warm and dry skin. Overdose victims should be taken to a hospital emergency room at once. ALWAYS bring the medicine bottle.

Special Information

Side effects of dry mouth, constipation, and sensitivity to bright lights can be easily relieved with candy or gum, a stool softener like Docusate, and sunglasses.

This medicine will reduce your tolerance to hot weather because it makes you sweat less than normal. Be careful not to become overheated in hot weather because of the chance of developing heat stroke.

If you forget to take a dose of Trihexyphenidyl Hydrochloride, take it as soon as possible. However, if it is within 4 hours of your next dose, skip the forgotten dose and go back to your regular schedule. Do not take a double dose.

Generic Name

Trimethobenzamide Hydrochloride

Brand Names

Tebamide Suppositories
T-Gen Suppositories
Tigan Capsules/Suppositories
Trimazide Capsules

(Also available in generic form)

Type of Drug

Antiemetic.

Prescribed for

Control of nausea and vomiting.

General Information

Trimethobenzamide Hydrochloride works on the "chemoreceptor trigger zone" of the brain, through which impulses are carried to the vomiting center. It can help control nausea and vomiting.

Cautions and Warnings

Do not use this drug if you are allergic or sensitive to it. Trimethobenzamide Hydrochloride rectal suppositories contain a local anesthetic and should not be used for newborn infants or patients who are allergic to local anesthetics.

Some drugs, when taken by children with a viral illness that causes vomiting, may contribute to the development of Reye's syndrome, a potentially fatal, acute childhood disease. Although this relationship has not been confirmed, caution must be exercised. Reye's syndrome is characterized by a rapid onset of persistent severe vomiting, tiredness, and irrational behavior. It can progress to coma, convulsions, and death—usually following a nonspecific illness associated with a high fever. It has been suspected that Trimethobenzamide Hydrochloride and other drugs which can be toxic to the liver may unfavorably alter the course of Reye's syndrome; such drugs should be avoided in children exhibiting signs and symptoms associated with Reye's syndrome.

Trimethobenzamide Hydrochloride can obscure the signs of overdosage by other drugs or signs of disease because of its effect of controlling nausea and vomiting.

Pregnancy/Breast-feeding

Do not use this drug if you are pregnant because Trimethobenzamide Hydrochloride may decrease your chances to have a successful pregnancy. No breast-feeding problems have been seen.

Seniors

Older adults may take this medication without special restriction. Follow your doctor's directions and report any side effects at once.

Possible Side Effects

Muscle cramps and tremors, low blood pressure (especially after an injection of this medication), effects on components of the blood, blurred vision, drowsiness, headache, jaundice (yellowing of skin or whites of the eyes). If you experience one of these side effects report it to your doctor. If you develop a rash or other allergic effects from Trimethobenzamide Hydrochloride, stop taking the drug and tell your doctor. Usually these symptoms will disappear by themselves, but additional treatment may be necessary.

Drug Interactions

Trimethobenzamide Hydrochloride may make you sleepy or cause you to lose concentration; therefore, avoid alcoholic beverages, antihistamines, sleeping pills, tranquilizers, and other depressant drugs which may aggravate these effects.

Food Interactions

This medicine is best taken on an empty stomach, but you may take it with food if it upsets your stomach.

Usual Dose

Capsule:
Adult: 250-milligram capsule 3 to 4 times per day.
Child (30 to 90 pounds): 100 to 200 milligrams 3 to 4 times per day.

Rectal suppository:
Adult: 200 milligrams 3 to 4 times per day.
Child (30 to 90 pounds): 100 to 200 milligrams 3 to 4 times per day.
Child (under 30 pounds): 100 milligrams 3 to 4 times per day.
Dose must be adjusted according to disease severity and patient's response.

Overdosage

Drug overdose effects are likely to be exaggerated drug side effects. Take the victim to a hospital emergency room for treatment.

Special Information

Severe vomiting should not be treated with an antiemetic

drug alone: The cause of vomiting should be established and treated.

Overuse of antiemetic drugs may delay diagnosis of the underlying condition or problem and obscure the signs of toxic effects from other drugs. Primary emphasis in the treatment of vomiting is on reestablishment of body fluid and electrolyte balance, relief of fever if present, and treatment of the causative disease process.

If you have taken Trimethobenzamide Hydrochloride, use special care when driving.

If you forget to take a dose of Trimethobenzamide Hydrochloride, take it as soon as you remember. If it is almost time for your next regularly scheduled dose, skip the one you forgot and continue with your regular schedule. Do not take a double dose.

Generic Name
Trimipramine Maleate

Brand Name
Surmontil

Type of Drug
Antidepressant.

Prescribed for
Depression with or without symptoms of anxiety.

General Information
Trimipramine Maleate and other members of the group known as tricyclic antidepressants are effective in treating symptoms of depression. They can elevate your mood, increase physical activity and mental alertness, and improve appetite and sleep patterns. These drugs are mild sedatives and therefore useful in treating mild forms of depression associated with anxiety. You should not expect instant results with this medicine: Benefits are usually seen after 1 to 4 weeks. If symptoms are not affected after 6 to 8 weeks,

contact your doctor. Occasionally other members of this group of drugs have been used in treating nighttime bed-wetting in the young child, but they do not produce long-lasting relief, and therapy with one of them for nighttime bed-wetting is of questionable value.

Cautions and Warnings

Do not take Trimipramine Maleate if you are allergic or sensitive to this or other members of this class of drug: Doxepin, Nortriptyline, Imipramine, Desipramine, Protriptyline, and Amitriptyline. The drugs should not be used if you are recovering from a heart attack. Trimipramine Maleate may be taken with caution if you have a history of epilepsy or other convulsive disorders, difficulty in urination, glaucoma, heart disease, or thyroid disease.

Pregnancy/Breast-feeding

This drug, like other antidepressants, crosses into your developing baby's circulation and may cause birth defects if taken during the first 3 months of pregnancy. There have been reports of newborn infants suffering from heart, breathing, and urinary problems after their mothers had taken an antidepressant of this type immediately before delivery. You should avoid taking this medication while pregnant.

Antidepressants of this type are known to pass into breast milk and may affect a breast-feeding infant, although this has not been proven. Nursing mothers should consider alternative feeding methods if taking this medicine.

Seniors

Older adults are more sensitive to the effects of this drug and often require a lower dose than a younger adult to do the same job. Follow your doctor's directions and report any side effects at once.

Possible Side Effects

Changes in blood pressure (both high and low), abnormal heart rates, heart attack, confusion (especially in older patients), hallucinations, disorientation, delusions, anxiety, restlessness, excitement, numbness and tingling in the extremities, lack of coordination, muscle spasms or tremors, seizures and/or convulsions, dry mouth, blurred vision, constipation, inability to urinate, rash, itching, sensitivity to bright light or sunlight, retention of fluids, fever, allergy, changes in composition of blood, nausea, vomiting, loss of appetite, stomach upset, diarrhea, enlargement of the breasts in males and females, increased or decreased sex drive, increased or decreased blood sugar.

Less common side effects include agitation, inability to sleep, nightmares, feeling of panic, peculiar taste in the mouth, stomach cramps, black coloration of the tongue, yellowing eyes and/or skin, changes in liver function, increased or decreased weight, perspiration, flushing, frequent urination, drowsiness, dizziness, weakness, headache, loss of hair, nausea, not feeling well.

Drug Interactions

Interaction with monoamine oxidase (MAO) inhibitors can cause high fevers, convulsions, and occasionally death. Don't take any MAO inhibitor until at least 2 weeks after Trimipramine Maleate has been discontinued.

Trimipramine Maleate interacts with Guanethidine, a drug used to treat high blood pressure: If you are prescribed Trimipramine Maleate and you are taking medicine for high blood pressure, be sure to discuss this with your doctor.

Trimipramine Maleate increases the effects of barbiturates, tranquilizers, other depressive drugs, and alcohol. Don't drink alcoholic beverages if you take this medicine.

Taking Trimipramine Maleate and thyroid medicine will enhance the effects of the thyroid medicine. The combination can cause abnormal heart rhythms.

Large doses of Vitamin C (Ascorbic Acid) can reduce the effect of Trimipramine Maleate. Drugs such as Bicarbonate of Soda or Acetazolamide will increase the effect of Trimipramine Maleate.

Food Interactions

This drug is best taken on an empty stomach, but you can take it with food if it upsets your stomach.

Usual Dose

Adult: 150 to 200 milligrams per day in divided doses or

as a single bedtime dose. Hospitalized patients may need up to 300 milligrams per day. The dose of this drug must be tailored to patient's need.

Adolescent and senior: Lower doses are recommended; for people over 60 years of age, usually 50 to 100 milligrams per day.

Overdosage

Symptoms are confusion, inability to concentrate, hallucinations, drowsiness, lowered body temperature, abnormal heart rate, heart failure, large pupils of the eyes, convulsions, severely lowered blood pressure, stupor, and coma (as well as agitation, stiffening of body muscles, vomiting, and high fever). The patient should be taken to a hospital emergency room immediately. ALWAYS bring the medicine bottle.

Special Information

Avoid alcohol and other drugs that depress the nervous system while taking this antidepressant.

Do not stop taking this medicine unless your doctor has specifically told you to do so. Abruptly stopping this medicine may cause nausea, headache, and a sickly feeling.

This medicine can cause drowsiness, dizziness, and blurred vision. Be careful when driving or operating complicated machinery.

Avoid exposure to the sun or sun lamps for long periods of time.

Call your doctor if dry mouth, difficulty urinating, or excessive sedation develops.

If you take Trimipramine Maleate several times a day and forget a dose, take it as soon as you remember. If it is almost time for your next regularly scheduled dose, skip the one you forgot and continue with your regular schedule.

Generic Name

Tripelennamine Hydrochloride

Brand Names

PBZ/PBZ-SR
Pelamine

(Also available in generic form)

Type of Drug

Antihistamine.

Prescribed for

Seasonal allergy, stuffy and runny nose, itching of the eyes, scratching of the throat caused by allergy, and other allergic symptoms such as itching, rash, or hives.

General Information

Antihistamines, including Tripelennamine Hydrochloride, act by blocking the release of the chemical substance histamine from body cells. Antihistamines work by drying up the secretions of the nose, throat, and eyes.

Cautions and Warnings

Tripelennamine Hydrochloride should not be used if you are allergic to this drug. It should be avoided or used with extreme care if you have narrow-angle glaucoma (pressure in the eye), stomach ulcer or other stomach problems, enlarged prostate, or problems passing urine. It should not be used by people who have deep-breathing problems such as asthma.

Use with care if you have a history of thyroid disease, heart disease, high blood pressure, or diabetes.

Young children can show signs of nervousness, increased tension, and anxiety.

Pregnancy/Breast-feeding

Antihistamines have not been proven to be a cause of birth defects or other problems in pregnant women, although studies in animals have shown that some antihistamines (Meclizine and Cyclizine), used mainly against nausea and vomiting, may cause birth defects. Do not take any antihistamine without your doctor's knowledge.

Small amounts of antihistamine medicines pass into breast milk and may affect a nursing infant. Nursing mothers should avoid antihistamines or use alternative feeding methods while taking the medicine.

Seniors

Seniors are more sensitive to antihistamine side effects. Confusion, difficult or painful urination, dizziness, drowsiness, a faint feeling, dry mouth, nose, or throat, nightmares or excitement, nervousness, restlessness, and irritability are more likely to occur among older adults.

Possible Side Effects

Occasional side effects include itching, rash, sensitivity to light, perspiration, chills, dryness of the mouth, nose, and throat, lowered blood pressure, headache, rapid heartbeat, sleeplessness, dizziness, disturbed coordination, confusion, restlessness, nervousness, irritability, euphoria (feeling high), tingling of the hands and feet, blurred vision, double vision, ringing in the ears, stomach upset, loss of appetite, nausea, vomiting, constipation, diarrhea, difficulty in urination, tightness of the chest, wheezing, nasal stuffiness.

Drug Interactions

Tripelennamine Hydrochloride should not be taken with a monoamine oxidase (MAO) inhibitor.

Interaction with tranquilizers, sedatives, and sleeping medication will increase the effects of these drugs; it is extremely important that you discuss this with your doctor so that doses of these drugs can be properly adjusted.

Be extremely cautious when drinking while taking Tripelennamine Hydrochloride, which will enhance the intoxicating effect of alcohol. Alcohol also has a sedative effect.

Usual Dose

Adult: 25 to 50 milligrams every 4 to 6 hours. Up to 600 milligrams per day may be used. Adult patients may take up to 3 of the 100-milligram long-acting (PBZ-SR) tablets per day, although this much is not usually needed.

Infant and child: 2 milligrams per pound of body weight per day in divided doses. No more than 300 milligrams should be given per day. Older children may take up to 3 of the extended-release (long-acting) tablets per day, if needed.

Overdosage

Symptoms are depression or stimulation (especially in children), fixed or dilated pupils, flushing of the skin, and stomach upset. Patients taking an overdose of this drug must be made to vomit with Syrup of Ipecac (available at any pharmacy) to remove any remaining drug from the stomach. Call your doctor or a poison control center before doing this. If you must go to a hospital emergency room, ALWAYS bring the medicine bottle.

Special Information

Antihistamines produce a depressing effect: Be extremely cautious when driving or operating heavy equipment.

If you forget to take a dose of Tripelennamine Hydrochloride, take it as soon as you remember. If it is almost time for your next regularly scheduled dose, skip the one you forgot and continue with your regular schedule. Do not take a double dose.

Brand Name

Tuinal

Ingredients

Amobarbital
Secobarbital

(Also available in generic form)

Type of Drug

Hypnotic combination.

Prescribed for

Daytime sedation; sleeping medication.

General Information

This drug is a combination of a short- and intermediate-acting barbiturate. The combination takes advantage of the fast-acting nature of Secobarbital and the longer duration of action of Amobarbital (about 8 hours). Although the combination works well, it can be addicting if taken daily for 3 months in sufficient doses (about 100 milligrams). Larger doses will result in addiction in a shorter period of time.

Cautions and Warnings

Tuinal is classified as a barbiturate; long-term or unsupervised use may cause addiction.

Barbiturates are neutralized in the liver and eliminated from the body through the kidneys; consequently, people who have liver or kidney disorders—namely, difficulty in forming or excreting urine—should be carefully monitored by their doctor when taking Tuinal.

If you have known sensitivities or allergies to barbiturates, if you have previously been addicted to sedatives or hypnotics, or if you have a disease affecting the respiratory system, you should not take Tuinal.

Pregnancy/Breast-feeding

Regular use of any barbiturate during the last 3 months of pregnancy can cause the baby to be born dependent on the medicine. Also, barbiturate use increases the chance of bleeding problems, brain tumors, and breathing difficulties in the newborn.

Barbiturates pass into breast milk and can cause drowsiness, slow heartbeat, and breathing difficulty in the newborn.

Seniors

Older adults are more sensitive to the effects of barbiturates, especially nervousness and confusion, and often require lower doses than younger adults to do the same job. Follow your doctor's directions and report any side effects at once.

Possible Side Effects

Drowsiness, lethargy, dizziness, hangover, difficulty in breathing, skin rash, and general allergic reaction such as runny nose, watery eyes, and scratchy throat.

Less common side effects include nausea, vomiting, diarrhea. More severe adverse reactions may include anemia and yellowing of the skin and eyes.

Drug Interactions

Interaction with alcohol, tranquilizers, or other sedatives increases the effect of Tuinal.

Interaction with anticoagulants (blood-thinning agents) can reduce their effect. This is also true of muscle relaxants, painkillers, anticonvulsants, Quinidine, Theophylline, Metronidazole, Phenmetrazine, birth control pills, and Acetaminophen.

Food Interactions

This medicine is best taken on an empty stomach, but may be taken with food if it upsets your stomach.

Usual Dose

Up to 200 milligrams.

Overdosage

Symptoms are difficulty in breathing, decrease in size of the pupils of the eyes, lowered body temperature progressing to fever as time passes, fluid in the lungs, and eventually coma.

Anyone suspected of having taken an overdose must be taken to the hospital for immediate care. ALWAYS bring the medicine bottle so the emergency room physician can quickly and correctly identify the medicine and start treatment. Severe overdosage of this medication can kill; the drug has been used many times in suicide attempts.

Special Information

Avoid alcohol and other drugs that depress the nervous system while taking this barbiturate.

Be sure to take this medicine according to your doctor's

direction. Do not change your dose without your doctor's approval.

Tuinal may slow down your physical and mental reflexes, so you must be extremely careful when operating machinery, driving an automobile, or performing other potentially dangerous tasks.

Call your doctor at once if you develop fever, sore throat, nosebleeds, mouth sores, unexplained black-and-blue marks, easy bruising, or bleeding.

If you forget to take a dose of Tuinal and you remember within about an hour of your regular time, take it right away. If you do not remember until later, skip the forgotten dose and go back to your regular schedule. Do not take a double dose.

Brand Name

Tussionex

Ingredients

Hydrocodone
Chlorpheniramine

Type of Drug

Cough suppressant-antihistamine combination.

Prescribed for

Relief of cough and other symptoms of a cold or other respiratory condition.

General Information

This drug may be prescribed to treat a cough or congestion that has not responded to other medication. The cough suppressant ingredient (Hydrocodone) in this combination is more potent than Codeine.

Cautions and Warnings

Do not use Tussionex if you are allergic to any of the ingredients. Patients allergic to Codeine may also be allergic to

Tussionex. Long-term use of this or any other narcotic-containing drug can lead to drug dependence or addiction. Both ingredients in Tussionex can cause drowsiness, tiredness, or loss of concentration. Use with caution if you have a history of convulsions, glaucoma, stomach ulcer, high blood pressure, thyroid disease, heart disease, or diabetes.

Pregnancy/Breast-feeding

Narcotics like Hydrocodone have not been associated with birth defects, but taking too much of any narcotic during pregnancy can lead to the birth of a drug-dependent infant and drug-withdrawal symptoms in the baby. All narcotics, including Hydrocodone, can cause breathing problems in the newborn if taken just before delivery.

Antihistamines like Chlorpheniramine may pass into your developing baby's circulation but have not been the source of birth defects.

Nursing mothers should use an alternative feeding method while taking this medication.

Seniors

Seniors are more likely to be sensitive to both the Hydrocodone and Chlorpheniramine in this combination. The Hydrocodone may have more of a depressant effect on seniors than on younger adults. Other effects that may be more prominent are dizziness, light-headedness, or fainting when rising suddenly from a sitting or lying position.

Also, antihistamines may produce confusion, difficult or painful urination, a faint feeling, dry mouth, nose, or throat, nightmares or excitement, nervousness, restlessness, or irritability.

Possible Side Effects

Light-headedness, dizziness, sleepiness, nausea, vomiting, sweating, itching, rash, sensitivity to light, excessive perspiration, chills, dryness of the mouth, nose, and throat.

Less common side effects are euphoria (feeling high), weakness, agitation, uncoordinated muscle movement, minor hallucinations, disorientation and visual disturbances, loss of appetite, constipation, flushing of the face, rapid heartbeat, palpitations, faintness, difficult urination, reduced sexual potency, low blood sugar, anemia, yellowing of the skin or whites of the eyes, blurred or double vision, ringing or buzzing in the ears, wheezing, nasal stuffiness.

Drug Interactions

Do not use alcohol or other depressant drugs because they will increase the depressant effect of the Tussionex.

This drug should not be taken in combination with monoamine oxidase (MAO) inhibitor drugs.

Food Interactions

This medicine is best taken on an empty stomach, but you may take it with food if it upsets your stomach.

Usual Dose

Tablet or capsule: 1 every 8 to 12 hours.
Suspension: 1 teaspoon every 8 to 12 hours.

Overdosage

Signs of overdose are depression, slowed breathing, flushing of the skin, upset stomach. In case of overdose, bring the patient to a hospital emergency room. ALWAYS bring the medicine bottle.

Special Information

Be careful while driving or operating any equipment.

The liquid form of Tussionex does not contain any sugar.

If you forget to take a dose of Tussionex, take it as soon as you remember. If it is almost time for your next regularly scheduled dose, skip the one you forgot and continue with your regular schedule. Do not take a double dose.

Brand Name

Tussi-Organidin DM Liquid

Ingredients

Dextromethorphan Hydrobromide
Iodinated Glycerol

Other Brand Names

Iophen DM Liquid   Tussi-R-Gen DM Liquid
IoTuss-DM Liquid   Tusso-DM Liquid
Tusside Liquid

(Also available in generic form)

Type of Drug

Cough suppressant and expectorant combination.

Prescribed for

Relief of coughs due to colds or other respiratory infections.

General Information

Iodinated Glycerol, an expectorant, increases the production of mucus and other bronchial secretions. Diluting thick secretions helps by making them easier for the body to deal with. Expectorants do not suppress your cough. The cough suppressant effect of Tussi-Organidin DM is due to the presence of Dextromethorphan, the most effective of all non-narcotic cough suppressants.

Many experts in the field of upper respiratory medicine are skeptical about the effectiveness of this medication, especially for removing mucus that accumulates in serious respiratory conditions like bronchitis, bronchial asthma, emphysema, cystic fibrosis, and chronic sinusitis.

Cautions and Warnings

Do not take Tussi-Organidin DM if you know you are allergic or sensitive to the Dextromethorphan ingredient.

People allergic to Iodine-containing products and those who must avoid Iodine for any other reason should not take this product.

People with a history of thyroid disease should use this medication with care.

Children with cystic fibrosis are more likely than other children to develop an enlarged thyroid gland after taking Iodinated Glycerol. They should not use this product Tussi-Organidin DM.

The Iodinated Glycerol ingredient in Tussi-Organidin DM may worsen an existing case of acne.

Pregnancy/Breast-feeding

Tussi-Organidin DM should not be taken by women who are or might become pregnant. The Iodinated Glycerol ingredient can interfere with the development of the baby's thyroid gland, resulting in an enlarged and possibly underactive thyroid.

Nursing mothers should not take Tussi-Organidin DM. It passes into breast milk and may cause a rash and an underactive thyroid gland in the nursing infant.

Seniors

Older adults may take Tussi-Organidin DM without restriction. Follow your doctor's directions and report any side effects at once.

Possible Side Effects

The most frequent side effects are nausea, vomiting, diarrhea, and stomach pains.

Prolonged use of Iodinated Glycerol may cause skin rash that can, rarely, become severe or fatal. Prolonged use of this drug may also result in an underactive thyroid. Symptoms of this are dry skin, swelling around the eyes, unusual sensitivity to the cold, tiredness or weakness, and weight gain. Other side effects of long-term use are bruning of the mouth and throat, severe headache, increased salivation, runny nose, sneezing and cold symptoms, irritation of the eyes or swelling of the eyelids, a metallic taste in the mouth, and soreness of the teeth and gums. Swelling of the neck may indicate thyroid enlargement.

Drug Interactions

The combination of Iodinated Glycerol with either Lithium or an antithyroid medicine may reduce thyroid function. This combination should be used with caution.

Food Interactions

Tussi-Organidin DM should be taken with a full glass of water or other fluid to get the best effect from the medicine.

Usual Dose

1 to 2 teaspoons every 3 or 4 hours as needed for relief of cough.

Overdosage

There have been no reports of any serious problems with Tussi-Organidin DM overdose. Call your local poison center or hospital emergency room for more information.

Special Information

Call your doctor at the first sign of nausea or vomiting, drug allergy (fever, joint pains, skin rash, hives, or swelling of the face or lips), chills, headache, loss of appetite, sore throat, swelling of the neck, tiredness, weakness, sensitivity to the cold, or weight gain. Other side effects should be reported if they are particularly bothersome or persistent.

Drink a full glass of water with each dose of Tussi-Organidin DM to help thin mucus secretions.

If you take Tussi-Organidin DM 3 or more times a day and forget a dose, take it as soon as you remember. If it is almost time for your next dose, take one dose as soon as you remember and another in 3 or 4 hours, then go back to your regular schedule. Do not take a double dose.

Brand Name

Tussi-Organidin Liquid

Ingredients

Codeine Phosphate
Iodinated Glycerol

Other Brand Names

Bio-Tuss C   IoTuss Liquid
Iophen C Liquid   Tussi-R-Gen Liquid

(Also available in generic form)

Type of Drug

Cough suppressant and expectorant combination.

Prescribed for

Relief of coughs due to colds or other respiratory infections.

General Information

Iodinated Glycerol, an expectorant, increases the production of mucus and other bronchial secretions. Diluting thick secretions helps by making them easier for the body to deal with. Expectorants do not suppress your cough. The cough suppressant effect of Tussi-Organidin is due to the Codeine present in the mixture.

Many experts in the field of upper respiratory medicine are skeptical about the effectiveness of this medication, especially for removing mucus that accumulates in serious respiratory conditions like bronchitis, bronchial asthma, emphysema, cystic fibrosis, or chronic sinusitis.

Cautions and Warnings

Do not take Tussi-Organidin if you know you are allergic or sensitive to the Codeine ingredient. Use this drug with extreme caution if you suffer from asthma or other breathing problems. Long-term use of Codeine may cause drug dependence or addiction.

People allergic to Iodine-containing products and those who must avoid Iodine for any other reason should not take this product.

People with a history of thyroid disease should use this medication with care.

Children with cystic fibrosis are more likely than other children to develop an enlarged thyroid gland after taking Iodinated Glycerol. They should not use Tussi-Organidin.

The Iodinated Glycerol ingredient in Tussi-Organidin may worsen an existing case of acne.

Pregnancy/Breast-feeding

Tussi-Organidin should not be taken by women who are or might become pregnant. The Iodinated Glycerol ingredient can interfere with the development of the baby's thyroid gland, resulting in an enlarged and possibly underactive thyroid.

Nursing mothers should not take Tussi-Organidin. It passes into breast milk and may cause a rash and an underactive thyroid gland in the nursing infant. The Codeine can affect the infant's breathing and general respiratory function.

Too much (large amounts taken for a long time) of any narcotic, including Codeine, taken during pregnancy and breast-feeding may cause the baby to become dependent on the narcotic. Narcotics may also cause breathing problems in the infant during delivery.

Seniors

Older adults are more sensitive to the effects of the Codeine in this drug. Follow your doctor's directions and report any side effects at once.

Possible Side Effects

The most frequent side effects are light-headedness, dizziness, sedation or sleepiness, nausea, vomiting, diarrhea, stomach pains, and sweating.

Prolonged use of Iodinated Glycerol may cause skin rash that can, rarely, become severe or fatal. Prolonged use of Iodinated Glycerol may also result in an underactive thyroid. Symptoms of this are dry skin, swelling around the eyes, unusual sensitivity to the cold, tiredness or weakness, and weight gain. Other side effects of long-term use are burning of the mouth and throat, severe headache, increased salivation, runny nose, sneezing and cold symptoms, irritation of the eyes or swelling of the eyelids, a metallic taste in the mouth, and soreness of the teeth and gums. Swelling of the neck may indicate thyroid enlargement.

Less common side effects, associated with Codeine, are euphoria (feeling high), weakness, sleepiness, headache, agitation, uncoordinated muscle movement, minor hallucinations, disorientation and visual disturbances, dry mouth, loss of appetite, constipation, flushing of the face, rapid heartbeat, palpitations, faintness, urinary difficulties or hesitancy, reduced sex drive and/or potency, itching, rashes, anemia, lowered blood sugar, and yellowing of the skin and/or whites of the eyes. Narcotic analgesics may aggravate convulsions in those who have had convulsions in the past.

Drug Interactions

Codeine has a general depressant effect and can affect breathing. Tussi-Organidin should be taken with extreme care in combination with alcohol, sedatives, tranquilizers, antihistamines, or other depressant drugs.

The combination of Iodinated Glycerol with either Lithium

or an antithyroid medicine may reduce thyroid function. This combination should be used with caution.

Food Interactions

Tussi-Organidin should be taken with a full glass of water or other fluid to get the best effect from it.

Usual Dose

1 to 2 teaspoons every 3 or 4 hours as needed for relief of cough.

Overdosage

Symptoms are difficulty breathing, extreme tiredness progressing to stupor and then coma, pinpoint pupils of the eyes, lack of response to stimulation such as a pin prick, cold and clammy skin, slow heartbeat, low blood pressure, convulsions, and heart attack. The patient should be taken to a hospital emergency room. ALWAYS bring the medicine bottle.

Special Information

Codeine is a respiratory depressant and affects the central nervous system, producing sleepiness, tiredness, and/or inability to concentrate. Be careful if you are driving, operating machinery, or performing other functions requiring concentration.

Call your doctor at the first sign of nausea or vomiting, drug allergy (fever, joint pains, skin rash, hives, or swelling of the face or lips), chills, headache, loss of appetite, sore throat, swelling of the neck, tiredness, weakness, sensitivity to the cold, or weight gain. Other side effects should be reported if they are particularly bothersome or persistent.

Drink a full glass of water with each dose of Tussi-Organidin to help thin mucus secretions.

If you take Tussi-Organidin 3 or more times a day and forget a dose, take it as soon as you remember. If it is almost time for your next dose, take one dose as soon as you remember and another in 3 or 4 hours, then go back to your regular schedule. Do not take a double dose.

Brand Name

Tuss-Ornade Spansules/Liquid

Ingredients

Caramiphen Edisylate
Phenylpropanolamine Hydrochloride

Other Brand Names

Ordrine AT Extended-Re-
    lease Capsules
Rescaps-D S.R. Capsules
Tuss-Allergine Modified T.D.
    Capsules

Tuss-Genade Modified
    Capsules
Tussogest Capsules

(Also available in generic form)

Type of Drug

Decongestant; expectorant.

Prescribed for

Relief of cough, nasal congestion, runny nose, and other
symptoms associated with the common cold, viruses, or
other upper respiratory diseases. The drug may also be used
to treat allergies, asthma, ear infections, or sinus infections.

General Information

Tuss-Ornade is one of almost 100 products marketed to relieve the symptoms of the common cold and other respiratory infections. These products contain ingredients to relieve
congestion, act as an antihistamine, relieve or suppress
cough, and help you to cough up mucus. They may contain
medicine for each purpose or a combination of medicines.
Some combinations leave out the antihistamine, the decongestant, or the expectorant. You must realize while taking
Tuss-Ornade or similar products that these drugs are good
only for the relief of symptoms and do not treat the underlying problem, such as a cold virus or other infections.

    The liquid formulations contain 5 percent alcohol.

Cautions and Warnings

This drug can cause you to become over-anxious and nervous and may interfere with your sleep. It should be avoided if you have diabetes, heart disease, high blood pressure, thyroid disease, glaucoma, or a prostate condition.

Pregnancy/Breast-feeding

This drug crosses into the blood circulation of a developing baby. It has not been found to cause birth defects. Pregnant women, or those who might become pregnant while taking this drug, should not take it without their doctors' approval. When the drug is considered essential by your doctor, the potential risk of taking the medicine must be carefully weighed against the benefit it might produce.

This drug passes into breast milk, but has caused no problems among breast-fed infants. You must consider the potential effect on the nursing infant if breast-feeding while taking this medicine.

Seniors

Older adults are more sensitive to the effects of this drug. Follow your doctor's directions and report any side effects at once.

Possible Side Effects

Dry mouth, blurred vision, difficulty passing urine, (possibly) constipation, nervousness, restlessness, inability to sleep.

Drug Interactions

Taking Tuss-Ornade with a monoamine oxidase (MAO) inhibitor can produce severe interaction, so consult your doctor before combining them.

Do not take this drug with sedatives, tranquilizers, antihistamines, sleeping pills, thyroid medicine, or antihypertensive drugs such as Reserpine or Guanethidine.

Since Tuss-Ornade contains ingredients which may cause sleepiness or difficulty in concentration, do not drink alcoholic beverages while taking this drug. The combination can cause excessive drowsiness or sleepiness and result in an inability to concentrate and carry out activities requiring extra concentration and coordination.

Food Interactions

Take with a full glass of water to remove excessive mucus from the throat and reduce stomach upset.

Usual Dose

Spansule (capsule): 1 every 12 hours.

Liquid: 1 to 2 teaspoons every 4 hours as needed for relief of cough, nasal congestion, runny nose, or other symptoms associated with the common cold or other upper respiratory diseases.

Special Information

If you forget to take a dose of Tuss-Ornade, take it as soon as you remember. If it is almost time for your next regularly scheduled dose, skip the one you forgot and continue with your regular schedule. Do not take a double dose.

Generic Name

Ursodiol

Brand Name

Actigall

Type of Drug

Gallstone dissolver.

Prescribed for

People with cholesterol gallstones readily identifiable by X-ray examination who refuse gallstone surgery or in whom surgery might be risky.

General Information

Ursodiol is a natural bile acid that suppresses the production of cholesterol in the liver and interferes with the absorption of dietary cholesterol through the intestine. It will not dissolve gallstones that are encased in calcium, stones that are not visible on X-ray, or non-cholesterol stones. Your doctor should examine your gallbladder every 6 months to see if

the drug is working. Most people who show progress at the
first 6-month evaluation are likely to lose their gallstones.
No change in the stones at 12 months is a sign that the
treatment is not likely to work at all.

Cautions and Warnings

Before taking this drug, it is important that your doctor perform a complete gallstone examination, including X-ray
tests, to be sure your bile duct is functioning normally. Bile
acids, including Ursodiol, may be weakly linked to the development of colon cancer among people who have had gallbladder surgery. People with chronic liver disease or who
are allergic to bile acids should not take this product.

Pregnancy/Breast-feeding

Four women, part of a pre-approved study, accidentally took
Ursodiol during the first 3 months of their pregnancy, and
they all delivered normal babies. Nevertheless, Ursodiol
should not be used by women who are or might become
pregnant.

It is not known if Ursodiol passes into breast milk. Nursing
mothers must observe their babies for any possible drug-
induced effect.

Seniors

Seniors may take this medicine without restriction.

Possible Side Effects

The most common side effects are nausea, vomiting, upset
stomach, abdominal pain, bile pain, gallstone pains, a metallic taste, constipation, stomach gas, and diarrhea. Itching,
rash, dry skin, sweating, and hair-thinning may occur. Ursodiol may also cause headache, fatigue, anxiety, depression, sleep disturbances, joint, muscle and back pains,
cough, and runny nose.

Drug Interactions

Aluminum-based antacids, Cholestyramine, and Colestipol
may interfere with the absorption of Ursodiol.

Food Interactions

Follow your doctor's instructions for dietary limitations while being treated with Ursodiol for gallstones. For best results, take Ursodiol with meals.

Usual Dose

3.5 to 4.5 milligrams per pound of body weight per day, divided into 2 or 3 doses.

Overdosage

The most likely result of an Ursodiol overdose is diarrhea. Call your local poison control center for more information.

Special Information

Take this medicine for the full course of treatment, even if you begin to feel better. If you stop treatment, your gallstones may not dissolve as quickly as possible, or they may not dissolve at all.

Months of Ursodiol treatment are required to dissolve most gallstones, and some may never be dissolved. Success with this drug depends on the size of the stones and their cholesterol content. Age, weight, and sex do not influence the dissolving of gallstones.

Half of all people who use this drug to dissolve their gallstones may experience another gallstone attack within 5 years.

People with severe, uncontrollable gallstone attacks, bile duct obstruction, inflammation of the pancreas, or other serious problems should not depend on this drug to dissolve their stones; surgery is more appropriate. Your doctor will determine which is the proper course of action for you.

Report any severe side effects to your doctor, especially pain in the abdomen, severe right-upper-abdominal pain that travels to your shoulder, nausea, and vomiting.

If you forget to take a dose of Ursodiol, take it as soon as you remember.

If you take this medicine twice a day and forget a dose until it is almost time for your next dose, take one dose as soon as you remember and another in 5 or 6 hours, then go back to your regular schedule.

If you take Ursodiol 3 times a day and forget a dose until

it is almost time for your next dose, take one dose as soon as you remember and another in 3 or 4 hours, then go back to your regular schedule.

Generic Name

Valproic Acid

Brand Names

Depakene
Depakote

(Also available in generic form)

Type of Drug

Anticonvulsant.

Prescribed for

Various seizure disorders.

General Information

Valproic Acid is used to treat absence, mixed, myoclonic, partial, and grand mal seizures. It can also be used for the special kind of seizures called petit mal.

Cautions and Warnings

Do not take Valproic Acid if you are allergic to it. Take this drug with caution if you have a history of liver problems. Some cases of liver failure have occurred in people taking Valproic Acid, especially children under 2 years old.

Pregnancy/Breast-feeding

Valproic Acid crosses into the blood circulation of a developing baby and is reported to have caused birth defects after having been taken during the first 3 months of pregnancy. Most mothers, though, who take this medicine deliver healthy, normal babies. If you are pregnant, discuss the relative risk of taking this medicine with your doctor.

Valproic Acid passes into breast milk and may affect a nursing infant. No problems have been found among breast-fed infants of mothers taking this medication, but you should discuss the possibility of using an alternative feeding method with your doctor.

Seniors

Older adults with poor kidney function are more likely to develop side effects from Valproic Acid, since the drug passes out of your body through the kidneys.

Possible Side Effects

Nausea, vomiting and indigestion, sedation or sleepiness, weakness, skin rash, emotional upset, depression, psychosis, aggression, hyperactive behavior. Valproic Acid can cause adverse effects on the blood system. The frequency of side effects increases as your dose of Valproic Acid increases.

Less common side effects include diarrhea, stomach cramps, constipation, appetite changes (either increase or decrease), headache, loss of control of eye muscles, drooping eyelids, double vision, spots before the eyes, loss of muscle control and coordination, tremors.

Drug Interactions

Valproic Acid may increase the depressive effects of alcohol, sleeping pills, tranquilizers, or other depressant drugs.

If you begin taking Valproic Acid while taking Phenytoin, your Phenytoin dosage may have to be adjusted. Use of Valproic Acid together with Clonazepam may produce a certain kind of seizure. This combination should be used with extreme caution.

Valproic Acid may affect oral anticoagulant (blood-thinning) drugs. If you begin taking Valproic Acid and have been taking an anticoagulant, your anticoagulant dose may have to be changed.

Aspirin may increase the chances of toxicity due to Valproic Acid.

Valproic Acid may cause a false positive interpretation of the test for ketones in the urine (used by diabetics).

Food Interactions

This medicine is best taken on an empty stomach, because food prolongs the time it takes for the medicine to be absorbed into the bloodstream. Nevertheless, you may take it with food if it upsets your stomach.

Usual Dose

7 to 27 milligrams per pound per day; up to 250 milligrams per day.

Overdosage

Call your doctor or take the patient to a hospital emergency room immediately. ALWAYS bring the medicine bottle.

Special Information

This medicine may cause drowsiness; be careful while driving or operating machinery.

Do not chew or crush Valproic Acid capsules or tablets.

Valproic Acid can cause mouth and throat irritation.

All seizure patients should carry special identification indicating their disease and the medicine being taken for it.

If you take Valproic Acid once a day and forget your dose, take it as soon as possible. If you don't remember until the next day, skip the forgotten dose and continue with your regular schedule.

If you take the medicine 2 or more times a day and forget a dose, and you remember within 6 hours of your regular time, take it as soon as possible. Take the rest of that day's doses at regularly spaced time intervals. Go back to your regular schedule the next day.

Brand Name

Vaseretic

Ingredients

Enalapril
Hydrochlorothiazide

Type of Drug

Antihypertensive combination.

Prescribed for

High blood pressure.

General Information

This medicine is a combination of a thiazide diuretic and a member of the class of drugs known as ACE inhibitors, which work by preventing the conversion of a potent hormone called Angiotensin 1. This directly affects the production of other hormones and enzymes which participate in the regulation of blood pressure. The blood-pressure-lowering effects of the 2 drugs add to each other to produce a result greater than could be expected from either ingredient.

Cautions and Warnings

This drug can cause kidney problems, especially loss of protein in the urine.

Patients taking Enalapril should have the amount of protein in the urine measured during the first month of treatment and monthly for the next few months. The drug can also cause a reduction on white-blood-cell count, leading to a potential for increased susceptibility to infection. Enalapril should be used with caution by people who have kidney disease or diseases of the immune/collagen system (particularly lupus erythematosus), or who have taken other drugs that affect the white-blood-cell count.

Do not take this combination if you are allergic to either ingredient or to sulfa drugs. You may be sensitive to Hydrochlorothiazide if you have a history of allergy or bronchial asthma.

Pregnancy/Breast-feeding

The effect of Enalapril on a developing fetus is not known. Hydrochlorothiazide crosses into the developing baby's blood system and can cause jaundice, blood problems, and low potassium. Women who are, or might become, pregnant while taking this drug should discuss the matter with their doctors.

It is not known if Enalapril passes into breast milk and if it will affect a nursing infant. Hydrochlorothiazide passes into breast milk but no problems have been reported in nursing infants.

Seniors

Older adults may be less sensitive to the blood-pressure-lowering effects of this drug combination than younger adults, but they may be more sensitive to its side effects. Dosage must be individualized to your needs.

Possible Side Effects

Dizziness, tiredness, headache, diarrhea, rash (usually mild), and cough are the most common side effects.

Less common drug side effects are itching, fever, temporary loss of taste perception, stomach irritation, chest pain, low blood pressure, heart palpitations, difficulty sleeping, tingling in the hands or feet, nausea, vomiting, jaundice and liver damage, excessive sweating, muscle cramps, (male) impotence, and muscle weakness. Some people experience unusual reactions after taking the first dose of the drug, including facial flushing and swelling, swelling of the arms and legs, and closing of the throat.

The Hydrochlorothiazide ingredient can cause a loss of body potassium. Signs of low potassium are dry mouth, thirst, weakness, lethargy, drowsiness, restlessness, muscle pains or cramps, muscle tiredness, low blood pressure, low urine production, abnormal heart rate, and upset stomach. Your doctor may prescribe a potassium-rich diet or a potassium supplement to counteract this problem, although Enalapril, which may increase potassium levels in your blood, can counteract the Hydrochlorothiazide.

Drug Interactions

The blood-pressure-lowering effect of Vaseretic is additive with that of beta blockers. Other drugs that cause rapid drops in blood pressure should be used with extreme caution because of a possible severe drop when taken together with Enalapril.

Enalapril may increase potassium levels in your blood, especially when given with potassium-sparing diuretics and/or potassium supplements.

People taking oral antidiabetic drugs who start taking Vaseretic may have to have their antidiabetic dosage adjusted. The chance of Lithium toxicity may be increased by Hydrochlorothiazide.

Food Interactions

This drug is best taken on an empty stomach, usually 1 hour before or 2 hours after a meal.

Usual Dose

1 tablet a day. Some people may take their total daily dosage in 2 divided doses.

People with poor kidney function have to take less of the medicine to achieve reduced blood pressure.

Overdosage

The primary effect of Vaseretic overdosage is a rapid drop in blood pressure, as evidenced by dizziness or fainting. Take the overdose victim to a hospital emergency room immediately. ALWAYS remember to bring the medicine bottle.

Special Information

Call your doctor if you develop fever, sore throat, mouth sores, abnormal heartbeat, or chest pain, or if you have persistent rash or loss of taste perception.

Vaseretic may cause dizziness when you rise quickly from a lying or sitting position.

Avoid strenuous exercise and/or very hot weather because heavy sweating and/or dehydration can cause a rapid drop in blood pressure.

Do not stop taking this medicine without your doctor's knowledge.

Avoid nonprescription medicines such as diet pills, decongestants, and stimulants that can raise your blood pressure.

If you forget to take a dose of Vaseretic, take it as soon as you remember. If it is almost time for your next regularly scheduled dose, skip the one you forgot and continue with your regular schedule. Do not take a double dose.

Generic Name

Verapamil

Brand Names

Calan/Calan SR   Verelan
Isoptin/Isoptin SR

(Also available in generic form)

Type of Drug

Calcium channel blocker.

Prescribed for

Angina pectoris and Prinzmetals's angina; high blood pressure; asthma; Raynaud's disease.

General Information

Verapamil is one of several calcium channel blockers available in the United States. These drugs work by blocking the passage of calcium into heart and smooth muscle. Since calcium is an essential ingredient in muscle contraction, blocking calcium reduces both muscle contraction and oxygen use by the muscle. This is why Verapamil is used in the treatment of angina, a kind of heart pain related to poor oxygen supply to the heart muscles. Verapamil also dilates the vessels that supply blood to the heart muscles and prevents spasm of these arteries. Verapamil affects the movement of calcium only into muscle cells; it does not have any effect on calcium in the blood. Verapamil brands with "SR" after their name are sustained-release formulas. They should be used only for high blood pressure.

Cautions and Warnings

Verapamil may cause lowered blood pressure in some patients. Patients taking a beta-blocking drug who begin taking Verapamil may develop heart failure or increased angina pain. Do not take this drug if you have had an allergic reaction to it.

Pregnancy/Breast-feeding

Pregnant women should only use this drug if absolutely necessary. This drug may cause birth defects or interfere with your baby's development. Check with your doctor before taking it if you are, or might be, pregnant.

Although taking Verapamil during nursing has not been shown to cause problems, nursing mothers should use the drug only if absolutely necessary.

Seniors

Older adults are more sensitive to the effects of this drug. Follow your doctor's directions and report any side effects at once.

Possible Side Effects

Low blood pressure, swelling of the arms or legs, heart failure, slowed heartbeat, dizziness, light-headedness, weakness, fatigue, headache, constipation, nausea, liver damage, especially in patients with previous liver damage.

Less common side effects include confusion, tingling in the arms or legs, difficulty sleeping, blurred vision, muscle cramps, shakiness, leg pains, difficulty maintaining balance, hair loss, spotty menstruation. In addition, some patients taking Verapamil have experienced heart attack and abnormal heart rhythms, but the occurrence of these effects has not been directly linked to Verapamil.

Drug Interactions

Long-term Verapamil use will cause the blood levels of Digitalis drugs to increase by 50 to 70 percent. The dose of Digitalis drugs will have to be drastically lowered.

Disopyramide should not be taken within 48 hours of taking Verapamil because of possible interaction.

Patients taking Verapamil together with Quinidine may experience very low blood pressure.

Verapamil's effectiveness may be decreased by taking calcium.

Food Interactions

Take this drug 1 hour before or 2 hours after meals.

Usual Dose

240 to 480 milligrams per day. The dose must be individualized to patient's need.

Overdosage

Overdosage of Verapamil can cause low blood pressure. Symptoms are dizziness, weakness, and (possibly) slowed heartbeat. If you have taken an overdose of Verapamil, call your doctor or go to a hospital emergency room. ALWAYS bring the medicine bottle.

Special Information

Call your doctor if you develop swelling in the arms or legs, difficulty breathing, increased heart pains, dizziness, lightheadedness, or low blood pressure. Do not stop taking Verapamil abruptly.

If you forget to take a dose of Verapamil, take it as soon as you remember. If it is almost time for your next regularly scheduled dose, skip the one you forgot and continue with your regular schedule. Do not take a double dose.

Brand Name

Vicodin

Ingredients

Acetaminophen
Hydrocodone Bitartrate

Other Brand Names

Amacodone	Duradyne DHC
Anexsia	Hydrocet
Anodynos-DHC	Hydrogesic
Bancap HC	Hy-Phen
Co-Gesic	Lortab
Damacet-P	Norcet
Dolacet	T-Gesic
Duocet	Zydone

Type of Drug

Narcotic analgesic combination.

Prescribed for

Relief of mild to moderate pain.

General Information

Vicodin may be prescribed for anyone who is allergic to, or
cannot take, Aspirin or who requires a narcotic pain reliever
more potent than Codeine. This combination will relieve virtually any kind of pain, but is probably not effective for pain
caused by arthritis or other inflammation because the Acetaminophen ingredient does not produce an anti-inflammatory effect. A better choice would be a drug that contains
Aspirin instead of Acetaminophen.

Cautions and Warnings

Do not take Vicodin if you are allergic to Acetaminophen or
to Codeine or any other narcotic pain reliever. People with
asthma or other breathing problems should use this combination with caution. The long-term use of Vicodin can lead
to drug dependence or addiction. Hydrocodone Bitartrate is
a respiratory depressant and affects the central nervous system, producing sleepiness, tiredness, and an inability to
concentrate.

Pregnancy/Breast-feeding

Neither Acetaminophen nor Hydrocodone has been associated with birth defects. However, taking too much Hydrocodone, or any other narcotic, during pregnancy can lead to
the birth of a drug-dependent infant and drug-withdrawal
symptoms in the baby. All narcotics, including Hydrocodone, can cause breathing problems in the newborn if taken
just before delivery.

Vicodin has not caused any problems among nursing
mothers or their infants.

Seniors

The Hydrocodone in this combination product may have
more of a depressant effect on seniors than on younger
adults. Other effects that may be more prominent are dizzi-

ness, light-headedness, or fainting when rising suddenly from a sitting or lying position.

Possible Side Effects

Light-headedness, dizziness, sleepiness, nausea, vomiting, loss of appetite, and sweating. These side effects usually can be controlled by taking a preparation with a lower narcotic dose.

Less common side effects include feeling "high," weakness, headache, agitation, loss of coordinated muscle movements, minor hallucinations, disorientation, blurred vision, dry mouth, constipation, facial flushing, rapid heartbeat, faintness, urinary difficulty or hesitancy, reduced sex drive and/or potency, itching, rash, anemia, low blood sugar, and yellowing of the skin or whites of the eyes. Narcotic drugs may aggravate convulsions in those who have had them in the past.

Drug Interactions

Alcohol, tranquilizers, sleeping pills, antihistamines, and other medicines that can depress the central nervous system should be avoided if you are taking Vicodin, because of the possibility of severe difficulty breathing. This interaction can be severe enough to make you stop breathing or can result in death.

Food Interactions

This combination may be taken with food or meals if it upsets your stomach.

Usual Dose

1 tablet every 6 hours.

Overdosage

The major signs of Vicodin overdose are extreme tiredness progressing to stupor and coma, difficulty breathing, pinpoint pupils of the eyes, loss of response to simple stimulation such as the prick of a pin, cold clammy skin, and reduced heart rate. Massive Acetaminophen overdose or chronic use of the maximum daily dose of Acetaminophen can result in liver failure, indicated by yellowing of the skin or whites of the eyes, nausea, vomiting, abdominal pain, and diarrhea.

Victims of Vicodin overdose, if discovered within 1 hour of the incident, should be given Syrup of Ipecac to induce vomiting to remove any remaining drug from the stomach. Call your doctor or a poison control center before doing this. DO NOT try to induce vomiting if the victim is unconscious or having convulsions. If Vicodin overdose is discovered later than 1 hour after the medicine is taken, the victim will have to be taken to the hospital for treatment of narcotic overdose. Acetaminophen poisoning takes 24 to 36 hours to develop and requires continuous monitoring by a doctor. ALWAYS bring the medicine bottle with you.

Special Information

Use care while driving or doing anything else that requires concentration or alertness. Avoid alcohol and other nervous system depressants while taking Vicodin.

Call your doctor if you have trouble breathing normally or if this product causes nausea, vomiting, constipation, or any other side effect that becomes unusually severe.

If you forget to take a dose of Vicodin, take it as soon as you remember. If it is almost time for your next regularly scheduled dose, skip the one you forgot and continue with your regular schedule. Do not take a double dose.

Generic Name

Warfarin Sodium

Brand Names

Carfin   Panwarfin
Coumadin   Sofarin

(Also available in generic form)

Type of Drug

Oral anticoagulant.

Prescribed for

Anticoagulation (thinning of the blood). This is generally a secondary form of treatment for other diseases—such as blood clots in the arms and legs, pulmonary embolism, heart attack, or abnormal heart rhythms—in which the formation of blood clots may cause serious problems.

Under investigation is the use of Warfarin to reduce the risk of recurring heart attack or stroke. It may also be of benefit in the treatment of lung cancer.

General Information

Anticoagulants act by depressing the body's normal production of various factors which are known to take part in the coagulation mechanism. If you are taking Warfarin it is absolutely essential that you take the exact dose in the exact way prescribed by your doctor. Notify your doctor at the earliest sign of unusual bleeding or bruising (that is, the formation of black-and-blue marks), if you pass blood in your urine or stool, and/or if you pass a black tarry stool. The interactions of this class of drugs are extremely important and are discussed in detail below.

Warfarin can be extremely dangerous if not used properly. Periodic blood tests of the time it takes your blood or various factors in your blood to begin to coagulate are required for proper control of oral anticoagulant therapy.

Cautions and Warnings

Warfarin must be taken with care if you have a preexisting blood disease associated with coagulation or lack of coagulation. Other conditions in which the use of Warfarin should be discussed with your doctor are threatened abortion, Vitamin C deficiency, stomach ulcers or bleeding from the genital or urinary areas, severe high blood pressure, disease of the large bowel, such as diverticulitis or ulcerative colitis, and subacute bacterial endocarditis.

People taking Warfarin should be extremely cautious about being exposed to cuts, bruises, or other types of injury which might cause bleeding.

Pregnancy/Breast-feeding

If you are pregnant or think that you may be pregnant, you must discuss this with your doctor immediately: Warfarin can cause problems with the mother and will also pass into the fetus. It can cause and has caused bleeding and death of the fetus.

A nursing mother should be careful, since Warfarin will appear in her milk.

There are situations where the potential benefits to be gained from the use of Warfarin or one of the other anticoagulants may outweigh possible negative effects of these drugs in the pregnant patient: The decision to use one of these drugs is an important one which should be made cooperatively by you and your doctor. Often pregnant women who need an anticoagulant are treated with Heparin because it does not cross into the developing baby's blood system.

Seniors

Older adults may be more sensitive to the effects of Warfarin and other anticoagulant drugs. The reasons for this are not clear but may have to do with a reduced ability to clear the drug from their bodies. Seniors generally require lower doses to achieve the same effect as younger adults who must take this medication.

Possible Side Effects

The principal side effect experienced by patients taking Warfarin or other oral anticoagulant drugs is bleeding, which may occur within therapeutic dosage ranges and even when blood tests normally used to monitor anticoagulant therapy are within normal limits. If you bleed abnormally while you are taking anticoagulants and have eliminated the possibility of drug interactions, you should discuss this matter immediately with your doctor: It may indicate the presence of an underlying problem.

Less commonly, people taking oral anticoagulant drugs have reported bleeding from peptic ulcers, nausea, vomiting, diarrhea, blood in the urine, anemia, adverse effects on components of the blood, hepatitis, jaundice or yellowing of the skin and whites of the eyes, itching, rash, loss of hair, sore throat and mouth, and fever.

Drug Interactions

Warfarin and other oral anticoagulant (blood-thinning) drugs are probably involved in more drug interactions than any other kind of drug. Contact your pharmacist or doctor to discuss any other medications which you may be taking, in order to avoid serious adverse interactions, which may increase the effectiveness of Warfarin to the point of causing severe bleeding or hemorrhage or decrease its effectiveness to the point of causing formation of blood clots. Your doctor and your pharmacist should have records of all medications which you are taking.

Drugs that may increase the effect of Warfarin include broad-spectrum antibiotics such as Neomycin or others which will act on the normal bacterial contents of the stomach and intestines to eliminate Vitamin K, the body's natural antidote to Warfarin; mineral oil; Cholestyramine; Phenylbutazone; Oxyphenbutazone; Clofibrate; Indomethacin; sulfa drugs; Chloral Hydrate; Ethacrynic Acid; Mefanamic Acid; Nalidixic Acid; Aspirin; oral antidiabetic drugs (Tolbutamide, Chlorpropamide, Tolazamide); Chloramphenicol; Allopurinol; Nortriptyline; Methylphenidate; alcohol; Cimetidine; Disulfiram; Chlortetracycline; Quinidine; Haloperidol; Ascorbic Acid in large quantities; monoamine oxidase (MAO) inhibitors; Meperidine; and Thyroid Hormone and the antithyroid drugs, such as Propylthiouracil and Methylthiouracil.

There are fewer drugs that will decrease the effect of Warfarin, but the potential interaction can be just as dangerous with barbiturates, Glutethimide, Ethchlorvynol, Meprobamate, Griseofulvin, estrogens, oral contraceptive drugs, Chlorthalidone, corticosteroids, Phenytoin (see the Phenytoin profile for interaction resulting in Phenytoin toxicity), Carbamazepine, Vitamin K, and Rifampin.

No matter what the interaction, it is essential that you discuss all medications you are taking with your doctor or pharmacist, including not only prescription drugs but over-the-counter drugs containing Aspirin or other ingredients which may interact with Warfarin. Consult your physician or pharmacist before buying any over-the-counter drugs.

Food Interactions

Vitamin K is the antidote for Warfarin. Therefore, you should refrain from eating large quantities of foods rich in Vitamin K, such as green leafy vegetables.

It should also be noted that any change in dietary habits or alcohol intake can affect Warfarin's action in your body.

This medicine is best taken on an empty stomach because food slows the rate at which the drug is absorbed into your blood.

Usual Dose

2 to 15 or more milligrams daily; dose is extremely variable and must be individualized for maximum effect.

Overdosage

The primary sympton is bleeding. A laboratory test will show longer blood-clotting time, and bleeding can make itself known by appearance of blood in the urine or stool, an unusual number of black-and-blue marks, oozing of blood from small cuts made while shaving or from other trivial nicks or cuts, or bleeding from the gums after brushing the teeth. If bleeding does not stop within 10 to 15 minutes, your doctor should be called. He or she may tell you to skip a dose of anticoagulant and continue normal activities or to go to a local hospital or doctor's office where blood evaluations can be made; or your doctor may give you a prescription for Vitamin K, which antagonizes the effect of Warfarin. The latter has dangers because it can complicate subsequent anticoagulant therapy, but this is a decision that your doctor must make.

Special Information

Some people have had problems with changing brands of Warfarin. Do not change brands without your doctor's knowledge.

If you forget to take a dose of Warfarin, take it as soon as you remember, then go back to your regular schedule. If you don't remember until the next day, skip the dose you forgot and continue with your regular schedule. Do not take a double dose. Doubling the dose may cause bleeding. Tell your doctor if you miss any doses.

Generic Name

Zidovudine

Brand Name

Retrovir

(Also known as AZT, Azidothymidine, and Compound S)

Type of Drug

Antiviral.

Prescribed for

AIDS.

General Information

Zidovudine was the first drug approved for use in the United States under a special government program for drugs considered essential for the treatment of specific diseases. Drugs in this program are released to the public before they have been completely tested for safety and effectiveness because of the concern for the severity of the disease they are designed to treat.

Zidovudine inhibits the production of several viruses, including the AIDS virus. It works by interfering with specific enzymes within the virus that are responsible for essential steps in the reproduction process. Zidovudine has not been proven to reverse the course of AIDS, but it has been able to slow the process of the disease and add to the life span of AIDS victims. Zidovudine is prescribed for adults as soon as there is evidence of immune system problems. It may be prescribed for children with AIDS-related symptoms or laboratory evidence of the disease.

Cautions and Warnings

Zidovudine should be taken with caution by people with bone marrow disease or those whose bone marrow has already been compromised by other treatments. Zidovudine can cause anemia and reduced white-blood-cell counts. Your doctor should take a blood count every 2 weeks, and the drug dosage should be reduced if problems develop.

Pregnancy/Breast-feeding

It is not known if Zidovudine can harm a developing fetus or whether the drug affects a woman's capacity to have a baby.

It is not known if Zidovudine passes into breast milk. Nursing mothers taking this medication should use an alternative feeding method.

Seniors

Older adults may be at a greater risk of Zidovudine side effects because of reduced kidney function.

Possible Side Effects

The most common side effects are anemia, reduced white-blood-cell count, headache, nausea, sleeplessness, muscle aches.

Less common side effects include body odor, chills, swelling of the lip, flu-like symptoms, greater susceptibility to feeling pain, back pains, chest pains, swelling of the lymph nodes, flushing and warmth, constipation, difficulty swallowing, swelling of the tongue, stomach gas, flatulence, bleeding gums, mouth sores, bleeding from the rectum, joint pains, muscle spasms, tremors, twitching, anxiety, confusion, depression, emotional flare-ups, dizziness, fainting, loss of mental "sharpness," cough, nosebleeds, runny nose, sinus inflammation, hoarseness, acne, itching, rash, double vision, sensitivity to bright lights, hearing loss, painful, difficult urination, frequent urination.

Drug Interactions

Combining Zidovudine with other drugs (Pentamidine, Dapsone, Amphotericin, Flucytosine, Vincristine, Vinblastine, Adriamycin, and Interferon) that can damage your kidneys will increase the chances of loss of some kidney function.

Probenecid may reduce the rate at which your body eliminates this drug, increasing the amount of drug in your blood and the chances for drug side effects. Other drugs that can reduce the liver's ability to break down Zidovudine are Acetaminophen, Aspirin, and Indomethacin. This can lead to increased drug toxicity.

Acyclovir, often used in combination with Zidovudine to combat opportunistic infections in AIDS victims, may cause lethargy or seizure when taken together with Zidovudine.

Food Interactions

This medicine is best taken on an empty stomach, but you may take it with food if it upsets your stomach.

Usual Dose

Adult: For symptomatic AIDS, 100 to 200 milligrams every 4 hours around the clock, even if sleep is interrupted. Your dosage may be reduced if signs of drug toxicity develop. Asymptomatic AIDS may be treated with 100 milligrams every 4 hours during waking hours.

Child (3 months to 12 years): up to 200 milligrams every 6 hours.

Overdosage

The most serious effect of drug overdose is suppression of the bone marrow and its ability to make red and white blood cells. Overdose victims should be taken to a hospital emergency room at once. ALWAYS bring the medicine bottle with you.

Special Information

This drug does not cure AIDS. It does not decrease the chances of your transmitting the AIDS virus to another person.

Be sure to take this drug exactly as prescribed (every 4 hours around the clock) even though it will interfere with your sleep. Do not take more than your doctor has prescribed.

People taking Zidovudine may continue to develop illnesses associated with AIDS even though they are taking the medication.

See your doctor if any significant change in your health develops. Periodic blood counts are very important while taking Zidovudine to detect possibly serious side effects.

Avoid Acetaminophen, Aspirin, and other drugs that can increase Zidovudine toxicity.

If you miss a dose of Zidovudine take it as soon as possible. If it almost time for your next dose, space the missed dose and your next dose by 2 to 4 hours and then continue with your regular schedule.

Drugs and . . .

DRUGS AND FOOD

The increased interest of many Americans in diet and nutrition has focused attention on how diet affects drug therapy and the effect of drugs on diet and nutrition.

How Does Diet Affect Drug Therapy?

Foods can interfere with the ability of drugs to be absorbed into the blood through the gastrointestinal system. For this reason, most medications are best taken at least 1 hour before or 2 hours after meals, unless specific characteristics of the drug indicate that it is better taken with or immediately following meals. Each drug profile contains a section on "Food Interactions" that tells you the best time to take your medicine and what foods, if any, to avoid while taking your medication. Check with your doctor or pharmacist if you are unsure about how to best take your medicine.

Some drugs which are taken with meals because the food reduces the amount of drug-related stomach irritation are Indomethacin, Phenylbutazone, and Oxyphenbutazone. Other drugs such as Amoxicillin may not be affected at all by food.

Some food effects interfere with a drug by reducing the amount of medication available to be absorbed. Juice or milk taken to help you swallow drugs can interfere with them. Many fruit juices, because of their acid content, break down Penicillin-G, Erythromycin, and other antibiotics. Milk or milk products (like ice cream) can interfere with the absorption of Tetracycline antibiotics through the gastrointestinal tract.

Investigators have questioned the seriousness of such effects, and it is generally difficult to prove that people who experience these food-drug interactions don't get well as fast as others who did not. There probably is some effect, but its extent is not known.

Some medications react with specific diets. People taking anticoagulant (blood-thinning) drugs should avoid fat-rich foods because they may reduce anticoagulant effectiveness. People taking Levodopa (L-dopa) should avoid high-protein diets rich in Vitamin B+ (Pyridoxine), which can reduce the effectiveness of Levodopa. Some raw vegetables, such as cabbage and okra, contain Vitamin K, which interferes with oral anticoagulant drugs. This interaction can contribute to the development of potentially fatal blood clots.

An ingredient in licorice can cause you to retain sodium and lose potassium. This can be dangerous if you have high blood pressure (increased sodium = increased water = higher blood pressure) or if you are taking a digitalis drug for your heart (less potassium = more digitalis drug side effects).

Many foods interact with monoamine oxidase (MAO) inhibitors.

Foods containing potassium can be useful to people taking diuretics who need to add potassium to their diet:

Apricots (dried)	Peaches (dried)
Bananas	Prune juice
Cantaloupe	Raisins
Dates	Steak
Figs (dried)	Turkey
Milk	Watermelon
Orange juice	

How Do Drugs Affect Diet and Nutrition?

Drugs can affect your appetite. Some medicines that can stimulate your appetite include tricyclic antidepressants and phenothiazine tranquilizers.

Drugs that can cause you to lose your appetite include antibiotics (especially Penicillin) and any medication with a possible side effect of nausea and vomiting.

Many drugs can interfere with the normal absorption of one or more body nutrients:

Antacids	Colchicine
Anticholinergics	Glutethimide
(e.g., Atropine)	Isoniazid
Anticonvulsants	Methotrexate
Barbiturates	Neomycin Sulfate
Cathartics (laxatives)	Oral contraceptives
Chloramphenicol	Sulfa drugs
Clofibrate	

Drug Interactions with Food

In general, food will either interfere with or prolong the time it takes for a drug to be absorbed into the bloodstream. This happens because food prevents the drug molecules from getting to the wall of the intestine or stomach, where drug absorption takes place. In most cases, the absorption of drugs is only delayed, not prevented or decreased. You should try to take your medication on an empty stomach to avoid any interference caused by food. However, drugs that are irritating to the stomach and intestines should be taken with food because this will reduce the irritating effect.

Some foods can directly interfere with the absorption of drugs from the gastrointestinal tract. The drugs most often involved are antibiotics. In the case of the tetracyclines, any food product that contains large amounts of calcium interferes with the drug's action, because a complex is formed between the antibiotic and the calcium. This interaction can be avoided by simply separating your dose of antibiotic from the time that you eat ice cream, milk, or other dairy products by about 2 hours. This will allow sufficient time for the drug to be absorbed. Other foods do not contain enough calcium to effectively interfere with the drug's action.

Another important drug-food interaction involves foods that contribute to the body's manufacture of chemicals that control central-nervous-system activity. Some drugs affect the enzyme system most responsible for breaking down these chemicals and removing them from the nerve endings. This enzyme is called monoamine oxidase (MAO).

Warfarin, an anticoagulant, or blood-thinning drug, works by interfering with chemical reactions in the blood coagulation mechanism that depend upon the presence of Vitamin K. The effect of Warfarin and other oral anticoagulant drugs can be completely reversed by taking Vitamin K. In fact, Vitamin K is given by injection as an antidote to an overdose of these anticoagulants. We get most of our Vitamin K from microorganisms in the gut that manufacture it. However, we can also get Vitamin K from some raw vegetables, such as cabbage and okra. If you eat too much of these vegetables, the Vitamin K content can interfere with the anticoagulant effect of Warfarin.

DRUGS AND ALCOHOL

Drug interactions with alcohol, itself a potent drug, are a significant problem and can be experienced by anyone, even those who avoid drinking near the time that they take prescription pills. Many over-the-counter medicines are alcohol-based and have the potential to interact with prescription drugs: There are more than 500 pharmaceutical items that contain alcohol, some in concentrations up to 68 percent. Alcohol is used to dissolve drugs, as in vitamin tonics and antitussive-decongestant liquids, and also to enhance sedative effects. Alcohol is found in almost all decongestant cold-suppressing mixtures.

Alcohol's action in the body is simply that of a central nervous system depressant. It may either enhance or reduce the effect of a drug. In some drug interactions, the amount of alcohol consumed may not be as important as the chemical reaction it causes in your body. Small concentrations can cause excess stomach secretions, while larger amounts can inhibit stomach secretions, eroding the stomach's lining. Use of over-the-counter alcohol-based products by seniors is especially dangerous, since their systems may be more sensitive to alcohol. People with stomach disorders such as peptic or gastric ulcer should be fully aware of the alcohol levels in products they use.

The effects of alcohol on your prescription are described in each drug profile.

One drug, Disulfiram (Antabuse), is used to treat alcoholism. Alcoholics using this medication will experience abdominal cramps, nausea, vomiting, headaches, and flushing if they drink any alcohol, including beer, wine, whiskey, or medication with alcohol base such as cough medications. These effects help alcoholics abstain from drinking. Some other drugs also produce this effect, but they are not used in primary treatment programs. They include the oral antidiabetics and Metrondiazole.

DRUGS AND SEXUAL ACTIVITY

Sexual activity is usually not limited by drugs; however, some drugs can have an effect on sex drive, and their side effects can lead to impotence. This is especially true in men taking some high-blood-pressure drugs or beta blockers, which affect the central nervous or circulatory system. It's important to discuss such effects with your doctor: A simple reduction in dosage or the change to another drug in the same class may solve the problem.

Many antihypertensives can impair potency and cause retrograde ejaculation in the male. Antidepressants, amphetamines, and sedatives have similar effects on sex drive and can reduce potency. Oral contraceptives have been linked to reduced sex drive in some women. Anticancer drugs don't affect sex drive but will reduce sperm count in many men.

Some drugs, such as Levodopa, have been reported to increase sex drive; note that this is age- and dose-related.

DRUGS AND PREGNANCY

Today we are acutely aware of the potential damage to a fetus from drugs of all kinds. In order for a drug to affect the fetus, it must cross the placental barrier from the mother's bloodstream to that of the fetus. Once in the baby's bloodstream, the drug may affect any of the normal growth and development processes. Because a fetus grows much more rapidly than a fully developed human, the effects of a drug on this process are exaggerated. Adverse results can range from physical disfigurement to severe mental and/or physical damage to death.

An illustration of the damage caused by drug use during pregnancy is the discovery of the latent effect of DES (Diethylstilbestrol). This hormone, given to many women during the 1940s and 1950s to prevent miscarriage, has been linked to vaginal cancer in the daughters of the women who used it. The Thalidomide scandal of the 1960s was caused by a drug which was intended to help pregnant women but which resulted in birth defects and deformities in children. This led to a complete reevaluation of the use of drugs during pregnancy.

Most obstetricians recommend that pregnant women avoid all unnecessary medication during pregnancy and after birth while lactating. This includes analgesics such as Aspirin. Unfortunately, potential damage to a fetus is greatest during the first three months of pregnancy, when a woman may not be aware that she is pregnant. If you are considering becoming pregnant, it is wise to curtail any drug use immediately and discuss it fully with your ob/gyn specialist.

Today, most doctors suggest that pregnant women use only vitamins or iron supplements and limit their alcohol, tobacco, and caffeine intake.

The Food and Drug Administration has classified all prescription drugs according to their safety for use during pregnancy. Every profile in *The Pill Book* contains specific information on drug safety for pregnant and breast-feeding women.

DRUGS AND CHILDREN

Medications for children should be given only on direct orders from a pediatrician or other doctor. Of course, children suffer from colds and runny noses and there are many over-the-counter medicines which parents use frequently. Parents should be aware of the ingredients of such products—for example, the alcohol content))and of possible side effects.

Children are at greater risk for drug side effects and interactions because their body systems are not fully developed. This is especially true of infants and young children. Some drugs like the tetracyclines have been linked to serious side effects in children and should be avoided. It's wise to ask your doctor whether side effects such as fever or rash are to be expected when he or she prescribes a drug for a child.

Some drugs have opposite effects on adults and children. Ritalin, which is given to children to calm hyperactivity, acts as a stimulant in adults.

Drug doses for children are usually lower and are often determined by body weight. Be sure you know all there is to know about a drug before you give it to your child. If you can, check with your doctor about over-the-counter products unless you've used them before and are sure they can't interact with other drugs the child is taking.

DRUGS AND SENIORS

Changes in the body caused either by age or disease make older adults 3 times as likely to have adverse drug reactions—nausea, dizziness, blurred vision, and others—as younger people. Drug interactions are another potential source of great danger for seniors. Since many older adults are on multiple drug regimens for more than one chronic condition, the potential for drug interaction is much greater.

Older adults often suffer from "asymptomatic drug reaction," silent undetected reactions caused by slowly building amounts of drugs that are not being properly metabolized by the older, less efficient systems.

Two-thirds of people over the age of 65 take prescription drugs regularly; in fact, 30 percent of all prescriptions are filled for older customers, who make up only 15 percent of the population. Many spend several hundred dollars a year to get an average of 13 prescriptions filled. The 1.5 million seniors in nursing homes are also at great risk for drug interactions: 54 percent of them take 6 or more pills per day, and some receive as many as 23.

Studies have shown that 70 to 90 percent of seniors take pills and over-the-counter medicines with little knowledge of their dangerous effects. Often older adults who have speech or hearing problems, are absentminded, or are experiencing other symptoms we attribute to aging are really suffering from drug reactions. This condition is called reversible dementia.

Seniors are often victims of overdose, and not necessarily because of mistaken dosages. Often body weight fluctuations and normal changes in body composition lead to overdose unless the dosage of a drug is altered accordingly.

Antihistamines, phenothiazines, and tricyclic antidepressants are known to cause frequent adverse reactions in seniors. Older people are sometimes unknowing victims of a drug reaction that causes another disease state. For example, gout can be precipitated by certain diuretics, and kidney disease can be caused by long overuse of anti-inflammatories like Aspirin.

It's important to make sure that older adults understand their drugs completely. Follow the tips for safe drug use on pages 983 to 984 to assist an older person in managing drug intake properly. Install a drug control system which lists the pills prescribed, the sequence in which they should be taken, the time of day, how they should be taken, and a place to indicate what was taken. Every drug profile in *The Pill Book* contains specific information on drug use by older adults.

DRUGS AND AIDS

In 1978, the federal Centers for Disease Control (CDC) in Atlanta, Georgia, observed that gay men had a much higher than expected incidence of an otherwise rare tumor called *Kaposi's sarcoma*. But it was not until 1981 that the medical community became generally aware of AIDS, when CDC published the observation that gay men in Los Angeles were found to develop a fungus infection called *pneumocystis carinii* much more often than other people. In the beginning, it took 18 months for CDC to collect the first 1000 cases of AIDS. Since then, AIDS has become the most important infectious disease in the world, infecting about 1000 people a week.

There are 2 varieties of the AIDS virus, also known as the Human Immunodeficiency Virus, or HIV. HIV-1 is responsible for almost all of the AIDS infections in America. HIV-2 is found primarily in west Africa. Many patients develop one or more symptoms of AIDS 7 years after initial infection. Despite the progress made in understanding AIDS and the

HIV virus, it is estimated that fewer than 15% of people with AIDS live for more than 3 years after developing the disease.

HIV attaches to cells called helper T-cells, which carry a protein known as CD4. The virus also attaches to other important white-blood-cell elements. HIV infects a wide variety of other cells, but CD4 cell counts are important because the number of CD4 cells serves as a direct indicator of the progress of the disease, patient condition, and the need for drug treatment. Once diagnosed by a series of skin and blood tests, including CD4 cell counts, treatment for AIDS or one of many associated diseases or complications may be started.

Anti-HIV Therapy

As of this writing, only 2 drugs are approved for use as anti-HIV agents: Zidovudine, also known as AZT, and ddl. It is reasonable to expect that other agents with anti-HIV effects—including ddC, d4T, AZdU, Foscarnet, and others—will also be approved to treat the virus as time passes. Until then, they may be available under research protocols to limited numbers of people with AIDS.

Zidovudine interferes with an enzyme known as *reverse transcriptase* that is essential to the reproduction of the virus. All of the other anti-HIV treatments work in a similar way; they may help some patients for whom Zidovudine is not effective because of individual differences in response. When Zidovudine was first used in patient care, it was given only to adults whose CD4 count had fallen to 200 or less because these people were judged to be at the greatest risk. Today, the starting point for Zidovudine and ddl anti-HIV treatment is a CD4 level of 500 or less, and treatment has been extended to infants as young as 3 to 6 months old infected with the virus. This more aggressive approach has helped to extend the lives of people with AIDS and to delay the development of AIDS-related complications.

When it is first started, Zidovudine is given in daily doses of 500 to 600 milligrams, about 1/2 the range at which Zidovudine was given when it first became available. Larger doses may be given as the disease progresses.

ddl is given to people who cannot tolerate Zidovudine or

for whom Zidovudine has lost its effectiveness. ddI is taken every 12 hours in a dosage that depends on body weight. It is manufactured as regular and chewable tablets and as a powder that can be dissolved in water and drunk.

Both Zidovudine and ddI can affect white- and red-blood-cell production in the body and are often given together with other drugs intended to raise cell counts and extend the time that the antiviral drug can be given. Erythropoietin may be given by injection to raise red-blood-cell levels, and drugs known as colony stimulating factors (G-CSF and GM-CSF) may be given to raise white-blood-cell levels.

Ganciclovir and TMP/SMZ, treatments for some complications of AIDS, may interact with Zidovudine to increase its effects on red and white blood cells. For this reason, other treatments may be used, or a decision may be made to stop Zidovudine treatment for a time.

Complications of AIDS

Because of its effect on the human immune system, AIDS exposes patients to a variety of bacterial and fungal infections that non-AIDS patients can easily fight on their own. These conditions—including candida, herpes, pneumocystis, syphilis, toxoplasmosis, CMV disease, and Kaposi's sarcoma—are known as opportunistic conditions: They are seen as flourishing because of the opportunity they find in an immune-deficient person. Other complications of AIDS include chronic hepatitis, sinusitis, brain damage and dementia, bone marrow failure, and other immune deficiency disorders.

Pneumocystis pneumonia   Pneumocystis, one of the first complications associated with the AIDS epidemic, can be deadly. Preventive therapy is normally begun for all people with AIDS whose CD4 counts fall to 200 or less. The treatment of choice has, for many years, been Pentamidine, which is inhaled directly into the lungs in doses of about 300 milligrams monthly. Controversies over the drug's cost and some of its complications have caused physicians to re-examine one of the original preventive treatments for pneumocystis, the antibacterial combination of Trimethoprim and Sulfamethoxazole (TMP/SMZ, Bactrim, Septra). The most common preventive dose of TMP/SMZ is one double dose taken 3 times a week. This drug has the advantages of low cost, the ability to be taken by mouth, and equal effectiveness to Pentamidine.

When pneumocystis develops, the same drugs are used for treatment in higher doses. Prednisone may also be given together with an antifungal drug to control inflammation within the lungs. Other, as yet unapproved, treatments like Trimetrexate or Dapsone may be given if Pentamidine and TMP/SMZ do not work.

Candida infection   Candida infections are rarely fatal in AIDS patients, but they can be extremely troublesome. Any number of standard anti-fungal drugs may be given to treat candida of the mouth (thrush), including Nystatin suspension, Clotrimazole tablets dissolved in the mouth, Ketoconazole, and Fluconazole. Fluconazole is the newest and most effective remedy against candida that is resistant to other drugs.

Sexually transmitted diseases   All sexually transmitted diseases, including syphilis, chlamydia, and gonorrhea, are especially problematic for people with AIDS, but recurrent herpes is a major problem. Herpes can be present together with candida and must be treated. Acyclovir is the drug of choice for treating herpes infections. Many AIDS patients may require intravenous doses of the drug to get large quantities of it into their systems. Most people with AIDS take 800 milligrams of Acyclovir daily to prevent recurrence of herpes.

Central-nervous-system infections   People with AIDS are particularly susceptible to meningitis and other nervous system infections caused by fungal organisms that are rarely associated with this kind of infection in people not infected with HIV. This creates the need for suppressive therapy with Flucytosine or Fluconazole and treatment with large doses of these drugs combined with sulfa drugs. Clindamycin may also be used in these situations.

Sinus infections and pneumonia   People with AIDS are subject to severe respiratory infections that may become chronic as time passes. As in other kinds of infections, the kinds of organisms involved create a more serious situation and require more potent and toxic drug treatment.

Cytomegalovirus (CMV) infection   CMV infection is one of the most serious complications of AIDS. It affects about one-quarter of people with the virus. CMV, which is a member of the herpes family of viruses, can infect almost any part of the body, but is particularly serious when it affects the eye. CMV retinitis, as the eye infection is known, is the leading cause of blindness among people with AIDS. It is treated with 2 drugs: Ganciclovir, which has been available for some time, or Foscarnet, which was approved in late 1991 by the FDA. Of the 2, Foscarnet, which must be given by intravenous injection, is the better therapeutic alternative. It is as effective as Ganciclovir in slowing the progression of the infection but also contributes to life extension for 2 reasons: It does not interact with AZT, allowing the continuation of antiviral treatment, and it has some anti-HIV effects of its own.

Diarrhea   Diarrhea is common among people with AIDS and can be due to any of a variety of causes. The diarrhea, which may become serious, is treated with general-purpose antidiarrheal drugs like Lomotil and Imodium because they provide general relief, regardless of the cause. Sometimes, more potent antidiarrheal products like Paregoric or Morphine Sulfate may be employed if the other medications don't work. If the exact cause of the diarrhea can be determined, another drug may be added to fight the specific cause of the problem.

Tuberculosis   AIDS increases the risk of tuberculosis. People with AIDS who develop tuberculosis usually respond to standard antituberculosis drugs like Ethambutol, Isoniazid, or Rifampin, but these treatments do not cure the infection. For many people, the side effects of drug treatment may be more serious than the tuberculosis infection, so decisions must be made about how aggressively to treat the tuberculosis based on the general condition of the patient. People who show few symptoms related to the tuberculosis should probably not be treated. Those who are losing weight, running a chronic temperature, and feeling sickly should be treated.

Kaposi's sarcoma   There is no treatment for this problem. Interferon and a variety of anticancer drugs have been tried with limited success. Some drugs that have been tried are Adriamycin, Bleomycin, Vincristine, and Vinblastine, but the side effects of these drugs, normally hard for anyone to tolerate, are especially difficult for people with AIDS. The basic problem is that people with AIDS who develop Kaposi's sarcoma have very low CD4 cell counts, reflecting a poorly functioning immune system. Because these drugs depend on a functioning immune system to bolster their effect, many of them end up making people who are already sick even sicker.

Dental problems   People with AIDS may develop a variety of oral problems, including mouth sores, warts, Kaposi's sarcoma, candida and other fungus infections, and gum disease. These are treated with many of the same drugs used to treat similar complications in other parts of the body or oral disinfections.

Skin problems   People with AIDS can develop a variety of common bacterial and fungal skin infections, including impetigo and hair follicle infections, or it may be possible to develop any of a host of rare skin infections requiring extraordinary treatments. Most common infections can be treated with standard antibacterial or antifungal creams, and ointments are used to fight many of these infections. Oral drugs may be needed when these infections become more widespread or unusually severe.

The treatment of AIDS is a complex and difficult problem. Researchers are still struggling with finding the best ways to deal with HIV and its many complications. In the end, the ultimate treatment for AIDS will likely be a vaccine against the virus or a series of drugs that bolsters the immune system. But progress comes in small, slow steps, and, although there are a number of vaccine products in development, all of them are years away from being proven effective.

Twenty Questions to Ask Your Doctor and Pharmacist About Your Prescription

1. What is the name of this medicine?

2. What results can be expected from taking it?

3. How long should I wait before reporting if this medicine does not help me?

4. How does the medicine work?

5. What is the exact dose of the medicine?

6. What time of day should I take it?

7. Can I drink alcoholic beverages while taking this medicine?

8. Do I have to take special precautions with this medicine in combination with other prescription drugs I am taking?

9. Do I have to take special precautions with this medicine in combination with nonprescription (over-the-counter) drugs?

10. Can I take this medicine without regard to food or mealtimes?

11. Are there any special instructions I should have about how to use this medicine?

12. How long should I continue to take this medicine?

13. Is my prescription renewable?

14. For how long a period can my prescription be renewed?

15. Which side effects should I report and which can I disregard?

16. Can I save any unused portion of this medicine for future use?

17. How should I store this medicine?

18. How long can I keep this medicine without its losing strength?

19. What should I do if I forget to take a dose of this medicine?

20. Is this medicine available in a less expensive, generic form?

Other Points to Remember for Safe Drug Use

- Store your medicines in a sealed, light-resistant container to maintain maximum potency, and be sure to follow any special storage instructions listed on your medicine bottle, such as "refrigerate," "do not freeze," "protect from light," or "keep in a cool place." Protect all medicines from excessive humidity.
- Make sure you tell the doctor everything that is wrong. The more information your doctor has, the more effectively he or she can treat you.
- Make sure each doctor you see knows all the medicines you use regularly, including prescription and nonprescription drugs.
- Keep a record of any bad reaction you have had to a medicine.
- Fill each prescription you are given. If you don't fill a prescription, make sure the doctor knows it.
- Don't take extra medicine without consulting your doctor or pharmacist.
- Follow the label instructions exactly. If you have any questions, call your doctor or pharmacist.
- Report any unusual symptoms that you develop after taking medicine.
- Don't save unused medicine for future use unless you have consulted your doctor.
- Dispose of unused medicine by flushing it down the toilet.
- Never keep medicine where children can see or reach it.
- Always read the label before taking your medicine. Don't trust your memory.

- Consult your pharmacist for guidance on the use of over-the-counter (nonprescription) drugs.
- Don't share your medicine with anyone. Your prescription was written for you and only you.
- Be sure the label stays on the container until the medicine is used or destroyed.
- Keep the label facing up when pouring liquid medicine from the bottle.
- Don't use a prescription medicine unless it has been specifically prescribed for you.
- When you travel, take your prescription with you in its original container.
- If you move to another city, ask your pharmacist to forward your prescription records to your new pharmacy.
- Carry important medical facts about yourself in your wallet. Such things as drug allergies, chronic diseases (diabetes, etc.), and special requirements can be very useful.
- Don't hesitate to discuss the cost of medical care with your doctor or pharmacist.
- Exercise your right to make decisions about buying medicines:
  1. If you suffer from a chronic condition, you can probably save by buying in larger quantities.
  2. Choose your pharmacist as carefully as you choose your doctor.
  3. Remember, the cost of your prescription includes the professional services offered by your pharmacy. If you want more service you will have to pay for it.

THE TOP 200 PRESCRIPTION DRUGS IN THE UNITED STATES

RANKED BY NUMBER OF PRESCRIPTIONS DISPENSED FROM OCTOBER 1990 TO SEPTEMBER 1991

(Generic products are followed by manufacturer name in parentheses.)

1. Amoxil
2. Premarin
3. Zantac
4. Lanoxin
5. Xanax
6. Synthroid
7. Seldane
8. Ceclor
9. Procardia
10. Vasotec
11. Cardizem
12. Dyazide
13. Tenormin
14. Naprosyn
15. Ortho-Novum 7/7/7
16. Capoten
17. Calan
18. Prozac
19. Tagamet
20. Proventil (Schering 28111)
21. Augmentin
22. Mevacor
23. Lopressor
24. Ventolin
25. Cipro
26. Tylenol w/Codeine
27. Provera
28. Ortho-Novum
29. Dilantin
30. Micronase
31. Lasix
32. Voltaren
33. Amoxicillin (Biocraft)
34. Darvocet-N
35. Trimox
36. Polymox
37. Halcion
38. Triphasil
39. Theo-Dur
40. Vicodin
41. Inderal
42. Humulin NPH
43. Lopid
44. Coumadin
45. IBU
46. Feldene
47. Anaprox
48. Diabeta
49. Lo/Ovral
50. Glucotrol
51. Micro-K
52. Maxzide
53. Hismanal
54. Duricef
55. Pepcid
56. Zestril
57. Valium
58. PCE
59. Propoxyphene Napsylate w/Apap (Mylan)
60. Estraderm

61. Timoptic
62. Nitrostat
63. Pamelor
64. E-Mycin
65. Hydrocodone w/Apap (Barr)
66. Ceftin
67. Motrin
68. Terazol
69. Monistat
70. Zovirax
71. Penicillin V (Mylan)
72. Prinivil
73. Macrodantin
74. Tavist-D
75. Carafate
76. Lotrisone
77. SMZ-TMP (Biocraft)
78. Trental
79. Tegretol
80. Pen-Vee K
81. Veetids
82. Retin-A
83. Ansaid
84. E.E.S.
85. Lozol
86. Lortab
87. Entex LA
88. Acetaminophen w/Codeine (Lemmon)
89. K-Dur
90. Demulen
91. Corgard
92. Tri-Levlen
93. Amoxicillin (Warner-Chilcott)
94. Nicorette
95. Ativan
96. Triamterene w/Hydrochlorothiazide (Rugby)
97. Acetaminophen w/Codeine (Barr)
98. BuSpar
99. Beconase AQ
100. ERYC
101. Atrovent
102. Slow-K
103. Hytrin
104. Slo-Bid
105. Acetaminophen w/Codeine (Purepac)
106. Vancenase AQ
107. Isoptin
108. Orudis
109. Klonopin
110. Transderm-Nitro
111. Erythromycin Base (Abbott)
112. Propacet
113. Furosemide (Rugby)
114. Iletin NPH
115. Thyroid (Forest)
116. Percocet-5
117. Ventolin
118. Cephalexin (Biocraft)
119. Acetaminophen w/Codeine (Halsey)
120. Nordette
121. Intal
122. Ery-Tab
123. Proventil (Schering 28113)
124. Cyclobenzaprine HCl (Danbury)
125. Sinemet
126. Ovcon
127. Hydrochlorothiazide (Rugby)
128. Fiorinal w/Codeine
129. Nitro-Dur II
130. Suprax
131. Flexeril

132. Furosemide (Mylan)
133. Dolobid
134. Wymox
135. Bumex
136. Axid
137. Nolvadex
138. Persantine
139. Bactroban
140. Cephalexin (Apothecon)
141. Furosemide (Lederle)
142. Deltasone
143. Cleocin
144. Erythrocin Stearate (Abbott)
145. Tenex
146. Tenoretic/100
147. Dipyridamole (Rugby)
148. Isordil
149. Phenergan
150. Rogaine
151. Fiorinal
152. Noroxin
153. Catapres
154. Lorazepam (Mylan)
155. Restoril
156. Tri-Norinyl
157. Keflex
158. K-Tab
159. Sumycin
160. Azmacort
161. Ogen
162. Proventil (Schering 28112)
163. Peridex
164. Prilosec
165. Donnatal
166. Klor-Con
167. Minocin
168. Clinoril
169. Prednisone (Rugby)
170. Penicillin VK (Warner-Chilcott)
171. Betapen-VK
172. Compazine
173. Elavil
174. Humulin Regular
175. Vanceril
176. Loestrin Fe
177. Tobrex
178. Reglan
179. Keftab
180. Lotrimin
181. Fioricet
182. Achromycin V
183. Amoxicillin (Mylan)
184. Estrace
185. Beepen VK
186. Lorcet Plus
187. Apap w/Codeine (Rugby)
188. Zovirax
189. Ritalin HCl
190. Premarin Vaginal
191. Tussi-Organdin DM
192. Questran
193. SMZ-TMP (Rugby)
194. Hydroxyzine HCl (Rugby)
195. Tylox
196. Anusol-HC
197. Norinyl
198. Medrol
199. Amitriptyline HCl (Rugby)
200. Minipress

Data supplied by Walsh America-PDS, Scottsdale, Arizona.

Index of Generic and Brand Name Drugs

Note: Generic drug names are indicated by bold type.

Index of Drug Types

ABOUT THE MEDICAL WRITERS

GILBERT I. SIMON, SC.D., is Director of the Department of Pharmacy at Lincoln Medical and Mental Health Center, the Bronx, New York. From 1961 to 1982 he was Director of the Department of Pharmacy at Lenox Hill Hospital, New York City. Dr. Simon received his B.S. from Fordham University; his M.S. from Long Island University; his Doctorate, Honoris Causa, from the College of Pharmacy Sciences, City of New York (Columbia University); and his MPA in Health from Pace University. He was an associate professor of pharmaceutical sciences at Columbia University from 1964 to 1976. Dr. Simon has served as president of both the New York State Council of Hospital Pharmacists and the New York City Society of Hospital Pharmacists. In 1973 he was honored with the Award of Merit from the latter group for his contribution to the practice of institutional pharmacy. He has been a member of the Pharmacy Advisory Committee of the Greater New York Hospital Association and the Governor's (NYS) Medical Advisory Committee and has served on committees of the Hospital Association of the State of New York. Dr. Simon has served as a consultant to the pharmaceutical industry, publishers, advertising agencies, and the government. He has been a principal speaker throughout the United States and in Europe. In 1975, Drs. Simon and Silverman co-authored MED FILE, a book on common non-prescription drugs and their interactions. Dr. Simon lives in Westchester County, New York with his wife, Shelia.

Educated at Columbia University, DR. HAROLD SILVERMAN has been a hospital pharmacist, author, educator, and consultant to the pharmaceutical industry. He currently directs the health care practice for the Washington, D.C. office of Hill and Knowlton, an international public affairs consulting firm. As an author, his guiding principle is that health reference books should help people understand why medicines are prescribed and how they can get the most from them. In addition to THE PILL BOOK, Dr. Silverman is co-author of THE VITAMIN BOOK: A No-Nonsense Consumer Guide and The MED FILE Drug Interactions System. He is the author of THE PILL BOOK GUIDE TO THE SAFE DRUG USE, THE CONSUMER'S GUIDE TO POISON PROTECTION, THE WOMAN'S DRUG STORE, and TRAVEL HEALTHY. Dr. Silverman's contributions to the professional literature include many articles, research papers, and textbook chapters. He is a member of many professional organizations and has served as an officer of several, including the New York State Council of Hospital Pharmacists, of which he was president. He has taught pharmacology and clinical pharmacy at several universities and won numerous awards for his work. Dr. Silverman resides in a Washington suburb with his family.